THE PAPERS OF
WOODROW WILSON

VOLUME 7
1890-1892

SPONSORED BY THE WOODROW WILSON
FOUNDATION
AND PRINCETON UNIVERSITY

THE PAPERS OF

WOODROW WILSON

ARTHUR S. LINK, *EDITOR*

JOHN WELLS DAVIDSON AND DAVID W. HIRST

ASSOCIATE EDITORS

JOHN E. LITTLE, *ASSISTANT EDITOR*

JEAN MACLACHLAN, *CONTRIBUTING EDITOR*

M. HALSEY THOMAS, *CONSULTING EDITOR*

Volume 7 · 1890-1892

PRINCETON, NEW JERSEY

PRINCETON UNIVERSITY PRESS

1969

INTRODUCTION

THIS seventh volume of *The Papers of Woodrow Wilson* chronicles the first two years—1890-1892—of Wilson's professorial career at Princeton. The book is rich in materials relating to Wilson's development as a teacher and to the history of the university during this period. Numerous documents illustrate his immediate success in the classroom and as a faculty colleague at Princeton. His plan for a School of Law, printed and described for the first time, reveals his innovative thinking about advanced legal education, while other documents show how he laid the foundations of an undergraduate curriculum in legal studies. Wilson's minutes of the Discipline Committee, of which he was an original member and secretary for many years, shed new light on undergraduate life in the 1890's, and excerpts from the minutes of the faculty reveal the day-to-day work of Princeton professors at this time.

Other documents illustrate the broadening scope of Wilson's professional activities and reputation. The notes that he used for a course on administration at The Johns Hopkins University, printed herein for the first time, demonstrate the advanced and pioneering nature of his work in this field. Additionally, this volume follows Wilson's progress in his first endeavor in historical scholarship, *Division and Reunion*, his continuing success as a public lecturer, his skill as a monographist and reviewer, and his growing nation-wide reputation as an educator sought after by other institutions.

Finally, Volume 7 abounds in materials illustrative of Wilson the husband and father, the teacher and friend. Long series of letters between Wilson and his wife, Ellen, trace the deepening relationship between them and also illuminate the atmosphere and social life of the village of Princeton during the early 1890's.

There have been no significant editorial innovations in this volume. As in earlier ones, the Editors have printed texts *verbatim et literatim*, repairing words and phrases only when necessary for clarity or ease of reading. However, in reproducing typed *copies* of letters, they have silently corrected what seemed to be obvious errors made by the typists who copied them.

Readers are reminded that *The Papers of Woodrow Wilson* is a continuing series; that persons, institutions, and events that figure prominently in earlier volumes are not usually reidentified in subsequent ones; and that the Index gives cross references to fullest earlier identifications.

This seems an appropriate time to acknowledge the past, continuing, and always cheerful assistance of Frederick Lawrence Arnold, Assistant Librarian for Reference of the Firestone Library, and his assistants, particularly Miss Eleanor Weld. M. Halsey Thomas, in his capacity as Archivist of Princeton University, contributed greatly to this and following volumes relating to Wilson's professorial career. Special thanks are due to Frances Hazen Bulkeley for making available letters of Wilson to her grandfather, Azel Washburn Hazen, D.D., and to George Lee Haskins for making available letters of Wilson to his father, Charles Homer Haskins.

The Editors are grateful to Mrs. Bryant Putney of Princeton University Press for copyediting and other assistance. Miss Marjorie Sirlouis and Colonel James B. Rothnie, U.S.A., Ret., have continued to decipher Wilson's shorthand expertly.

THE EDITORS

Princeton, New Jersey

April 14, 1969

CONTENTS

Introduction, vii
Introduction, xv
Abbreviations and Symbols, xvii

The Papers, September 5, 1890–June 8, 1892

Editorial Notes
    Wilson's Teaching at Princeton, 1890-91, 5
    Wilson's Plans for a School of Law at Princeton, 63
    Wilson's Lectures on Administration at the Johns Hopkins,
        1891-93, 112
    Wilson's Teaching at Princeton, 1891-92, 291
    "Democracy," 344
    Wilson's Lectures on Administration at the Johns Hopkins, 1892,
        381
    Wilson's Lectures at the New York Law School, 470
The Johns Hopkins University: Documentary Material
    Notes for Lectures on Administration, Jan. 1891-Feb. 1894, 114;
        Feb. 1892-Feb. 1895, 381
    Required Reading List for a Minor in Administration, 167
    Minutes of the Johns Hopkins Seminary of Historical and Po-
        litical Science, 168
Letter from Charles Kendall Adams to Albert Shaw, 160
Letter from Stockton Axson to Ellen Axson Wilson, 369
Letter from Louisa Cunningham Hoyt Brown to Ellen Axson Wilson,
    451
Letter from Davis Rich Dewey to Daniel Collamore Heath, 239
Letter from Florence Stevens Hoyt to Ellen Axson Wilson, 469
Letter from William Burhans Isham, Jr., to Robert Bridges, 78
Letter from Francis Landey Patton to Cornelius Cuyler Cuyler, 611
Letters from Francis Landey Patton to James Waddel Alexander,
    192, 630
Letter from Ellen Axson Wilson to Stockton Axson, 178
Letters from Wilson to
    Herbert Baxter Adams, 101
    Charles Augustus Aiken, 74
    Stockton Axson (notes), 510
    Charles Fisk Beach, Jr., 173
    Robert Bridges, 61, 95, 102, 105, 179, 194, 290, 309
    Francis Fisher Browne, 318
    James Bryce, 370
    Thomas Chrowder Chamberlin, 224
    Elijah Richardson Craven, 48, 57
    Richard Heath Dabney, 233
    Winthrop More Daniels, 606, 634, 636, 637
    Alfred Pearce Dennis, 83
    The Editors of The Princetonian, 373
    Daniel Coit Gilman, 3, 182, 191, 630
    Albert Bushnell Hart, 210, 221, 274, 285, 375, 555
    Azel Washburn Hazen, 228, 642
    Daniel Collamore Heath, 70, 76

Frank Irving Herriott, 627
John Franklin Jameson, 226, 273, 371, 444
Francis Bazley Lee, 181
Cyrus Hall McCormick, 158
Francis M. McKay, 632
Arthur W. Partch, with Enclosure "To Whom It May Concern,"
    241
The Postmaster of Rosemont, Pennsylvania, 240
Horace Elisha Scudder, 165, 211, 236, 309
Albert Shaw, 62, 75, 93, 183, 225, 243
Edwin Oscar Smith, 322, 342
Ellen Axson Wilson
        March 1892
                445, 447, 450, 457, 461, 466, 470, 480, 482, 486, 490,
                491, 494, 495, 500, 502, 506, 509, 519, 520, 524, 526,
                528, 532
        April 1892
                536, 537, 540, 543, 545, 549, 551, 553, 556, 559, 562,
                564, 567, 569, 572, 575, 578, 581, 584, 585, 587, 592,
                594, 597, 600, 602
        May 1892
                605, 608, 611, 616, 618, 621, 624, 627
Letters to Wilson from
    Herbert Baxter Adams, 93, 104, 320
    Mary Jane Ashton, 103
    Stockton Axson, 45, 50, 56, 278, 504, 639
    Robert Bridges, 69, 78, 92, 193, 242, 289, 308
    Howard Allen Bridgman, 240
    Francis Fisher Browne, 310, 440
    James Bryce, 343
    Thomas Chrowder Chamberlin, 222
    William Calvin Chesnut, 241
    John Bates Clark, 49, 51, 68, 75
    Seward Vincent Coffin, 171, 243
    Elijah Richardson Craven, 48, 58
    Cornelius Cuyler Cuyler, 219
    Charles Force Deems, 97
    George A. Denison, 75
    Alfred Pearce Dennis, 440
    Robert Ewing, 277
    Max Farrand, 222
    Philena Fobes Fine, 222
    Ella Ralston Flemming, 287
    Daniel Coit Gilman, 189, 203
    John Frelinghuysen Hageman, Jr., 441
    Albert Bushnell Hart, 175, 213, 272, 276, 286, 377, 438
    Azel Washburn Hazen, 181, 289
    Daniel Collamore Heath, 175, 239, 302
    D. C. Heath and Company, 172
    George Henderson, 209
    James Bayard Henry, 378
    Thomas Wentworth Higginson, 288
    Annie Wilson Howe, 47, 51, 79, 82

George Howe, Jr., 70, 80, 248
Thomas Alexander Hoyt, 57
Edmund Janes James, 96, 106, 203
George Francis James, 246
John Franklin Jameson, 238, 270, 442
Percy Lincoln Johnson, 79
Adrian Hoffman Joline, 54
John Hanson Kennard, Jr., 223, 235, 247
Theodore Monroe MacNair, 46
Cyrus Hall McCormick, 379, 613
John Dale McGill, 188, 215
Francis M. McKay, 601
Charles Edmund Merrill, 49
Philippus William Miller, 104, 377, 381
Wilfred Pirt Mustard, 217, 247
Charles Bertram Newton, 342
Frank Mason North, 8
Edwin Curtis Osborn, 207
Arthur W. Partch, 237
Francis Landey Patton, 106
James Burton Pond, 376
Bradford Paul Raymond, 68, 191
Horace Elisha Scudder, 164, 166, 234, 240
Albert Shaw, 71, 92, 159, 187, 194, 229
Edward Wright Sheldon, 310
William Milligan Sloane, 166, 204, 443
Samuel White Small, 180
Edwin Oscar Smith, 314
Frederic William Speirs, 166
Andrew Stephenson, 205
James Monroe Taylor, 321
Albert Harris Tolman, 188
Henry Nevius Van Dyke, 440
Ethelbert Dudley Warfield, 441
John Howell Westcott, 437
William Royal Wilder, 269, 270, 380
Jesse Lynch Williams, 303
Ellen Axson Wilson
    March 1892
        446, 448, 450, 459, 466, 468, 481, 485, 488, 491, 493,
        494, 497, 501, 507, 511, 519, 522, 525, 527, 533
    April 1892
        537, 538, 541, 544, 546, 551, 552, 558, 560, 563, 566,
        567, 570, 573, 578, 580, 583, 584, 586, 591, 592, 595,
        599, 601, 603
    May 1892
        606, 609, 614, 617, 619, 623, 625, 628
Joseph Ruggles Wilson, 10, 52, 82, 105, 168, 174, 195, 204, 206,
    219, 237, 269, 284, 287, 311, 322, 489, 531, 636
Joseph R. Wilson, Jr., 3, 55, 77, 84, 97, 220, 248, 324, 380, 441,
    612
Caleb Thomas Winchester, 189, 314, 321
William Alphonso Withers, 246

James Woodrow, 286
Hiram Woods, Jr., 214
Marginal Notes, 169
New York Law School: Documentary Material
   Lecture on "The General Nature of Constitutional Law," 472
   Lecture on "Sovereignty and the Nature of Government," 512
Outline of "The Philosophy of Politics," 99
Outline of the Preface to "The Philosophy of Politics," 98
Princeton University: Documentary Material
   First Notes for a Course in Public Law Described, 7
   Revised Notes for a Course in Public Law Described, 7
   Minutes of the Princeton Faculty, 11, 51, 84, 96, 108, 192, 294,
      322, 342, 373, 531, 545, 566, 640
   Announcements in *The Princetonian*, 69, 104, 173, 178, 179,
      180, 187, 189, 379, 445, 598
   Notes for an Advanced Course in Political Economy Described,
      83
   News Items in *The Princetonian*, 84, 219, 310
   Final Examination in the History of Political Economy, 107
   Final Examination in Public Law, 161
   Notes for a Course in American Constitutional Law Described,
      174
   Notes for an Elementary Course in Political Economy Described,
      177
   Special Examination in the History of Political Economy, 193
   Final Examination in Administration, 208
   Final Examination in Constitutional Law, 212
   Examination for the Theodore Cuyler Prize, 215
   Final Examination in Political Economy, 216
   Wilson's Minutes of the Discipline Committee, 294
   Notes for a Course in Jurisprudence Described, 303
   Notes for Classroom Lectures on the Outlines of Jurisprudence,
      304, 312
   Examination in the Outlines of Jurisprudence, 436
   Examination in the History of Political Economy, 439
   Notes for a Course in International Law Described, 453
   Notes for a Classroom Lecture on International Law, 453
   Reading Recommended for Undergraduates, 594
   Special Examination in Jurisprudence, 633
   Examination in International Law, 635
   Examination in Elements of Political Economy, 638
Prospectus on University Extension Courses, 1891-92, 223
Public Addresses and Lectures
   Talk to the Philadelphian Society at Princeton University, 58, 61
   Address on "The Evils of Democracy" to the Connecticut Valley
      Economic Association at Springfield, Massachusetts, 80
   Address on "College Work and the Legal Profession" to the
      Princeton Alumni in Philadelphia, 161, 164
   Address to the Princeton Alumni in New York, 176
   Notes for a Chapel Talk at Princeton University, 187
   "Political Sovereignty," 325
   Remarks to the Southern Club Banquet in New York, 342
   "Democracy," 345, 374

Remarks to the Princeton Alumni in Baltimore, 443
Remarks to the Princeton Alumni in Philadelphia, 444
Reviews of *The State*
    Berlin *Deutsche Litteraturzeitung* (Siegfried /Brie), 59
    New York *Presbyterian and Reformed Review* (Richard Heath
       Dabney), 85
Telegrams
    Cyrus Hall McCormick to Wilson, 612
    Ellen Axson Wilson to Wilson, 509
Translation and Digest, with Commentary, of Merkel's "Elemente
    der allgemeinen Rechtslehre," 249
Translation of a Boudoir Scene, 462
Writings
    "The English Constitution," 12
        I. General Characteristics, 12
       II. History, 18
      III. The House of Commons, 29
      IV. The Cabinet, 34
       V. The Executive Departments, 37
      VI. The Sovereign, 39
     VII. The House of Lords, 39
    VIII. The Courts, 40
      IX. Local Government, 41
       X. Summary, 42
    Review of Taylor's *Origin and Growth of the English Constitu-
      tion*, 87
    Review of Mason's *Veto Power*, 185
    Review of Burgess's *Political Science and Comparative Constitu-
      tional Law*, 195
    Review of Boutmy's *Studies in Constitutional Law*, 275
    "The Study of Politics," 278
    Review of Sidgwick's *The Elements of Politics*, 318
    Review of de Chambrun's *Droit et Libertés aux États-Unis*, 534
Index, 645

ILLUSTRATIONS

Following page 326

Wilson as a young professor at the College of New Jersey
Princeton University Library

Ellen Axson Wilson in the 1890's
Princeton University Library

Jessie Woodrow Wilson and Margaret Wilson
Eleanor Wilson McAdoo (ed.), "The Priceless Gift"

Eleanor Randolph Wilson
Princeton University Library

The Wilsons' home at 48 Steadman Street, later Library Place
Princeton University Library

Nassau Hall
Princeton University Archives

The front campus of the College of New Jersey about 1890
Princeton University Archives

*Francis Landey Patton, President of the College of New Jersey
and Princeton University, 1888-1902*
Princeton University Archives

*William Milligan Sloane, Professor of History at Princeton, 1883-
1897*
Princeton University Archives

*James Ormsbee Murray, Dean of the Faculty of Princeton, 1883-
1899*
Princeton University Archives

TEXT ILLUSTRATIONS

*The first page of Wilson's revised notes for his course in public law,
typed on his Caligraph, 9*

*Wilson's table of the derivation of terms for "Law" used in his course
in jurisprudence, 306-307*

ABBREVIATIONS

ALI	autograph letter initialed
ALS	autograph letter(s) signed
API	autograph postal initialed
att(s).	attached, attachment(s)
EAW	Ellen Axson Wilson
ELA	Ellen Louise Axson
enc(s).	enclosed, enclosure(s)
env.	envelope
hw	handwriting or handwritten
hwLS	handwritten letter signed
JRW	Joseph Ruggles Wilson
L	letter
sh	shorthand
T	typed
TCL	typed copy of letter
tel.	telegram
TLS	typed letter signed
WW	Woodrow Wilson
WWhw	Woodrow Wilson handwriting or handwritten
WWsh	Woodrow Wilson shorthand
WWT	Woodrow Wilson typed
WWTLS	Woodrow Wilson typed letter signed

ABBREVIATIONS FOR COLLECTIONS
AND LIBRARIES

Following the National Union Catalogue of the
Library of Congress

CtW	Wesleyan University Library
CtY	Yale University Library
DLC	Library of Congress
Ia-HA	Iowa State Department of History and Archives, Des Moines
MdBJ	The Johns Hopkins University Library
NjP	Princeton University Library
RSB Coll., DLC	Ray Stannard Baker Collection of Wilsoniana, Library of Congress
ViU	University of Virginia Library
WC, NjP	Woodrow Wilson Collection, Princeton University Library
WHi	State Historical Society of Wisconsin, Madison
WP, DLC	Woodrow Wilson Papers, Library of Congress
WU	University of Wisconsin

SYMBOLS

[Sept. 8, 1890]	publication date of a published writing; also date of document when date is not part of text
[*Sept. 8, 1890*]	latest composition date of a published writing

THE PAPERS OF
WOODROW WILSON
VOLUME 7
1890-1892

THE PAPERS OF
WOODROW WILSON

From Joseph R. Wilson, Jr.

My dearest brother: Clarksville, Tenn.   September 5th 1890.

I have time for only a few lines this afternoon, for I am in my office with only a few minutes "between acts" so to speak. You know I have been connected with this paper as a reporter for some months.[1] Our City Editor left us about two weeks ago, and I was promoted. I now, therefore, am City Editor of the "Progress." . . .

Father reached home about two weeks ago and we are still holding forth in our little cottage and have gone back to the Arlington Hotel to board. It is much improved under an entirely new management. Father and I are both pretty well.

What would you think if I were to tell you I am engaged? Well, this is about the truth of it. I have fancied many girls as you know, but during the entire time I have felt that no one of them could come up to what I would so much wish. You may remember Miss Kate Wilson who sings in the choir? Well, I am very much of the opinion that Kate Wilson will always be her name, although her station in life may be changed. Kate seems to be of about the same opinion. She is all in all to me now, and is as true a little Christian woman as ever was. I know you will love her now for *my* sake and after you know her for her *own* sake. Love unbounded to dear sister E., the chicks and your dear self. Please write very soon. You have not written to me since Spring.   Your aff. bro.   Joseph.

ALS (WP, DLC) with WWhw sums and WWsh notes on env.
   [1] See J. R. Wilson, Jr., to WW, April 25, 1890, Vol. 6.

To Daniel Coit Gilman

Princeton, New Jersey[1]

My dear Mr. Gilman,   10 September, 1890

A business letter will, I fear, be hardly an acceptable greeting to you after your year of relief from business, and yet it is a hearty greeting that I want it to convey. I sincerely hope that your year of travel,[2] of which we have had so many delightful accounts from yourself, has been full of the best refreshment for you and that you feel like taking the Hopkins as far in the next fourteen years as you have taken it in the last fourteen—not to speak of equal periods to follow.

I have delayed writing about the matter of business of which I want to speak for fear of being unduly prompt in subjecting you to the annoyances of your office; and now that I am about to broach it, I shall be brief. My brother-in-law, Mr. Stockton Axson, graduated from Wesleyan this year. I induced him to come on from the University of Georgia to Wesleyan in order to be under Prof. [Caleb Thomas] Winchester, whom I have come to regard as a very extraordinary man in the teaching of English literature. I knew my brother-in-law's devotion to English studies, and I guessed that he was held back only by pecuniarly limitations from preparing for a college chair of English. The year at Middletown brought him out wonderfully. Prof. Winchester, who has all the New England reticence and judicial judgment, praised his work in the highest terms and is ready to stand by him to any degree of recommendation. He regards him as one of the very best men he has ever had under him.

My plan for him is to spend next year in Baltimore, in order to get his bearings thoroughly in the philological world and get his grip upon German—for his training heretofore has been exclusively in literature—to spend the year after next in Germany, beginning with the summer semester of 1891; and his third year in Baltimore again, seeking his degree in 1893. But in order to carry out this programme without wearing anxiety and sacrifice he needs pecuniary assistance. Can he obtain a scholarship? I can say with the greatest confidence that he deserves one and will ornament it; but is there one available?[3] I feel sure, with Prof. Winchester, that he will distinguish himself as a writer.

With warmest regard

Sincerely Yours,   Woodrow Wilson

P. S.   I am the more anxious about this matter because he is offered pecuniary assistance at Harvard, and has heard so much about that well-known centre of superior learning and consummate effort to obtain students (that fling at H. caused me a blot)[4] that he is naturally hesitating, though inclining to take my advice because of his own preference for J. H. U.

Faithfully,   W.W.

ALS (D. C. Gilman Papers, MdBJ).
    1 The Wilsons had moved to Princeton on about September 1, into a house

at 48 Steadman Street (now 72 Library Place). See Marsh and Wright to WW, June 9, 1890, Vol. 6.
² See C. H. Haskins to WW, May 25, 1890, n. 12, Vol. 6.
³ Gilman's reply is missing, but in it he must have said that all fellowships and scholarships for 1890-91 had been awarded. Stockton Axson did go to the Hopkins in early October, but not as a fellow or holder of a scholarship.
⁴ Wilson refers to an ink blot on the page.

EDITORIAL NOTE
WILSON'S TEACHING AT PRINCETON, 1890-91

This guide to the documentary record of Wilson's first year of teaching at Princeton might well begin with the copy that he wrote, probably in the early autumn of 1890, for the Princeton *Catalogue* for 1890-91:

Jurisprudence and Political Economy.
PROFESSOR WOODROW WILSON.

1. Public Law, its historical derivation, its practical sanctions, its typical outward forms, its evidence as to the nature of the state and as to the character and scope of political sovereignty. Lectures, recitations, collateral reading. Two hours a week, first term, alternate years, alternating with Course 2. Given 1890-91. Junior and Senior elective.

2. General Jurisprudence, the philosophy of law and of personal rights. Lectures, recitations, collateral reading. Two hours a week, first term, alternate years, alternating with Course 1. To be given in 1891-92. Junior and Senior elective.

3. American Constitutional Law, state and federal. Lectures, recitations, collateral reading. Two hours a week, second term, alternate years, alternating with Course 4. Given 1890-91. Junior and Senior elective.

4. International Law. Lectures, recitations, collateral reading. Two hours a week, second term, alternate years, alternating with Course 3. To be given 1891-92. Junior and Senior elective.

5. Administration. Lectures and collateral reading. Two hours a week, second term, alternate years, alternating with Course 6. Given 1890-91. Senior elective and open to Graduate students.

6. English Common Law. Lectures and collateral reading. Two hours a week, second term, alternate years, alternating with Course 5. To be given 1891-92. Senior elective and open to Graduate students.

7. Political Economy. Elementary course. Recitations (Walker's Elementary Political Economy) and lectures. Two hours a week, second term. Required of Juniors.

8. Political Economy. Advanced Course. Lectures and recitations. Collateral reading. Two hours a week, first term. Senior elective.¹

As the notes of Wilson's lectures on administration at the Johns Hopkins in early 1890, marginal comments, and other documents printed in Volume 6 show, Wilson was deeply immersed in the lead-

¹ *Catalogue of the College of New Jersey . . . 1890-91* (Princeton, N.J., n.d.), pp. 33-34.

ing authorities in the field of public law by the late summer of 1890. He planned his Princeton course, the first that he had an opportunity to give exclusively on public law, with extreme care since he envisaged it, along with a course on jurisprudence, as the cornerstone of his undergraduate program in the philosophy and history of law. As a beginning, he wrote out, in the first of the pocket diaries described at December 28, 1889, Volume 6, a course plan with twelve topics and twenty-five lectures. Then, perhaps near the end of the summer of 1890, Wilson prepared a new list of lecture topics.[2] Finally, on October 6, 1890—after he had begun his lectures—Wilson set down a revised plan of lectures in the pocket diary mentioned above.

Wilson, undoubtedly in the summer of 1890, prepared the first body of notes on public law described at September 15, 1890. These were handwritten, sketchy outlines, and Wilson soon revised and expanded them into the second body of notes described at September 15, 1890. These notes, which he used again with some revisions and additions in 1892-93, are not printed.[3] However, the topics listed in the second body of notes and the final examination printed at January 30, 1891, give a good view of his coverage. Additional evidence may be found in the *Syllabus on Public Law. 1891* (n.p., n.d.), printed by Princeton undergraduates and covering lectures through January 15, 1891, and in the notes, covering lectures between November 20, 1890, and January 14, 1891, kept by Lawrence C. Woods, '91. Both documents are in the Wilson Papers, Library of Congress.

A description of Wilson's notes for his second-term course on American constitutional law is printed at March 10, 1891. A conspectus of the coverage and nature of this course may be obtained by referring to the lecture topics printed in this description, to the announcements and reading assignments printed at January 21 and April 3 and 10, 1891, and to the examination printed at May 21, 1891.[4]

For his course on administration in the spring of 1891, Wilson used selectively the notes that he had just prepared for his lectures at the Johns Hopkins. The marginal markings on these notes, printed at January 26, 1891, show which notes Wilson used at Princeton. The announcements printed at January 21 and March 13 and 20, 1891, and the examination printed at May 13, 1891, give further evidence about the coverage of and assignments in this course. There is also a full set of classroom notes taken by Lawrence C. Woods in the Wilson Papers.

The spring-term elementary course in political economy was the first such that Wilson had ever given, and he prepared the new set of notes described at March 13, 1891. The text assignment printed at January 21, 1891, and the examination printed at June 1, 1891, give a good view of Wilson's emphases and coverage.

Wilson devoted his first-term advanced course in political economy

2 *"Topics of Lectures: Princeton, 1890-'91:—,"* two-page WWhw MS. in notebook inscribed (WWhw) on cover: "Notes on *Public Law*   Woodrow Wilson" (WP, DLC).

3 Wilson's much revised and expanded notes on public law, prepared largely in 1894-95, will be printed in Volume 9.

4 Wilson used these notes when he gave constitutional law again in 1893. He completely revised them in 1894, and they will be printed in Volume 8.

to a history of economic thought and modern socialism. Pulling the notes described at October 3, 1887, Volume 5, from his files, he used these for lectures on economic thought from ancient times to the German historical school of his own day. Turning to socialism, perhaps around December 15, 1890, he began to use the notes described in this volume at that date. The examinations printed at January 23 and April 22, 1891, provide an almost complete outline of this course.

It might not be amiss to add that Wilson rarely if ever did anything haphazardly, and that this generalization applies most particularly to his courses. Volumes 5 and 6 of this series have already revealed how Wilson planned and used his courses from 1885 to 1889 insofar as possible to prepare himself to write *The State*. At Princeton, as at Bryn Mawr and Wesleyan, he was obliged to give certain courses to satisfy curricular needs. But as Professor of Jurisprudence at Princeton, Wilson was free to plan and develop a course program that would achieve the two academic objectives that were now paramount in his mind: first, his own self-training in the study of law, preparatory to writing his projected *magnum opus*, "The Philosophy of Politics,"[5] and, second, the development at Princeton of the core of a course program for the School of Law that he expected soon to found there and to head.[6] Hence the inclusion in his first plan for Princeton of courses in public law, jurisprudence, American constitutional law, international law, administration, and English common law.

[5] See the Editorial Note, "Wilson's First Treatise on Democratic Government," Vol. 5.
[6] See the Editorial Note, "Wilson's Plans for a School of Law at Princeton."

First Notes for a Course in Public Law

[c. Sept. 15, 1890]

Contents:
    (a) WWT and WWhw title page: "Lectures on Public Law (I) Princeton, Sept., 1890–January, 1891."
    (b) WWhw notes for lectures on the following topics: "I. *Place and Significance of Law as a University Study.*"; "II. *The Several Branches of Law: Their Character, Content, Inter-relationship and Community.*"; "III. *Public Law: Its Actual Origins and Development.* (1)"; "IV. *Public Law: Its Actual Origins and Development.* (2)"; "V. *Chief Steps in the Constitutional History of France.*"; "VI, VII. *Sources of Public Law*"; "VIII. *Written Constitutions.*"; "IX, X. *The State as the Source of Law.*"

Loose sheets (WP, DLC).

Revised Notes for a Course in Public Law

[c. Sept. 15, 1890–c. Dec. 1, 1892]

Contents:
    (a) WWT with some WWhw and WWsh notes for lectures on the following topics, with composition dates when given: "*Introductory:*

Place and Significance of Law as a University Study."; "II. *The Sevei oa Branches of Law: Their Character, Content, Inter-relationship, and Community.*"; "*Topics of the Course*"; "I. *Public Law: Its Actual Origins and Development.*"; "I. *Its Actual Origins and Development* (2).*"; "I. Its Actual Origins and Development.* (3).*"; "II. *The Several Sources of Public Law.*"; "III. *Written Constitutions*: Documentary History of Public Law in Typical Instances."; "IV. *The State Itself as a Source of Law.*"; "SOVEREIGNTY: Its History."; "SOVEREIGNTY: Its Nature. (*The Unitary State*)"; "5. *First of the Federal State:*"; "VI. *Organs of Sovereignty*: I. *The Head of the State.*"; "*The Actual Administration*"; "*Law and Ordinance.*" (Dec. 2, 1890); "*The Organs of Sovereignty. II. The Law-making Body.*" (Dec. 12, 1890); "*The Organs of Sovereignty. III. The Courts*" (Jan. 14 and 19, 1891). The foregoing all contain emendations made in 1892-93, when Wilson used them for a second time.

(b) WWT notes for topic, "*Law and Ordinance.*" (c. Dec. 1, 1892).

Loose sheets (WP, DLC).

From Frank Mason North[1]

My dear Professor: Middletown, Conn. Sept. 15th 1890.

You were so kind in making the second long trip to our summer hospital that it has been on my mind both to thank you and tell you that Eric is slowly convalescing.[2] We brought him home on Monday after you called and he is still in bed or in arms—though the fever was apparently conquered ten days ago. We are greatly relieved about him though typhoid is so treacherous that we are not yet free from anxiety.

It was a strange ending to our vacation.

Please assure Mrs. Wilson that it was one of our disappointments that we were unable to return your kind call—or rather that we were unable to put you in our debt by calling first as we had fully intended to do.

I sincerely hope your work will open to your mind—if you will pardon the possible implication in the phrase—and that all your economics—domestic as well as political may be satisfactory. We shall miss you greatly here. Your place in our thoughts is a warm & comfortable one and we have no desire to put anyone else in it. Our satisfaction in knowing Mrs. Wilson and yourself is entirely non-professional and absolutely uncollegiate. We deeply regret on our own account that we shall not have you while we continue here.

It would add to our pleasure & mitigate our regret if we might believe that the future holds for us some opportunities for the ripening of our relation into more genuine friendship. We hope Princeton will not rob us altogether of your thought and interest.

P U B L I C   L A W.

Introductory:

Place and Significance of Law as a University
   Study.

I. Law is everywhere else being made a University
   study, and must become such in the United
   States.
       Princeton plans: to make it an academic topic,
   as part of a philosophical study of society.

2. Law usually made an exclusively technical study,
   wheras, properly conceived, it is a study in
   political science.
       That is, of the new, historical, political
   science, not of the old, speculative, a priori political science. Speculation has its
   effect upon Law, but it is not itself a direct source of Law. Law is derived from concrete conditions. (Law, says Thorold Rogers,
   "is a practical condition of social life")

3. This preeminently an age of social questions,
   most of which lie within the domain of political economy. They lie also, however, (if Lav-
   eleye's definition of P. E. be accepted), indirectly within the domain of Law.
       "Social questions" are within the sphere of
   social dynamics, whereas law studies are studies in statical conditions: How power, force,
   may be made to serve permanence.
       In so far as social reformers endeavour to
   establish institutions, however, they are bound
   by the conditions of the life of Law: the conditions of its derivation, sanction, and workability.

4. Law is a growth, and the result of growth. It is
   the growth of society recorded in institutions
   and practices.

*The first page of Wilson's revised notes for his course
in public law, typed on his Caligraph*

Mrs. North joins me in the heartiest expressions of goodwill which your own apt pen could possibly set down—for Mrs. Wilson, yourself and the wee Wilsons all.

Yours Faithfully,   F. M. North.

ALS (WP, DLC).

[1] Pastor of the Middletown Methodist Church, 1887-92, whom Wilson had come to know well in the Conversational Club of Middletown. North later achieved prominence in national church affairs, holding, among other positions, the offices of President of the Federal Council of Churches of Christ in America, 1916-20, and of Secretary of the Board of Foreign Missions of the Methodist Episcopal Church, 1912-24. He was also the author of the hymn, "Where Cross the Crowded Ways of Life" (1903).

[2] His son, Eric McCoy North. The "summer hospital" was at or near Sagaponack, Long Island, where the Norths and Wilsons had vacationed in August.

From Joseph Ruggles Wilson

My beloved Woodrow—   Clarksville, Tenn., Sep. 15/90

I have waited to hear of your actual removal to Princeton before writing again. And then I wished to learn something as to our dear Marion's orphaned children,[1] in order to confer with you as touching their welfare. As yet, however, I have learned nothing except that Annie[2] has taken to her home the little Jessie, and that probably an uncle on the Kennedy side[3] would take one of the boys[4] to live with his family somewhere in South Carolina. This would leave two of the children at Batesville with the Longs,[5] about whom I have been vainly hoping that Dr. L. would communicate with me. I presume, however, that he and his wife are having these in their tender keeping, there being enough means left for their support without burdening those kind people. Still, I am in the dark; and when light appears I shall let you know.

My stay here will be continued I suppose until next June. The number in my classes is now too small to make it much more than a farce to maintain this school in their behalf; and I look to a suspension of it at the end of the present collegiate year. There will probably be only *seven* theological students during the coming winter & spring—4 in one class, 3 in another. Of course I cannot reasonably blame myself for this meagre showing. It is due to a number of causes, but especially to the fact that we have here no theological faculty in any true meaning of the latter word; and accordingly those young men who naturally belong to us go to the *real* institutions where the apparatus of instruction is indefinitely [infinitely] more complete; and no one can well find fault with them for their decision—especially as they are offered scholarships such as are entirely beyond our means. I might go on to mention other causes that operate to our damage, but will not bother you therewith.

I hope soon to hear that you are all pleasingly "fixed" in your new home. To that home I send many of my best thoughts, and my most ardent prayers are offered for God's blessing upon the loved ones gathered there. Let me beg of you, my darling son, that you will so arrange your affairs as that overwork may not pull down your constitution and shake the foundations of your health. I know of course that you cannot but fill your time with labors that shall tax your strength. Nevertheless you have a future as well as a present to consult. And I am sure that your own thoughtful wisdom will serve to provide for both, so as to ensure a success which shall not be achieved at the cost of a too-burdened mind and a broken body.

Josie[6] promises well in the discharge of his new duties. He does not get much money, but he is learning to cultivate habits of industry which will stand him in good stead in the days to come. He has not time for close study or large reading; and unhappily he does not as yet see the necessity for great application in such directions. But he will do well as a practical business man one of these days.

Our health is good. I preached yesterday, and found myself as strong as when in my youth.

Love, big & broad, to dearest Ellie, and to yourself my unbounded heart   Your affc   Father

ALS (WP, DLC).
    [1] Joseph Leland, William Blake, Wilson Woodrow, and Jessie (identified more fully in WW to EAW, Aug. 13, 1886, n. 1, Vol. 5), children of A. Ross and Marion Wilson Kennedy, both of whom had died in recent months.
    [2] Woodrow Wilson's sister, Annie Wilson Howe, of Columbia, South Carolina.
    [3] A. Ross Kennedy's brother, John W., President of the Presbyterian College of South Carolina in Clinton, 1888-90.
    [4] Joseph L. Kennedy.
    [5] Dr. and Mrs. Isaac Jasper Long. Dr. Long was president of Arkansas College in Batesville and a brother-in-law of A. Ross Kennedy.
    [6] Joseph R. Wilson, Jr.

From the Minutes of the Princeton Faculty

3 P.M., Wednesday, Sep. 17th 1890.

... *Resolved* That the arrangements of the hours for the Classes in Political Economy be referred to the Committee on the Schedule and Prof. Wilson.

College of New Jersey, "Minutes of the Faculty, 1888-95," bound ledger book (University Archives, NjP).

An Essay[1]

[October 1890–January 1891]

THE ENGLISH CONSTITUTION.

I. GENERAL CHARACTERISTICS.

Take it all in all, the English Constitution must be conceded to be at once the most interesting and the most important in existence, whether for the student of history or for the student of politics. It has certain irresistible claims to pre-eminence. It is by many centuries the oldest among free constitutions. Its history leads the student by slow, orderly, and easily distinguishable stages, out of the antique polity of the Teutonic[2] races, through the complex order of the Middle Ages, to the institutions now everywhere in vogue among advanced nations, as if it had been planned beforehand as an object-lesson in normal political development. And its structure and principles have accordingly become models for the imitation of all who, less privileged in the conditions of growth, have in these latest times felt it needful to have like generous measure of political liberty and to adopt like open and efficient organization of popular power.

It was natural that the Constitution of England should be chosen as a model by European reformers. It is in one sense essentially a European constitution; it differs from other European constitutions chiefly in having been left freer to grow along normal lines than they were. It got its full development before the age of railways and steam navigation brought nations close together despite distances once formidable and seas once dangerous, before there was talk of bridging or tunneling the Channel; there had been water enough, therefore, between it and the Continent to give it leave to be independent and individual in its growth. It was not separated from European influences; these reached it and enriched its life in as great abundance and with as complete potency as could have been desired; but it was separated from European disaster. A sea stood between it and the fell sweep of European wars and revolutions. It sufficed that

[1] This essay, the original manuscript of which does not seem to be extant, was originally printed in four installments. They have been combined here; repetitive editorial headings have been omitted; and Wilson's footnotes, which follow, have been numbered consecutively. For earlier correspondence relating to this essay, see T. L. Flood to WW, April 25 and 30, 1890, Vol. 6.

[2] (Teu-ton'ic.) "Before the political history of Germany began, or a distinct German nation appeared, Germanic races molded the political organizations of the north and west of Europe, and Germanic languages either superseded or modified the speech of the previous inhabitants. Ethnologists sometimes classify the Germanic races under the general name of Teutons, as a main division of the Slavo-Germanic branch of the Aryan or Indo-European family of nations."

England should become a naval power; it was not necessary that she should become a military encampment. Civil war she did not escape; revolutions she did undergo; but she was delivered by nature from that international compulsion which forced France to become a centralized military despotism. The parties which contended for supremacy within her sea borders were not able to get effectual foreign assistance such as every civil war on the Continent showed to be inevitable where impassible natural barriers did not give imperative pause to neighborly jealousy and rivalry. In short, England had the inestimable advantage of being an easily defensible island, and of being privileged, in consequence, to live her own life in her own way.

Accordingly it has been common to say that England had the development which most of the countries of Western Europe might have had, had they been so fortunately protected as she was from outside interference and international exigency. The English people were of the same family stock as the German peoples of the Continent; had much the same blood and habits at the first as the dominant element in France. The race movements of the fifth century, which sent Teutonic races across every frontier of the Roman Empire and everywhere substituted Teutonic for Roman masters, of course put Teutonic institutions everywhere in the place of Roman, and the chief countries of Western Europe received the same infusion of Teutonic politics that England received when conquered by the Angles and Saxons.

It is true that England became an English land much more thoroughly, much more literally, than France became a Frankish land, for the English became the dominant race in Britain numerically, as well as the dominant race in power, as the Franks[3] did not in Gaul. Indeed it was for a long time supposed, by very learned historians, that the earlier inhabitants of Britain had been utterly exterminated by the English, or had retired before them into Scotland and Wales and Ireland, and that all blood was English in England. In Gaul, on the contrary, there was a thorough fusion of races, but hardly an absorption of one by the other. The Gauls[4] of the country which the Franks conquered, moreover, had been thoroughly Romanized; Gaul was dotted with Roman cities, and most of its civil habits were in the

[3] A confederation of German tribes which in the third and fourth centuries crossed into Gaul—now France—and finally in the fifth century wrested it from the Romans.

[4] "It is generally believed that the Gauls, who are undoubtedly a branch of the great Indo-European family, left their Asiatic homes before the dawn of European history and occupied the western regions on the Rhine, Seine, Rhone, and Garonne, Ebro and Tagus, as well as the islands of Britain when the Roman state was still in its infancy."

possession of Roman law. The Franks were not a little changed by their contact with things Roman and things Gallic. The contact of the Teutonic peoples with Rome, indeed, dated from times long preceding the period of their triumph over Rome. They had felt the force of Roman example in many ways before ever they crossed the Rhine, and they came to their conquests already in part prepared to adapt themselves to new conditions. The English, therefore, were in every way much more German than the Franks. They were freer, too, to work out Teutonic institutions on a national scale than were even the peoples who remained in the original German home-land beyond the Rhine; for these were prevented by internecine strife and international jealousy from forming any stable national government at all.

While it is in a general way true, therefore, that the nations of Western Europe started upon their course of development with much the same political institutions and habits that the English had when they made their beginnings in Britain; and while there is a good deal that is plausible in the claim that in adopting English institutions during the present century, these nations have only been importing what they might have had of their own make, had they been set apart on islands like Britain, it is none the less true that some half a thousand years have passed since England and Western Europe were politically near of kin. English institutions were the best to copy; were, indeed, the only free institutions in existence from which to take example; but Europe could not take them into her constitutions as we could here in America, as simply her own institutions developed on a perfected scale. Sir Henry Maine[5] once said that there must be offset against the great service which philology had done for historical and literary scholarship, the serious disservice it had done to the undeveloped races of India, which it had taught to claim kin with the Aryan peoples of Europe. "If of the same stock as the English, why then equal to the English," has been the logic of the awakened Hindoo mind, to the neglect of such differences of habit, and consequently of capacity, as have been produced by a few paltry thousand years of history. The stiff mold of the caste system has not failed to produce forms of character and thought which not all the free exercises of the nineteenth century can quickly change. Nothing but long habit will avail to steady and energize free institutions. You can teach

[5] (1822-1888.) An English jurist. For some years he was professor of civil law at Cambridge, and later professor of jurisprudence at Oxford. He was the author of several works, among which are "Roman Law and Legal Education," "Ancient Law; its Connection with the Early History of Society," and "Lectures on the Early History of Institutions."

a savage in a single day how to use a rifle; but not even a hundred years of persistent practice has taught Frenchmen how to behave in a House of Commons. It has proved dangerous to copy institutions representing radical peculiarities of historical development.

Another danger, besides, hardly less great, has attended all efforts to reproduce features of the English Constitution on foreign soil. All the *made* constitutions of these last hundred and one years of systematic political reform have been *written* constitutions, either summary single documents like our own Federal Constitution or groups of "constitutional" statutes such as France has built her present government upon. They are one and all attempts at a systematic formulation of the principles and methods of government which they seek to establish. And to formulate English institutions, or any part of them, in this summary fashion, is to interpret English history; for the English Constitution is not written. It is scattered up and down English legal history, in some half dozen documents unlike each other in character and sanction, formulated at different and widely separated periods, products, therefore, of quite dissimilar occasions and to be read in as many different historical lights. More than that, the constituent parts of this singular Constitution lie scattered throughout English parliamentary practice, as well as among the several chief documents of English legal history; and that parliamentary practice has never in its most important parts taken the form of statutes. The English Constitution without much inaccuracy might be described as consisting (1) of the liberties which Englishmen have established their right to exercise, and to most of which they have, at one time or another, given the formal expression and sanction of written law, and (2) of the methods of conducting the government which in course of time have been established under the dictation of Parliament, the representative legislature of the kingdom.

Such a body of occasional law and accumulated (if not even yet accumulating) custom, it is very manifestly difficult, if not impossible, to formulate, to codify. And yet any one who nowadays undertakes to copy English institutions must undertake to codify them, and must run all the complicated risk of misinterpreting them. He must attempt to photograph *tendencies* and give complete and formal application to still growing principles. That is what the framers of our Federal Constitution attempted; and that is what the constitution-makers of Europe also undertook. Of course our own constructive statesmen had a great and inestimable advantage over those who ventured like tasks of construction in Europe. Our people were English. They had all the English experience in self-government, all the English habit of liberty and self-possession in the exercise of power. The convention of 1787 stood throughout most of its work on the safe ground of our own colonial practice in politics. It was generalizing from English experience in government and codifying English institutions; but English institutions were our own institutions, and the convention was handling familiar stuff. It is noteworthy, moreover, that even this assembly of English men, bred in English politics, fell into one or two radical misinterpretations of English practice at just those points where that practice had not been made vivid and real to their minds by colonial experiment. So difficult is it to codify and appropriate the experience of somebody else!

And, of course, the difficulties which beset the task of formulating English institutions for use in Europe were tenfold greater. No European people had shared English experience; no European statesman was capable of thinking easily or correctly in the terms of English political principle. No transplantation could be successful until a soil of political habit had been prepared such as England had. Stimulating and instructive, therefore, as English principles of liberty and self-government have been to the people of Europe, they have as yet proved rather too strong drink, have often acted as intoxicants where they were intended to serve as tonics merely. So closely does the English manner of conducting government inhere in the particular experiences of English history that to generalize from it is in almost all cases to misunderstand it. The English Constitution is not a constitution which has been reasoned out, but one which has been wrought out by living. It is just as much a thing of accommodation and widely-observant experience as are the manners of good society.

It is much in point, therefore, and much to our present purpose, to observe that these very circumstances make the study of the English Constitution an undertaking of no little difficulty. We are in the same case with those who would codify English institutions for their own uses. We have some of the advantages of the framers of our federal constitutions, for we are Americans, and our own institutions are at almost every point closely like the English institutions, from which, of course, they were derived. But we have not all of the advantage which our constitution-making convention had. It was *making* a constitution and its members were privileged to depart from their model where they would, whether from mistake or from design. We, on the contrary, must see to it that we understand what they misunderstood, see what they did not see in the English Constitution; for our only business is to understand it, to see it as it is. And, unfortunately for us, some of the very parts of that constitution of which our political forefathers did not clearly discern the real character, and of which we have had no experience, therefore, because we have had no copy of our own, are the very parts which have now come to be most prominent and important in English political life. We are assisted to their comprehension by the unfailing interest with which Americans read English political news, and have read it ever since the Revolution, hardly less than before; but we are not assisted by any similar experiences of our own.

The English Constitution, as of course follows from what I have already said of its peculiar development, is hardly separable at any point from English history. It cannot be understood at all except in the light of how it came to be what it is. A man's traits are interesting often when you cannot at all account for them, but they are comprehensible only when you know how he came by them. It is interesting to observe this characteristic fact about the growth of English institutions, that it is seldom possible to say exactly at what period any single feature of them came into existence. To those who have "no memory for dates" it is extremely gratifying to find that, previous to the present century at any rate, the English Constitution has had no exact dates. Its growth by date may be said to have begun with the Reform bill of 1832. This almost insensible development from age to age, this slow accommodation to circumstance in place of formal statutory amendment, has meant, of course, great flexibility. Whatever right Englishmen have proved stout enough to assert and stand by until it was established in the law of the land, whatever method or power in dealing with ministers or sanctioning legislation the House of Commons has successfully forced into acceptance as a binding precedent, that has become a part of the English Constitution.

To those who look at it now, that constitution, though not a little irregular in many points of detail, seems a symmetrical structure enough, with its all-powerful legislature, its planning, responsible ministry, its ancient and dignified throne and aristocracy, and its several agencies of government proceeding forth from these. And yet much of the development which has given it these apparently balanced parts with their nice theoretical co-ordination has been a quite unconscious development. There was no planning for symmetry in it, no deliberate purpose to have a balanced adjustment of parts. For English capacity in politics has been an eminently practical capacity, a capacity for systematic action in politics rather than for systematic thought about it. In this the English have been like the Romans, the other ruling race of history. They have never been "thorough" in making changes, but have reconstructed institutions piece-meal, by slow and partial modifications, not abolishing out of hand parts that had become useless or cumbersome, but letting them slowly fall into disuse or decay and drop away from the Constitution in their own time. This is practical sagacity. No state can safely develop by revolution. You can acquire speed in thought, but not speed in the change of habit; and the use of institutions is a thing of the common habit. Institutions cannot be worked out simply by being thought out, cannot be invented or enacted. They must gain a hold upon the national habit slowly and by parts, by a process of conservative experiment.

II. HISTORY.

The history of the English Constitution, as has already been said, begins with primitive Teutonic institutions. Of the character of these we have no detailed information. Caesar, in a few compact sentences of his Commentaries, sums up what he had learned from the Gauls of the institutions of the German tribes; Tacitus, writing a century and half later, gives a much fuller, though generalized, account of the life and government of the Germans, who were much better known in his time than in Caesar's; we have the accounts of much later writers like Bede and Nithard[6] of the knowledge current in their day of Saxon institutions; we have codes of law possessed by Teutonic peoples in times near enough the century in which the Angles and Saxons conquered Britain to render it safe to search them for fragments and suggestions of a polity still more antique. Viewed in the light of such sources of information, it is plain that the Teutonic peoples that conquered Britain in the fifth and sixth centuries, had been organized in their home-lands into more or less distinct and independent tribes, often co-operating, sometimes confederated, conscious of kinship, and gradually suffering themselves to be forced into some sort of coalescence or consolidation by pressure from without or by common efforts of conquest; but still separately organized, in some points differently organized, and maintaining each its virtual independence.

Each tribe, when maintaining a life of its own, possessed its distinct domain, its own broad clearings, round about which the country was laid waste, to hold all rival neighbors at arm's length.

6 (Ne-tar.) (790-853.) A French historian; the grandson of Charlemagne.

The characteristic unit of organization within the tribe was the village community, a settlement, doubtless, of a group of kinsmen or of closely related families whose lands were cultivated in accordance with the customary rules of some equitable system of apportionment, as common property allotted for certain periods to individual freemen for their separate use. Each village had its own assembly, through which the land allotments were effected, local by-laws passed, and all strictly communal administrative affairs attended to. But, although thus freely self-governed in small things touching only its own interests, it was in all larger matters subject to the authority of the tribe. Some tribes had kings, others had none; and even where there were kings the kingly office was one of more dignity than power. The king, of course, took precedence of all others in dignity; he presided in the general council, for he represented the unity of the tribe; he received special gifts, and was distinguished by a special retinue. But, whether there were a king in the tribe or not, authority rested with the great tribal council. This consisted of all the free men of the tribe, gathered, with their arms in their hands, in the open air at some sacred rendezvous. It elected the magistrates, or chiefs, who were to preside over the administration of the several villages and other divisions of the tribal domain. It chose the king himself, as the tribe's general representative head. It made sovereign decision of all great questions. Trivial matters of mere administration were determined by the elected chiefs of the several districts, acting as a sort of national board; and to this board belonged also the function of preparing the business which was to come before the council itself.

For judicial purposes, the villages were combined into areas larger than the single villages,—areas which the Latin writers call *pagi* and which resemble the later "hundreds" which we shall find in England. For each of these districts a court sat, whose president was one of the local magistrates elected by the tribal council and in which committees of the whole body of free landowners of the district served as judges and jurors combined. In such courts, made up of the representative free villagers, were all important disputes between man and man adjudged, all crimes declared and punished.

We have here, certainly, a very attractive type of free constitution. It shows us a manly, self-reliant race, observant of individual equality and independence, combining for common purposes without subserviency to a central power, possessing an easy capacity of informal and yet efficient combination, wedded to communal self-government and yet conscious of tribal unity and subordinated in all major interests to tribal authority, singularly cohesive and yet notably free.

Free and democratic as was the primitive Teutonic constitution it early developed germs of change which were to give it a character of a very different sort. The village assembly, the district court, the tribal council, were all bodies of free men and spoke a direct democratic power. But not every one was free even in those primitive communities. There were those who, though not slaves, were not their own masters but were bound to the soil which they cultivated, forced tenants, so to say, bound to their holdings and obliged to turn over to the masters of the soil a fixed proportion of its produce. Below this half servile class, again, were numbers of veritable slaves, prisoners of war or men condemned for debt or crime.

Nor were all free men equal in social status or privilege. Some were *eorls*, distinguished by reason of descent from god or hero or by reason of special service to the tribe; others were *ceorls* merely, simple freemen, of the rank and file of freedom. The *eorl* received more land in the allotment than did the *ceorl* and probably commanded the services of a larger number of the half servile class by which the land was tilled. It was doubtless generally an *eorl* who was picked out by the tribal assembly to exercise magisterial authority in the village or to preside over the courts. Although thus privileged and distinguished, however, in virtue of his noble blood, the *eorl* was not more free than the *ceorl*. His privileges were vouchsafed him by custom and election only, and his political rights were no whit greater than those of the humblest *ceorl*. His precedence was honorary, like that of the king. Whoever was elected by the tribal assembly, however, to be chief magistrate of his village, president of his neighborhood court, at once attained to privileges of very substantial advantage. He could maintain his *comitatus*, his household of personal followers. It was the habit of the young men of the tribe to attach themselves to such chiefs as their personal following, apprentices in arms and in the public service. The relationship thus established was exceedingly close and intimate. The members of a *comitatus* entered the household of their leader, ate at his board, did him household service. He fitted them out for the field of battle, where they were at once defenders of his person and rivals of his prowess in arms. Their adhesion to him was voluntary; the chief of most liberality and repute had the largest *comitatus*, and herein was the germ of an ascendency which needed only opportunity to overwhelm the democratic principle of the older polity.

When the tribal assembly declared war it also elected a commander of the host and gave him authority for the campaign. Commonly, no doubt, the man chosen was already a chief, the trusted leader of a numerous *comitatus*. His election to supreme command would naturally swell his following and increase his opportunity for influence and power. Similar elections picked out the leaders who were to head organized expeditions for plunder or in search of new settlements. Hengest and Horsa the notable chiefs of the great expedition which represents for us the beginning of the conquest of Britain by the tribes which were to make it English land, we may regard as just such leaders, men of first repute in arms, of tested courage and unfailing resources, of quick, unhesitating, unerring initiative, and therefore chosen leaders, followed with devoted ardor, heeded with trustful obedience, and yet fellows among the men of their host, not masters.

But conquest quickened many momentous tendencies and inaugurated a profound transformation of the entire polity of the conquerers. The authority of the leaders could not be taken away so soon as the first struggle for a foothold on the island was over: it was necessary that it should continue undiminished in order that the work of conquest might be extended and made good. The invaders were for a long time an encamped host in the new land, not peaceful settlers privileged to resume their wonted practices of simple communal self-rule. Their leaders were virtual kings from the first; they established kingdoms, not commonwealths, in Britain; and the polity which they founded there has ever since been crowned by a throne.

The change was not sudden, but gradual, no doubt at the time imperceptible. Every freeman of the host received his share, of course, of the land he had helped to win, and the old forms of settlement and government were very faithfully continued. The territory was divided upon the basis of the immemorial division of the host into hundreds,—to every hundred warriors and their families so great a district; and this districting of the land among the hundreds served to reproduce the old judicial system. The districts themselves came to be called "hundreds," and for each hundred there was a court to try all cases whether civil or criminal. Within the hundred, as its constituent parts, were "townships," in whose organization and functions the primitive self-governing village-community re-appears. Each township had its own town *moot*, or meeting, and its own elected magistrate, the reeve, and was in all things of local concern self-directed, a wee democratic commonwealth. Its priest, its reeve, and four men selected in town-meeting represented it in the membership of the hundred court. Above and combining township and hundred was the great *folkmoot*, the assembly of the kingdom to which all freemen were at liberty to go, in which every freeman was at liberty to vote.

This is unquestionably the old Saxon constitution over again; but it is that constitution with a difference. The royal and aristocratic elements are beginning to assert themselves. In the old home lands in Germany it used to be true that to hold land was simply a badge of freedom: every free man was sure of his allotment because he was free; now, on the contrary, the rule is being turned about: no man is free unless he has land, and some are left, or are likely to be left, landless. For, although some of the newly acquired land is held in common and is subject to allotment, much of it is held separately and permanently, and those who are noble and powerful have obtained much more than has fallen to the simple *ceorl*. The leader, he who has become permanent king of his people, has naturally obtained most and by bestowing lands upon his *comitatus* is creating a superior rank of nobles out of his personal following. For rank and its privileges are now beginning to go with land. The time is approaching when the mere possession of land will confer rank, when the *ceorl* who can get his five "hides" of land (six hundred acres, in our measure) will be reckoned no longer a *ceorl* but a noble, a *thegn* (thane).

The word "thegn" meant servant. Such was the frank title which was finally assumed by all who attached themselves to any man as his *comitatus*. There were thegns who served the king, and thegns who served the *eorls*, or *ealdormen*, as they were called in England. And every man who could boast such a following rewarded his thegns with gifts of land. There came to be a recognized and invariable connection, therefore, between thegnhood and the possession of land. No thegn could maintain his dignity, moreover, it was thought, with less than six hundred acres of land, a full five "hides." More than that, the possession of land became hereditary, and with the land passed the titles to which it gave consideration; so that presently it came about that thegnhood lost its once invariable association with personal service and became simply a concomitant of land-ownership. Whoever could obtain possession of five hides of land could assume the title of thegn. The thegn was the prototype of the country gentleman, "the squire." The idea of a landed aristocracy is rooted fully twelve centuries deep in English politics.

Along with these developments of rank there went radical changes in the whole system of society also. Gifts of land made by the king or by some lesser magnate only bound the thegn so much the closer to his lord from whose hands the gift had come. The land was given upon condition of continued fealty and service, and society in no long time came to have lines of personal dependence running through it in all directions, and from the highest to the lowest ranks. The lord owed his thegn protection in return for service; the thegn, in his turn, owed protection to and received service from less persons who held land of him: wherever a relation of tenure was established, there a relationship of personal dependence was established also. The principle was not slow to grow up that "every man must have his lord." If a man, though free, was landless and thus without a lord, he was without protection, was to all intents and purposes an outlaw; he must "commend" himself, that is, *submit* himself to some lord, and so fall into some recognized place in the new order of things. This new order is what we know as the *Feudal System*. It was radically unlike the old democratic order and threatened to destroy it altogether.

Meanwhile the national parts of the English Constitution were growing, and these were destined after a while to give to the old principles of popular self-rule a new life and potency. When the Angles and Jutes and Saxons first made their settlements in Britain they established, not one kingdom, of course, but a group of small kingdoms. To these the Danes afterward added others. The great problem of the early centuries of English history, as everybody knows, was how to make out of these several separate and hostile powers a single national whole. Before the Normans came, in 1066, that problem had been solved: England had been united and needed only the compulsion and the organizing skill of the greater kings of the new foreign line, like William the Conqueror and Henry II., to give to her life and her politics a veritable national unity. Each petty Saxon or Anglian kingdom had had its *folkmoot*; when the several kingdoms were united there sprang into existence, as the council of the united realm, a great *Witenagemot*. The constituent kingdoms, many of which became the modern shires of England, retained their own councils, but these were presided over by ealdormen, chosen by the Witenagemot and by sheriffs who were deputies of the king. The Witenagemot (whose name signifies a meeting of the *Witan*, wise) consisted, possibly, in theory at least, of all the possessors of freehold land who chose to attend, after the model of the folkmoot of the smaller kingdoms; but, as a matter of fact, it was attended only by "the king, the ealdormen, or governors of shires, the king's thegns, the bishops, abbots, and generally the *principes* and *sapientes*[7] of the kingdom," who often made up a body of from ninety to a hundred members. Ecclesiastical members had been very early admitted to such councils. The church, with its uniform and centralized organization, unbroken by any line of division between kingdom and kingdom, had been England's first pattern of unity. Churchmen had become extensive landholders, and the bishop as well as the ealdorman had his thegns. Bishops and abbots were in reality of the nobility, as well as of the hierarchy of the church. The bishops were even associated with the ealdorman and the sheriff in the presidency of the *shiremoots*.

The powers of the Witenagemot were very great in theory, and in the presence of a weak or complaisant king very great, no doubt, in practice also. The old principle was persistently maintained that the king must owe his throne to election, and sometimes the election was more than a form. There were grants to be made from the public lands; there were great offices, like that of ealdorman, to be filled; there were taxes to be levied, high crimes and misdemeanors to be tried, disputes among the greater nobles to be adjudged; there was law to be created, and in all these things the advice of the Witenagemot carried more or less imperative weight. The king, however, grew more and more powerful; the common lands, once known as folk land, gradually came to be known as *crown* lands; such great offices as did not become hereditary were filled generally as the king would; in most matters the Witenagemot had only a power of sanction instead of a power of determination; still it did not become a mere shadow, and it was in the fullness of time to grow into a parliament.

When the Normans came they changed the substance of many things but they preserved the old forms. William wished to seem to come to the throne by lawful succession and submitted to the form of election by the Witenagemot. He hastened and completed the feudalization which already had gone so far, establishing the principle that every man held his land of the king; and by wholesale confiscation of the estates of all Englishmen who seriously resisted the establishment of his rule he filled the chief holdings with Normans. The council he drew about him, therefore, and in which he doubtless sought to preserve the organization of the Witenagemot, was a council of Norman barons and of the chief officers of the Norman court, more like a continental gathering of great feudatories than like the Saxon body which it had displaced. This Council, however, whether we see in it a continuation of the Witenagemot or not, is in one sense the most

[7] The chief men and the wise men.

interesting and important body of English constitutional history. It contained within itself, in germ at least, all the chief parts of the present English Constitution. From it were to spring, in course of time, the Courts of Law, Parliament, and the Cabinet of Ministers which directs the business of Parliament and is the responsible executive body of the modern realm, the modern empire of England.

An outline of this evolution may be briefly given. Although the custom of summoning the Great Council, as we must now call the successor to the Witenagemot, continued to be observed reign after reign, it was manifestly impossible, on grounds of convenience, that so large and miscellaneous a body should be frequently summoned or made to serve as an ordinary council to give advice upon the daily conduct of the public business. It very naturally came to be the practice of the king to consult upon such matters those members of the Great Council who were constantly near his person, the thegns and officials of the court. These advisers were constantly accessible, not only, but were also, of course, familiarly acquainted with the greater part of the affairs to be decided. There sprang up thus, almost inevitably, an inner circle of councilors, a smaller Permanent Council. Scarcely had this Permanent Council come into existence, moreover, when again naturally and in obedience to the dictates of convenience, a further specialization of functions began. Some members of the Council were assigned specially to business connected with the finances; others were given separate charge of the judicial determination of cases coming up to the king for decision; and the several high officers of the Royal Household began to be associated with these several committees according as their functions were of the one kind or the other. It was in this way that the courts of law as we know them sprang into existence. At first very much resembling committees of the Permanent Council, they gradually acquired a complete separateness from that body and a complete independence of it, having a membership peculiarly their own and a jurisdiction much enlarged beyond that of the body to which they had once belonged. They were, moreover, separate from and independent of one another. A Court of King's Bench followed the king wherever he went within the kingdom, hearing all cases not specially assigned to other tribunals and supervising the local administration of justice; a Court of Common Pleas heard all suits between subject and subject; a Court of Exchequer all suits in which the Crown was directly interested, and a Court of Chancery supplied all with remedies for whom the other courts had no means of redress.

The Cabinet of Ministers was evolved out of the Permanent Council in a very similar manner. Even the Permanent Council proved to be inconveniently large for frequent consultation; some of its members, moreover, enjoyed the king's confidence in a higher degree than did others and were often selected by him as his advisers in affairs of special secrecy or importance. He thus, by slow, almost insensible, accretions of practice, drew about him still another "inner circle"—this time an inner circle of the Permanent Council, not of the Great Council—which was in course of time distinguished as the Privy Council. The Permanent Council as a council thus disappears, superseded on the several sides of its activity by its parts. Nor was that the end of the differentiation process. The same forces that created within the Permanent Council a Privy Council produced within the Privy Council a Cabinet which in course of time has absorbed all executive function and left the greater body from which it was derived without any thing to do which it as a whole can insist upon doing. The Cabinet, like the Privy Council, was at first simply a small body of persons selected by the sovereign for special confidences out of the general body of his accredited counselors. Its name came to it because of the fact that this committee of special advisers was generally closeted with the king in a small room, or "cabinet," apart from the large chamber in which sat the Council itself. To this day, although the Privy Council, which still exists in name, is never called together as a whole or consulted in any matter, the Cabinet in theory owes its authority in executive matters to the fact that its members are members also of the Privy Council.

None of these developments took place suddenly or abruptly, of course, but in the slowness of time. The differentiation and development of the courts began early in the twelfth century and were not complete till the middle of the fourteenth. The Privy Council does not emerge from the Permanent Council until about the middle of the fifteenth century (time of Henry VI.). The Cabinet comes very slowly into view. It does not assume definite shape before the reign of Charles I., does not assume its present functions before the time of Sir Robert Walpole,[8] and has not attained its present organization and importance or been subjected to its present complete responsibility to Parliament before the close of our own revolution. It was the Cabinet as a link between the Crown and the legislature that our constitution-

---

[8] See [James Richard Joy] "Outline History of England" [New York, 1890], page 274.

makers did not understand when they copied the English Constitution in the Convention of 1787.

Meanwhile the Great Council from whose history we turned to trace the development of the Permanent and Privy Councils and of the Courts of Law, had had its own growth, its own changes of composition and character, and that enlargement of sphere and power which were to make it over into the modern Parliament. The Great Council was at first, so to say, all House of Lords; there were no commoners in it, but only the earls and the greater barons, and the high officials of state and church; and this constitution of the national body was suffered to suffice for more than a century. Then, however, a distinct effort was made to bring the rest of the nation into representation in it. The barons made John promise in Magna Charta (A. D. 1215) that he would summon the lesser nobles, as well as the greater, to his parliaments; but the lesser barons would not come; they were not interested enough, and it was too expensive. Representation was resorted to, therefore. The county courts (the successors of the old shiremoots) elected representatives from the county gentry to go up as "Knights of the Shire" and attend Parliament. In 1265 Simon of Montfort, having temporarily triumphed over Henry III. and assumed control of the government, summoned Parliament and directed that representatives (burgesses) be sent from the towns as well as from the counties, because he knew that the towns-people would support him. Edward I. continued the arrangement because he wanted representatives of the towns to be present in Parliament to promise him taxes. It was in this way, not at all deliberately planned beforehand, that Parliament obtained the present elements of its membership. At first the lesser clergy also were privileged to send representatives to Parliament, but the privilege was not much or long used. The clergy preferred to sit apart in their own separate "convocations" and there vote the taxes they were called upon to contribute. Only the bishops retained their place in Parliament.

The evolution of the part played by Parliament in legislation is both curious and interesting. In the early days the laws were said to be enacted by the sovereign with consent of his Great Council. It is still, indeed, the form in England to regard the Crown as the source of law and to describe Parliament, not as making, but as assenting to legislation, although it has now been a very long time since this form corresponded with the facts. At first it did correspond with the facts fairly well; it came to be an established principle that all laws which the king proposed should be sanctioned by the lay and ecclesiastical magnates of the kingdom gathered in the Great Council. And when the representatives of the counties and towns were called to Parliament they were not at once put upon a footing of equality with the bishops and barons in this great function. It was not until the fourteenth century that two separate Houses were developed, a House of Lords and a House of Commons. During a long transitional period the several classes of members, new and old, would seem to have sat together. Probably, however, they did not vote as a single body; and not even after their differentiation into two Houses were the knights and burgesses who composed the Commons participants in law-making. It was still for a long time the Lords, and the Lords only, who assented to laws. The Commons only assented to taxation and petitioned for such laws as they desired to see enacted. In due course, however, the power of the Commons increased, for they could withhold taxes till their wishes were heeded; and English constitutional history became a history of the rise of the Commons to that pre-eminence of power in the state which has made it the most influential legislative body in the world.

The stages of the rise of the Commons to pre-eminence of power in the state are well enough marked. Petitions for legislation could be made effective by withholding grants of money to the Crown, and were well enough when heeded in good faith; but it very often happened that after a petition had been favorably answered by the king and a grant of taxes voted, the legislation, actually drawn up in accordance with it and promulgated in the name of the king and lords, differed in essential points from that which had been asked and promised. Statutes were even sometimes collusively changed in phraseology by the judges whose duty it was to transcribe them into the statute-book. Aroused at length by such frauds, the Commons again used their money-grant weapon and forced the Crown to accede to the demand that their petitions should be carried out without change or addition, and the statutes thus framed accurately transcribed by the judges. Still, however, they had no real control over the matter; the statutes were promulgated after their money votes had been passed.

It was necessary to occupy and hold a still more advanced position. The Commons, therefore, demanded that no statute should be passed without consent of the whole Parliament, the Commons included; and, after a struggle, gained what they demanded, as usual. Only two more steps and the omnipotence of Parliament, together with the full participation of the Commons in that omnipotence, would be fully established. As a still further security against fraudulent practices by the judges in transmuting petitions into formal statute by transcription into the statute-book, the practice was established of submitting proposed laws to Parliament in the form of bills, in the form, that is, which it was proposed they should retain when made into statutes by vote of Parliament, so that Parliament might examine even the phraseology which the law was to wear, and, if it chose, change it until it was to its mind before giving it a vote of sanction.

These steps had all been taken by the end of the fifteenth century. The final step was taken in the celebrated Bill of Rights, whose date is 1689. The Tudors and Stuarts had assumed great and arbitrary powers as toward the laws. So old a writer as Bracton[9] had said that it was part of the Constitution of England that the king himself should be subject to the laws. But the more arbitrary monarchs had claimed the right to suspend what laws they chose (the right of *dispensation*, it was called) and their pretensions in this matter were given additional color by the fact that the Reformation in England had made the king head of the church in the place of the pope, and had thus made him apparent successor to the pretended right of the pope to dispense with obedience to human law. But after James II. had been thrust out, in 1688, Parliament gave an imperative and final negative to all that. No law, said the Bill of Rights, can be either suspended or in any way changed except by the same authority as that which enacted it. It had taken a long while to establish the principle, but henceforth Parliament was omnipotent.

III. THE HOUSE OF COMMONS.

The Revolution of 1688, as we have seen, finally established the supremacy of Parliament. It is evident to any one who considers the details, or even the general features, of the long process by which this result was brought about, that what had been growing all the while was the power and influence of the Commons rather than of the House of Lords. It was the Lower House that had all along forced the fighting and won the victories. Indeed, the fighting was at first as much against the exclusive privileges of the Lords in law-making as against the power of the Crown. The Commons began by forcing its way to a place of equality beside the Upper House and then straightway proceeded to use its power to gain complete ascendancy over that House and become itself to all intents and purposes the whole of Parliament.

[9] Henry D., Lord Chief Justice of England in the time of Henry III. He was the earliest writer on English law, his work being the famous book "Concerning the Laws and Customs of England." He died about 1270.

It was from the first equipped with a power which was in the long run always irresistible. It represented the great body of the tax-payers and could withhold supplies from the government. It was necessary to keep it always in a good humor; and it was in a good humor only so long as its power was growing. Sunderland, when minister of William III., showed that eye for essential fact and commanding tendency which marks the statesman, by advising the new sovereign brought from over seas, to recognize the Commons as the vital member, the active partner, in Parliament, and choose his ministers from the party which had the majority in that House. William took the advice, and so set in motion by a single practical act one of those slow revolutions so characteristic of English constitutional history.

The English Cabinet Ministers are now always chosen from the majority in the House of Commons, whether that majority consist of the adherents of a single political party, or of one party and a wing of another combined, as at present. If defeated, that is outvoted, upon any important matter, they must resign their offices and give place to others who shall represent the new majority. The old weapon of the Commons was *impeachment*. When they did not like the course taken by a minister they accused him of "high crimes and misdemeanors" and he was tried by the House of Lords, the inheritor of the judicial prerogatives of the Great Council from which it directly, the Commons only by adoption, is descended. It was this great and formal process of impeachment that fixed the attention of our constitution-makers in 1787 and was borrowed by them to be put among our own constitutional machinery, to be used, if necessary, even upon the head of the state, as it could not be used in England. They did not perceive that the new and less drastic way of controlling ministers was to outvote them in Parliament, after making it necessary for them to act always through Parliament.

This new kind of responsibility of the Ministers to the Commons, like every thing else in English constitutional practice, came slowly into existence, and in coming, brought with it no great revolution in the character of the government. The government of England was never, except for one or two comparatively short periods (for example, during the reigns of William the Conqueror, Henry II., Henry VIII., and Elizabeth) a veritable monarchy. It has rather been, during much the greater part of its history, an aristocracy whose characteristic part was the House of Lords. It kept this character during the whole of the last and the early part of the present century in spite of the fact that the House of Commons had become its characteristic organ, because the Crown and the Lords in a very mischievous way controlled the composition of the Lower House, were able, that is, to dictate who should be elected to it.

It was determined in the reign of Henry VI., in the first half of the fifteenth century, that no one in the counties should vote for the county members of Parliament (the knights of the shires) who did not possess a freehold estate worth forty shillings a year; forty shillings were worth then as much as eighty pounds ($400) would be now, so that the qualification was put pretty high. But it remained the same till the present century, and the shilling meantime declined very greatly in value; so that the qualification became liberal enough, and the county members were real representatives, no doubt, of a considerable, certainly of a respectable, body of voters. But with a great many of the borough members the facts stood very different. They represented nobody but a few influential noblemen. The franchise was determined in most of the towns by their charters, which were of mediæval dates and patterns, liberal enough, perhaps, for the times in which they were drawn up, but not liberal enough for the times which were to follow. They generally vested all privilege in certain mediæval classes or associations whose membership became very much narrowed as the mediæval system of town life passed away, until the choice of members of Parliament, like all other municipal functions, was restricted at last to a very few persons, easily to be gotten at and influenced.

Many of the parliamentary towns, moreover, decayed and almost passed away, when modern industrial influences began to draw population away from the south of England to the manufacturing middle and western counties; for the statutes which bestow the parliamentary franchise, bestow it upon particular places, not upon the principle that it is to be retained so long as those places remain entitled to it by virtue of possessing a certain population, but to be retained until withdrawn. A few towns, therefore, like the celebrated borough of Old Sarum,[10] actually passed out of existence without losing their right to send members to Parliament. These and others greatly decayed became so-called "pocket boroughs," their franchise being virtually pocketed by the lords and the country gentlemen who owned the

[10] This extinct city of Wiltshire, two miles north of Salisbury, was, during the times of the early Britons, of the Roman occupation, and of the West-Saxons, a most important place. King Alfred made it a bishop's see in the eleventh century; but the cathedral was removed in the reign of Henry III., and the place, in time, became utterly deserted. There remains of it now only the ruins of its walls, castle, and cathedral. The proprietor holding the estate, however, had the right of sending two members to the House of Commons, after the borough had lost all of its inhabitants.

estates covering or contiguous to them. The towns which sprang
into existence in the middle and western counties, moreover the
great commercial marts like Liverpool and great manufacturing
centers like Manchester and Birmingham, meantime remained
without representation in the Commons.

So far as the borough franchise was concerned, it began to
look as if, not the people of England at all, but only influential
individuals and petty, close corporations were to be represented
in legislation. It is said that four hundred and twenty-five out of
the six hundred and fifty-eight members which the House of
Commons contained in 1801 were returned "on the nomination
or on the recommendation of two hundred and fifty-two patrons,"
and that "three hundred and nine out of the five hundred and
thirteen members belonging to England and Wales owed their
election to the nomination either of the treasury or of one hundred and sixty-two powerful individuals." In short, a majority of
the members of the Lower House were nominees either of the
government, the ministry of the day, or of members of the landed
aristocracy. No wonder patriots in America got so little sympathy,
so few concessions, from Parliament! The English government
was then, not a government by the House of Commons but a government by the Crown and the Lords through the House of
Commons.

It had become very clear to every man of public spirit before
the end of the last century that such a system needed immediate
and thorough reform. But just as that reform was about to be
undertaken, the French Revolution came; and that Revolution
seemed to all who were timid, an object-lesson in the terrible
risks of systematic constitutional reform. The conservative classes
everywhere took fright. England kept still and held her breath;
entrusted her government to all sorts of safe commonplace men;
enjoyed reaction for a full generation, nay longer, and tried to
forget parliamentary reform. But the disfranchised classes refused to let her forget it, and in 1832 she had to begin to make
the Commons really representative. The "rotten," decayed boroughs were disfranchised, representation was given to the new
towns which had sprung into importance, and the franchise was
everywhere extended so as to include at least the middle, well-to-
do classes, the small traders, and the substantial tenants of town
and country. In 1867 another re-distribution of seats and widening of the franchise took place, and in 1884-85 still another. As
the law stands now, the franchise, though still based upon a
property qualification, is very liberal; indeed, it could hardly be
extended further without being made "universal." Every person,

whether resident in a county or in a borough, who is a house-holder, and every lodger whose lodgings cost him ten pounds ($50) annually, is entitled to vote for members of Parliament.

Such reforms, in making the House of Commons really representative of the nation, made it also unquestionably the predominant power in the state. Its will is now conclusive, irresistible. The assent of the House of Lords to all laws is as necessary to their validity now as it ever was; but the House of Lords would now no longer dare withhold its assent to any measure about which the House of Commons had clearly made up its mind. The House of Commons governs England, and the ministers are its servants.

The House of Commons has six hundred and seventy members, of whom four hundred and ninety-five represent England and Wales, one hundred and three Ireland, and seventy-two Scotland. It sits in a beautiful but not spacious chamber of oblong shape which is devoted entirely to legislative business and debate. The members are not provided with chairs and writing desks, as the members of our legislative bodies are; they must do their writing in a comfortable reading room near at hand. In the House itself there are only cushioned benches, running the length of the hall, four rows, or tiers, rising one above another on each side of a wide central aisle. The main doors to the House open at one end of this aisle; at the other end of the aisle which they face, rises the canopied seat of the speaker, below and in front of which are the seats and tables of the clerks and a broad table running some distance down the aisle, holding among other things, the boxes in which petitions are put and the great mace which is the symbol of the speaker's authority. Above the speaker's chair is the gallery set apart for reporters; opposite his seat is a gallery reserved for special classes of visitors; on either hand are the galleries which, the speaker's permission being obtained, any one may enter.

The benches of the House are not of sufficient sitting capacity to accommodate all the members; when they crowd into it to hear a great debate or to be ready for a critical vote many must stand, some are even forced to find places in the galleries. But, inasmuch as a full attendance is exceptional, it has been thought better to keep the House small enough for business than to make it large enough for comfort and convenience.

After all, the real use of it is, not to seat the members, but to sift and discuss the public business. The purpose of having a hall is to secure debate, not to furnish a place to sit or vote simply; and the most efficient and fruitful discussion, oftentimes, is that which is informal and conversational, such as would be impossible in an immense chamber. If you are really going to understand the public business and subject it to a thorough talking over, you must be content to sit close to your fellow-members and make it possible for commonplace men with untrained voices, as well as for the great orators, to express their opinions easily and audibly.

When members are in their places they sit in party groups. The party which is in the majority sits on the benches which rise to the Speaker's right, the minority on the benches opposite. There is a still further classification, also, always more or less formally and consciously observed. Narrow aisles, or "gangways" as they are called in the House, divide the rows of benches on either side into two sections. The Ministers sit on the front bench immediately to the Speaker's right, having the long table that holds the mace and the petition-boxes before them; and on the front benches just opposite to them sit the recognized leaders of the "Opposition," that is, the minority. Directly behind the Ministers usually sit their stanchest supporters, the men who can be counted on to speak and vote as they do; while directly behind the leaders of the minority opposite, sit the like "thick-and-thin" party men of the Opposition.

All these are "above," that is to say on the Speaker's side, of the gangways. Below the gangways on either side sit those who hold themselves more or less at liberty to vote against their party, in accordance with their own independent interests or opinions. Most of the Irish members, for example, now that the Conservatives are in office, sit on the benches below the gangway on the Liberal side of the House. With this key to the usual arrangements, the marshaling of the party hosts for parliamentary battle is easily understood.

IV. THE CABINET.

Most of the legislation considered is contained in bills framed and brought in by the Ministers, who are now virtually responsible both for legislative measures and for the conduct of executive business. The Ministers, rather than the sovereign, constitute the Executive. The negative, or veto, of the Crown upon legislations has fallen entirely into disuse; or, rather, to speak with greater historical correctness, the real initiative of the Crown itself in legislation no longer exists. It is still the theory of legislation in England that laws originate with the Crown, whether or not upon the petition or suggestion of Parliament, and are assented to or negatived by the Houses. This places the *veto*, if there can be said to be any such thing in English constitutional law, in the hands of Parliament rather than in the hands of the monarch. But the monarch acts through his Ministers, and it is now incumbent upon him, by virtue of a practice nearly two hundred years old, to choose his Ministers from the majority in the House of Commons, and Ministers so chosen will not submit to Parliament any measures which they know to be displeasing to the party they represent. Should they propose any measure and be defeated, moreover, they cannot insist upon it, but must resign. This is explanation enough of the fact that the will of the sovereign has not been pressed upon Parliament in matters of legislation these two hundred years. This is what is meant when it is said that the Crown no longer exercises its right of veto. The ministers are practically "the Crown," and of course "the Crown" does not negative what it itself proposes.

The Ministers, I have said, must resign if defeated upon any important measure in the Commons; but they need not resign without "an appeal to the country." The legal term of each House of Commons is seven years. It may well happen that a House elected in 1885 is not in sympathy with the majority of the voters in 1890. If the Ministers lose their majority, therefore, if, that is, they are outvoted in a House of Commons which began its life by giving them its favor and support, and they think that opinion "out-of-doors," that is, among the voters, is on their side, they may advise the sovereign to "dissolve" the House and order a new election. This the Crown has a perfect right to do, and is constrained by precedent to do whenever the Ministers advise it. If the majority of the new House is favorable to the Ministers, they stay in office, and feel bolstered up by a direct "verdict of the country"; if the majority of the new House be against them, they of course resign, and new Ministers are chosen from the new majority. The defeated Ministers and their party change sides in the House and become the "Opposition."

The subordination of the Ministers to the Commons is, therefore, very complete. They must submit all financial matters to it, get its sanction for all schemes of revenue, its specific votes for all expenditures of money; they are expected to see all needs for legislation, to propose measures suited to meet them, and to stand or fall according as those measures are carried or lost in the Commons. At the same time it would be radically erroneous to say that the action of the Executive is wholly subjected in England to the will of the popular House of Parliament. The Ministers govern an extended empire as well as a central kingdom and many things of the very greatest consequence depend upon their initiative concerning which Parliament cannot possibly insist upon being consulted or heeded beforehand. They may do what they will in the field of foreign affairs and in the administration of such colonies as India without any previous consultation of Parliament whatever, without the knowledge of Parliament, indeed; may negotiate and conclude treaties of whatever import; may increase and use Indian armies and finances; may assume financial obligations,—may commit England to courses of action which may embarrass her for generations. The Commons, of course, may show its displeasure afterward and turn them out of office with a direct vote of want of confidence; but what has been done in such cases generally cannot be undone; the next Cabinet must carry out all the engagements made by its predecessors.

All the prerogatives of the Crown, in brief, are at the disposal of the Ministers, to be employed as they think best, and by no means all of those prerogatives connect themselves with measures which must be submitted to the Houses. There are some matters, indeed, of too delicate a nature to be publicly discussed in Parliament; some plans, particularly of foreign policy, would be simply frustrated by being prematurely disclosed,—prematurely put at the mercy of the Opposition. A certain wide discretion must be allowed the Ministers as to the matters they will make public.

The Cabinet,—the Ministers, that is, chosen from the majority in the Commons and standing responsible to that House for the conduct of the government and the progress and character of legislation,—consists, according to circumstances, usually of from fourteen to sixteen members. These members are always either heads of executive departments or of distinct branches of the public business, executive or judicial. There are eleven officials who are always members of the Cabinet, namely, the First Lord of the Treasury, the Chancellor of the Exchequer, the Lord Chancellor, the Lord President of the Council, the Lord Privy Seal, the five Principal Secretaries of State (for Home Affairs, for Foreign Affairs, for the Colonies, for India, and for War), and the First Lord of the Admiralty. To these are generally added several others, upon the general rule that every interest which is likely to be prominent in the debates and proceedings of the House of Commons ought to have a Minister of Cabinet rank to speak for it and to offer the House responsible advice concerning it. The President of the Board of Trade is often a member of the Cabinet, therefore; sometimes, as at present, the Chief Secretary for Ireland; and frequently the president of the Local Government Board.

V. THE EXECUTIVE DEPARTMENTS.

The English executive departments have been no more symmetrically developed than the other parts of English constitutional machinery; they have come into existence slowly and by pieces, as they were needed. The principal department is that of the Treasury, which is always represented in the Cabinet by two officers, the Chancellor of the Exchequer and the First Lord of the Treasury. The First Lord is the nominal head of the department; the Chancellor of the Exchequer the real, the working head. The office of First Lord almost always is assumed by the leading minister, the Prime Minister, who, by occupying an office having none but nominal executive duties connected with it, is left free for the arduous and delicate task of leading his party in the Commons. The Chancellor of the Exchequer submits the budget[11] to Parliament and is in all things the Finance Minister.

There are five great Offices of State, whose development furnishes the best possible illustration of the manner in which institutional growth has taken place in England. There was, to begin with, a single Principal Secretary of State, who, first, served the sovereign in any matter of special secrecy or importance, then had specific duties assigned him, and finally had so much to do that it became necessary to double him and have another Principal Secretary of State. This multiplication of the office, which is still in theory a single office, went on until there were five Principal Secretaries of State, and virtually, of course, five great Offices of State: the Home Office, which superintends the police and the local magistrates of the kingdom, advises the sovereign with reference to the granting of pardons to criminals, administers certain statutes regulating the employment of labor, etc.; the Foreign Office, which has charge of foreign relations and corresponds to our Department of State; the Colonial Office, to which go all questions affecting any of the colonies except India, for the oversight of whose administration there is a special India Office; and the War Office, which directs the discipline, equipment, and use of the army. The naval department is called the Admiralty and is administered by a commission of six, consisting of a chairman, bearing the title of First Lord of the Admiralty, and five Junior Lords. All statutes concerning commercial matters, the oversight of railways, the inspection of passenger steam-

[11] The annual financial statement which gives the House of Commons a general view of the national income and expenditure, the taxes and salaries. The word is derived from the French word *bougette*, a bag; and this use of it arose from the custom of bringing in a leathern bag the reports of these different matters into the House, where the *budget* was opened. The name of the receptacle soon came to be applied to its contents.

ers and merchant vessels, the maintenance of harbors and lighthouses, the regulation of pilotage, the providing of standard weights and measures, the coining of money, are executed by the Board of Trade, which is a board only in name, being conducted by a President. The Post-Office, also, is a subdivision of the Board of Trade. The administration "of laws relating to the public health, the relief of the poor," and the multitudinous and important affairs of local government is supervised by the Local Government Board, which, although in name a board, is not such in reality, but, like the Board of Trade, may be said to consist of a President.

Scotch affairs are represented in Parliament by a Secretary for Scotland, Irish affairs by an official whose full title is Chief Secretary to the Lord Lieutenant, "who, though in titular rank a subordinate of the Lord Lieutenant, is by virtue of his relations to the Cabinet and to Parliament, in effect his master." The Lord Chancellor is both a legislative and a judicial functionary, presiding over the sessions of the House of Lords and acting as the chief officer also of the system of courts, which I shall presently describe. There are other executive offices; but these are the chief, and will serve as a type of the rest.

All the heads of these departments, even the Lord Chancellor, who is not in strictness an executive officer at all, go out of office with a defeated ministry. The method of reconstituting the executive upon such an event is interesting and characteristic of the system by which the ministers are made responsible to Parliament. When a Cabinet resigns, the sovereign sends for the leader of the Opposition and directs him to form a ministry. There is generally no difficulty at all in determining who is the leader; there is almost always some one man who, by sheer force in statesmanship and debate, has pushed his way to the front of his party in all parliamentary battles and won recognition as unquestionably the man upon whose initiative his party waits. Such a man, being summoned to form a ministry, first consults representative men of his party in the Commons, and then, acting upon the results of that consultation, nominates leading men among his party associates for the vacant executive offices. These the sovereign appoints as a matter of course, and a new ministry takes its place on the front bench to the Speaker's right in the Commons, or in the corresponding seats of authority in the Lords. Lords as well as Commoners become ministers, of course, though precedent always assigns the chief financial office, the Chancellorship of the Exchequer, to a member of the Commons.

VI. THE SOVEREIGN.

What place remains for the sovereign in a system which assigns the control of the government to a Ministry which must obey the House of Commons? A place, not of command, but of great influence and weight—a weight proportioned to character and intellectual endowment. The sovereign is a permanent minister, unaffected by parliamentary votes, yet in a position to insist upon being consulted in all affairs of weight; in a position, too, to become uncommonly acquainted with the public business in its continuity; identified with the dignity and credit of the nation as a whole; under no necessity to be a partisan; and with every opportunity to obtain consideration for every earnest word of advice uttered from such a vantage ground. The sovereign has only to be diligent in business, not slothful in spirit, to become a very potent factor in the conduct of the government.

VII. THE HOUSE OF LORDS.

It was convenient to postpone the consideration of the House of Lords because its legislative functions, not now as important as they once were, are associated with functions which are strictly judicial, and which, therefore, connect it with the courts, which, must be described last in our order of topics.

The House of Lords consisted during the parliamentary session of 1888 of four hundred and seventy-six English hereditary peers (dukes, marquises, earls, viscounts, and barons); the two archbishops (of Canterbury and York) and twenty-four bishops, holding their seats by virtue of their offices; sixteen Scottish "representative peers," elected for the term of Parliament by the whole body of Scotch peers, of whom there are eighty-five; twenty-eight Irish peers, elected by the one hundred and seventy-seven peers of Ireland to sit for life; and three judicial members, known as the Lords of Appeal in Ordinary, sitting, as life peers only, by virtue of their office. It is necessary to specify the session in giving the number of English peers, because that number is by no means fixed, but changes from time to time. Two-thirds of the present peerages[12] of England were created during this century; thirteen

12 The term peer from the Latin *par*, equal, was applied originally, in feudal times, to all vassals of the same lord, because all were equally bound to his service. In England at the present time it is used to denote a lord of Parliament, all of whom are known as the king's peers, not because they are equal with him, but because they form his highest court, and because whatever the degree of their nobility, they are all equal in the discharge of official duty, as in their votes in Parliament and in impeachment trials, and all share alike in privileges. The different degrees of nobility in the order of precedence are given in the article. "The two most striking features in the later history of the peerage are the amazing increase in its numbers, and the unreserved admission to its ranks of men of distinction in every honorable employment,—soldiers, lawyers, diplomatists, bankers, tradesmen, manufacturers."

of them were created in the single year 1886. The Crown can create English peerages whenever it chooses, that is, whenever the Ministry chooses; the other elements of membership, however, are fixed by statute and do not change.

Of the legislative function of the House of Lords almost enough has been said already. Although in legal theory upon a footing of perfect equality with the Commons in lawmaking, it does not venture to oppose measures which have a large vote of the Lower House or a pronounced public opinion back of them; and its chief value is as a chamber of revision and as a forum[13] for the speeches of the peers who are prominent in the Government or in Opposition. While its proceedings lack the vigor and excitement which kindle orators in the House of Commons, its leisurely ways of doing business and its quiet atmosphere afford time and appropriate encouragement for very complete and effective speeches, which will have their due effect "out-of-doors." The House of Lords does not control legislation, but it may very sensibly affect it. It is much more important, however, as a judicial tribunal than as a branch of the legislature. It is the supreme court of appeal for England, having never lost the supreme judicial function of the ancient Great Council[14] from which it is directly descended. This function of supreme court it does not, however, any longer exercise as a whole, as a House. It hears all law cases through a committee consisting of the Lord Chancellor and the three Lords of Appeal in Ordinary, who are learned judges appointed life-peers especially to serve in this capacity. So separate in character the House of Lords when acting as a court has become from the House of Lords when acting as a House of Parliament that its sessions as a court can be held at any time, whether Parliament be sitting or not, whereas its sessions as a branch of the legislature can be held only when the Commons also are sitting.

VIII. THE COURTS.

The several law courts evolved out of the Permanent Council[15] retained their separate existence and their separate jurisdictions until 1873. Between 1873 and 1877, however, the judicial system was thoroughly reorganized; or, rather, a system was created where there had been no system. The general courts of the kingdom are now all combined as branches of one Supreme Court of

13 A tribunal or court. This general use of the word is derived from the specific name of the Roman market-place or public square, where causes were tried and orations delivered before the people, the *Forum Romanum*, or Roman Forum.

14 See "Outline History of England," page 85.

15 See *The Chautauquan* for November [1890], page 152.

Judicature, which is divided, however, into two practically distinct and independent parts, a High Court of Justice and a Court of Appeal. The High Court of Justice has its Chancery Division, its Queen's Bench Division, and its Probate, Divorce, and Admiralty Division, and these divisions take the places of the old courts of similar names,—have absorbed the jurisdiction also of the old Courts of Exchequer and of Common Pleas, which have been done away with. The Court of Appeal consists of the Master of the Rolls and five Lord Justices, and of the presiding judges of the three Divisions of the High Court of Justice. Three judges constitute a quorum, and it is the practice to hold the court in two sections, three judges acting in each, thus doubling its working time and capacity. Appeals go from the several Divisions of the High Court to the Court of Appeal, from the Court of Appeal to the House of Lords.

IX. LOCAL GOVERNMENT.

We have been so long discussing the development of Parliament and the courts out of the original English-Norman constitution and in setting forth the present make-up and powers of the Houses and the Executive as almost to have lost sight entirely of those local organs of self-government which are, after all, the most important to the life and vigor of political liberty. We have yet time, perhaps, to take a glance at their history.

As I have said, the old folk-moots became shire-moots, county courts. They were composed of delegates from the townships and the hundreds, and were presided over by the bishop, the ealdorman, and the sheriff. But early in Norman times their character began to undergo a radical transformation. Ecclesiastical jurisdiction was separated from civil, and the bishop retired from the court. The sheriff was the king's officer, and the Norman and Plantagenet kings made him a real servant of the crown, and the ealdorman's importance was completely overshadowed; the county court became the sheriff's court. Then its functions began to slip away from it. The king's justices rode circuit through the counties and drew to themselves the judicial jurisdiction that had given it importance; its financial functions came to be quite independently exercised by the sheriff on his own authority. Then, the sheriff having grown too great to be any longer made easily subservient to the Crown, his powers began to be curtailed. The chief administrative functions of the county passed, with local judicial power, by degrees into the hands of officers known as Justices of the Peace. These officers continued to be the principal governing authorities of the counties until 1889, when, in accordance with the law of 1888, their administrative powers passed to County Councils elected by the tax-payers.

The old township courts gave way before the manor courts of the great feudal estates and the few functions that remained with the people of the manors passed into the hands of the vestry, which was the people of a parish gathered in church meeting.

While these old forms of local government have been falling into decay and disappearing, others have been found to take their place, so that self government has by no means been lost. In matters of general legislation it of course has grown with the power and the representative character of the House of Commons; in matters of local interest it has been secured in the towns and boroughs by statutes which have substituted popular for mediæval charters and given the city councils a truly representative character, and in the counties by an organization modeled upon that of the boroughs.

X. SUMMARY.

The outline I have given of the historical development and the existing organs of the English Constitution, I hope will prove sufficient to display the general features of that singular system of law and precedent. In the main, its foundations are laid in tradition rather than in statute; its strength lies in national habit and the precedents of immemorial practice rather than in the commands of written law. So far as it rests upon written law, its history may be said to begin with the Great Charter which the barons wrung from John in 1215. There had been charters before, but none so specific as this. Henry I. had assented to a charter of liberties; many there were, indeed, who in the days of oppression which followed the Conquest, looked back with longing to the "laws of Edward the Confessor," at whose hands men had received justice and a recognition of their liberties. Those liberties, should habit and tradition be received as authoritative, were as old as English history. But not till John's day did they receive exact and specific enumeration and statement. The charter obtained from John stated at length the rights of Englishmen, "their right to justice, to security of person and property, to good government." It set forth how and where the courts should sit, under what conditions Englishmen should be put in jeopardy of life, liberty, or property. It directed how the Great Council should be constituted, and denied the right of the king to tax without that Council's consent. It abolished abuses and re-constituted orderly government. It may, thus, be said to stand at the center of the first period of constitutional development in

England, not creating new law, but summing up what had gone before, and preparing what was to follow. Among the most noteworthy of the documents which preceded it were the so-called Constitutions of Clarendon (laws passed in the Council at Clarendon, A. D. 1164), in which the supremacy of the Crown over the church, already more than once asserted, was re-established, and the ecclesiastical made subordinate to the civil courts, and the Assize of Clarendon (1166) concerning the organization and action of the civil courts, by which the system of presentment by grand jury, now so central to our administration of criminal justice, was established.

Besides the Great Charter, the most important fundamental documents of English constitutional history are (1) The Petition of Right, presented by Parliament to Charles I. in 1628, in which those rights and liberties are set forth which the Stuarts had wantonly violated and prayer is made that the laws be observed; (2) The Habeas Corpus[16] Act, passed by Parliament in 1679, in which provision is made against the arbitrary imprisonment of any person without speedy trial and legal proof of his guilt; (3) The Bill of Rights, passed in 1689, which summed up as law the rights which James II. and his predecessors had violated, and swept away as illegal all the powers which they had assumed for the purposes of their tyranny; and (4) The Act of Settlement, of 1700, whereby the Roman Catholic branch of the Stuart family was denied succession to the throne, and the Protestant branch of Hanover substituted which was to give England, Anne and the four Georges, William IV. and Victoria. Perhaps there should be added to these great documents the reform bills of the present century (1832, 1867, and 1884) by which the House of Commons has been made the governing power in England by being made the truly representative organ of the constitution.

These documents one and all differ conspicuously from our own constitutional laws in this, that they are either royal ordinances, like Magna Charta, or acts of Parliament, like the Bill of Rights or the laws reforming the system of representation in Parliament. Our own constitutional provisions of like character and importance are invariably contained in documents which have been submitted to a vote of the people, and, by reason of adoption by them, given a specially formal and sacred character. An act passed by Parliament may also be repealed by Parliament;

---

16 "The exact meaning of this Latin expression is 'You are to produce the body.' That is, you, the accuser, are to bring before the judge the body of the accused that he may be tried and receive the award of the court; and you, the accused, are to abide by the award of the judge."

a royal ordinance also may be set aside by statute; our fundamental laws can be altered only under certain conditions and by
special assent of the people to the change. This difference between our constitutional provisions and the laws which under-lie
the English Constitution have seemed to many to render English
institutions unstable as compared with ours. Such an inference,
however, is for the most part false and misleading. Parliament
dare not tamper with any fundamental law which public opinion
regards as sacred, for Parliament is dependent upon public opinion. That opinion is very conservative in matters of fundamental
principle; the constitution is, therefore, very stable, resting upon
the common thought and the common habit as fully and truly
as ours.

This is nowhere more conspicuously evident than in those
parts of the English system which rest wholly upon precedent,
such, for example, as the practices of ministerial responsibility to
the House of Commons. Such parts of the system have proved
quite as lasting and quite as safe from sudden or whimsical
change as have those other parts which rest upon written law,—
quite as stable as our own constitutional provisions. The institutions of any people, if derived from, and carefully adjusted to,
their historical circumstances and character, will be found to
change, in the absence of passionate revolution, as slowly or as
fast as the people themselves and their habits of life and thought.

In one sense the English is the most practical of existing constitutions. So soon as you formulate a constitutional system as a
whole, in a single document or group of related contemporaneous
documents, you subject yourself to certain necessities of logic:
you must prove every subsequent change proposed to be, not incompatible but harmonious and consistent with the symmetry
of the whole. English institutions have enjoyed an incomparable
flexibility and freedom of development because they have not
been subject to this law of theoretical consistency, but have been
put together piece by piece as practical conditions and new needs
have demanded. They have been put together by the forces of
national development, not in accordance with the suggestions of
any abstract logic of political theory.

Printed in *The Chautauquan*, xii (Oct. 1890-Jan. 1891), 5-9, 149-54, 293-98,
and 430-34.

From Stockton Axson

Dear Brother Woodrow: Baltimore, Md.   Oct 3 1890.

Please excuse me for writing with pencil, for I have no ink in the room.

I got your letters for which I am ever so much obliged and should have answered them before, but I have been waiting to try to get something definitely settled. I dont feel that even my boarding house arrangements are yet settled. I met Dr. Warren[1] on the train (the Dr. Warren of the Romance department) and he was exceedingly kind to me and desired to take me at once to his boarding house. I put him off however as I wanted to find out something for myself. The day after I got there he met me again and insisted that I should go and look at the room in his house, which I did. I told him about Miss Ashton's[2] and he frightened me away from there by telling me that she had had trouble with her boys last year and they had all left her. Finding that whatever arrangements I made I should be compelled to be civilized since there are no large student boarding houses here, so far as I can discover, I decided to go with him and am now domiciled at Mrs. Carey's.[3] . . .

Your name has been a passport to me every where. I dont know what I should have done without it. Everyone has been exceedingly kind to me and I hope that the year will be a profitable one. . . . So as I see things now I am inclined in this course—major, English (the literature, philology and all is classed as one study); first minor, German; second minor, English History. What do you think of that course? You see the English History is not only something in which a man made of flesh and blood can feel some little interest, but it is also a thing which will be of great value to me in the study of English *Literature*. In fact it is about the *only* thing in this dreary curriculum which will have any bearing on the real work which I love and hope to be able to do some day. I have been debating between history and philosophy, but think that possibly the history will be the best. Notwithstanding the delightful course which I had under you in American History[4] (and it was certainly one of my most delightful) I wish very much that I could have had your other course, the English History, for I should then have some preparation for something. . . .

I miss you all more than I can say and am already looking forward to the Christmas holidays when I can see you again. I hope the house matters are progressing. Thanking you for the letters and all the world of other things which you have done for me I am with warmest love for all

                Affectionately yours,   Stockton Axson.

Address c/o Johns Hopkins, still.

ALS (WP, DLC) with WWhw notation on env.: "Ans. Oct. 12/90."
    [1] Frederick Morris Warren, Associate in French and German at the Johns Hopkins.
    [2] Mary Jane Ashton, at whose boardinghouse on McCulloh Street Wilson usually stayed while in Baltimore.
    [3] Martha Ward Carey.
    [4] That is, at Wesleyan University, 1889-90.

From Theodore Monroe MacNair[1]

Dear Wilson,   Tōkyō Japan   Oct. 7th 1890

I am very glad to know that you are established in Princeton and I've been intending for a good while to write and tell you so; but I've been kept somehow from doing it until now I have an excellent chance. I want some information and take the liberty of seeking it through you—thus mixing my request with the congratulation to you on your change which, further, gives Princeton the benefit of your not being any longer somewhere else.

I am told that in the library the card system of cataloguing is used (as nearly everywhere now I suppose) and I would like to know about the system in detail. The reason is that I have just become librarian of the college here with upwards of 6000 books to look after and I naturally wish to know how to do the work in the best way. Will you kindly get for me such points as I ought to have and a copy of the various cards, more or fewer, that are necessary to the system. I hope that I shall not greatly inconvenience you. I venture to risk doing so in view of my needs and in spite of my knowing that you are not a man of large leisure.

I have been much interested in reading your book on "The State." I like it so well that I venture on the further liberty of choosing to use it as a text book with my classes. I'm greatly obliged to you for the opportunity.

I hope that the football men are getting into proper shape to repeat last autumn's performances. If, like [Alexander] Johnston your predecessor, you are on speaking terms with the football field, just convey my cordial regards and sympathy to the fellows. I happen to know how painful it is to beat Yale and so can sympathize in advance.[2]

With regards to Magie and Davis[3] (when you see them) and also, if I may send them, to your wife.

I am   Yours Sincerely   Theodore M. MacNair.

ALS (WP, DLC) with WWhw notation on env.: "Ans. 7 Nov/90."

[1] The Rev. Theodore M. MacNair, a member of Wilson's class at Princeton. He was a Presbyterian missionary to Japan until his death in 1915 and taught economics, history, and anthropology at the Meiji Gakuin in Tokyo from 1884 to 1895.

[2] MacNair's exploits as a member of the Princeton football team became legendary. As *Fifty Years of the Class of 'Seventy-Nine* (Princeton, N.J., 1931), p. 48, puts it: "He played three years against Yale ('77, '78 and '79) and never lost a game. The characteristics of his playing were several. He was a mighty kicker, a swift runner, and an 'artful dodger' who puzzled and confused his opponents in a most bewildering fashion. Many regard MacNair as the greatest football player Princeton ever produced."

[3] William Francis Magie, then on the Princeton faculty, and John D. Davis, then teaching at the Princeton Theological Seminary. Both were members of the Class of 1879.

From Annie Wilson Howe

My darling Brother,   Columbia, Oct. 8th 1890

I have wanted to answer your letter before this, but have been so unwell that it seemed impossible to write. I wanted too, to accept your cordial invitation if I could arrange matters so that I could leave home. When I got your letter, Gussie Waltham was with us. She left this morning, and Mr. Craig[1] writes us that he will be here on Friday, to make a short visit. If it were not for Jessie [Kennedy] I could go just as soon as Mr. Craig leaves—but I cannot go without Jessie. She needs so much attention that I do not feel that I ought to leave her to Dr. George.[2] She has just commenced school, and I do not think I ought to take her away. I do want to see you all, more than I can say, and I am not going to say positively that I cannot go—because, I *may* be able to make some arrangement in a week or so, but I am afraid I will have to give it up. Uncle James [Woodrow] says you are all looking well. It must have been very hard for you to manage with your studies before you got into your own home. I hope you are comfortably settled by this time. We can sympathise with you, as we have been in an unsettled state for the past six weeks. The carpenters, painters & paper hangers having possession of most of the house. The painters are still at work, but, as they are outside of the house, we do not mind them much.

I will write again, in a few days, and let you know positively what I am going to do. I think I am better than I was—and hope soon to be myself again. Dr. George unites with me in warmest love to dear Ellie and your dear self. Kiss the children for me. George[3] is at school or he would send some message. Write soon.

Your devoted sister,   Annie.

ALS (WP, DLC).

[1] The Rev. Dr. John Newton Craig, Secretary for Home Missions of the southern Presbyterian Church.

[2] Her husband, Dr. George Howe, Jr. Jessie Kennedy was then eight years old.

[3] Her son, George Howe III.

To Elijah Richardson Craven

My dear Sir,   Princeton, New Jersey, 9 October, 1890

Will you be kind enough to have a copy made and sent to me of the memorandum of the prize in United States history recently established by Mr. Joline of New York.[1] The supply of old catalogues is exhausted; a new catalogue must be issued at once; and the committee is importunate for copy. If you would have the memorandum sent me at an early date, therefore, you would greatly contribute to my peace of mind.

I have entered upon my work here with not a little gratification at being once more in Princeton and in the service of the College; and I already feel at home.

With much regard,
                    Most respectfully Yours,   Woodrow Wilson

ALS (University Archives, NjP).
[1] See A. H. Joline to WW, July 9, 1890, n. 2, Vol. 6.

From Elijah Richardson Craven

My Dear Prof. Wilson: Philadelphia   Oct 11th 1890

The reception of your note this morning drove me, at first, completely to sea—without chart, compass, or rudder. I knew of no prize in *United States* History, & I had never heard the name, *Mr Josline of New York*.[1]

It suddenly struck me, however, that "Mr Joseline" might be "the generous friend of the College" mentioned in the "Regulations concerning the Boudinot Fellowship (or Prize) in History"—& that it had been decided by the Faculty to require the Fellow to direct his attention to *United States* History.

Acting on this supposition I send you a copy of the "Regulations" referred to. If the paper enclosed be not the one you desire I must acknowledge that I am still at sea.

I am pleased to learn that you are pleased with your new position, & that you feel "at home.["] Trusting that all things may continue pleasant, I remain,
                    Truly Your Friend,   E. R. Craven.

ALS (WP, DLC) with WWhw notation on env.: "Ans." Enc.: handwritten memorandum, "Regulations Concerning Boudinot Fellowship in History."
[1] Craven, Clerk of the Board of Trustees of the College of New Jersey, had misread the name of Adrian H. Joline in Wilson's letter. Joline had written to the Board (A. H. Joline to the Board of Trustees, College of New Jersey, June 30, 1890, Trustees' Papers, University Archives, NjP), saying that he wanted to establish a prize in American history. His letter had been received in Princeton and endorsed by Edwin Curtis Osborn, Treasurer of the College. President Patton informed the Board of Joline's gift at its meeting on November 13, 1890.

From Charles Edmund Merrill

Charles E. Merrill & Co.   Publishers

Dear Sir: New York Oct. 13, 1890.

We have thought of publishing a fourth volume of Lalor's Political Cyclopedia, bringing the work down to date. We have in mind a volume about uniform in size and exactly corresponding in style with the other three volumes.[1]

While, as you know, this work has taken very high rank, only a very small part of the money invested in it has ever been returned, or, under the most favorable circumstances, ever can be. One reason for this is that the first volumes cost more than they ought to have done.

Before definitely committing ourselves to the scheme above outlined, we wish to get as nearly an accurate estimate of its cost as possible. We suppose the volume will contain about 800 pages. (We may add that we expect to issue a supplementary volume once in ten years, immediately after each census is available.)

As the successor to Prof. Johnston, we have thought you would be interested in the matter, and that perhaps you would be willing to write the articles on U. S. History, continuing his work down to date.

Will you please let us know whether you are disposed to consider such an undertaking, and if so, what you would charge us per page for your contributions?

Yours truly,   Chas E Merrill

TLS (WP, DLC) with WWhw notation on env.: "Ans., (No) 17 Oct./90."
[1] John Joseph Lalor (ed.), *Cyclopaedia of Political Science, Political Economy, and of the Political History of the United States* (3 vols., Chicago, 1881-84). Apparently Merrill never published a fourth volume, for a three-volume edition appeared in 1888-90 and again as late as 1904.

From John Bates Clark[1]

Dear Professor Wilson   Northampton, Mass.   Oct. 14 1890

We are delighted that you can come.[2] The meeting is on Monday about the middle of Nov. I will send exact date. I want to have you spend Sunday and Monday with me here, if you can do it. The meeting is at Springfield. Come if possible on Saturday and give me the little visit.

Yours Very Truly   J. B. Clark

ALS (WP, DLC) with WWhw notation on env.: "Ans. (Yes) 17 Oct./90."
[1] At this time Professor of Political Science and History at Smith College.
[2] Clark refers to Wilson's acceptance of an invitation, presumably made by Clark personally while visiting Wilson in Princeton, to address the Connecticut Valley Economic Association.

From Stockton Axson

Dear Brother Woodrow: Baltimore, Md. Oct 15/90

I have been trying for a week to get a chance to write to you but somehow when I am in my room I have so much to do and do it so slowly that it is almost impossible to get any time for writing.

In regard to my curriculum: I am taking only English and German this year. I gave my name to the history department for a minor in history but upon examining my schedule I find that the three things will give me seventeen hours a week of work and I am strongly advised not to take more than twelve. The professors say that it is impossible to do justice to my work when I have seventeen hours of it. So I now have thirteen hours with the two studies.

I shant say now how I feel about my course here and its prospects for I am entirely too blue over it to dwell on the subject yet awhile. I have just put aside my German books after spending three steady hours in preparing one third of tomorrow's recitation.

My professors are Drs. Bright and Learned[1] (fortunate names for college professors). Of course it is too soon yet for me to form any just opinion of them, but certainly merely as *lecturers* I have heard better; their candles burn feebly before, at least, three of the men whom I sat under at Wesleyan. I have great hopes however that I am going to get a good deal in time from Dr. Learned. He realizes that there is such a thing in the world as *literature* and I should say, though of course I am a poor judge, that he knows German Literature very thoroughly. Dr. Bright is only a scientist and that in the strictly modern sense— *not* as Novalis[2] was.

To my surprise I find that there is quite a number of students in the English department. They say it grows larger every year.

I am still at Mrs Carey's where where [*sic*] I shall have to stay now until Christmas, at least. In the mean-time Harrison[3] has gotten a room-mate. The fare at his house is really not bad—plain but wholesome and abundant.

It is very pleasant here at Mrs Carey's however. I never see anybody except at the table and then it is a very jolly crowd. . . .

Almost everyone whom I meet asks most kindly about you. I know that it would gratify you, and Sister even more, to hear their pleasant remarks about you. With warmest love for all

Affectionately yours   Stockton Axson.

ALS (WP, DLC) with WWhw notation on env.: "Ans. 26 Oct./90."
    [1] James Wilson Bright, Associate in English, and Marion Dexter Learned, Associate in German.

2 Pseudonym of Friedrich Leopold, Freiherr von Hardenberg (1772-1801), a poet and theorist of the Romantic period.

3 Thomas Perrin Harrison, Fellow in English, to whom Axson had referred in an unpublished portion of his letter to Wilson of October 3, 1890.

From John Bates Clark

Dear Professor Wilson   Northampton, Mass.   Oct. 18 1890

I am delighted that you can come on Saturday. The public is invited but a small part of it comes to our meetings. The dependence is mainly the members of the Conn. Valley Branch. I hope we may get a selected representation of outsiders. There is a hesitation about accepting our invitation on the part of men who do not pay a fee; hence the small attendance. What there is will be of the best. We ought to have fifty people. The papers give wide currency to the chief points in the discussion and they do much good.   Yours Very Truly   J. B. Clark

ALS (WP, DLC).

From the Minutes of the Princeton Faculty

5 5' P.M., Friday, Oct. 24, 1890.

. . . Profs. Young,[1] Marquand[2] and Wilson were constituted the Committee on the Senior Class.[3]

1 Charles Augustus Young, Professor of Astronomy.

2 Allan Marquand. Born New York City, Dec. 10, 1853, son of Henry Gurdon Marquand, a wealthy New York banker and patron of art. A.B., College of New Jersey, 1874. Studied at Princeton Theological Seminary and at Union Theological Seminary in New York. Studied philosophy at the University of Berlin, 1877-78, and at the Johns Hopkins, 1878-80, where he received his Ph.D. in 1880. He spent his entire academic career at Princeton as Tutor in Latin and Lecturer on Logic, 1881-83; Professor of Archaeology and the History of Art, 1883-1905; Professor of Art and Archaeology, 1905-24; and Director of the Museum of Historic Art at Princeton, 1890-1921. Died Sept. 24, 1924.

3 An *ad hoc* committee appointed to consider the protests of seniors, set off when certain members of the senior class were ousted from their customary seats in Marquand Chapel at "chapel stage" speaking (about which, see Vol. I, p. 220, n. 1) and forced to sit with the sophomores. The special committee quickly restored the dispossessed seniors to their rightful places. See *The Princetonian*, xv (Oct. 27, 1890), [2].

From Annie Wilson Howe

My darling Brother,   Columbia, S. C.   Oct. 24th 1890

Mr. Craig has gone, and Joe Kennedy, who came just after Mr. Craig left, has gone, but I find it is impossible for me to get off. I have tried in every way to arrange matters, so that I could make you a little visit. I want to see you all *so* much, and think the trip would do me good. If it were not for Jessie I could have gone on with Mr. Craig, as far as Washington. Dr. George thinks it would not do for me to take Jessie. She requires so much of my time and attention—and there is no one to leave her with. I would as soon ask *Mrs. Girardeau*[1] to take her, as to ask Marion Woodrow.[2] So I will have to put off my visit to you. It is a dreadful disappointment to me. It was very sweet in you to give me such an urgent invitation—and I had set my heart on accepting it. . . .

Both Georges join me in warmest love to you both, and kisses for the babies.   Your devoted sister,   Annie.

ALS (WP, DLC) with WWhw notation on env.: "Ans. 2 Nov./90."
  [1] The wife of the Rev. Dr. John Lafayette Girardeau, a professor at the Columbia Theological Seminary and an old antagonist of Joseph Ruggles Wilson.
  [2] Daughter of Dr. James Woodrow.

From Joseph Ruggles Wilson

My precious son: Clarksville, Octr 25/90
    I am hoping that letter-writing is not about to become a lost virtue so far as we are concerned. It *is* a virtue I suppose, as may be proven by one of virtue's characteristic sign: a thing hard to practise; at least to bring to perfection. Certainly even love itself, which is usually so ready with its affirmations, never feels like lagging except when urged to make up for its epistolary deficiencies: and here its ingenuity in inventing excuses is something phenomenal. Indeed it now and then shamelessly lies, in the endeavor to cover up its conscious delinquencies—although the lie is as easily detected as the falling of night. But do not accuse me of falsehood, I pray you, when I say that I have not written to my darling Woodrow for many weeks, simply and alone for the reason that I did not wish to put him to the pains of answering my letter whilst he was in the midst of the discomforting hurries of his new beginnings in his new home. This is the precise fact. So that if you send me no reciprocating words—until you are quite at leisure, be this ever so far off—I shall not complain. Indeed my trust in your affection is too firmly fixed to be shaken by any supposable possibility: it is a part of my creed, and is insusceptible of revision, God be thanked. All the same, my dear one, your letters, when they do come, serve to brighten my life to an extent you might hardly credit.
    Your last communication I have thought over, long and deeply. I allude especially to the expression of your fear as touching the possibility of my quitting the position I am now holding—the fear

that I should suffer from lack of congenial employment. No doubt this is a rational apprehension, and I know not how to shake it off my mind. Yet—yet—it cannot be long before the crisis must come. It is every day becoming more and more probable that circumstances will compel my removal from this place, whether I shall wish it or not. For the certainty gets plainer that this divinity school cannot continue much longer. A scheme is being inaugurated—has indeed taken definite shape—a scheme for establishing a theological seminary at Louisville, under the direction of the Synod of Kentucky and with the sympathetic help of some of the very Synods which are at present the sources of our chief patronage here.[1] Next fall this new enterprise is to be set practically afoot. And if we of this college do not fall in with it—as we have been invited to do—it will all the same go forward without us: and the competition, already so formidable everywhere about us, could not long be successfully resisted, or resisted at all. All this is not a mere *scare*, such as ought not to frighten thoughtful and earnest men. It is a substantial reality. Of course I could still stay on where I am, teaching, with what heart I might, a few students who would possibly come to us in any event. But *ought* I to do so, merely for the sake of maintaining a school that is not needed, or of enjoying a salary which I must reluctantly and mortifyingly demand?—and until I should be respectfully asked to vacate?

Besides I am longing for that rest which at my time of life is well-nigh imperative, and which whilst health measurably remains I would so keenly prize, if indeed it might be that sort of *active* rest which would consist in writing, and perhaps preaching where opportunity would present an opening, as it must do in some centre of population. I constantly pray for direction to Him in whose hand are all my ways, and to whose will I shall in all things patiently submit.

Josie is getting on with his work as a co-editor—making very little money but acquiring experience, such as may help to lift him higher. He is in love, and this hinders him a good deal— for much of his time is spent with his Kate whom he thinks is the foremost of her sex, and who is in fact quite a fine girl I believe. He sends love to you all, & much of it.

You will have noticed that your Uncle James Woodrow is again in the midst of a contention. The Charleston Presbytery has refused to receive him upon his letter from Presby[y] of Augusta[2]—for reasons contained in the enclosed resolutions which you may not have seen.[3] I regret this exceedingly, both on his account and of [on] the church's. What asses Presbyterians are capable of becoming—whose ears extend to all the earth!

But I must close and go to bed. I send love unbounded both to yourself and to dearest Ellie.

Your affectionate   Father

ALS (WP, DLC) with WWhw notation on env.: "Ans. 1 Dec./'90."

¹ Southwestern Presbyterian University, organized in 1874 on the foundation of Stewart College of Clarksville by the Synods of Alabama, Arkansas, Memphis, Nashville, Mississippi, and Texas, had established a Theological School in 1885, with Dr. Wilson as its head. The Synod of Kentucky had refused to support the enterprise. For later developments in this matter, see JRW to WW, Nov. 7, 1891, n. 2.

² Charleston Presbytery, meeting at Allendale, South Carolina, from October 7 through October 9, 1890, considered the letter of the Presbytery of Augusta dismissing Dr. Woodrow to Charleston Presbytery. The examination of Dr. Woodrow, conducted by the Rev. Dr. Robert Alexander Webb, pastor of Westminster Presbyterian Church of Charleston, continued from October 8 through October 9. At the conclusion of the examination, Dr. Webb moved that Charleston Presbytery decline Dr. Woodrow's application for membership because his life had become too secularized for the ministry and because he had "seriously reflected upon the honor, the sincerity, and veracity of this body" in his weekly newspaper, the *Southern Presbyterian* of Columbia. The motion carried by a vote of seventeen to six. "Records of Charleston Presbytery. Beginning October 1889. Ending November 1899," bound minute book (NcMHi). See also the Charleston *News and Courier*, Oct. 11, 1890, and the Columbia *Southern Presbyterian*, Oct. 23, 1890.

Through his old friend and supporter, the Rev. Dr. J. William Flinn of Columbia, Dr. Woodrow asked the Synod of South Carolina, which met at Yorkville (now York) on October 21, 1890, to reverse Charleston Presbytery's verdict. The Synod rejected the appeal by a vote of ninety to fifty-two. Columbia *Southern Presbyterian*, Oct. 30, 1890.

This was only one incident in Dr. Woodrow's long fight for moral vindication after his removal as the Perkins Professor of Natural Science in Connection with Revelation at the Columbia Theological Seminary. For a good summary of this controversy, see Clement Eaton, "Professor James Woodrow and the Freedom of Teaching in the South," *Journal of Southern History*, XXVIII (Feb. 1962), 3-17.

³ The enclosure was an undated clipping printing Dr. Webb's motion.

From Adrian Hoffman Joline

My Dear Sir: New York, Oct. 25 1890.

I have yours of the 24 inst. The subject of the prize was formulated by Professor [Theodore Whitefield] Hunt. He very kindly put it in proper shape, and I supposed that in a letter which, at his suggestion, I addressed to the Trustees,¹ I had sufficiently stated the purpose. That letter ought to be in the possession of some one connected with the college. I will try to recall the exact form of the proposition—and will, if you wish, forward it to President Patton—only, having once written on the subject, it makes me appear rather ridiculous to be writing again.

With regard to a subject for the essay, I should prefer to leave it entirely with you, knowing your familiarity with the field. I am willing however to make suggestions—but please consider them only as suggestions, not to be followed if you think of something more calculated to attract or interest.

The Origin and Growth of Political Parties in the U. S.

Development of the Judicial Department of the Federal Government—1787-1820.

The Jay Treaty—& its History.

The Diplomatic Relations of the U. S. with England & France under the Admst of Adams.

The X. Y. Z. Letters & Edmund Randolph.

The Annexation of Louisiana & its Consequences

The Financial History of the Administration of Washington.

The Organization & Development of the Executive Departments of the Government.

The Kentucky & Virginia Resolutions of 1798-9.

The Embargo of Jefferson's Administration.

The Genesis & Development of the Republican or Strict Construction Party.

The History of Federalism & the Federalists.

The Alien & Sedition Laws.

Some of these topics are of course trivial in comparison with others. I think however, something could be done with them by anyone who would care to try.

Yrs very truly   Adrian H Joline

ALS (WP, DLC).
1 See E. R. Craven to WW, Oct. 11, 1890, n. 1.

From Joseph R. Wilson, Jr.

My dearest Brother: C'ville, Tenn., Oct. 26th 1890.

Possibly I should not feel so, but I do feel just a wee bit hurt at not receiving any answer to my last letter for I told you therein of a matter of such vital importance to me and about which I wanted your sympathy. My engagement to Kate gives me much real happiness, and I want those who are nearest and dearest to me to feel happy with me. Last Wednesday evening I put the finishing touch on the affair by calling on Kate's father. He gave me perfect satisfaction in the matter, and now we consider it all settled. Father knows all and seems satisfied. Kate's folks evidently like me quite well and, as Mr. Wilson told me, consider me as one of the family—and Kate and I love each other "muchly" and after prayerful consideration feel that with each other in a home of our own we will be perfectly happy and well contented. We do not expect to make our future home in Clarksville for here no opportunity is given me of advancing in my profession. Brother, you are more or less influential with some of the largest publishers in the country. Could you help me to rise in my profession? I want to become connected with some big journal. Cannot you give me some advice on the subject? Please do if you can. You see I must hurry now and win the prize I am striving for. To do this I must call upon my influential kin people for without such a support comparatively little can be done you know.

Father and I are both suffering with colds—he with a cold in his sholder which he calls rheumatism—and I with a cold in my head which bothers me considerably as I have to bend over my office desk and write so much. We will both be well shortly, however, I hope.

Love unbounded from us both to you all. Please write to me as soon as you conveniently can, dear brother.

Your aff. bro.   Joseph.

ALS (WP, DLC) with WWhw notation on env.: "Ans. 2 Nov./90."

From Stockton Axson

Dear Brother Woodrow: [Baltimore, c. Oct. 28, 1890]

... I appreciate your letter, which I received yesterday afternoon, so much. I shall not allow myself to be utterly discouraged but it is hard to keep from it in the Seminary and Journal meetings.[1] I dont believe that you have any conception of the dullness of the transactions there. Certainly I never had. Without exaggeration the work of the German critics, of which I read a little last year, is piquant and luminous—almost lucid in comparison with the work of the Hopkins students in English.

My best love for all. I have been intending for a fortnight to write to Sister, but somehow I havent.

Affectionately yours   Stockton Axson.

ALS (WP, DLC) with WWhw notation on env.: "Ans. 2 Nov./90."
  [1] "The Seminary," the English Department's section in the Hopkins catalogue explained, "is divided into two branches, the Seminary proper and a Journal Meeting. This division affords the double advantage of restriction and of freedom. In the Seminary proper, attention is given to the continuous study and investigation of a definite subject or a group of related subjects for a more or less extended period of time. The end in view is minute accuracy and scholarly completeness within the selected domain. Each student takes part in the investigation. On the other hand, a stimulus to more extended study is furnished by the Journal Meeting. The primary purpose of this meeting is the presentation of reports, by the instructors and the students, on the current scientific and literary periodicals and other recent publications relating to English." The Johns Hopkins University, *Register for 1890-91* (Baltimore, 1891), p. 76.

To Elijah Richardson Craven

My dear Sir, Princeton, N. Jersey., 29 October, 1890

The prize to which I referred in my last letter to you was one which Mr. Adrian H Joline, of New York, wishes to establish in U. S. History,—a prize of $50.00 for the best essay written by a Senior on some topic in American History between the dates 1789 and 1825. When I heard that you had no note of it, I wrote to Mr. Joline requesting that he would formulate a statement of the prize and send it to Dr. Patton, that it might get into the Catalogue through the regular official channels as soon as might be. He replies that he wrote a *letter* stating his purposes touching the prize "to the Trustees"; and now I come back to you quite bewildered. I find that Dr. Patton knew nothing about it either.

I was put in correspondence with Mr. Joline last summer by Prof. Hunt, to whom he had first communicated his design of offering the prize; but I know very little more than I have stated.

I hope that you will pardon my troubling you further about the matter. I do so in the (forlorn) hope that you may not have recollected Mr. Joline's letter to the Trustees and because Mr. Joline is evidently just a little piqued that he should have been asked to formulate the prize again. If you do not recollect his letter, I will try to make out a statement myself for the Catalogue, with Prof. Hunt's assistance

Respectfully and Faithfully Yours, Woodrow Wilson

ALS (University Archives, NjP).

From Thomas Alexander Hoyt

My dear Woodrow— Phila Oct. 29, 1890.

Your Aunt Saidie[1] has returned & we are at home again.

We hope you & Ellie will come to see us soon.

Saidie & I will run over to see you & Ellie some day before long, provided you are established.

I have tied up the books for you—Schlosser's 18th Century, & will forward them—8 vols.[2]

I am gratified to hear of the sensation you have created at Princeton.[3] Mr. Wm. Brenton Greene, whose family live there told me yesterday that your Lectures excite great enthusiasm among the students.

Give my love to dear Ellie—I wrote her some time since. Kiss the Babies for me. All send love to all.

Sincerely yours—T. A. H.

ALI (WP, DLC) with WWhw notation on env.: "Ans. 2 Nov./90."

1 Mrs. Thomas A. Hoyt.

2 Friedrich Christoph Schlosser, *History of the Eighteenth Century and of the Nineteenth till the Overthrow of the French Empire*, trans. by David Davison (8 vols., London, 1843-50). This work is in the Wilson Library, DLC.

3 Dr. Hoyt was referring to the sensation caused by the enrollment of 146 students (out of a total of 238 juniors and seniors in the Academic Department) in Wilson's junior-senior elective course on public law—a fact noted by *The Princetonian*, xv (October 13, 1890), [3], and the *Princeton Press*, October 18, 1890.

Notes for a Talk[1]

[c. Oct. 30, 1890]

These, *simplifying texts.*

> With a single postulate (that *God is maker and ruler*) they furnish a *scientific* basis for life. ("Hitch your wagon to a star")—Conemaugh Jane[2]
>
> But it is something *more than a science*—it is a *philosophy* of life that we seek. "Honesty *is* the best policy," but it can have no stable existence if it be *merely* a policy. What is politic seems to vary—what is righteous stands fast.
>
> These texts mean *the cultivation of character*—of permanent motives and frames of mind.
>
> The *first text equivalent*, upon analysis, to the second: "Fear God"—be sensitive regarding his judgments—have a moral regard for him, and ∴ keep his commandments, *because* this is "the whole of man"
> Seek the kingdom of God and his righteousness
> It is *character*, not mind, *that loves truth.*

WWhw MS. (WP, DLC).

1 These notes, although undated, seem to have been the ones that Wilson used for the talk reported in the news item printed at Nov. 1, 1890.

2 A cue for an anecdote.

From Elijah Richardson Craven

My Dear Prof. Wilson   Philadelphia, Oct. 31 1890

Your letter of the 29th inst was received this morning. In it you give me the name of the gentleman who wishes to establish a prize in U. S. History—namely Mr Adrian H. Joline.

With this new clue in my hand I have gone carefully through the minutes since June 1888 inclusive. I have not been able to discover any mention of the name of Mr Joline, nor any reference to any such prize as you indicate. I have also examined the files of the meetings held during the last year, which happen just now to be in the Trustees valise which I keep in Philadelphia. In those files I place every official letter that comes into my hands, every scrap of paper that has been before the Board. I have been unable to find a letter or paper having on it the name of Mr Joline.

I shall be much obliged if you will ascertain from Mr Joline the name of the gentleman to whom he addressed his letter stating his intention to establish a prize, & also the date or approximate date of that letter. Such information might enable me to trace the matter. Mr Osborn, the Treasurer, may be able to throw some light on the subject.

I regret exceedingly that there should have been any misunderstanding or neglect in reference to this matter, but at present I am utterly unable to remove the difficulty.

I remain   Yours most truly   E. R. Craven.

ALS (WP, DLC) with WWhw notation on env.: "*Ans.* 31 Oct/90."

Siegfried Brie's[1] Review of *The State*

[Nov. 1, 1890]

WOODROW WILSON, The State. Elements of historical and practical politics. A sketch of institutional history and administration. Boston, Heath and Co., 1889. XXXVI, u. 686 S. 8°. $ 2.

Der Verf., welcher sich bereits in seiner Schrift über »Congressional Government« als scharfen Beobachter der politischen Factoren und Zustände seines Heimatlandes erwiesen hatte, gibt in dem vorliegenden interessanten Buche eine allgemeine Statslehre auf geschichtlicher und rechtsvergleichender Grundlage.

Dic Arbeit ist das Product eingehender und umfassender Studien und enthält eine Fülle belehrenden Stoffes. Voran gehen vorzugsweise an H. S. Maines Forschungen und deren Resultate sich anschliessende Erörterungen über den wahrscheinlichen Ursprung und die wahrscheinliche älteste Entwickelung des States. Es folgen Skizzen der griechischen Statswesen und des römischen States, bezw. Reiches und Rechtes, sowie eine Charakteristik der germanischen Stats- und Rechtsbildungen im Mittelalter. Hieran reihen sich sehr concise, durch kurze historische Rückblicke eingeleitete Darstellungen der gegenwärtigen Statseinrichtungen der wichtigsten oder als typisch zu betrachtenden Culturstaten: Frankreichs, des deutschen Reichs und Preussens, der Schweiz, Oesterreich-Ungarns und Schweden-Norwegens, Englands und seiner Colonien, der Vereinigten Staten von Amerika. Die Verwaltungsorganisationen der verschiedenen Staten sind ebenso sorgfältig berücksichtigt wie das Verfassungsrecht. Vielfach sind die in Marquardsens Handbuch des öffentlichen Rechts der Gegenwart enthaltenen Darstellungen des Statsrechts der einzelnen Länder benutzt; selbständigen Wert haben namentlich die Abrisse des britischen und des nordamerikanischen Statsrechts (vergl. über die auch besonders veröffentlichte Bearbeitung des letzteren v. Holsts Kritik in dieser Zeitschr., 1890 Nr. 22). Dass die Angaben des Verfs. in Einzelheiten zuweilen unrichtig sind, wird man bei der Fülle des verarbeiteten Stoffes begreifen und entschuldigen (so beruht augenscheinlich auf einem Versehen die Notiz, S. 250, dass der deutsche Bund eine Armee von 30 000 Mann unterhalten habe; so ist irrig die Behauptung, S. 271 und S. 499, dass im jetzigen deutschen Reiche die Naturalisation von Ausländern nicht durch Reichsgesetz normiert sei; S. 272 in der Anmerkung ist das Datum der geltenden preussischen Verfassungsurkunde falsch angegeben).

Nachdem der Verf. in einem kurzen Kapitel (S. 575—592) die hauptsächlichen Uebereinstimmungen und Verschiedenheiten, welche sich aus der vergleichenden Betrachtung der von ihm vorgeführten statsrechtlichen Bilderreihe ergeben, zusammengefasst hat, beschliesst er sein Werk mit allgemeinen Erörterungen über Wesen und Formen des States und über Begriff und Entwickelung des Rechtes, über die statlichen Functionen und über die rationellen Grenzen und Ziele der Statstätigkeit.

Die Methode Wilsons ist eine entwickelungsgeschichtliche, gemäss seiner Ueberzeugung, dass die statlichen Weiterbildungen sich im Wege conservativer Anpassung, durch Umwandelung alter Gewohnheiten in neue, durch Modificierung alter Mittel zur Erreichung neuer Zwecke, vollziehen. Wie es insbesondere für einen Angehörigen der Vereinigten Staten natürlich ist, sieht er eine allgemeine und durchgreifende Geltung demokratischer Einrichtungen voraus. Die moderne Demokratie aber unterscheidet sich nach seiner Auffassung von der antiken dadurch, dass der Stat für die Individuen—nicht diese für den Stat—existiert und daher auch sich gegenüber Rechte der Individuen anerkennt. Dennoch ist Ws. Standpunkt kein rein individualistischer, sondern vielmehr zugleich, wie er selbst S. 658—659 ausführt, ein in gutem und gemässigtem Sinne socialistischer, insofern insbesondere der Stat die individuellen Rechte mit den socialen Pflichten in Einklang zu setzen berufen sei.

Nach dem Vorwort soll das Werk ein Lehrbuch für die nordamerikanischen Studierenden sein. Wenn es diesen, mit der vorausgesetzten Hilfe des Lehrers, gelingt, den Inhalt und Geist des Buches sich anzueignen, so werden sie in vielseitiger Kenntnis und richtigem Verständnis der statlichen Einrichtungen und Probleme die grosse Mehrzahl ihrer deutschen Genossen weit übertreffen.

Breslau.   Brie.

Printed in the Berlin *Deutsche Litteraturzeitung*, XI (Nov. 1, 1890), 1618-19.
    [1] Professor at the University of Breslau, author of many works in political science, and an Imperial Privy Councillor.

A News Item

[Nov. 1, 1890]
    Prof. Woodrow Wilson addressed the Philadelphian Society[1] on Thursday evening [October 30].

Printed in the *Princeton Press*, Nov. 1, 1890.
    [1] The Philadelphian Society, founded in 1825, was an association of Princeton undergraduates "for the promotion of the religious interests of the College." Devotional meetings, usually conducted by members of the faculty, were held on Thursday evenings; business meetings, on Saturday evenings. The Philadelphian Society had its own building, Murray Hall (erected from a bequest of Hamilton Murray, '72), which contained a hall for public worship and a reading room supplied with religious books and periodicals. Wilson addressed the Philadelphian Society many times in the coming years.

To Robert Bridges

My dear Bob,   Princeton, 2 Nov., 1890
    This is to notify you that it is high time for you to come down and spend Sunday with me. At last I may say that we are settled in our house; and there is a spare room in it aching to be occupied. No one has slept in it yet,—and I want you to come down and christen it for us: we want you to be our first guest. Now you can't decline that,—and, in order to accept you must come soon, for there's an uncle and aunt[1] that may come to see us any time.
    I learned from "the Freshman," John,[2] that you had your mother with you in New York; and I was heartily glad at the thought of it. I know what a pleasure it must have been to you, and how much good the pleasure of it must have done her.
    Do instruct the Freshman to come to see me. I find it hard to catch sight of him and keep up with his *status* and prospects. I want to help him in every way he will let me. He's a capital, lovable fellow, as you said he was. He said to me the first night I met him: "That uncle of mine is more than my life to me."
    I saw Mr. Brownell[3] when he was here the other day, but that queer distant manner of his prevented my doing more than speak to him.
    Let me hear that you are coming soon. Mrs. Wilson joins me in all cordial messages. As ever
              Most affectionately Yours,   Woodrow Wilson

ALS (WC, NjP).
    [1] The Thomas A. Hoyts.
    [2] John Miller Bridges of Carlisle, Pennsylvania, a "Special Student" (not a

candidate for a degree) in the John C. Green School of Science of the College of New Jersey during the academic year 1890-91.

[3] William Crary Brownell, literary critic and editor for Charles Scribner's Sons, 1888-1928.

To Albert Shaw

My dear Shaw: Princeton, New Jersey. 3 November, 1890.

I have not yet made up my mind exactly how I feel about your election to the Cornell chair.[1] I am heartily glad, as you know, that you are going into college work: I believe that you will enjoy it; and I feel confident that it will greatly strengthen and, so to say, facilitate your influence. But I am sorry you are going to Cornell, simply because I want you to come to Princeton.

And that's what this letter is about. It is written unofficially: I can commit no one to anything; but I do write with the President's knowledge and private sanction to ask how you would feel about a call to come to Princeton next year. Our President is not only an extraordinary man intellectually, deserving the admiration he gets from every man in Princeton, and of every man of brains outside of Princeton who knows him—a man most liberal too in his whole mental attitude, outside church battles; but he is also a man to tie to,—a lovable man, and a man whom it is good to work with: I mean to make my praise of him unstinted. But he is an extremely cautious man and feels perhaps overmuch the need of caution in the head of an institution representing a board of trustees and a constituency as conservative as ours. When I wrote to him last winter about you and my desire to have you here, he did not know apparently (to speak in all frankness) how well-known a man you are, and how sure of a reputation of the first order.[2] Since then, I find, he has been looking you up, so to speak,—opening his ears and his eyes to your fame; and he is now, so far as I can judge, in "a coming-on mood." As for Sloane he is thoroughly for you. Now, as for Princeton itself. Now that I am on the ground and see the new Princeton at the threshold of her university career, I believe more thoroughly than I did when I wrote to you last even that her materials for success are infinitely superior to those of most of her younger competitors: I mean that there's the finest stuff in the country in the classes from which she draws her students; that her strategic position, outside of self-centred New England— of whose self-regarding narrowness I now know much—and yet in the heart of this East of commerce and old wealth (young strength and old resources) is incomparable; that her resources, already splendid, promise every needed increase. I feel here in my teaching like a man feeling the bit of a spirited horse, capable of any speed and with wind for any race. Dr. Patton is, in his intellectual sympathies, of our faculty altogether. The next thing he means to have after filling the chair I want to see you take is a Law School,—not a duplicate of those already in full blast all over the country, but an institutional law school, so to speak, in which law shall be taught in its historical and philosophical aspects, critically rather than technically, and as if it had a literature besides a court record, close institutional connections as well as litigious niceties,—as it is taught in the better European universities.[3] We shall also certainly have additional instruction in History. In brief, the future is with us.

The chair I am thinking of for you is to be a chair of Economics. If we can get you, I will be glad to surrender to its occupant so much of my own domain as would cover municipal government in all its bearings: and the rest of the work of the chair you could mould to your own preferences. They prefer short courses here to long ones—I think wisely—half-year courses to whole-year, and I do not think that your work would need to exceed four hours a week. That is my own quota. Freedom for original work, therefore, and time for writing a man could have in fullest measure—in an atmosphere of companionship and warm mutual helpfulness that is already making me love the place from this side, as I used to love it from the other as a student.

In short, this letter is to sound you: to ask you if you would come down and join us in making Princeton a place to be proud of,—in keeping up her extraordinary records—recognized by New York men today—as a mother of men of affairs in the high and influential sense. Please read the letter I wrote you before[4] as well as this and then write me your whole thought about the matter. I feel that my own success here depends in no small degree upon getting you here. At any rate you can and must stop here with me next time you head for Baltimore and see the place. Sincerely yours, Woodrow Wilson

TCL (in possession of Virginia Shaw English).
[1] Wilson is replying to Albert Shaw to WW, June 6, 1890, Vol. 6.
[2] See F. L. Patton to WW, May 13, 1890, Vol. 6.
[3] See the Editorial Note below.
[4] WW to Albert Shaw, May 5, 1890, Vol. 6.

EDITORIAL NOTE
WILSON'S PLANS FOR A SCHOOL OF LAW AT PRINCETON

Wilson's reference in the letter to Albert Shaw, just printed, to a School of Law at Princeton is a reminder of discussions and plans in which Wilson was already deeply involved by the autumn of 1890.

The College of New Jersey had more or less maintained a law school from 1847 to 1855 and there had been talk at Princeton from time to time about re-establishing a law school ever since the expiration of the ill-fated institution. President Patton, in his inaugural address in 1888, had called for the founding of a chair in jurisprudence and looked forward to the possible establishment of a full-fledged law school.[1] Patton, uncharacteristically, wasted little time in trying to implement his plans. In July 1889, he opened discussions with Wilson concerning Wilson's early appointment to the new chair of jurisprudence and the formation of a "School of Political Science" upon which he would seek to build a School of Law.[2]

Wilson had, in fact, in 1888 worked out a plan for a school of public affairs to be affiliated with The Johns Hopkins University.[3] Thus he came to Princeton not only fired with new hopes by President Patton, but also with his earlier abortive Hopkins plan much in mind. As the Editorial Note, "Wilson's Teaching at Princeton, 1890-91," has already pointed out, he set up his basic undergraduate courses with the specific objective of developing, at the very least, a core program to prepare undergraduates for the new Princeton School of Law and other law schools as well.

Wilson's letter to Albert Shaw of November 3, 1890, makes it clear that by this date Wilson and Patton had discussed the project of a law school again at greater length soon after Wilson's arrival in Princeton and, more important, that they were in full agreement about the kind of institution that Princeton should have. Later evidence indicates that Patton had also asked Wilson to draft a plan of organization for the law school and to join him in a campaign among the alumni for an endowment.

Wilson went to work furiously. First, he probably studied the catalogues of leading law schools and departments in the United States, as well as the curricula of some leading European universities.[4] Next he sketched out a preliminary scheme of organization, listing departments and subjects to be taught.[5] Then he wrote out a new and slightly more elaborate plan of organization, as follows:

School of Law:

Chair I: *Public Law.*
    Constitutional Law
    Administrative Law
    International Law
    General Jurisprudence
    History of Law
    History of Legal Philosophy
    Public Corporations
    Conflict of Laws.

---

[1] *The Inauguration of President Patton* . . . (Princeton, N.J., 1888), pp. 35-36.
[2] WW to R. Bridges, July 23, 1889, Vol. 6.
[3] See Wilson's plan printed at May 22, 1888, and WW to D. C. Gilman, May 22, 1888, both in Vol. 5.
[4] For example, he copied out a brief summary of the law curriculum of the University of Erlangen in the first of the pocket diaries described at Dec. 28, 1889, Vol. 6.
[5] WWhw five-page MS. (WP, DLC) beginning "I. *Public Law.*"

Chair II. *Real Property.*
    The Common Law
    Wills and Successions
    Real Property.
Chair III. *Private Law*
    Personal Relationships not of Contract.
    Contracts not affecting Realty
    Personal Property
    Partnership
    Private Corporations.
Chair IV. *Roman Law and Equity.*
    Roman Law
    The Civil Law
    Equity
    Commercial Law
Chair V. *Criminal Law and Civil and Criminal Practice.*
    Criminal Law
    Civil Practice and Pleading
    Criminal Practice
    Evidence
    Admiralty.[6]

This was a time when the entire enterprise of legal education in the United States was in momentous transition. For one thing, what had been "law departments" in various universities, with one or two professors who taught mainly from a few commentaries, were becoming reconstituted as law schools affiliated with universities often only in a nominal sense. More important, these new law schools were concentrating more and more on the technical and practical aspects of the law (in this respect actually continuing the main tradition in American legal education) to the virtual exclusion of the study of law in its broad philosophical, historical, and moral aspects. The rapid spread of the so-called case method of study, which had been introduced at Harvard by Professor Christopher Columbus Langdell in the early 1870's, had provided the method for the new "scientific" study of law.[7]

The question of legal education was the subject of much discussion and controversy in the 1880's and 1890's. One group, of whom President Patton was himself a member, said that legal education in universities should concentrate exclusively upon law in its broader aspects. Another group, increasingly the majority, argued that law schools should turn out men with a mastery of the law in its practical details, not philosophers.

Wilson, in his plan of organization for a School of Law and in subsequent comments in letters and speeches,[8] made it indelibly clear where he stood in the great debate.

It is a risky kind of statement to make, because so few original ideas emerge anywhere in the world at any given time, but it seems possible that Wilson had made an intellectual breakthrough and was

[6] In the first of the pocket diaries described at Dec. 28, 1889, Vol. 6.
[7] Albert J. Harno, *Legal Education in the United States* (San Francisco, 1953), *passim.*
[8] For a complete guide, see the Index.

envisaging something new, or relatively new, when he laid out his plan for a School of Law at Princeton. What he conceived was nothing less than an institution that would combine the best features of European and American legal education.

His law school, like the law faculties of Scottish and Continental universities, would provide instruction in all the historical and philosophical branches of law. He was of course well acquainted with the curricula of these universities because of his wide reading in the works of leading European legal scholars and in European legal journals. In 1891, after he had already begun his campaign for a School of Law at Princeton, Wilson copied in shorthand the following excerpt from a review of James Lorimer's *Studies, National and International* (Edinburgh, 1890) in *The Juridical Review*, III (1891), 72:

> In accordance with the wider notion of it, universally prevalent on the Continent, and vigorously urged in this volume, an Academic Faculty of Law should provide a liberal education in the different branches of social, jural, and political science, as well as instruction in the technical branches of positive law. In other words, our Faculties of Law should prepare their students not merely for the practice of the legal profession, but for every part of the broad field in which they may be called to lead and direct their fellow-citizens. . . . It is not the province of a University to heap up in the student's mind a heterogeneous mass of details, and "points," rather that province is, and such has been the tradition of the professional chairs in Scottish Universities, to give the student some knowledge of legal principle, to aid him in forming the details into a system, to exhibit the mutual relations of different rules, and to sketch the process by which the law in its present shape has been slowly developed.[9]

This statement summarized Wilson's own passionate conviction, which he had voiced many times before reading Lorimer's review. As Wilson would say over and over in the future,[10] he was primarily interested in turning out lawyers who could be wise administrators, learned judges, and statesmen, as well as practitioners at the bar who would give leadership in adapting the law to new necessities as the United States moved from a rural economy into an urban, industrial way of life. Only lawyers with a deeply informed *Zeitgeist* could perform this indispensable function.

However, it is just as important to note that Wilson made ample provision in his curriculum for courses that would fit lawyers for the common, day-to-day business of their profession. Such knowledge European law students usually obtained, not at university, but in various sorts of apprenticeships. Wilson would provide such training in his law school, and there is no evidence that he would have objected to the use of the case method of study in practical courses. It is interesting that Wilson omitted from his curriculum any course specifically on torts. Perhaps this reflected his long-standing distaste, going all the way back to his experiences as a fledgling lawyer in

[9] Transcript of WWsh in the first of the pocket diaries described at Dec. 28, 1889, Vol. 6.

[10] Particularly in the addresses printed at July 26, 1893, and Aug. 23, 1894, both in Vol. 8.

Atlanta in 1882-83, for the grubby work ordinarily involved in damage suits.

It is only a slight exaggeration to say that the School of Law for Princeton was an obsession with Wilson all during the period 1890-93. As the documents in this volume and the next will show, he used what influence he had among wealthy alumni to raise the money for an endowment. He went on the alumni circuit in 1891, 1892, and 1893 at great inconvenience to himself in order to generate wider interest and support. He was probably responsible for the decision of the officers of the Class of 1883 to give a library in political science and jurisprudence as the class's decennial gift to the College.[11] As Wilson put it in a letter to Richard Heath Dabney as early as July 1, 1891, everything was ready for the realization of his plans but the money.

The money was the rub, primarily because President Patton, while always generously encouraging Wilson's plans, did virtually nothing to support them. Patton's ordinary languidness was accentuated during this period by intermittent illness. Moreover, his problems and priorities were different from Wilson's. When a correspondent suggested that Princeton use the windfall of the Fayerweather Bequest[12] to underwrite a law school, the President replied that Princeton first had to strengthen her academic departments, and that "then the coming giver will see that the Law School is his great opportunity." He did not know who the donor would turn out to be, Patton continued, but he was surely alive and would reveal himself "in due time."[13]

At no time between 1890 and 1895 did Patton ever propose to the Trustees the establishment of a law school. Moreover, a search of Patton's letter books for this period reveals no effort whatsoever to raise an endowment for the institution. On the rare occasions when he mentioned the matter in correspondence—and always in reply to suggestions or inquiries—Patton would respond with bland statements such as that he was "living in hope" of a donor,[14] or that the law school was "the next & most logical & needed stage in our development."[15] Insofar as is known, only once during the period 1890-95 did Patton add his voice to Wilson's public appeals—when they both spoke to the Philadelphia alumni on January 30, 1891.[16]

Patton did bestir himself slightly in 1896, by very cautiously suggesting a law school to a wealthy alumnus as one of several projects that might be realized once Princeton should become, formally, a university at her Sesquicentennial.[17] But he did not press the cause unduly, and it fell out of sight during the last years of his presidency.

Wilson meanwhile had lost hope for a School of Law after 1893 and had to content himself with offering what he thought was the right

[11] See the Editorial Note, "Wilson and the Class of 1883 Library of Political Science and Jurisprudence," Vol. 8.
[12] See WW to EAW, March 14, 1892, n. 2.
[13] F. L. Patton to Henry Wynans Jessup, March 14, 1891, Patton Letterpress Books, University Archives, NjP.
[14] F. L. Patton to H. W. Jessup, April 13, 1894, *ibid.*
[15] F. L. Patton to Moses Taylor Pyne, Dec. 14, 1894, *ibid.*
[16] See the news report printed at Jan. 31, 1891.
[17] F. L. Patton to Isaac C. Wyman, March 6, 1896, Patton Letterpress Books, University Archives, NjP.

kind of undergraduate program for pre-law students. However, Wilson never abandoned the dream. Among the projects for Princeton's development that he mentioned in his first report to the trustees as President of Princeton University, in 1902, Wilson included a "School of Jurisprudence," with a needed endowment of $2,400,000.

From Bradford Paul Raymond

My dear Professor Wilson: Middletown, Conn., Nov. 3 1890

Yours of the 1st of November at hand. Enclosed find receipt.[1] You need make no apology for the delay of payment. I have been there myself. Stephenson and Commons,[2] are here and as far as I know are doing well. Stephenson has just begun work, having had an engagement at Bucknell University to fill. The work is starting pleasantly, and with a large Freshman class, (76) large for us, and quite an increase in our other classes, making in all an increase of 23, we are expecting a good year. I was at Pennington last week and tempted to come over and call on you & see Princeton, but concluded I had not time. I shall hope to do this at some time, and let me assure you, we shall all be very glad to see you in Middletown at any time. Mrs. Raymond joins me in kindest regards to yourself & Mrs. Wilson.

                    Sincerely yours,   B. P. Raymond.

ALS (WP, DLC).

[1] This enclosure, which is missing, was probably a receipt for Wilson's last rent payment for the house in Middletown that he had rented from Wesleyan University.

[2] Andrew Stephenson, Associate Professor of History, and John Rogers Commons, Tutor in Economics and Social Science at Wesleyan, who was just beginning his distinguished career as an economist.

From John Bates Clark

Dear Professor Wilson   Northampton, Mass. Nov. 3 1890

These circulars have just come to me. I see the Sec. has put all the meetings on Tuesdays. They used to be on Mondays. Now can you not come on Saturday as proposed, and stay with me over Sunday and Monday? It would give me the very greatest pleasure. We can visit Amherst on Monday. It is wholly an off day with me at the college. If the day, Tuesday, is in any way a bad one for you we must try to get it changed. I suppose our secretary[1] is kept at his editorial work on Monday and released on Tuesday. What would please me best would be what I first suggest.   Yours Very Truly   J. B. Clark

ALS (WP, DLC) with WWhw notation on env.: "Ans. Nov. 4/90." Enc.: Printed circular of the Connecticut Valley Economic Association announcing an address by Wilson, "How to Prevent Legislative Corruption," on Nov. 18, 1890.

¹ George A. Denison, Assistant City Editor of the *Springfield* (Mass.) *Republican*.

An Announcement

[Nov. 3, 1890]

CONDITION EXAMINATION

I shall hold an examination for students conditioned or unexamined in Political Economy in the English room¹ at seven o'clock on the evening of Wednesday, November 12; and an examination for students conditioned or unexamined in Constitutional Law, at the same hour and place on the evening of Tuesday, November 18.   Woodrow Wilson.

Printed in *The Princetonian*, xv (Nov. 3, 1890), [1].
¹ A large lecture room in Dickinson Hall.

From Robert Bridges

Dear Tommy: [New York] 8 pm Nov 4 '90

The worst kind of returns is coming in while I am writing, and Scott has just left the Club feeling that he is defeated. Unless there is a big change in present indications Tammany will be easy victors.¹

Sprague and I have been dining together, and the one bit of satisfaction in the situation is the probability that at last Sprague's faction has downed the "Wicked Gibbs."²

I shall only take a minute to thank you for your invitation to come to Princeton soon, and to say that I cannot accept for this Sunday, as my sister Mrs. Witherspoon, will be in the city.

I hope, however, to make an early trip to Princeton.

Thank you for all you have or may do for John. He has an examination in French on Nov. 8—and I should like you to stir him up to hard work in it. I want very much that he shall be admitted regularly, and not remain a *special* student.

Your friend   Robert Bridges

ALS (WP, DLC).
¹ Revelations of corruption in the Tammany administration of Mayor Hugh John Grant led a reform group, the People's Municipal League, to nominate Francis Markoe Scott to oppose Grant in the mayoralty election on November 4, 1890. Although Scott had the endorsement of the Republican party, he lost to Grant by a vote of 92,435 to 115,843.
² Frederick S. Gibbs, whom the *New York Times* habitually referred to as "the wicked Gibbs," and Henry L. Sprague headed rival Republican factions in the Thirteenth State Assembly District of New York City. On September 26, 1890, Gibbs's slate of delegates for the Republican county convention defeated

a slate headed by Sprague in what the *Times* characterized as an obviously fraudulent election. The county convention, at its meeting on October 6, ousted the Gibbs delegation and seated the one led by Sprague. The Gibbs faction retaliated four days later by nominating Gibbs for assemblyman in the Thirteenth District at a rump primary meeting from which the Sprague men were locked out. The Sprague faction nominated James A. Cowie for assemblyman that same evening. The acting County Clerk, a Tammany Democrat, ruled that Gibbs's name should go on the ballot in the Republican column. James H. Southworth, the Tammany-Democratic candidate, defeated Gibbs in the election on November 4, 1890. See the *New York Times*, Sept. 27, Oct. 7, 11, 15, and 21, and Nov. 2 and 5, 1890.

To Daniel Collamore Heath

My dear Mr. Heath,   Princeton, New Jersey, 4 November, 1890

I have examined the copy for the circular concerning the "State" very carefully; and believe I have only one comment to make,—a comment which I shall put in the form of a query: Is it safe, do you think, or "in good form," to use the favorable part of the *Nation's* notice[1] when that is so much the smallest part? Will it not make a bad impression? For a great many readers of your circular will be readers of the *Nation* also.

Will you not be kind enough to send me a copy of your last impression of "The State," for my own use? I have none but the first impression, with none of the errors corrected.

What is the sale of the book now? Has the list of institutions using it increased since this college year opened? I should be glad to know all you can tell me about it.

I return the circular "copy."

In haste,   Sincerely Yours,   Woodrow Wilson

ALS (Clifton Waller Barrett Coll., ViU).
[1] That is, the New York *Nation's* highly critical review of *The State*, printed at Dec. 26, 1889, Vol. 6.

From George Howe, Jr.

Dear Woodrow,   Columbia, S. C., Nov 5 1890

Your last urgent invitation to Annie has moved her exceedingly. She gave you a reason for not visiting you, the fact of Jessie's presence, with the inconvenience of taking her along or leaving her behind. There is another reason which her modesty prevented her from mentioning. She is now four months enciente, and she feels that the world will soon know that which she and I only know. She fears her presence with you in her condition may prove embarrassing to you and Ellie and herself. Her condition is not obvious except to those very familiar with her figure. Now it is for you to say whether a visit from her will be perfectly agreeable under the circumstances. You must be freely candid. "Mum is the word" to all others just now[.] There is a possible contingency which may prevent her going[.] My sister Mrs Green[1] has been ill for weeks. A letter received to day makes it possible that she may not recover. If she does not she will be buried here and Annie would have to be at home.

Annie is very anxious to make the visit to you. She would have gone to you earlier, but Craig came along from the far west, and made us a visit which put and [an] end to the matter.

I hope Ellie is perfectly well and over the ill effects of her burn[2] Love to her, the children and yourself.

Yrs affly   Geo Howe

ALS (WP, DLC) with WWhw notation on env.: "Ans."
    [1] Sarah Emily Howe Green, wife of the Rev. Dr. Edward Melvin Green, pastor of the Presbyterian Church of Danville, Kentucky. Mrs. Green died soon afterward. See Annie W. Howe to WW, Nov. 17, 1890.
    [2] For numerous references to this episode, see the Index to Vol. 6 under Wilson, Ellen Axson.

From Albert Shaw

My dear Wilson: Minneapolis, Nov. 6. 1890.

Yours of the third inst. came this afternoon; and I think it well to reply immediately. Let me hasten to explain just the position I am in. Several weeks ago Mr. W. T. Stead of London wrote to me explaining the remarkable success his *Review of Reviews* had attained (a circulation exceeding 100,000 copies within the first year) and offering me the position of American editor, with office at New York, his plan being to issue an American edition containing a good deal of original matter and adapted throughout to an American circulation, tho' retaining its character and identity. Mr. Stead came to know me quite well when I was in London, and I wrote somewhat for the Pall Mall Gazette. He had also been familiar with my articles in the Contemporary Review and elsewhere. He offers me a large salary, and puts the thing in a favorable light. I replied that I was disposed to give the matter careful and probably favorable consideration. Just then President C. K. Adams wrote me that the Cornell trustees were about to meet, and asked me to telegraph whether I would accept a chair of Pol. & Municipal Institutions if elected. I replied explaining the situation. They proceeded however to elect me, giving me time to consider the Stead matter. My work in any case would not begin at Cornell until next fall. I should have said that there were some contingencies in the *Review* business, depending upon publication arrangements in New

York. But those matters seem now to have been adjusted favorably; and last night I received a cablegram from Mr. Stead asking me to come to London immediately if possible. It would of course be necessary for me to see him personally in order to arrange in detail the American work. I think it wholly probable that I shall arrange to go within a few days. President Adams has written me that there would be no objection whatever to my combining the two things, provided it were feasible to do the *Review* work at Ithaca and to do it without neglect of the duties of the chair. But I do not think that it would be possible—or, rather, advantageous—to try to do Mr. Stead's work at Ithaca. It had been my thought that if I finally accepted Mr. Stead's proposition I should live in one of the New Jersey suburbs,— Montclair for instance. And now, since your letter has come, it occurs to me to wonder whether it might not be possible for me to take Mr. Stead's work to Princeton if I should be wanted there. Of course much would depend upon the kind and amount of work the *Review* would require from me. My impression is that it could be so organized, with assistants doing the routine and drudgery, that my part would be no more arduous than the literary or journalistic work that many an industrious professor accomplishes as a side task. Further, it is my impression that the *Review* will have such a character and standing as a periodical and a library accessory that its connection in some sense, through its American Editor, with a college or university would be favorable rather than otherwise to the institution. It is not according to my observation that a certain amount of identification with current outside matters detracts from the live work and thorough work of a college professor. Princeton is so near New York that it would be easy to run in and out as often as necessary. The *Review* work would be well in hand a good while before the professorial work would begin, and assistants could have been trained to their duties. The writing of a few pages each month of the introductory editorial "Progress of the World" would be congenial and appropriate work for me.

But, as to the professorship itself. I have a very high regard for Princeton and much faith in its future. While I do not count myself a deep scholar, I think that I possess to some extent the knack of imparting instruction in a clear way, and that I could make my classes feel a genuine interest in their study. I count my practical experience as valuable, especially, for class-room work in political economy, etc.

The other day President [Cyrus] Northrop of the University of Minnesota came to me and said that he did not want me to leave Minneapolis and that if I would accept he would take steps to create a chair for me here. Our University is coming up very brilliantly, and in Professors [William Watts] Folwell and [Harry Pratt] Judson it has two admirable men in political, economic and historical lines. I mention this matter not to take any credit to myself but simply to show that here, where I am well known in my everyday character and work, I am considered fit for a university chair. You will appreciate the fact that it is a pretty severe test when I remind you that I am most commonly known here, necessarily, as a writer upon a partisan newspaper, and that our western universities, through the pressure of politics and various interests, are not likely to create a chair of political science for a local newspaperman unless he stands pretty well. I appreciate the compliment highly. I do not know what account Princeton would take of the tariff views of a professor of political economy. You remember, I think, that I lean more strongly to the protectionist side than many of our friends do. Yet I am not aware that my views would so prejudice me as to vitiate or unfairly bias my teaching. Such pronounced free-trade economists as Henry C. Adams, [Frank W.] Taussig *et al.* have never been afraid of me as a possible professor of political economy on the score of my tariff notions. The Univ. of Mich. through Prof. Adams has asked me if I would give a course of lectures next spring on Protection and Free Trade. Prof. E. J. James, for the Univ. of Penn'a, has written asking if I would be able to repeat in the Wharton School my J. H. U. course (that you have seen announced) on American city gov't etc. I am invited to lecture in an important course at Chicago, and at the Univ. of Wisconsin.

I should have written none of this, but for the fact that it is perfectly right from the business point of view that President Patton should know to what extent I have begun to attain an academic standing. Such little reputation as I may have obtained is far more than I deserve, and I have no wish to dilate upon it. The writing I have done is a good deal scattered; but you know something of it. It would have been much more extensive (I mean the more careful writing) but for the vast quantity of newspaper editorial composition that has absorbed my time and energy. But I have a good deal of writing yet to do, I hope. I may very possibly have gone east before this reaches you; but I will ask you to venture a line of reply. Perhaps, however, it will be better that you should write to me in care of Dr. John C. Fisher,—Warsaw, Wyoming Co. New York,—whom I shall visit briefly on my way. Dr. F. (who, by the way, is a Princeton graduate) is my brother-in-law, and my mother now lives in his family.

I cannot say absolutely at this moment that I would accept the Princeton chair if it were offered me; but I should consider it very earnestly. And if it were agreeable all around for me to bring to Princeton a connection with Mr. Stead's enterprise, the argument would be doubly strong for me.

It is not yet known outside that Mr. Stead has made me this offer, and of course it will be well to keep it confidential; and the same is true of Pres. Northrop's offer to arrange a chair in the Univ. of Minnesota. But you are at liberty to communicate anything in this letter to Pres. Patton,—or to anyone else so far as you may have occasion.

I need not explain that it would greatly help me to arrange my plans all around if I could know in the early future whether or not Princeton would be likely to want me. The Cornell place has many attractions, and I shall not decline it without reasons that shall seem ample and convincing. This letter is painfully egotistical. But it could hardly have been otherwise under the circumstances. I am delighted that you find your Princeton life so congenial. It would be a source of constant pleasure and inspiration to me to have you at hand; but I'm afraid you wholly overestimate my desirability as a colleague.

Sincerely Yours,   Albert Shaw.

P.S. Perhaps I can run over to Princeton and call on you when I go to N. Y. *en route* for England.

ALS (WP, DLC).

To Charles Augustus Aiken[1]

My dear Dr. Aiken,   [Princeton, N.J.] 7 November, 1890.

So far as I know none of the Seminary students is attending either of my courses at the College. Both my courses are undergraduate courses; I shall not given [give] any course intended specifically for graduate students[2] until next half-year, though of course students from the Seminary are welcome in any of the classrooms.   Very truly Yours,   Woodrow Wilson

ALS (WC, NjP).

[1] Professor of Oriental and Old Testament Literature and of the Relations of Philosophy and Science to the Christian Religion at Princeton Theological Seminary.

[2] He meant, actually, "open to graduate students." He had not planned any courses "specifically" for graduate students.

From George A. Denison

My Dear Sir,   Springfield, Mass.   Nov 8 1890
Professor Clark has sent me your note of the 4th. If Monday the 24th would be a more convenient date for you we can as well hold our meeting then as a week earlier. The objection to your coming the 17th is that Stanley[1] is to lecture here on that evening, and I fear that our attendance would not be so large as we would wish. As to the title of your address if you prefer, "The Evils of Democracy," we shall be as well pleased. Will you kindly advise me if the 24th is satisfactory to you, and also your decision about a subject, and much oblige
Yours Truly   Geo. A. Denison
Secy Conn Valley Economic Assn.

ALS (WP, DLC) with WWhw notation on env.: "Ans. 10 Nov./90."
[1] Henry Morton Stanley, the famous reporter and explorer.

From John Bates Clark

Dear Professor Wilson   Northampton, Mass.   Nov. 10 1890
A letter has come from our Sec. saying the meeting will be changed to 24th inst. Will that be convenient for you? I hope so, and will count, in that case, on your coming to Northampton on the 22d. We can take in a drive to Amherst on the morning of the 24th or we can have Prof. Morse[1] come over and dine and spend the afternoon with us here, going with us to the meeting in the evening.
Yours Very Truly   J. B. Clark

ALS (WP, DLC) with WWhw notation on env.: "Ans. 11 Nov./'90."
[1] Anson Daniel Morse, Professor of History and Political Economy at Amherst College.

To Albert Shaw

My dear Shaw: Princeton, New Jersey.   11 November, 1890.
Your letter reached me yesterday and has given me a great deal of solid satisfaction: for it seems to me to create a very strong probability of your coming to Princeton. I took the letter to Dr. Patton last night (he was out of town during the day) and had a long talk with him about it. I can sum up the impression left on my mind by the interview thus (with all the more confidence because of Dr. Patton's straightforward frankness in everything). He is himself distinctly in favour of calling you, saying that he has every reason to believe that you are just the

man we want for the place, and, like President Adams, he sees no objection at all to your combining editorial work of the kind you have now in mind with professional duties, provided, of course, it could be so arranged that the latter duties would not suffer because of the former, but take precedence of them. On the contrary, he sees the advantage which would accrue both to you and to the College from the combination. But of course he wants to sound the men back of him (the Trustees); wants to assure himself that the necessary funds shall be forthcoming, etc. In the meantime, he is genuinely anxious to meet you, and begged me to urge you to come down and make the visit you half promise in your letter. Come by all means, my dear fellow, for my sake, for his, and for the sake of "the situation," or— if for no other reason—only to see Princeton. Let me know what time you will come so that I may make sure that Patton will be here,—and Sloane, for he will want to meet you again. I am sincerely glad of your fine prospects in the Stead matter, and don't wonder that you want to avail yourself of so unusual an opportunity. But we'll talk of that when you come. It weighs not a little with Patton that we could, under the circumstances, take you without discourtesy to Cornell, inasmuch as you could not manage to run the *Review* from Ithaca and could easily manage to run it from Princeton.

Mrs. Wilson sends her regards and joins most heartily in urging you to come.

As ever   Sincerely yours,   Woodrow Wilson

TCL (in possession of Virginia Shaw English).

To Daniel Collamore Heath

Princeton, New Jersey,

My dear Mr. Heath,   12 November, 1890

You seem to have misunderstood me about the use of the *Nation's* notice of "The State."[1] I meant to advise simply that you use none of it,—not that you use all of it. I don't think it worth using at all.

I think the notice in the *Deutsche Litteraturzeitung*[2] very fair indeed. Prof. Brie is a very considerable authority.[3] You will probably want to use some of his sentences in the circular (?)[4]

Very sincerely,   Woodrow Wilson

ALS (Clifton Waller Barrett Coll., ViU).
   [1] Heath's letter to which this is a reply is missing.
   [2] This review is printed at Nov. 1, 1890.
   [3] He is identified in n. 1 to the review just cited.
   [4] Wilson translated parts of Brie's highly favorable review on both sides

of two small pages (WP, DLC), writing both in longhand and shorthand. He then recopied the extracts on a separate page or pages and enclosed them with this letter. The enclosure is missing. Whether Heath used any of Brie's comments in the circular is unknown, as the files of D. C. Heath & Company for this period are not extant.

From Joseph R. Wilson, Jr.

My dearest brother: Clarksville, Tenn., Nov. 14/90.

I am going to write you a long business letter. Please answer it at your earliest possible convenience for the matter becomes more and more important to me day by day.

To begin with—in what business is your Nashville friend[1] engaged? Please tell me all you can about it. I am rather disposed to remain a newspaper man if possible, that is, unless I can better myself considerably in another business. My relation to Kate makes it all the more necessary for me to grasp the first chance which presents itself to me, so that I may make a home of my own.

In the second place, I want to ask your opinion on a scheme I have found. You say the South is the place for me. To this I say 'amen' for I would prefer remaining in the South. As to Tennessee—I feel satisfied to remain in this state. I know of none I would like better. As for a place to *settle* in Tennessee, why not Clarksville if I can do so without a sacrifice? Although only a large town at present, during the five years and over we have been living here, Clarksville has grown greatly. She is still growing with a steady, healthy growth that is of the lasting kind, her citizens believe. An acquaintance of mine, an old newspaper man, and I formed the idea of starting a morning daily. This plan has been pretty well given up, for a *morning* daily would hardly pay at present with two afternoon dailies in the field. The *"Progress"* is only a little country paper, but a paying institution to its owner, L. W. Gaines. This acquaintance of mine and I have thought of trying to purchase this paper. We have found that the editor would sell, but we know not his price as yet. Another plan was proposed to me today by a banker friend in this place—i.e. for me to purchase an interest in the Progress. The present proprietor is a pushing, active young man although not a first class editor by any means. In either of the two latter plans father, I am sure from what he has said, would aid me if by doing as I have proposed I could secure a good and reliable income. An income of $1,200 would support me well here, I believe, with board not over $40.00 per month for two and housekeeping not exceedingly expensive. Now, as Clarksville is an enterprising town, a growing town, would not such a plan as I propose be nice *if* I can secure the interest I mention at a re[a]sonable price and *if* my income after securing that interest would be equal to about $1,000 or $1,200 per year? There are several *"ifs"* in this, I know, but I will probably be able to answer fully all questions on the above mentioned points, in a few days. In the mean while, please give me your views in the matter and some information concerning your Nashville friend's business.

My present plan is this—If Mr. Grant (the acquaintance mentioned above) and I cannot *buy* the Progress, I will see what I can do towards securing an *interest* in the paper.

Father and I are both pretty well, I believe. This is about all the news I know concerning either of us. Kate seemed much pleased with your messages.

With unbounded love to you, sister Ellie and the children,

Your aff. bro.   Joseph.

Please write soon.

ALS (WP, DLC) with WWhw notation on env.: "Ans. 1 Dec./90."
    [1] Wilson, in a letter to his brother of November 2, 1890, which is missing, had undoubtedly mentioned Robert Ewing of Nashville, Ellen Wilson's first cousin-in-law, as someone who might help Joseph R. Wilson, Jr., in his search for a position. Ewing was at this time connected with the city government of Nashville.

From Robert Bridges, with Enclosure

My dear Tommy: New York   Nov 17 1890
    I reached my desk about 9:45 to find the enclosed note from Billy Isham: I shall expect you to accept his invitation, and stay with me. Please write to Billy soon, as he is always uneasy.

With my regards to Mrs Wilson

Your friend   Robert Bridges

ENCLOSURE

William Burhans Isham, Jr., to Robert Bridges

My dear Bob,   5 East 61 Str [New York, c. Nov. 17, 1890]
    I always like to give the fellows a dinner[1]—& will you come on Tuesday Nov 25th to my home & see what I can do for you? If you can keep our dear old friend Tommy Wilson would you just enclose this to him & tell him I hope he will come, now that he knows the way. dinner at 7.15

Yours 79ly   Wm B Isham Jr

ALS (WP, DLC).
    [1] About the "Isham dinners," see WW to EAW, May 6, 1886, n. 1, Vol. 5.

From Annie Wilson Howe

My dearest Brother,   Columbia, S. C.   Nov. 17th 1890

You must think it strange that I have not written before this. Just after receiving your telegram, Dr. George got one from Mr. Green, telling him that Emilie was *very* ill, and begged that he would come to see her before she died. He left home on Monday morning, and returned on Friday. In the mean time a telegram came telling us of Emilies death. They brought her body here, and the burial services were held on Sabbath morning. Mr. Green, Eddie, George and Marion, are all here, and will probably remain for a week. Isn't it strange that I have been stopped so often. I expected to be with you tomorrow. I expect now to leave home the first of next week—if that time will suit you. Jessie will not go with me. We will send her to her aunt, in Clinton.[1]

Dr. George's trip was just such a one as I took to Arkansas.[2] It was very trying. Mr. Green is broken down—having nursed Emilie constantly for four months. I have not time to write more just now—but will let you know exactly what day to expect me. With warmest love to Ellen & your dear self from us both,

Your devoted Sister

ALS (WP, DLC).

[1] Mrs. John W. Kennedy. Her husband had just died.

[2] When she went to Batesville in August 1890, just before the death of her sister, Marion Wilson Kennedy.

From Percy Lincoln Johnson[1]

Dear Sir: New Haven, Conn.   Nov 20th 1890

It has for some years been the custom of the Yale Kent Club, a debating society open to the members of the Yale Law School, to give a course of six or more lectures during the winter term. This course is open to this department and to as many members of the university at large, as we are able to accommodate with seats.

The course will open, this year about Jan 20th. We have secured the services of Hon. Theodore Roosevelt of New York, and we hope and expect to add the names of Hon. Edward J. Phelps[2] and the Rev. Dr. J. M. Buckley.[3] We would very much like to have you help us out this year.[4] We are embarrassed somewhat, at being unable to offer any substantial remuneration, but are so situated that we can only pay the expenses of our speakers.

We should expect to serve your convenience as to dates, with a preference for Wednesday evening. As to a subject we would prefer to leave the choice to you.

Hoping that you will be able to serve us,

I remain,   yours very truly,
P. L. Johnson   For Committee.

I heartily concur in this invitation & shall be greatly gratified with its acceptance

Francis Wayland   Dean of Law Faculty

ALS (WP, DLC) with WWhw notation on env.: "Ans. Dec. 15/90."

1 A Wesleyan graduate of the Class of 1889, Johnson was at this time a student at the Yale Law School and received his LL.B. in 1891.

2 Edward John Phelps, former Ambassador to Great Britain and at this time Kent Professor of Law at Yale.

3 The Rev. Dr. James Monroe Buckley, Methodist minister, editor of the New York *Christian Advocate*, and a well-known orator.

4 Wilson accepted and delivered "Leaders of Men" (printed at June 17, 1890, Vol. 6) in Osborn Hall on March 18, 1891.

From George Howe, Jr.

Dear Woodrow   Columbia, S. C., Nov 24 1890

Annie expects to leave for Princeton to-morrow Tuesday night. She will probably lie over in Washington Wednesday night and reach Princeton sometime Thursday forenoon. I dislike to send her off alone but I think she will have no trouble.

Thank Ellie for her kind and sympathetic letter, which was received to-day.   Yrs affly   Geo Howe

ALS (WP, DLC).

A Newspaper Report of an Address
in Springfield, Massachusetts

[Nov. 25, 1890]

The Connecticut Valley economic association mustered an audience of finest quality last evening for the lecture by Prof Woodrow Wilson of Princeton university, who came up to see the foot-ball game Saturday and has since been the guest of Prof J. B. Clark at his home in Northampton. This meeting was the annual one, adjourned from September. . . . Rev Dr Walker, the newly-elected president, took the chair after the business had been settled and Prof Wilson was introduced. His talk was an ampli[fi]cation of this skeleton.[1]

The function assigned me is an ungracious one; to criticise the political faith upon which the institutions of the country rest. And yet it does not seem as if that were the faith of the men who framed the federal constitution. That constitution was not by intention democratic. It has been made so by subsequent changes —by presidential nominating conventions and by the widening everywhere of the franchise. It is significant that it has been proposed that the choice of the people with regard to senators be declared by ballot. There are four assumptions upon which democracy is based: First, that the will of the majority is the general will, or the will of the people. The truth of this assumption depends upon whether you regard "the people" as an organized whole, or as merely a crowd. If the latter, why of course a mere show of hands will suffice; but if the former, the majority is not decisive without the second assumption, that questions of government of every sort that come to vote are generally understood; whereas they are understood and realized in their true bearings only by a minority. Evidence is excluded from most minds by reason of haste or preoccupation. Third, that the average judgment (the uninstructed, instructive judgment), is the best and the final judgment. Fourth, that there is always one prevalent opinion in existence which can be called for whenever there is occasion to decide any matter.

As for the dogma of popular sovereignty, government means guidance, initiative, conduct of affairs, and for none of these things is "the common will" fitted. There is no apparent contradiction between democracy and the concentration of authority, of command in the hands of one or of a few. The apparent logic of popular power is that the impulse of authority must be imparted through various independent channels, that the variety of the nation may be watched [matched] by the variety of its political organs and its political determinations compromise determinations in all their stages. Thus comes the weakening of authority and consequently of obedience, which is the cohesive principle of society, the perfect freedom. The law of growth, of political faith and progress, is not fixed order, but ordered change. Democracy as a principle is closely kin to socialism. As a form of government, it is simply in line with political development in general, and may be made to give a decided negative to socialism. It differs from socialism in this,—both are[2] postulate government by the people, but democracy means this in a less organic sense, socialism meaning the community. History warrants and necessitates government for the people, but it has not made possible government by the people. Sovereignty must still be lodged, intelligent and independent. Civil-service reform, for example, is eminently wise and imperatively necessary for good government, but it is not democratic in idea—at least, not in the modern idea of democracy. It substitutes for the average man or "the man of the people," the man of the schools; that is, the instructed and fitted man. A self-instructed man like Lincoln is not a "man of the people" (any more than Washington was), but a man come out from the people and elevated above them.

Printed in the *Springfield Republican*, Nov. 25, 1890; editorial headings omitted.
[1] The following report virtually reproduces Wilson's own outline, a five-page, handwritten MS. entitled *"The Evils of Democracy,"* WP, DLC. The reporter, who was undoubtedly George A. Denison, obviously had Wilson's manuscript in hand when he wrote his account.
[2] Wilson wrote "both postulate"; "are" was inserted in error in the printed report.

From Joseph Ruggles Wilson

My Precious Son,   Clarksville, Decr 13/90
 I cannot put upon paper those half-undefined thoughts which press upon me in view of my probable changes of life. I have therefore resolved to make you a call during Christmas week, that we may, over dishes of talk and in goblets of counsel, canvas the whole subject. I am to go first to New York, and shall, with God's favor, be with you about Tuesday the 23d—to remain during some hours at least. I only hope that this will be accomplished, and that you will not be inconvenienced. Great love to dear Ellie & your dear self. I am yours most affy—
                                                    Father.

ALS (WP, DLC).

From Annie Wilson Howe

My darling brother,   Columbia, Dec. 14th 1890
 I got home this morning at half after six—very tired—but not sick. I cannot begin to tell you how thouroughly I enjoyed my visit to your lovely home. Of course I knew what *you* would be in your own home, and I knew that Ellie was very lovely, but I did not know *how* lovely she is, until I saw her for myself at home. I am so glad I can now think of you all as you are every day. As for the dear children, I never saw lovelier ones anywhere. I stopped in Charlottesville from half after three on Friday until yesterday afternoon, at the same hour. Mr. and Mrs. Sampson were very pleasant and cordial. Wilson[1] looks well, and seems to be satisfied. I met there a young man named Bridges—a cousin of your friend Bob Bridges. He is not staying there, but was spending a day & night with the boys—on his way home.
 I hope Ellie's gloves got to Princeton in time, and suited her.

I got them as soon as possible after I got in—and took them to the office myself. Were the handkerchiefs all right?

I found everything all right at home—except that Dr. Geo. has a severe cold. I hope your cold is better. I will write again, and tell you of my trip home, in a few days. Dr. Geo & George jr. unite with me in warmest love to you & dear Ellie, and please kiss the precious children for me.

Your devoted sister   Annie

ALS (WP, DLC) with WWhw notation on env.: "Ans. 22 Dec/90."
[1] Her son, James Wilson Howe, who was presumably attending some preparatory school in or near Charlottesville.

Notes for an Advanced Course in Political Economy

[c. Dec. 15-Jan. 20, 1891]

Contents:

WWhw and WWT lecture notes with the general heading, "*Socialism.*" and the following topical headings, with composition dates when given: "*Its Nature, Foundations, Opportunities, Tendencies and Status.*"; "*Theoretical Basis of Socialism.*"; "*Saint-Simon: Bazard.*" (Jan. 7, 1891); "*1813) Louis Blanc (1882*" (Jan. 15, 1891); "*Views of Rodbertus, Marx, and Lassalle Contrasted.*" (Jan. 19 and 20, 1891).

Loose sheets (WP, DLC).

To Alfred Pearce Dennis[1]

Dear Mr. Dennis,   [Princeton, N.J., c. Dec. 18, 1890]

Will you not be kind enough to say, in the "Here and There" of the *Princetonian* that I was unable to meet my classes this week on account of sickness?[2]

I have been suffering[3] in a way that made me feel very much more like *de*-composition than composition.

Very truly Yours,   Woodrow Wilson

ALS (photostat in RSB Coll., DLC).
[1] Born Worcester County, Md., Jan. 10, 1869. A.B., College of New Jersey, 1891; A.M., 1893; Ph.D., 1894. Instructor in History, Princeton, 1893-94; Professor of History, Wesleyan University, 1894-95; Professor of History and Politics, Smith College, 1898-1907. Later engaged in mercantile business. Commercial Attaché, American Embassy at Rome, 1918-21, and at London, 1921. Member United States Tariff Commission, 1925-31. Died Aug. 29, 1931. His memoir, *Gods and Little Fishes* (Indianapolis, 1931), pp. 84-117, includes an unflattering portrait of Wilson as a teacher.
[2] Dennis was Managing Editor of *The Princetonian*.
[3] From "la grippe," or influenza. See WW to R. Bridges, Jan. 9, 1891.

A News Item

[Dec. 19, 1890]

Prof. Woodrow Wilson has been unable to meet his classes in Public Law and Political Economy this week on account of sickness.

Printed in *The Princetonian*, xv (Dec. 19, 1890), [3].

From the Minutes of the Princeton Faculty

5 5' P.M., Friday, Dec. 19th, 1890.

. . . Professors Sloane and Wilson and Mr. Miller[1] were appointed a Committee to select a *Question* and to report *Judges* to the Faculty for the *Debate* on February 22nd, 1891.[2]

Resolved, That the Question be announced *three weeks* before the Day of the Debate.

[1] Marion Mills Miller, Instructor in English and Oratory.

[2] That is, the debate for the Class of 1876 Memorial Prize. This prize, consisting of the interest on $1,000, was given to the winner of a debate on a subject of current interest in American politics held on Washington's birthday. Each class chose a competitor. The committee drafted the question, "Resolved that the Reform of Indian affairs demands the transfer of their control to the War Department"—a timely subject in light of the Ghost Dance uprising of the Teton Sioux on the Black Hills Reservation then in progress and reminiscent of the first debate in the Liberal Debating Club in 1877, about which see Vol. 1, p. 255.

The debate for the Class of 1876 Memorial Prize occurred on February 23, 1891, because Washington's birthday fell on a Sunday, and was won by Samuel Semple, '91, who defended the affirmative side of the question. The account in *The Princetonian*, xv (Feb. 25, 1891), [1], does not mention the names of the judges.

From Joseph R. Wilson, Jr.

My dearest Brother: Clarksville, Tenn.   Dec. 23rd 1890

There is no telling what elegant presents I would send my dear ones if it were not "for the stringency of the money market." Since money is so high, even presents less elaborate than my *feelings* would prompt me to give, are beyond my reach. These facts being sad but nevertheless true, I must do the next best thing—write a Christmas letter. Any body, even the poorest of the poor, may write Christmas letters to those they love, or, if they cannot write themselves, can soon find some kind hearted individual who will undertake the task for them, but few can express as much love and as many heartfelt wishes for a very joyous Christmas and a glad New Year as I can. Why? Well, the answer is easily given. Those to whom others have to write Christmas letters are not worthy of so much love and esteem as I think my loved ones are. Of course I am a partial judge in this matter. Please accept herewith my best and most sincere wishes for yourself, sister Ellie and the children. May your Christmas be very joyful and your New Year glad. That God's richest blessings may be showered upon you and yours is the prayerful wish of your brother.

I suppose dear father will be with you at the time you receive this epistle. How I wish I could be with you all. My Christmas will be well spent, however, for I will eat dinner and spend most of Christmas day with the Wilsons. I know Kate can make me happy. Good-bye dear brother. Love unbounded to dear father, yourself, sister Ellie & the children.

Your aff. bro.   Joseph

ALS (WP, DLC) with WWhw notation on env.: "Ans."

Richard Heath Dabney's Review of *The State*

[January 1891]

THE STATE: Elements of Historical and Practical Politics. By WOODROW WILSON, Ph.D., LL.D., author of *Congressional Government*. Boston: D. C. Heath & Co., 1889. Pp. xxxvi, 686.

When Dr. Wilson's *Congressional Government* appeared in 1885, it was hailed as a work of great importance—an original contribution to American political thought. Rejecting the conventional bookish theories of the Constitution, the gifted young author endeavored to penetrate beneath the surface and to discover its real nature; and, while some might doubt the efficacy of his prescription for the maladies of our body politic, few competent judges would deny that his diagnosis was both acute and profound.

His second work, *The State*, is of a very different nature. The facts which it contains—and their name is legion—are not new facts; and those persons (so numerous nowadays) who deny originality to all who fail to grub up a new fact from some unexplored corner of the universe, might say that the work was a mere compilation. But facts alone are comparatively useless things; and those who look upon the work of the architect as higher than that of the brickmaker or the hodcarrier, will see that *The State*, though built with bricks made and collected by others, is a structure by no means devoid of originality. It would be strange if, in so comprehensive a work, there were no views with which a reviewer might differ. We, for example, believe that Dr. Wilson, in endeavoring to account for the democratic and aristocratic character of New England and Virginia society respectively, lays too much stress upon the difference between these sections in soil and climate. Soil and climate undoubtedly had their influence; but the fact that the original settlers of New England came mainly from the lower and middle classes of English society, while a very large cavalier element settled in Virginia, is of far more importance. Nor do we think that he displays his usual scientific carefulness of statement in asserting that the Civil War has made this country "homogeneous," and that there is now "no longer any obstacle to our being in reality one great nation." Not to speak of the Chinese, Hungarians, Russians, Irish, and other heterogeneous elements which immigration is pouring into our midst, or of the enormous economic diversities between such States as Massachusetts and Texas, or Florida and Nevada, the simple presence of the negro race in the Southern States is sufficient to prevent homogeneity between the North and the South, and is surely an obstacle to perfect unity of feeling between the sections. But, despite the few defects which the work contains, we emphatically recommend it as the best manual of historical and practical politics in the English language, and believe that, if it could gain a million readers, this country would be greatly benefited thereby. The practical politics it teaches is, of course, not the variety cultivated by Tammany braves; and yet we wish it could be read by such of the braves as can read at all. True practical politics is politics based upon a study of the past. "History," says Mr. Freeman, "is past Politics and Politics present History." Only upon the basis of historical facts and conditions can a sound policy be founded; and, recognizing this truth, Dr. Wilson has not attempted to evolve from his inner consciousness any Utopian panacea for political and social ills. Neither the by-gone sophisms of a Rousseau, nor the modernisms of a Bellamy or a Henry George can blind him to the fact that "one rule there is which may not be departed from under any circumstances, and that is the rule of historical continuity. In politics nothing radically novel may safely be attempted. No result of value can ever be reached in politics except through slow and gradual development, the careful adaptations and nice modifications of growth. Nothing may be done by leaps." Equally free from the shallow doctrines of extreme *laissez faire* and from the fantastic absurdities of those would-be reformers who imagine that human nature can be utterly changed by legislative nostrums, he declares that "Society, it must always be remembered, is vastly bigger and

more important than its instrument, Government. Government
should serve society, by no means rule or dominate it. Government should not be made an end in itself; it is a means only—
a means to be freely adapted to advance the best interests of the
social organism. The State exists for the sake of society, not
society for the sake of the State."

The scope of the work is very wide. Beginning with a discussion of the probable origin of government, the author rejects the
various *a priori* hypotheses and adopts the only historically
grounded theory, that the family, viz., was the original State,
and that the modern State "may be regarded as in an important
sense only an enlarged family." Discussing next the probable
early development of government among primitive tribes, Dr.
Wilson goes on to discuss historically and critically the governments of Greece and Rome. Mediæval governments, as evolved
from the fusion of Roman, Christian and Teutonic ideas and
customs, are next passed in review. The governments of important modern States are then taken up, the government of
France, the various governments of Germany and Switzerland,
those of the dual monarchies, Austria-Hungary and Sweden-
Norway, and, in still greater detail, those of England and the
United States. All these governments are historically treated,
special attention, however, being given to their present forms,
and not merely to their national Constitutions, but to the various
state, county, district, department, town and village institutions.
The work is a cyclopædia of valuable and interesting facts, and
is recommended both to teachers and the public generally. It
would be well if it could be read and studied by all who think
politics can be understood by any male of twenty-one years and
who imagine that the only necessary qualifications for statesmanship are the capacity to "fix" primaries and mouth upon
the stump.

University of Virginia.   R. H. DABNEY.

Printed in the New York *Presbyterian and Reformed Review*, II (Jan. 1891), 177-79.

A Review   [January 1891]

THE ORIGIN AND GROWTH OF THE ENGLISH CONSTITUTION. An
   Historical Treatise, in Which is Drawn Out, by the Light of
   the Most Recent Researches, the Gradual Development of the
   English Constitutional System, and the Growth out of that

System of the Federal Republic of the United States. By
HANNIS TAYLOR. Boston, 1889. Vol. i, pp. xl, 616.[1]

This volume justifies its title. It is a careful *resumé* of the
scholarly material, so various and so important, which has accumulated in recent years touching the history and development of the English Constitution. It is more than that. It is also
a discriminating *resumé*. Mr. Taylor is a lawyer of Mobile, Ala.
His work was conceived and begun, he tells us, before the appearance of Green's *Short History of the English People* and Taswell-Langmead's *Constitutional History*.[2] It has developed under
his hands slowly; his materials have grown thrice familiar to
him, becoming parts of the stealthy, unhurried accretions of his
thought before making their way into his manuscript. They
have, in a sense, been reconceived, therefore, and the book is
Mr. Taylor's own, not a compilation merely. There is evidence
at many points of independence of judgment; once and again,
indeed, the author has been able, because of his training in the
law and his knowledge of the best discussions of legal and constitutional principles and of legal history, himself to contribute
clarifying suggestions regarding matters of critical interest. The
Introduction, which occupies some eighty pages, is an eminently
satisfactory setting forth of his thesis as a whole, and a serviceable mirror of his method and point of view, while the Summary,
which occupies the last twenty-eight pages of the volume, is a
piece of writing which it would be conventional to call "masterly," but more discriminating to characterize as instinct with a
clarified appreciation of the subject as a whole. It preserves a
fine sense of proportion at the same time that it gives distinct
enumeration to every essential element of the constitutional
development under examination. As a whole, the book deserves
a most cordial welcome and appreciation. A work of minute carefulness, it is at the same time vital and engaging. It makes
available to the student a vast amount of matter before scattered
and unharmonized—except for the somewhat similar work of
Taswell-Langmead—and for this students cannot fail to be
grateful.

But, unhappily, as Mr. Bagehot says, it is not the business of
the critic to be grateful, and it is necessary to join to very generous praise of this book a statement also of its limitations.

---

[1] The second part (not volume) of this work was published in Boston by
Houghton Mifflin in 1898.

[2] The reader is reminded that *The Papers of Woodrow Wilson* is a continuing
series, indexed with cumulative cross references. All authorities and works cited
by Wilson in this review have been mentioned, in most cases many times,
in bibliographies, essays, lecture notes, etc., in preceding volumes.

These, although not to be too much insisted upon as against the general merit and value of the work, are nevertheless radical. In the first place, the promise of the Preface, that the subject will be unfolded "in the light of the latest researches—English, German, French and American," is not fulfilled, except to a limited extent. The author chooses a certain set of authorities and follows them quite absolutely, and that without being always careful that they are in complete agreement among themselves. The extremely important opinions of Prof. Gneist, whose studies have lain almost exclusively in the field of English constitutional and administrative history, widely diverge at more points than one from the views which Mr. Taylor accepts without question from Prof. Freeman and Bishop Stubbs, but they receive, at least in this first volume, hardly any consideration at all. For instance, at page 240, where Mr. Taylor is setting forth the views of the two great English writers touching the virtual derivation of the Norman Council from the Saxon Witan, we are simply told, with all possible brevity in a foot-note, that "Gneist denies the continuance of the witan as a feudal council." This is an issue between almost equally great authorities upon a question central to the whole of English institutional development, and it is fairly startling to find it passed by with so great indifference. Not a little of the "light of the most recent researches" is thus summarily quenched. Of the irreconcilability of the authorities relied upon there are several instances. Perhaps the most notable occurs in the discussion of our Federal Supreme Court. Mr. Taylor there accepts, as he should, Mr. Bryce's demonstration that the powers of constitutional interpretation vested in our Federal judiciary are perfectly normal developments from long-established English principle of judicial function, and find a virtually complete parallel in the judicial systems now existing in all the more important British colonies, systems capped by the Judicial Committee of the Privy Council as a national Supreme Court; and yet he follows a *dictum* of Sir Henry Maine's in asserting that "the Supreme Court of the United States has no prototype in history." If Mr. Bryce's exposition of the character and derivation of our national judiciary be correct—as it indisputably is—the statement of Mr. Taylor that our Supreme Court has no prototype can be true only in a formal sense. He cannot be right with both Bryce and Maine, unless he hedge his statement about with qualifications which he entirely omits.

Another important limitation to the permanent value of the book is found in its incomplete and therefore quite inconclusive scientific analysis of institutions. Here again, apparently, the author errs through obedience to his leading authorities. Mr. Freeman (to be specific) is not strong in scientific analysis, and it is Mr. Freeman's analysis which he accepts in his discussion of the nature of "federalism as a system of government"–the best example that can be given of his method. In endeavoring to differentiate confederations of the loose type exemplified in our own federal arrangements under the Articles of Confederation, and in the Swiss Confederacy as it existed under the Pact of 1815, from compacted federal States such as our own present Union and the present German Empire, he fastens upon the single question whether the federal authority acts directly upon individuals or only indirectly, through the States, as the conclusive criterion. If the federal authority acts directly upon individuals, we have a "perfect or ideal federal government," a "composite State" (Mr. Freeman's phrase); if the federal authority acts upon individuals indirectly, by requisition upon the several States of the federated group, it is an imperfect federal government. This is the criterion first suggested by Hamilton in the *Federalist*, though Mr. Taylor does not seem to derive it from him, but from Mr. Freeman. When examined, however, this criterion proves to be, not the essential, but only an accidental feature of the perfected federal State. It is noteworthy that Mr. Taylor does not cite the federal example of the present German Empire in his discussion of this point. That Empire is unquestionably a perfected federal State, more compacted and energized in many respects than our own federal government or that of Switzerland. Its structure has furnished writers like Laband and Jellinek with the most perfect analysis of the essential character of the *Bundesstaat* yet offered. And yet this great federal State acts in many things, not by commanding individuals, but by requisition upon the States which are its members. This is an awkwardness, a weakness, in organization, but it does not deprive it of the character of a perfected federal State. "The federal State has, as contrasted with a confederation, these distinguishing features: (*a*) a permanent surrender on the part of the constituent communities of their right to act independently of each other in matters which touch the common interest, and the consequent fusion of these communities, in this respect, into what is practically a single State. As regards other States they have merged their individuality into one national whole; the lines which separate them are none of them on the outside, but all on the inside, of the new organism. (*b*) The federal State possesses a special body of federal law, a special federal jurisprudence in which is expressed the national authority of the compound State. This is not a law agreed to by the constituent communities; as regards federal law there are no constituent communities; it is the spoken will of the new community, the Union. (c) There results a new conception of the exercise of sovereignty.["] There exists in the federal State no single completely sovereign body. "In certain spheres of State action the authorities of the Union are entitled to speak the common will, to utter laws which are the supreme law of the land; in other spheres of State action the constituent communities still act with the full autonomy of completely independent States." The central criterion is the existence of a common sovereign will which is not compounded of the consenting judgments of the constituent communities, but is separate and independent, speaking the individuality of the Federal State. Whether that will be or be not exercised directly upon individuals is, though an important accident, only an accident of the federal character.

Mr. Taylor, of course, necessarily falls into inconsistencies in holding both the ordinary view that the colonies became sovereign States upon the establishment of their independence and the view of Von Holst that the second Continental Congress constituted a national government, but this has its close connections with the incomplete analysis of institutions to which reference has already been made, and space forbids its further discussion here.

The author's method is, in places, too much the method of the digest, and one feels once and again that this book, like Mr. Freeman's perfected federal government, is "composite," rather than all of a piece. But a just judgment of the book, when spoken in sum, must give greatest prominence to praise, not to blame.

Princeton. WOODROW WILSON.[3]

Printed in the New York *Presbyterian and Reformed Review*, II (Jan. 1891), 179-81.
[3] It is difficult to say precisely when Wilson wrote this review. There is no correspondence concerning it in the Wilson Papers because the chief editor of *The Presbyterian and Reformed Review*, Benjamin B. Warfield, was a professor at Princeton Theological Seminary, and Wilson presumably responded to Warfield's oral request for a contribution. Wilson's copy of the Taylor volume (Wilson Library, DLC) is inscribed "Sept. 1889." It seems likely that Wilson read the book thoroughly during the summer of 1890 while writing his essay, "The English Constitution," printed at Oct. 1, 1890, even though he had made some use of Taylor while preparing his Johns Hopkins lectures on administration in early 1890. He probably wrote the review soon after coming to Princeton.

Wilson made a few marginal comments while reading the Taylor volume and, after finishing the book, wrote a two-page longhand and shorthand summary and critique. These sheets he tucked in between pages 298-99.

From Robert Bridges

Dear Tommy: New York   Jan 3 1891

There was a panic precipitated the other day by the receipt of a note in my brother's family from Registrar [Henry N.] Van Dyke warning them in language diplomatic but vigorous that John was in danger of failing to pass English, German, and Algebra in the coming mid-year examination. The note was a printed blank with the subjects filled in. As I was not familiar with that particular blank in my college days, I am a little in the dark as to its seriousness. Perhaps you can, without too much trouble, give me light? Is it sent out to most of the "fourth division" men or is it reserved for "incorrigibles" who are in danger of the judgment?

I fear John has been loafing, though he assures me he has tried very hard. I suppose he really thinks he has been working, but he does not know how. He has changed his club[1] to a new house on the street near Duff's.[2] Do you know anything about that particular Club? I hear that there are four freshmen Clubs in the house, and all of them very noisy.

Please dont put yourself to any trouble about these questions, but take your time to answer. I shall make a personal investigation in a week or two.

Here's wishing you a happy new Year—with all the success that is sure to be your's.

With my regards to Mrs. Wilson

                    Your Friend   Robert Bridges

ALS (WP, DLC) with WWhw notation on env.: "Ans. 9. Jan'y, '91."
    [1] The Catch as Catch Can Club, a freshman eating club which survived only for the academic year 1890-91.
    [2] John Thomas Duffield, Dod Professor of Mathematics, who lived at 23 University Place, Princeton.

From Albert Shaw

Dear Wilson: [New York] Wed'y evening.   Jan. 7, 1891

I got in today per the "Bothnia," in good condition. I am about to catch a train for Warsaw N. Y. where I shall stay a day or two—perhaps until Monday—with my mother and sister. The upshot of my visit to England is—in brief—that I shall take charge of the Am. edition of the *Review of Reviews* upon terms highly favorable in every way for me. But my hand will not appear for a month. I must break this news to Pres. Adams of Cornell. On some accounts I am a little anxious to know what is the "lay of the land" at Princeton. You will, I am sure, understand perfectly that I am, in no manner whatsoever, presuming upon anything from that quarter; but I feel a pretty strong drawing thitherward, and if I should be honored with an invitation to undertake a professorship there I should probably deem myself "effectually called." Possibly there is nothing more for me to know than I knew on Nov. 21; but in any case I am going to ask you to send me a line, care of Dr. J. C. Fisher, Warsaw, New York. I should like, if possible to hear from you before communicating with Pres. Adams. My engagement with the *Review* is not irrevocable; but I am fully persuaded that it is best in view of the whole situation, for me to undertake the work.

I had a pleasant time in London and Paris.

With regards to Mrs Wilson, I am, as ever,

Sincerely Yours　　Albert Shaw.

ALS (WP, DLC) with WWhw notations on env.: "Ans. 9 Jan'y '91" and "Gneist: History of the Eng. Const. 2 vols (letter-press ed. limited) $8.oo (Net) G. P. Putnams."

From Herbert Baxter Adams

My dear Dr. Wilson:　　　　　Baltimore, Md., January 9, 1891.

When can you come to us this year to give your lectures on Administration? We are planning for various short courses of lectures in our department and it is very desirable to fix the dates for each lecturer. I am preparing another circular for the Historical Department and should be glad to announce any special topics which you may desire to treat in your promised course.　　　　　Very sincerely yours,　　H. B. Adams

TLS (WP, DLC) with WWhw notation on env.: "Ans. 12 Jan'y, '91."

To Albert Shaw

My dear Shaw:　　　　　Princeton, New Jersey.　9 January, 1891.

I was sincerely glad to get your letter, and to know that your trip had been in every way satisfactory to you. I feel every confidence in your ability to make the Review 'go' in a way satisfactory both to the eyes and the minds of readers on this side, and I believe that you will enjoy the work.

I wish that the matter of our chair of Economics here could be concluded in an equally prompt and satisfying manner; and, if we had as much money as Mr. Stead now commands, it could and would be. You may be sure that I have canvassed the matter here very thoroughly; for I feel that I simply must have you as a colleague; that it is necessary to me in every view of the case, social or intellectual; and I now believe, from all indications, as I believed when I wrote to you from Middletown, that I shall have you as a colleague if only you are free and willing to come when we conservatively managed people down here are ready to move in the matter. It is a case of money, and stands thus: the general income of the college would bear, with a little skimping in administration, the salary of another professor; but the only prudent way in which to administer a college trust is to have every chair endowed and independent of the ups and downs (the possible ups and downs) of the general income from tuition and dormitory rents. Dr. Patton wants to establish the new chair of Economics by endowment and he believes that he can secure the endowment very soon provided his leverage on the generosity of our friends be not lessened by the fact that we have already such a chair and are somehow managing to pay its incumbent a salary. In short, as you will have no difficulty in seeing, it will be much easier to get money to create the chair than to get money to relieve the general income of the college of a charge which it is nevertheless showing itself able to bear. That is the financial situation; and, although impatient on personal grounds of any causes of delay, I cannot say that the reasons are not cogent ones: for it is imperatively necessary that all the elasticity of the college funds should be reserved to cover the necessary increase of instruction in departments in which no one can be made interested enough to be brought to the point of endowment.

Now, as to the situation from a personal point of view. There is no doubt in my mind that you are the only man seriously considered for this chair, which must come soon, even if it come without endowment. Dr. Patton and Professor Sloane are already both of them your strong supporters, and all of the trustees who have been consulted, so far as I know, are strongly inclined to the opinion that we ought to have you if and when we can get you. In brief, it seems to me that, if you should be willing to wait for a call here, so far as your plans are academic plans, there is little or no doubt that the place will be yours. This of course is my own judgment in the matter. I can commit no one else: I can only tell you in confidence what I know and have heard. I know the heartiness of Sloane's and Patton's endorsements of you, so far as they personally are concerned; and the financial situation Dr. Patton explained to me last night, knowing that I had come to find out how I was to answer your letter.

My temperament is probably not the cautious executive temperament: I should prefer to act when the situation and the man both seem to be ready. At any rate in a confidential letter like this to a dear friend I can show no diplomatic circumspection; I must lay bare the whole inside of the affair for your private consideration. And I am going to add that I hope that, if this delay on Princeton's part, well-advised and necessary as it seems from the Administration's point of view, involves any definite risk of our permanently losing the chance to get you, you will let me know it very distinctly.

Mrs. Wilson joins me in the very warmest regards; and you are always sure of the affection of

Your sincere friend　Woodrow Wilson

TCL (in possession of Virginia Shaw English).

To Robert Bridges

My dear Bobby,　　　　　　　　Princeton, 9 January, 1891

I was obliged to wait till the term opened to find any one who could give me a satisfactory account of the sort of notice sent to John's parents. Even yet I have not been able to see any one who can tell me about his particular case: that I hope to be able to do to-night at Faculty meeting. In the meantime, however, rather than keep you waiting longer for a reply, I make what preliminary report I can. It isn't much, but it answers your questions.

At about this period of the term the Freshman Committee, for the academic freshmen, the School of Science Committee, for the scientific freshmen,[1] go through the roll of the class, examining records so far as determinable, select the men, be they few or many, whose records indicate that the term examinations may trip them, and send notices to that effect to their "parents or guardians," in order that the boys may receive warning in the most effective way—through the most impressive channels—and have a period of grace in which to take a 'brace.' John, therefore, is probably, not alone in his danger. But I shall try to make a more particular report on his case within a day or two.

In the meantime, Bobby, a word with you. Don't ever again dare to speak of 'troubling' me about any affair which in any way concerns you. Even if I did not like John for his own sake, it would be enough for me that he is your nephew, and nothing I could do for him would be any 'trouble' at all, but only and wholly a pleasure. But I do like him, heartily—and have but one complaint to make of him: that I have never yet been able to persuade him to make a confidential friend of me. I always have to hunt him up and thrust questions and advice upon him.

I was ill with the 'grippe' (or words to that effect) for the two or three weeks immediately preceding the Christmas recess, and am not quite 'chipper' yet: but I am in fairly good trim again. What bears most heavily upon me is the want of funds to secure our Law School and the indispensable Stockton Estate (now for sale cheap) on which to put it.[2] With warmest regards from Mrs. Wilson and love from myself,

Your affectionate friend,   Woodrow Wilson

ALS (Meyer Coll., DLC).
[1] The College of New Jersey at this time was divided into two departments, the Academic Department, for students working for the A.B. degree, and the John C. Green School of Science, for students working for the B.S. degree in the physical sciences and various branches of engineering.
[2] Wilson was referring here to the ancestral Stockton mansion, "Morven," and its large lot. "Morven" was sold soon afterward by the trustees of Samuel Witham Stockton to Professor Charles Woodruff Shields for $30,000. See Alfred Hoyt Bill, *A House Called Morven* (Princeton, N.J., 1954), p. 149.

From the Minutes of the Princeton Faculty

5 5' P.M., Friday, Jany. 9th, 1891.

. . . The Dean[1] having called attention to the habit of demanding exorbitant prices for the furniture of rooms in College it was thereupon

Resolved That a Committee be appointed to take into consideration the matter of the allotment of rooms in College to the students and the disposal of furniture.

Professors Duffield, Packard,[2] Murray, Ormond[3] and W. Wilson were appointed the Committee.[4]

[1] James Ormsbee Murray, Dean of the Faculty and Holmes Professor of Belles Lettres and English Language and Literature. Born Camden, S.C., Nov. 27, 1827. A.B., Brown University, 1850; instructor in Greek at Brown, 1850-51. Was graduated from Andover Theological Seminary in 1854 and held pastorates in Massachusetts and New York, serving as pastor of the Brick Presbyterian Church of New York City, 1873-75. Elected Holmes Professor at Princeton in 1875, he became the first Dean of the Faculty in 1883 and served in this post until his death on March 27, 1899.
[2] William Alfred Packard, Kennedy Professor of Latin Language and Literature and the Science of Language.
[3] Alexander Thomas Ormond, Stuart Professor of Mental Science and Logic.
[4] For their report, see the Princeton Faculty Minutes, Jan. 24, 1891.

From Edmund Janes James

Annals of the American Academy
of Political and Social Science.
My Dear Prof. Wilson: Philadelphia, Jan. 10/91

Can you not present a paper to the Academy in the course of the winter, possibly at the next meeting in February, upon legal

education in the United States.[1] I should like very much to have
the Academy take up this subject, and push it along; and, of
course, whatever you may print in the Annals will give you a
permanent place to refer to for whatever subsequent work you
may wish to do in carrying out your schemes at Princeton.

Very truly yours,   Edmund J. James[2]

TLS (WP, DLC) with WWhw notation on env.: "Ans. 12 Jan'y, '91."
  [1] There is nothing in the *Annals of the American Academy* for 1891-92 to
indicate that Wilson returned a favorable reply.
  [2] Professor James was editor of *The Annals* as well as a professor at the
Wharton School of the University of Pennsylvania.

From Charles Force Deems[1]

American Institute of Christian Philosophy.

Dear Sir,   New York, 10 Jan 1891

It gives me pleasure to be permitted to communicate the wish
of our Institute that you will be one of our lecturers at our
Fifteenth Summer School next August.

Avon-by-the-Sea is a very charming Summer resort.

The honorarium is not tempting but the service to truth seems
to so many learned men a compensation that we have had a
very distinguished list of lecturers, to which we greatly desire to
add your name. Please fix the subject and the date in your reply
if you can. Please make an early return of the enclosed that we
may know your decision.[2]

With great regards,   Yours truly,   Charles F. Deems

Ps. If not prepared with subject now that can be given later.
Be good enough to suggest other lecturers.

TLS (WP, DLC) with WWhw notation on env.: "Ans. 12 Jan'y '91." Att.: typed
contract, unsigned.
  [1] Lecturer and author of many books on religious subjects.
  [2] Wilson undoubtedly declined the invitation.

From Joseph R. Wilson, Jr.

My dearest Brother: Clarksville, Tenn., Jany. 11/91.

I have been one of the busiest fellows during the past week
that you ever heard of. As you saw by the marked copy of the
Progress I sent you a few days ago, I have purchased the plant
of the Clarksville Democrat. I gave $500.00 cash and bal. will be
paid in 6, 12, & 18 months. Cost of plant $2,100.00. The Clarks-
ville Democrat is an old weekly paper. When I say old I mean
that it has been long established. It has quite a reputation in
this and surrounding counties and has a large subscription list.

A well fitted job office is connected with the Democrat. This newspaper plant I have consolidated with the Daily Progress and commencing tomorrow, The Progress-Democrat afternoon and weekly, will be issued, Gaines & Wilson proprietors. L. W. Gaines, proprietor of the Progress, will do duty as business manager of the firm and a good business man he is, too. I will be managing editor and will have under me a local editor who will take my place as City Editor. . . .

Father has been rather unwell during the last three days, but is much better today. It was only a short spell of sickness. I am in statu quo. We both send much love to you all.

Your aff. bro.   Joseph.

I enjoyed your last letter muchly as did Kate also.

ALS (WP, DLC).

An Outline of the Preface to "The Philosophy of Politics"[1]

[c. Jan. 12, 1891]

The Democratic State

Preliminary:

1. Present estimation of democracy
   Immense importance of understanding it.

2. The sort of philosophy wanted
   Grounds of dissatisfaction with past Commentaries

3. The historical method and the *organic theory*

The essence of the matter is in the nation itself. Loose constitutions would be as unstable as they have been in France.

4. Opposition between written constitutions and the organic conception. *Is* the constitution *essential*?

Our theory unorganic, our practice organic.

5. Effects of written constitutions upon thought and practice. The rule of lawyerly conceptions and *formalism*. Difficulty, springing hence, of reading the growth of national sentiment in the U.S.—are they speaking of the law of constitutions or of the laws of politics and national development?

6. Analysis sufficiently complete: what is needed is, *synthesis*. The possible line of synthesis.[2]

WWhw and WWsh one-page MS. (WP, DLC).

[1] For a general essay on Wilson's projected study of modern democracy, which he now usually called "The Philosophy of Politics," see the Editorial Note, "Wilson's First Treatise on Democratic Government," Vol. 5.

[2] This outline seems to be the document to which Wilson refers in the next document.

An Outline of "The Philosophy of Politics"

(Next after what is written). 1/12/91

Proposition: It is diffusion of vitality and diversification of habit
and capacity that make for structural and functional
strength and for individual liberty. (Here adapt passages
from old P.o.P. *mss.*[1] on the character of English as contrasted with French self-government,—by way of explanation and illustration of what I mean by diffusion of vitality
and diversification of habit and capacity). A statement of
the real historical nature of individual liberty:

Political liberty (i.e. individual liberty) not contrasted with or
antagonistic to the powers and eminences of the body
politic, but the logical complement thereof: i.e. political
progress consists in vital differentiation, that is, in the
greatest diffusion of power and diversification of habit and
vitality consistent with wholeness; and individual liberty is
simply the crown of the process: the utmost possible diffusion of power and diversification of habit and capacity
among the individuals who make up the state. In other
words, that the commune should to the greatest possible
extent choose its own life and supply its own means is a
principle carried but one step further in the proposition that
the individual also, the smallest unit of society, should to
the utmost possible extent be given choice of his own life
and left to supply the means of it. His liberty is *in direct
line* with political progress.

Inquiry: What has produced and what can be counted on to produce vigour and variety of life throughout the whole structure, and what sort of vitality and diversification produces
good democratic stuff?

Illustrative contrast between ancient and modern democracy:
Complexity of modern political life and of modern government as compared with ancient simplicity of life and of
government.

> *The Case of Athens*, where the simplicity was of two kinds:
> (1) of social elements and political structure;
> (2) of geographical size and constitution, so that Athens
> was not only all of a single piece, but also so put together
> and collected for immediate action as to be able to do all
> things,—and anything,—upon a single resolution and at
> once.

[1] Here Wilson refers to "The Modern Democratic State," printed at Dec. 1,
1885, Vol. 5.

Simple states much more liable to error and sudden disaster than complex states,—states complex both in elements and structure.

Historical Survey:

A. *Ancient political society*: its structure, elements, and operation.

B. The transformation and diversification effected by *the Middle Ages*:

All elements, old and new, and more than ever in the world before (whose history had been characterized by exclusion rather than by combination), thrown into the pot. A new mass produced, needing a new differentiation and development.

Two products: on the one hand, complexes like England in one sort and Germany in another; on the other simple states of great mass hammered into a compact and mechanically homogeneous whole by the processes of the later feudal monarchies,—like France.

C. *The industrial and educational revolution* of the last and the present centuries (having begun, germinally, of course, in the Renaissance).

Has not been of the same benefit to the simplified state, such as France, because the energies of such a state are still to a great extent undifferentiated, still exercised as a mass, with unparted functions, a dangerous unity of structural action and impulse.

D. *The modern democratic state*: its various antecedents, forms, and conditions; its elements of strength and of weakness; the conditions of its development in the future.

PART I.

History of Self-government.

Chap. I. Development of a diffused political vitality and diversification of the governing habit and capacity in *the classical states of antiquity.*

II. *The Middle Ages*: the elements; their combination; the new differentiation and development.

III. Development of a diffused political vitality and diversification of the governing habit and capacity in *England.* Examination of English local government from the test point of view under the regime of *the Justices of the Peace.* Are the new counties constituted with the right organization, when judged from the same point of view?

IV. *In the United States.* History of local government in the U. S. Organized in accordance with English types of an

earlier time, and developed along different lines,—lines more in keeping with or [our] test standard, of differentiation and diffusion of vitality.
V. *In Germany*. Destruction of local government proper, but preservation of local differentiation of a certain not unvital sort in the division of the country into a congeries of petty states, with just enough unity to promise unity with vital variety in the future.
VI. *In France*. France, though large, made as simple an organism, and therefore as undeveloped and dangerous (as direct, eager, impetuous, and much more tremendous), by this feudal monarchy, as was Athens or Rome.
VII. The political training of *the Russian nation*. Illustrates the test principle by contraries.
VIII. *The Forces* that make for Political Development.

PART II.
The Democratic State in Action.
Chap. I. *The Structure* of the Modern Democratic State.
 II. *The Law and the Legal Character* of the Modern Democratic State. (Historically and practically considered)—
 A. Its *Public Law*;
 B. Its Relations to *International law* and action;
 C. Its *Private Law*.
 III. *The Ends and Functions* of the Modern Democratic State.[2]

WWT MS. (WP, DLC).
 [2] A second briefer outline is printed at Aug. 28, 1892, Vol. 8.

To Herbert Baxter Adams

My dear Dr. Adams, Princeton, New Jersey, 12 January, 1891.
 I owe you an apology for not having written sooner concerning the time to be appointed for my lectures on Administration; but I have been taking it for granted that they were to be given, as heretofore, at the beginning of your second semester. That is the time for which I have planned and for which I have arranged an absence from my work here. I should like to begin at the very earliest possible date after the twenty-third (23) of January. That is the date at which our mid-year examinations begin here; and if I could do part of my work at the Hopkins during the ten days of those examinations, it would be with just that much less sacrifice of my courses here. Of course, however, your own convenience must be served, and I will come just when your second semester opens, if you prefer. I would be much

obliged if you would arrange for a five weeks' course, as last year (that is, for five lectures a week insted of only four).[1]

I don't believe that I have any topics for the course which would bear separate announcement.[2] I have carefully worked out my scheme for the course;[3] but I have been careful to give the topics such a close integration that few, if any, of them would have much significance if separately announced.

I expect to transport my family and household gods to Baltimore this time for the weeks of my stay; and I therefore look forward to my engagement with you with even more than ordinary pleasure.

I hope that I shall find you quite well and the department in its usual vigour. I trust that Dr. Ely's health is quite restored. Be kind enough to give him my warm regards.

I am enjoying immensely the opportunity given me here to work exclusively in my own lines.

With sincerest regard,
        Very cordially Yours,   Woodrow Wilson

WWTLS (H. B. Adams Papers, MdBJ).
    [1] As it turned out, Wilson lectured for six weeks, between January 26 and about March 6, 1891.
    [2] Wilson did, however, send a general description of his projected lectures on administration to Adams, the text of which was published in The Johns Hopkins University, *History and Politics* [n.p., n.d.].
    [3] A topical outline for a new three-year cycle, typed on three half-sheets (WP, DLC), and printed in the Editorial Note, "Wilson's Lectures on Administration at the Johns Hopkins, 1891-93."

To Robert Bridges

My dear Bobby,   Princeton, New Jersey, 14 January, 1891

I have seen the chairman of the Committee of the School of Science about John's case, and I have seen John himself and administered proper stimulants. The case, though not desperate, is serious. The boy has certainly been very negligent in several of his studies; and I have tried to tell him how critical the situation is, and to show him how to meet it. I believe that a determined effort will get him through everything,—perhaps even through German, though that looks a trifle desperate; but it will need a *continuous* effort from now till the end of the term. I tried to encourage, as well as to scare, him in my talk with him the other day; and he certainly left me in the proper frame of mind for a determined 'brace.'

Come down a[nd] spend next Sunday with me, Bob., not only to see the boy and add your exhortations to mine, but also to give us the cheer and pleasure of your company. This is *urgent,* from both Mrs. Wilson & me;–& I shall expect you unless I hear from you to the contrary.

Affectionately Yours,   Woodrow Wilson

ALS (WC, NjP).

From Mary Jane Ashton

Dear Mr Wilson,   Balto. Jan 15–91.

Your letter received–and would have been answered sooner had I not been waiting on one of the young men in the house to decide as to what he is going to do. He told me last week he thought of going back to Harvard College this week–and if he does–that will give me a vacant room. The young men in the house say they will arrange matters and you can have one room & I will give you the room over the dining room. So the best we can do for you will be to give you the third-story front-room– & second-story back-room. They both have double-beds–& the second-story room has also a cot. If you think the rooms will suit you–will you kindly write me which you would rather occupy yourself. The one on the second floor has a big window–but not very light, but would be very convenient for the children on account of being so near the bath-room, and also for them going up & down the stairs. I shall be very glad to have you all–if you think the arrangements will suit. As for the children being troublesome I have no fear of that. I have been used to them all my life–and am very fond of them. Mrs Hills rooms are all filled–& I would not advise you to go there if they were not– for they hate children–and are always finging [finding] fault with everyone who boards there. I sent her the young man whose name you semi-circuled–but he was a stranger. I would not send her anyone that I took an interest in. Is your nurse white or colored–does anyone of the children sleep with her. I am sorry I can't give you communicating rooms. I don't know of anyplace where you can get rooms & board in a private family. I suppose you will want to be near the University[.] Please let me know– what you think of my offer and oblidge.[1]

M. J. Ashton

ALS (WP, DLC) with WWhw notation on verso of letter: "Maggie Hutton to date of leaving $16.70[.] Maggie Foley to date of leaving $6.29," and WWhw notation on env.: "Ans. 18 Jany, '91."

[1] The Wilsons took rooms at Miss Ashton's boarding-house at 909 McCulloh Street in Baltimore.

From Herbert Baxter Adams

My dear Mr. Wilson: Baltimore, Md., January 17, 1891.

We can arrange for you to begin your lectures on Monday, January 26 at 10 A.M. and to continue at that hour on Tuesday and at 11 o'clock on Wednesday, Thursday, and Friday until the close of your course.

Hoping that this arrangement will be entirely satisfactory, I remain   Very cordially yours,   H. B. Adams

TLS (WP, DLC) with WWhw notation on env.: "Ans. 19 Jan'y."

From Philippus William Miller[1]

My dear Tommy,   Philadelphia, Jany. 17th 1891

I meant to write you a formal letter, but it seems impossible, so I have put it in more familiar shape. We have our Alumni Dinner on Friday Jan. 30th and we want you to represent the Faculty and give us a talk. Wont you please oblige us? At a meeting yesterday of the Executive Committee of the Association, of which I am Chairman, you were unanimously chosen as the representative of the Faculty at this year's Dinner and it is the earnest desire of of [sic] the Committee and of others of the Alumni that you accept. We will send you your toast in ample time, or if you prefer it you can select your own topic. We will see that you are accommodated here, and try to make you comfortable. I expect an affirmative answer.[2] If it is any inducement you will be welcomed by such as Ridge Wright, Job Trotter, Charlie McFee[,] Katie Vanuxem[3] and others including
        Yours Sincerely   Philippus W. Miller

ALS (WP, DLC) with WWhw notation on env.: "Ans. Jany 20/91."
  [1] Born Philadelphia, Oct. 18, 1859. A.B., College of New Jersey, 1879; LL.B., University of Pennsylvania, 1882. Spent his life in the practice of law in Philadelphia. A member of the executive committee of the Princeton Alumni Association of Philadelphia, 1882-97, he was the first president of the Princeton Club of Philadelphia, 1897-1900. Died Feb. 3, 1941.
  [2] Wilson returned one. His address is printed at Jan. 30, 1891.
  [3] All members of the Class of 1879.

An Announcement

[Jan. 21, 1891]
PROFESSOR WOODROW WILSON'S CLASSES
FOR THE SECOND TERM.

Prof. Woodrow Wilson will be absent from Princeton during all of February and a portion of March, and makes the following announcements concerning his classes for the second term:

He will expect the Junior required class in Political Economy to read during his absence Walker's First Lessons in Political Economy (Holt), and to be prepared to be examined upon it during the third week of March.

He will expect his elective class in American Constitutional Law to read, during the same time, Cooley's Principles of Constitutional Law (Little & Brown), and to be prepared to be examined upon it during the third week in March.

And he will expect his elective class in Administration to read "The Central Government," by H. D. Traill, (in the English Citizens Series of Macmillan), and to be prepared for an examination upon it during the third week in March.

Printed in *The Princetonian*, xv (Jan. 21, 1891), [1].

From Joseph Ruggles Wilson

My dearest son   Clarksville, Jan. 21/91
I enclose a draft on N. York for $200.00 at your request. I fully appreciate the motive for this loan, and thank you for your perfect trust in one who has never forsaken the boy he loves with all his soul and never will. What I have is yours, until all is gone & then—we can get on quite joyously just the same. I have been very ill since getting *home* (?)—rather since *leaving* home: i. e. your house. I was laid up for about 10 days. All is as it sh'd be again, however, and I am at work as usual. My danger was not much, but my *suffering* was considerable. I don't know what the matter was, and of course the doctors do not. Josie is well, & would send lots of love were he present; but he is at his office.

Be sure, my precious Woodrow, that I love you and yours more even than you can well understand, just yet. Kiss darling Ellie for me, & the sweet children.
                               Your affc   Father & *Friend*.

This money is to be without interest for as long as you want— if *never* paid, all right: for *we are one*. Only acknowledge receipt

ALS (WP, DLC) with WWhw and WWsh brief research note on env.

To Robert Bridges

My dear Bobby,   Princeton, N. J., 21 January, 1891
Alas, Saturday night will see us *all* in Baltimore. My lectures there are to begin next Monday, the 26th, and the family must be taken down on Saturday. I am deeply disappointed—*we* are

deeply disappointed. I specially wanted to see you; and I am very jealous indeed of having you stay in any house but mine. But this time I *must* turn you over to [Henry Nevius] Van Dyke,—for there's no choice. In haste (of preparation), disappointment, and affection,   Yours as ever,   Woodrow Wilson

I am to speak at the Phila. and Chicago[1] alumni meetings, I'm sorry to say.

ALS (WC, NjP).
  [1] See WW to C. H. McCormick, Jan. 27, 1891.

From Francis Landey Patton

Dear Professor Wilson   [Princeton, N. J.] Jany 22 [1891]
    I went to the Library Com yesterday for the special purpose of presenting the claims of your department. I found that the sub-com. had recommended an appropriation of $50 for Jurispru-dence in addition to the appropriation for Political Economy. It is a very small amount but it is the best we can do.
    If it is possible I will get something outside for your depart-ment so as to get a start: but I dislike to assume obligations of this kind & to make promises for I find that sometimes I can't so easily meet them. I will do what I can however, you may be sure.   Sincerely   Francis L Patton

ALS (Patton Letterpress Books, University Archives, NjP).

From Edmund Janes James

My dear Sir: Philadelphia, Jan. 23/91
    The American Academy of Political and Social Science will shortly complete its first year. We have had unusual success, and have begun a work which in many respects, we believe, is destined to prove valuable and helpful. Owing to certain circum-stances in the course of the year our printing has not been kept in as forward a state as we should have liked to keep it.
    The third number of the Annals will be out shortly, to be followed by two supplements within a short time, constituting with the 4th No. of the Annals to be issued in April the first volume of the proceedings, making in all between eight and nine hundred pages of printed matter for the first year of operations.
    It is proposed now to publish the proceedings, instead of in the form of a quarterly with supplements, in the form of a bi-monthly without supplements, paging each number by itself, and also with a continuous pagination on the inside of the page, covering

the whole proceedings for the year. This will make about six volumes of proceedings of an average of 150 pages to be issued in the course of each twelve-month. The indications are that there will be no lack of co-operation on the part of scholars, nor any lack of good things that we may be able to do for the benefit of the cause.

I should be pleased if you would indicate what you think of this plan of issuing a bi-monthly form instead of a quarterly form with supplements.

The proceedings of the Academy now reach a very wide public. We shall send out to members alone over 1600 of the January number, which will shortly appear. It has received a wide notice abroad, and will become, we believe, a more and more valuable place to put valuable matter into which specialists and the general public, interested in the economic and social affairs, would like to see.

It will be seen that the Academy has published and will continue to publish chiefly matter which the existing journals or series can not or will not take, and yet which ought to be put within the reach of all persons interested in economics and politics.

We should be glad of any contribution to the work of the Academy either from you or from your friends.[1]

Very truly yours,   Edmund J. James.

TLS (WP, DLC).
[1] Wilson apparently responded to this request with the review printed at April 1, 1891.

A Final Examination

January 23, 1891.

EXAMINATION IN THE
HISTORY OF POLITICAL ECONOMY.

1. Criticise the statement that the history of Political Economy is merely the history of error. What is the true significance of that history?

2. Why were ancient times barren of the science? Why was its development delayed until modern times? And why was it natural that the Mercantilist system should be the first to arise?

3. (a) Contrast Mercantilism and the doctrines of the Physiocrats and explain the rise of the latter school; (b) name the French statesman whose career is most prominently associated with Mercantilism, and the chief Mercantilist writers; (c) name the principal Physiocratic writers.

4. What was Adam Smith's method in Political Economy? What relation does he bear, on the one hand, to the school of thinkers represented by Ricardo, and, on the other hand, to the modern historical school?

5. Characterize the "economic man" of the school of Ricardo. State Ricardo's doctrines of Rent and of Wages.

6. Outline Frederick List's ideas of national economic development and policy.

7. State and criticise the theoretical basis of Socialism.

8. To what five conditions does Roscher ascribe the rise of communistic and socialistic movements?

9. State and connect the views of Rodbertus and Karl Marx.

10. What is the Social Democracy and what are its ideals?

Printed examination (WP, DLC).

From the Minutes of the Princeton Faculty

5 5' P.M., Friday, Jany. 23, 1891
... The Committee on the Allotment and Rental of Rooms and the Disposal of Furniture in the Rooms by the Students made a Report which was read and its recommendations were considered seriatim and adopted in part. The further consideration of it was then postponed until the meeting to be held to-morrow (24th inst.) at noon.

12 5' P.M., Saturday, Jany. 24th, 1891.
... The Report of the Committee on the Allotment and Rental of Rooms was again considered, amended and adopted and is as follows, viz:

Report of the Committee.
Rules Governing the Allotment and Rental of Rooms.

I. Rooms shall be assigned for occupation during the following College Year between the 15th of May and the 1st of June of each year.

II. This assignment shall embrace all rooms occupied by students whose connection with the College will terminate at the end of the College Year and all rooms occupied by such other students as have not renewed their leases (Vide *Rule V.b.*).

III. An allotment may also take place at the close of the first Term of each College Year for the purpose of assigning such rooms as may then fall vacant.

IIII. *a.* The assignment of rooms shall in all cases not herein specially excepted take place in such a manner that specific rooms shall be assigned by lot.

b. The rooms to be assigned shall be classified according to the amount of their rental in five groups as follows:

(1.) The first group shall embrace rooms whose rental is from $25 to $35, inclusive;

(2.) The second, those whose rental is from $40 to $66, inclusive.

(3.) The third, whose rental is from $70 to $100, inclusive.

(4.) The fourth, those whose rental is from $105 to $140, inclusive.

(5.) The fifth, those whose rental is from $155 to $180 inclusive.

c. The applicants for rooms shall be divided into corresponding groups, each applicant being required to inform the Curator in writing before the 10th of May or the 20th of January, as the case may be, both of his intention to enter the drawing and of the group in which he wishes to be placed.

d. Each drawing shall begin with the first group and proceed from that group through the other groups successively in the order given above. Any applicant who does not obtain a room in the group to which he first asked to be assigned may be allowed to draw in any higher group.

e. If there be any rooms remaining unas-[signed] after a drawing, such rooms may be assigned by subsequent allotment, at such time before the end of the year or of the term as the Curator may appoint; such supplementary allotment to be made under the same rules as the principal allotment with this exception, that the rooms disposed of by means of it may be classified [as] above or not at the discretion of the Curator.

f. Priority in the drawing shall be determined by the length of time the applicants shall have been resident members of College. The first drawing shall include the names of all applicants who have been resident members of College for more than one year. A second drawing shall include the names of all applicants who have been resident members of College one year or less.

g. New students shall have choice of any rooms remaining vacant at the time of their entering upon residence in the order of their application after under-[going] the entrance examinations for full standing, upon condition of immediately signing the lease required in all cases. (See Rule V.*a.*)

h. Double rooms shall be separately classified and alloted in accordance with the above regulations. Only such suites as consist of a study and two bed-rooms shall be considered double rooms within the meaning of this clause. No double room shall be assigned to a single individual, nor shall it be within the privilege of any single individual to draw for a double room. Every application for a double room must give the names of the two persons who intend to occupy the room together and who undertake to be jointly responsible for the rent of the same.

i. Whenever, for any reason, one of the occupants of a double room is permitted or obliged to cancel his room lease, the remaining occupant must vacate the room at the end of the current College Term, unless he agrees to pay the whole rent, or provides a room-mate who shall join him in signing a new lease for the remainder of the College Year.

When one of the occupants of a double room is a member of the Senior Class, the room shall become vacant when the Senior is graduated, and become subject to allotment as above unless the joint occupancy has continued for at least one College Year.

V.a. The tenure and liabilities of those to whom rooms are assigned under these rules shall be the tenure and liabilities expressed in the following lease, which must be signed in the case of each room allotted by the student who is to occupy it and by his parent or guardian. This lease must be signed and delivered to the Curator in each case within ten days of the allotment, except in the case of new students, provided for under Rule *IV.g.*

This agreement, made the   day of   , 189 , between the Trustees of the College of New Jersey and   of   witnesseth that the said Trustees of the College of New Jersey do hereby lease unto the said   Room No.   , in the   Entry of   to hold for one year from the date hereof, paying therefor during the said term unto the said Trustees of the College of New Jersey the yearly rent of $ in two equal payments, to be made, the one the first   days of the first Term of the College Year, the other within the first   days of the second Term of the College Year.

And the said   covenants to pay the said rent in the manner and at the times aforesaid and to deliver up the said premises to the said Trustees of the College of New Jersey or its legal representative at the end of the said Term in as good condition as the same now are or may be put into by the said Trustees of the College of New Jersey, reasonable use and wear and tear thereof, and fire and other casualty excepted. The said lessee also covenants that he will not do or suffer to be done any damage in the leased premises, and that, if any damage beyond reasonable wear and tear be done, he will cause the same to be made good as soon as possible at his own expense, employing for that purpose the proper College workmen, and paying the cost thereof at once to the College Treasurer, it being understood that the damage here meant includes the breakage of glass whether by accident or design. The said lessee further covenants that he will not sublet the same or any part thereof, nor permit any other person or persons to occupy the same or any part thereof, nor make nor suffer to be made any alteration therein without the consent of the said Trustees of the College of New Jersey for that purpose in writing first had and obtained. And the said lessee further covenants that the said Trustees of the College of New Jersey through their authorized representatives may enter the said premises for the purpose of viewing or making improvements therein at any reasonable times in the day time, or at any other time for the legitimate purposes of College discipline.

b. Any occupant of a College room may retain his room until the end of his College or Graduate Course provided he annually notify the Treasurer of his intention of retaining it, and sign a new lease, before the 1st of May. Otherwise his room shall be considered vacant and shall be included in the next allotment. In case an occupant of a double room be left without a roommate at the end of the College Year, he may renew his lease upon condition of naming another student of the College who will become joint lessee with him for the following year.

It shall also be the privilege of any occupant of a College room to renew his lease at the end of his own tenure in the name of his brother, when that brother is to enter College immediately.

c. All rooms taken at any allotment shall be taken subject to the provisions of Rule *VI.*

d. The right to occupy a room is not transferable and terminates with the expiration of the lease. Any attempt on the part of the occupant of a College room to sell or transfer, directly or indirectly, his right of occupancy shall be deemed a fraudulent transaction, and may be dealt with by the Faculty as a grave breach of College law.

e. The occupant of a College room shall deposit with the Treasurer the sum of twenty five (25) cents for each key to his room that may be furnished him by the College; and all amounts paid under this clause shall be refunded upon the return of the key or keys furnished.

VI. Students vacating College rooms shall be allowed to store any furniture not disposed of in a room designated by the College authorities, under the charge of a salesman appointed by the College, where it may be offered for sale. Furniture remaining unsold at the end of four (4) months after the date of storage shall be disposed of at public auction to the highest bidder.

VII. No exchange of rooms shall be allowed unless formally sanctioned in writing by the Curator; and then only upon terms explicitly stated in a written application signed by both parties to the proposed exchange, and not in contravention of the spirit of these rules. Such applications shall be kept on file in the Treasurer's Office.

VIII. When rooms are vacated during (*in*) a term the rent shall be paid to the end of the term.

An occupant of a College room who expects to be absent on leave for a term may be released from the obligations of his lease, provided he notify the Treasurer before the beginning of the term during which he expects to be absent, and give up the room; but no abatement or drawback of room rent shall be allowed for any period less than a College term, except by express direction of the Faculty.

Temporary Rule.

The foregoing Rules shall go into operation in regard to all dormitories except the Albert B. Dod Hall at the drawing in June, 1894. In regard to the Albert B. Dod Hall they shall go into operation at once.

Resolved, That the report as adopted be communicated to the Committee on Grounds and Buildings of the Board of Trustees and that Professors Duffield & Packard be appointed a Committee to present these Rules as expressing the views of the Faculty and to represent the opinions of the Faculty upon the subject to the Committee.[1]

The Faculty then adjourned.

[1] These regulations, approved by the Trustees' Committee on Buildings and Grounds on February 9, 1891, were printed in *Catalogue of the College of New Jersey at Princeton . . . 1891-92* (Princeton, n.d.), pp. 146-50. WW to C. H. McCormick, Jan. 27, 1891, indicates that Wilson was the principal autnor of the new regulations.

EDITORIAL NOTE

WILSON'S LECTURES ON ADMINISTRATION

AT THE JOHNS HOPKINS, 1891-93

Having already made his intellectual breakthrough in early 1890 by defining administration as a branch of public law,[1] Wilson set about with confidence inspired by this new understanding to plan a new three-year cycle of lectures for the Johns Hopkins. Probably

[1] See the Editorial Note, "Wilson's Lectures on Administration at the Johns Hopkins, 1890," Vol. 6.

near the time that he wrote his letter of January 12, 1891, to Herbert Baxter Adams, Wilson typed on half sheets the following outline:[2]

Johns Hopkins University

ADMINISTRATION, (1st. Series).

Topics:

1. Nature, Scope, and Method of Study.
2. Place and Content as a Department of Public Law.
3. The Idea of the State and of its Functions.
4. The Theory of the Division of Powers.
5. The Actual Division of Powers.
6. The Character, Forms, and Sources of Administrative Law.
7. The Relation of Administrative Acts to the Laws.
8. The Relations of Administrative Action to Personal Rights.

Johns Hopkins University

ADMINISTRATION, (2nd. Series).

Topics:

Resumé: Administrative Functions.

1. Division and Coordination of Administrative Powers and Functions,—Central and Local. General Questions of Theory and Expediency.
2. A Professional or a Non-professional Service? The technical tasks and the training of experts.
3. Central Administrative Organization, its conditions, principles, and (historical) development.
4. Central Administrative Organization in England.
5.   "   "   "   in France.
6.   "   "   "   in Prussia.
7.   "   "   "   in Italy.[3]
8.   "   "   "   in the United States.
9. Summary of Central Administrative Organization.

Johns Hopkins University

ADMINISTRATION, (3rd. Series).

Topics:

Resumé of topics of first and second series.

1. Local Administrative Organization, its conditions, principles, and (historical) development.
2. Local Administrative Organization in England.
3.   "   "   "   in France.
4.   "   "   "   in Prussia.
5.   "   "   "   in Italy.
6.   "   "   "   in the United States.

---

[2] Loose pages (WP, DLC).

[3] As Wilson's notes for lectures in 1892 and 1893 will themselves make clear, he failed to cover Italy in this series and the next, even though E. Brusa's monograph, *Das Staatsrecht des Königreichs Italien*, in the Marquardsen series, had been available since 1888.

7. Summary of Local Administrative Organization.
8. The Administration of the Modern Industrial City.
9. Administration of the Courts: Administrative Justice.[4]

The notes for the first series are printed immediately below. The notes for the second series are printed at February 1, 1892; for the third, at January 26, 1893, Volume 8. Wilson's own composition dates, the typing itself, and the bibliographical references make it clear that he revised and added to some of these notes when he lectured at the Hopkins during the third and final complete cycle, from 1894 through 1896. This is particularly true of the notes for 1891, which Wilson very considerably reworked in 1894.

In his letter to Albert Bushnell Hart of June 22, 1891, Wilson described his administration notes as mere skeletons of his lectures. Fortunately, this characterization is not entirely correct. The notes themselves are so full as to constitute the elaborate outline of a book which, if Wilson had published it, would have secured his reputation as the father of the study of administration in the United States, if not as the pre-eminent scholar in the entire field. Moreover, Wilson annotated his notes so conscientiously as to make it unnecessary to comment on his sources. Full bibliographical information about authors and titles cited can be found either in Wilson's own bibliography at the end of the first lecture in the 1891 series, or else in the bibliographies printed at March 27, 1890, Volume 6, and in the Editorial Note, "Wilson's Working Bibliography on Law," in Volume 8.

In reproducing these notes, the Editors have followed Wilson's format insofar as possible. All notes are by Wilson unless otherwise indicated.

In 1891, Wilson began his lectures on January 26, lectured four times a week for six weeks, and completed this series on about March 6. As he noted in letters to Horace E. Scudder (February 7, 1891) and to John Franklin Jameson (June 29, 1891), Wilson went to Baltimore with notes for only one lecture in hand and prepared the balance of his notes from day to day.

4 Wilson made another copy of this prospectus. It is a one-page WWT MS. entitled "Johns Hopkins University. Seventy-five Lectures on Administration," dated Dec. 29, 1891 (WP, DLC).

Notes for Lectures at the Johns Hopkins

(First Year Course). [c. Jan. 26, 1891-Feb. 27, 1894]

ADMINISTRATION

I. *Nature and Scope,—Method of Study.*

Introduction.   Political Science is so rich in topics which afford broad outlooks over the very greatest questions of social organization and progress that we might, at first sight, seem to be making ourselves voluntarily poor in confining our attention to matters of mere executive management, wh. concern primarily, not the greater meanings of the life of the state, but only the mechanism of government. But, in reality, Administration cannot be divorced from its intimate connexions with the other branches of Public Law without being distorted and robbed of its true significance. Its foundations are those deep and permanent principles of Politics which have been quarried from history and built into constitutions; and it may by no means properly be considered apart from constitutions.

1. *Definition*: Consider what Administration really is:

> *It is the continuous and systematic carrying out in practice of all the tasks which devolve upon the State*; and these tasks the State has had laid upon it *by reason of its history, thr. Law*, which is the product of what it has learned regarding liberty and authority, regarding right and obligation.

In its more general sense.

The administration of a trust organization for that purpose.

No topic in the study of government can stand by itself,—least of all, *perhaps, Administration, whose part it is to mirror the principles of government in operation*. It is not a mere anatomy of institutions. It deals directly, indeed, and principally with the structural features and the operative organs of state life; but it at every point derives its motive and significance from the essential qualities and the vital institutions of government. It must constantly turn to these for its explanation and its sanction.

> *The organs of government are nothing without the life of government, and the organs of each* State must advertise, in their own peculiarities, the individual characteristics of the State to which they belong.

2. *Administration national*, whatever may be said of Political Economy. *The problems* of Administration are also, *however*, in a very real sense *universal*, international. A wide examination of governmental organs will discover, *not only* the *differences* which may exist between government and government, *but likewise* the general *likenesses* between them. It is one of the main objects of comparative studies in Administration to reveal and discuss these two things: viz., these individual differences and these common likenesses.

If that object be at all adequately attained, there will be *opened to us a main door to* that greatest question of Politics, *the Nature of Government*;—and, whether we care to enter that door now or not, it will remain upen [open] to us so long as we retain a just conception of the usual province of the State as revealed in Administration.

3. *Legislation and Administration, Distinction* between:—Various *criteria* suggested. For legislation also, as well as Administration, may be described as the active promotion of the ends of the State.
(a) Distinction between *Will* and *Deed*. (Stein).

(b) Distinction between *general rules* and the *particular application* of them.

(c) Distinction between *Independence of will* & *Subordination* of will; between *origination* with its wide range of choice, and *discretion* with its narrow range of choice. (*Sarwey*, O v., "Allgemeines Verwaltungsrecht,"—Marquardsen, II, ii,—pp 5 et seq.).

This *a distinction not at all developed in our* own constitutional *literature*. Very vague idea conveyed, even to the legal mind, by the announcement of a course of lectures on 'Administration.'

Full realization of its field and importance all the more necessary. (See subsequent lecture).

4. *Field of Administration*, the field of *organization*, of *effective means for the accomplishment of practical ends*. It may and should be made to answer the question, *What is feasible?* Purely political questions and considerations being waived, what promising schemes are workable, which not workable. (Frame a bill; *organize a commission* or a bureau under the law).

"Man is an animal with hands."

Administration, therefore, sees *government in contact with the people*. It rests its whole front along the line which is drawn in each State between *Interference* and *Laissez faire*. It thus touches, directly or indirectly, the whole practical side of social endeavour.

5. *Its Questions are questions of adjustment*, the adjustment of means to ends, not only, but of governmental function *to historical conditions*, to liberty. Here lie, of course, the test qns. as to the success or failure of government. There is *an organization which vitalizes*, and there is *an organization which kills*. If government energizes the people by the measure of assistance which it affords, it is good; if it decreases the energy and healthful independence of individual initiative, it is bad,—bad just to the extent it does this.

Absence of these qus. of life fr. most of the books.

6. *Its Method, comparative and historical.*
Like other branches of Political Science, must undertake the study of the general political development and experience of the race.

While Administration should unquestionably regard scrupulously in all its principles and methods of action both national habit and national sentiment, its methods may, in so far as they are mere *matters of business effectiveness*, be treated as universal, international, *E.g.*, *Audit and Account*, the *differentiation and integration of Depts.*, &c., can have but *a single best way*.

Historical in method, because the development of Admin. Law has gone hand in hand during this century with the development of constitutional theory. *The following topics*, ∴, must be the hinges of our discussions:

I. *Place and Content* of Administrative Law in the general field of Public Law. *Topics*:

II. The *Tasks of the State*

III. *The Idea of the State* and of Its Functions, including *What Is a Constitutional Government?*

IV. *Theory of the Division of Powers*

V. *Actual Process and Extent of Division.*

VI. *Character, Sources, and Forms of Administrative Law.*

VII. *Theoretical and Actual Relationship of Administrative Acts to the Laws.*
The Administration and the Courts.

VIII. *Personal Rights and Administrative Action.*
The Nature of Political Liberty.

7. *Age and Development of Our Study*:

The youngest branch of Political Science, although we have a systematic work upon its main topics (the work of *Justi*) as early as 1756. And it has, until within a very few years, been *a European study entirely*, not an English study.

Reason: It *waited upon the development of Public Law.* Public Law got its main subjects only after the *development of the modern definitive constitutions*; these were built upon popular rights; and it was the effort to effect *a systematic balance between private right and public power* that produced the Science of *Administration.* So long as government could do anything it chose or deemed wise, there could be no science of Administration; for their [there] can be *no science of choice or wisdom.* *A birth of liberalism.*

In England, where popular rights were early and consciously developed, the science was unnecessary because of *parliamentary control*; because the Ministers were also members of Parliament, and had both their own and all their party's constituents to please.

Now necessary everywhere by reason of the great growth of *positive Administrative Law.* (The various sources of this portion of positive law to be discussed in a later lecture.).

8. *Stages of Development in Germany: Three* in number,

(1) *Stage* when it was based upon *empirical theory*, the theory which dominated *early political liberalism*, viz., that *Politics* was *a struggle* between two opposing forces, the government and the governed: *law the balance* established between these two forces: Administration the guardianship, interpretation, and enforcement of the law. *An Instinct.*

No actual State being found whose structure and functions tallied with this theory, *an arbitrary list of additional* and exceptional (?) *powers* was tacked on, including certain so-called *sovereign rights* (*Hoheitsrechte*), rights of *eminent* domain (*Gebietshoheit*), of *military, financial,* and *police* supremacy, etc., which could be brought under no common rubric and had simply to be catalogued.

A Theory.

(2) *Stage* when it was based upon the *conception of the state as a mere legal institution,* a mere *Institute of Law (Rechtsstaat).* This stage marked by the great treatise of *Von Mohl,* which broke a road and determined the whole future course of the study. He *recognized Administrative Law and Constitutional Law* as *two parts of one and the same science,* viz. *Staatsrecht,* or *Public Law,* and in this his example has been decisive.

But he was prevented from seeing the full significance and scope of Administrative Science by *his conception of the State as an Institute of Law,* the representation of the people as merely a means of protecting their rights, etc.

A Convenience ("A Condition")

(3) *Stage* when based upon *empirical fact,*—the facts of the development of *positive enactment in Germany,* and the facts of the development of study in the various parts of the field of Political Science, the development of *separate "Disciplines,"* e.g., Political Economy and Finance, Adjudication, Military Science, etc. (*See post*).

The organic conception of the State necessitates principles (and perhaps divisions of the field) of quite another kind. (This to be discussed subsequently).

9. *The Literature of the Science.* I shall give under this head *only the main authorities:*

OLD: *Justi,* "Grundsätze der Polizeiwissenschaft," Göttingen, 1756.

Sonnenfels, "Grundsätze der Polizei, Handlung und Finanzwissenschaft." Vienna, 1765 (7th. ed. 1804).

Berg, "Handbuch der Deutschen Polizeirechts," Göttingen, 1799 (2nd. ed. 1802).

Mohl, R. von, "Die Polizeiwissenschaft nach der Grundsätzen des Rechtsstaates," Tübingen, 1832 (3rd. ed., 1866).

---- - ---, "System der Präventiv-Jurtiz," Tübingen, 1834. Published with the above in three volumes, Freiburg i. B., 1890.

MODERN: I. *German:*—

Stein, L. von, "Verwaltungslehre," 8 vols., Stuttgart, 1865-1883.—.

----- - ---, "Handbuch der Verwaltungslehre und des Verwaltungsrechts," 1 vol., Stuttgart, 2nd. ed., 1876.

Gneist, R. von, "Der Rechtsstaat," 2nd. ed., Berlin, 1879.

----- - ---, "Selfgovernment, Kommunalverfassung, und Verwaltungsgerichte in England," 3 ed., 1 vol., 1871.

------ - ---, "Das englische Verwaltungsrecht der Gegenwart in Vergleichung mit dem deutschen Verwaltungswesen," 3 ed., 2 vols., 1883 & 1884.

------ - ---, "Englische Verfassungsgeschichte," Berlin, 1882.

Rösler, "Lehrbuch des Verwaltungs-Rechts," vols., 1 & 2, Erlangen, 1872-'73.

Sarwey, O. von, "Allgemeines Verwaltungsrecht," in Marquardsen's "Handbuch des Oeffentlichen Rechts der Gegenwart," I., ii., monograph I. Freiburg i.B., 1884.

------ - ---, "Das Oeffentliche Recht u. die Verwaltungsrechtspflege," Tübingen 1880.

Meier, E. von, "Das Verwaltungsrecht," in Holtzendorff's "Encyklopädie der Rechtswissenschaft" 5 ed., 1890, pp. 1157 et seq.

Schönberg, G., (ed.), "Handbuch der Politischen Oekonomie," Part III, "Verwaltungslehre," by Rümelin, Gg. Meyer (the theory and general principles), L. Jolly, and E. Löning.

Bornhak, C., "Preussisches Staatsrecht," 3 vols., (vols. 2 and 3 devoted to Prussian administration), Freiburg i.B., 1889.

Stengel, K. Freiherr von, "Wörterbuch des deutschen Verwaltungsrechts," 2 vols., Freiburg i.B., 1889-1890.

Meyer, G., "Lehrbuch des deutschen Verwaltungsrechts," vol. 1, Leipzig, 1883.

Loening, C., "Lehrbuch des deutschen Verwaltungsrechts," vol. 1, Leipzig, 1884.

Jellinek, Georg., "Gesetz und Verordnung." Freib., 1887

MODERN, II. *French*:—

Haas, C. P. M., "Administration de la France, Histoire, et Méchanisme des grands pouvoirs de l'État, Fonctions publique, Conditions de l'administration et d'avancement dans toutes les Carriers, Privileges, et Immunities," 4 vols., 2 ed., Paris, 1861.

Chéruel, "Dictionnaire historique des Institutions, Moeurs, et Coutumes de la France," 2 vols., 6 ed., Paris, 1884.

Laferriére, E., "Droit Administratif," 5 ed., 1860.

--------- -, "Traité de la Juridiction administrative et de recours contentieux," 2 vols., 1887 & 1889.

Batbie, "Cours de droit administratif," 1869.

Aucoc, L., "Conferences sur l'administration et le droit administratif" 3 vols., Paris, 1882.

Ducrocq, "Cours de droit administratif" 2 vols., Paris, 1881.

Dufour, G., "Traité général de droit administratif appliqué," 3 ed., 8 vols., Paris, 1869-'70.

Pradier-Foderé, "Précis de droit administratif," 7 ed., Paris, 1872.

Bloch, Maurice, "Dictionnaire de l'administration française," 2 ed., Paris, 1877, and annual Supplements 1878-'82.

Lébon, André, "Das Staatsrecht der französischen Republik," in Marquardsen's "Handbuch des Oeffentlichen Rechts der Gegenwart," Freiburg i.B., 1886.

Ferron, H. De, "Institutions municipales et provinciales comparées," Paris, 1884.

MODERN: ENGLISH,

The only systematic work in English devoted distinctively to Administration as a separate "discipline":

Goodnow, Frank J., "Comparative Administrative Law," 2 vols., New York, 1893

II. *Place and Content as a Topic in Public Law*:

1. *The Division* of Law *into Public and Private*:—

Public Law is that which concerns the organization, authority, and functions of the State, and the relations of the State to individuals, or of individuals to the State.

Private Law is that which concerns the relations of individuals to one another. It, much more than public law, a field of choice, and of non-imperative law.

Analysis:—

Private Law
- Civil Law
  - *Personal relationships* not of contract, as parent & child, guardian and ward.
  - *Contracts.*
  - *Property*, Real & Personal, incl. Wills and Successions.
  - *Torts* (Civil wrongs not breaches of contract[)
- *Commercial and Maritime Law* (incl. Banking).
- *International Private Law.*

Public Law:
- *International Public Law.*
- State Law: { *General* or Comparative *or* *That of some one State.* } {
  - *Constitutional* Law
  - *Administrative* Law
  - *Criminal* Law (incl. Criminal Procedure)
  - *Civil Procedure.*
  - *Ecclesiastical Law.*
}

2. *In its widest sense Administration includes* a side of Justice and most of Finance, and even some parts of military and international affairs. *In the practical cultivation of the field* of Political Science, however, these several topics or branches of inquiry have gained separate standing, and *Administration, coming last into*

the field, has been left to deal with everything else not legislative. *It is limited, therefore,* on the one hand *by* the domain of *Finance,* which, after having been a topic under Political Economy, has come to be almost a separate science in itself; of *military administration,* which has been given over to the soldiers, but which has, nevertheless, a side of strictly civil administration; of *Justice,* which has been resigned to the lawyer; and of *international intercourse,* even whose administrative parts have become parts of diplomacy.

> Weather Bureau (U. S.)

It is thus *limited to "innere Verwaltung"* alone, which *includes "sicherheitspolizei,"* i.e. Police in the narrow sense of the term, *and "Wohlfartspolizei,"* the active promotion of individual activities, etc.

3. *Limited also on many sides by Constitutional Law:* With *topics such as the following* constitutional law, and constitutional law only, has to do: *viz.,* the natural foundations of the State and of legislation, together with the scope and validity of the legislative act; the acquisition and exercise of the governing or *executive* power; the representation of the people, its constitution, make-up, summoning, duties, methods of business, its relations to the head of the State and to the organs of the State subordinate to him; the representation of the State abroad; the rights of individual liberty, and the special privileges and subordinations of the several classes of society, in case the law recognizes classes; Etc., etc.

> As distinct from dominion.

From all of these topics *must Administration refrain; but not from* that great question, with us so central to all discussions of constitutional law,

4. *The Question of the Functions of Government:* Upon this ground *constitutional and administrative theory meet,* and enjoy possession in common. In a sense legislation and the constituent law must determine the functions of government; and yet, looked at from another point of view, *the functions of government are in a very real sense independent of legislation,* and even of constitutions, because as old as government and inherent in its very nature. *The bulk and complex minuteness of our positive law,* which covers almost every case that can arise in Administration, *obscures for us the fact* that *Administration cannot wait upon legislation,* but must be given leave, or take it, to proceed without specific warrant in giving effect to the characteristic life of the State.

Administration, too, rests upon customary as well as upon positive law, upon the habit of the community as well as upon the deliberate expressions of its will.

> 'Common' Pub. Law.

5. *In this country Administrative not separated from constitutional*

Law; the existence of the distinction hardly recognized, except in so far as it is perceived that outside of and beyond the questions of constitutional adjustment, there lies a region of business regulation and clerical differentiation.

The importance of the distinction for us is just here: *It may deliver us from the too great detail of legislative enactment; give us administrative elasticity and discretion;*[1] free us from the idea that checks and balances are to be carried down through all stages of organization; and give us some sort of gradation of command and obedience, instead of equality of central and local officers, complete independence in origin and authority of each office, etc.

6. *Query: Have we not* in this country *an opportunity to recast the whole science* of Administration for ourselves? Are there not reasons why we should depart from European models, inasmuch as the development of the science in Germany has been in a sense arbitrary, empirical, accidental? *E.g.* the close connection in the U. S. between the courts and administrative action suggests *the reclamation of Justice* as a topic within the field of Administration. And if in one particular why not in another? May not a division line of principle be run between con'stitutional and administrative law? *Is Finance*, to take another example, *irrevocably lost* to Administration?

College chairs of "Finance & Admin."

7. *Main Divisions of the Study:* (*Comp. Sarwey*, pp. 42, 43, fine print)

   (1) *The actual tasks of administrative organs,* and the scope and character of administrative law.

   (2) *The limitations set by law* to administrativ[e] action by reason of the recognition of a sphere of individual will and right.

   (3) *The organization of the Administration.*

   (4) *Administrative Justice.*

8. *The Tasks of the State:* Specific *Subdivisions:*

   I. *In the first place,* the *State conditions* both *the existence* and *the competence of the individual,*

     (a) *authenticating his birth,* his *marriage,* his *death,* —indirectly, and in some states directly, *his name,* —by *registration;* determining the *age of full capacity* (majority), and in some states *authenticating it* by administrative process.

---

[1] "The laws reach but a very little way. Constitute government how you please, infinitely the greater part of it must depend upon the exercise of powers, which are left at large to the prudence and uprightness of ministers of state. Even all the use and potency of the laws depends upon them. Without them your commonwealth is no better than a scheme upon paper; and not a living, active, effective organization"—BURKE.

(b) *Artificial persons* (corporations) the State entirely equips, after creating.

(c) *It requires of the individual certain services* (of hand, knowledge, sword, and purse) *as a condition of its recognition of his independent existence* and rights.

II. *In the second place, the State gives society the means of its self-knowledge* through Statistics, social, economic, financial, *and its means of self-management* through local subdivision and organization.

III. *The State protects society and the individual* against disorder and dangerous persons (Here come in all questions as to *the repression of* such movements as *the socialistic*) and against the *dangers threatened by natural forces*, such as fire, water, explosive substances, dangerous structures, deleterious processes of manufacture, etc.—*inspection of steam vessels, etc.*, etc.

IV. *Promotes the health of the individual* by
   (a) *Sanitation;*
   (b) *Authentication of physicians*, apothecaries, etc.
   (c) *Establishment and Maintenance of Hospitals;*
   (d) *Public Slaughter Houses*, etc.

V. *Stands economic guardian to the individual* in
   Poor relief,—insurance, (pensions and other,)—*savings banks,* etc.,*—Forestry, game,* and *fishing,* laws.

VI. Stands *spiritual god parent* in
   Education (including the education of the poor and neglected classes;)
   Repression of vice (prostitution, gaming, etc.).

VII. *Promotes* the *economic and other activities* of society by means of
   1. Establishment and policing of *public roads* and waterways;
   2. Establishment of *posts, telegraph, (telephone)* etc.
   3. Maintenance or supervision of *railways.*
   4. *Coinage* of money and exclusive regulation of the money standard;
   5. Regulation of *weights and measures.*
   6. Establishment of institutions of *credit.*
   7. Regulation and promotion of horse and cattle *breeding.*
   8. Maintenance of *public markets* and warehouses.

VIII. *Protects* (and ensures) *property* by
   1. *Administration of estates* of minors and incapables, and oversight of the administration of *cestuis qui trust.*

2. Regulation or facilitation of *irrigation and drainage*.
3. *Patents*.
4. *Protection,—reciprocity,—*free trade.
5. *Public insurance*.

Sarwey,
64-93.

III. The Idea of the State and of its Functions:

1. *The real Nature of the* (Historical) *State.*

("Die Idee des Staats ist das Gewissen der Verwaltung"—*Stein.*)

Every State is the historical form of the organic common life of a particular people, some form of organic political life being in every instance commanded by the very nature of man. No nation has ever been without an organic common life; nor can any nation ever break the continuity of that organic common life without instantly ceasing to be a nation.

The State, therefore, *is an abiding natural relationship*; neither a mere convenience nor a mere necessity; neither a mere voluntary association nor a mere corporation; nor any other artificial thing created for a special purpose, but *the eternal, natural embodiment and expression of a higher form of life than the individual*, namely, that common life which gives leave to individual life, and opportunity for completeness,—makes individual life possible and makes it full and complete.

2. *Each nation has its own State*, i.e., its own form of organic life, its own organic and functional characteristics, *produced by its own development*, expressive of its own character.

Einleitung,
p. 4.

The *principal species of States* (to use *Mohl's* classification) have been: (*1*) *the patriarchal*, in which the family or tribal life was of preponderating importance (Note the clan principle of life and standard of ethical judgment in the Scotch Highlander). —(2). *the theocratic*, in which a religious principle served as at once the object and the law of the organic common life of the people;—(*3*) *the patrimonial*, in which authority rested upon possession, and which devoted itself to the protection of the private life and the private acquisition characteristic of the fundamental principle of possession;—(4) *the State of classical antiquity*, which sought to realize in the highest possible degree the common life, to the complete subordination and absorption of the individual;—(5) *the despotic*, in which a single man, wielding an unrestrained authority, based upon physical force, uses all things for the accomplishment of the purposes of his own will;—(6) *the State of our own time*, whose aim it is to effect such a rational ordering of the public power as will best promote individual development and the development of society as a whole.

Whether a State should have one or another of these forms

of political life has always *depended upon its stage of culture,*
its *circumstances* of *age,* of *stress,* of *strength,* of *belief,* etc.,
etc.,–of *education and political consciousness.*

3. *The Powers of the* STATE: The several theories (*the rationale*)
of the State's authority, and of its (more or less extended) scope.

The *critical fact* about every form of government is, that *power
is* of necessity *entrusted to individuals*: a few govern; the great
mass must obey. *Power must* also, under whatever polity, *be applied,*–applied in the compulsion of individuals.

When certain forms of state organs, therefore, *have outlived*
their usefulness, *their suitability* to the age of culture and political conscious-[ness] at which the nation has arrived,–when,
i.e., they have *ceased to express the organic life* and will, and
tend to represent only their own will and love of authority,–*a
feeling of antagonism towards them* inevitably springs up on the
part of the mass of the community.

The so-called liberal spirit in politics manifests itself in power
only after the unfitness of the organs of the State to embody the
common life and purpose has penetrated society and a new
phase has become necessary in the organic life. *The ideas of the
"Weal State"* (in themselves true, but unsuited to an unreformed
government) *give way,* therefore, *to the ideas of the "Law State,"*
–the ideas of free state action, to ideas of strictly prescribed
and circumscribed state action.

4. *The "Weal State" (or "Police State"):–The idea* which underlay   *Theories:–*
this conception of the State was an idea, *not of organization, but
of motive.* All functions were legitimate for the State *whose object was the promotion of the interests of the State and of its
members*; but *no new or certain means of determining the common good was provided*: all was left to the *discretion of an un-
checked Administration.*

This is the State with full powers of discretionary administration, *the "Police State"* of the German writers

"The *word Police* (πολιτεία–*politia*) *originally* signified *the
sum total of political relationships. First ecclesiastical affairs*
were separated from it," the antithesis *politica, ecclesiastica*
was established, and the expression Police came to signify the
temporal power, the government and its discipline. "*Then,* by
degrees, police affairs were differentiated from *the affairs of
justice,* of *financial administration,* and *military management,*
so that the word *Police became* the technical expression for
the whole interior administration, the offices of interior administration became known as police offices, and *the Science of*

Administration, as *Police Science"—E. v. Meier* (in Holtzendorff) 1158-1159.

Under this conception *the Administration* was *the embodiment
of* the judgment and power of *the community*: its powers extended to any and every act which would quicken the development of the community as a whole. There lurked here *the de-
lusion of a benevolent despotism.*

Criticism: *the idea* was at bottom *unimpeachable*: *the State is an
instrumentality for quickening in every suitable way* (there has
been a long history of disastrous experiment) *both collective and
individual development.* BUT you must *take care that there is
really an intimate organic connection between the Administration and the Community as a whole*, with its diverse and complex interests, *that* the *Administration* is in very truth *an organ*,
and *not an outside power* (however benevolent), holding the
people in tutelage. *The motive must come from the whole*; but in
the time of the theory did not.

5. *The "Law State,"* to which the Weal State gave way in the development of political thought, *represented an effort after greater
cohesion*, and gave more perfect expression to the organic character of the State (though at first sight this is not evident).

> *Such was not the idea* or purpose *of those who sought to
> establish this view* of the State. It was their idea to hold "the
> government" in restraint, as something foreign, and even
> hostile, to the people,—*to build bulwarks about popular rights*,
> —to effect a "balance" between opposing forces,—*to establish
> a system of checks.*

Its real effect was, in some measure, *to bind people and Administration together* in a common system of law,—to establish, as the
phrase went then, *"a government not of men but of laws."* Com-
munity and government were to be *integrated* by being brought
under a common power, the power of law: the people to have
their legal rights, the Administration only its legal powers.

*Criticism: The life of the State cannot be summed up and ex-
hausted in its laws*, but has an inherent character outside of
them, to the realization of which the laws must give leave. "The
laws reach but a very little way" and every government must
be a government of and by men. *Laws may guide, balance, define, determine; but they only reflect life, they do not contain it.
Life must integrate, must effect the organic.*

This is the conception of the State *which we have* ourselves
adopted, and upon which we have constructed our written constitutions, together with *our immense and complex body of positive administrative law*, with its characteristic *exclusion of* an

administrative *hierarchy* (of 'men') and its *minute prescriptions* of official duty and responsibility. With us the State is in all parts a legal institution.

6. *The Constitutional State* developed in Europe under the dominating *influence of English experience.*
Our own specialized idea of a constitution.
What is a constitution? When and *how* did the idea arise of *a separate and distinct body* of constitutional law?
  A Power outside the Government.
  When we speak of the "constitution" of *a State* which existed *before the modern time* (before the *regime* of liberalism) we generally mean only *a make-up and method,* not an authoritative body of limitations or a grant of powers fr. without.
England's a test case.
  The States of Europe got the "constitutional" form of state life (so far as they have in fact really developed it) *by imitation of English institutions.*
  The *English reached it thr. a long process*[2] wh. (*a*) made the will of the Commons supreme in legislation; (*b*) brought the ministers directly under parliamentary control; (*c*) made the Commons at length truly representative of the commonwealth; and (*d*) secured to the judges an independent tenure.
  "The English constitution has no real existence"—Tocqueville.
  What can Parliament change? And what, exactly, is there to prevent its taking any revolutionary course it pleases?
  In all States, at all times, the power and authority of the Government has rested upon the consent of the governed; but generally that consent has been vague, its extent defined and ascertained only by experiment. A "constitutional" state is one in which that consent—that agreement of will between Govt. and community has been made definite in content and purpose.
The State vs. the Government. Origination of the State outside constitutional, or other positive, law.[3]
  Written constitutions make the existence of the State more definite, self-conscious, explicit,—but not more real. (See *post*).
Definition: *A constitutional State is a self-conscious, adult, self-regulated* (democratic) *State.*[4]
Characteristic Elements:
  1. *A law-making body representative of the State,* not of the

---

[2] A process of adjustment between the Gov't. and the Community.

[3] *Historically,* the chief instrument in the creation of a State has been the Govt.—it was when it was otherwise that a written const., creating a Govt., became a necessity.

[4] A *"constitutional"* Government is one concerning whose powers there is a definite understanding with the Community—between whose powers and the life of the State there is a definitive adjustment.

Government: set to direct and control the Gov't. With this body, however, *the Head of the State shares* the law-making power.

2. *An Administration subject to the laws*; but not necessarily energized and commissioned by the laws in respect of all its acts.

3. *A Judiciary equipped with* a wide range of *independent powers* and *secured*, by an independent tenure, *against corrupt* or other improper *influences*.

4. *A more or less careful and complete formulation of the rights of individual liberty*, i.e. the rights of the individual against the Gov't. A pledge taken by the Community of the Gov't.

7. *Federal Constitutional Law* transitional? A vehicle for the unification of habit and law,—for the national sentiment and purpose.

Our own constitutional law is a complex of historical pieces, *to be interpreted*, as Marshall interpreted it, *by the logic of history.*

8. *Written Constitutions.*

Formulations of the relations of the Government to the State: a product of the self-conscious and deliberate stage of state life, and generally of circumstances wh. necessitate the creation of a Govt. by the State, instead of the opposite, wh. is the historical, process.

Note the very inadequate nature of our constitutions as the originative source of institutions. E.g., they do not in every instance create the arrangements of *local government*, but simply presuppose and at most regulate them.

They emphasize our definition of a "constitutional" government, as a government watched and restrained in the interests of liberty, viz. in the interest of the freest (*i.e. the best adjusted*) relations between man and man, and bet. man and Gov't.

Our constitutions are vehicles of experience and purpose. *In reality, constitutions of liberty*[5] in all their parts—meant to effect the adjustments which we deem favourable to liberty.

Conclusion (of Theories): Law, ∴, limits, defines, adjusts the functional life of the State; but it creates neither State nor Govt. It alters no necessity of life.

9. *The Logical Position and Scope of Administration in a Constitutional State*:

We we [sic] thus make plain the fact that *"constitutionality" does not alter the nature of the* (historical) *State*, we see that *the scope of Administration* is, in every case, *all the necessary*

---

[5] Const. of Gov't. vs. Const. of Liberty

and characteristic functions of the State, largely defined and
regulated and always limited, as a matter of fact, by the laws,
to which it is of course subject; but *serving the State, not the
law-making body* in the State, and *possessing a life not resident
in statutes.*

The administrative organs of the Community thus become
organically whole, vigorous, and full of purpose.

Revised, 31 Jan., 1 Feb'y, 1894

IV. The Theory of the Division of Powers.

1. *Division of Powers vs. Division of Organs:—The literary theory*
   (given its classical form by *Montesquieu*) is in fact *a theory of
   the division of organs,* taking for granted the existence of a
   corresponding division of functions: a theory, in brief, *of an
   actual based upon an abstract division* of functions. (*Vide* the
   Federalist; our various *state constitutions,* the *cantonal constitutions,* etc.)[6]

   The usual expression of the theory is, that the powers of the
   State are of three kinds, legislative, judicial, executive, and that

[6] No. XLVII. The *Federalist* himself (in this case *Madison*) is *not deceived.*
Montesquieu, he says, meant "not that these departments ought to have no
partial agency in, or no *control* over the acts of each other. His meaning . . .
can amount to no more than this, that when the *whole* power of one department
is exercised by the same hands which possess the *whole* power of another department, the fundamental principles of a free constitution are subverted."
And *the care taken* to prove and enforce this *shows the prevalence of a radical
misunderstanding.*

Madison quotes both the constitution of Mass. and that of Va. (as well as
several others). The *constitution of Mass:* "The legislative department shall
never exercise the executive and judicial powers, or either of them: the executive shall never exercise the legislative or judicial powers, or either of them:
the judiciary shall never exercise the legislative or executive powers, or either of
them." *Virginia:* "The legislative, executive, and judiciary depts. shall be
separate and distinct; so that neither exercises the powers properly belonging to
the other; nor shall any person exercise the power of more than one of them
at the same time; except that the justices of the county courts shall be eligible
to either House of Assembly."

Poore [*The Federal and State Constitutions, Colonial Charters, and Other
Organic Laws of the United States* (2 parts, Washington, 1877).], II., 1729,
par. 29. *Const. of Coahuila and Texas,* 1827: "The supreme power of the State
is divided for its exercise, into Legislative, Executive, and Judicial, and never
can these three powers, nor two of them, be united in one corporation of person,
nor the legislative power deposited in one individual."

Poore, I., 501 *Nebraska,* 1875: "Except as her[e]inafter expressly directed or
permitted." *Indiana, 1816:* "The powers of the government of Indiana shall be
divided into three distinct departments, and each of them shall be confided
to a separate body of magistrates, to wit: those which are legislative, to one;
those which are executive, to another; and those which are judiciary, to
another. And no person or collection of persons, being one of these departments,
shall exercise any power properly attached to either of the others, except in
instances her[e]in expressly permitted." Art. III

Schaffhausen, Art. 26: "Die gesetzgebende, die vollziehende, und richterliche
Gewalt sind grundsätzlich getrennt." *Similarly twelve other Swiss cantons.*
[Wilson is quoting from the constitution of the Canton of Schaffhausen. Eds.'
note]

[i.e., below]
Post, 4, (3).

these should be separated in use. (*Locke* spoke also of a *federative* power). *Some* confusion, or rather *inadequacy, of thought* is apt to result *from the words* used in this classification, *particularly from the term 'executive.'* It implies that the *administrative* organs of the government (for such is their proper designation) are simply agents of the law-making, organ, that they simply execute its will. As a matter of fact *the administrative power* is considerably wider and *much more inclusive than the 'executive'* power of the theory. *Besides the duty of executing positive law,* there rest upon the administrative organs of every State those duties of *provident protection and wise coöperation* and assistance which, though nowadays generally explicitly enjoined by enactment, would be,—as they have always been,—part of the State's normal and essential function, *whether so enjoined or not.*

There is a notable *example* also of functions necessary, with or without commission of the laws, in the *management of foreign relations.*

Comp.
Laband, "Das
Staatsrecht
des deutschen
Reiches"
I., 671-684
(2d. ed.,
1888).

2. *Theoretical Basis of the Division of Functions*: distinctions in the nature of the Functions:—

1. *Distinction between Legislation and Adjudication*: *Legislation*, the binding enactment of a rule of law, the establishment of an abstract legal rule; *Adjudication*, the binding determination of a concrete legal relationship, the recognition, denial, determination of a legal claim: the setting up of a concrete legal judgment. *Creation vs. conclusion*, a logical process.

L[aband].,
P. 675.

2. *Distinction between Adjudication and Administration*: *Administration*, the actual carrying into effect of the purposes or judgments of the State; *Adjudication*, one of the judgments to be carried out: *an action vs. a logical process*. *Adjudication*, the subsumption of a particular set of facts under an already established rule, which serves as the major premiss in the reasoning.

Pp. 676-677.

3. *Distinction between Legislation and Administration*:—*Legislation*, the delimitation of the rights and duties of subjects towards one another, or of their rights and duties as towards the State itself. (*It presupposes more than one will*, and the possibility of a conflict of wills). *Administration* (where it comes nearest to Legislation in its apparent character), a regulation of the carrying out of the functions of the State.

P. 681.

E.g., the laying out of a *railroad* or a *canal*, the contraction of a *loan*, the preparation of an *expedition*, or of an *exhibition*, a *scientific investigation*, the *acquisition of property,* like forest lands (Yellowstone, Niagara), etc., etc.

In doubtful cases (of ordinances which seem to confer rights or impose duties on individuals, etc.) *the form* should be taken as *decisive*: if promulgated under the forms of legislation, it may be regarded as a legislative act. If not, it may be regarded as a mere administrative instruction or regulation.—*Examples of doubtful cases*: measures organizing administration or adjudication, creating new instrumentalities, or expanding or changing old ones.

The difficulty about drawing the line of distinction *here* lies in the fact that *not every administrative act* is *direct*: there is often a long series of commands, proceeding from one set of administrative organs to another, (becoming differentiated, too, and complicated as they pass from the category of general to the category of particular instructions),—and the characteristic act comes last; comes sometimes in various places, through various processes. *The first step in command* or instruction may *often* (See later lecture) be *taken by the law-making body*, though, none the less on that account, an administrative act. Pp. 678-683.

3. *Legislation in the formal vs. Legislation in the essential sense* of the Term: v. Sarwey, Pp. 24 et seq

Law in its essential significance we have just contrasted with administrative determinations. *Laws in the formal sense* of the term are *acts or measures in their nature administrative* which are nevertheless, for one reason or another *given full form and authentication as enactments*, and thus made commands of the legislat[i]ve organs of the State.

Confusion arises (1) Out of Law State (2) Out of taking over by popular representation bodies of dominant functions belonging to the old govt. legislatures.

They differ from administrative acts sanctioned by the legislature but *not given the form of enactments* also in this, *that they have the full force of enactments*, being valid and binding whether in agreement with previously existing law or not.

Theory of the constitutional state should enable us to make the distinction practical.

The essential characteristic of law in the formal sense, in v. Sarwey's view, is, that, as the will of the highest organ of the State, *it is binding without limitation,* as no administrative act or judicial judgment can be.

The example used by v. Sarwey is a resolution of the legislative body that the claim of an individual against the State is not valid. This has no force as against a judicial judgment. But a formal law that the claim shall not be allowed is conclusive and binding.

Omit, Princeton

4. *Scientific Development of the Idea* of a Division (whether of Powers or of Organs.):

Comp.
Jellinek,
"Gesetz u.
Verordnung,"
Freiburg, i.B.,
1887, Part I,
Chs. I-VIII.
Pp. 3-130.

    1. *In ancient times. Aristotle* clearly *recognizes the essential difference* in character between legislative acts, administrative acts, and judicial determinations; *but* he insisted upon a *corresponding division of organs* as little as did the Greek constitutions of his day. *The unity of the State* generally meant, in the logic which the ancient thinkers derived from the constitution of the society about them, *the concentration of all species of authority* in the hands of a single person or body of persons,—but they recognized the difference between the several species of power.

    2. *The mediaeval State* exhibited the phenomonon of *authority concentrated*, in a way almost without precedent in Europe, *in the hands of the feudal Prince*; and the mediaeval theorist (of whom *Bodin* is a representative type) addressed himself, not to singling out the several species or pieces of the Prince's power, but to discerning *the nature and scope of that power as a whole*: the nature and sources of *Sovereignty*: *What law was*, & whether the Prince was bound by it: *Whether there were individual or class rights* which the Prince was bound to respect as limitations upon his sovereignty. These were the central questions of legal theory for him.

    3. *In England* the *scientific development* of the theory of the division of powers *has advanced pari passu with the* several stages of the concrete *struggle for power* in the State. The debate between *Filmer*, on the one hand, and *Sidney* and *Locke*, on the other, was *the old mediaeval debate*, as to the source of law and the degree to which the Prince was subject to it. Sidney wrote before the Revolution of 1688, *Locke* after it: the first is fighting absolute power; the second, constructing a philosophical excuse for its (accomplished) overthrow.

(1632-1704.)

    With Locke the powers of the government are, when essentially differentiated, (the judicial being excluded) *the law-making power, the executive,* and *the federative.* Among these *the law-making power* is, by its very nature, *supreme; but* great play is given the federative power because law-making can but slightly affect foreign relationships (at least directly); and not a little play to the executive power because the law-making power can neither always foresee exceptional or occasional cases nor always remain in session to deal immediately with matters as they arise, and such cases must be administratively dealt with.

    The principle, again, *of the separation of judicial* from executive functions has been, in England, a question of the *separation of organs* rather than of functions, and was the *outcome of* the struggle to guard *individual rights* against administrative encroachment.

If *Blackstone's views* are to be taken as the sum of scientific thought in this field up to his day, the theory of the division of powers had lagged very far indeed behind the fact of the division of organs, *the king* being *still conceived* of as *the source both of law and of justice.*

4. *In France* the history of the distinction practically *begins with* (1689-1755.) *Montesquieu* (by whom we have ourselves been principally affected), to be *subsequently* much affected by *Rousseau* and *the modern French constitutions. Montesquieu,* standing further away from English institutions than Locke did, conceived *the division of organs* differently in an essential particular. *He maintains the equality of the several powers,* giving them equal weight and rank, and conceiving the idea of *a balance,* each power (i.e. lodged power; organ) restraining the others from excess or error. And yet the independence of these organs consisted in nothing concrete except their exterior separation.

According to Rousseau, there is *no theoretical, but only a* (1670-1741) *practical, necessity for a separation of powers.* Political power (i.e. *Sovereignty*) is *indivisable,* and belongs to the People, who are the law-makers: executive (and judiciary) act only *ad interim* and for the purpose of the particular applications or adjustments of the law made necessary by circumstances.

The earliest constitutions of the revolutionary period were made under the influence of the conceptions of the *Contrat Social,* and embodied the statement that the *executive* was the *mere agent* or minister *of the law-maker.*

Finding it *necessary to deposit genuine administrative discretion somewhere,* the Rousseauite constitution-makers *committed it to the communes* and to the newly made Departments. To them was entrusted the *widest powers of police ordinance,* of oversight in the execution of the laws, the whole equipment of administrative energy and choice of means. The 'executive' was put into commission, *as under our own state constitutions.*

Jellinek (p. 89) pronounces the result *"anarchy."* "With a will-less kingship there had been created a will-less State."

Subsequent French constitutions, however, have recognized more and more completely a separate administrative sphere.

In modern French constitutional theory the distinction between laws proper and laws formal, which are in fact administrative determinations, is fully established, and *a further distinction* obtains, on the active side of state function, between (a) *the Gouvernement*, the guiding political power both at home and abroad, (sphere of policy, sphere of Cabinet), and (b) *the Administration*, whose function it is to give effect to the laws (capped by the Council of State), but which is not itself without its own range of discretion.

Note the stiff and quite absolute theory of the division of of powers.

5. *In Germany* we need not go back of the time when *the liberal spirit* manifested itself in politics, and all effort was directed towards a *curtailment* of power (at least *of arbitrary power*) by means of the theory of the *"Law State,"* already discussed, which of course inisited [insisted] upon a differentiation of organs and a close definition and limitation of their powers,— *protection of one against the others*, and of the individual against them all.

Finally, however, has come *the historical school*, with its explanation of *the actual differentiation* of organs, and of the abstract logical differences between them in respect of the classes of function undertaken by them, by no means reproduced in the actual development of any state. *Hence the* modern conception of the *Constitutional State*.

6. *In the United States* the theory of the *division of organs* has taken the stiffer and more *artificial form* (which seems to be indicated by Montesquieu, but which did not exist in his model, England) of the idea of coordination and a resulting system of *checks and balances*, a system which extends with us, as under no other constitutional government, to *making the courts*, the 'Judiciary,' *one of the active checks*, one of the effective offset powers.

This theory is not different from the ordinary except in its greater concreteness and formality.

Its theoretical basis is that of the older liberalism, viz., *Individualism vs. State Power*.

2-5-'91.

V. *The Actual Division of Powers*:

That *the actual division of functions between the several organs of government by no means corresponds in any existing government with the theoretical division* which we have discussed will be made evident by a study of,

1. *The Administrative and Judicial Acts of Legislatures*: W. C.,[7]
   I. *Administrative acts*: illustrative examples:
   1. *Private bills*, when not judicial in nature.
   2. *Appropriations* of money for all purposes not creative of rights (as, perhaps, appropriations for land purchase would be).
   3. *Incurring of debts* by the State.
   4. *Undertaking of public works* (buildings, roads, canals, railways); in short, internal improvements.
   5. *Acquisition or alienation of public property* (including the exercise of eminent domain, the acquisition of water rights, easements, etc.).
   6. *Creation of new army corps* (this simply *a type* of many acts).
   7. *Creation of commissions or* scientific institutions or agencies. (Department of Agriculture, Smithsonian Institution, etc.).
        Under our own division of functions, all administrative *departments* are *created by statute*, under most *foreign* systems, by *administrative decree*,—the legislature controlling only indirectly, by *appropriation*.
   8. *Changes of national boundaries.*
   9. *Acts of incorporation.*
   10. *Election of administrative or judicial officers* (the French President, Swiss Bundesrath, judges in many States, federal Senators).
   11. *Counting the vote* for President and Vice President; (also judicial: *see post*).
   12. *Naturalization* (in England and elsewhere).
   13. *Auditing* of public accounts.
   14. *Organization, adjournment*, etc.
   II. *Judicial Acts of Legislatures* (Examples).
   1. *Impeachment* of public officers (supplanted in Eng.).
   2. *Decision of contested election cases.*
   3. *Counting the votes* for President and Vice President. (*See ante*, 11).
   4. *Granting of divorces* (now for the most part a disused function).
   5. *In Switzerland*, the Houses hear *appeals* from the *Bundesrath in administrative cases* and upon religious ("confessional") questions.
   6. *The Swiss Federal Assembly* (*Bundesversammlung*) acts as *a court of conflicts* as between federal authorities.

[7] Wilson's abbreviation for "wherein consider." [Eds.' note]

7. *The Swiss Federal Assembly* also exercises the *semi-judicial function of pardon.*

Attainder of private persons, and bills working *forfeiture of private property*, though now disused, or at any rate discredited, ought to be mentioned in this connection.

2. *Legislative and Judicial Acts of the Administration:*

Here, of course,—more perhaps than anywhere else,—is the place to keep firmly in mind *the distinction* between *legislation in the formal* and *legislation in the essential sense* of the term.

I. *Legislative Acts:*

1. *Provisional measures*, needing the subsequent sanction of the law-making body, including both suspensions of law (to be covered by a subsequent act of indemnity) and positive regulations meant to meet an exigency.

E.g., opening of *the Irish ports* to the importation of grain, 1848; suspension of *specie payments.*

Here, unquestionably, *the Administration acts in the rôle of permanent member of the law-making body*, acting *ad interim*. This principle of permanent membership recognized in our presidential veto; *but note* the absence of anything analogous to the Eng. Orders in Council.

2. *Acts under 'empowering clauses' of statutes.*

A statute may not only *confer* large powers of *discretion* on the executive, but may also, "by express words, be operative until annulled by royal proclamation"; *not operative until* made so by proclamation, etc., etc.

E.g., *Act* of the 50th. Congress *empowering the President to stop the shipment of goods* through the United States to Canada under bond; the clause of the *"McKinley Bill"* empowering the President to establish and proclaim *reciprocity*, etc.

Locke's "federative" function.

3. *Treaties* which do not need ratification by the representative body.

4. *Measures in the main administrative in character* which nevertheless create new rights or duties, although they do not need the sanction of the Legislature.

E.g., creation of *new administrative authorities* (as contradistinguished from mere clerical arrangements or rearrangements) which usually give to individuals new subordinations or new contacts with the Administration, or,—etc. Machinery often involves rights.

E.g., *changing local boundaries.*

5. *Effectuation of the laws* may itself involve individual right or duty.

E.g., *postal regulations*, where the Administration is given free discretion with regard to them. Ditto *sanitary regulations.*

6. *The making of Bye-laws* by local authorities.

7. *Administration of* such branches of the public service as *the army*, where large discretion is given, may involve regulations regarding recruiting, promotion, etc., which involve individual right and duty on a wide enough scale to deserve mention here.

Note the very significant *abolition of the system of purchase in the British army* by an Order in Council.

8. *The Swedish "economic laws."*

In Sweden the Crown may "formulate what are there denominated 'economoc laws,' administrative laws, namely, regulative of *trade, commerce,* and *manufacture,* and of *mines and forests.* He is, moreover, the sole and sovereign author of *police regulations,* and of laws controlling *vagrancy*; he has power to make rules concerning the *erection of buildings* and to originate ordinances touching *sanitary precautions* and protection against *fire."–"The State,"* sec. 625.

Similarly, all *police regulations* of a restrictive or permissive character, where such do not need the sanction of statute.

E.g., Regulating *explosives, nuisances, large gatherings,* etc.

II. *Judicial Acts of the Administration*:

1. *Pardon.*

Not judicial as mere clemency, but clearly judicial as a remedy in cases where new evidence has been discovered, or evidence obtained which was not obtainable at the time of the trial, etc.

2. *Military Justice,* under every system of government made separate, as part of the necessarily peculiar discipline of the army and navy.

3. *Administrative Justice* in civil cases arising out of collisions of public power and private interests.

This ceases, however, to belong to this classification so soon as the judges of administrative cts. cease to be in any real or distinctive sense officers of administration and become like the ordinary judges in qualification, appointment, separateness, and tenure, as well as like them in function, etc. *It is quite possible to secure impartiality* while keeping the administrative constitution of these tribunals,—*by organization*; *but—*

4. *Interpretation of Statutes.*

E.g., statutes appropriating moneys, affording relief, awarding pensions, etc., etc.

5. *Adjudication of claims* made on the various Departments of the government.

The German Bundesrath affords the best example of the union (the advantagious union) of legislativ, administrative, and judicial functions. (*Read* the "*State,*" secs. 407-410).

Comp. Laband I. 685, 686.

III. *Action and Reaction of Law-making and Administration:*

Administration is indirectly *a constant source of public law*. It is through Administration that the State makes test of its own powers and of the public needs,—makes test also of law, its efficiency, suitability, etc.

Law is always a summing up of the past: its result, the conclusion from its experience,—and valid conclusion comes only after a series of impressions and experiences. *Administration*, on the other hand, is *always in contact with the present*: it is the State's experiencing organ. It is *thus* that it becomes a *source of law*: *directly*, by the growth od [of] administrattive practice or tradition,—as customary (common) law grows up out of the changing, accommodating practices of individual intercourse,—*or indirectly*, by way of suggestion or initiative. This *one of the most useful* because most practical, *means of developing public law.*

Immediate control of function of administration as between legislation and adjudication

Historical instances of the administrative creation of law cited by *Laband* (686):

The *jus civile* of the Romans succumbed to the official *decrees of the Praetors and Aediles*, to the *jus honorarium.*

The *ancient folk law* of the Germanic race disappeared before the official instructions promulgated by the Merovingian and Carolingian kings in their *Capitularies.*

The *common provincial law* of the later Middle Ages (*Landrecht*) was in the profoundest manner changed, transformed, developed through the *ordinances of city magistrates.*

The law received from the Middle Ages gave way to entirely new law created by means of the *instructions issued by feudal lords* to their agents and ministers and to their courts of justice.

IV. *Close organic relationship between legislation and adminis-* Comp. La-
band, p. 686.
tration in the normal State:

The propriety of *administrative initiative in law-making* made sufficiently evident by considerations stated above. The propriety of the *participation of representatives of the people in certain acts of administration* is made equally clear by these, and by all constitutional history.

Means of their participation: (a) *Impeachment*; (b) *Cen-* Organic opin-
ion and
sure*; (c) *Budget*; (d) *Formal legislation*, ordering and practice. The
administra-
tive and
regulating administrative action. organic
method.

3. *Administrative and Legislative Acts of the Judiciary*:

I. Administrative Acts:

1. *Administration of estates*, trust, intestate, etc., their partition, investment, etc.

2. *Guardianship*. ("The guardian I of pretty young maids in Chancery").

3. *Record and registration* (titles, encumbrances, etc.). Tendency to become separate administrative process— Indiana

4. *Incorporation.* Copyrights
granted un-
der our old

5. *Naturalization* (in the United States). law by the

6. *Appointment* (e.g., appraisers, receivers, supervisors of district
courts. election, etc.).

7. *Statistics* of crime and of litigation, etc.,—of all the social phenomena to be gotten out of court records. (E.g., the supreme courts of many of the *Swiss cantons*; *See "The* "*The State*"
secs. 1189,
State," sec. 562). 1190. *Maine*,
"Ancient

II. *Law-making Acts of the Courts*: Law," II.,

1. *Direct*: Equity, ancient and modern; court rules. III. Con-
tempt of

2. *Indirect*: Case law;—fictitious cases, colusive suits. court.

4. *Actual History of the Division of Powers*: *Omit*,
Princeton.

1. *In Athens* we see that *unity and solidarity* so fundamentally See 5. characteristic of ancient state life. In the *duties of the Archons* administrative, judicial, sacerdotal functions are united.

In the Senate and Ecclesia, legislative, administrative, and judicial functions were united also. *The only differentiation* was *in the forms* under which these several functions were exercised. *The sovereign Council* (the Senate of Four (Five) Hundred) was, *in the earlier days*, entrusted with the decision of all but the weightiest matters, without consultation with the Popular Assembly. *In later times* it kept the initiative in all things, and retained the administrative control of finance, the navy, the army.

It prepared all the non-legislative business of the pop-

ular *Assembly* under the form of provisional resolutions (προβουλεύματα): with reference to all matters save legislation proper, *the procedure was*: προβούλευμα, (amendatory motions being permissible in the Assembly); ψήρισμα.

Legislative procedure (in which the Senate had, apparently, no part): (*a*) *In the first Assembly* of the year, the question put: Shall motions be allowed looking towards the extension or alteration of existing laws? *If "Yes,"* such motions must be made carefully public. (b) *Third Assembly of the year* arranged for the constitution of *a commission* (*Nomothetae*) to consider such motions. (c) *All such motions considered and dealt with by this commission*, special counsel being appointed to defend the existing laws. (Number of the commission probably often about one thousand).

> *Chosen* (in what manner we do not know) *from* among the *Heliasts* of the year; who were over thirty years of age, and *already under oath* to perform their function with fidelity.

The decisions of these commissions were *conclusive*; there was *no subsequent submissions of a report* to the Ecclesia.

Strictly prescribed forms for all other business, too, such as the examination and discipline of magistrates, judicial determinations, ostracism, etc.

The Judiciary: (*a*) *the thesmothetae*, who adjudged all cases arising between private individuals, subject to appeal to the heliastic courts. (*b*) *The Helioea* (chosen from the several Phylae: acting in sectional courts, etc.) who considered all criminal,—in general, all public,—cases, and heard appeals from the Thesmothetae in private causes (finally by degrees in great measure absorbing original jurisdiction here also).

> *These heliastic courts*, let it be noted, *not essentially different from* the popular Assembly (*Ecclesia*).; and the legislative commissions identical with them in membership.

> *Further connection between courts and legislation, in judicial tests of constitutionality.*

> *Objection* could be made to a legislative motion when it was first offered; after it was accepted, or even after the Nomothetae had acted on it,—*at any stage*, that is,—on the ground of illegality, and an *appeal* taken to the courts. *During this* appeal legislative proceedings were to be suspended. The courts appealed to were the *heliastic courts*.

2. *In Rome*, the same *unity and solidarity*, but much *less symmetry and logical analysis in method*. Law and decree were mixed together without essential differences of procedure.

Any act passed by the people (whether the *Comitia Tributa* or the *Comitia Plebis Tributa*) *upon the initiative of a magistrate* was a formal law, *whether its purpose was* the extension or alteration of existing *law* or merely some *administrative adjustment* or judicial determination.

The formal sanction of the Senate was *at first* necessary *before* a magistrate could submit a law (or bill) to the people; and *for long* the *subsequent assent* of the Senate *to all measures* passed. *But finally* the practical outcome was the self-sufficiency of the *plebiscite*.

In adjudication the general principle of Roman practice was, that *civil actions* were for *private* settlement. *For all* private (civil) *actions not affecting real estate*, there was the process of *magistrate and judex. For real actions* involving Quiritary rights there was reference, not to a judex, but to *a centumviral court* (*chosen by* the Praetor, three from each of the thirty tribes, and presided over by the decemviri(?)).

Criminal cases were originally regarded as in most instances affecting individuals only, and to be dealt with by private process, vengeance, or civil damages. *If,* however, "a man committed *a wrong so heinous* that it seemed improper to leave it to individuals to pursue by a civil remedy, *or* one (e.g. treason) for which there was *no remedy at all in the civil courts,* he was solemnly tried by by [sic] the people under legislative forms, analogous to the English *bill of attainder*." *Comitia Centuriata.*

Towards the end of the Republic, however, a series of statutes affecting *particular classes of crimes* established a series of *permanent courts* or commissions for their trial, prescribing procedure and punishment. *E.g., Repetunda.* There were also *sometimes special commissions* for the trial of particular cases. These special or permanent commissions were *composed of jurors taken* from (a) the *Senatorial* class; (b) the *equestrian* (Gracchus to Sulla). *Smith's* Dictionary of Antiquities, (ed. 1890), p. 563.

3. *In England:*
    1. *The original Teutonic constitution,* in which the popular assembly or court both declared and altered the law and took administrative resolution.
    2. *The Witenagemot,*—the Great Council,—the differentiation into Parliament,—the Permanent Council,—the courts,—the Privy Council,—the Cabinet.
    3. *The House of Lords* and the *Privy Council* retain judicial functions; the Cabinet has legislative authority, etc.
    4. *The history of local government* has centered in the *Jus-*

tices of the Peace, at once judicial, executive, administrative (ordinance-making) authorities.

4. *In France*:
   1. *Same original Teutonic materials* as in England, with the addition of *Roman elements* much more powerful than in the case of England. *Same feudal elements* also.
   2. *Failure of the States General* to develop into a Parliament like the English.
   3. *The concentration of all powers* in the hands of a single absolute monarch.
   4. *Growth of the modern system,* with its administrative courts; its pre-consideration of legislative proposals by an administrative body (the Council of State); its dependence of the administration upon the Chambers, etc.

5. *In Prussia*: need consider only *modern history*:
   1. *The General War Commissariat*, the *General Finance Directory,*—the War Commissariats and the Domains Chambers,—*fusion*: The General Supreme Financial Directory for War And Domains.
   2. The *present "Administrations."*
   3. The principles of *Prussian city government*.
   4. The *administrative courts*.

5. *General Conclusion*:

The *object sought* is, not the effectuation of a system of mechanical, or artificial, checks and balances, but only the facilitation and promotion of *organic differentiation*, with its accompanying diffusion of vitality and accession of vigour. *The modern constitutional State* seeks to support this differentiation with the positive sanctions of law.

No part is to be *overworked*, but every part is to be disciplined and rendered skilful by specialization. *Each* is to be *coördinated* with and assisted by the others. *Each* is *an organ*, not to serve a separate interest, but *to serve the whole. The argument for a division of functions is simply an argument from convenience,* in the highest sense of that term.

2-11-'91.

VI. *Character, Sources and Forms of Administrative Law.*

When we set out upon this course *we recognized* four more or less distinct *divisions of the subject*:

(1) *The actual tasks* of administrative organs, and the scope and character of administrative law in its various sorts.

(2) *The limitations set* upon administrative action *by the law*, in the recognition of a sphere of individual will and rights.

(3) *The organization of the Administration*, including the matters of authority, subordination, etc.

(4) *Administrative Justice*.[8]

At this stage of our discussion we must recognize these several divisions as all *summed up together* under "Administrative Law."

1. *Administrative Law, What?*

"*The sum of the legal rules obtaining in a State in respect of the public administration*"; that is, the whole body of rules, however derived, which determine the powers and moles [modes] of action of administrative authorities, on the one hand, and, on the other, the obedience or submission of individuals to administrative action   *Sarwey, P. 42.*

"With *the organic separation of legislation and administration*, the point of departure of *the constitutional State*, the germ of the development is created whose product is *administrative law*"—Sarwey, p. 33.

We are not primarily *concerned here with* the application of the *distinction between formal and substantive law*. Substantive law in innumerable instances contains *items or inferences of administrative regulation*. Throughout the whole body of law,— alike public and private,—there are provisions which either give tasks to Administration or take them away from it.

We are concerned, moreover, also *with rules* which lie quite outside law, both formal and substantive, proceeding from administrative self-determination.

This leads directly to a consideration of the

2. *Sources of Administrative Law*:

(1) *The free self-determination of the State* in the protection or realization of its own individuality, within the sphere of self-determined activity which the State shares with the individual. E.g., in *foreign affairs*, in the management of *public property*, in the promotion of *science and art*, in the interior administration of *education*, etc. In these things the State may be regarded as an individual, possessing and exercising an individual's freedom of choice.

(2) *Laws formal or substantive*: W. C.,

1. *Constitutional laws* contain,

A. *In general*: (1) provisions touching the general structural differentiations of the government which directly affect (condition) administration;

E.g., When it is said, in the Constitution of the U. S., that "*the judicial power* of the United States *shall be*

---

[8] (*See pp. 16, 17*). [Here Wilson refers to Lecture III, sections 3 and 4, in his own manuscript. Eds.' note]

vested," etc., it is taken to mean that no power not judicial shall be exercised by the federal courts.

(2) grants of specific, as well as general, powers; (3) general or specific statements of the qualifications for office; (4) general rules as to the apportionment of representatives in the legislative body; (5) general election laws; (6) financial regulations, as to the voting and expenditure of money; (7) some provision touching the conduct of foreign affairs; (8) a more or less extended enumeration (Bill) of individual rights and immunities; (9) often provisions concerning geographical divisions of jurisdiction in matters administrative.

(*10*). Federal constitutions, moreover, generally contain some general regulations touching the administrative relations of state and federal authorities.

B. *In Particular*, as to the contents of individual constitutions, in addition to the matters mentioned:

Omit, Princeton[.] See 2. post, p.

(*1*) *The Constitution of the United States* gives Congress [control] over the District of Columbia,—provides that the discipline of the militia may be prescribed by Congress,—forbids money to be taken from the Treasury except in accordance with appropriations, and commands that regular statements and accounts of all receipts and expenditures of public money shall be published from time to time,—regulates the choice of presidential electors, and the manner of counting their votes in the Houses,—lays down certain rules touching the President's salary,—makes provision for the conduct of the executive branch of the government in the event of the death or disability of the President and Vice President,—confers upon the President specifically the office and powers of commander-in-chief of the army and navy,—regulates one point at least of his relations to the executive Departments (may require written opinions),—provides for all grades of appointments to office,—specifically bestows and circumscribes the treaty-making power,—commands annual messages or speeches to Congress by the President—(indeed, virtually the whole of Article II is administrative in character)—,—directs that full faith and credit be given in each State to the official acts of the other States,—provides means of reclaiming those who flee from justice from one State into another,—protects citizens against the quartering of troops in times of peace and against arbitrary or general search narrants [war-

Amends. III., IV.

rants],—regulates procedure in indictments and trials for crime,—and prescribes trial by jury in certain civil cases. v., vi. vii.
(2) *The German Imperial Constitution* goes very much more into administrative detail than does any other leading constitution.

It prescribes in detail the organization of the *Bundesrath*, particularly its several commottees [committees] or Commissions, which are administrative rather than legislative in their functions,—equips the Bundesrath with numerous important administrative functions,—provides for 'execution' against a delinquent State,—declares that government officials "shall not require leave of absence in order to enter the Diet,"—outlines the main territorial arrangements with regard to the administration of the customs duties,—directs that the collection and administration of customs duties be left with the States severally, but that the Emperor shall appoint certain imperial officers of oversight to see that the imperial laws are properly carried out,—provides (Art. 38) for the disposition of the customs receipts, and for the rebates and reductions to be allowed from the gross total,—prescribes (Art. 39) quarterly summaries of receipts by the revenue officials of the States,—regulates (Arts. 41-45, 47) railways and posts and telegraphs (Arts. 48-51),—makes provision for the recruiting of the army and navy (Art. 53),—prescribes military and naval service (See especially Art. 63),—directs in various details the application of the revenues (Art. 70), etc., etc.

Land forces and fortifications; naval affairs; tariff and taxation; trade and commerce; railways, posts, and telegraphs; justice; accounts; foreign affairs.

(3) *The English Constitution* affords meagre (documentary) materials: *I. Magna Charta*:—common pleas to be holden in some certain place, not to follow the court,—fines by the Crown regulated,—distraint also, and purveyance, restricted,—enclosure of commons forbidden,—uniform commercial standards of measure to be provided,—only capable and trustworthy persons to be appointed justices, constables, and sheriffs,—forest laws regulated. *II. Bill of Rights*:—denies royal power of suspending or dispensing from laws,—secures against cruel and unusual punishments,—source of our own bills of rights. (IV. [*sic*] Act of Settlement contains nothing additional illustrative of the present topic).

(4) *French Constitution*:—provides that the President shall promulgate the laws,—that his acts shall be countersigned by a minister,—that the Council of Ministers

shall act as Executive ad interim when for any cause the presidential office is vacant,—and provides for the Bureaux of the Chambers, their composition, election, etc. (5) *Constitution of Pennsylvania*:—designates election districts,—arranges for the apportionment of representatives,—prescribes the detail of legislative procedure, in the matter of references to committees, etc.,—commands that stationery be furnished the Legislature, and the public printing be done by contract, under certain safeguards against corrupt jobs,—provides for the keeping of the public records, etc., by the Secretary of the Commonwealth,—sets forth in detail the powers of the Governor, and in general terms the powers of the Secretary of the Commonwealth, of the Secretary of Internal Affairs, of the Superintendent of Public Instruction, the Auditor General, and the State Treasurer,—commands reports by certain officials,—regulates the conduct of elections, limits the debt-contracting powers of the local authorities,—prescribes the payment of local debts within a period of thirty years from the time of their contraction,—determines the organization of local government; etc., etc., etc.

Resume here, Princeton.

2. *Criminal Law and Police Regulations*: E.g., warrants, searches, seizures, arrests, posses;—regulation of gatherings, parades, etc.,—granting of licenses, inspection of places of bad repute, etc., etc.

3. *Procedure*: E.g., competence (qualification in particular cases) of judges; appeal; places and times of holding court; court organization; clerk's office hours; filing of papers; service of notice; publications; hours and circumstances of serving process; etc., etc.

4. *Private Law*: Registers (E.g., of births, marriages, deaths; trade associations, etc.); records of titles, mortgages, liens, etc.; probate of wills; etc., etc. (*See* ante, under "*Administrative Functions of the Courts*").

5. *Laws distinctively and wholly administrative* in character and content, i.e., explicitly meant for the determination of the organization or action of administrative authorities in any matter. E.g., the *Judiciary Act* of 1789; the various acts erecting the several executive Departments of the federal government, etc., etc.

3. *Various Forms of Administrative Law*:

(1) *Self-determinative*, including *Ordinances* or decrees, *Warrants, Decisions, Orders,* or other Measures adopted in connection with the execution of administrative functions.

Ordinances include those (decrees, Orders in Council, etc.) wh. proceed *from the head of the State* and bear the countersignature of a minister, or *from a royal council* and bear its seal; those issued *by ministers severally* as general departmental regulations, etc.; those issued by lesser administrative authorities, but still by way of general regulation; and those issued *by the organs of local self-government*. It is only these latter that are given the distinctive designation, Ordinances, in this country.

Ordinances differ from warrants, decisions, orders, etc., in the following particulars: (*1*) An Ordinance *establishes a rule*; the other administrative acts named apply only to individual cases, personr [persons] or occasions. (2) The Ordinance, like the law, is *given general publication*, at least general publication within a certain district, whereas the others need be made known, usually, only to the persons directly affected,—in writing or by word of mouth merely.

(2) *Imposed from without,* i.e., laws, whether formal or substantive, *regulative or suggestive* of administrative action.

2-19-'91.

VII. Relationship of Administrative Acts to the Laws.

1. *The Question and What it Involves*: We have considered the character, sources, and forms of positive administrative law; the question now arises, *How far does* this various body of *law circumscribe*, as well as effectuate administrative action? Are laws a ring fence or a motive power? *Is the sphere of administrative action as wide as the sphere in which it may move without infringing the laws*; or is it only as extensive as specific legislative provision makes it?

   Involves the question of the *nature of the State,* and takes us back to the theory of the "Law State." That theory we criticised on the ground of its inconsistency with actually existing phenomena.

2. *Turns, perhaps, on the distinction between positive and conventional (or customary) law.* Certainly it turns upon the distinction which may be drawn between *positive and inherent* law,—i.e., the law of existence which inheres in the thing, government, and in the very nature of its several functions,—a nature determined by historical circumstances and development. *What is "positive" law?*

   E.g., the historical derivation and significance of terms, employed in constitutions or statutes. Take as a sample the competence of Congress to limit *punishments for contempt of court,* when the whole theory of contempt of court is one of the chief weapons of self-defence (historically derived and developed) possessed by the courts, a co-ordinate branch of the government. (*The Fields-Terry case*).[9]

3. *Relation of the Question to Prerogative*: In one sense it *is* the qn. of Prerogative; in another sense it is very much wider than the qn. of Prerogative. *Historically wider.* Prerogative the question of the powers and privileges of a particular organ,–the Sovereign. The present question *affects*, on the other hand, *the whole operative part of governmental action. Powers taken from the King have not,* in most instances, *ceased to exist,* or to be administrative. They have usually passed into other hands, simply (Into the hands, e.g., of our state legislatures: Supreme Court).

4. *To be Answered separately for each Government*, according to the characteristic development of law ther[e]in. But govts. of several leading classes may be discussed as follows:

(1) *In the case of our own governments,* both state and federal, we have already several times noted the effort to realize the theory of th[e] *"Law State." We have even excluded* from our federal law, *the Common Law*, which all the States possess. *Have we also excluded that common public law* which determines, historically, the nature and powers of our governmental organs? The tenour of many *decisions of the Supreme Court of the United States* would seem to indicate that we have not. That court has habitually determined questions of privilege and competence, where distinct constitutional provision was lacking, upon *grounds of historical analogy,* upon *English precedent,* upon the *meaning of terms in English constitutional and political usage.*

Take, e.g., (an extreme case, no doubt, and yet symptomatic) the course of reasoning in *Juillard vs. Greenman* (110 U.S., 421), wh. has been summarized as follows: "The right to issue such notes has been regarded as one of the usual powers of government. It is not

---

[9] A case that achieved considerable national notoriety during the 1880's. It concerned the drawn-out attempts of David S. Terry, a former judge on the California bench, and his wife, Sarah Althea Hill Terry, to obtain a share of the estate of the wealthy mine owner, banker, and former United States senator, William Sharon, whose friend Mrs. Terry had been before her marriage. At one stage of the proceedings both Terrys were imprisoned for contempt of court. Terry sought unsuccessfully to have his term reduced through petition of the United States Circuit Court and the Supreme Court and by appealing to friends in Washington, including President Cleveland. Stephen J. Field, Associate Justice of the United States Supreme Court, presided over at least two sessions of the Circuit Court in which claims of the Terrys were denied. On August 14, 1889, shortly after the last denial, an embittered Terry assaulted Field in a restaurant in Lathrop, California, and in the ensuing struggle Terry was killed by a Deputy Marshal. [Eds.' note]

expressly forbidden by the Constitution. The issue of such notes was of the greatest use, if not an actual necessity, in putting down the rebellion. Like crises may arise again, even in peace. The power, therefore, is one of the means which Congress in its discretion may use in aid of the purposes it is expressly authorized to accomplish."—*Chas. A. Kent*, "The Supreme Court since 1864," in "The Constitutional History of the United States as seen in the Development of American Law," 1889, p. 223.

President Grant informed Congress that he would not carry out certain appropriations for rivers and harbours contained in a Bill which he signed August 14, 1876, not regarding the Act as obligatory because of the language employed in its first paragraph.[10] *How far could this be carried?* What would be the available remedy?

(2) *In the case of the English government* it is the question, in the last analysis, of *Prerogative*, which is now defined and limited on many sides by both statute and customary law, the so-called conventions of the constitution. *Outside* the question of *Prerogative*, it is the question of *the relation of the Ministers*, in their composite character as Executive, *with the Commons*, in its character as authoritative censor. I.e., not a question of positive law so much as a question as to which body shall suggest administrative action. (*Hence the necessity among us* in this country for greater detail of law, other means of control being lacking).

(3) *In the case of European Governments in general*, substantially common historical considerations affect the scope and authority of administrative action. *Everywhere the "Police State" stands back of the modern constitutional state*; and administrative authority is unimpaired where there is no specific constitutional restriction

This *conditioned*, of course, *upon the historical age, antecedents*, and *character of the government*. E.g., *the federal gov't of Germany* has no historical basis or precedent save such as it derives from the constitution of *the North German Confederation* and the present constitution of *the German Empire*, and from the brief practice under t[h]ese instruments.

5. *In the case of the Historically Normal Government*, we may say that, in the absence of specific legal developments to the contrary, the presumption is in favour of the principle, that *the*

---

10 *Mason*, "The Veto Power," p. 104. [Wilson's review of this monograph is printed at April 1, 1891. Eds.' note]

sphere of administrative authority is *as wide* as the sphere in which it may move *withiut* [without] *infringing the laws*, statutory or customary, either in their letter or in their reasonable inferential meaning.

6. *Means of Securing Legality in Administrative Action*:

(1) *Through administrative organization*, i.e., oversight and control: hierarchy, subordination.

Under this head it is necessary to consider *the scope* which is to be *given to inferior officials* in judging the legality of the acts which they are directed to perform, and in refusing obedience to their superiors. Where is the line to be drawn?

Possibly *where the French draw* their line, between "authorities" and mere agents.

And, if subordinate authorities are to have this discretion, *how are conflicts* between them and their superiors *to be determined*? Should there be a system of disciplinary courts, as in the continental countries?

Connection of this question with that of a permanent (merit) service: i.e., irremovable except by judicial process. To be discussed under a subsequent title.

(2) *Resistance by individuals*, in challenge of, subsequent, prosecution.

(3) *Complaint*, which is provided for as of course under foreign systems, but which is quite *irregular (and offensive) under our own*,—except indirectly, through the newspapers,—being made, usually, in person and under the influence of anger.

(4) *Legal, i.e., judicial, determination*, accomplished through two different methods: (*a*) *the English-American*, under which officers acting illegally may be indicted for crime or sued for civil damages (not being regarded as officers when acting beyond their legal powers); (*b*) *the European*, of administrative courts, formal accusation, trial under appropriate process, etc.

(5) *Parliamentary Control*, effected either through the "political responsibility" of the Ministers or through one or other of the following processes: (*a*) *question*, (*b*) *interpellation*, (*c*) *investigation* (usually through a special committee), (*d*) *impeachment*. This is *a central topic of constitutional history*.

7. *Here again* we come upon *the topic of the integration and organic life of government*. This life is not summed up in enacted or adjudicated law, or in the application of it.

2/24/91

VII. (Continued) *The Administration and the Courts.*

1. *The Courts under a Constitutional Government.*
   The radical *separation of constituent and law-making functions*
   is *peculiar to us*, among independent States.—*Found also in the*
   British colonies.—By no means necessary to a written constitu-
   tion, or invariable in connection with written constitutional law.
   On the contrary, it is exceptional.

   Made improbable, indeed, in the nature of the case, *by reason*
   of the inherent weakness of the Judiciary.

2. *General English Principle*: *Parliament itself subject* to the laws,
   unless it repeal them. (*Stockdale* vs. *Hansard*)

   The *Commons supreme only since* they became constituent
   (*1688*):

   > Burke: "The House of Commons was supposed orig-
   > inally to be no part of the standing government of this
   > country. It was considered as a control issuing imme-
   > diately from the people, and speedily to be resolved into
   > the mass from whence it arose. In this respect it was
   > in the higher part of the government what juries are in
   > the lower."
   >
   > "The House of Commons cannot take cognizance of
   > particular men's complaints, nor can it give satisfaction
   > in damages." *Ashby vs. White*, Smith's Leading Cases,
   > 251.
   >
   > "The king hath no prerogative but that which the law
   > of the land allows him." *Case of Proclamations*, 12 Coke,
   > 74.
   >
   > "Proclamations are of great force which are grounded
   > upon the laws of the realme,"—*Coke.*
   >
   > "Proclamations are binding upon the subject, where
   > they do not either contradict the old laws or tend to
   > establish new ones; but only enforce the execution of
   > such laws as are already in being, in such manner as the
   > king shall judge necessary." *Blackstone*; "yet," he adds,
   > "the manner, time, and circumstances of putting those
   > laws in execution must frequently be left to the discre-
   > tion of the executive magistrate."

   Laws of all kinds come to the Courts to be enforced: the Courts
   must, ∴ , in each instance, if necessary, determine the validity
   and authority of the law, whether it proceed from Executive of
   [or] from Legislature.

3. *Restrictions which our Courts impose upon themselves in all*
   cases:

1. The question of authority must be *necessary* to the determination of the case.

2. The question must be *raised by a party in interest*, that is, by a party directly interested in the determination of that question.

3. There can, in the case of a law, be *no other ground of invalidation except inconsistency with the Constitution*.

4. There must be *plain conflict*.

The doctrine of legislative (political) *discretion*. (*McCullough vs. Maryland*).

4. *The Courts and the Executive*:

General Principle: The courts *will not interfere with the Executive in the exercise of its judgment or discretion*; and they will construe 'discretion' most liberally, as including all ordinary executive or departmental functions. They *will not command executive officers* to the performance of their duties *except in* cases of *acts merely ministerial* in character.

> "*The province of the court* is, solely, to decide on the rights of individuals, not to inquire how the Executive, or execution officers, perform duties in which they have a discretion. Questions in their nature political, or which are, by the constitution and laws, submitted to the Executive, can never be made in this court." *Jay*,[11] *Marbury vs. Madison*.

The Secretaries are proxies of the President, and thus members of the constitutional Executive.

> "*A mandamus would not lie* to the Secretary of the Navy to compel him to pay to the plaintiff a sum of money claimed to be due her as a pension under a resolution of Congress. There was no question as to the amount due if the plaintiff was properly entitled to the pension; and it was made to appear in that case affirmatively (this is the language of the court in *Brashear vs. Mason*, quoting *Decatur vs. Paulding*) that the pension fund was ample to satisfy the claim. The fund also was under the control of the Secretary, and payable on his own warrant. . . . The court say that the duty required of the Secretary by the resolution was to be performed by him as head of one of the executive departments of the government, in the ordinary discharge of his official duties,"

and reiterate the general principle stated above.

5. *How far are other Departments bound by the decisions of the*

---

[11] This is an obvious slip. The quotation is taken directly from Marshall's famous opinion in Marbury *v.* Madison. [Eds.' note]

Courts? Only to the extent of their legal conscience and political responsibility. "The decisions even of our higher courts are accepted as final only in relation to the particular cases with which they happen to deal, and their judgments do not impose compulsory limitations upon the action of any other department."—*Ordronaux*, "Constitutional Legislation," p. 420.[12]—*Quote Lincoln.*

6. *Bluntschli's objections* to administrative decisions by the ordinary law tribunals *obviated*.

21 Feb'y, 1894

VIII. Relations of Administrative Action to the Rights of Individuals.

1. *Bills of Rights*: *How far does the mere statement* or enumeration of individual rights in a constitution avail to *make* them *positive rights*? It is not true that when these rights are stated in their most abstract or general terms (e.g., as *"inviolability of person"*) they constitute an absolute check on administrative action. *Their validity depends upon the admission and definition of exceptions*: upon the careful running of definite lines of positive law which shall separate those invasions of individual right by executive power which are necessary to the order and energy of the State from those which are unnecessary, arbitrary, and tyrannical. *Positive law must make all such invasions regular* (i.e., deliberate, and just and uniform in process), and must confine them to necessary cases.

Following v. Sarwey. pp. 119-149.

> *Note the* specific, and generally negative, *form of* the items of our constitutional *bills of rights*,—their tendency to take the form of particularized administrative provisions: No quartering of soldiers in time of peace, *"except in a manner prescribed by law"*; *no unreasonable* seizures or searches of persons or premises, *except upon warrant*, issued upon probable cause, supported by the oath or affirmation of the person asking for it, designating a particular person, place, etc.; no criminal prosecution *except under certain definite safeguards*; etc., etc.

Such Bills, having once been defences against unjust exercises of royal power, are *now*, Sarwey suggests, *safeguards against arbitrary* partisan exercises of power by *majorities*.

The definitions and exceptions embodied in positive administrative enactment are *necessary in supplement of the general terms* of constitutions in order also that local or temporary circumstances may be provided for.

2. *It is Personality which is sought to be Protected* by Bills of Rights;

---

12 John Ordronaux, *Constitutional Legislation in the United States* (Philadelphia, 1891). [Eds.' note]

and this personality has *two general aspects*, the one sole, the other social.

Under the first fall (*a*) *Being* or existence, (*b*) *Will*, (*c*) *Possession; under the second* fall all social rights and duties, where the individual is not sole but coöperative.

This classification may be made to carry the following discussion:

.3. *Individual Rights: How far restraints* upon administrative action? Here our view is confined to *the first general aspect of individuality* (*Being, Will, Possession*):

I. *Inviolability of person.* Of this we may say that it does not prevent the use of force by administrative agents for the accomplishment of any of the legitimate objects of government. It *simply prevents malicious, unreasonable, arbitrary, unregulated* direction of *force* against individuals. As *legitimate exceptions*, note the forcible overcoming of passive resistance, the use of corporeal punishment in the public schools, compulsory vaccination, the occasional employment of manacles or fetters; etc., etc.

II. *Personal Liberty*, including

1. *Freedom from personal detention*, except after cause shown (*Habeas Corpus*), in pursuance of *subpoena,* etc.

2. *Liberty of settlement*, subject to limitations based either upon *considerations of public safety*, as, e.g., prevention of expatriation in time of war by those subject to military duty, or at any other time on the part of those needed for witnesses in court, etc.,–upon *principles of citizenship* and local governmental duties,–upon *systems of poor relief*.

(1) *In Austria* there is compulsory communal residence as the basis of citizenship, one commune to be exchanged for another only under certain rigid restrictions; (2) *In France* (*Italy and Spain*) there is practically no restriction in this matter whatever; (3) *In England and Germany* there are sundry restrictions upon free movement and settlement, based upon a system of communal (parish) poor relief.

Sanitary regulations also, such as Quarantine (internal), may be considered in this connection.

3. *Restrictions placed upon the Right to Marry.* In addition to the civil (private) law restrictions in this matter, based upon consanguinity, bodily unsoundness, etc.,

Inter-state "commerce" includes the carrying of passengers, and is protected by federal law.

some States condition the right of marriage upon *proof of means of support, personal blamelessness, etc.*

4. *Freedom of Economic activity* is limited under every system of government in greater or less degree. In its most general statement, it is the right of the individual to make his living in any way he pleases. But, as *examples of limitations,* consider: (1) *Compulsory Education,* whose economic aspect is this, that the parent may be compelled to put the child upon a higher plane of economic endeavour, or of general self-development: i.e, that one generation shall not determine the grade of occupation of the next.

 The "School Duty" is *put by Sarwey upon this basis,* "that the duty of the representatives of growing youth to give them the elements of intellectual culture indispensable for their further development, up to a certain grade attainable by all, is a moral duty which the State, as the natural protector of incapable persons, and because of the influence of the education of the individual upon the total national power, is called upon to give effect to as a legal duty." [p.] 128.

(2) *System of requiring professional licenses* in law, medicine, etc. (including requirements of legal or technical training on the part of those who would enter certain grades of the public service). (3) *The regulation of occupations,* as, e.g., requiring licenses or permission in cases where the occupation is dangerous in greater or less degree to others; requiring trades or undertakings involving risks, inconweniences, or nuisances to the community; provisions regulating manufactures, etc., in the interest of the labouring classes: e.g., forbidding the truck system of paying wages, forbidding work on Sundays or holidays, regulating the length of the labour day (especially with reference to the labour of women and children); prohibiting certain businesses or arrangements inimical to health, etc., enforcing the observance of certain safeguards (e.g., the fencing in of machinery), insurance of various sorts an[d] degrees; etc., etc. (4) *Compulsory labour of the able-bodied poor* who become a charge upon the public funds.

5. *Intellectual Liberty, including* (1) *Freedom of belief,* now in almost all countries practically unlimited, (2) *Freedom of the press* subject to greater or less restriction

under *the law of libel*: e.g., under certain regulations with regard to the registration of the name and character of the publication, the name of the publisher and of the (responsible, citizen) editor; and under police regul[a]tions or criminal law touching the publication of political matter of a particular sort; etc. (3) *Right of combination*, subject to corporation laws, to provisions touching objects of combination, places of meeting, bye-laws (made subject to inspection, sanction, etc.).

6. *Secrecy of the Post, and Home Privacy*, subject to such limitations as seek to exclude obscene matter from the mails, or matter which tends to stir up sedition (?); and, in the case of home privacy, subject to such (regulated) invasions as are necessary in searching for stolen goods, for criminals, etc., in breaking up gaming, making tax assessments, sanitary inspections, etc., etc.

7. *Limitations put upon the use of common or public property*, or upon the use of the property of public corporations, based upon general grounds of convenience, decency, order, the general good., etc., etc.

III. *Inviolability of the Rights of Property: Limited* to any extent by any general provisions of law, particularly, e.g.,

(1) *By forest, mining,* hunting, fishing, building *laws,* and by various agricultural regulationr [regulations];

(2) *By* certain *duties or contributions* due by individuals to State;

(3) *By cases of necessity* (to be set forth and conditioned as carefully as possible by legislation) in which the Administration cannot act without a violation of property rights in the performance of its necessary duties (e.g., tearing down houses to prevent the spread of fire, etc.).

(4) *By the right of eminent domain or expropriation,* with or without compensation, according as the appropriation of property by the State is permanent, temporary, casual, or etc. This of course depends upon positive enactment.

4. *Individual Rights: How far dependent upon administrative action for their realization:* how far created or enlarged by administrative action? *Here we are dealing with personality* in its second aspect (see ante), *its social aspect,* in which its sphere is a sphere of rights and duties. Here it is that personality is bettered

and enlarged, is rendered nobler than the personality of the brute or the savage.

I. *Social Rights*:

 1. *Citizenship*: *i.e.*, general title to equal consideration with others, and equal privileges under the law. Includes such rights as that to protection, etc.
 2. *Communal citizenship*, with aspects chiefly economic.
 3. *Special social rights*, as, e.g.,

 (1) The right to use *public ways and places*;
 (2) The right to make use of *public institutions* and all public instrumentalities;
 (3) The right to enter *certain employments*;
 (4) The right to claim *compensation for certain services* rendered in furtherance of public objects;
 (5) Right to share in the use of *communal property, privileges, and institutions*.

II. *Social Privileges, subject to* laws as to *qualification*, etc.

 1. The *electoral privilege*, and the privilege of candidature;
 2. The *privilege of office*;
 3. Special *class privileges*, noble titles, honours, etc., etc.

III. *Social Duties*: military and official service (compulsory under some systems, as, e.g., in the case of "select citizens" under the Prussian system of city government), the giving of information, assistance in apprehension of offenders, appearance to answer charges, assistance in warding off public dangers, contributions to the support of the government.

5. *Extraordinary Powers of the Administration*, to meet exigencies, etc. E.g., suspensions of *Habeas Corpus*, the state of siege, suppression of riots, defence against invasion, provisional regulations of various sorts, etc., etc.

2-26-'91.

VIII. (Continued) *Nature of Political Liberty.*

1. *Misconception* (re-called), *That government is a necessary evil*, and that Liberty consists in having as little of it as possible. *The State is a higher form of life* than the individual.—*Quote Ruskin.*[13]

---

[13] Since a proper conception of the State limits its functions at the point where the *necessity* for universal *coöperation* ceases, political progress is conditioned upon the utmost encouragement of individuality outside the limits of necessary universal coöperation.

"How false is the conception, how frantic the pursuit, of that treacherous phantom which men call Liberty! There is no such thing in the universe. There can never be. The stars have it not; the earth has it not; the sea has it not; and we men have the mockery and semblance of it only for our heaviest punishment.

"The enthusiast would reply that by Liberty he meant the Law of Liberty. Then why use the single and misunderstood word? If by liberty you mean

Life, liberty, property, the pursuit of happiness—all dependent upon the State.

2. *Constitution of Government vs. Constitution of Liberty:*
Organization vs. Delimitation of Sphere, accommodation of elements.

> *Differences,*
>
> > (1) *In Age.* Ancient constitutions distributed powers, but did not recognize individual rights.
> > (2) *In Character:* Organization-Restraint.
> > (3) *In Source:* A power outside government the source of the constitution of liberty.
> > (4) *In necessary Distinctness.*

3. *Legal Aspects of Socialism:* Socialistic schemes *reverse the historical order*, strengthening and consolidating gov't. in order to realize liberty. Gives liberty over again into the keeping of government.

> A *"constitutional" government* is not one which has a constitution or organization, but *one which is restrained by the recognition of Liberty.*

4. *Political Liberty* is, *not the negation of order, but the perfection of it,*—the equable and coöperative play of elements, the harmonious correlation of forces. *It is action within the best order.* Like health, it depends upon a nice balance of functions

27 Feb'y, 1894

---

chastisement of the passions, discipline of the intellect, subjection of the will; if you mean the fear of inflicting, the shame of committing a wrong; if you mean respect for all who are in authority, and consideration for all who are in dependence; veneration for the good, mercy to the evil, sympathy with the weak;— if you mean, in a word, that service which is defined in the liturgy of the English church to be "perfect Freedom," why do you name this by the same word by which the luxurious mean license, and the reckless mean change;—by which the rogue means rapine, and the fool, equality; by which the proud mean anarchy, and the malignant mean violence? Call it by any name rather than this, but its best and truest test is, Obedience."—*Ruskin.*

[Wilson's comment and the quotation from Ruskin were found on two loose sheets. He had earlier written the Ruskin extract (from *Seven Lamps of Architecture*, Chap. 7, Sects. 1 and 2) in his Confidential Journal described at Oct. 20, 1887, Vol. 5. Eds.' note]

To Cyrus Hall McCormick

My dear McCormick,   Baltimore, Md., 27 Jan'y, '91

I am afraid that I have seemed very rude indeed in having so long delayed my acknowledgements of your kind invitation to stay with you while in Chicago.[1] The truth is, that when your first letter reached me I was in the midst of my preparations to bring my family here for the six weeks of my annual lecture course at the Johns Hopkins, besides having in charge some very engrossing faculty business.[2] Until to-day I have been almost literally without opportunity for a *deliberate* letter of any kind. Now, however, I have both ease of spirit and quiet of body sufficient to express the gratification I feel at being able to accept the invitation you so kindly extend me. I shall enjoy thoroughly the opportunity to meet Mrs. McCormick again and to have some long talks with you.

I can't say just at this moment when you may expect me; but, unless you hear later to the contrary, count upon my being in Chicago at 9:45 Monday morning the 9th, the time mentioned in your second letter, forwarded to me to-day. I have no doubt I shall be able to make the schedules from Baltimore fit the programme you suggest. With warmest regards,

Sincerely Yours,   Woodrow Wilson

ALS (WP, DLC).

[1] As WW to R. Bridges, Jan. 21, 1891, discloses. Wilson was planning to go to Chicago to speak to what was officially called the "Princeton Alumni Association for the Northwest." It is extremely doubtful that he was able to fulfill this engagement. All correspondence concerning the proposed meeting, except for this letter to McCormick, is missing. The sole reference in future documents appears in Wilson's notes for his speech to the New York alumni on March 12, 1891 (see the newspaper report dated March 13, 1891, n. 2). However, Wilson in this instance could have been referring to the notes that he had prepared for the Chicago dinner, not to the affair itself. What might be called the negative evidence that Wilson did not go to Chicago in February 1891 is very impressive. No account of any Princeton alumni dinner appears in the Chicago dailies during February and early March 1891, and these newspapers reported such affairs in great detail. Moreover, Wilson's father, in a letter to his son of February 26, 1891, said that he was glad that Woodrow had been such a success in his speech to the Philadelphia alumni (on January 30, 1891) and did not mention a Chicago meeting. It seems likely, therefore, that once he arrived in Baltimore Wilson discovered that he could not arrange his lecture schedule to permit the extended absence that the trip to Chicago would entail.

[2] The new regulations governing the allotment and rental of dormitory rooms at Princeton. See the Princeton Faculty Minutes printed at Jan. 24, 1891.

From Albert Shaw, with Enclosure

My Dear Wilson: Minneapolis, Minn., Jan. 28th, 1891.

I enclose to you a letter from President Adams of Cornell, which will show you that you are very much in people's minds.

It is of course not my business to speak for you in any matter, and yet in my reply to President Adams I shall say that it is my impression that you are exceedingly happy in your relations at Princeton in every way, and that your plans and thoughts are quite bound up in the idea of permanent work and residence where you are. I do not know anybody whom I should like to take the liberty to recommend to President Adams, but perhaps you know of the right man and very likely Professor Herbert Adams would have in mind a list of the men most eligible.

I shall be in New York next Monday morning. We are not crowding matters desperately in undertaking the Review work, but everything comes on hopefully and the prospect is wholly satisfactory. My temporary address in New York will be #160 Broadway, care of D. O. Eshbaugh. In a very few days we shall probably have secured offices of our own.

As ever, sincerely yours,   Albert Shaw

TLS (WP, DLC).

E N C L O S U R E

Charles Kendall Adams to Albert Shaw

My dear Dr. Shaw: Ithaca, N. Y.   January 23/91.

It was with great regret that I received and read your letter. While I am quite able to see your point of view, and to appreciate your reluctance to abandon a class of work in which you have been so preeminently successful, it is a matter of great regret that you have decided not to unite your fortunes with ours. I cannot but have a lingering feeling that [if] we could have talked matters over it would have been found possible to do the work here and in New York at the same time; but evidently you have canvassed the matter and think that the distance is too great. Without knowing what the Review of Reviews definitely promises I cannot measure accurately the weight of the reasons which have led you to the decision. I shall certainly be very happy to talk the matter over with you, if you should find it convenient to pay a visit to the University.

I am quite at a loss to know which way to turn for a man to take the work of the chair left vacant by Professor Tuttle's tran[s]fer.[1] Do you have any person in mind whom you could warmly recommend? Do you know whether Professor Woodrow Wilson is completely satisfied and happy in the chair which he now holds? I do not know whether his tastes would lead him to change. The work here will consist very largely of the Institutes of Politics, that is of the Organization of Political Institutions, considered in their nature and in their historical development, and also the nature and organization of Civil Governments. We can get along without having the International Law or the English Constitutional History taught by that chair.

I am,   Very truly yours,   C. K. Adams.

P.S. omitted. TLS (WP, DLC).

[1] Herbert Tuttle, who had given up his position as Professor of the History of Political Institutions at Cornell in 1890 to become Professor of Modern European History in the same institution.

A Final Examination

January 30, 1891.

EXAMINATION IN PUBLIC LAW.

1. Define and give the main subdivisions of Private Law, on the one hand, and of Public Law, on the other. At what stage in the development of political society did the distinction emerge as a fact?
2. Name and describe the several sources of Public Law. Are these sources to be distinguished in the history of written constitutions?
3. Outline the contest, in its several steps, by which the Commons in England gained control of legislation.
4. Define Sovereignty. Discuss its nature, covering in the discussion, Austin's conception of sovereignty and its application to the case of a written constitution; the attributes of sovereignty; and the questions, whether sovereignty is susceptible to limitation, and whether it is susceptible of division.
5. Apply this discussion to the case of a federal state, taking Germany and the United States as illustrative examples; and discuss the question whether sovereignty is necessary to statehood.
6. Give the main points of Dicey's comparison between sovereign and non-sovereign law-making bodies.
7. What is law, in the light of the distinction between law and ordinance? Illustrate this by the analysis of a budget. Is prerogative derived from the laws, or is it simply limited by them and supplementary to them? Contrast prerogative in England and in the United States.
8. What is the theoretical legal basis of representation in representative legislatures? Mention and characterize the various kinds of laws. What kinds of laws are imperative, which not imperative?

Printed examination (WP, DLC).

An Address to the Philadelphia Alumni

[Jan. 30, 1891]

College Work and the Legal Profession

This is a solemn toast,—and I am a solemn fellow—so solemn that I once, without changing countenance, emptied a very large dinner hall by an after-dinner speech, and did it quickly.[1]

So clean-shaven is my solemnity, that at the Irish end of the town, I've been taken for a Catholic priest: and sentimental young ladies prefer to identify me as an actor—while in the midst of all the masquerading I retain the simple heart and unsophisticated opinions of a college prof.

I suppose your committee sent for me out of a sort of kindly curiosity to see the freshman of the faculty, but it was a mistake of judgment, which even Committees will sometimes make, for I am in a position to make a damage [damaging] revelation, and I mean to make it: I could not in conscience refrain. *Hazing prevails in the faculty*, and to a dreadful extent, the Pres. himself taking part in it. I have been a victim. They call it committee work, but in reality it is very much worse than that: it is a form of torture, prolonged and horrid,—and, to say the best of it, consumes valuable time which might much more profitably be otherwise employed, in the service of one's fellow-men.[2] But, that's a painful subject, and does not lead to my toast.

I've been connected with college work for some time, and I was once connected with the legal profession: I'm therefore a party in interest on both sides. I was connected with the legal profession for a single brief but instructive year—one's first year at the bar always is instructive, I believe: but I left the bar after getting my experience, for reasons which, I feel, will enlist your sympathy. I felt that I had something to say—I *did* feel so *then*—but I anticipated difficulties: I knew how hard it was to get an audience,—how hard, when you once got one, to keep it: and it occurred to me (it might have occurred to anyone) that if I went into college work the curriculum would furnish me with an audience, and the system of marking absences would enable me to keep it. What more natural than that I should go into college work, then? I went. And again I was in for experience, and lots of it. I first taught in a woman's college, w[h]ere the audiences had the dearest confidence possible in everything I said. Then I taught for two years in what a class-mate of mine picturesquely calls a bi-sexual institution. Finally I bring up in an institution all male,—male-clad, in sweaters and blazers. All through the absence system has stood nobly by me: I have kept my audiences! and I feel confirmed in my opinion as to my own sagacity in choosing a profession.

And yet a college audience has its drawbacks. You generally know more than a college audience, and it believes almost everything you say,—at least almost everything,—and then a year or two after its graduation it looks back upon you as a theorist. One has, in the presence of these facts, to comfort oneself with thinking upon the good sides of a college audience. A college audience is earnest and it will take enthusiasm, if you offer it straight and without sweetening. Even the loafer allows himself to become comfortably warm for a minute and to credit rumours of a purpose in life. And there's a grimmer kind of earnestness in the class-room nowadays, it seems to me, than there used to be in days gone by. The new methods of education which are putting new topics of practical moment into the college curriculum are creating the useful impression among students that life has already begun before they leave college. The impression nowadays gaining ground in college is, that when a fellow is in college he is simply doing systematically and daily what he will all the rest of his life try to do in such odd snatches of opportunity as come in his way, *viz.* to come at the world's thought in the great things of speculation and practice which have given us the world and its business as we see it, and which must be improved upon in order to give to our children the world and its business as we hope they may see them. He is simply looking the world over more widely than he ever can again: simply looking about for his chief interest and in a good way to find it.

But, what has that to do with the legal profession? It has a very great deal to do with the legal profession. I am old-fashioned enough to believe that that man is the best lawyer who knows the most law, and knows it deepest down in him,—and I believe that the best knowledge of the law has to be built up very much as law itself was built up, out [of] a thorough understanding of the circumstances and ideas which produced it. That's the reason we want and mean to have a law-school at Princeton and mean to let a man begin to head for his profession as a lawyer from his junior year on in the choice of electives which explain law and give life even to the details of it. (Anecdote about the 'nighest' road and the 'sightliest' road) And so the nighest road to a complete mastery of the law—such as would make a man a fit judge and a lasting text-writer—is the sightliest road too, for it lies along high ground and commands many outlooks. If it would retain its high influence in the country, it must remain a learned profession, and not become content with mere expertness in a technical business.

WWhw and WWsh MS. (WP, DLC).
[1] A reference to his address to the New York alumni on March 23, 1886. See the Editorial Note, "Wilson's 'First Failure' at Public Speaking," Vol. 5, and the text of this address printed at March 23, 1886, *ibid.*
[2] Another reference to his recent work as a member of the special committee on the rental and allotment of rooms at Princeton.

A Newspaper Report of Wilson's Address to the Philadelphia Alumni

[Jan. 31, 1891]

The Alumni Association of Philadelphia held its banquet last night.[1] Judge Craig Biddle presided.[2] Dr. Patton was one of the guests. He made an appeal for the proposed department of jurisprudence, and incidentally suggested that a million dollars should be raised somehow. Dr. Patton was followed by Professor James MacAllister, of Harrisburg,[3] who spoke about "Sister Colleges," and then Professor Woodrow Wilson, of Princeton, class of '76 ['79], arose. He referred to himself as the baby member of the Fasulty [Faculty], and accused the latter of hazing him, at which Dr. Patton looken [looked] surprised. This hazing consisted in giving the baby member a great lot of committee work, which is an imposition and makes him tired. . . .[4]

Printed in the *Princeton Press*, Jan. 31, 1891.
[1] At the Bellevue Hotel.
[2] John Craig Biddle, '41, Presiding Judge, Court of Common Pleas, Philadelphia County.
[3] James MacAlister, new-elected president of the Drexel Institute of Philadelphia.
[4] This report of the Philadelphia meeting is fuller than any in the Philadelphia newspapers.

From Horace Elisha Scudder

Editorial Office of *The Atlantic Monthly*,
My dear Wilson   Boston.   4 February 1891

It is long since I have heard from you or written to you. Is your work congenial? Is there too little of it? Don't you want to write an unsigned article for the Atlantic on Burgess's book?[1] If I could have a paper of four or five pages by the middle of next week I could use it in the April number; but I wont harry you, and three weeks later will suit me for May.

I hope you read the Atlantic for if you do I am pretty sure you will be prompted by some things in it, as Hart's paper on The Speaker as Premier in the March number, to write me a signed paper.[2] Come! what are you thinking about? Are you thinking a thought eight pages long on public affairs? if so, I am the person to whom you ought to send it. I am going to New York to-morrow, to lecture in Brooklyn Monday evening. If you are to be in the city, look me up at 11 E. 17 St.

Sincerely yours   H. E. Scudder

ALS (WP, DLC) with WWhw notation on env.: "Ans. 7 Feb'y, '91."
[1] John W. Burgess, *Political Science and Comparative Constitutional Law* (2 vols., Boston, 1890-91). Wilson's review is printed at May 1, 1891.
[2] Albert Bushnell Hart, "The Speaker as Premier," *Atlantic Monthly*, LXVII (March 1891), 380-86.

To Horace Elisha Scudder

My dear Mr. Scudder, Baltimore, Md., 7 Feb'y., '91

Your letter of the 4th had to follow me here, where I am going through my annual six weeks course of lectures, and reached me only last evening.

I don't know whether I ought to accept the office of reviewer in the case of Burgess's book or not. If you happen to remember a conversation we once had about Burgess & his opinions, you will see why I hesitate. I shall open the book expecting to find a great deal in it to disagree with and criticise, and I suppose that that is a frame of mind which would make my purpose to be impartial,—to admire what is admirable even in a writer of an opposite school—rather awkward to carry out. Still, I mean to read the book and to appreciate it, and, if you think that even under the circumstances, you could trust me to criticise it by means of a fair test of thought, rather than an unfair test of prepossession, I will write the notice you propose with pleasure. But not for the April number, I am afraid I must say. For I have never yet turned over a barrel of lectures: I am still writing from day to day the lectures which I from day to day deliver. I could not read the volumes and consider and prepare the notice within the time you mention; but doubtless I could get it done by the end of the first week in March.

It is a sincere pleasure to get a letter from you,—and to feel that you trust me sufficiently to ask of me an article for the *Atlantic*. I *am* a constant reader of the Atlantic, and I shall of course read Hart's article. You may be sure, too, that, should I be moved to write an article, you will be at any rate the *first* editor to see it. But alas! the name Hart reminds me! I am booked for one of the volumes in the Epochs of American History which the said Hart is editing,[1] and on my heart that task is sitting, never flitting, &c.—one chapter done, after a fashion—and no more.

I feel that I am likely to profit every way by my move to Princeton. The work there, though engrossing, is not too heavy, and the prospects for development there in the lines of work in which I have the deepest interest are most encouraging. I wish I might have a chance to talk with you about certain plans maturing there.

With warmest regards,

Faithfully Yours, Woodrow Wilson

Be kind enough to have Burgess's book sent to me here.

TCL (RSB Coll., DLC).
  [1] For a review of the writing of this book, see the Editorial Note, "Wilson's *Division and Reunion*," Vol. 8.

From William Milligan Sloane

My dear Wilson: Princeton, N. J. Feb. 12, 1891

We will be glad when you return to us. Do not work too hard. I return Joline's letter[1] and suggest for the choice of subject "The annexation of Louisiana, etc" We have had essays on all the others within my time. I have started a "Seminar" instead of the course for which no time could be found.

If the theme suits you will you send it to the Princetonian to be announced.[2]   Yours faithfully   Wm M. Sloane.

ALS (WP, DLC).
  [1] A. H. Joline to WW, Oct. 25, 1890.
  [2] The announcement, which Wilson sent in at once, appeared in *The Princetonian*, xv (Feb. 16, 1891), [1], as follows:
  "Joline Prize in U. S. History.
  "The subject assigned for the essay for the C. O. Joline prize in American Political History is 'The History and Consequences of the Annexation of Louisiana.' The essays for this prize must be handed in on or before the first day of May."

From Horace Elisha Scudder

My dear Wilson   Boston.   13 February 1891

I have directed the Burgess books to be sent you, and should have sent them earlier, as well as written, but that I have been away for a week. Tis always a toss-up, whether you will get a friend or an enemy to review the book. On the whole Id rather trust a conscientious enemy, when it is a matter of politics, and I have no fears that you will not be equal to a whole House of Burgesses.

I hope before the spring to find my way to Philadelphia, and if I do I certainly shall make Princeton a stopping place.

If I have your review—say four or five pages—by 9 March, it will be in season for May, but even so do not distress yourself. Immediacy is not essential, though of course I like to get my hand in as early as may be.

                    Sincerely yours   H. E. Scudder.

ALS (WP, DLC).

From Frederic William Speirs[1]

Dear Sir: Vermillion, So. Dak., Feb. 18, 1891.

I am contemplating a return to the Johns Hopkins next year

to finish my work for a degree. I wish to make administration a second minor. I took your lectures for two years, and hope to get full notes of this present course. I should like to do the necessary reading this summer, and take the examination at the beginning of the academic year. I shall be obliged to you if you will at your convenience furnish me an outline of the required reading on the subject.[2] I read neither French nor German with ease, but can handle them quite successfully with the aid of a lexicon.

I enjoyed the privilege of listening to your commencement address at Worcester, last June.[3] I am sure your vigorous exposition of your subject aroused some of the conservative citizens of that conservative old town to a realization of present conditions.

The University library here is wretchedly poor. My copy of "The State" is the only book accessible upon administration, and the volume is sadly overworked, but always equal to the occasion.

Very truly yours,   Fred W. Speirs.

ALS (WP, DLC) with WWhw notation on env.: "Ans."
    [1] At this time Instructor in History at the University of South Dakota.
    [2] Wilson apparently responded with a copy of the reading list printed below.
    [3] A newspaper report of this address, on municipal reform, is printed at June 27, 1890, Vol. 6. Speirs was from Worcester.

A Reading List

[c. Feb. 21, 1891]

Required Reading
For Minor in Administration, 1891.

1. *v. Sarwey*, O., "Allgemeines Verwaltungsrecht," (in *Marquardsen's* Handbuch des Oeffentlichen Rechts) J. C. B. Mohr, Freiburg im B., (Price 5 marks.)

    or
    Stein, L. v., "Handbuch der Verwaltungslehre," Stuttgart, 1876.
2. *Wilson*, W., "The State."
3. *Schönberg*, "Handbuch der Politischen Oekonomie," Vol. II: Verwaltungslehre, II, "Die Behördenorganisation der Verwaltung des Innern," by *G. Meyer*. (36 pp.)
4. *Pradier-Fodéré*, "Precis de droit administratif," Première Partie, Chapitre Premier. (48 pp.).
5. *Bryce*, Jas., "The American Commonwealth," The chapters on Local Government.
6. *Traill*, H. D., "Central Government" (English Citizen Series).

WWhw MS. (WP, DLC).

From Joseph Ruggles Wilson

My precious Son,   [Clarksville, Tenn.]   Feb 26/91

I wrote you about the time of your last writing to me. But not knowing your Baltimore address I sent to the care of Dr. Gilman. If you never get it the loss will be nothing,[1] for it was a poor sickly note the object of which was to ascertain your precise address. You may partly guess how glad I was to hear from you after so long a silence. Of course I know how you are hurried and worried; and our dear Ellie would of course never think of writing when you cannot! But maybe she is lecturing, too!

I am truly glad—without being surprised—that you had a successful time at Philadelphia in the matter of the alumni meeting. How I should like to hear my darling boy on such an occasion! But, indeed, I thought for some days about two weeks ago, or less, that I never should see you again[.] My stroke of sickness was like a sword run through me. I[t] has left me very weak, although I manage to get to my classes—riding when the weather is at all inclement.

I dare not write more just now; and send this mainly to express my gratification at the receipt of your sweet letter. All its loving sentiments I fully reciprocate, it is hardly necessary to say. Josie is well, & doing the best he can: i.e. he works hard day by day and yet no money, not near enough to pay all current expenses!

Love to Ellie, and thanks to her for *intending* to write me which I am sure was the fact!   Your loving   Father

ALS (WP, DLC).
[1] WW apparently never did receive it.

From the Minutes of the Johns Hopkins Seminary of Historical and Political Science

Bluntschli Library   Feb. 27, 1891

The Historical Seminary convened at eight oclock, Dr. Adams presiding. The address of the evening was given by Dr. Woodrow Wilson, who spoke on "The Literary Politician" (Walter Bagehot). . . .[1]   Emory R. Johnson, Secretary.

Hw entry, bound ledger book (MdBJ).
[1] Here follows a long summary of Wilson's paper, which is printed at July 20, 1889, Vol. 6, the date of its first delivery.

Marginal Notes

John W. Burgess, *Political Science and Comparative Constitutional Law* (2 vols., Boston, 1890-91).

Vol. I, 36:
In the third place, the empire must suppress all local autonomy. Law and ordinance must be one and the same in every district and for every part of the population.

Vol. I, 37:
Fourth and last, we come to consider the political psychology of those nations which may be termed the political nations *par excellence, viz;* the Teutonic; and if the peculiar creations of these nations may be expressed in a single phrase, it must be this: that they are the founders of national states. It is not possible to divine whether this great work could have been accomplished by them without the training in Roman ideas received by them in the Carolingian Empire and the Roman Christian Church. The Teutons strove most earnestly and determinedly, during the earlier, pre-Frankish period of their political history, against even the necessary organization of the state, and came to the consciousness of their mission as the founders of national states, only after half a century of life in the European Empire of the great Charles; but education can only develop what already exists in seed and germ, and we may therefore conclude that no amount of Roman discipline, which was distinctly anti-national in its universality, could have evolved the national idea unless this had been an original principle of Teutonic political genius.

Vol. I, 39:
The national state permits the participation of the governed in the government. In a national state the population have a common language and a common understanding of the principles of rights and the character of wrongs. This common understanding is the strongest moral basis which a govern-

Transcripts of WW Shorthand Comments
[c. March 1, 1891]

Was this in fact true under the Roman imperial organization?

What of the original singleness of stock between Teuton, Celt, Latin, and Greek? If education did not make these several parts of the same race different in capacity what did? And if education gave them different faculties, why could it not give them the same faculties again?

In every instance, or only in the most modern times[?] Was not the French state national before the Revolution?

ment can possibly have; and, at the same time, it secures the enactment and administration of laws whose righteousness must be acknowledged, and whose effect will be the realization of the truest liberty.

Vol. I, 62:
And should we examine carefully into the sources of that readiness to obey law which has characterized the true American citizens of this republic, we should without doubt find ourselves ultimately face to face with the early religious discipline of New England.

Does this mean that the true American citizens were to be found only in New England?

Vol. I, 145:
But we become confused upon the still more important point as to whether the sovereignty is in the United States or in the commonwealths; and we are led to misconceive the real character of the commonwealths, and to think of them really as states instead of merely as governments. This is also true, in some degree, when the ratifying bodies are conventions of the people resident within the commonwealths; but it is much easier to comprehend that these bodies, created directly by the constitution of the United States and solely for United States purposes, are institutions of the United States, than that the legislatures of the commonwealths are such, even when acting in this capacity only.

Still, they are exactly like the constituent bodies, familiar to the states, by which the state constitutions are framed or amended. In other words, they are normal pieces of the state machinery.

Vol. I, 179:
Should the legislative and executive powers conspire against the judiciary, or the legislature fail to hold the executive to his duty by impeachment, the sovereignty within the constitution may be appealed to, so to amend the constitution as to prevent the nullification of its intent by its governmental servants. It is difficult to see how the guaranty of individual liberty against the government itself could be made more complete.

How appealed to except under revolutionary methods?

Vol. II, 12:
This is a highly practical form of government. In the first place, it is conservative. It fixes the weight of responsibility upon a single person; and there is nothing like this to produce caution, deliberation, and an impartial regard

for all interests concerned. In the second place, it is energetic. One capable person can come to an agreement with himself, while a half-dozen or more are haggling over questions of precedence and procedure. In the third place, it is powerful. That one poor commander is better than two good ones is the *bon mot* often quoted, of one of the most powerful commanders whom the world has ever produced.

Vol. II, 14:

This [parliamentary system] is in some respects, and under certain conditions, an admirable system. Its chief excellence is that it maintains permanent harmony between the different branches of the government; but in gaining this result, it sacrifices entirely the independence of the executive, and destroys practically the independence of one of the two houses of the legislature. Legislation is thus made comparatively easy; but at the risk of an unsteady and an inconsistent administrative policy. Another great advantage which this system offers is the better information of the legislature upon all subjects concerning which it must act, through the presence and voice of the heads of the administration in the chambers. Legislation is neither initiated nor shaped, as in the other system, by the heads of a half-hundred legislative committees—by men, that is, who are commonly inexperienced and often visionary.

This is rather *a priori* than founded upon the principles of presidential government.

Better some administrative policy than none.

If it is to be made of actual existing systems, administrative policy is in both in all real features subject to the will of the legislature; and it is equally answered or achieved in both, in the presidential at stated intervals, in the parliamentary at uncertain intervals.

From Seward Vincent Coffin[1]

My dear Friend,   Middletown, Conn., March 1, 1891.

In pursuance of a plan proposed nearly a year ago, we have a committee, representing the faculty, undergraduates & alumni of Wesleyan, charged with the duty of inventing a plan whereby the athletic interests of the college can be made more of a unit.

Your humble servant is unfortunate enough to be of this committee; & I write to ask you for a few "pointers" if you can spare the time to give us any.

My idea has been to have some sort of a board, composed

perhaps of one professor & two alumni, with power to step in & prevent evil results at critical times,—in some such fashion as the Princeton managers did when Poe was substituted for Ames as foot ball captain.[2] And, on the financial side, to have if possible a graduate treasurer to whom the managers & treasurers of the various associations should report &c. These ideas are not the result of mature thought on my part, but only schemes that have presented themselves to me as perhaps advisable.

You are undoubtedly familiar with the entire system at Princeton; &, having had some practical experience with our present system, you can readily tell what there is in the Princeton arrangement that would be practicable for us here. Any ideas & information that you may send me will be thoroughly appreciated, I assure you.

Max Farrand,[3] of your Foot Ball Association, is a firm friend of mine; & perhaps he might give me the details of Princeton foot-ball management; but you understand *our* situation & needs so well, that I prefer writing to you. I trust it may not be too great a tax upon your time to give us suggestions that I know will be valuable.

It may be of interest to you to know that the college boys still talk of the time when you & "yours truly" were on the foot ball board, & speak of it as a time when "everybody was satisfied."

Please give my kindest regards to Mrs. Wilson, & believe me
Very sincerely yours,   Seward V. Coffin.

ALS (WP, DLC) with WWhw notation on env.: "Ans 1 July/91."
  [1] Wesleyan University '89, who had served with Wilson as a director of the Wesleyan University Foot-Ball Association in 1889-90.
  [2] *The Princetonian*, XIV (Oct. 11, 1889), Supplement, announced that the Graduate Committee of the Foot Ball Association had advised a change in the captaincy of the Princeton football team. The only reason given was the committee's belief that leadership of the team, "in view of the close contest we are expecting in November [*i.e.*, the game with Yale]," had to be "intrusted to some member of the team who has perfect coolness and self-command in critical moments." This same special issue announced the resignation of Knowlton Lyman Ames, '90, as captain. Edgar Allan Poe, '91, elected captain on October 17, led the team to an undefeated season.
  [3] Born Newark, N. J., March 29, 1869. A.B., College of New Jersey, 1892; A.M., 1893; Ph.D., 1896. Student at the Universities of Leipzig and Heidelberg, 1892-96. Instructor in History, Wesleyan University, 1896-98; Associate Professor of History, 1898-1900, and Professor of History, 1900-1901. Professor of History, Stanford University, 1901-1908. Professor of History, Yale University, 1908-25. General Director, Commonwealth Fund, 1919-21; adviser to the same foundation, 1921-27. Director, Henry E. Huntington Library and Art Gallery, 1927-41; Research Associate, 1941-45. Author and editor of many scholarly works on American history. Died June 17, 1945.

From D. C. Heath and Company

Dear Sir,   Boston, Mass.   Mar. 3, 1891.
  Enclosed is royalty statement, which should have gone to you

before, and would, had it not been for the fact that we have been unusually crowded with details this year, and the added fact that we could not sooner get returns from our Chicago office. We wish for your sake, as well as ours, that the sales had been three times as large.[1]

In view of the usual feeling that the author gets about one-tenth as much on the sale of books, as the publisher, it may interest you to know that last year we paid our authors in royalties over three thousand dollars more than we made ourselves, and the prospect is that this year the difference in favor of the author will be even larger. It may also interest you to know that we have given away during the past year over forty thousand books as samples.   Yours very truly,   D. C. Heath & Co.

TL (WP, DLC) with WWhw notation on env.: "Royalty Statement Jan'y '91."
Enc.: royalty statement dated Dec. 31, 1890.
[1] The royalty statement reported sales during the last six months of 1890 of 194 copies of *The State* and of 1,606 copies of *State and Federal Governments of the United States*, and total sales through December 31, 1890, of 1,644 copies of the former and of 2,384 copies of the latter.

To Charles Fisk Beach, Jr.[1]

My dear Sir,   Baltimore, 3 March, 1891
    Your letter of Feb'y. 28th,[2] addressed to Princeton, has been forwarded to me here. The address on Bagehot to which you refer has not been printed; had it been, I should be very glad to send you a copy. I am very much interested to learn that you too are specially interested in Bagehot. For me he has a great and enduring fascination.
                    Very sincerely Yours,   Woodrow Wilson

ALS (WC, NjP).
[1] A New York lawyer and legal scholar.
[2] It is missing.

An Announcement

[March 4, 1891]
PROF. WOODROW WILSON'S CLASSES
    Prof. Woodrow Wilson expects to return to Princeton this week and will meet his classes hereafter according to the catalogued schedule, beginning Tuesday, March 10, at 8.30 a.m. All his classes will meet in the English Room.

Printed in *The Princetonian*, xv (March 4, 1891), [1].

From Joseph Ruggles Wilson

My precious son—   Clarksville, Tenn., March 7/91

I am afraid that you noticed a thin mist of bad humour in the last two letters I wrote you, and which you received at B. In thinking over the said epistles it was "borne in upon me" that there was something of the sort, although I was not conscious of the aforementioned mist at the time of writing. But I was feeling very weak, and very solitary, and very old (having age-shakes throughout my mental structure), and quite in an upset condition generally. So that I imagined, in this downed condition, that my Woodrow was forgetting me somewhat! *Would* you have believed that even my imagination, which is vivid and morbid enough normally, could have taken such a flight as this? But don't you think that every one has at times a crazy fit: and when all the world seems to be cracked or awry except himself? Certainly solitude is not best for *me*. It raises spectres. It moulds self-love into shapes that are far from being pretty. It thins the skin of sensitiveness, so that needles wound more than bludgeon-blows ought to. And it makes me feel ashamed of myself many a time, as now I feel when thinking that I have no excuse for momentarily doubting your love except my own—cussedness (I mean nothing in the least profane, but there is no other word)

Well I have at any rate made a clean breast, which affords a sort of relief—and said dirty breast will not have to be again cleaned of a similar defilement. Now therefore do you and Ellie—please—put your arms about my neck and say to me this: 'Well, you are a poor old stick after all; and there is no telling what a turn your worn-out thoughts may next take; but all the same we love you with our whole hearts, and intend hereafter to discipline you so as to make you more and more worthy of our love!' But ah, I must now stop—for I am actually crying—and that won't do, you know—because crying is catching and you two dear ones might be guilty of a similar softness! So, good night with a father's truest love for you both.   Affy yours—F.

ALS (WP, DLC).

Notes for a Course in American Constitutional Law

[March 10, 1891-May 16, 1893]

Contents:

(a) WWT notes, with some WWhw, for lectures on the following topics, with composition dates when given: "I. *The Character of Constitutional Law in general   Of our own Constitutional Law in particular.*" (March 10, 1891); "II. *Constitution of Government,—Consti-*

tution of Liberty." (March 17, 1891); "III. *Genesis of Our Constitutions of Government, State and Federal.*" (March 31, 1891); "IV.
History of Bills of Rights" (April 22, 1891); "V. *The Executive,—
State and Federal.*" (April 28, 1891); "VI. The Executive (continued),
—American and Foreign." (May 5 and 6, 1891); "VII. *The Legislature,—State and Federal.*" (April 25, 1893); "IX. The Courts,—State
and Federal." (May 16, 1893).

(b) A few loose pages with notes and bibliographies.

Loose sheets (WP, DLC).

From Daniel Collamore Heath

Dear Prof. Wilson: Boston, Mass. 3/11/1891.

Yours of the 9th received,[1] and I return with this Mr. Wenzle's
MS.[2] He is a young man, working his way thro' college, and is not
burdened with money: he hopes you will indicate the points
which he can look up just as well as you, also the sources, as he
wants to make the charge as little as possible for the correction.
Perhaps after looking the MS. thro' a little you can tell about
what time it will take and therefore what the charge will be.
He thinks he would like to know.

We did not contemplate binding it with The State, but in a
separate pamphlet, to be used with The State where anybody
cared for it.

We tho't the statement' of sales would please you. The larger
part of the sales for the United States were in the Grammar
Schools of Washington, where we gave one-half of all money we
received for getting the book introduced; so you can see that we
did not get rich out of the transaction, but it will be a good advertisement for the book in other places.

Yours Truly,   D. C. Heath.

TL (WP, DLC).
1 It is missing.
2 This study guide for *The State* was published as John Wenzel, *Comparative
View of the Executive and Legislative Departments of the Governments of the
United States, France, England, and Germany,* by D. C. Heath and Company in
1891.

From Albert Bushnell Hart

Dear Prof. Wilson: Cambridge, Mass.   March 12, 1891

It is a long time since I have written you about the Epochs.
Vol I is out and of course you have received it.[1] I should like
much to have your judgment upon it, for my own private edifica-
tion, and also any suggestns which might be useful in my own
volume. I expect to go to press September 1 with Vol II.[2]

Your plea for time is of course most unimpeachable, and I do not write to urge or hurry you. But what is the prospect on Vol III?[3]

The Colonies has been well received. Tyler, McLaughlin at Ann Arbor, Prof Salmon at Vassar[,] Turner at Madison speak well of it.[4]

I send you one of my screeds on federal government[.][5] Did you see an article in the March Atlantic on the Speaker? I mention it because it, in a way, grew out of your Cogressnal Governmt. That is, I have tried to elaborate one phase of a development which I first learned from that work

Sincerely yours, Albert Bushnell Hart

ALS (WP, DLC) with WWhw notation on env.: "Ans."
[1] Reuben Gold Thwaites, *The Colonies, 1492-1750* (New York and London, 1891).
[2] It was A. B. Hart, *Formation of the Union, 1750-1829* (New York and London, 1892).
[3] That is, Wilson's *Division and Reunion* in the "Epochs of American History" Series, which Hart edited.
[4] Moses Coit Tyler, Andrew Cunningham McLaughlin, Lucy Maynard Salmon, and Frederick Jackson Turner.
[5] Hart's enclosure is missing.

A Newspaper Report of Wilson's Address to the New York Alumni

[March 13, 1891]

About sixty members of the Princeton Club of New York attended their regular meeting last evening in the ballroom of the Hotel Brunswick, and . . . the President, Mr. James W. Alexander, called the meeting to order at 9 o'clock. . . .

The President stated that the course at Princeton would never be shortened, but that, on the other hand, it would doubtless be broadened and made more comprehensive. He said that Princeton was sadly in need of an increased Faculty force, and that the college should be made more useful in academic lines.

Prof. William Libbey[1] was to have addressed the club on the recent Government work done by Princeton men, and he was also to have described the work of the Lumholtz expedition in Central America, of which he was a member, but owing to a sudden attack of the grip he was unable to fill his engagement. As the speaker of the evening Mr. Alexander introduced Prof. Woodrow Wilson, the well-known writer on political science, as "the last but by no means the least addition to the Princeton Faculty."

Prof. Wilson spoke generally upon the needs of Princeton and the necessity of extending the work of the college.[2] The Princeton of to-day, he said, was totally unlike the Princeton of yesterday. When he graduated the student applied what he had to further and broader study, but now the demand was for a practical course which would prepare the student for life. Consequently some radical changes were needed in the present course.

Princeton, he said, was in a very critical condition. She must make great advancement, and unless there was rapid progression there would certainly be rapid retrogression. The present needs of the college were a Law School and additional professorships in Political Economy and History.

Mr. [Hugh L.] Cole offered a resolution that the President, on behalf of the club, in the current effort to establish an Alumni fund for the college, appoint a committee to co-operate with other Alumni associations engaged in the same matter. Dinner was then served and the meeting came to an end.

Printed in the *New York Times*, March 13, 1891; editorial headings omitted.

[1] William Libbey, Jr., born Jersey City, N. J., March 27, 1855. A.B., College of New Jersey, 1877; A.M. and Sc.D., 1879. Studied at Berlin and Paris, 1878-80. He spent his entire career at Princeton as Assistant Professor of Natural Science, 1882-83; Professor of Physical Geography and Histology, 1883-98; and Professor of Physical Geography, 1898-1921. Active in the New Jersey National Guard, he served in the United States Army during the First World War and was discharged in 1919 with the rank of colonel. Long active in civic affairs in Princeton, he was also an officer in many scientific, learned, and patriotic societies. Died September 6, 1927.

[2] Wilson's notes for this talk are on two loose pages in WP, DLC. The following extract provided the cue for the heart of his speech: "Princeton just now in transition. . . . The real chance of the age (Chicago dinner) *et seq.* An institution of law and literature,—to convey the spirit of institutions along with the spirit of the age. Spirited and confident, but conservative, progress[.]"

Notes for an Elementary Course in Political Economy

[March 13-May 7, 1891]

Contents:

(a) WWT title page: "Lectures on Political Economy (Elements)."[1]

(b) WWT, WWhw, and WWsh notes for fifteen lectures on the following topics, with composition dates when given: "*Significance.—Province.—Method.*" (March 13, 1891); "II. *Public and Private Economy Contrasted.*" (March 13, 1891); "III: *Production: Its Nature and Varieties.*" (March [April] 3, 1891); "IV. *History of Production.*" (April 3 and 10, 1891); "V. *The Industrial Revolution: Capitalistic Production.*" (April 17, 1891); "VI. '*The Postulates of English Political Economy.*'" (May 7, 1891).

Loose pages (WP, DLC).

[1] Wilson wrote a "*Provisional Scheme of Lectures,*" with some eleven topics and envisaging eighteen lectures, in a notebook in the Wilson Papers, DLC, inscribed on the cover "~~Political Economy~~ Woodrow Wilson." Only the cover and two pages remain of this notebook.

An Announcement

[March 13, 1891]

JUNIOR AND SENIOR ELECTIVES.

. . . Professor Wilson. Administration. Lectures will be on nature and scope of study, place and content of administration in the general field of public law, and the development of the idea of a state and its functions. The only reference outside of the French and German authorities is an article on the "Study of Administration" by Woodrow Wilson in the first volume of the Political Science Quarterly. There is no announcement in constitutional law.

Printed in *The Princetonian*, xv (March 13, 1891), [1].

Ellen Axson Wilson to Stockton Axson

My dear Stockton,   Princeton Mar. 15/91.
. . . We had a good sermon from Dr. Taylor of New York today.[1]

W. went Thursday night to the meeting of the Princeton Club in N. Y. He was "the guest of the evening" and he made a speech that "took" tremendously. It was chiefly about the law school, and one of the trustees who was present has written to him since asking for an interview on the subject, saying much in praise of his "interesting, able and masterly" address, and adding that they all felt that in Woodrow the school had its best chance of success.[2] He wants to know how much money it will take to start it. Encouraging, is it not? But Woodrow says the most encouraging thing was the unanimity with which the numerous lawyers present agreed that such law schools were the very sort needed and that Princeton would be inaugurating a great reform by leading the way in that direction. We thought that most of the lawyers would be too "practical" to see it in that light. . . .

But I must say 'Goodnight.' You don't know how much we *all* miss you, dear, old & young alike. If I could only see you settled here in the college *how* happy I should be! I wonder if that is one of the things too good to come true[.] With *warmest* love from all
                          Your aff. sister   E. A. W.

ALI (WP, DLC).
[1] The Princeton newspapers do not reveal who Dr. Taylor was or where he preached. He may have been the Rev. Dr. Charles H. Taylor of Brooklyn. The church was presumably the Second Presbyterian Church, which the Wilsons formally joined in 1897.
[2] This letter, probably from Wilson's warm supporter, James W. Alexander, is missing.

An Announcement

[March 20, 1891]
JUNIOR AND SENIOR ELECTIVES.

. . . *Professor Wilson*. Administration. The lecture will be on the development of the idea of a state and its functions. The sole reference is the article on the "Study of Administration" by Woodrow Wilson in the first volume of the Political Science Quarterly. There is no announcement in constitutional law.

Printed in *The Princetonian*, xv (March 20, 1891), [1].

To Robert Bridges

My dear Bobby,   Princeton, 20 March, 1891
    There's no use in your coming down, I deeply regret to say. John came into my lecture room this morning just as I was about to set out in search of information about his case. I went to see, not Rockwood, but Cornwall,[1]—Billy Magie sent me to him; and he says, kindly, but with evident sincerity, that the "drop" is final,—that it would be unwise, because useless, to make any effort to reopen the case again;—and that because when the boy was given another trial, at your request, it was their understanding that the new trial was to be the final one, decisive of the case. There's nothing for us to do, therefore, it would seem, but to swallow the bitter disappointment as best we may.
    I think your Dickinson plan[2] the best possible under the circumstances, and am glad that the boy is to be here once more next year.
    I am to see him again before he leaves of course, and will be of what use I can to him.
    I am in a peck of trouble myself:—for I have come back to find Mrs. Wilson and all three of the children ill with the *grippe*. I have not undressed since I saw you. The cases, however, though distressing, are not in any important sense serious, I hope.
    I must stop now to prepare questions for "a written," to be held presently.   More very soon.   As ever
                    Faithfully Yours,   Woodrow Wilson.

ALS (WC, NjP).
    [1] Charles Greene Rockwood, Jr., Professor of Mathematics, and Henry Bedinger Cornwall, Professor of Analytical Chemistry and Mineralogy.
    [2] Apparently John Bridges planned to enroll at Dickinson College for a term or two.

From Samuel White Small

My Very Dear Sir: Philadelphia, March 25, 1891.

I have the honor, with the added personal pleasure, of notifying you that, at the annual meeting of the Board of Directors of the UTAH UNIVERSITY[1] of the Methodist Episcopal Church, you were unanimously chosen a member of the

BOARD OF VISITORS

of that Institution of Christian Learning and the Liberal Arts.

To-day I forward the parchment certificate of your election, duly sealed and signed.

In due time a copy of the Charter, Functions of the Board of Visitors, and other documents of information, will be transmitted to you.[2]

Trusting the above action may be agreeable to you and that our Institution may be largely profited by your distinguished co-operation, I have the happiness to be

Your obedient servant,
Samuel White Small, President.

(Eastern Address, 1905 Diamond St., Philadelphia, Pa.)

TLS (WP, DLC).

[1] Utah University was never much more than a paper organization. A contract was let for a building to house the institution in Ogden in November 1889, and the Reverend Samuel White Small was elected President by the Board of Directors in June 1890. Only the basement of the building was completed when the directors were sued for failure to pay their bills. The Methodist Mission in Utah then recommended that the enterprise be liquidated, and this was done later in 1891. See Henry M. Merkel, *History of Methodism in Utah* (Colorado Springs, Col., 1938), pp. 195-96.

[2] Utah University did not survive long enough for these to be forthcoming.

An Announcement

[March 25, 1891]

CUYLER PRIZE IN ECONOMICS[1]

The subject of the essay for this prize will be "The Nature of Wages," with especial reference to the relation between Wages and Profits. Due June 1st.[2]

Woodrow Wilson.

Printed in *The Princetonian*, xv (March 25, 1891), [1].

[1] The Theodore Cuyler Prize in Economics, consisting of the interest on $1,000, presented by Wilson's classmate, C. C. Cuyler. It was given "to that member of the Senior class who shall present the best thesis and pass the best examination in June, 1891, on some subject in Political Economy, to be assigned by the Professor in charge of the Department of Political Economy." *Catalogue of the College of New Jersey at Princeton 1890-91*, p. 131. The examination is printed at June 1, 1891.

[2] The winner in 1891 was Thomas Ferguson McNair.

From Azel Washburn Hazen

My dear Friend: Middletown, Conn.   26 March, 1891.

When I heard that you were coming to speak in New Haven,[1] my heart began to flutter with the hope that you might run up here. You can hardly imagine what a pleasure it would have been to see you. But it has given me joy to hear directly from you through Prof. Winchester. Mrs Wilson's letter to Mrs Hazen also refreshed us. Her manner of speaking of me was so cordial and generous that *I* want to *thank* you both for her words, with my own hand.

It is a constant pain to me to pass your old home here, which has still on its front the doleful sign *"To Rent."* Yet the house is no more vacant than your place in the College and the Community seems to be. Two small men are "rattling around" in your department,[2] to be sure, but the idea of *filling* it has never been conceived by anybody.

For myself, I do miss beyond all telling your presence and worshipful spirit in the Church, as well as your loyal, inspiriting friendship always.

Now, my dear friend, I say these things to gratify myself, not to lay upon you the burden of a response to my poor words. Mrs Hazen joins me in love to Mrs Wilson & yourself, also in remembrances to the children and the young gentlemen.[3]

With sincere affection,

Very truly yours,   A. W. Hazen

ALS (WP, DLC) with WWhw notation on env.: "Ans. July 1/91."
  [1] To deliver "Leaders of Men" before the Kent Club of the Yale Law School on March 18.
  [2] Andrew Stephenson and John R. Commons.
  [3] Stockton Axson and Edward Axson, who had lived with the Wilsons in Middletown. At this time Edward was at the Bingham School in North Carolina.

To Francis Bazley Lee[1]

My dear Sir,   Princeton, New Jersey, 27 March, 1891

I am sorry to say that I cannot be of much service to you in the matter about which you inquire, inasmuch as I have never yet given any especial attention to the history of the Belgian constitution. In Müller's "Political History of Recent Times" (Harpers), pp. 112 *et seq.*, you will find a good brief account of the circumstances under which the constitution was framed; there is a "Histoire politique interne de la Belgique" by E. *Poullet,* published in Louvain in 1879; the *Nation* has from time to time had excellent editorial matter touching constitutional questions in Belgium; and Poole's Index doubtless contains references to magazine articles which would either give you what you want or guide you in finding it.

I am quite aware that I am not answering your question; but this is the best I can do under the circumstances.

Very truly Yours,   Woodrow Wilson

ALS (WC, NjP).

¹ At this time studying law in the office of a Trenton attorney. He later wrote a history of New Jersey.

To Daniel Coit Gilman

[My dear Mr. Gilman,]   [Princeton, N.J., c. March 29, 1891]

I knew Prof. Winchester at Wesleyan rather more intimately than any other colleague at Wesleyan and my brother-in-law, Mr. Stockton Axson, was a pupil in all his classes. I had, therefore, the best means of knowing both the personality of the man and his methods as a teacher. I shall speak of the latter first, though I by no means esteem personality a secondary matter in the case of a teacher.

The essence of Mr. Winchester's method as a teacher may be said to be, not instruction, in any narrow sense of the word, but work by the pupil under direct guidance and stimulation. He deals with his older classes quite after the Seminary method, though his Seminar resembles that of a German university rather than our own in this, that its members are selected by special tests, not admitted because of mere academic stage of progress. He gets as much work out of his students, and as much intelligent work, as any man I have known, both sending them to work up the best sources of literary criticism and subjecting their reports of results to a keen critical examination wh. at once corrects mistakes and furnishes the incomparable stimulation of points of view to be found only by the mature critic,—and discovered to the pupil in his case in a manner which is itself a model of literary form and matter.

Mr. Winchester's scholarship in the subjects proper to his chair I believe it would be hard to parallel among university professors: I mean his acquaintance with our literature, old and new, big and little, his knowledge of the best criticism, his feeling for form and comprehension of substance, his perception of relative values both in our own literature and as between our own and other literatures. He is what a professor of Eng. lit. ought to be: both a born critic and a made critic. He not only has keen powers of appreciating literature of the most varied and even opposite types, but also that salt of sanity—a sense of humour,—which could be proved to be derived from a sense of proportion.

His personality, you hardly had a good opportunity to judge: it comes out only upon intimate association, such as is offered to pupils and colleagues. I know from personal experience how much, and yet subtly, he can stimulate—how subtly one, so to say, *experiences* his knowledge by association with him, and with what pleasure one takes his points, put with such finesse, humour, and suggestiveness. You yourself felt the charm of his public address. He is much the same in conversation, and in the class-room.

I have spoken enthusiastically because I did not in this case know any other way to speak that would express my sober sentiments. When one knows a genuine man, with the equipment he should have for his calling and station, it is right for one to say so,—as I have now done.

I ought to say, however, that, while in his public lectures you get the charm of manner which he carries into all his utterances, you do not get the strength, the thoroughness, the depth of his class-room method. Admirable as his public lectures are, they are designedly popular, designedly devoted to the more obvious aspects of his subjects. His class-room discussions, on the contrary, have a scope and thoroughness which his popular discourses hardly suggest.

[Faithfully yours,   Woodrow Wilson]

WWhwL (draft) (WP, DLC).

To Albert Shaw

My dear Shaw: Princeton, New Jersey.   29 March, 1891.

I write this afternoon to make a request which involves some display of cheek, and therefore (I hope you will believe) costs me some effort. I write to ask whether you have a place on the *Review of Reviews*, present or prospective, for a fellow whose only journalistic experience was a brief connexion with a country newspaper, but who is uncommonly able and whom I can back to any extent you may demand. To be explicit: I have a brother-in-law, twenty-three years of age, Stockton Axson by name, who graduated at Wesleyan last June, and who is spending this year at the Hopkins, in the English Department. He means to be a professor of English literature; but English literature, as you know, is not taught in Baltimore. He wants, therefore, to stay out a year, if he can find some means of supporting himself during that time, in order to give the Hopkins authorities time to find a man to fill the Donovan chair,[1] recently endowed but never established.

He studied at Wesleyan under Winchester, whom you probably don't know, but who, it seems clear to me after two years' association with him, ought to be the Donovan professor, as I told Mr. Gilman with full conviction. Winchester pronounced Axson one of the ablest fellows he had ever had under him, especially as a writer, and is ready indeed to back him with something like affectionate enthusiasm,—as I myself would, most assuredly. Axson has also had some business experience. He could serve you, I feel pretty confident, in a variety of ways, should you choose to use him variously. Bob. Finley[2] knows him and could tell you something of his personality. He is here with us now for a few days, and means to come up to see Finley the latter part of this week. It was my idea alone, of course, to write to you,—not his,—though Finley has, I know, been looking for a summer job for him in New York. I mean to give him a note of introduction to you, so that you may take a look at him, if you choose. If you have nothing to try him in yourself, you may know of some like job that you could suggest him for.

Now, that's all of that: let's change the subject,—it's always an effort for me to ask a favour, even when I ask it of a close friend, who will, I know understand me perfectly.

I enjoyed immensely the little glimpse I had of you the other day,—my only objection to it was its brevity; but I'm in New York not infrequently and can see more of you next time. I am booming you upon every occasion for our coming chair of Economics, and hope with some confidence that things will be in good shape before you have very long felt settled in your new establishment. You see I am working for myself in the matter, in fact, because it would hearten and refresh me mightily to have you as a colleague. I feel a great confidence that we could remain young together, as well as older and wiser and more learned.

Mrs. Wilson joins me in very warm regards, and also in the very earnest wish that you would run down and spend a Sunday with us. Try it once and you will find how easy it is to do and will let yourself be persuaded to do it often. You can come by a train that leaves New York at 5 p.m. and you can very comfortably be back in New York by eleven Monday morning.

As ever

Cordially and affectionately yours,   Woodrow Wilson

TCL (in possession of Virginia Shaw English).
    [1] A professorship in English literature, endowed in 1889 by Caroline Donovan.

Lecturers were invited on the foundation from time to time, but a professor was not appointed until 1905.

2 Robert Johnston Finley, assistant editor of the New York *Review of Reviews*, formerly a student at the Johns Hopkins.

A Book Review

[April 1891]

MASON'S VETO POWER. Harvard Historical Monographs, No. 1. "The Veto: Its Origin, Development, and Function in the Government of the United States (1789–1889)." By EDWARD CAMPBELL MASON, A.B. Paper, pp. 232. Boston: Ginn & Co., 1890.

Harvard, following the example of several other Eastern universities, has adopted the plan of publishing some of the theses produced by her more advanced students of history and politics; and of this plan the publication of Mr. Mason's excellent monograph on *The Veto Power* is the first fruit. It is certainly a most creditable piece of work, painstaking, thorough, and well arranged; written in a businesslike style, which loses no time; indicative also of a clear-sighted appreciation of the significance of its subject as a topic in political science, of its bearings and uses in studies of a wider scope. Mr. Mason has searched the public records, not only for all the vetoes, but also for all the Presidential protests touching legislative action between 1789 and 1889; he has classified the vetoes as those affecting the form of government, those affecting the distribution of the powers of government, and those affecting the exercise of the powers of government, and has discussed each of these classes separately; he has analyzed carefully the constitutional procedure as to vetoes; he has sketched the genesis of the veto power, and has outlined its political development; and he has added six valuable appendices, giving chronological lists (occupying more than seventy pages) of all the vetoes and protests, with references to documentary sources, as well as of the vetoes sent to the Confederate Congress by President Davis; a tabulated view of the vetoes of the several Presidents, a condensed statement of the provisions of State Constitutions relative to the veto, and a list of the books he has used in the preparation of the monograph.

This would seem to leave little to be desired, even in the absence of the chapters on the workings of the veto in the States, and on the veto power in other modern constitutions, which, we are told in the editor's preface, were crowded out by the unexpected bulk of the matter here published; and, from one point of view, nothing more ought to be desired. The thoroughness and exactness of the record here made of the use of the veto in the first hundred years of our present federal government must command hearty admiration from everyone who understands just how much industry and how much intelligence such thoroughness and exactness indicate. No one can fail to see how much one important topic is simplified by Mr. Mason's monograph for all future students of constitutional machinery. From another point of view, however, the work is by no means so satisfactory in respect of what it accomplishes—and that the very point of view which the author himself seems to have sought to occupy in its preparation—the point of view, namely, of historical and comparative politics. The historical matter contained in those portions of the book which seek to explain the genesis of the veto power, and to sketch its development as a political factor, is thin and unsatisfactory; not inaccurate, except by reason of what is omitted; inconclusive, because meagre; without body, and consequently without weight. It is true, for example, that the veto in England remained with the Crown as the mere negative half of the once round and complete power of legislation at first exercised by the Sovereign; and it is true that the veto has been disused since Anne's time; but it is also true that it is just within the period since Anne's time that the initiative in legislation has, under the guarantees of ministerial responsibility, passed to the Cabinet: that when, nowadays, we say the Crown, we mean the ministers; and that the part of the English executive in legislation, and in the positive, formative, aggressive side of it, is just as important now as it ever was. That is the reason that the negative part of the executive power in legislation has not been used since Anne sought to have ministers to her own liking. We copied the disused power, the veto, and omitted—wisely or unwisely—the initiative of the Crown.

Again, Mr. Mason refers to the characteristics of disposition or of policy which determined the attitude of the several Presidents toward legislation, but his references lack color and reality, and make no impression. He discusses constitutional points, but so slightly as to leave a sense of weakness. But it would be unfair to insist upon these defects, as if they marred the real value of the sketch to those who shall use it to base conclusive commentary upon. Criticism with insight may be based upon it, and history that tells its whole story; and those who thus use Mr. Mason's clear matter will know best how valuable, how indispensable it is. WOODROW WILSON.

Princeton.

Printed in the *Annals of the American Academy of Political and Social Science*, I (April 1891), 694-97.

An Announcement

[April 3, 1891]

JUNIOR AND SENIOR ELECTIVES.

. . . In Constitutional Law, Prof. Wilson during the next week will take up the derivation of the Federal Constitution and also the constitutions of the Admitted States. The works announced as bearing on these subjects are as follows: The Genesis of a New England State, by Alexander Johnston in the Johns Hopkins Uhiversity [University] Studies, first series, eleventh monograph; A. V. Dicey's "The Law of the Constitution," chap. on Non-sovereign law-making bodies; John Fiske's "The critical period of American History," pp. 211-222; Alexander Johnston on the First Century of the Constitution in the New Princeton Review, vol. 4, pp. 175-190.

Printed in *The Princetonian*, xvi (April 3, 1891), [1].

From Albert Shaw

My Dear Wilson: New York, Apr 4. 1891.

It has been a genuine pleasure to meet Mr. Axon, and we all like him immensely. There is nothing (to speak of) in the literary line, not already provided for, that is to be done on the R. of R; but I think we can arrange some business functions,—with more or less writing incidentally,—that will fill in your brother's vacant year opportunely. He seems inclined to cast his lot with us. Of course the thing is not princely, for new periodicals are seldom rich. Mr. Gates, my friend and business manager, has taken a strong fancy to Axon, and of course Finley and I will be delighted to have him helping us. We shall appreciate him if he comes, and I shall sympathize to the full in all his plans of work and study for the future. I send you the *Review*. Judge it leniently. I never did anything under a greater stress of difficulties—chiefly mechanical. But in two months things will be well organized.

Give my most cordial regards to Mrs. Wilson. I shall hope to make her a call in the early future.

As ever yours: Albert Shaw.

ALS (WP, DLC).

Notes for a Chapel Talk[1]

Chapel, April 5, 1891.

Read Job, XXVII

John III, 7: "Let no man deceive you: he that doeth righteousness is righteous, even as he is righteous.["]

Genuineness, manly fidelity (wh. is *manliness*) a *specially appropriate theme for a college audience.*
Youth ingenuous, but college life artificial, full of temptations to disingenuousness.
   You may safely appeal to the generous, manly motives of a college audience,—but too often you *have to appeal.*
Genuineness (*"Doeth"*=achieveth, accomplisheth).
   (1) *Interior*—of structure, motive, etc. (Analogy of a building, "fitly joined together")
      Native or acquired
   (2) *Exterior,* of *action*=just, upright, truthful.
Antithesis between '*righteous*' and '*good*' ("For scarcely for a righteous man will one die: yet peradventure for a good man some would even dare to die.")
Result of effort, of *attitude*:
   "*Blessed are they* which do hunger and thirst after righteousness: for they shall be filled."

WWhw MS. (WP, DLC).
   1 Delivered at the afternoon Sunday service in Marquand Chapel on April 5, 1891.

From John Dale McGill

Dear Sir: Jersey City, Ap. 6, 1891
   Pardon the delay in answering your letter. An epidemic of "grip" has consumed all my time lately. You are perfectly welcome to make any repairs to the bath-tub you please.
   I have somewhere a key to the safe in dining room—which you can have to duplicate.
   The paraphernalia of the fire-places is also at your disposal for use in the house.
                              Very Respectfully   J D. McGill

ALS (WP, DLC).

From Albert Harris Tolman[1]

Dear Sir;   Ripon, Wisconsin, April 6, 1891.
   I see by the Springfield (Mass.) Republican that the chair of English Literature in the new University of Chicago has been offered to Professor Caleb T. Winchester of your University. If Professor Winchester shall leave you,[2] I desire to be a candidate for his present position. I shall be very much obliged to you if you will let me know to whom I should make application, if there should be any occasion to go so far in the matter.

It has been easy for me to keep you in mind since the time when we shared the hospitality of good Miss Ashton's home in Baltimore. I occupy a settee here, not a chair, and your book on *Congressional Government* is a constant help to me in my capacity of "acting" (the word has special significance) Professor of Civics. . . .

Hoping that you are prospering in every way, I am

Yours sincerely,   A. H. Tolman.

ALS (WP, DLC) with WWhw notation on env.: "Ans."
¹ A former fellow-graduate student of Wilson's at the Johns Hopkins, Tolman was at this time Professor of English Literature and Rhetoric at Ripon College.
² Tolman addressed his letter to Wesleyan University.

From Daniel Coit Gilman

Dear Professor Wilson   Baltimore.   Ap. 7. 1891

I was very much gratified by your letter in respect to Prof. Winchester, and I wish that every body could have so clear & strong an exponent of the good that is in him. I have shown what you said to Prof. Gildersleeve & to two others of my colleagues, and we are *considering*—with no little anxiety, what it is best for us to do.   Yours Sincerely   D. C. Gilman

ALS (WP, DLC) with WWhw sums on env.

An Announcement

[April 10, 1891]

JUNIOR AND SENIOR ELECTIVES.

. . . In Constitutional Law.—The lectures of next week will deal with a comparison of the Executive, seen in the status of the United States, the several States and the constitution of foreign States. References same as before.

Printed in *The Princetonian*, xvi (April 10, 1891), [1].

From Caleb Thomas Winchester

My dear Professor Wilson,   Middletown, Conn., Apr. 14th 1891.

In some perplexity of late, I have often wished that I might consult with you: it occurs to me that you may not think I'm presuming too much if I ask by letter your opinion and advice. Of course I refer to this Chicago invitation. You, more than any one else I know, are in a position to give an unbiased opinion.

The matter has, indeed, much against my wishes and I am

sure not by my fault, got into the papers in a more definite form that the facts justify. Dr Harper[1] could say, with truth, that he had not formally offered me the headship of a dep't in his new Univ. at a salary of $5000.00; he *hasn't* done that, exactly. Yet it suffices to say here that that *is* the proposition I have to consider. I think it would be formally made if I intimated that I should accept it. I would rather, however, that you wouldn't state as much as this to any one.

As to compensation our trustees have urged me to stay here on a salary of $3500.00; and that here is nearly as good, I find, as $5000.00 in Chicago: so that, if I consent to accept a higher salary than my colleagues here, the financial inducements will be nearly the same in the two places. And I should be the less unwilling to accept an advanced salary here, from the fact that, I think, by the time the advance would begin, 1892-3, the salary of some other members of the faculty here will probably be lifted.

The inducements to go to Chicago, aside from financial ones, are obvious. It is probably to be a large institution in a comparatively new field. I should have the opportunity to extend my reputation and influence, get the stimulus that comes from larger responsibilities, the intellectual and social advantages of life in a large city, etc.

On the other hand there are, to my thinking, strong reasons for hesitation. It counts for something that I'm anchored here, pleasantly situated, and feel a natural reluctance *quieta movere. That*, however, is mere inertia. It counts for more, that I've just got my dep't divided here, my hours of class work reduced, my tools fairly into my hands and ready to work. I think that with our new man Meade[2]—who is really a very bright fellow—to look after the philological side of the dep't. we are in condition to do some decent work in English here. If I remain here I ought to be able to develop my dept well, and to write and print a little soon.

And it counts for most of all in my hesitation that I'm not at all sure what sort of a thing the Chicago Univ. is to be when it is born. That it will be big and have a certain kind of success, I don't doubt. But I mistrust a good many of Harper's ideas. It seems to me he is planning a big cramming machine. I don't feel at all certain that it is to be a University. Is Harper himself, with all his power to organise and to "push things" a *scholar*? And for myself, I fear that if I went there with twelve hours a week of class-room work, and the care of organizing and administering the dep't, I should get little time for that kind of work which makes a man *grow*—at least in the next five or ten years.

This I would rather not have mentioned.

Thus you see I am in a quandary, inclining a little I think to stay where I am, but some way from a decision. And I venture, in these circumstances to ask how the thing looks to you.

We've all been saddened here by hearing that the Armstrongs have lost their baby.[3] It will be a gloomy return for them here, and I'm afraid their new home on High St. will be very lonely.

Mrs. Winchester joins me in kindest regards to Mrs. Wilson and yourself. We very much wish it were possible to see you oftener.   Yours very sincerely   C. T. Winchester

ALS (WP, DLC) with WWhw notation on env.: "Ans. 16 April, 1891."
  1 William Rainey Harper, President of the University of Chicago.
  2 William Edward Mead, who had been appointed Associate Professor of the English Language at Wesleyan in 1890.
  3 The Rev. and Mrs. Andrew Campbell Armstrong, Jr. Armstrong had been Professor of Philosophy at Wesleyan since 1888. Mrs. Armstrong, a daughter of Dean Murray of Princeton, had probably gone to her parents' home to have her baby.

From Bradford Paul Raymond

My dear Professor Wilson: Middletown, Conn., April 16th 1891
  I do not believe you can afford to pay us an extra month's rent, and I therefore enclose a check for $38.25. You gave up the house Sep. 1 and have paid rent until Oct. 1. You must credit the discovery of this to Miss Van Vleck.[1] She brought it to my attention a few days ago and as I am teaching ethics, I tell her we must be honest, especially when we are likely to be found out. I hope you and family are well. We have not heard from Prof. Armstrong since the death of his babe, but trust he is recovering rapidly. With kinds regards to Mrs. Wilson
                    Sincerely yours,   B. P. Raymond.

ALS (WP, DLC) with WWhw notation on env.: "Ans. 17 April/91."
  1 Probably Clara Van Vleck, daughter of Professor John Monroe Van Vleck. She seems to have worked in the Treasurer's office of Wesleyan University.

To Daniel Coit Gilman

My dear Mr. Gilman,   Princeton, New Jersey, 16 April, 1891
  I am afraid that when you find that this is another letter about Prof. Winchester you will be reminded that there is a perseverance which is *not* of the saints; but I write because of a critical circumstance. Prof. Winchester has just written me a long letter asking my advice as to whether he shall go to Chicago or stay at Wesleyan at a very considerable advance of salary; and I long to give him a hint to wait till it be seen what is to be done towards filling the Donovan professorship: for he knows nothing, of

course, of his having been considered in that connexion. I feel
so fully convinced that he is an admirable man to give the English
department just the breadth and inspiration of culture that it
needs that I am sincerely anxious he should not be captured by
the "rival enterprise" in Chicago. If you can give me leave, therefore, to convey, even though it be but the barest hint, I shall have
my way very much cleared up.

If this be presumption, pray forgive it, and construe it as
what it is, mere zeal for the Hopkins and for an admired—
admirable scholar.

In haste,   Faithfully Yours,   Woodrow Wilson

P.S. The fact that the Wesleyan trustees have offered him a
much larger salary was, I ought to say, communicated to me in
confidence by Professor Winchester.   Yours,   W. W.

ALS (D. C. Gilman Papers, MdBJ).

From the Minutes of the Princeton Faculty

5 5′ P.M., Friday, April 17, 1891.
... The President appointed Profs Murray, McCloskie, McMillan,[1]
Cornwall & W. Wilson the Committee on the Difference in the
"Passing Mark" &c.[2]

[1] George Macloskie, Professor of Biology, and Charles McMillan, Professor of
Civil Engineering and Applied Mathematics.
[2] "The matter of the difference in the 'Passing Mark' in the Academic Department (=50) and in the Scientific Department (=60) was made the first order
of business at the next meeting, a Committee to be appointed in the mean time
to consider the matter." Princeton Faculty Minutes, April 10, 1891.

Francis Landey Patton to James Waddel Alexander

My dear Mr. Alexander: [Princeton, N. J.] April 20th [18]91
If you will suffer the infliction of a long letter I think I can say
some things that will lead you to take a less pessimistic view of
our college situation. . . .

I am sorry to hear that Pres Low[1] has his eye on Wilson &
McCay.[2] I had not heard it before. But again, let us consider:—

I suppose I am more responsible than any one else for bringing Wilson here. I fought for him against apathy in the Faculty
& opposition in the Trustees: & went to no end of trouble to
assure myself that he was the right man. I am proud of him.
He is a brilliant & unqualified success. But when the salary question was raised I did not feel that it would be just to other men
to offer him more than $3000[.] He ought to have $3400 & if

his friends will take care of his chair even to partial endowment
we could make the salary $3,400[.] But I have quietly told him
he could go on for the present with his lectures at Johns Hopkins; he gets I suppose $500 in this way. I think he ought to be
allowed to do this at least till we give him more salary. Of course
if he should be offered 5 or 6,000 in New York we would
probably lose him: tho' I think that he would be wise to consider whether he could live as well on what he would get in N. Y
as on what he does get here. . . .

I would like then to see Wilson's chair taken care of: then
the way will be clear to call a Prof. of Polit. Economy; then
with Sloane, Wilson & X in the Dept. of Political Science &
History that Dept would be well manned: & if need be we could
give them a tutor besides. . . .

Very faithfully   Francis L. Patton

ALS (Patton Letterpress Books, University Archives, NjP).
  1 President Seth Low of Columbia College.
  2 LeRoy Wiley McCay, Assistant Professor of Analytical Chemistry and
Mineralogy.

From Robert Bridges

Dear Tommy: New York   Apr 22 1891
I expect to go to Princeton Saturday afternoon to "investigate
the curriculum" for the Princeton Club. I want to stay with you
unless you are still full of household troubles over the grip—
which I heard had seized you all. Van Dyke urges me to come
to the "monastery"[1]—so that I hope you will not let me stay with
you if it will put you to any inconvenience. I know that your
illness must have interfered seriously with your work.

Faithfully Your friend   Robert Bridges

ALS (WP, DLC).
  1 His residence at 53 University Place, Princeton.

A Special Examination

Special in History of Political Economy
L. Adams, '91 (22 Apr. 1891)

1. Why should the Political Economy of one time be different
   from that of another?
2. What influences and facts determine the topics and methods
   of the science now?
3. How did Aristotle regard wealth? How does the modern political economist regard it?

4. What part of the Physiocratic ideas did Adam Smith adopt?
5. What is Ricardo's doctrine of Rent? What Jones's criticism upon it.
6. Who the principal writers of the historical school? In what respects do they differ from former writers—how much—wherein?
7. Why does the socialist object to the modern wages system?
8. Character, life, and system of Louis Blanc.
9. Contrast any three writers.

WWhw examination (WP, DLC).

To Robert Bridges

My dear Bobby,   Princeton, 23 April, 1891
   Of course you come to us. We are all much better, and the pleasure it will give us to have you will do us a lot of good. There are a score of things I want to talk over with you, which will perhaps be *à-propos* of an "investigation of the curriculum." Why can't you come Friday and see the Dramatic Association in Po-ka-hon-tas?
   In haste and affection,
                      Yours as ever,   Woodrow Wilson

ALS (WC, NjP).

From Albert Shaw

My dear Wilson: New York, April 23, 1891.
   I am writing you on an errand for a friend. A very competent Minnesota professor writes asking me if I know whether arrangements have been made for preparing the volume on Minnesota in the "American Commonwealths" series.[1] I don't happen to know anything about it and I feel some delicacy in inquiring directly from Houghton, Mifflin & Co., because it might seem as if I were a candidate myself. Inasmuch as you have relations with the house of Houghton, Mifflin & Co., it occurred to me that perhaps you would not mind sending them a line asking whether they had made arrangements for a Minnesota volume. If they have, of course the matter ends there. If they have not, I shall inform my friend in Minnesota and negotiations can begin. I happen today to be quite too rushed to add anything to this rerequest [request], except that matters are going on here as well as could be expected.
                      Sincerely yours,   Albert Shaw   per I.

TLS (WP, DLC).
  [1] See H. E. Scudder to WW, Feb. 27, 1885, Vol. 4, p. 309.

From the Minutes of the Princeton Faculty

5 5′ P.M., Friday, April 24th, 1891.

. . . Profs. Sloane & W. Wilson & Mr. Miller were appointed a Committee to nominate *Judges* & select a *Question* for the *Lynde Debate*.[1]

  [1] About the Lynde Debate, see Wilson's undergraduate diary, entry for June 23, 1876, n. 1, Vol. 1, p. 145. The committee's question was "*Resolved*, That Reciprocity in Trade with European States is more desirable than with American States." *The Princetonian* did not divulge the names of the judges appointed, but it did report in its issue of June 10, 1891, that Samuel Semple, '91, won the first prize; James C. Meyers, '91, the second prize; and George Riddle Wallace, '91, the third prize.

From Joseph Ruggles Wilson

My precious Woodrow—   Clarksville, April 30/91

I had hoped to receive a postal at least as touching the health of the dear ones whom you reported some time ago to be very ill. My anxiety finds relief in the thought that *no* news is *good* news; but all the same it would be comforting to receive a direct assurance—even of a line—to the effect that the household is upon its feet again. I have just returned from Presbytery where every one was as pleasant as possible, and where some good work was done for the great kingdom. My health, too, seemed better whilst there. It is not in a *very* bad condition now, at any time, with the exception of my eyes which alarm my fears. After Genl Assy[1] I will visit George, and get him to make a complete examination of my person all over.

Josie is quite well, and attending to his business with commendable diligence, and does not seem to be discouraged.

Present my love to dear Ellie & the other little ones—and receive for your darling self every big thing in my heart.

Affy Your Father

ALS (WP, DLC).
  [1] The General Assembly of the southern Presbyterian Church met in the First Presbyterian Church, Birmingham, Alabama, on May 21, 1891.

A Book Review

[May 1891]

A SYSTEM OF POLITICAL SCIENCE AND CONSTITUTIONAL LAW.[1]

Mr. Burgess has produced a work possessing conspicuous

  [1] *Political Science and Comparative Constitutional Law*. In two volumes. By John W. Burgess. Boston: Ginn & Co. 1891. [WW's note]

merits and conspicuous faults. It will both command admiration and provoke criticism; and it will be fortunate if the criticism does not overcrow the praise which it must receive. For the very fact that its good and its bad points are equally accentuated tends to make its bad points seem more prominent than any just estimate should pronounce them. It will serve the purposes alike of specific appreciation and specific criticism if, at the outset, a general chart be made of Mr. Burgess's method and thought, and an outline of the excellences and defects which must be examined and estimated before his work can be appreciated as a whole.

Its excellences are excellences both of method and of thought. There is the utmost clearness and adequacy of analysis throughout the book: nowhere in the two volumes does one lose his way in the subject, or doubt for a moment concerning the bearings of what he reads upon the subject-matter as a whole. There is also, of course, what successful analysis always secures, namely, perfect consistency everywhere; there is almost complete logical wholeness in the exposition. The reader enjoys the satisfaction, so rare in this day of easy writing, of being nowhere in doubt as to the author's meaning.

These are excellences of a high order, and are excellences, obviously, not of method only, but of thought as well. The thought is for the most part clear, consistent, and certain. There is accurate knowledge throughout, also, and thoroughness in setting it forth.

The faults of the work, though equally evident, are not so easy of statement: the mind of the reader finds them distinct and irritating, but his vocabulary may find them subtle and difficult of explicit exposure. Stated in the plainest words that come to hand, they consist in a mechanical and incorrect style, a dogmatic spirit, and a lack of insight into institutions as detailed expressions of life, not readily consenting to be broadly and positively analyzed and classified.

We have now our scheme for a more minute and just examination of the contents of the work, whose importance no one can deny without fortifying his judgment by not reading it. The title of the work indicates at once the principal distinction upon which its treatment is based: one portion of it is devoted to those topics touching the nature and operations of the state which the author conceives to fall mainly within the domain of political science; another and quite distinct portion embodies such topics as fall exclusively within the domain of constitutional law. A sharp line of division is run between these two domains. Political science deals with those processes, whether legal or revolutionary, and with those conceptions, whether juristic or lying entirely outside the thought of the lawyer, by virtue of which states come into existence, take historic shape, create governments and institutions, and at pleasure change or discard what forms or laws they must in order to achieve development. Constitutional law, on the other hand, has a much narrower scope. It deals only with such part of political life as is operative within the forms of law, and obedient to its commands and sanctions. Juristic method scrutinizes laws, examines their contents, ponders their meaning, seeks to elicit from them their logical purpose; does not concern itself with what they ought to contain, but only with what they do contain. The method of political science is much broader and freer. It does not hesitate to question laws as to their right to exist, to indulge bold speculations as to their foundations in the historical development and purposes of the people which has produced them, to account revolution just and necessary upon occasion, to say that laws are valid only so long as they contain some part of the national life and impede no essential measure of reform. Political science, in short, studies the forces of which laws are only the partial and temporary manifestations, while constitutional law is a study of conditions wholly statical.

Almost all that is most individual and important in Mr. Burgess's thought lies within the first portion of his work, which deals with the greater topics of political science. The two topics which stand forward most prominently in his treatment, as including all the rest, are Sovereignty and Liberty. The cardinal questions of systematic politics are, first, With whom does supreme political power rest, where is sovereignty lodged? and second, What liberty does the sovereign vouchsafe to the individual, and what are the guarantees of that liberty? But neither of these questions, nor any other questions whatever, either of political science or of constitutional law, can be discussed with any assurance of success without a most careful and consistent observance of the distinction between the state and the government. This is a distinction fundamental to every portion, great or small, of Mr. Burgess's thought. Always, under whatever constitution, distinguishable in thought, the state and the government are in most modern constitutions distinguishable also in fact. Back of the government, or else contained in it, is that other entity in which there persists a life higher than that of the government, and more enduring: that entity is the state, which gives to the government its form and its vitality. State and government are never identical except in mere point of organization; they may have the same organs, but they are not on that account the same thing. It is the state which is sovereign; whatever person or body of persons constitutes the sole vital source of political power in a nation, that person or body of persons is the state, and is sovereign. In those periods of the history of politics in which the will of a king or of a prince has been decisive of law and conclusive as to individual liberty, the monarch has himself been the state. Wherever minorities have established themselves as a ruling class, obeyed by all organs of government, there minorities have wielded sovereignty, have been the state. Whenever majorities command, the nation has itself become sovereign, has been made the state.

So much for the fact of the state as a thing separable from the forms of government, and merely operative through those forms. The organization of the state is another matter. Its organization may be identical with the organization of the government, as it practically is in England, where the House of Commons is sovereign; or it may be distinct from the organization of the government, as it is among ourselves, where our constitutions are not changed by ordinary legislative process, but by other machinery specially arranged for the purpose. Only the state is superior to the laws; the government is subject to the laws. The state makes constitutions; governments give effect to them. Whatever power can change the constitution, that power is the state organized. Thus in England the government is organized in the Queen, the Lords, and the Commons; but the state is organized in the House of Commons alone, whose will, whenever it is clearly determinate, is supreme. In France the state is organized in the National Assembly sitting at Versailles; the government, in the Chamber of Deputies, the Senate, and the President and Ministers. In Germany the government consists of the Emperor, the Reichstag, and the Bundesrath; but sovereignty resides in the Reichstag and a majority of the Bundesrath great enough to include at least forty-five out of the fifty-eight votes of that body. In the United States, while the government is organized in the houses of Congress and the President, the state has an alternative organization, represented by the two alternative methods of amending the Constitution permitted by Article V. of that instrument.

Nor does the significance of this distinction between state and government stop here. It is carried much further, to the upsetting of not a little familiar phraseology; for it invades that portion of Mr. Burgess's book which is devoted to comparative constitutional law, and commands his discussion of the forms of government. We can no longer speak of a federal state, but only of a federal government; neither does there exist any dual state, though dual governments there may be and have been. Every state is single and indivisible, let governments have what duality or complexity they may. The sovereign body which can make or unmake constitutions is in every case a single body; but the governments which give effect to constitutions may be made up of as many distinct and balanced parts as constitution makers may succeed in giving them. Sweden-Norway, for example, is not a dual state, for there is no such thing, but two states bound together in some important matters under a common government, which you may, if you choose, call a dual government.

If it be asked, Why must the sovereign will be always conceived of as single and indivisible,—why may it not be dual or treble, or multiple? the answer is ready and emphatic: Because sovereignty is by very definition supreme will, and there can be but one supreme will. This is an old answer, sometimes supposed to have become long ago axiomatic; only the reasoning here built upon it contains anything that is new.

Such is the theoretical side of the book, such its structure of thought. The importance and serviceableness of such an analysis will not for a moment be doubted. It is only in the application of it to the actual facts of political life, the actual phenomena of state growth, that difficulty enters. Mr. Burgess himself does not seem to feel that there are any difficulties. He is as confident in his application of this analysis as in his construction of it. It is characteristic of him to have no doubts; to him the application of his analysis seems the perfect and final justification of it. His thoughtful readers, however, will experience much more difficulty and have many more doubts. For he makes specific application of his analysis to the governments of the United States, England, France, and Germany,—governments with which every student of politics is familiar, and whose history is known in detail. It is in his treatment of the history of these governments— a treatment in every instance as brief as it is confident—that our author is at his boldest in making trial of his theories. He subjects them to great risks in the process, and they by no means escape damage. Or perhaps it would be more just to say that, in seeking a very absolute exemplification of the truth of his theories at every stage of complex national histories, like those of Germany, France, and England, he displays an extraordinary dogmatic readiness to force many intricate and diverse things to accommodate themselves to a few simple formulas. He believes that he can specifically identify on the one hand the state, and on the other the government, in each period of the manifold development of these great nations,—that he can point out exactly, that is, the real possessors of sovereign influence or authority during each principal age of their political growth; and the attempt must give every reader accustomed to deal with the multiform and delicate phenomena of such growth a distressing impression of crudeness and dogmatic presumption.

Perhaps the most striking example of this quality is afforded by Mr. Burgess's confident analysis of our own national history in the terms of his theory. Without touch of hesitation, he formulates our history as follows: A national "state" came into existence among us in 1774 with the assembling of the first Continental Congress; so long as the Continental Congress continued to sit, it represented that state in organization; when that state, thus in Congress assembled, consented to the formation of the Confederation, under the Articles framed in 1777 and put into operation in 1781, it consented to its own dissolution, for those Articles attributed statehood to the several commonwealths, denying in every provision the existence of any single national sovereign will; but in the Constitution of 1789 the national state reasserted itself and regained organization, while the commonwealths lost their statehood, and became once again merely governments. These conclusions Mr. Burgess reaches, not as a lawyer, of course, for they are without sanction in our legal history, but as a political scientist: they are the "facts" of the case as contradistinguished from the law of the case,—a distinction upon which he is careful to insist. The distinction is indeed valid,—nay, obvious enough; but many there be that are betrayed into singular error in the use of it. For the facts have to be determined; and while it is generally easy enough to determine what the law is, political fact is subtle and elusive, not to be caught up whole in any formula. It is a thing which none but a man who is at once a master of sentences and a seer can bring entire before the mind's eye in its habit as it lived, so many-sided is it and so quick to change.

It is always necessary to ascertain, therefore, just what a writer means by the antithesis between law and fact. Mr. Burgess believes, as we have seen, that a "state," with a single sovereign will, sprang into existence, however imperfect its organization, with the assembling of the Continental Congress of 1774. He evidently, therefore, excludes opinion altogether from the category of "fact"; for he quite certainly would not undertake to prove that in contemporary thought there was any real recognition of the occurrence of so momentous an event. He admits, indeed, with perhaps a touch of regret, that "the dull mind of the average legislator cannot at once be made conscious of such changes"; and he would probably admit also that even legislators who were not dull, like Madison and Hamilton, for example, were quite unconscious that a state had been born in 1774, and destroyed in 1781. The truth is, of course, that political fact is made up largely of opinion. Opinion is no less a fact than is heat, or cold, or gravitation. It is a determining force, and for that reason a controlling fact; in political development it is the fact of facts. If Mr. Burgess could but appreciate this, it would give life and significance to his theories such as in his own hands they do not possess. The national "state," with its sense of unity and of a common purpose, if democratic in structure, comes always slowly into existence, with the habit of coöperation and the growth of the national idea. The commonwealths of 1774 esteemed themselves states, and were states; adding nothing to their independence and dignity, assuredly, by the arrangement of 1781, but on the contrary consciously curtailing their privileges thereby. States they remained both in consciousness and purpose when they entered the union consummated in 1789. The national "state" has come into existence since then by virtue of a revolution of ideas, by reason of national union and growth and achievement, through a process also of struggle and of civil war. A state cannot be born unawares, cannot spring unconsciously into being. To think otherwise is to conceive mechanically, and not in terms of life. To teach otherwise is to deaden effort, to leave no function for patriotism. If the processes of politics are unconscious and unintelligent, why then this blind mechanism may take care of itself; there is nothing for us to do.

The truth seems to be that Mr. Burgess does not keep the method of the jurist and the method of the political scientist quite so distinct as he supposes. The juristic method is the method of logic: it squares with formulated principles; it interprets laws only, and concrete modes of action. The method of political science, on the contrary, is the interpretation of life; its instrument is insight, a nice understanding of subtle, unformulated conditions. For this latter method Mr. Burgess's mind seems unfit; the plain logic of concrete modes of action is much more natural to him than the logic of circumstance and opinion. Where he employs the forms and expressions of induction, therefore, he will often be found using in reality the processes of a very absolute deduction. He has strong powers of reasoning, but he has no gift of insight. This is why he is so good at logical analysis, and so poor at the interpretation of history. This is why what he says appears to have a certain stiff, mechanical character, lacking flexibility and vitality. It seems to have been constructed, not conceived. It suggests nothing; it utterly lacks depth and color. As a matter of fact, these defects do not invalidate in the least the serviceable analysis upon which the whole work is founded, neither do they rob its very excellent and lucid discussions of comparative constitutional law of their significance; but they do put the author at a great disadvantage with his reader by creating the impression that the whole matter of the volumes has been arbitrarily conceived.

Mr. Burgess, constructing thus, does not write in the language of literature, but in the language of science. The sentences of the scientist are not sentences in the literary sense,—they are simply the ordered pieces of statements; they are not built upon any artistic plan, but upon the homeliest principles of grammatical joinery, which cares nothing for color, or tone, or contrast, but contents itself with mere serviceable construction out of any materials that will hold together mechanically. There is no "style" about such writing; words are used simply as counters, without regard to the material out of which they are made, or to the significance which they bear in their hearts. A book thus constituted may be read much and consulted often, but can itself never live: it is not made up of living tissue. It may suggest life, but it cannot impart it. Doubtless the artificers of such writings do not pretend to be making literature, but they have no choice; if they do not write literature, they do not write truth. For political science cannot be truthfully constructed except by the literary method; by the method, that is, which seeks to reproduce life in speech. Constitutional law may perhaps dispense with the literary method in its expositions, but political science cannot. Politics can be successfully studied only as life; as the vital embodiment of opinions, prejudices, sentiments, the product of human endeavor, and therefore full of human characteristics, of whim and ignorance and half knowledge; as a process of circumstance and of interacting impulses, a thing growing with thought and habit and social development—a thing various, complex, subtle, defying all analysis save that of insight. And the language of direct sight is the language of literature.

It would not be possible to criticise these volumes in detail without criticising them in very great detail. The strong ideas that stand out in them will prove eminently serviceable to subsequent writers in the great field which they seek to occupy, and will doubtless pass into the literature of the subject; but Mr. Burgess's specific judgments upon the political history of the four great nations with whose institutions he chiefly concerns himself, his judgments also upon races and upon race development in the opening chapters of the work, every attempt that he makes to unfold the interior meanings of national political development, must provoke sharp dissent and criticism. Perhaps this, in the absence of a suggestive method of treatment, will be the book's means of stimulation. Its very dogmatism, indeed, will prove not unpleasant to those who have experienced a touch of *ennui* in this age of cautious, timid writing. It is an agreeable shock to hear once more the old confident phrase, "I have demonstrated." You may not agree, but you may possibly admire the boldness of temperament which makes such phrases possible.

Mr. Burgess will not have done a bad thing if he hearten us once more to get clear ideas and put muscle into their defense. That is one way to rouse truth, though it may not be the gentlest or the best way.[2]

Printed in the *Atlantic Monthly*, LXVII (May 1891), 694-99.
[2] Wilson wrote rather extensive longhand and shorthand notes for this review in a two-page MS. with the WWhw heading "Burgess," tucked into the second volume of the Burgess work in the Wilson Library, DLC. Wilson's marginal notes on the book are printed at March 1, 1891. [Eds.' note]

From Edmund Janes James

My dear Wilson,   Philadelphia, May 4, 1891.

Your cordial invitation of May 1st came to my hands upon my return from the sea shore where I left Mrs. James. I am not quite sure when she will return but as soon as she does return I will let you know, and then I shall certainly make arrangments for our visit. I am afraid I shall have to send her for a day or two and run up for over night myself.[1]

Yours very truly,   Edmund J James.

TLS (WP, DLC) with WWhw notation on env.: "James (Ans.)."
[1] Margaret L. James to WW, May 26, 1891, ALS (WP, DLC), expressed regrets that they were unable to accept the invitation.

From Daniel Coit Gilman

Dear Professor Wilson   Baltimore, Md.   May 5, 91

I was very grateful to you for your notes in respect to Professor W. They were so discriminating & frank as to be of much value & they added to the respect I already felt for him. But our authorities are not prepared to appoint a Donovan professor at present; so yesterday they voted to give to Dr. Browne[1] the title & work of Associate Professor of English Literature & to Dr. Bright[2] the title & work of Associate Professor of English Philology. Mr. Murray[3] was made Librarian

Yours Sincerely   D. C. Gilman

ALS (WP, DLC).
  [1] William Hand Browne.
  [2] Identified earlier in this volume. Appointed as the first Donovan Professor in 1905.
  [3] Nicholas Murray, Librarian of the Johns Hopkins, 1891-1908.

From Joseph Ruggles Wilson

My precious son   Clarksville, May 6, '91

Your very interesting and important letter has come to hand and been considered as fully as could be done in the circumstances. Your plan with respect to securing a lot and building thereon is good, so far as I am competent to understand the situation.[1] *Precisely* what *I* am expected to do in the premises I cannot quite gather. Certainly I shall help to the fullest extent that is possible with what means are left for future support. I say this, however, that should you conclude to "swim in" to this business, your R. F.[2] will hold himself prepared to meet the payment of the first instalment on the purchase of the lot, which would be, let us say, $1000.00, and after that we can put our wise heads together and see. Will this do for the nonce?

I am about as usual and am preparing to leave for the Assembly at Birmingham whither I shall wend on the 18th inst. As to my classes I have now nothing to do except *"examine"* them (on the 12th).

Present my best love to dear Ellie. I am grateful that she and the "annuals"[3] got through safely. Josie sends love also. And I remain always your *loving Father* + a good deal besides

ALS (WP, DLC) with WWhw notation on env.: "Ans. 9 May/91."
  [1] See JRW to WW, May 11, 1891, n. 2.
  [2] Their abbreviation for "Revered Father."
  [3] That is, the children.

From William Milligan Sloane

My dear Professor Wilson: Princeton, May 8, 1891

Will you read the essays or hold the examination for the Atwater prize?[1] If all one to you I would like this year to judge the essays for I have been deep in that subject.

Pray tell me also who are the five first men in your work this year and your choice for the historical fellowship—two names in order of merit. We should I think give it to a man wishing to make history and political science his life work.

We have a superb man for Queen's[2] place next year—Daniels[3] —and we want the best we can get for the place which Gibby[4] has rattled around in this year.

Faithfully yours   Wm M. Sloane

P.S.   Irvine[5] will pass his oral examination this evening[,] the last he has for Ph.D.[,] at 8 P. M. in the Faculty Room. Perhaps you would like to see what his mettle is.

ALS (WP, DLC) with WWhw notation on env.: "Ans. 11 May, '91."
   [1] The Lyman H. Atwater Prize in Political Science, established by the Class of 1883 in memory of Professor Atwater and consisting of the interest on $1,000. It was awarded annually to a senior for the best examination and essay on topics to be set by the professors of political and social science. The subject for the examination in 1891 was state socialism; the subject for the essay, pensions and the public service. The winner in 1891 was James Henry Dunham.
   [2] John Wahl Queen, Princeton, '87; Ph.D., '89, South East Club University Fellow in Social Science, 1890-91.
   [3] Winthrop More Daniels, who resigned the South East Club Fellowship to accept an instructorship at Wesleyan University. Born Dayton, Ohio, Sept. 30, 1867. A.B., College of New Jersey, 1888; A.M. 1890. Instructor in Economics and Social Science, Wesleyan University, 1891-92. Assistant Professor of Political Economy, Princeton, 1892-95; Professor of Political Economy, 1895-1911. Member, Board of Public Utility Commissioners of New Jersey, 1911-14. Member, Interstate Commerce Commission, 1914-23; chairman, 1918-19. Professor of Transportation, Yale University, 1923-24; Thomas DeWitt Cuyler Professor of Transportation, Yale, 1924-36. Author of numerous articles and books. Died Jan. 2, 1944.
   [4] William Dwight Gibby, Princeton, '90; Boudinot Fellow in History, 1890-91.
   [5] William Mann Irvine, Princeton, '88; Ph.D., 1891.

From Andrew Stephenson

Dear Professor: Middletown, Conn., May 8 1891.
   It is decided to hold the examination for the prize in "the State" on the 8th day of June. I will look for your list of questions any time between now and then that will suit your convenience.[1] I am exceedingly obliged to you for so kindly consenting to furnish the questions and make the award.[2]

And let me here thank you for your kind suggestions to me in regard to the work here. I have more than realized the truth of these suggestions. I have fallen into many errors and have attempted to do many things which appeared very feasible to me but which have been almost failures owing to the fact that our young men here are seemingly unwilling to spend any time in studying authorities or developing lectures. I shall leave the most of such work hereafter to bide its time and shall work on an entirely new plan. I have no reason to complain as I have really done better than I thought. Another year I shall be doubly armed and believe that, with hard work, I shall get out into the sunshine.

Will you have your new book[3] ready for use next year? Longman, Green & Co. write me that you will. I am going to introduce Thwaites Hist. of the Colonies and sincerely hope you will have your work ready for use. I have been reading, very carefully, your Congressional Government and honestly think it the *best thing of its kind I ever read.* This notwithstanding some things therein very hard for me to assent to. These I shall mention when I am surer of my ground

Most sincerely yours,   Andrew Stephenson

ALS (WP, DLC) with WWhw notation on env.: "Ans."
    [1] Wilson responded with a copy of the WWT MS. entitled "Examination in 'The State'" (WP, DLC).
    [2] That is, Wilson had agreed to read the papers and choose the best one. He did not go to Middletown to make the award.
    [3] That is, Wilson's *Division and Reunion.*

From Joseph Ruggles Wilson

My precious son—   Clarksville, Tennessee May 11/91
    It would be a *strain* were I to invest $1,500 just now in the Princeton property. When I proposed to own the land on which the house might be built,[1] my imagination did not fly so far as $3,000—for I had no idea you were likely to buy so much land. Still, if you think it best, all right. You may depend upon the 1,500: but it w'd hardly be *possible* for me to meet another payment of this size within a year. You see I have Josie to carry. He owes about $2,000 upon the purchase of the printing office which so far is bringing him in almost nothing, owing I cannot but think to the bad selfishness of his partner. By 1st July therefore I must pay on Josie's account some $600—for I have endorsed his notes in the hope of setting him up in business once for all. Two other notes will fall due in 6 mos & 12. I have already paid out some $700.00 for the boy[.] So, my dear, you see that my money condition is by no means lovely[.] Nevertheless—and I wish you to understand that in business matters I always mean *just what I say*—and especially as between *you and me* who are really *one person*—draw upon my purse for the 1,500 to which you refer. Only I thought it was fair to us both for me to state the exact condition of my affairs. Now, shall I have to beg of you to throw aside hesitation and *go on*, with the help I am able to give. When the 2nd payment will be [due] to be made, then you and I can put our heads together[.] Besides

if the worst with me come to the worst, it will be *your* loss, for then I shall go and billet myself upon you, bag and baggage, for the residue of my life!

Now, darling, you know me well enough to be assured of my complete sympathy in all your undertakings and of my full help up to the measure of my ability. *Tell me when to send the money.* Indeed I think I will send it at once; and if you shouldn't need it you can return it. So, please find enclosed a N. Y. draft for $1,500. Please acknowledge receipt at once.

Love to dear Ellie.

Your affectionate and admiring   Father

P.S.   Be careful to see that the *title* to said land is perfect[2]

ALS (WP, DLC) with WWhw notation on env.: "Ans."

1 Dr. Wilson, in JRW to WW, March 27, 1890, Vol. 6, had first suggested that he would like to help his son build a house in which he, Dr. Wilson, might have a small apartment. Dr. Wilson and Woodrow and Ellen had undoubtedly talked about this matter when Dr. Wilson visited in Princeton over Christmas.

2 As subsequent documents will reveal, and as other documents not printed also show, the following events concerning this subject occurred during the period covered by this volume and the next.

Wilson purchased a lot from George A. and Sarah W. Bayless of Princeton on June 20, 1891, for the sum of $3,651.23. Situated on Washington Street (now Washington Road), the lot was a large one. Beginning some 203 feet from Prospect Avenue, its front ran along Washington Street for some 386 feet to what is now Ivy Lane. The lot was, roughly, 245 feet deep. The adjoining lot on the corner of Prospect Avenue and Washington Street, with a house numbered 5 Prospect Avenue, was owned by Mrs. Andrew F. West. See general warranty deed, George A. and Sarah W. Bayless to Woodrow Wilson, June 20, 1891 (WC, NjP). The Wilsons borrowed $1,800 from Mary C. Olden, then of Princeton, on June 26, 1891, securing the loan with a mortgage on the lot that ran for three years at 5 per cent. See "Bond. Woodrow Wilson to Mary C. Olden," dated June 26, 1891, printed form with handwritten entries, attached to Mary C. Olden to WW, May 24, 1893, Vol. 8, and printed mortgage form with handwritten entries, dated June 26, 1891, also attached to Mary C. Olden to WW, May 24, 1893.

Professor John Howell Westcott, in February 1892, asked Wilson to sell him a lot eighty feet wide next to Mrs. West's property. J. H. Westcott to WW, Feb. 2, 1892. Wilson refused. However, he did sell a two-hundred-foot frontage on the Prospect Avenue side to Jenny Davidson (Mrs. John Grier) Hibben on April 19, 1893, for $4,500. Printed purchase agreement with handwritten entries, dated April 19, 1893 (WP, DLC).

As Mary C. Olden's letter to Wilson of May 24, 1893, will show, Wilson paid the $1,800 balance due her soon after selling the lot to Mrs. Hibben.

From Edwin Curtis Osborn

Dear Sir: Princeton, May 12th. 1891.

As a member of the Committee on Rules Governing the Allotment and Rental of Rooms, may I trouble you for your opinion in the following case:

J. W. Easton '92 and Alfred North, Special, have applied to me to enter the Drawing for Dod Hall room under the new rules. Easton lives in Town, at his home and *does not* intend to occupy the room at night, but wants it as a stopping place during the day. This is his story, but I think I see another purpose; North being a special, cannot draw in the first drawing and uses Easton for that purpose. North expects a brother to enter '95. If Easton draws a room, he will be a nominal tenant for the year and then surrender his interest to the North Brothers.

I claim that as Easton does not intend to occupy the room as rooms in all Dormotories are occupied, he is not a bona fide occupant and cannot enter the drawing unless he will so occupy the room he may draw; further, he being a resident of the Town and an upper classman, his roommates being underclassmen, the intent is to act for them in the drawing, thereby giving them a priority over others in the class in which his roommate would draw: if Easton did not act for them.

Kindly let me hear from you at once if possible as I am obliged to decide this point tomorrow or next day.[1] I am sorry to trouble you, but I want your advice as a Lawyer as well as a member of the Committee. I do not enclose a retainer, but we can adjust that matter at some later time.

Very respectfully,   E C Osborn   Treasurer.

TLS (WP, DLC).
[1] Wilson may have given Osborn an oral reply, or Wilson may have answered in a letter which is not extant in the Princeton University Archives. North did secure a room in Dod Hall, but Easton did not.

A Final Examination

13 May, 1891.

College of New Jersey.

EXAMINATION IN ADMINISTRATION.

I. Lectures

1. Define Administration and Administrative Law; outline the field and proper methods of administrative study; and indicate the nature of the questions which it involves.

2. Distinguish Administration from Legislation, on the one hand, and from Adjudication, on the other; and differentiate Law in the formal sense from Law in the essential sense of the term.

3. Specify the main functions which Administration performs for Society, giving one or two examples under each.

4. Discuss (a) the theory of the Weal State, (b) the theory of the Law State, and (c) the theory of the Constitutional State.

5. What is the relationship of administrative action to the laws

(a) in the United States, (b) in England, and (c) in the continental states; and what are the several means of securing legality in administrative action.

II. Traill.

6. Explain carefully the relations of the English Cabinet to Parliament.

7. Describe the process of granting money to the Executive in England, and of securing its application to the specific objects for which it is granted.

8. How is the English Local Government Board organized, and what are its principal duties?

9. What part does the Privy Council play as a branch of the Executive?

10. What does Mr. Traill consider to be the main tendencies of central government in England.

Printed examination (WP, DLC).

From George Henderson

The American Society for the Extension
of University Teaching[1]

My dear Sir: Philadelphia   May 18th, 1891.

By concurrent mail I send you one or two pamphlets explaining the nature and character of our work, but suppose you are already well informed upon that subject. We are just about to make arrangements for courses for next season, and I write to ask if you could not offer some of six lectures each. I am well aware that you are extremely busy, but earnestly hope that you will at least consent to give one course, for I can assure you that the demand is far greater than the supply, and we already foresee that we shall have difficulty in securing lecturers.

The fees fixed for the work are $20 per lecture and expenses.

Hoping to hear that you can assist us,[2] I am

Very truly yours   George Henderson[3]

TLS (WP, DLC) with WWhw notation on env.: "Ans. June 24/91."

[1] Organized in Philadelphia in 1890 by William Pepper, Frederick B. Miles, George Henderson, and others, and modeled after the Lecture Syndicate of Cambridge University, the London Society for the Extension of University Teaching, and the University Extension Delegacy of Oxford University. The American Society for the Extension of University Teaching had its own small staff of lecturers and invited others, usually from the academic world, to give short lecture courses from time to time. Edmund J. James was president of the American Society from April 1891 to November 1895. See American Society for the Extension of University Teaching, *Ten Years' Report . . . 1890-1900* (Philadelphia, 1901).

[2] Wilson's reply of June 24, 1891, is missing. In it, however, he seems to have said that he would like to participate and to have enclosed a copy of the

"Memorandum" printed at June 24, 1891. The publications of the American
Society for the Extension of University Teaching make it clear that Wilson did
not participate in 1891-92, the reason probably being the lack of demand. Wilson
was to give an Extension series in 1895-96 entitled "Great Leaders of Political
Thought," with lectures on Aristotle, Machiavelli, Montesquieu, Burke, de Tocqueville, and Bagehot. See the Editorial Note, "Wilson's Lectures on Great Leaders
of Political Thought," Vol. 9.

³ Henderson was the General Secretary of the American Society.

To Albert Bushnell Hart

My dear Prof. Hart,   Princeton, New Jersey, 19 May, 1891.

Doubtless you have 'opined' that it was a conscience not void
of offence that kept me so long from answering your last letter.¹
In part it was that; but it was much more. For more than two
months after the receipt of that letter everybody,—literally everybody,—in my little household, myself alone excepted, was suffering, for most of the time acutely, with the *grippe*. I was not
only exhausted at the end of the siege with anxiety and fatigue,
but my work was piled in huge arrears; and the pile is only now
resuming normal proportions.

I have at last a definite plan with reference to completing
the Epoch. The preliminary chapter, a survey of the state of the
country and of parties at the opening of my period, I have had
done for some time, and my head, as well as numerous scraps
of paper, is full of notes for pretty much all the rest of the
volume. I am going to stay here in Princeton this summer and
(such is my hope and purpose) write the whole of the volume
in outline, putting in all the main strokes and doing all the constructive part of the composition of it; and after that is done
the filling in and completion can be left to the scattered moments
of opportunity which occur during the winter. I found that I
could not construct the book during such occasional opportunities, such separated spaces of leisure; but I hope that I can fill
in as they permit.

Your article on "The Speaker as Premier"² interested me very
much indeed; but I believe that I must take exception to it upon
a fundamental point. It does not seem to me that any officer who
belongs wholly to the legislature can ever reproduce for us the
functions of the English Prime Minister. For it seems to me that
the essential feature of the Premier's leadership is that he is,
while he leads the House, himself constantly in the midst of
administrative business, and that the value of ministerial initiative lies in the fact that the ministers are all the time in contact
with the practical tasks of government, always making experiment of the workability of statutes already passed and experiencing the need of statutes as yet unenacted. In short it is the

close association of administration and legislation that seems to me to constitute the admirable feature of English Cabinet government. Our Speaker can never, therefore, become in any closely analogous sense our Premier. Moreover the guidance of a body of men in some sort at least constituting an *outside* body with *other* responsibilities besides the merely legislative, seems to me a safe body to exercise leadership; while the leadership of one man supreme within the legislature, with no responsibility for administration, seems to me an unsafe leadership. I should be glad to know what you think as to this.

With warm regard,

Very sincerely Yours,   Woodrow Wilson

TCL (RSB Coll., DLC).

[1] A. B. Hart to WW, March 12, 1891.

[2] That is, Hart's "The Speaker as Premier," *Atlantic Monthly*, LXVII (March 1891), 380-86.

To Horace Elisha Scudder

My dear Mr. Scudder,   Princeton, New Jersey, 19 May, 1891

When you open and examine the essay which I send you to-day by express,[1] I am afraid that you will be provoked with me. You have asked me several times to send you something on some topic in my own line, and I have each time pretended to be too much driven by lecture-writing to prepare anything; and yet now, as if in impudence, I send you an essay which is evidently a product of leisure—and of leisure spent in wandering afield when I ought to have been doing what you had requested me to do!

The fact of the matter is, that I am afraid to keep constantly intent upon my special topics of study. It is my creed that literary training and method are as essential to the production of good political science as to the production of good poetry or valid criticism. It is my practice, consequently, to try my hand, whenever I can, at various sorts of writing as unlike my professional tasks as possible. The essay I send you is one of my 'exercises.' If I am mistaken in believing it suitable for publication, I'm sure you'll know it, and save me the mistake.

Will you consider me impertinent if I ask whether the "Commonwealth Series" is to contain a volume on Minnesota, and, if so, whether that volume has been assigned? I know a man who wants—and is doubtless competent—to write it: but if you say none need apply, I shall try to prevent him.[2]

With warmest regards,

Very sincerely Yours,   Woodrow Wilson

ALS (in possession of Henry Bartholomew Cox).
¹ "The Author Himself," printed at Dec. 7, 1887, Vol. 5. For the provenance of this essay, see the Editorial Note, "Wilson's Desire for a 'Literary Life,'" Vol. 5.
² See A. Shaw to WW, April 23, 1891.

A Final Examination

21 May, 1891.

College of New Jersey.

EXAMINATION IN CONSTITUTIONAL LAW.

I. Cooley.

1. Enumerate the checks and balances of the federal system. What has been the working of the system of presidential electors?

2. In what respects are the constitution, laws, and treaties of the United States the supreme law of the land?

3. By what law is the franchise regulated? What does the federal constitution say concerning the suffrage by which members of the federal House of Representatives shall be elected? What other provisions touching the franchise does the constitution contain?

4. Upon what principles may powers not specifically granted by the constitution be implied? What are the powers of the Executive?

5. How may the courts restrain the Executive? How may Congress restrain the Executive or the courts from illegal action?

6. How may the constitution be amended? What two classes of amendments have been added?

II. Lectures.

7. Expound the nature of constitutional law by means of the distinction between 'the state' and 'the government,' and explain the special function of a written constitution.

8. State the differences and the relations between 'the constitution of government' and 'the constitution of liberty.'

9. What was the difference between the derivation of the constitutions of the original states and the derivation of the federal constitution?

10. Discuss the historical position of the modern executive, indicating the apparently permanent features and the apparent political tendencies of the office.

———

1. What are the principles established by the Constitution respecting laws impairing the obligation of contracts? Do they affect State or federal legislation?

2. What is the meaning and scope of the federal guarantee to the States of a republican form of government? In what way does it affect constitutional changes in the States?

3. What protection does the Constitution secure to persons accused of crime? What are *Ex post facto* laws? What is treason under federal law? What is the writ of *Habeas Corpus*?

Printed examination (WP, DLC).

From Albert Bushnell Hart

My dear Professor Wilson: Cambridge   May 24, 1891.

Yours of the 19th is at hand, and I am much pleased that the Epoch volume is so far advanced. My own plan is little farther along. I expect to begin in a few days, and to get my MS. in by about Sept 1st[.] Yours will follow in excellent season. Of course the editor's task will be a formality. The exigencies of the series call for division into paragraphs, such as is shown in Vol. I., and for a classified bibliography at the beginning of each chapter. Might it not also be made a feature of your volume to devote one chapter to the government of the Confederacy 1861-65?

About maps I will write you later: they are the only part of the series for which I assume all the responsibility i.e. for their historical accurracy. Of course your wishes are to be consulted as to the selection for your volume.

In regard to the Speaker as Premier I should like to write more than is possible tonight. I recognize as well as any one can the undesirability of making the moderator of a great assembly a parliamentary leader: my point of view is rather that of one who sees an institution which has arisen and which cannot be destroyed—i.e. the Speaker's political power: having arisen, I think it better that it should be recognized and its possessor held to responsibility. My article was rather one on fact than on theory. Your other point, about the alteration of defective statutes, is one that had never occurred to me, and it has great weight[.] Next year I undertake a new course "Government and Administration in the United States, national[,] state and municipal." Are your J. H. lectures of this year reprinted in any form? Or could I get a set of student's notes on them?

Further, one practical question in which every one of my correspondents is interested—what type-writer do you recommend? Yours seems to be a superior machine, and I am in the market.   Sincerely yours,   Albert Bushnell Hart

ALS (WP, DLC) with WWhw notation on env.: "Ans. Jun 22/."

From Hiram Woods, Jr.

My dear Tommy: Baltimore, May 29, 1891.

You doubtless remember my writing to you a year or more ago, when you were in Connecticut, in behalf of my friend Fay, who then wanted a place as teacher of Sanskrit.[1] This letter is in behalf of the same individual. He has been teaching at Ann Arbor this year, but seems to think there is no future there for him, & is anxious to get away. A letter arrived from him this A. M. contains the following:—"I am going to apply at the University of South Carolina for the chair of Ancient Languages. Dr. Woodrow's influence will probably be very great. Can't you get Wilson to help me to it?" This remark, as you will probably observe, is clear and self-explanatory. Its meaning somewhat resembles the celebrated Richard Cobden:—you will probably note the resemblance.

Seriously, however, you will be doing an act of kindness, almost of charity, if you can help Fay get a good place. He has gotten to his present position in the face of many difficulties, and deserves success if ever a fellow did. He is trying to educate a younger sister, and denies himself a great deal for her good. What's more, from all I can learn he is a good teacher and well able to fill the place he seeks. I am sure Bloomfield[2] and his other teachers at Johns Hopkins will speak well of him. I will greatly appreciate any effort you may make in his behalf.

I am a grass-widower just now, Mrs. Woods and the little ones being at Frank's[3] home in Providence on a visit. I expect to go up there after them next month. Do you know anything about the Decennial Record of our class? I sent Billy Wilder a check for a copy in February 1890. It is scarcely necessary to say that Billy did not acknowledge its receipt, but the check came back endorsed all right, so he evidently got it. Of the Record, however, I have heard nothing. Is it out?[4]

Please present my regards to Mrs Wilson.

Sincerely Yours: Hiram Woods, Jr.

Fay's full name and address is: Edwin W. Fay, 37 S. Ingalls St., Ann Arbor, Mich.

ALS (WP, DLC).
  [1] H. Woods, Jr., to WW, May 12, 1890, Vol. 6.
  [2] Maurice Bloomfield, Professor of Sanskrit and Comparative Philology at the Johns Hopkins.
  [3] The Rev. Frank Churchill Woods of Providence, Hiram Woods's brother.
  [4] The decennial record of the Class of 1879 was apparently never published.

A Prize Examination

Examination for the Theodore Cuyler Prize.[1]

1 June, 1891[2]

1. State the fundamental differences between exchanges of commodities and exchanges of services which make it necessary to distinguish Distribution and Exchange.

2. How far is Distribution necessarily a contest between antagonistic classes? In what respects have landlord and capitalist an economic advantage, and how is it possible to neutralize that advantage?

3. Under what historical circumstances is the economic doctrine of rent applicable?

4. Does rent form a part of the price of agricultural products? Can the same reasoning be applied to the question whether profits swell the price of commodities? What differences are there between the two cases?

5. How do rents differ in respect of the sorts of land or the sorts of natural resources rented; and where are speculative values most likely to appear?

6. Discuss the economic results and the political equity of the confiscation of rents upon the ground of unearned increment in land values.

7. Distinguish entrepreneur and capitalist. What differences are there between the law of interest and the law of profits?

8. What influences principally affect the rate of wages? What importance among these influences would you assign to a protective tariff?

9. How would you criticise the theory that wages constitute the residual share in Distribution?

10. Analyze the effects of cooperation (a) upon labour, (b) upon the accumulation of capital.

11. What other shares are there in Distribution besides interest, profits, rent, and wages?

WWT MS. (WP, DLC).
[1] See the announcement printed at March 25, 1891.
[2] Wilson used this same examination in 1892, changing the "1891" to "1892."

From John Dale McGill

Dear Sir: J[ersey] City   June 1st 91

If the repairs you mention were within the limit of our agreement you are authorized to deduct them from the quarterly rent due today. I have every confidence in your good faith in this matter.

As to the lightning rods on the house I am under the impression that they are quite serviceable; it is possible however that I may be mistaken.

You know that the lightning rod man is a famous character in rural districts where he is ubiquitous, and his brazen importunity a matter of note.

Nothing delights his soul so much as to give him a carte-blanche order to protect a house from lightning, he will cover every square foot of the roof and the gables with lightning rods and gilded points that invite the thunder-bolts to strike. If the lightning-rods are really defective they must be fixed—but I should wish to have a more reliable opinion in the matter than that of a lightning rod man. I have already spent over $1,000 in repairs to the house and dont care to add to that sum needlessly.

Yours Respectfully   J. D. McGill

Tall trees about a house are a better protection than lightning rods.

ALS (WP, DLC).

A Final Examination

1 June, 1891.
College of New Jersey.

EXAMINATION IN POLITICAL ECONOMY.

Answer briefly and put in no irrelevant matter.

I. Text Book.

1. (*a*) Define Political Economy.

(*b*) Name the four chief divisions of the study, and outline some of the topics under each of those divisions.

2. (*a*) What are the functions of money; and what do you understand by a tabular standard of deferred payments?

(*b*) For the use of what is interest paid?

(*c*) What is the difference between 'bank money' and inconvertible paper money?

(*d*) What is Bi-metallism?

(*e*) What causes depreciation in the value of money?

3. (*a*) What are the functions of banks; and to what extent are they indispensable to the modern industrial system?

(*b*) What is a Clearing House?

4. Expose the error involved in the word Over-production when

used as an explanation of industrial crises; and suggest the true explanation.

5. (*a*) Distinguished real from nominal wages. What considerations must enter into the computation of real wages?

(*b*) State the grounds upon which Mr. Walker bases his theory that wages are the *residual share* in Distribution.

(*c*) What are the conditions of free competition between labor and capital; and how far are those conditions realized under the present system of industry?

6. What is the theoretical law of profits, and how assimilated to the law of rent? For what, theoretically, does the entrepreneur receive profits?

II. Lectures.

7. What have been the various stages in the history of production? (Give a brief characterization of each stage, and include a statement of the stages of production from the point of view of Exchange.)

8. Describe the industrial organization of the mediæval city and point out its advantages and disadvantages.

9. State the causes and the results of the break-up of that organization.

10. Criticize the theory of the transferability of Capital.

The following questions are for those who did not attend the written recitation of March 20, 1891.

1. Discuss normal price. What, normal price being the standard, are the characteristics of market price and customary price?

2. What is meant by the 'unearned increment' of land? What equity is there in the claim that rents belong to the community?

3. What is the object of industrial coöperation? What are its difficulties, in what sorts of undertakings most felt, and why?

Printed examination (WP, DLC).

From Wilfred Pirt Mustard[1]

My Dear Sir: Balto. Md.   June 4th 1891

I have survived all my examinations—the much dreaded Oral among them—and get my Ph.D. on the 11th. By making my Degree in two years' attendance here I have broken the record for the Classical Dept. Very few men get through in three years— only one man has done so since I came to Baltimore.

I have not yet accepted any offer for next year: I have only decided *not* to go to one or two places,—to Nebraska e.g. I am waiting for a decent position. You may remember my asking you about the University of Wooster when you were in Baltimore. I had a letter from the President—Rev. Sylvester F. Scovel—this week asking me for testimonials, references &c. and I put you down among my references as to 'personal character.' The vacancy out there is in the Professorship of Greek, and Gilder-sleeve, Warren[2] & Bloomfield have all promised to write enthusiastic letters in my favor. So that I may hear more of it. There is a vacancy also at Bowdoin. One of my friends in the Latin Seminary here—a Bowdoin graduate—offered to tell the President[3] all about me this week, and try to get him to make inquiries about my scholarship &c, if I would give him some references. He says that Johns Hopkins sent up two men a few years ago who had very little tact—who were bookworms of the most pronounced type—and didn't 'get on.' He therefore thinks that something more than Hopkins backing (which, I may say, another man is receiving,) is necessary to secure the Latin Professorship up there, for they want a man, who is likely to 'get on' with the students and people generally. I told him he might refer the President to you as an authority on such matters. It is just possible that you may hear from him.

The object of this letter is not, as you may suppose to warn or prepare you for inquiries about me from either of these sources. May I ask you to write President [Thomas Chrowder] Chamberlin of the University of Wisconsin and say what you can in my favor. The Professor of Latin out there[4] is leaving and going to Brown. A few weeks ago President Chamberlin was in Baltimore, and among other business he was looking for an Instructor in Latin. Haskins[5] had asked him to look me up, and I had a short interview with him. He is exceedingly non-committal, and said nothing except that he was glad to have met me. I think Dr. Warren had frightened him off, by hinting that I was not likely to accept the low salary he had to offer. I did most of the talking and tried to impress on him the fact that I was too good for $1000 a year. The vacancy in the chair of Latin out there is a later development. Dr. Warren told me today that he was going to recommend me to the Wisconsin people—(I have been Scholar & Fellow in Latin here.)—and if you will write to the President in my favour I shall be greatly obliged.

Our 'Fratres in Urbe'[6] are coming up to the Chapter-House next Saturday night for what they call a Symposium. I wish you were within easy reach of Baltimore for the occasion.

                                        Yours sincerely   Wilfred P. Mustard

ALS (WP, DLC) with WWhw notation on env.: "Ans. June 19/91."
1 A.B., University of Toronto, 1886; Ph.D., the Johns Hopkins, 1891. Professor of Latin, Colorado College, 1891-93; Instructor to Professor of Latin, Haverford College, 1893-1907; Professor of Latin, the Johns Hopkins, 1907-32.
2 Minton Warren, Associate Professor of Latin at the Hopkins.
3 William DeWitt Hyde.
4 Charles Edwin Bennett.
5 Charles Homer Haskins, at this time Instructor in History at the University of Wisconsin.
6 Of Wilson's fraternity, Phi Kappa Psi.

A News Item

[June 6, 1891]

CALEDONIAN GAMES[1]

The Annual Caledonian Games for the inter-class championship and the Peace Cup took place this morning on the University Grounds. A large audience assembled for the sports while the day itself was excellent. The track was in good condition and a number of records were broken. The cup was won by '93 with '94 second. The officers of the day were as follows:

Referee.

Professor Woodrow Wilson. . . .

Printed in *The Princetonian*, xvi (June 6, 1891), [1].
1 An annual track and field meet for undergraduates.

From Joseph Ruggles Wilson

My precious son—   New York, June 18 1891

I am here and will be *there* soon—I don't mean to tell you by what train so as to give you no trouble—for I can drive right up to the house[.] It will probably be in the evening of to-morrow (Friday) or pretty early on Saturday—more likely the latter. I shall stay at Princeton only until Monday morning, because I *must* go out West,[1] starting Monday night probably.

Love to dear Ellie

Your loving & everything-ing   Father

ALS (WP, DLC) with WWhw names and sums on env.
1 To Nebraska, to attend to the affairs of the Estate of Janet Woodrow Wilson. See M. R. Hopewell to WW, Oct. 25, 1889, Vol. 6.

From Cornelius Cuyler Cuyler

My dear Wilson,   New York   June 19th 1891.

I am in receipt of your favor of June 18th, contents of which carefully noted.

I thank you for your kind expressions of friendship and also for the interest you manifest in regard to the "Inn."[1] I believe, after full consideration, that you are correct in the position you have taken, but I bespeak for this enterprise your continued thought, and trust you will advise me of anything that you may see in regard to the construction, when once under way, that does not strike you as entirely proper and suitable.[2]

Necessarily, being at a distance, I will be at a disadvantage in following the work closely and we must rely on our good friends at Princeton to keep us posted on the progress of the work and the general manner of the construction.

With kind regards, I remain,

yours very truly,   C C Cuyler

HwLS (WP, DLC).
　[1] The Princeton Inn, near the juncture of Stockton Street and Bayard Avenue (now Lane). The Inn, being built by several alumni of the college who had purchased land for the site from the Stockton Estate, was opened in 1893.
　[2] Wilson, who passed the construction site while walking between his home and the college, had obviously heard or seen something which he thought was amiss.

From Joseph R. Wilson, Jr.

My dear Brother:　　　　Idaho Springs [Tenn.], June 21/'91.

I am away from home on a *"spree"* or rather a *rest*. I felt rather worn out so on last Saturday I came out here, about 4 miles from home, and will remain at this quiet summer resort until next Wednesday morning next. Kate is out here consequently I care not how quiet the place may be, having all the company I care for.

You have probably had father with you before this and he has told you of my change of plans concerning my business.[1] This is the only way out that I can see. I know that our generous father would help me as much as I might ask, but this help I must not take for he has been so liberal during the past six months. I commenced business on my own hook too soon I fear and it will be best for me to work on salary for a few years to come.[2] If my plans pan out then I hope to have my wishes carried out—in other words I hope to be able to marry and not only establish thereby a home for myself but give dear father a comfortable place where he will be so much more happy during the next college year.

I will write only a short note this time. More anon.

Much love to sister Ellie, the children and a liberal share for yourself. Write soon.　　　　Your aff. bro.　Joseph.

ALS (WP, DLC) with WWhw notation on env.: "Ans. June 29/91."
　[1] The venture described in J. R. Wilson, Jr., to WW, Jan. 11, 1891, had failed.
　[2] He was remaining as managing editor, on salary, of the Clarksville *Progress-Democrat.*

To Albert Bushnell Hart

My dear Professor Hart,   Princeton, New Jersey, 22 June, 1891.

Your letter reached me when we were in the throes of the final examination period; now at length calm has returned, with vacation (or what is vacation with those happy mortals who do not have to write Epochs), and I can write to you.

Your letter interested me very much. The suggestion about a chapter on the government of the Confederacy is one of those suggestions which one accepts at once, on sight, as he would good money. There is only one proviso,—provided there be room for such a chapter. I see from the outset that the problem of getting even an outline of sixty such years as 1829-1889 into 250 tiny pages is to be the controlling problem throughout.

Like yourself, I have so much to say upon such a subject as *The Speaker as Premier* that I could not say any important part of it in a letter. I continue to hope that the meeting we have so often wished for may come under circumstances which will enable us to exchange views with some fulness.

I wish that my J.H.U. lectures on Administration were of such a character, and in such shape, as to be of service to you in your preparation of a course on Government and Administration. But my course of this year, prefatory for the most part, as it was, being the first portion of a three years' course, was general in character and had no specific or systematic reference to our own administrative arrangements. It concerned, rather, the general, theoretical questions of administrative science. Next year and the year after I shall get down to concrete systems and practical discussions. In the next place, I never write out a lecture, so that I have merely skeleton notes. These would be themselves at your disposal should you care for them in any case.

As for type-writers, this is a No. 2 Caligraph, which I have been using since 1883 with not a little satisfaction. And yet, having my due share of human nature, I am not satisfied after all. I suspect that the Hammond is a better machine for 'literary fellers,' because of its variety of type and visible writing.[1]

I shall let you know in due season what my ideas are as to the maps needed for my Epoch.

With much regard,

Very sincerely Yours,   Woodrow Wilson

TCL (RSB Coll., DLC).

[1] Wilson did eventually purchase a Hammond, but not until January 1893.

From Thomas Chrowder Chamberlin

My dear Sir: Madison.   June 22, 1891.

I have the pleasure of acknowledging your kind favor of the 19th inst. relating to the qualifications of Dr. Mustard. He appears to me to be an able man. We have, however, already called to the chair of Latin Professor George L. Hendrickson of Colorado College, and to the instructorship in Latin Dr. Herbert C. Tolman of Yale University.

I brought away from Princeton and have carried every [ever] since an exceedingly pleasant memory of the evening I spent with you and of the many valuable suggestions you made on various subjects, and especially relative to our department of civics. The Board of Regents had been thinking upon the subject independently and had come to a strong desire to develop a department devoted to commercial and financial economy. At their recent meeting they decided to establish a chair of Commercial Economy and Finance. I have Dr. Falkner[1] uppermost in my mind, as his work seems to more immediately fit him for the position. Can you aid me in any way in securing him or an equally excellent man? It will greatly add to my already great obligations.   Very truly yours,   T. C. Chamberlin

TLS (WP, DLC) with WWhw notation on env.: "Ans. June 26/91."
    [1] Roland Post Falkner, at this time Instructor in Accounting and Statistics, Wharton School, University of Pennsylvania.

From Max Farrand

My dear Prof. Wilson,   99 Spruce St. [Newark] June 22, 1891.

I expect to run down to Princeton either this week or next, but wish to do so on some day when I can see you for a few minutes. Will you be at leisure Wednesday morning of this week? or if not will you kindly let me know what day of next week I can find you.   Yours very sincerely   Max Farrand

ALS (WP, DLC) with WWhw notation on env.: "Ans. June 22."

From Philena Fobes Fine

My dear Mr. Wilson,   Syracuse.   June 22. '91.

I enclose a draft for five hundred dollars which will reduce the note somewhat.[1]

I did not realize that every thing had been settled.[2] I have such a horror of interest. I shall certainly pay the rest as soon as possible.

Harry[3] is having a beautiful time and is now in Gottingen and expects to spend a short time in Berlin and Leipsic and then home.

My sister is so ill that I could not get to Princeton during Commencement. I hope to get back by Sep first

You are very kind to have taken so much trouble[.] I am only sorry I was so stupid as to take the matter so lightly and wish I had the whole sum at liberty just now.

With love to Mrs. Wilson and Jacks[4] best remembrance to the babes I am most sincerely   Lena Fobes Fine

Has the Cottage Club broken ground yet

ALS (WP, DLC) with WWhw notation on env.: "Ans. 23/June '91."
    [1] This letter is the only extant evidence concerning this loan.
    [2] That is, that Wilson had purchased the lot on Washington Street.
    [3] Henry Burchard Fine, born Chambersburg, Pa., Sept. 14, 1858. A.B., College of New Jersey, 1880; A.M., 1883; Ph.D., University of Leipzig, 1885. Married Philena Fobes, Sept. 6, 1888. Spent his entire academic career at Princeton as Tutor and Assistant Professor of Mathematics, 1881-84, 1885-90; Dod Professor of Mathematics, 1891-1928; Dean of the Faculty, 1903-12; and Dean of the Science Departments, 1911-28. Author of several treatises on mathematics. LL.D., Williams College, 1909. Died Dec. 22, 1928.
    [4] Her son, John Fine.

A Prospectus

[c. June 24, 1891]

Memorandum

University Extension Courses offered, 1891-'92.
    I. The Renaissance.
    II. The Comparative Study of Modern
        Political Constitutions.
    III. Socialism and Democracy.
    IV. Six Great Political Writers (Aristotle,
        Machiavelli, Montesquieu, Locke, Burke,
        Bagehot).

WWhw MS. (WP, DLC).

From John Hanson Kennard, Jr.

My Dear Friend: New Orleans, La.   June 26th, 1891
    Replying to the long and complete letter, which you should have written, in answer to my last communication,[1] and did not, I beg to convey my kindest regards to yourself and family, and to say that if you have a schedule for the summer, and do not wish to keep it a secret from me, I will be glad to know what it is, that I may see whether or not I can meet you sometime before

next season commences, and abuse you as you deserve, for having been silent so long. If you are too lazy to write to me, at least send me a copy of the Princeton Catalogue, as I still think of sending my small brother there, if I can stand the expense. I wrote you, as you have undoubtedly by this time conveniently forgotten, a letter, asking you all manner of questions, about the probable expense of carrying a boy through Princeton, but you did not honor me with an answer.

I suppose however, I will have to forgive you as usual, and be glad to see you, if an opportunity presents itself, which will enable me to be with you again.

Mrs. Kennard joins me in the kindest remembrance to Mrs. Wilson and yourself. My small brother encloses a letter, stating how far he has gone, and if you have time and can tell, do me the favor to look over it, and see whether you think he can make the Sophomore Class, at your University. He completed, last year his Sophomore year at Roanoke College Va.

Very Truly,   Your Friend.   John Hanson Kennard

TLS (WP, DLC) with WWhw notation on env.: "Ans. 29 June/91." Enc.:
F. C. Kennard to WW, c. June 26, 1891, ALS (WP, DLC).
1 This letter is missing.

To Thomas Chrowder Chamberlin

Princeton, New Jersey,
My dear Dr. Chamberlin,   26 June, 1891.

I have received your kind letter of the 22nd, and am sincerely delighted to think that you enjoyed as much as I did our brief conversation in my parlor. I hope that it is indeed true that I may have been of some use to you in fomulating your plans for the university.

I was very much disappointed that Mustard did not win the election, for he seems to me in every way a fine fellow; but I shall not hesitate to do what I can to help you fill the chair of Commercial Economy and Finance even if I did fail to help you fill the chair of Latin.

My impressions of Falkner are very favorable indeed. I don't know what his prospects for promotion may be where he is; but I imagine that they are not such as would prevent his giving a very favourable consideration to a call from Wisconsin. If you will tell me how I can be of service to you in the matter, I will do all I can.   Very sincerely Yours,   Woodrow Wilson

WWTLS (President's Files, WU).

To Albert Shaw

My dear Shaw:　　　　　Princeton, New Jersey　26 June, 1891.

I promised you a long letter when I sent you that postal card[1] which accompanied the photograph of Patton for the University Extension article;[2] but now that I have the leisure to write it I find that I don't know what to say. What I wanted to say concerns (what is all the time uppermost in my thoughts) the filling of that chair of Economics: the situation with regard to that chair, I am deeply chagrined to say, has changed very radically; and what the change is I could tell you either indirectly and diplomatically, or directly and without any attempt at circumlocution. I believe that we know each other well enough to make the latter method the only tolerable one: that you know my affection and admiration for you well enough to make it unnecessary for me to apologize for plain speaking. You will understand when I am speaking my own judgments, when the judgments of others.

Up to within a few weeks past you were not only the man most prominent in the minds of our trustees for that chair; you were also practically the only man seriously considered. But lately there has been a strong (and, so far as my and Sloane's forces are concerned, an irresistible) reaction caused, of course, not by anything you have said or done, but simply by what our masters here choose to consider the character of the *Review of Reviews*. Of course since they began thinking about you they have taken to reading the Review, and the very first number of it that appeared under your editorship did the business for most of them; for it contained Mrs. Besant's article on Bradlaugh and Mr. Stead's on Wesley.[3] Both of those articles, as you no doubt realized, were calculated to shock conservative people very much. Stead's was in his most flippant style, and our friends here began to realize how much his connection with the Review (at which they had winced from the first, whenever they thought of connecting the Review with Princeton) might mean. Mrs. Besant's article praised almost everything which they despise. And all this dissatisfaction brought out and endowed with undue importance other objections which had already been made to a periodical of that character: the objections, namely, with which you are doubtless only too familiar, which are made on the ground of its alleged secondary, unoriginal character.

So far as I am concerned, I need hardly assure you, these matters count as nothing: I not only believe that you are the man, and the only man, for the place: I not only feel that if you are not chosen to occupy it it will be a deep personal loss and disappointment to me; but I also know that the American edition of the Review will presently express your taste and personality, not Stead's, and will become accordingly only what every man of sense would appreciate and admire. But unhappily my opinions, and Sloane's, just now count for very little in the matter as against the prejudices which have been aroused. What we have to meet is not a theory but a situation, a condition. And it is in fairness both to you and to myself that I have stated thus pointedly and bluntly what that situation is.

What I want very much, is that you should reply to this letter in as direct and frank a style. Hit whom you please, and as hard as you like, for you will not be hitting me,—you will not, I may add, be hitting Dr. Patton. He does not change his preferences; but he has to play his trustees, and secure their liking, as well as his own, for the candidate he prefers. My object is nothing less, and nothing else, than to get you elected. I've set my heart on that, and shall say some very plain things if it is not accomplished. Won't you tell me just what impression all this makes upon you,—just what you would say, were you a candidate on your own hook, instead of being, as is the case, a candidate through me?

Mrs. Wilson joins me in warmest regards,

Awaiting your reply with as much solicitude as confidence and affection,

Sincerely and faithfully yours,   Woodrow Wilson.

TCL (in possession of Virginia Shaw English).
   1 It is missing.
   2 It appeared in Herbert Baxter Adams, " 'University Extension' and Its Leaders," New York *Review of Reviews*, III (July 1891), 593-609.
   3 Annie Besant, "Charles Bradlaugh," New York *Review of Reviews*, III (April 1891), 235-49; William T. Stead, "St. John of England. On the Centenary of the Death of John Wesley," *ibid.*, pp. 250-61.

To John Franklin Jameson

My dear Jameson,   Princeton, New Jersey, 29 June, 1891

If I should attempt to excuse my long and (you must think) extraordinary silence, I should fail: at least I should fail to prove that such a silence is compatible with the deep and genuine affection I bear you. The simple truth of the matter is, that, this having been the busiest twelvemonth of my life (I devoutly hope I shall never have a busier), I have husbanded my strength by writing no letters save such as were absolutely necessary in the business sense of the word. I have no doubt that I have alienated some acquaintances, and I have more than once feared that I was straining the indulgence of my friends. It is a very

cheap and easy expedient to trust to being forgiven for the wrongs
you do: and I feel that I have sinned against you in this matter
in an especial degree. I value your friendship and esteem as I
value few others: I should feel it an irreparable loss should it
prove that I had done anything to cause you to abate your affection for me. All I can say is, that I have not done you this wrong
through mere self-indulgence, or without suffering many acute
pangs of regret, and apprehension: I have been afraid about my
health,—having no margin of energy after my regular tasks were
performed, I have deliberately spent such spare moments as I
could command in as complete inaction as possible. But I have
heart-sickness, as a consequence, whenever I think of you and
others whom I may have offended; and I now believe that I kept
my physical condition at too great a cost. I can only beg you to
forgive me, and re-instate me in your affections. If you cannot,
there will be a great deal that we rejoice in taken out of the
lives of both Mrs. Wilson and myself. I shall be almost as busy
again next winter as I h[a]ve been this (indeed I am almost
as busy now, writing at that Epoch of American History), but I
will not again do my own heart so much damage. Please write
to me soon to say how it stands.

Everybody in Baltimore who knows you agrees with me, I find,
in thinking that the biggest mistake the Hopkins has made it
made in letting you go; and since I have read of Scharf's gifts
to the University[1] I have been thinking about it even more than
before. I have an ardent desire to see the history of the South
studied as you would study it, and I simply cannot give up the
idea of your making a life work of it as you intended to do. It
gave me not a little comfort to see that you had chosen Southern
constitutional history as the theme of your Hopkins lectures of
last month;[2] but I fear that you cannot command the materials
you will need unless you return once more to a Southern latitude.
Would you go back to Baltimore if they were to call you?

I need not tell you that Mrs. Wilson and I enjoyed exceedingly
meeting and knowing Mrs Carey as we were able to do while
we were in Baltimore. I went to Baltimore with only one out of
my twenty-four lectures prepared, and had, as a consequence,
as you may well imagine, almost no time at all for going out;
but I did force myself to go out a little, and nowhere did I enjoy
myself so much as at Mrs. Carey's. Did she not tell me that you
were going to spend a little time in the South this Summer in
search of some materials? If so, what I want to say is this: we
are spending the Summer here at home, and nothing would
cheer and delight us so much as a visit from you, whenever you

return this way. Even if you were not coming this way, can't you come some time during the vacation, if for nothing else, just to show how magnanimous you can be?

The year here has done me good, I believe. I have opportunity to do work of as high an order as I am capable of doing, and it has benefited me to have a try at the best things, hard as it has been to get through so much new work without overstraining myself. But I have been lonely, and that has been the worst feature of the year. There are many fine men here who command my entire admiration, and many of them are men of my own age; but I have not yet found the companion I want: and there is the more need, as I selfishly reckon, that you should come to see me. Princeton is such a place as you could very easily stand for a little while even in mid-summer. At any rate, if you write to me, please fill your letter with personal detail about yourself.

Mrs. Wilson sends her warmest regards.

Sincerely and affectionately,   Woodrow Wilson

WWTLS (J. F. Jameson Papers, DLC).
    1 John Thomas Scharf, a prolific writer on Maryland local history, presented his great collection of Americana, including much material relating to southern history, to the Johns Hopkins in 1891.
    2 They were ten lectures on the constitutional and political history of the southern states.

To Azel Washburn Hazen

Princeton, New Jersey,
My dear Friend,   30 June, 1891

I am astounded, as I open it again, to find your letter dated so long ago as the 26th of March! A letter like that never gets old: it is as fresh in my mind, and in my heart, as if it had been received every day: and I have not answered it until now because I did not have the sort of time—the sort of heart leisure,—one wants to write a love letter in.

I cannot tell you how it gratifies and heartens me that you should think of me as you do. Even when your words lead me to fear that I have somehow imposed upon you, assuming parts that I could not play for long together, they give me deep pleasure, for it cannot do you any *harm* to think of me more highly than I deserve, and it does me infinite good.

It was a keen disappointment to me that I could not run up to Middletown when I went to New Haven to speak, but it was my duty to come home immediately: I had to crowd the lecture in between two class exercises here.

If you miss me in church, how much more do I miss you, do you suppose? Last Sunday I had to hear a man preach who made the most dismal failure imaginable trying to do the very thing in which you always succeed to admiration.[1] He tried to give us a summary of one of the books of the New Testament. *You* can take selected texts and make them, each contributing its own note, speak a meaning whole and vital, as if they had been combined according to their nature; while he holds his texts apart, and gives them to you lifeless fragments, torn from their places in some commentary! Its' sad work listening—and it provokes in my heart an un-Christian envy, of the congregation of the First Church in Middletown.

I never had a harder year's work than this last; but I have come out of it with good health, and we have enjoyed our first season in Princeton. We have a pleasant home and have made many delightful friends. But new friends are not like old friends—and you and Mrs. Hazen we reckon *old* friends, measuring time by the amount of affection that has been excited. We love you both sincerely, and our hearts turn to your home in Middletown—and to our own home there—with the instinct of those who seek strength and joy.

Affectionately and sincerely Yours,   Woodrow Wilson

ALS (in possession of Frances Hazen Bulkeley).
  [1] The name of this minister, apparently a visitor, is, perhaps fortunately, lost to history.

From Albert Shaw

My dear Wilson: Minneapolis, July 1. 1891.
Your letter of June 26 has been forwarded to me. I have been doing trustee duty at Iowa College, and am now spending three or four days in my old home.[1] Let me thank you heartily for the frankness of your letter;—there is nothing so beautiful as plain truth. In reply I hardly know what to write. The fact is, you see, that I *also* am one of those instinctively conservative people who like good form, and upon whose ears all manner of revivalist shrieking in the furtherance of reform and all journalistic flippancy do jar unpleasantly. And I also was somewhat scared by the Bradlaugh article, which wasn't to my taste, (—though in my soul I believe there was a lot of truth in it in spots.). How then can I resent the disapprobation of Princeton? I understand the position exactly. But the fact is that what alarms your friends is not so much just what has happened as what, in their apprehension, might possibly happen in the future. To you I may say that such apprehensions are practically needless for several reasons. The April (Bradlaugh-Wesley) number was improvised in great

haste. I had advertised the Am. edition. I was obliged by circumstances to use the English materials largely. But I am not under any obligation to print from month to month any material from the English edition that appears to me unwise for the American edition. After a few months I shall have in hand enough reserve matter to make it easy to substitute a safe thing for an unsafe thing, on a moment's notice. Let me illustrate. You will probably by this time have received the July number, with the "University Extension" article as its leading feature.[2] That article was not prepared until I had received copy of a long Blavatsky character-sketch from London.[3] I promptly wrote Mr. Stead that Blavatsky would not do at all for our leading feature, and I immediately arranged with [H. B.] Adams to prepare the educational article as a substitute. I finally decided, in order to keep the two editions from too great divergence, to cut down Blavatsky to less than half its original length and use it in small type. With our "Progress of the World" review, our Univ. Extension article, the Ballot-law article, the Analysis of the Encyclical, and the "Food-aided education" article,[4] it is hardly correct to regard us as a periodical that does not publish "original" matter. The fact is that we print as much (possibly more) strictly original matter every month as the *Forum*. Of course the *Review* is journalistic and popular in its tone. But there is no virtue in being ponderous and stupid. With all its grave faults,—so sharply detected at Princeton, the *Review* is getting a wonderful hold upon the serious people of this country. By far our most numerous class of subscribers thus far are ministers;—and I think the Presbyterians are as numerous as the Methodists. As for Mr. Stead, let me tell you, my dear Wilson, that he is the man of all the men I have ever known who is most fearlessly and unselfishly devoted to the service of God and of truth. Men of his intense personality and peculiar temperament some times make mistakes, and they almost always make the correct and conforming world feel uncomfortable. Mr. Stead is forever making me slightly uncomfortable by his intensity and his so-called eccentricity. I have the honor to know very well some scores of American Doctors of Divinity; and several of them are as good Presbyterians (I happen to be a Congregationalist, you know) as any you have at Princeton. But Stead impresses me as a better Christian than any of these reverend Doctors. He is ready to sacrifice even his reputation and his standing among his Christian brethren for the love of the truth as he sees it. I have never met so chivalrous a man as Stead. And yet, at times, we should have to classify him as "a crank." And we are always a little bit afraid of cranks. But as for me, whatever other faults and shortcomings I have—and they are abundant, of course—I think nobody ever suspected me of even a latent capacity for behaving like a crank. I am sympathetic intellectually; and tolerant; and extreme men almost always like to talk to me because I hear them and am deferential. But if I understand myself at all, it is a certain quality of "saneness" and even balance that is my best working equipment. It is this quality alone that makes it possible for me to work with Stead. I am *elastic within limits*! Having undertaken to put the American *Review of Reviews* on its legs and soundly establish it, of course it is my present duty to carry out that work. I cannot regard it as my principal life work, tho' it seems to me my most important immediate task,—chiefly, however, a business task. With such assistance as I can now hope to command, it seems to me entirely feasible for me to give editorial supervision to the *Review* while doing other and more personally congenial work. For some reason, the *Review* has not offended college authorities elsewhere as it has yours at Princeton. I have been simply astonished by the great chorus of academic appreciation that the American edition has aroused. Apparently it does not seem an undignified thing to most college men. Its best friends in this country are seventy-five or a hundred college presidents,—men of candor and intelligence. I do not intend to give them cause to think less of the magazine. The *R of R* believes that the stirring contemporary life of the world, and the turbulent—often misguided and shallow—thinking and utterance of of [*sic*] the people of today, summed up as we mean to do it, are not wholly unworthy of the notice of the academicians.

My own lines of work are in the direction of political and economic science, and I shall not abandon them. I have a great deal of writing to do, and sooner or later, if I live, I shall do it. As for a professorship at Princeton, that would be very attractive on many accounts, yet my heart is not set upon any place or position. I am not and have never been an applicant, in any sense of the word. The only thing I ever applied for was a country school one winter when I was about eighteen. I got the school, and the traditions of my administration, as I found last week, are still cherished in the district. Princeton could hardly be a congenial place for me if I felt that I was a suspect. It happens that, young as I am, I have been accustomed for years to have men much older come to me for my judgment about men and things,—pastors for churches, professors for colleges, reporters for newspapers, etc, etc. And I have been equally accustomed to having young fellows come to me for counsel as to their studies and especially for advice as to their future work. This sort of thing has not turned my head; but it has thoroughly accustomed me to being considered a safe and discreet man; and to be doubted at these points amuses me a little because it gives me a novel sensation. I should prefer a far more obscure place than Princeton, with the consciousness that I was *wanted* and *trusted*, and with a sense of full liberty to do my outside work in accordance with my own honest judgment. From what you say, it is apparent that I should not be *persona grata* at Princeton among precisely the class of men whose confidence and esteem it has been my good fortune to enjoy elsewhere. Your own too appreciative friendship and good offices I shall always remember gratefully, and I can only beg of you now that you will not let my name be made a bone of contention. I never have any uneasiness about my reputation; and yet I should feel a trifle touched in my pride if any man should ever point at me as a rejected candidate at Princeton. Do not let me be put in a false position like that. Princeton can easily find economists—scores of them—who would be glad of a place and who would be free from all embarrassing personal alliances. As for me, it is not improbable that I shall in due time feel myself justified in retiring from editorial work to enter upon educational—i.e. professorial—life in the West, where somehow my heart insists upon staying.

After extremely trying and engrossing work for several months in getting the *Review* officed, and printed and organized in New York, I am delighted to find myself in unusually good health. I shall return within a week, and shall hope to see you some time this summer.

Please glance at my Paris article, appearing today in *The Century Magazine*.[5]

With cordial regards to Mrs. Wilson, who is, I hope, in good health, I am   Sincerely yours: Albert Shaw.

ALS (WP, DLC) with WWhw notation "Ans. 14 July 1891" and WWhw address "J. P. Parker   Arlington Hotel   Cobourg, Ont." on env.

[1] He was writing from Grinnell, Iowa, where he grew up. Iowa College was later re-named Grinnell College.

[2] See WW to A. Shaw, June 26, 1891, n. 2.

[3] William T. Stead and A. P. Sinnett, "Madame Blavatsky," London *Review of Reviews*, III (June 1891), 548-57. The same article was abridged under the title "Two Views of Madame Blavatsky" in the New York *Review of Reviews*, III (July 1891), 613-17.

[4] The articles not cited heretofore were "The Progress of the World," New York *Review of Reviews*, III (July 1891), 569-83; William B. Shaw, "American Ballot Reform," *ibid.*, pp. 609-12; "The Pope's Encyclical on the Labor Question," *ibid.*, pp. 622-28; and "Food-aided Education," *ibid.*, pp. 618-21.

[5] Albert Shaw, "Paris, the Typical Modern City," *Century Magazine*, XLII (July 1891), 449-66.

To Richard Heath Dabney

My dear Heath,   Princeton, New Jersey, 1 July, 1891.

Will you pardon me if I write you a letter on my type-writer? The only pen that I can write with is half a mile away, in the summer study[1] which I have established in one of the college buildings, and I don't want to delay writing to you until I can fetch that pen. I have not written to you this long time past because I was (I feel quite certain) the hardest worked man in the United States; but now that I can write I am in a hurry to do it.

I have not forgotten that handsome review of "The State," which you wrote for the Presbyterian and Reformed Review[2] (even the criticisms of which I enjoyed, for I had no doubt they were just): for that I owe you hearty thanks. Your appreciation of my work went straight to the right place and heartened me immensely. I hope that there was not too large a modicum of the leniency of affection in your praises of the book. I am curious, too, to know whether you have heard any one speak of his experience with the book as a text for class use.

I feel very lonely sometimes to think of you away off so many, many miles from me and of all the stimulation and comfort I might get, if I could but renew our old comradeship. Distance and prolonged separation do not cool friendships, at least not friendships that struck deep as ours did, but they do sadly curtail opportunities for the sort of growth which is to be had only by intercourse with those whose minds and whose hearts alike you can repose perfect confidence in. How do I know that a fellow who is not my friend and intimate is not talking for effect?

Apparently it must still be several years before I can get away from home easily even in vacation, so much work have I, and so many engagements of one kind or another. This summer I am pegging away at that 'Epoch of American History' which I have had to postpone writing until now because of new class work constantly pressing for first attention. But cannot you get this far, even if you have to bring some work with you? I am not too busy to spend half the day with you, and it would do us both a world of good to see you once again. Think about it, old fellow, and try. There are a thousand and one things it would do us both good to talk about.

My work here is proving very stimulating indeed: it is like lecturing constantly to cultivated audiences, for my electives number about 160 men each; and it stimulates me immensely to have to interest so many minds in the more abstruse topics of jurisprudence. Political Economy, which at present I have charge of, I shall presently get rid of, for we are to have a special chair of Economics. Then I shall be lecturing wholly within the special field of my choice, and shall expect to grow into some sort of power and success, especially if my dearest scheme, the establishment of a law school here on the Scotish and European plan of historical and philosophical, as well as technical, treatment, should become a realized plan. And everything is ready for its realization, except the money!

By the way, you have generally been in Washington when the Economic Association was in session: what men among its younger members have made the best impression on you,—such an impression as men of real thoughtfulness and of teaching ability ought to make?

Write to me soon to prove that you forgive my long silence; accept the most affectionate messages from us both; and come soon to Princeton.

As ever of old,

Affectionately Yours,   Woodrow Wilson

WWTLS (Wilson-Dabney Correspondence, ViU).
  [1] Wilson was using Professor John Howell Westcott's room, 12 West Witherspoon Hall.
  [2] It is printed at Jan. 1, 1891.

From Horace Elisha Scudder

My dear Wilson   Cambridge   4 July 1891

When your letter and paper came I was just submerged in a sickness which forbade my seeing letters, papers, *MS*, anything save the doctor, the nurse, the spoon and such like. Now, I am once more playing with my work, though I do not go much to town.

I have read your paper with genuine pleasure and feel like signing my name under yours as a sort of joint author. I hope to print it in the October number.[1]

I am afraid you must discourage your Minnesota historian, for I have called a halt on the Commonwealth, or rather the publishers have, and I shall make no new engagement at present.

But do you think he would be capable of giving me a really valuable study of the two cities of St. Paul & Minneapolis? In confidence, I have been aiming to get studies of a few of our cities, regarded as personalities. I don't want statistics of grain elevators, but if any one can depict for me the *spirit* of these two cities, he is my friend. I have some hopes of securing what I want for Chicago, and in order to help the writer to absolute frankness, I tell him I am ready to publish his paper anonymously, and to go down to my grave with the secret in my letter book.   Ever sincerely yours   H. E. Scudder.

ALS (WP, DLC) with WWhw notation on env.: "Ans. 7 July/91."
   1 Wilson's essay, "The Author Himself," appeared in the *Atlantic Monthly*, LXVIII (Sept. 1891), 406-13.

From John Hanson Kennard, Jr.

My dear Wilson: New Orleans, La.   July 7th., 1891
   Your letter of the 29th., ultimo was followed by the catalogue, which you saw addressed to me, by your Registrar, and my brother and myself have spent considerable time in going over it to see if there was not a place where he could "crawl through the bars" if he cannot get "over the fence." I am very much afraid that his deficiency in Greek would prevent his going to Princeton. His Latin and Mathematics he might make up by work this summer, and during the coming Session, but he has never studied any Greek at all, and while I would strain a point to let him be with you three years, I do not feel justified in starting him at the beginning of the Freshman year, so as to give him a four year's course. Certainly the expense is quite an item, but I should be willing to stand it, for the sake of the increased good a course at Princeton would do him, if he could get through in three years. Is your Greek course a four year one? If it be only a three year course, might it not be possible for a boy to be Freshman Greek, but Sophomore everything else? Is your Math., a four year's course, and if it is a three year's course, would it be possible for a man to be Freshman Math., Freshman Greek and Sophomore everything else? You see I am still pestering you with questions, but would not bother you, if the Catalogue covered the points I mention. However, I have no doubt you need exercise badly, and to furnish me the information I require, you will have to trot around considerably, I doubt not, and I excuse myself for the trouble I am giving you by the thought, that perhaps I am helping to preserve your health.
   Our plans for this summer are very uncertain. . . . I certainly do intend however, if everything favors it to run on to New York some time in the early Fall, and if I do so, may or may not be able to take Mrs. Kennard with me. If she can go along we will give you due warning, and if it suits your convenience, will drop in on you. If Mrs. Kennard cannot come, if you will give me a fair share of the welcome you intend for us both, I will stop in to see you. I appreciate so fully the advantage it would be for my brother to be at Princeton with you and Mrs. Wilson to be

kind to him, that I shall not give up the idea until I see that it is throughly impracticable.

With kindest regards to Mrs. Wilson and yourself and with many thanks for your attention to the matter, about which I wrote,
    I remain,
                Very Truly, your friend,   John Hanson Kennard

TLS (WP, DLC) with WWT notation on env.: "Ans. 13 July, 1891."

To Horace Elisha Scudder

My dear Mr. Scudder,   Princeton, New Jersey, 7 July, 1891
    I hope that you will pardon my writing to you in this mechanical fashion, on a type-writer; but the only pen in the world that I can use with any degree of speed or comfort is half a mile away in one of the college buildings where I have established a summer study, and I want to write at once, having just received your kind letter of yesterday.

I am sincerely distressed to hear of your illness, and I fear from what you say that it must have been serious. It is reassuring to know that you are well out of it, and that you were already well enough on the first of the month to read that address at Williams.[1] I sincerely hope that you are indeed all right again.

I read that address with deep interest and pleasure: "them's my sentiments" exactly. I please myself by believing that there is occuring, in most of our eastern colleges at any rate, just about as much reaction against the scientific excesses as you would like to see. I should like very much to know whether that is your impression also. I meet a good many college men who think that they have observed such a tendency. It is certainly in the interest of health and symmetry. Please make as many addresses of that kind as you can.[2]

I am glad you liked the essay. It's a subtle compliment you pay me when you say that you feel like adding your own name to it, and a compliment which pleases me very deeply. I have a much higher opinion of the piece now than before receiving your letter.

I do not know who the man was who wanted to write the Commonwealth volume on Minnesota; the question was put to me through Albert Shaw of the *Review of Reviews*, who is a "chum" of mine. Shaw, by the way, would be an ideal man for the character sketch of Minneapolis and St. Paul. He is an old resident of the former twin, and is in my opinion a master-hand at the sort of writing you indicate.

Most cordially and sincerely yours,   Woodrow Wilson.

TCL (RSB Coll., DLC).
1 It was Scudder's address at the dedication of Mark Hopkins Memorial Hall, Williams College, July 1, 1890. Scudder must have enclosed a reprint, *Address at the Dedication of Mark Hopkins Memorial Hall. By H. E. Scudder* (n.p., n.d.), in his letter to Wilson of July 4, 1891.
2 Wilson was referring to a passage in which Scudder, after paying due obeisance to modern science, said: "But though science in its relation to thought and in its relation to material well-being has yet many victories to achieve, I suspect that in relation to education it has, for the present, reached its limits, that the claims which it makes upon the academic life are now to be considered carefully and to be readjusted; that there is, in fact, growing up, under the multiform energy of scientific study, a peril which needs to be met not so much in the world at large as in the college world which exists for the sane and symmetrical training of the human mind. For you will note that the enthusiasm of science is leading men into a constantly greater respect for minute specialization, a greater impatience of generalization unless it rests upon an enormous accumulation of independent facts, the observation of an increasing number of isolated phenomena. The tendency is of the utmost value as a corrective of superficial hasty conclusions, the habit which it engenders is a menace to inaccuracy and feebleness; but if we permit this extreme scientific temper to dominate college work we are imperilling the education not only, I am bold to say, of the general student, but of the embryonic scientist himself. . . . I . . . raise the question if it be not most wise, most philosophical, for us here to lay our plans in the future with special reference to what, in the older technical phraseology, we term the Humanities."

From Arthur W. Partch

Dear Friend,   Hiawatha, Kan.   July 7, 1891.
I have applied for two or three positions as teacher of Political Economy; and I would be very grateful if you could write a testimonial for me. The year after leaving college,1 I taught a class in Political Economy at the Hiawatha Academy, using Chapin's "First Principles of Political Economy." It is a most excellent little compend. We had some very interesting discussions in the class, especially over the author's free-trade theory. I have about settled upon Sociology for my collateral specialty through life. I expect to preach, you know, but I want also a line of study outside of my profession. Garrett Biblical Institute (which I attended last year) has under consideration the establishment of a chair of Political Economy.   Very truly,   Arthur W Partch.

ALS (WP, DLC) with WWT notation on env.: "Ans. 13 July, 1891."
1 He was graduated from Wesleyan in 1889.

From Joseph Ruggles Wilson

My precious Woodrow—   New York,   July 8 1891
I went to the West—but got no further than Chicago because (1) my money gave out, and (2) the floods in Nebraska were preventive of travel. After getting back to New York I accepted an invitation to Norwood Park (a kind of suburb of Long Branch) where is [I] was royally entertained for some days by my friend

Rev. Dr. McLean, Secretary of Am. Bible Soc.[1] His wife was very pleasant, as was he himself—& everybody else—for I saw a good many nice people. I even made a 4th July speech to certain members of the G. A. R! who marched to Norwood in compliment to its owner Mr. Munro. The latter part of this week, or early next, I am expecting to go to Saratoga—to remain about one week: this in obedience to George's[2] direction as to Congress water[3] being likely to affect favorably my eyesight. As I hear nothing from you I cannot be quite sure of your whereabouts. But presuming that this note will be forwarded I send the same with assurances (unnecessary) of my extreme love for you both & for the little ones. I expect to bore you soon again but maybe you are already full of visitors or will be?   Your affectionate   Father

ALS (WP, DLC) with WWhw notation on env.: "Ans. July 9/91."
    [1] The Rev. Dr. Alexander McLean, Secretary of the American Bible Society, 1874-98.
    [2] His son-in-law, Dr. George Howe, Jr.
    [3] That is, the springs at the famous Congress Hotel.

From John Franklin Jameson

                              Bladensfield, Richmond Co.,
My dear Wilson: Virginia, July 8, 1891.
    I will be as honest as I believe you to be, and say that in fact it *was* a source of much regret to me that the wires seemed to be down between your house and mine. But I believe every word you write, and so all's well. And for proof that my affection for you has not been damaged by your being in reality too busy to write, I hereby declare that it would give me very great pleasure to stop over at Princeton and see you and Mrs. Wilson, and that I mean to do it. It can be only for a day, I think, but it will give me much satisfaction and refreshment, I know.
    This will be near the end of this month, if you happen to be at home then, when I am returning from the Virginian trip which, as you see, I have actually entered upon. It is very good of you to expect much of me in the way of Southern history. How it will turn out I don't know; but at any rate I mean to try to do something with Virginian history during the most important period. So I got off early this year, lectured at Baltimore on the general Southern field, and then made my way to Richmond. There I toiled over papers and talked with men for two or three weeks. The two or three since have been spent in many different places in eastern Virginia, in old houses and towns, searching for materials. I have got many notes, but the best acquisition has been an understanding of Virginian life and character which,

however imperfect, I value highly and could not have got otherwise. I see how ignorant we Northern historical students have
been concerning many matters of primary consequence, and am
resolved to do something toward relieving such ignorance. Meanwhile, I have enjoyed the Virginians very much.

I will tell you more of what I have seen when I meet you, and
more of my year. The chief achievement of it was raising the
odd $8500 of the Diman Fund.[1] Now we have $1000 a year for
books in history. At my last news from Andrews[2] it looked as if
I were to have an assistant, but I have not heard the conclusion
yet.

But I must close. Please remember me most kindly to Mrs.
Wilson, accept my thanks for your kind invitation, and believe
me, with every sort of friendly feeling,

Sincerely yours,   J. F. Jameson.

ALS (WP, DLC) with WWT notation on env.: "Ans. 13 July, 1891."
[1] The Diman Memorial Fund for the purchase of books in medieval and
modern history, in honor of Jeremiah Lewis Diman, one of Jameson's predecessors at Brown University. See Elizabeth Donnan and Leo F. Stock (eds.), *An
Historian's World* (Philadelphia, 1956), p. 52, n. 62.
[2] Elisha Benjamin Andrews, President of Brown University.

From Daniel Collamore Heath, with Enclosure

Dear Mr. Wilson: Boston, Mass.   July 9, 1891.
The enclosed from Dr. Dewey, of the Inst. of Tech., will interest
you. Glad to see that the President is using his leisure hours in
reading the best books. There is hope for him yet.

Yours Truly,   D. C. Heath.

TL (WP, DLC).

ENCLOSURE

Davis Rich Dewey to Daniel Collamore Heath

My dear Mr. Heath,   Boston, June 26 1891.
Are you responsible for making up the "ad." of Wilson's book
which I presume you are floating?[1] It is the most ingenious and
subtle enterprise yet received, and I congratulate you.

Yours sincerely   Davis R. Dewey

ALS (WP, DLC).
[1] The files of D. C. Heath and Company for this period are no longer extant,
and the Editors have been unable to find this advertisement, which presumably
quoted President Benjamin Harrison on *The State*.

From Horace Elisha Scudder

Dear Mr. Wilson   Boston.   9 July 1891
    Of course. Shaw is just the man. I have the highest regard for
his work though I never have had the pleasure of meeting him.
I am quite sure I should have thought of him sooner or later,
and your note makes me think of him sooner. I have written
him. Don't think I wanted to palm off an old address for a new
one on you. I gave the Mark Hopkins address *last* year. But in
educational matters a year doesnt always matter.
                              Yours ever   H. E. Scudder

ALS (WP, DLC).

To the Postmaster of Rosemont, Pennsylvania

My dear Sir,   Princeton, New Jersey, 10 July, 1891
    Will you not be kind enough to inform me what is the present
address of Mary Freeman,[1] an Irish woman who has a married
sister at your post-office, and whose address, up to two years
ago at any rate, was Rosemont?
    Enclosed you will find a stamped envelope.[2]
                              Very truly Yours,   Woodrow Wilson

WWTLS (WP, DLC).
    [1] One of the Wilsons' former servants in Bryn Mawr and, occasionally, in
Middletown.
    [2] The reply, Ida M. Hunter to WW, July 15, 1891, ALS, was written at the
bottom of Wilson's letter. The writer said that she herself did not know Mary
Freeman and could not supply any information.

From Howard Allen Bridgman

My dear Sir,   The Congregationalist, Boston.   July 10, 1891.
    In making our plans for next year, we hope to get two or three
articles which will stimulate national and municipal patriotism.
We know your interest in this subject, and we would request an
article from you, not to exceed 1600 words, along this general
line.[1]
    It need not be written until the first of 1892, but we should like
the promise from you that we may announce it in our prospectus
to be issued early in the fall. Some such taking title like "How
can we make our boys Patriots?" or "What is true Americanism?"
may serve you as a general index of what we should like; or
select any phase of the subject which you please.

    Hoping for an early and favorable reply, I remain
        Very truly yours,   H. A. Bridgman.   Man. Editor

TLS (WP, DLC) with WWT notation on env.: "Ans. Yes, 13 July, 1891."
1 Wilson contributed "The True American Spirit," printed at Oct. 27, 1892, Vol. 8.

From William Calvin Chesnut

Dear Sir,   Baltimore, July 11, 1891.

At the last regular meeting of the Hopkins House of Commons of '91, I, as clerk of the House, was instructed to inform you that the House had had on the whole a very satisfactory year and has great hopes for next year.[1] The average attendance for about ten meetings after you so kindly instilled new life into it was about 25. Though small for a Univ of 450 students yet you can doubtless appreciate the disadvantages under which it labored. The last meeting was held about the last week of April when the near approach of the "*finals*" compelled us to abandon all else for them. I must personally beg pardon—both yours and that of the House—for my negligence in not writing earlier but it has not been from a lack of sense of duty but inability to find a convenient time. Also please excuse the informality of this letter which the present absence of the minutes of the last meeting necessitates.

Yours respectfully,   W. C. Chesnut,   J. H. U. '92.
Clerk Hopkins House of Commons.

ALS (WP, DLC) with WWhw notation on env.: "Ans. 23 July, '91."
1 For a note about the organization of the Hopkins House of Commons by Wilson in 1884, and Wilson's attempt in 1891 to revive it, see WW to ELA, Dec. 15, 1884, n. 3, Vol. 3, p. 544.

To Arthur W. Partch, with Enclosure

My dear Mr. Partch,   Princeton, New Jersey, 13 July, 1891

It was a sincere pleasure to hear from you again, and to know that you are well. I enclose a testimonial such as you ask for, which I have written with genuine pleasure, and which I hope may serve your purpose. In the haste of a very busy man, but with much deliberate regard,

Very sincerely Yours,   Woodrow Wilson

E N C L O S U R E

To Whom It May Concern

Princeton, New Jersey, 13 July, 1891.

I take pleasure in saying that I have the highest regard for Mr. Partch both as a man and as a student of Political Science. His success as a student under my instruction at Wesleyan University was remarkable; and I feel very sure that he will prove abundantly able to teach Economics wherever he may seek the opportunity to do so.

Woodrow Wilson
Professor of Jurisprudence and Political
Economy in Princeton College

TCL (in possession of Henry W. Bragdon).

From Robert Bridges

Dear Tommy: [New York] July 13–91
   You were very good to write me a long letter.[1] I was glad to hear that you were at work on the *Epoch*, and envied you the long quiet mornings in Witherspoon.
   I have just returned from a two days outing a[t] Southampton (by the sea) where I had a beautiful time—riding, sailing, swimming, driving, and walking. [Harold] Godwin has a cottage opposite the house where I was a guest, and yesterday we had a long ride through the woods together. He is very well, has a son and a daughter, and also a mustang of which he is equally proud.
   On my return I found Burlingame[2] back from his European trip (as I expected) very much refreshed—and I am relieved of much extra duty. At the same time I have been saddled with jury duty which may keep me in New York for the rest of this month. I have tried to get excused, but only succeeded in getting one week off. Consequently my vacation plans are all in the air. I have been thinking some of a five-weeks' trip to Europe, but think it wiser to wait till next spring—though I may change my plans after a short visit home.
   I am thirty-three years old today—and am not very well-satisfied with the result—though I have a suspicion that I have been building on a broader basis than appears on the surface, with some stability and accumulation of friendships back of it all that ought to count for something. At any rate I have never doubted that it is a good thing to live, and to live with enthusiasm, with faith in the better things that other men are capable of.
   This would be twaddle to any other man than you, who knows me.
   As I was up at six o'clock this morning, and have had a hot and busy day, I find I am tired and incoherent.
   So good-night, and the best of luck for the new book. With regards to Mrs. Wilson.   Your friend   Robert Bridges

ALS (WP, DLC) with WWhw notation on env.: "Ans. 22 Sept. '91."
   1 This letter is missing.
   2 Edward Livermore Burlingame, editor of *Scribner's Magazine* since 1886.

From Seward Vincent Coffin

My dear Prof.,   Middletown, Conn., July 14, 1891.

Your very welcome letter of the 1st inst. was duly received. After your abject apology I surely cannot do otherwise than forgive you for not writing me more promptly. I can pardon you the easier since I feel that I owe some sort of apology to *you*. I was much chagrinned to find that I failed to send you any sort of formal announcement of my marriage. Notwithstanding that we spent four months, off & on, at our "list,"–we occasionally think of some good friends omitted.

Now if Mrs. Wilson & yourself will overlook *my* oversight, we'll "break even" and start fresh!

I am obliged to you for the little book on Princeton Athletics.[1] One was promised me last fall by Max Farrand, but I presume he forgot about it. I think it will form a good basis for us at Wesleyan.

It makes me "tired" to think of trying to evolve a *satisfactory* & *effective* code; but there is a crying need for *something*, & we must take the bull by the horns.

Do you know of a Princeton man, first class foot-ball coach, who would take charge of our team next fall? I am not *authorized* on this matter, but I think nothing has been done, so I am feeling about on my own hook.

With sincerest regards from myself & my "better half,"

I remain,   Most cordially yours,   Seward V. Coffin.

ALS (WP, DLC) with WWhw notation on env.: "Ans. July 31/91."
[1] *The Athletic Organizations of Princeton University; Their Histories, Records and Constitutions, June, 1891* (Princeton, N. J., 1891).

To Albert Shaw

My dear Shaw: Princeton, New Jersey.   14 July, 1891.

Your letter has filled me with various emotions,–chiefly admiration, for I never read a better letter,–but also concern, because it gave me some reason to fear that my letter, to which it was an answer, had been by no means the best of its kind. To begin with (besides reiterating that you are not and shall not appear to be a candidate,–anybody's candidate but my own) let me assure you that you could not come to Princeton as a 'suspect.' When I told you of what was thought about the Review of Reviews, and uneasily felt about Mr. Stead, I did not mean to convey the impression that such were the thoughts of Princeton. A certain too influential group of men in our Board of Trustees have a great deal to do with our government in some respects, but they do not constitute Princeton: if they will consent to your election, Princeton will receive you with cordial appreciation. And, another thing. It was perfectly natural that you should think that the men I alluded to must be clergymen, and doctors of divinity; but they are not. On the contrary, they are business men, the moneyed men of the corporation; which makes it all the more singular,—and all the more awkward. Hard-headed, narrow men,—that's the breed.

They are, however, I believe, reasonable men in the long run. And, inasmuch as you have complete control of the American edition of the Review, I feel quite safe in letting the long run take them to the right conclusions. Already there are signs of sanity. Dr. Patton told me the other day that he was going to invite you to give a course of lectures here next February while I am in Baltimore,[1] some one having given him some money with which to secure outside lecturers for short courses; and I most sincerely hope that you will accept. The only part of the scheme I don't like is, that you are to be asked to come during my absence. I should like to be here to welcome and entertain you. You will receive a most cordial greeting, and I shall count upon you to come. Let me say, by the way, that I had no part whatever in the origination of this plan: it comes spontaneously from Dr. Patton, who is thoroughly your friend; and it will be carried out in such a way that you need have no fear of candidature.

In brief, things look now very much less foolish than they did when I wrote you last, and I want you to feel altogether rid of the impression that, even as things then stood, you would feel out of place in Princeton itself: you could not wish for a freer academic air,—or expect it in an old and conservative college. Indeed my own impression is that Princeton is the very place for men like you and me: for the description you give of your own type of conservatism (with its tolerant and even sympathetic understanding of radicalism) would serve excellently to describe my own mental temperament,—and the general temperament of all but the (inevitable) fossils of our faculty here. I am the more anxious that you should realize this because, while I understand and honour your love for the West and your desire some day to return to it, I believe that you will do your best service in the East,—just because you are of the West. What each of the sections needs is liberalization and variety; eastern faculties ought to contain many men from the South and West; Western faculties, many from the East and South; Southern faculties, many from the North and West. Too much breeding-in is fatal to the strain,—too much sympathy with the section in which you work and think, blinding and deadening. Send some of our stiff Eastern fellows to the colleges you believe in in the West, and yourself accept a chair in some typical college here in the East, and so mix elements and variegate strength.

I read, not only with appreciation, but even with emotion, what you said of Mr. Stead,—and I am quite willing to accept your judgment with regard to his moral qualities: I must accept it, for I feel that you speak with knowledge. At the same time, I am glad that you leave me room to doubt as to his wisdom. Whenever I think of such men I remember that passage in which Burke says, "When I see a man acting a desultory and disconnected part, with as much detriment to his own fortune as prejudice to the cause of any party, I am not persuaded that he is right; but I am ready to believe he is in earnest." I have a social instinct which leads me to deem the free lance mistaken; which gives me the conviction that we are not at liberty to advance social reform by exalting our own points of view above that of those with whom we ought to associate. Persuasion and cooperation are better forces than antagonism and exasperation; and the road that lies over the sensibilities of others is not the road that leads to lasting reform. But I am growing quite ludicrously sententious and writing what may make you say buzz, buzz!

Your article on Paris I have not yet read because our reading rooms are in summer chaos and I have not been able to get hold of the *Century*; but, in the meantime, I hear nothing but praise of it from those who have read it, and who wonder that 'facts' can be made to serve as both exposition and argument.

You probably think that I forgot all about your request to find out from Mr. Scudder about the Commonwealth Series and the volume on Minnesota, but I did not. I wrote to Mr. S., but he was ill when the letter reached him, and did not answer for a long time—until just the other day. The publishers, it seems, have called a halt on the series and no more engagements are to be entered into for the present!

Mrs. Wilson joins me in warmest regards,—in pleasure at your good reports of your health,—and in the strong hope that you will soon be down to see us: we shall be here all summer, and you and I must needs have a talk.

Yours with cordial affection,   Woodrow Wilson.

TCL (in possession of Virginia Shaw English).

1 Patton, who was notoriously dilatory, apparently never got around to writing this letter. In any event, no letter from Patton to Shaw about this subject has survived in the Patton Letterbooks in the Archives of Princeton University (some of the letterpress copies have faded entirely), and Shaw did not deliver a series of lectures at Princeton in 1892.

From William Alphonso Withers[1]

Dear Sir: Raleigh, July 16th 91
    Being an ex-Davidsonite and from North Carolina I take the
liberty of writing you for some information which I very much
desire.
    We are attempting in this state to organize an association of
the college and university Professors in this state. While it will be
a small body we shall probably do work of the character of the
college association in the middle states & in the New England
states. I do not know who are the secretaries of these two associations and I should be greatly obliged if you will be kind enough
to give me their addresses. I feel sure that the reports of these
meetings would be of great value to us.
    If you know of any other matter relating to the subject we
should be glad to know of this also if we may be pardoned for
imposing so much on your kindness.
    Assuring you we shall greatly appreciate your assistance, I am
                    Respectfully yours   W. A. Withers.

Address till Aug 20 Davidson, N. C.

ALS (WP, DLC).
    [1] Professor of Chemistry, North Carolina State College of Agriculture and
Mechanic Arts.

From George Francis James[1]

My dear Sir: Philadelphia.   July 21st, 1891.
    We are going to make University Extension a special feature
of the September number of "Book News" similar to the May
number. I should like very much to have you offer a discussion
on the Civil Government for this number, giving an indication
of the methods of treatment and the best literature on the subject
to be purchased by the centre if $25. were available or if $50.
or even $100.[2]
    Make the scope of the article as wide in its treatment as
possible. The article will be paid for at the rate of $15. per
thousand words. I hope that you can see your way clear to favor
us in this way and will send us the title and the probable length
of the article. The manuscript of the same will be needed some
time during the first week in August.
    Hoping to receive and [an] early and favorable reply, I beg to
remain,   Very truly yours,   George F. James,   Per S.

TLS (WP, DLC) with WWhw notation on env.: "Ans. 'Yes' 23 July, 1891."
    [1] Editor of the Philadelphia *Book News* and brother of Professor Edmund J.
James.
    [2] Wilson replied with "The Study of Politics," printed at Sept. 1, 1891.

From John Hanson Kennard, Jr.

My Dear Wilson: New Orleans, La., July 21st., 1891

Had I not partly anticipated the probable nature of your reply, it would have made me even more sorry, than it has, but all probability of my brother going to Princeton has been done away with. However, it is not your fault, and so I do not blame you at all in the matter, but have only to thank you for your kindness in replying so fully on the subject. I am just back from attending the Second Annual Meeting of the League of Southern National Building and Loan Associations, and it may please you to know that I was elected President of said League, to succeed General Fitzhugh Lee, who filled the position during the past twelve months. I left Mrs. Kennard at Monte Sano, which is just outside of Huntsville, in the hope that the cold weather would strengthen her for next winter's home duties. I share your hope most sincerely, that she will be able to go North with me in the Fall, when I expect to make my trip, but this is too far off for me to be certain about it now.

With many thanks from both my brother and myself for your kindness in writing so fully on the matter.

I remain,   Very Truly,   John Hanson Kennard.

TLS (WP, DLC).

From Wilfred Pirt Mustard

My Dear Sir—   Uxbridge, Ont.   July 22nd 1891

I am still disengaged for next year, and some of my friends at Toronto and Baltimore are booming me for the Greek chair at Lake Forest, which is vacant by Emerson[1] going to Cornell. I am sure that a letter from you would be of great service to me—if only because Princeton and Lake Forest are both Presbyterian institutions. Will you be so good as to write to the President— William C. Roberts, D.D., LL.D.—and say what you can in my favor.

The Wisconsin position, about which I last troubled you was filled very suddenly—before your letter could have reached President Chamberlin: the Lake Forest chair is, as far as I can learn, still vacant.

I hope you are having a very pleasant vacation, and am sorry to have to break in upon it in this rude way.

Yours sincerely   Wilfred P. Mustard

ALS (WP, DLC) with WWhw notation on env.: "Ans. July 30/91."
  [1] Alfred Emerson, who had just gone to Cornell as Associate Professor of Classical Archaeology.

From Joseph R. Wilson, Jr.

My precious brother: Clarksville, Tenn.   July 29, 1891

Your welcome letter of a recent date was received in due time. Yes, my dear brother, you have my full consent to try what can be done in Nashville.[1] I am very unwilling to leave Clarksville while father is here but it may be best for me to do so. I am feeling about me with a view to securing a position with a large iron furnace about to be started here and have met with some encouragement from Capt. Tracey a rich & prominent Clarksvillian who is at the head of the institution. Of course I would hate like everything to leave the town where Kate lives, but she, dear girl, would not lift a finger to keep me here if it would be to my interests to move away. She would, naturally, be unwilling to leave her family, but says she will gladly go with me wherever I think best. She talks just like the true sweet little woman she is. I do not agree with you in what you say about wasting my "talents" (?) in journalism. The work suits me exactly and if I could get with some city journal I would be O. K. I would give up my newspaper ambition, however, for a lucrative position where I would stand some chance for promotion, so please write to Mr. E. as soon as possible.

Stocton [Axson] has probably written you concerning his visit to Clarksville. I enjoyed his short stay here very much, as you can guess. We called on Kate, went to the cave and spent several pleasant hours together.

I am in statu quo now. Having just recovered from a severe attack of "misery in my midst" I am a little weak but feel better than I have in weeks.

Love unbounded to you all. Please write again soon to
                              Your aff. bro.   Joseph.

Kate is much pleased at the messages of love from my dear ones. Cannot you or sister Ellie write to her? Sister Annie has not done so yet & I feel *hurt* at it, too.

ALS (WP, DLC) with WWhw and WWsh and other jottings on env.
  [1] Woodrow Wilson, in a missing letter to his brother of June 29, 1891, had again offered to write to Robert Ewing of Nashville on Joseph's behalf.

From George Howe, Jr.

Dear Woodrow   Columbia, S. C., July 30 1891

Your letter with check for 154.00 came safely to hand to-day.[1] Geo. Wright has his family at Buena Vista. There are also several Augusta people there. The accommodation this season, consists in [an] old inn somewhat freshened up and a green cook. The new hotel is underway but will not be completed before November. It will be a very nice one when it is done. Wright says it is one of the finest locations he knows of in the Mts.

I send you the prescription you wish for your eyes. I am afraid that you are writing too much and thereby abusing your health. Don't do it all at once[,] spread it out a little & save yourself for some more. Annie unites with me in warmest love to you and Ellie.   Yrs affly   Geo. Howe

I send this morning's State, which has an advertisement of the Buena Vista hotel or inn.

ALS (WP, DLC).
¹ Wilson's payment for a lot adjacent to one purchased by the Howes in Buena Vista, a new development off the main road between Asheville and Hendersonville, N. C. For the background of this transaction, see George Howe, Jr., to WW, March 14, 1891, and W. Elliott Gonzales to G. Howe, Jr., April 4, 1891, both ALS (WP, DLC).

A Translation and Digest, with Commentary

[c. Aug. 1-21, 1891]

Notes on Jurisprudence.

From *Merkel*¹

Character of Law: Law is a principle of *order*. (2) It is also, and in equal degree, a principle of *freedom*, inasmuch as, by establishing order and setting bounds and rules about individual action, it in all other things sets individual powers free. (3) It is a principle of *peace*, obviously, obviating, as it does for the most part, individual collisions, or else checking and adjusting them.

The State and Law: The State does not pre-suppose Law; neither does Law pre-suppose the State: they are coexistent, inseparable concepts.

Not every expression of the will of the State is Law; and there can be law which is not of the State. Any association which may make independent determination of the relations of its members to each other and to itself may possess its own law, whether i[t]s authority be derived from the State, or dependent upon it, or not. E.G., the *Roman Catholic Church*.

Law is essentially imperative, though its *form* is sometimes not that of command. It is never merely polemical, didactic, philosophical in intent as might seem to be the case, e.g., with constitutional *bills*

¹ Adolf Merkel, "Elemente der allgemeinen Rechtslehre," in Franz von Holtzendorff (ed.), *Encyclopädie der Rechtswissenschaft* (Leipzig, 1890), pp. 5-44.

Merkel continued[2]

 of rights.) The imperative is in such cases is [*sic*] latent. Law's imperative need not, however, be the cause of its efficacy (e.g. when it confers rights or privileges.)

Primary and Secondary Commands. Secondary commands there often are which constitute the *sanction* of the primary, directing what shall be the punishment in case of infraction of its main commands, and commanding the process of punishment or remedy by the organs of the State's power.

To Whom is Law Addressed? Not to the officers of the State only: it is not all sanction,—but to all whom it may concern: to all who can put it in force or take advantage of it.

Law and Force: Force is a characteristic and indispensable sanction of Law; not of each law, but of Law. The force need not be physical: it may be moral, spiritual, a force of habit and opinion. Laws do not lose their character as such by ceasing to need even so much as a threat of force to secure obedience, by lacking all sanction; but in any case their sanction is the will of the Community, and where there is will there is force, of one kind or another.

 No law, indeed, can be said to be "valid" which must depend always upon force for its effectuation. A law which no one obeys

Still Merkel

except under compulsion is no law at all.

The Binding Force of Law: Consists in its alliance with those moral forces alive in the people from which there proceeds compulsion to obedience. A régime of force becomes a régime of law only when it has been accorded acceptance by the general moral sense, the sanction of the moral forces of the nation. *Force and wrong* may originate laws in this sense,—may originate rules which will in time establish themselves in the general habits and acquiescence, and thus *become* Law.

 On the other hand, there is a sense in which law may cease to be law: namely, when it ceases to keep pace with the moral development of the people, when it falls out of harmony with their moral sense and their developing judgments and habits. (Position of Seward and Chase).

 ("The question what the binding force of law is, and upon what dependent, has hitherto, in spite of its great

---

2 Wilson wrote a note of continuation such as this at the top of each page. Some were whimsical, some separated his own comments from his abstracts or summaries of Merkel. They have all been retained.

importance for the general theory of Law, received very limited scientific attention."[3] Very little attention, that is, to such generalizations as can be drawn from the concrete political and social experiences of the race. There has been speculation enough of an *a priori* nature touching the matter.)

Merkel again

Law as a Means to an End: Law is not, of course, an end in itself. Neither does it serve ethical purposes *because* they are ethical, though the ethical character of its commands has a great deal to do with their acceptability and consequent validity.

Righteousness (right-ness)—or such a conception of right as is held by the community concerned—may *condition* law, but it is not on that account necessarily the *object* of law. Many things condition the growth of a tree or the cure of a patient, but these things are not on that account objects of the tree's growth or of the physician's efforts. Moreover, the law may by no means be charged to undertake the accomplishment of everything that is right. In short, it is not right which is the object of law, but the best ordering of the material and (so far as wise and practicable) of the other spheres of the people's life.

The object of law may be said to be the creator or source of law. But it does not necessarily follow that the object or end served at present by any particular law was *its* source. It may have been produced by a complex historical process from which any conscious or unconscious search after its present service was altogether excluded.

Law as an Organ of Social Interests: "The operation of law displays an exercise of force on the part of the powers collected and organized in the state in the service of social interests." The qu., What objects are served may be resolved into the qu., Whose will and power express themselves in the rules of the law. The primary object of law is, to serve the

Merkel once more

purposes of the community—it is a means for the accomplishment of social aims. In one sense, .˙. , there is no such thing as private law: behind every rule applied in the interest of individuals stands, what is the commanding element in law, the interests of the community, and private

[3] The quotation marks, which are Wilson's, indicate direct translations of Merkel's text.

rights are such, in the eye of the law, only so far as they are coincident with general interests.

The community or society here spoken of is a *unit*, not an aggregate, a personality, not an abstraction. Its unity and personality cannot be proved (scientifically); and this conception of the state may very easily be exaggerated. The unity and national individuality which it attributes to law is relative only: the national spirit and character undoubtedly affect law, but they affect it only in part. There is a very large element of uniformity in the laws of different peoples, and the influences from which it springs are many, manifold, and complex, not few and simple. The national element in it should not be exaggerated.

The Compromise Character of Law: The interests served and furthered by law are by no means concurrent, harmonious, or even consistent: to a certain extent it is true that where one interest gains another must lose, and law is the result of a compromise between them.

Some interests gain through the very permanence and stability of law and of the public organs, whose energies, capacities, and sphere of activity remain for long periods together unchanged. Other interests gain a certain advantage

Merkel unfinished

from the free play of individual initiative and the unsuitability of the law to the regulation of certain classes of interests. Hence reforms and the opposition to reforms.

There is a tendency for rulers to substitute their own interests for those of the governed—and here again the compromise nature of law (which is generally formulated by rulers) is manifest. Hence the struggle for political predominance among interests and classes—a struggle for the possession of power.

The progress of civilization, in this view, postpones the unity and harmony of law; because it increases the variety and complexity of competing interests.

It is a mistake to suppose that to destroy this compromise nature of law is to get strength, that strength lies, for law, in consistency and simplicity. Its progress comes because of victories of strength on the part of one interest or set of interests at a time: its strength is the strength of struggle. (In society men have only such rights as their history, their character, their victorious struggles have entitled them

to: they *deserve* the positions they *gain*—a wholesome truth
for socialists and labour reformers.) Betterment—social betterment—will come, not when strife is abolished, but when
the means of strife become peaceful instead of warlike:
when victories are of debate rather than of arms.

The Positive Character of Law and of Rights: 1. Law was at first
not positive law at all: it was not looked upon as made,
but as received, from God or from divine ancestors. It was
the function of the magistrate simply to interpret and to enforce. Law, accordingly, was declared (e.g. in the ancient
Germanic system) by popular assemblies: for it was the
received tradition, not an enactment: the executive simply
enforced.

2. *Positive* law (law, i.e., eman-

Merkel persistent

ating directly from the conscious will of the state) came
later, and, even when it came, was regarded as subordinate
to the "natural" or traditional law: its function was supplement, not distinct creation.

3. In a third stage of the history of law the parts were
reversed: the will of the state came more and more prominently forward as the chief source of law; custom and tradition became subordinate to it, waited upon its sanction for
validity, became itself, in its turn, supplementary, additional. The making, interpretation, and enforcement of law
were separated in *personnel*, but they remained functions
of one and the same will, that will, namely, from which
the constitution sprang—the will of the organic state.

4. Then followed a period in which this positive law, this
self-determined order of the state, as spoken by the law-
maker, began to be contrasted with popular conceptions of
individual and social rights (—the law, so to say, became *too
positive*,—too much an enactment instead of a derivative of
the common thought). Abstract conceptions of right began
to furnish standards whereby to criticise and estimate law,
ground for revolution, bases for reform, and there sprang
up the ideal philosophy of the *Law of Nature*. This Law of
Nature, however, never became more than an outside, ideal
standard for the development of positive law. Wherever
applied, it was itself positive law, and can be shown to have
been derived from the particular historical circumstances
of peoples who applied it and of the time in which it was
applied.

History of Opinion Touching Rights: May be summed up in the
statement that conceptions of right (justice), like conceptions touching the origin and

Merkel even yet
sanction of law, depend upon the circumstances of the
life of each generation, upon the interplay of circumstances
and of social forces. The conception of rights, in short, like
law itself, which secures rights, *is an historical product,
rather than a logical product.* In proportion as nations have
been brought into contact with each other and made subject
to similar conditions (particularly, of late days, to similar
economic conditions) have certain common and almost universal conceptions of right sprung into prominence and
become effective in the creation of law. For example, the
weight and significance now given to *personality*, the freedom accorded to personal belief, the legal capacity ascribed
to every individual, etc.

Hence the principle that laws must emanate from, or
at least be directly or indirectly sanctioned by, the whole
body of citizens—must be the product of their sense of right,
i.e., in part at least, of their circumstances.

From such conceptions has sprung the untenable theory
of *Contract* as the sanction of the state's authority: a contract which presupposes a totally unhistorical and impossible
individual autonomy.

The development of views touching rights has advanced
pari passu with the spiritual life and consciousness of the
People.

The Conception of Rights: The conception of 'justice,' though
compounded of historical elements, derived from historical
conditions, conditioned upon

And yet once again Merkel
the stage of culture and development, has at its centre the
thought of the *worth of personality* and the relative significance of actions as measured by personality. Every judgment, in order to conform to personal right, to justice, must
be based (a) upon a correct view of the facts, (β) a correct
application of the law to the facts, and (γ) upon a law which
is consistent with the ethical judgments at which the community has arrived. E.G., we would not now tolerate laws
directed against belief or against scientific error, though a
former age would have regarded such laws as just. The
common judgments to which law must conform are not

theoretically derived, but are developed with our powers of mind and the interests of our social life, though they of course may be and are affected by speculation. The most important service performed by scientific thought is the dissipation of superstitions and prejudices.

The principal considerations which lie at the basis of our judgments as to justice are social considerations: the interests of the people, of the state, of social groups or classes. We may not, however, be always conscious of these considerations. It is an example of the principle that the present labour party rest their arguments upon their conception of the social rights of the labouring class.

Not only are social interests themselves affected by historical changes: they also change in their relative importance as regards our conceptions of justice.

As much as ever from *Merkel*

The Ethics of the modern world is not the same as that of the ancient: there is greater freedom of ethical conception; men do not regard their own race or nation only but draw their thought from wider sources; society is not supreme over the individual but must receive formative impulses from him.

Moreover, our ethical conceptions are deeply affected by the doctrines of Christ, which cannot be regarded as a mere reflexion of historical conditions.

Once more, our conceptions of justice are now sometimes opposed to some existing social interests, and those interests and these conceptions mutually affect one another.

Finally, there is no ground for the apprehension that a clear understanding of the conditions under which our conceptions of justice are developed—a clear perception of their dependence upon circumstances—will unsettle them, deprive them of their validity. Those conceptions rest upon what we are and perceive of our relations to others, and until these things change those conceptions will themselves not change.

(These considerations must throw a flood of light upon the qu. as to the legitimate means of winning for a class (as, e.g., the labouring class) a special recognition in the law: that class must establish its social worth and character and become entitled to a special place in a reformed law by making clear its veritable relation to other classes, its true

Myself, then Merkel

ethical status. It can do this only by itself taking care to regard other social interests than its own in its conceptions of what ought to be done. Law is a compromise, not a victory for one class; and no class can, consistently with the healthful life of society, be suffered to consider itself the whole of society, or its interests the dominant interests of society. The modern state is above all things else complex: compromise rather than harmony is all that can as yet be hoped for.)

Nature of the State: "A state is the organization of a people as a society, or the sum of the arrangements through whose regulated operation the life-associations of a people find their realization." "This operation presupposes a power which secures the ordering of the common life against disturbance and may ove[r]come resistance when occasion renders it necessary, and which constitutes the highest authority of the people concerned." This power must, according to the conception, be sovereign, i.e., have no other power set above it; and its activity must be directed towards preserving the unity of the state and advancing its general interests and standing.

At a certain stage of development the state is connected with a particular territory and has authority not only over

Merkel only

citizens but also over all within that territory.

There are no *legal* (jural) limits to the authority of the modern state, though there are, of course, actual limits.

There is a contrast between the ancient and the modern state in respect of these limits as regards individual privilege as well as in respect of the relations of the state to individuals. The modern state accords to the individual a freedom and a value as over against the state quite unknown to the ancient state.

The interests of the people with which the State concerns itself vary with the times and with prevalent conceptions: & this is particularly true of religious and economic interests. Here, as elsewhere, it is all a matter of ethical development.

As regards the forms of the state's activity, they are three: (1) The origination, alteration, and repeal of the rules of law through laws and ordinances; (2) The application of existing laws to existing interests through the action of courts; (3) The settlement of concrete affairs in the forms of administration or of legislation (in the formal sense of the word).

Ganz *Merkel*

Administration has in part the character of a carrying out of certain laws and in part the character of an expansion of the functions of the state within certain fixed limits of law.

Inasmuch as the development of the state mirrors the development of the people, their political and social conditions and necessities, etc., "the history of political constitutions is the history of the progressive application of public institutions to the needs and the relationships of power developed by the people." Alongside of these go ethical and social developments which in their turn exercise an influence upon political developments.

There is a certain degree of likeness and uniformity in political developments, because certain conditions are often quite similar upon an all but universal scale. For example, the modern organization of the administration of justice in its relations with the functions of legislation and administration. The efforts for a maintenance of order under the sanctions of law lead to efforts for the formation of the 'Legal State' in the higher meaning of that term. By a 'legal

Merkel abstracted

State' we mean one "in which a public law, established in safe operation, regulates the relations between public authorities and between these and individuals in every respect, and in which transgressions of these limits set by the laws can be cited before courts which furnish guarantees for an unpartisan application of the law."

The unity of the state's tasks bespeaks a unitary organization with a fixed middle point (centre of gravity) and a single will: hence there is usually a single organ—whether that organ be a person or a body of persons—in which the power of the state is centred. This is the "sovereign" power: in a monarchy possessed by one person, in an aristocracy by a minority, in a democracy or republic by the totality of the citizens of full political rights. The *German Empire*, as contrasted with these simpler forms, affords an instance of mixed form in which there are several equal organs independent of each other (?). Each of these draws its authority and derives its functions directly from the Constitution, which is the expression of the national will (?), and none has undivided power. For example, the Emperor, the *Bundesrath*, etc. Generally the constitutional monarchy is

Merkel resumed

characterized by such relations between its organs: there is, in form at least, an equality between the parliament and the administration, and the action of the state is determined by their co-operation.

Prevailing political theories insist that sovereign power is lodged always in some particular person or body of persons; but such theories are in contradiction with facts. How little unity of power is a necessity is witnessed by all the great federal states. Here organs and authorities with powers exclusively their own for the furtherance of functions necessary to the achievement of the ends of the nation as a whole exist alongside of organs having powers exclusively their own for the furtherance of the local and special functions of the member-states. It is a mistake to apply to the member-states, however, as well as to the federal state itself the name and conception of "state": there can be but one "state" for a single nation: the members are but parts of the state; only in conjunction can they perform the whole function of the state.

After Merkel

"The state is a jural person, that is a possessor of subjective rights and subject to jural conditions." To contend that it has no subjective rights because its 'objective rights' are identical with Law (Objective Right) itself is to induce confusion. The state is a personality of a special sort, which, as over against other personalities, has its own rights and duties. That its rights are self-determined is not in contradiction with this view.—Comparable with human personality.

The Founding of the State: 1. "The state was preceded by social formations of varied character; among which, as the most ancient, are blood-unions, associations in which a not very large number of members lived together in the relations of kinship. These latter unions divide themselves into two principal groups, in which either the '*Mutterrecht*' or the '*Vaterrecht*' prevailed. In the former kinship was determined by relationship to common female ascendants; the father played no rôle; the nearest of kin to the children among males were the brothers of the mother; and guidance fell to those of most consideration

Merkel translated

in respect of strength, wisdom, or experience; etc. In the
latter, on the contrary, relationship to a common father,
grandfather, etc., was determinate, and a *patriarchal regime*
existed. These latter associations represent an altogether
later form, but one which, at the same time, the nascent
state usually found in existence and made use of. All these
pre-political associations were held together by common
economic interests & common interests of peace and war,
in the higher stages by a common religion also.

2. "The view for a long time prevailed that the family, by
a progressive organic evolution had widened into a nation
organized as a state, and that thus, out of the family authority of the father, the power of the chief of the greater
community had come forth. The formation of states, however, does not in itself exhibit an organic growth. The latter
in itself leads only to a weakening of the bonds which hold
individuals together in primitive societies, to the embarrassment of a common economy, and to a division into narrower associations. The development of the

Merkel's own words

state presupposes operative conditions of an opposite tendency. It involves the subordination of a number of blood-
associations existing alongside of one another to a common
ruling power. Such (a power), however, has never come
into existence in the form of an organic development.

"3. The chief creator of states is War, and the manner in
which it exercises this function is three-fold. First to be considered are incessant feuds between neighbours, which,
leading to no results but mutual injuries, a common necessity for peace, and, by means of that, the beginnings of state
organization come into existence. Further, common interests
of defence and attack against common enemies. Finally
and especially, the forcible subjection of one clan by another;
and here the subjugation of the settled population of a
country by warlike hordes pressing in from without is of
primary importance. The necessity of holding the subjugated
masses in subjection, and the desire to make use of them
economically, lead, in connexion

Merkel Englished

with the necessity of preparation for war against hostile
tribes, to a closer combination of the ruling race and to the
development of the forms of a stable government.

"4. Within the state, although under manifold modifications, the old associations, especially the patriarchal blood-unions, maintain themselves. They come there in various ways into connexion with the new arrangements and rise to be bearers of political functions. Hence there are frequently to be distinguished in the constitution of the older states two formations interlaced with each other, one especially political, and one pointing back to pre-political conditions. Thus there persist in the families in which the organization of the ancient city states has its foundation the old associations, although in the manner of their limitation and in the duties laid upon them the influence of the state appears; while in the kingship and in the magistracy specifically political formations stand over against them.

Merkel, Anglicé

5. "The state appears also, in its creative activity and in its whole management, in a certain spiritual dependence upon these associations. Thus it develops its organs in many ways in accordance with precedent models; especially does the king lay claim to a power answering to the father's power in the patriarchally organized blood-unions. There is developed, besides, a state religion which is connected with the religious conceptions and usages which have already attained development in them. The state, in general, enters into the spiritual heritage of these associations and develops it according to its needs.

"6. The oldest religion is a worship of ancestors. In the state the great dead of the collective people take their place by the side of those of the kindred and become superior to them. The founders of the state and its energetic rulers are magnified in the fancy of the people into gods

The plain English of Merkel

or demigods. But such divinities as, like the Olympian, are derived from this source, or are of another and newer origin, unquestionably assume relations of kinship to subsequent generations. Great kings are reckoned as their descendents.

"7. The further developed religion generally advances in close connection with political arrangements and lends to them a higher consecration and a weightier element of power. These arrangements obtain as established by the gods and exist under their protection. They are, moreover, the guardians of the entire morale of the people, the representatives of the unity, and the bulwarks of the power and of the fame of the folk. They all stand over against the individual as a thing exalted, for which he should learn to stake power and wealth with gladness.

"Religion itself in this wise gains a more important

Merkel still speaks

content. As the state is built up by its aid, so it is itself expanded by the influence of the state. If we mean by the word religion developed conceptions and doctrines and precepts of an ethical intent, we may regard its most ancient forms as a creation of the State, and likewise the divine world, in so far as we mean thereby an exalted system expressing itself in binding commands and in a furtherance of the general welfare. In this sense Hobbes was right when he placed the birth of the immortal gods in closest connection with the birth of the mortal god, the State.

"8. The development of the conditions of political sovereignty and of the whole political law followed, for the rest, under the influence of various factors, above all of war and of economic needs, in three principal forms: that of a division of power among the elements contending for mastery; that of agreements and other determinations of the folk-as-

Merkel, as literally as possible

sociations concerned; and that of a longtime developing process, the form in which custom and the ethical conceptions which conditioned the efficiency of political arrangements were developed and changed under the influence of stable relations of political sovereignty, of newly-developed necessities and popular ideas. All these forms have already been noticed and will be returned to in what follows in connexion with a consideration of the various theories concerning the state.

The sovereign authority of the state is based by these theories either upon the subjection of the weaker by the stronger, or upon contract, that is, a constituent act of will on the part of the ruled, or, finally, upon an historical process of organic development and the spiritual forces operative, or conceived to be operative, in such. (a process).

"9. The foundation of the state is the most important example in the history of the division of human labour and in the

A rendering of Merkel
> evolution and differentiation of the various social functions.
>
> "With the differentiation of the activities of rulers and the ruled there is connected the emergence of law from out the domain of hitherto undistinguished usages in the form of a political administration of justice, and, in general, a differentiation of the forces regulated by the state from the unregulated social and individual activities. There is connected with it, further, a more intensive conduct of agriculture by the politically and economically dependent classes, etc."

Organic Conception of the State. "The state is not a mere theoretical unit or merely a special name for the aggregate of its members," but, instead, "a real vital unit," "which asserts itself and fulfils its aims through activities distributed in a fixed order among ministrant organs which undergo a constant renewal, and in which, on the one hand, a separation and change of

The English equivalent of Merkel
> fundamental elements is perceptible without any consequent change in the form of the whole or in the character and distribution of its activities, and, on the other hand, a process of growth and a manifold metamorphasis in the whole, with which corresponding changes in those elements are not incompatible which in the end develop their forms from within and manifest a capacity and a tendency to balance interior disturbances. All this has the state in common with the human organism. On the spiritual side a more remarkable correspondence manifests itself between volitional developments on the part of the State and volitional developments on the part of individuals. The spiritual powers which there come into play, when decisions of a determinate sort are to be taken, appear like those which find expression in the soul of the individual

Just what Merkel says
> under analogous circumstances (especially in personalities typical of a particular people). The conceptions which come into contact with each other in the discursive thoughts of the latter and receive test of prevalence, as well as the contending emotions of the heart which here precede weighty decisions, certainly have their specific counterparts in the domain of political life,—these are present in the political parties,—but the similarity and equivalence in the one case

and in the other of the occurences mentioned are not thereby excluded. There are also to be seen in the sequences of
resolution and effect which find expression in political transactions the same regularities as in the succession of these
phenomena in the individual.

"It would be to mistake the organic theory to regard the
individual as merely a member of the state (in the sense
of the Greek philosophy). Especially in the presence of the
prevailing conceptions of the modern world, we must regard the individual, not merely as not emanating from the

Substantially Merkel's language

state and existing because of it (that of course), but also as
a determining, as well as a determinate, element. The
members of the state have, and ought to have, an independent individuality and worth of their own. The sphere of
their self-determination, indeed, it is the distinctive service
of modern thought to have enlarged and promised still
further enlargement."

Rights (das subjektive Recht) and Jural Relationships.

Jural Relationships. The law orders the relationships of individuals to each other, defining the sphere of power belonging to each, and creating on the one hand capacity, on the
other safety, security. It creates in every case, in short, on
the one hand a duty and on the other hand a right; and
it never creates the one without creating the other. There
may be cases where there seems to be only a right, and no
duty on the part of any one, corresponding to the right,—
or a duty with no right anywhere vested; but this can be
only upon the surface: a right is dead without a corresponding duty: a duty in abeyance without

A la Merkel

a corresponding right vested in some one to insist upon
its performance.

The necessity for the elevation of life-relationships into
jural relationships increases with the independence of the
parties concerned and with the variety of separate interests.
Thus the "relations between elders and their dependent children are ordered by law to a much narrower extent than
those between them and those persons who do not belong
to their family."

From one point of view, both the right and the duty are
two-fold in character, having both an ethical and a material

side. In the case of a duty, there is, on the one hand, the
consideration of the wrong which will be done to those who
have the corresponding right, and, on the other hand, the
consideration of the public power which will be brought to
bear to enforce it. In the case of a right, there is always
the moral claim, and the privilege of commanding the
power of the state in its enforcement.

A *Right* (*das subjektive Recht*) is a determinate interest in the
power conferred by law: it is a power over some one else;—
there is no law which does not create a legal duty on the part
of some third person.

It is incorrect, therefore, to speak of a power over things
maintained

Thus far Merkel

by right, or of the obligation (or liability) of things in or
of themselves. As well speak of the duty of my fruit tree to
bear fruit, or of my right to demand that it observe my
wishes. The law does not concern itself with the relations
of things to our interests; and the power which it bestows
upon those who are not the owners of the things in question.

The view that a Right is the command which the individual exercises over the law, consisting of his privilege of
commanding the assistance of the law in the assertion of
certain claims, the law, without the exercise of his will, remaining passive, is shown to be incorrect by two considerations: (1) The law will often compel the observance of
rights without being called upon by the parties interested:
e.g. in the protection of life and health. It will often, also,
compel the assertion of rights by those, or at any rate
in behalf of those, who possess them. E.g., in the protection
of the rights of those who are subject to guardianship. In
both these classes of cases there is a connexion between
private rights and public interests. Some rights it is safe
to leave to be asserted by individuals; but in the assertion
of others the state must more or less

Still further Merkel

fully interest itself.

(2) In those cases where the law permits the individual
to do foolish or dangerous things, it prevents third persons
from interfering, but it holds the person who exercises the
right responsible in its exercise.

The definition of Right given above does not exactly
correspond with the meaning attached in juristic usage to

the phrase *das subjektive Recht.* That usage does not include in the word Right *every* case in which individual interests are supplied with means of protection or realization through the power of the law; but only those cases in wh. a definite part of that power is applied or adapted to a definite interest of a particular kind, and is thereby in a certain sense individualized,—where some specific interest becomes, as it were, a direct product of the law itself. This characteristic is easily recognized, for example, in the legal means of enforcing the claims of creditors, in the laws of property, in the political rights of electors and representatives, etc. These are made specific subjects of legal protection. But jurisprudence takes no notice of the 'right' to take a ride or to read the newspaper because the law affords such 'rights' no specific or special protection, but simply recognizes them *inter ceteros*, as incidents, perhaps, which are given special recognition or structure in the law.

Merkel's meaning

The Establishment of Jural Relationships: The function of law is not, in general, creative, but regulative. It constructs out of the existing circumstances of a people a system of ordered peace by means of which, while prevailing needs and convictions are observed, conditions will be developed and bettered in individual cases. Thus it gives to Possession and to relationships of power or authority the character of jural relationships, without regard to the manner of their creation; either recognizing them as they are, or with a view to their having a certain duration, or a certain growth, etc.

This is true, however, in varying degrees. The more law asserts itself within a certain sphere, and thought develops itself touching laws, and existing conditions attain a certain independence of jural existence, the more do considerations assert themselves concerning the way in which new relationships come into existence, the more is a critical standard applied to the means of their establishment; they are attacked and defended, and movement is sought in some direction which will express the common interests and convictions. In other words, law-making becomes a self-conscious means of development, and is conducted in accordance with standards established by means of a critical examination of existing conditions, of the circumstances under which those conditions came into existence, and of the normal di-

This is Merkel's

rection of change. Take, as an example under these statements, modern economic legislation.

Among the transactions in wh. jural relationships take their rise the dealings of those parties take the first place who are clothed with rights, or of those who are charged with duties. Among these there are *Rechtsgeschäfte* and breaches of law. The former are actions wh. are intended to establish, to satisfy (or to alter or abolish) certain legal relationships, in accordance with the intentions of positive law.[4] Breaches of law, on the other hand, are actions wh. withstand the laws, and the interests wh. are under their protection, and whose legal operation works against him who undertakes them.

Both in *Rechtsgeschäfte* and in breach of law there must be two things: an overt act and an intention..

The conception of *Attribution* calls for a closer examination. It has the same significance in all of the various spheres of law, even when its application is not similarly regulated for all cases, and not accompanied by the same consequences to the person concerned. Its application is relative to incidents which possess an objective importance for the interests protected. The attribution of such incidents, however, involves a two-fold judgment: viz. (a) a causal judgment, to the effect that these incidents can be referred to the will of a particular person, and (b) a distributive judgment, to the effect that, by reason of this causal relationship, these incidents shall be charged to the person from whose will they proceeded, and the claim of person damaged be reckoned, in proportion to the manner in wh. the interests of the latter have been affected.

Within the sphere of law, the word Attribution is used to denote acts wh. violate the legal interests of third persons, to wh. also a negative value is at-

Merkel's also

tributable. This use of the term excludes the ascription of *debt* on the part of the person to whom the offence is attributed. Debt arises out of the faithless conduct of a person, for which specifically he is brought to book. The conception of debt has nothing to do with the attribution of facts shown: it rests upon proof of a jural relationship already existing. There is a broad distinction between debt and damages.

[4] E.g. The agreements between lessor and lessee. [WW's note]

Attribution presupposes that the person to whom acts are attributed was at the moment of their commission in a condition to realize their significance, that he is capable of exercising his individuality and caring for his interests, and that he has freedom of will, etc., etc.

Many regard law solely as that which is brought into existence by the establishment of legal relationships and their connexion with legally significant actual conditions. According to this view, the consequences of legal transactions (*Rechtsgeschäfte*) have the same significance as the consequences of breaches of law, and liability to damages the same significance as liability to criminal punishment.

As a matter of fact, however, the creative power of law is very limited. Its real function is to furnish forms, measures (standards), criteria, and sanctions for those phenomena and transactions of society (with their ethical and purposeful incidents) wh. arise out of the natural play of existing interests and circumstances, and wh., at least in great part, even if imperfectly and precariously, would exist and take shape without its assistance, by virtue of the independent energy of individual and social forces.

The repeal, for example, of all laws respecting purchase and sale would not of a sudden destroy trade and

Merkel proceeds

commerce: it would only confuse, weaken, imperil their transactions by depriving them of all legal form or force. Should the law no longer concern itself with murder or arson, it would only throw society back upon its resources of self-help: it would not free murderers and incendiaries from punishment. Nowhere, however, are the selective, formative, and dignifying functions of law more conspicuous than in its organization of coöperation against such offences,—as to its original forms and its progressive development.

It follows that the connexion between actual conditions and the operations of law is not a merely arbitrary connexion. In the first place, real factors are operative in this connexion whose working follows psychological laws and cannot be arbitrarily set aside. In the second place, there is prevalent in this whole sphere a *naturalis ratio* whose interpreters are the people's conscience and the peoples understanding, and, in a broad sense, science and legislation; a *naturalis ratio*, indeed, touching which what has already been said about the relativity of legal truths holds good.

Among the points of view which possess importance, as a result of this *naturalis ratio* in respect of the connexion between facts and legal consequences, one may be given prominence. It concerns the qu., What sort of obligations shall result from legal transactions and breaches of law, as well as from other transactions, arising out of individual interests but possessing importance for the legal interests of third parties; and it issues in this, that conditions shall be realized between those who act and those whose interests are affected by the action under wh. the making good of

Merkel holds:

the interests and of the entire transactions of the former shall consist with the welfare of the latter, and under wh. the law may maintain its sovereignty and execute its decrees. This point of view contains a fundamental element of the legal thought of all peoples, and innumerable regulations of the law now obtaining among us range themselves under it. This is true of the entire contents of criminal law. So, too, of those rules of law wh. determine damages and the obligations of contract, and afford means of enforcing them.

The binding character of a contract depends, for the most part, upon the intentions of the contracting parties: a contract is binding because they will it to be so. Why, however, should not a subsequent inconsistent purpose have the same validity; why should the first declaration of purpose acquire the force of a legal duty? Because, not the purpose alone suffices to constitute a contract (that by itself is immaterial), but the means of its expression and the manner in which it affects the interests of the other contracting parties, and thus brings itself within the scope of the principles of law which protect interests thus created. It is not the mere purpose, but the transactions corresponding to the purpose and the relationships established between those transactions and the interests or welfare of others, that bind the individual. Not only breaches of contract, but all breaches of law do violence to rights: we are not at liberty to do anything wh. injuriously affects the life, health, safety, or property of others.

It is this principle wh. enters into all reckonings as to the consequences of breaches of law: the principle

Merkel

of the damage done, the judgment granting damages, commanding restitution, etc. etc. A similar principle lies at the foundation of criminal law. Breaches of law assume the character of crimes because of the peculiar or the universal character of their consequences to other persons, or to the community at large.

When we hold men responsible for a correspondence between their actions and the established legal order we do so upon the presupposition that we are dealing with accountable persons and imputable deeds. The general principle upon wh. accountability rests is *freedom of will*; and those who disagree with the general opinion with regard to freedom of the will fail to observe that this freedom underlies also all responsibility of action under Private, as well as under Criminal, law. The whole of law, indeed, is based upon the presupposition that the deeds of men proceed from their natures, and are connected with these natures by the law of cause and effect. Freedom of the will, the reflection of personality in action, the correspondence between intention and deed,—these are the fundamental concepts, the major premises, of legal responsibility,—and of law itself. There is no other conceivable basis for any part of the fabric of law.   21 August, 1891

WWhw translation in bound notebook inscribed on cover (WWhw): "Notes on *Merkel. Jurisprudence* Woodrow Wilson" (WP, DLC).

From William Royal Wilder

My dear Wilson: New York, August 4th, 1891
    Are you spending the summer at Princeton or somewhere along the shore, or are you occasionally in town. I would like to run across you sometime between now and September first for a few moments chat. I am here almost continuously, and can be found nights at a cottage near the Wilburton at Spring Lake and I am at all times,   Sincerely yours,   Wm. R Wilder

TLS (WP, DLC) with WWhw notation on env.: "Ans. Aug 5/91."

From Joseph Ruggles Wilson

                    Saratoga Springs, N. Y.
My precious Woodrow—   August 10 1891
    I am here you see—reluctantly but rightly no doubt. My stay need not be long; one week will probably be quite enough for all health-purposes, and as to any other I am indifferent. Besides the expense is great.
    I unexpectedly met your friend Hazen of Middletown. He

was very cordial, on your account no doubt; but would have been so on my own account were I half a[s] likeable as he is. He seems to love you with a true affection. Miss Russell[1] and some other Middletownians were with him, who all spoke of you and Ellie with enthusiasm.

The best preaching I have heard lately was by Dr. Cannon on yesterday, and the worst (nearly) by some one last night who has a Reverend piazzaing his name.[2] The crowd here is large and ever larger. And the annoyances to a quietly disposed individual are proportionally many. But anything may be endured when necessity puts the burden on. I hope that your book progresses as rapidly and as favorably as you can wish, and that all the residue will be as full of excellences as the portions finished. My headquarters are still at #33 East 22nd St., which is also my post-office address.[3]

Love to dear Ellie.

Yours with unbounded affection—Father.

ALS (WP, DLC) with WWhw notation on env.: "Ans. Aug. 14/91."

  [1] Undoubtedly Frances Ann Russell, niece of Samuel Russell, builder of the Russell House, now Wesleyan's Honors College.

  [2] "Dr. Cannon" was perhaps the Rev. Dr. John Franklin Cannon, pastor of the Grand Avenue Presbyterian Church of St. Louis. The name of the evening preacher is unknown, as the files of the Saratoga Springs *Saratogian* for this period are no longer extant.

  [3] The home of Dr. Wilson's friend, Elizabeth Bartlett Grannis, editor of the New York *Church Union.*

From William Royal Wilder

My Dear Wilson: New York, August 10th, 1891

Yours to hand; and I thank you most heartily for your kind invitation, which later in the season I will be most happy to accept, unless I have the good fortune to run across you here in the city. My engagements at the shore with my family are such that I cannot get away for a night with you at Princeton until after the 24th, when I will be glad to do business with you at the old classical stand, if you are still of the same mind.

Faithfully yours,   Wm. R. Wilder

TLS (WP, DLC).

From John Franklin Jameson

My dear Wilson: Woburn, Mass., August 10, 1891.

The New England summer has set in with its usual severity, immediately upon my arrival, and as Woburn is a warm town,

this is a warm house, and I have the warmest room in it, it is doubtful whether my fingers will long continue to hold the pen, or will melt and dissolve themselves into a dew. But I will at least remark that I am well and got here safely. I interrupted the journalistic toils of Shaw and Bob Finley during much of Monday, but did not find John Finley[1] or Alden[2] in. Munro, my assistant professor,[3] and his wife were on the Providence steamer, just from Europe. Harry Gardner[4] and his wife have got home by this time. Wilson[5] has just married, too, so that I shall be in a painfully small minority in our historical and political faculty. Tomorrow I go over to Providence to spend the rest of the week in preparation for next year and in other work. Soon after I shall go up to Kennebunkport to spend a week or two with my sisters and Mrs. Carey. Since I got here I have done no very active work,—just a little reading and writing; and have seen no one that you know, save that this morning, going to the Riverside Press on an errand about my little book,[6] I saw our exuberant friend Mifflin.[7] It was, I learn, not true that Adams had accepted the call of the exhibitionaries;[8] whether he has since done so I know not. George Howard, of the Univ of Kansas, has been called to the Stanford.[9] I have received Todd's[10] cards. Please give my kindest regards to Mrs. Wilson, and tell her I enjoyed my visit exceedingly; also to your father, who is better, I hope. Please kiss the girls for me,—meaning specifically your daughters,—and believe me
Sincerely yours,   J. F. Jameson.

ALS (WP, DLC) with WWhw notation on env.: "Ans, Aug. 14 '91."
  1 John Huston Finley, born near Grand Ridge, Ill., Oct. 19, 1863. A.B., Knox College, 1887; graduate student, the Johns Hopkins, 1887-89. Secretary, State Charities Aid Association of New York City, 1889-92. President of Knox College, 1892-99. Editor, *Harper's Weekly* and *McClure's Magazine*, 1899-1900; founder with Walter H. Page of *World's Work*. Professor of Politics, Princeton University, 1900-1903; President, College of the City of New York, 1903-13; Commissioner of Education, New York State, 1913-21. Associate Editor, *New York Times*, 1921-37; Editor-in-Chief, 1937-38. Prolific author and one of the promoters of the *Dictionary of American Biography*. Died March 7, 1940.
  2 Edmund K. Alden, an employee of the Century Company.
  3 Wilfred Harold Munro, who had in fact just been appointed Associate Professor of History at Brown University.
  4 Henry Brayton Gardner, at this time Associate Professor of Political Economy at Brown.
  5 George Grafton Wilson, at this time Associate Professor of Political and Social Science at Brown.
  6 *The History of Historical Writing in America* (Boston and New York, 1891).
  7 George H. Mifflin of Houghton Mifflin.
  8 Professor Herbert Baxter Adams of the Johns Hopkins had, during the spring of 1891, received several attractive offers from the University of Chicago. After considerable negotiation with both the Hopkins and Chicago administrations, Adams decided to remain at his post in Baltimore.
  9 George Elliott Howard, at this time Professor of History at the University of Nebraska, not the University of Kansas. He went to Stanford as Professor of History in the autumn of 1891.
  10 Henry Alfred Todd, at this time Associate in Romance Languages at the Johns Hopkins; he had been married on July 30.

From Albert Bushnell Hart

Dear Prof. Wilson: Cohasset, Mass., August 14, 1891.

A brief attack of illness has driven me to accept for myself the plan you suggested for your volume. I must write vol II as I go over the ground in lectures, and my copy will not be ready till well into the next academic year.

But my maps are nearly ready, and the publishers are desirous of issuing the whole series of maps, immediately, in advance of the publication of Vols II and III. The sketches are to be placed in their hands as soon as possible, and I should like therefore to settle with you the maps for your volume.

The Colonies contains, as I remember

No 1. Physical features

    2, 4. North America in 1650, 1750

    3 Colonies in 1700

Vol II will contain

No 1. Territorial gvm't of the U S 1775-1865

No 2. English Colonies 1763-1775

    3, 4 5, U S in 1783, 1801, 1825

For Vol III I propose as a frontispiece a novel map showing the states as to freedom or slavery of the parts of the U S from 1775 to 1865. This is a mere question of fact, except of course as to the legal effect of the Compromise of 1850, Kansas Nebraska Act of 1854, Dred Scott decision and Proclamation of Emancipation. Here the map and text should agree. I propose to treat each act as legally binding, so far as it goes: and to treat as free territory only that in which by positive law no person can be born a slave and none can be introduced from without and sold as a slave. It is all plain sailing on this basis to 1848. I propose to consider California and New Mexico as free (so Clay considered); New Mexico & Utah as not free by Comp. of 1850, the La. purchase not affected; by the Act of 1854 freedom lost to all territories west of the Miss.; by Dred Scott Decision freedom lost to the remnant of the N. W. Territory[.] Then I propose to show the effect of the admission of free states, of the Act of 1862 prohibiting slavery in the territories; then I propose to consider the Proclamation of Emancipation as operative within the limits which it announced: then to accept the abolition acts of Mo., West Va & Md (though of course we know that the Mo & Md acts did not represent the real will of the people); then to leave the 13th amdt to apply to Del. & Ky. If you differ from this view in any respect, please indicate your dissidence and its grounds. You see I mean to state only facts, accepting the legal effect of the acts and proclamation, although in a cooler time they might have been doubted, and they were doubted.

The other four maps I propose to make as follows, unless you have changes to suggest

No 2. N. E Boundary—N W Boundary—Texas Controversy (3 small maps)

No 3 U S Mar 4, 1851

No. 4 U. S. Mar 4 1863

No 5 U. S. Mar 4, 1891

If, as you have sketched the field in your mind, you wish to substitute another date for any of these, please indicate your wish. In the '63 map can be shown all necessary places for the Civil War—I take it that the military history will be very brief. 1851 shows the settlement by the Compromise of 1850

The publishers propose to put the 14 maps together in a cover, and sell them for fifty cents.

From all appearances the Epoch series is likely to be a good deal used.

An early answer, even out of your well-earned vacation, will much oblige,

Your sincere friend,   Albert Bushnell Hart

ALS (WP, DLC) with WWhw notation on env.: "Ans. 21 Aug/91."

To John Franklin Jameson

My dear Jameson,   Princeton, New Jersey, 14 August, 1891

I was glad to get your letter, though I grieved to learn that the hot weather had extended to the city of Woburn, and that you had to set off for Providence in the midst of it. I hope the relief has come to you by this time, as it has come to us.

I of course kept quietly on at my work, in spite of the intense heat: a fellow that's Epoch-making cannot afford to stop for a little weather! I should assuredly stop making Epochs, however, were all weather like that hereabouts,—and should begin making tracks.

Nothing, of course, happens here: every thing that happens comes to us by way of the newspapers: our news is common news. Still, we don't mind it: we keep busy and grow selfish in this cosey nook of a town: and wait for the students to come like a rush of wind from another sphere,—and wake us up. In the morning I write; in the afternoon Mrs. Wilson sketches—and that seems to us to complete the day.

My father left us the day after you did, and is now in Saratoga, where he hopes much from the waters, which usually do him much good. He gave me, by the way, one note for your bibliography. He says that some very excellent sketches of southern life before the war were contributed to a paper called the *South Western Presbyterian*, published at New Orleans, under the title "Plantation Life," by Rev. Dr. R. Q. Mallard.[1] A note addressed to the paper, or to Dr. Mallard would probably put you in the way of getting these. A letter addressed to Dr. R. Q. Mallard, New Orleans, La., would doubtless reach him: father could not give me any more specific address or the year in which the series of papers were published, but they were recent.

Give our warmest regards to Mrs. Carey when you see her, and remind your sisters of my having met them by giving them my regards. Please remember me also to your father and mother.

We enjoyed your visit thoroughly and trust that it may very speedily be repeated. Cordially Yours, Woodrow Wilson

ALS (J. F. Jameson Papers, DLC).
[1] Robert Q. Mallard's "Plantation Life Before Emancipation," published in twenty-five installments in the New Orleans *Southwestern Presbyterian*, Nov. 6, 1890-May 21, 1891, was published in book form under the same title in Richmond in 1892.

To Albert Bushnell Hart

My dear Prof. Hart,   Princeton, N. J., 21 August 1891

I should have answered your letter the day it came, had I not been suffering from a temporary illness (slight but immediately concerning my nerves) which rendered it painful for me at the time to write even a letter. I am sincerely sorry to learn of your own indisposition. I trust that you now feel quite recovered.

I have read your letter with care, of course, and quite agree to the plan proposed as to the maps. Amid the confused politics of the period 1848-'65 there is nothing to do, inasmuch as a map cannot be polemical, or hold a brief for a party, but to accept each act of Congress, each decision of the Supreme Court, and each formally valid act of State legislatures, as accomplishing what it purposed to accomplish. I shall so treat the questions involved in the text, too.

The small boundary maps will be all the more necessary and serviceable because I shall give questions of boundary no detailed discussion at all. Since it is necessary in so small a volume to pick and choose topics (I half wish I had time and the consent of the publishers to make two volumes out of my 'Epoch'—as I understand Burgess is to do in writing of the same period for the Scribner Epochs[1]) I shall confine myself to those which *make politics* and seriously affect development.

I have taken no vacation as yet—and do not mean to take any—if nature will but indulge me. Almost one-half my *mss.* is in some sort of shape: perhaps by the time college opens two-thirds of it will be.

With sincere regard,

Cordially Yours,   Woodrow Wilson

ALS (de Coppet Coll., NjP).
1 John William Burgess eventually published three titles in Scribner's "American History Series": *The Middle Period, 1817-1858* (New York, 1897); *The Civil War and the Constitution, 1859-1865* (2 vols., New York, 1901); and *Reconstruction and the Constitution, 1866-1876* (New York, 1902).

A Book Review

[*c. Aug. 22, 1891*]

Studies in Constitutional Law: France—England—United States.— By ÉMILE BOUTMY. Translated from the French by E. M. DICEY, with an Introduction by A. V. DICEY, D. C. L. New York: Macmillan & Co., 1891, pp. xiv, 183.

This stimulating and suggestive book, with its lively style, its strong individuality of method and of view, its surprising accuracy of information and certainty of insight, has been known and prized by specialists ever since its first publication in 1885: this translation of it makes it accessible to English readers, and ought to be the means of giving it the wide popularity it deserves. The first of the three essays it contains sketches briefly and rapidly, but with a very sure touch, with sufficient historical explanation, and with many acute comments, the various and diverse sources of English constitutional law and practice; the second analyzes, at considerably greater length, our own constitutional structure, its state and its federal, its documentary and its customary parts; the third rounds out the other two in a most interesting and suggestive way by discussing the spirit and historical genesis of English and American institutions in comparison with the spirit and history of French political developments.

There is a singular *naïveté* in the self-confidence with which M. Boutmy smiles, now at the ignorance, and again at the mental characteristics of his own countrymen, and acts as schoolmaster to other French students of constitutional law in the study of English and American political arrangements. But there is no touch of arrogance in the urbane and placid way in which it is all done, and M. Boutmy furnishes on almost every page abundant justification of the assumption that he knows what he is talking about.

Evidences are not wanting that he is himself a Frenchman, who sometimes finds it just a little difficult to occupy the

English or American point of view. It makes one stare to read in a preface written in 1888 that "the question of secession is not yet closed" in the United States, and that there is still a chance that we may have several federal republics upon this continent instead of one. It seems odd to us to find Georgia put along with Massachusetts, Connecticut, and Pennsylvania in a generalization as to density of population and rate of immigration when speaking of a period preceding the war (p. 132); we can hardly agree that our constitutional Declarations of Right were in the nature of commercial advertisements, meant to attract immigrants (pp. 129, 130); we wonder when we read (p. 10) that there was a time, not a hundred years ago, when the practical independence of Ireland might have been quickly accomplished; it is evidently out of keeping with the author's general (perfectly true) view of English constitutional development, that it has been a history of practical expedients and not a history of the carrying out of systematic plans, to say (p. 48) that the English "did not *intend* their Constitution to be a compact whole," and that constitutional items of law, "instead of being marked out and easily distinguished, are *purposely* mixed up with ordinary laws, and allowed to fall out of view." Many individual judgments contained in the volume may well be doubted.

But these are only incidents, perhaps we might say only accidents, in the general progress of an exposition almost uniformly admirable, and at some points,—notably in the third essay,—rising to quite unusual heights of excellence and suggestiveness. Under M. Boutmy's handling familiar institutions assume a new significance, are clothed with a new life. Those who do not read this little volume will have missed a principal source of information and inspiration.

The style of the translator is excellent. It is not exactly M. Boutmy's style; a rather surprising license of free translation is observable throughout. But the spirit of the original is very well preserved, and at almost every point its true significance.

WOODROW WILSON.[1]

Princeton University.

Printed in the New York *Educational Review*, II (Nov. 1891), 392-93.
  [1] As his reading date at the end of this book reveals, Wilson finished it on August 22, 1891. Handwritten notes and a shorthand draft of this review, tucked into the volume, indicate that Wilson wrote his review immediately after reading Boutmy, hence the composition date ascribed to it.

From Albert Bushnell Hart

Dear Prof. Wilson: Cohasset, Mass., Aug. 23, 1891.
    Yours of the 21st is at hand, and I am much pleased to learn

of the advance of Vol. III. I am myself quite well again, but shall not try to accomplish anything except the maps for the three volumes. I have sent the sketches to the publishers; and will ask them to send their first sketches to you for examination and suggestion. Please send them to me, as fast as you receive them, with any corrections that you find necessary or desirable. My address is *Cohasset, Mass.* (Lothrop Mansion) till Sept 10.

The limits of the series are narrow: for I think the plan of finishing it up in three volumes will ensure it a large use as a college text-book, which a longer series could not attain. There is great need for a *brief* history of the U. S. such as the three volumes will form

What do you know about the Scribner Series? I have heard various rumors about it, vox et praeterea nihil

Are you not coming up this way some time soon?

Sincerely yours,   Albert Bushnell Hart

ALS (WP, DLC).

From Robert Ewing

My dear Mr Wilson,   Nashville, Tenn. Aug 26 1891

Please pardon the delay in answering your letter received about two weeks since. Immediately on its receipt I applied to the party on the "American" newspaper here, whom I thought could get a place for your brother and until yesterday I had hoped for success; but another has been appointed and I delay no longer. The managing editor was about to retire on account off [of] ill health and it was the vacancy that his retirement would have caused that I hoped to have Mr Joseph fill, but they concluded to give the place to one who formerly held it, but who had been in Memphis for the past four years, at work on the Appeal-Avalanche. I regret this exceedingly, partly because I have been unable to oblige you and partly because your brothers residence here would have been a personal pleasure to us. I inferred from your letter that Joseph wanted to continue in the newspaper work and therefore tried in this line. If there was a possible opening in this Company, (with which I have just become connected)[1] I would do my best to obtain it for him, but the iron market has been so exceedingly dull, that we will shortly have to part with some salaried men we now have. I will do everything I can to aid your brother both on his account and yours.

Tell your good wife we have another little boy at our house. This puts us in the 9 hole. I wrote Mr Hoyt[2] that Mosaic & early Christian names "had done give out" and we had resorted to

fiction & called him Esmond. Hattie³ is recovering rapidly & looks
well. Stocktons visit to us was a genuine pleasure. We tried to
get him to steal a few days & give them to us, but he could not.
Give our love to E & children   Very Truly   R. Ewing

ALS (WP, DLC) with WWhw notation on env.: "Ans. Sept. 8/91."
    ¹ The Southern Iron Company of Nashville, of which he was vice president.
    ² His father-in-law, the Rev. Dr. Thomas Alexander Hoyt of Philadelphia.
    ³ His wife, Harriet Hoyt Ewing.

From Stockton Axson

The Review of Reviews   New York
Dear Brother Woodrow: Saturday Afternoon [Aug. 29, 1891]
    I have seen Uncle Randolph and Ellen¹—both are looking well.
They will leave for Princeton Monday afternoon if they can get
away but as their departure depends upon some tailoring which
Uncle R is having done it is possible that they will not leave before
Tuesday afternoon. If I can find out anything more definite I will
let you know.
    I saw Dr [J. R.] Wilson and he is *magnificent* in appearance.
He thinks of going to Princeton Monday. I will let him know of
Uncle R's arrival and they may all go down together.
    As matters stand I shall remain in New York this Sunday.
Dr Shaw is away and I am not disposed of yet.² In the mean time
I am helping to make the October number of the "R of Rs."
    Warmest love for all
                Affectionately yours   Stockton Axson

ALS (WP, DLC).
    ¹ Randolph Axson and his daughter.
    ² Stockton was about to leave for Wesleyan University for graduate study
in English literature under Professor Winchester.

An Essay

[September 1891]
THE STUDY OF POLITICS.

    I suppose that it is to be reckoned one of the very first duties
of the University Extension lecturer that he make his subject
vital and interesting; that he adapt his whole method to exciting
an intelligent and, if may be, permanent curiosity concerning the
topics of which he treats. If this be true, he must resist all
temptation to be doctrinaire. Nothing doctrinaire is interesting to
the man of the world, or, in politics, ought to be interesting to
anybody. The study of politics is a study of life; of the life of
States, the close organization of peoples into communities, their

wide organization into commonwealths, their united efforts towards the attainment of common ends. Nice theories do not fit the study of such things, for theories must be logical and life need not be, indeed, seldom is; it can be learned only by familiar association with it, can be penetrated only by insight, deciphered only by close and repeated scrutiny.

The first thing to be understood, therefore, in undertaking the study of politics is that it is not a mere study of facts—unless, indeed, we are to give to the word "facts" a meaning so wide as to include every aspect of life. Of course the play of my imagination is a fact (at least if it be allowed that I have one), but we do not call a study of the imagination a study of facts, but a study of mental processes, of the laws of thought. Nation differs from nation, in habits, aptitudes, ambitions, needs, desires, and a system of politics which will suit one nation may be eminently unsuitable for another, its neighbor. There is, accordingly, no one best system of government, but for each nation there is some sort of government which is best adapted to its wants and capacities, most appropriate and helpful in its present stage of development. When once this idea is fully accepted, as it must be by every student qualified to judge, it is impossible to be doctrinaire, to travel any longer the "high *priori*" road of political speculation.

The reason why one polity suits one nation and another, another is that institutions match the thought of the people to which they belong; revolution comes when the thought of the people has become intolerant of its form of government. It follows, therefore, that if we would know politics on the broad scale we must match patterns of thought with patterns of political structure, fit peoples into their institutions in our conceptions of systems, realize how those institutions are made up out of their ideals. Of course it is no easy matter to study the thought of a nation, for its thought is not a simple but an infinitely complex thing. Its way of looking at things is compounded of ancient prejudices most obscurely derived and constructed, of social conventions most variously acquired and based upon many partially hidden ideas, of a score of items most curiously extracted from a history full of variety and change. There is nothing in the life of a people which does not in some way affect its politics; there is nothing, consequently, in that life which is intrinsically foreign to the inquiries of the student of politics. But there are things which lie close to his subject and things which obviously lie remote from it, and he must limit himself to those things which afford him direct suggestion.

There are some things which directly affect the political spirit of a people—such, for example, as the family relationships, the laws of property and inheritance, the usages of local government, the personal characteristics and ambitions of the families which have ruled over them, the wars which have subjugated or the struggles which have liberated them. All these things are the proper theme of the student of politics. He may consent to a division of labor with the historian, and allow the latter to supply him with the facts he desires to found his reasoning upon; but he must know these things even if he be forced to discover them for himself. His own more than proper field of first-hand exploration is the political literature of the world, which, he will soon discover, is apt to lie as often in the poetry as in the systematic disquisitions of the people he is studying. There is as much Greek politics (between the lines) in Homer as in Aristotle; there is hardly less in Milton than in Burke; there is more, if only what is sound be reckoned, in several of the Victorian poets than in Bentham. The sentiments of a people are as of the heart stuff of their politics. Their principles are not formulas, but affections and beliefs. These may or may not be logical; they are seldom consistent.

Another important consequence of these doctrines, if they be true, is that to study one government alone is to understand none at all. I have often had my doubts about the possibility of making good citizens by the very simple process of filling the heads of schoolboys with an analysis of the Constitution of the United States. It is hard to imagine anyone gaining an affection for that distinguished document in that way. Patriotism and correct political principle do not enter the mind by way of the memoriter task. Their best vehicle must always be found in something that appeals to the heart and gives play to the practical imagination. It is the saving virtue of the historical and comparative method of teaching politics that it does give play to the practical imagination, and does excite sentiments of approval and disapproval. To some persons, we must admit, our own institutions do not seem either ideal or superexcellent in themselves; but to everybody, we may be sure, they must seem admirable by comparison with the institutions of other times and peoples which they have superseded, and the very difficulties which were overcome in their establishment ought to appeal to imaginations of every grade. There was such good fighting in the process of their upbuilding, such stubborn persistency, so many dramatic combinations and tragical situations! Other races have developed so much more slowly, and accomplished so much less. There is excitement and pride in the tale. We see it all only when we look away from our own institutions and history to those of other peoples whom we have outstripped.

All these things, the features of other polities, and the contrasts between those polities and our own, may be traced in broad lines or they may be traced in minute detail; in a course of six lectures, or in a course of reading planned for busy people, the lines must obviously be broad and general. But there is the broad outline of the mechanical draughtsman and the sketch of the artist; there is the inventory and the picture. The broad lines which are to tell must make choice of characteristic features, must suggest artistic groupings, must indicate color even where they cannot employ it. The method in University Extension—the method both of the lecturer and of the reader—must be the popular method, though only in the sense which is not inconsistent with scholarship. The greater the artist, the more popular his method; which, being translated, means that the consummate master of his materials, the employer of genius in the use of them, produces what will tell on all minds, what will be popular in the sense of being universally understood and appreciated.

The same is true in politics. Here the student studies, not what can be produced and modified in a laboratory, not elements which can be handled and experimented with, but the life, the powers and the subordinations, the habits and the capacities of the people themselves; and if these elements be not popular they cannot be political. Politics is as essentially popular as Shakespeare's thought is Shakespearian; and assuredly what inheres in the life of a people ought to be susceptible of being clearly and simply explained to them, and need not suffer deterioration in the process. It is essentially picturesque also, and ought not to be considered damaged for the uses of the laborious investigator when held up in its picturesque aspects.

This is an excellent and stimulating programme, no doubt; but what of the practicable and available means of carrying it out? Of the lecture part of it I shall not speak; each lecturer must, of course, adopt methods of exposition, approved by his own literary and artistic judgment. Of a course of reading it is less difficult to speak; for although there are few books ideally adapted for the purpose, there are some of the first order of excellence, and many of an order next to the first, and a short course need not go beyond these.

The shortest course I can think of would begin with Bagehot's "Physics and Politics." I venture to say that there is more stimulation in this book than in any other modern writing on the history of political development. It quickens and fertilizes the imagination—the scientific imagination—imparts a sense of reality to the obscure matter of the first formations of political society, and sets a pace for the student in his subsequent reading. This might very properly be followed by a very different book—the more different the better—Mr. John Fiske's "American Political Ideas." Because of its broad view, its lucid and effective style, its firm grasp upon commanding principles of development, this book engages the attention of the reader throughout, and throughout excites a healthy desire on his part to know more of the matters discussed. After this, again, let the reader take up Bagehot's inimitable work on the "English Constitution." That will give him an insight into the spirit and methods of English politics, and an understanding of the structure of the English government such as he can get nowhere else. Then let him return to Mr. John Fiske and read his little volume on "Civil Government in the United States," in which he has succeeded in setting forth with great felicity and good judgment the origins and operations of our complex federal system. Last of all, I would make bold to suggest that he read a book of my own entitled "Congressional Government." I venture to name it in this connection because it is the only brief treatise upon the practical spirit and method of our national politics.

These five books it might be well for each member of a local University Extension centre to own, as affording him a brief and general introduction to the study of politics. Their use will be one of stimulation rather than of formal instruction; they will excite his curiosity, and when that is done the rest of his reading will come without effort or difficulty, and will not need much guidance. He will search out for himself the books he wants upon the particular questions which have most arrested his attention, and will have become systematic in the best way. The best system is not that prescribed in a fixed course of reading, but a diligent satisfaction of intelligent curiosity; the system of the individual mind itself.

Below I give three lists of books: first, a list the books in which could be bought, I estimate, for about twenty-five dollars; second, a fifty-dollar list; and third, a hundred-dollar list. In the second and third lists I repeat the titles of the lists preceding, in a somewhat briefer form, for the purpose of showing the order in which, in my judgment, the books should be taken up for study. I have followed throughout in my choice of titles for these lists the same rule: to give preference to interesting and suggestive books and exclude those which are merely technical, or primarily intended for the student of detail; and I have, of course, laid the chief emphasis in my choice of subjects upon our own institutions and those of the mother country.

It should be the chief object of the student of politics to study the life of states, and, to that end, to comprehend their histories. And not to comprehend them merely, but also to get their spirit, if possible, into his brain, so that he may think of them as they think of themselves, perceiving the power of their ideals, feeling the compulsion of their fortunes, realizing the coherence and necessity of their characteristic developments. This is not easy, but it is delightful when once it has been fairly engaged in. The teaching of politics ought to be more easily accomplished, its study may reasonably be expected to prove more irresistibly attractive, in the United States than anywhere else in the world. For certainly when Aristotle declared man to be by nature a political animal he hit the character of the Americans who were to come after him as neatly as he hit the character of the Greeks, his contemporaries. The average American understands politics as instinctively as he understands bargaining; he is skilled in the rules of the game and has a quick imagination for all its turns and disclosures. If he cannot be interested in the systematic study of it, it must be the fault of the books or of the teachers he resorts to; it is not because he is not kin to the subject.

1. Twenty-five dollar list:

"Physics and Politics," by Walter Bagehot, (International Scientific series). $1.10

"Ancient Law," by Sir H. S. Maine. $2.60

"The Ancient City," by Fustel de Coulanges. $1.60

"The Spirit of Laws," by Montesquieu (Bohn's Library). 2 vols. $2.00

"The Rise and Progress of the English Constitution," by Sir Edward Creasy. $2.10

"The English Constitution," by Walter Bagehot. $1.50

"The Development of Constitutional Liberty in the English Colonies of America," by E. G. Scott. $1.90

"American Political Ideas," by John Fiske. 75 cents.

"Civil Government in the United States," by John Fiske. $1.00

"Congressional Government," by Woodrow Wilson. 90 cents.

"The American Commonwealth," by James Bryce. 2 vols. $1.75

The Clarendon Press Selections from Burke's Works. 3 vols. $3.25

"On Liberty," by John Stuart Mill. 90 cents

"Liberty, Equality, Fraternity," by Sir J. F. Stephen. $1.50

"State and Federal Government in Switzerland," by J. M. Vincent. $1.28

"France As It Is," by André Lebon and Paul Pelet. $1.90

"The State," by Woodrow Wilson for general reference. $2.00

2. Fifty-dollar list:

Bagehot's "Physics and Politics."

Maine's "Ancient Law."

Coulanges' "The Ancient City."

The "Politics of Aristotle." Welldon's translation. $1.90

Montesquieu's "Spirit of Laws."

"Two Treatises on Government," by John Locke (Morley's University Library). 30 cents.

"A Short History of Anglo-Saxon Freedom," by J. K. Hosmer. $1.50

Creasy's "Rise and Progress of the English Constitution."

"The English Constitution," by Émile Boutmy. $1.35

Bagehot's "English Constitution."

"The Central Government," by H. D. Traill (English Citizen series). 75 cents.

"Local Government," by M. D. Chalmers (same series). 75 cents.

"The Law of the Constitution," by A. V. Dicey. $2.60

Scott's "Development of Constitutional Liberty."

Fiske's "American Political Ideas."

"Studies in Constitutional Law," by Émile Boutmy. $1.35

Fiske's "Civil Government in the United States."

"Democracy in America," by A. de Tocqueville. 2 vols. $3.75
Wilson's "Congressional Government."
Bryce's "American Commonwealth."
"Henry Clay," by Carl Schurz (American Statesmen series). 90 cents.
"Federal Government in Canada," by J. G. Bourinot. 85 cents
"Problems of Greater Britain," by Sir C. W. Dilke. $3.60
Clarendon Press Selections from Burke.
Mill's "Liberty."
Stephen's "Liberty, Equality, Fraternity."
"Switzerland," by Hug and Stead (Stories of the Nations series). $1.10
"A Sketch of the Germanic Constitution from Early Times to the Dissolution of the Empire," by Samuel E. Turner (N. Y., 1889).
Vincent's "State and Federal Government in Switzerland."
"The Federal Government of Switzerland," by Bernard Moses. $1.50
Lebon's "France As It Is."
Wilson's "The State."

"The Puritan Revolution," by S. R. Gardiner (Epochs of Modern History). 75 cents.
Scott's "Development of Constitutional Liberty."
Fiske's "American Political Ideas."
Boutmy's "Studies in Constitutional Law."
Fiske's "Civil Government."
"History of American Politics," by Alexander Johnston. 80 cents
A. de Tocqueville's "Democracy in America."
Wilson's "Congressional Government."
Bryce's "American Commonwealth."
"Patrick Henry," by M. C. Tyler (American Statesmen Series). 90 cents.
"Alexander Hamilton," by H. C. Lodge (same series). 90 cents
"Thomas Jefferson," by J. T. Morse (same series). 90 cents
Schurz's "Henry Clay."
Bourinot's "Federal Government in Canada."
Dilke's "Problems of Greater Britain."
Selections from Burke.
Mill's "Liberty."
Stephen's "Liberty, Equality, Fraternity."

3. Hundred-dollar list:

Bagehot's "Physics and Politics."
Maine's "Ancient Law."
Coulanges' "The Ancient City."
Aristotle's "Politics."
"The Life of Cicero," by Anthony Trollope. 2 vols. $2.25
Montesquieu's "Spirit of Laws."
Locke's "Treatises on Government."
Hosmer's "Anglo-Saxon Freedom."
Creasy's "English Constitution."
"The Growth of the English Constitution," by E. A. Freeman. $1.35
Boutmy's "English Constitution."
"Walpole," by John Morley (Twelve English Statesmen Series). 45 cents.
"Henry II," by Mrs. J. R. Green (same series). 45 cents
"The Epoch of Reform," by Justin McCarthy (Epochs of Modern History Series). 75 cents
Bagehot's "English Constitution."
Traill's "Central Government."
Chalmer's "Local Government."
Dicey's "Law of the Constitution."
"The Origin and Growth of the English Constitution," by Hannis Taylor. $3.40

"The History and Origin of Representative Government in Europe," by M. Guizot (Bohn's Library). $1.00
"Germany, Present and Past," by S. Baring-Gould. $2.60
Turner's "Sketch of the Germanic Constitution."
"Life and Times of Stein," by J. R. Seeley (Tauchnitz).
Stead's "Switzerland" 4 vols. paper. $1.80
Vincent's "State and Federal Government in Switzerland."
Moses' "Federal Government in Switzerland."
"The Ancient Régime," by H. A. Taine. $1.90
"The Ancient Regime," by A. de Tocqueville. $1.10
"The French Revolution," by Bertha M. Gardiner (Epochs of Modern History). 75 cents.
Lebon's "France As It Is."
"Political History of Recent Times," by W. Müller. $1.50
Wilson's "The State."
"Johns Hopkins University Studies in Historical and Political Science." 8 vols.

Printed in the Philadelphia *Book News*, x (Sept. 1891), 36-39.

Two Letters from Joseph Ruggles Wilson

My precious son—   N. Y. Septr 2/91

I have of course been intending to run over to Princeton for a day or two more. I have however postponed the doing so until it is now too late. I leave for Tenn. day after to-morrow (i.e. 4th) hoping to get there (after a Sunday rest in Cincinnati,) by Tuesday, 8th, at latest. You will miss my visit the less by reason of Randolph's stay with you, which you must be enjoying—both of you—in so full a degree as to render you incapable of holding any more. He was so kind as to call upon me last Sunday, and I enjoyed the short moments of his sitting greatly. Also I have had the satisfaction and pleasure of seeing Stockton, twice; and I love him more every time I come into contact with the dear boy. My health is quite as good as I could have expected; and my home in N. Y. is very attractive—made the more so by its quietness as well as by the loving ministries of its amiable head. My stay "in town" has been prolonged by a necessity for waiting day after day upon my friend Dr. Moran[1] who last week seemed at the point of death for a day or so. Love to Ellie & affectionate regards to Randolph & his little Helen

Yours, unalterably,   Father

[1] The Rev. Dr. Robert Sanford Moran, a Methodist minister, presumably retired.

My dearest one   N. Y   Sept. 3/91
    Your telegram has just come (11.30). I am so sorry that it will not be possible for me to spend even one night more in Princeton. I have an engagement, of my own making, for this evening which cannot decently be foregone especially as it relates to a sick man who depends upon me for most of the comfort he gets. You know my love for you all, just the same. And the fact is, I would not care to endure the pain of a formal farewell, which, indeed would be no pain were it *merely formal*. I am all prepared to leave to-morrow—and now must say God bless you and yours with every large benediction!   Your affc *Father*.

ALS (WP, DLC).

To Albert Bushnell Hart

                                        Princeton, New Jersey
My dear Prof. Hart,   11 September, 1891
    Longmans, Green, & Co., have sent me maps 3, 4, 5, for Volume III; I have examined them, and now forward them to you. I have but one criticism of moment to make. I think that the description " '*Loyal*' Free States," " '*Loyal*' Slave-holding States," on Map 4, is unfortunately chosen for the volume I am writing. I am a thorough Unionist, but I do not regard the question as one of '*loyalty*.' If there *be* a constitutional question, that word comes perilously near begging it. If you are willing, I should very much prefer the neutral description *Union* Free States, *Union* Slave-holding States.
    A much smaller matter is the *colour* of the maps. It sadly hurts my eyes to find points in the midst of colouring which is so dark. The light greens and pinks and yellows seem to me much preferable.

Would it be practicable to have a small uncoloured map to show the points of Taylor's and Scott's operations in the Mexican war?

My *mss.* still advances: about two-thirds of it is now in pretty good shape—and I have hopes for the Winter.

Hoping that you are by this time quite yourself again,
                    Cordially Yours,   Woodrow Wilson

ALS (de Coppet Coll., NjP).

From Albert Bushnell Hart

My dear Prof. Wilson: Cambridge, Mass.   Sept. 12, 1891.

Yours of the 11th is at hand: I shall look for the maps tomorrow. Your suggestion in regard to "Loyal" shall be followed out. It was for just such points that I wished you to examine the maps.

As to the map sh[ow]ing the Mexican war, I'm afraid the publishers have gone to the extent of their willingness; none of the Epochs of Modern History have inserted maps, in the text: and the contract limit for each volume, of the folded-in maps, is five. I will try what I can do on later editions. The folds really cost a large sum. In map No 2 and one other I have inserted places as far south as Buena Vista.

The color of the maps will be less troublesome in the engraving: the sketches are of course less clear.
                    Sincerely yours,   Albert Bushnell Hart

ALS (WP, DLC).

From James Woodrow

My dear Nephew: Columbia, S. C., Sept. 12, 1891.

I have been away from home a few days, and therefore your letter of Sept. 1st has been unacknowledged. I reached home last night.

You send cheque for $318.[1] I did not intend that you should pay interest; but since you so prefer, I cannot refuse. I am glad the amount last year was of use to you.

It was with regret that I was forced to content myself with a distant view of Princeton as we whirled along the railway without even stopping at your station. But my visit to the North was cut short by letters I received in New York, and I was obliged to hurry home to attend to matters that could not wait.

From my pleasant recollections of Princeton, I would suppose it no great hardship to be obliged to spend a summer there;

except, indeed, that, if there is virtue in change, you did not get it by remaining at home.

I am glad to know that you and your dear ones have all been perfectly well. So have I and mine, except Lottie,[2] who is no worse.

With much love to you all,

Your affectionate uncle,   James Woodrow.

ALS (WP, DLC).
   [1] The circumstances of this loan remain mysterious.
   [2] His daughter, Mary Charlotte Woodrow.

From Ella Ralston Flemming

My Friend,   Washington, D. C.   Sept 12, 1891.

Our Son Ralston expects to enter the class of '95.[1] I hope it may be agreeable and pleasant to you and to him, to renew and continue the acquaintance formed at 1227 Conn Ave. some three years since.[2] And too, I trust, the acquaintance may ripen into a friendship fused by a tinge of kindred blood. We remember most kindly the short meeting and pleasant note afterwards received from you. Owing to Ralston's leaving, we have closed our house and gone to boarding, but the latch string of our 'apartments' will ever be out for 'Cousin' Woodrow Wilson.

With kindest greetings from Mr Flemming and a renewed hope that our boy may be a pride to all his friends, I am

Yours in friendship,   Ella Ralston Flemming.

Emma Larimore Gray and Marion were in Washington last summer.

ALS (WP, DLC) with WWhw notation on env.: "Ans. 18 Sept '91."
   [1] James Ralston Flemming, who entered Princeton in the autumn of 1891.
   [2] Actually, Mrs. Flemming had met her cousin, Woodrow, two and a half years before. See WW to EAW, March 18, 1889, Vol. 6.

From Joseph Ruggles Wilson

My precious son—   Clarksville 13th Sp./91

I reached this place on Tuesday morning last (8th) after a Sabbath spent in Cincinnati in order to break the long journey. It was a sore trial to me to come all this way without another call at Princeton. But it seemed to be unavoidable. In looking back I feel that I might have accomplished the desired visit by a little management; and no doubt would have done so at any rate only I somehow was impressed with the certainty that you would come to N. Y. to see me for a day or so. I am deeply sorry that we did not meet again[.] My heart was with you so constantly as to make it almost seem that my whole person was at your side. Indeed this is the case all the while; because my love knows nothing of distances: it always has you as near as the pulsations of my life.

I know that you must have enjoyed uncle Randolph's visit— that best of men—and his little daughter's, that nicest of children. You know perhaps that I had the satisfaction of a call from both in New York—a brief call which I enjoyed greatly notwithstanding its shortness. I am disposed to envy you in the having of him for days together. It is not often such true men turn up.

I would have liked to hear you read a few more chapters of your forthcoming book, and all the more because those you did read were so superb. I shall be relieved—along with yourself— when the whole shall have been completed and your nose freed from its contact with the grindstone.

My junior class is promising finely as to numbers. There will probably be 15 on my roll, the largest no. since my connection with this institution. But whether I shall be able to continue throughout the session to give the young men that instruction which they need, is measurably doubtful—for my health is not promising to hold out. Last night I was quite sick with something like the pains that attacked me twice last winter and over this summer. It is not to be accounted for seeing that I am full of prudence. But the onlook is not by any means reassuring.

I am unable to write more just now—but whether I write little or much, do not doubt as to my complete love for my darling son. Love to dear Ellie[.] Josie joins me in love to both.

Your affectionate   Father

ALS (WP, DLC) with WWhw notation on env.: "Ans."

From Thomas Wentworth Higginson

Dear Sir   Dublin, N. H.   Sept. 14, 1891

Allow me to express the pleasure with which I have read your paper in the *Atlantic*.[1] Your literary touch is so light and sure that you ought by no means to confine yourself to public questions which so many others are testing. We have few who possess the literary touch.

I should not venture to write this, but that the best reward of Literature lies in the acknowledgments it brings from strangers.

Cordially yours   Thomas Wentworth Higginson

ALS (WP, DLC) with WWhw notation on env.: "Ans. 18 Sept. '91."
    1 "The Author Himself," printed at Dec. 7, 1887, Vol. 5, which had just been published in the *Atlantic Monthly*, LXVIII (Sept. 1891), 406-13.

From Azel Washburn Hazen

My dear Friend: Middletown, Conn. 17 Sept 1891.

Your "love-letter" gave me joy in all my vacation. Its sweet music still vibrates in my heart. I *thank* you most sincerely for every utterance—too kind though many were. One cannot feel that his life is wholly useless, if he can win the esteem and affection of such a person as yourself. Your words as to my ministry encourage me to attempt better things than are yet achieved.

But I took my pen to tell you that I had a charming visit with your father in Saratoga, and you see how my emotions ran away with me as I began to address you! We met several times at the Congress Spring and exchanged calls. I need not say that your father was the same fascinating man that he was when in this city.

My vacation—a happy one—is now obscured by Mrs Hazen's illness. She came from the sea with a heavy cold, which has developed into typhoid fever. The form of it is as yet not aggravated, and the Doctor thinks she will conquer it. She was greatly cheered by Mrs Wilson's letter in July, & would have messages of love for you both if she knew I were writing you. Such messages I send for myself assuredly.

Ever cordially yours   A. W. Hazen[1]

ALS (WP, DLC) with WWhw notation on env.: "Ans. 22 Sept. '91."
  [1] Wilson's reply of Sept. 22, 1891, which was received too late to be included in sequence, is printed as an Addendum in this volume.

From Robert Bridges

My dear Tommy: [New York]   Sept 20 91

I have been trying for a week to write you how much I liked your *Atlantic* article. You hit the weak point of the present school of writers exactly. It is an affectation of "sophistication"—and it all comes from New England. They are ashamed of their best sentiments, and when they presume to admire a fine thing, they mildly make fun of themselves afterward.

But this is an old sermon to you. It does my heart good, though, to hear you preach Scotch individualism from the Yankee pulpit.

Even the "sophisticated" Burlingame said that he would have been glad to have that article for our magazine. (He volunteered the statement.) I hope you wont let us have the go-by when you write again in that vein.

I had a fine vacation, from Aug 13 to Sept. 8. Part of the time Strong, Blydenburgh[1] and I spent in the Maine wilderness, west of Moosehead Lake. But the true narrative of that expedition can be told only by word of mouth. We are prepared to give you fish stories that would astonish Walton or Munchausen.

My niece Eleanor is very ill, and Dr. Carr has gone to Carlisle to see her. He writes me cautiously but with some hope. It is a very doubtful case—resembling meningitis.

My regards to Mrs. Wilson, and to all my Princeton friends.

Yours faithfully   Robert Bridges

ALS (WP, DLC) with WWhw notation on env.: "Ans. 22 Sept. '91."
¹ Strong is unknown. Blydenburgh was Benjamin Brewster Blydenburgh, Princeton, '81.

To Robert Bridges

My dear Bobby,   Princeton, New Jersey, 22 September, 1891

Thank you very heartily for your praise of my *Atlantic* article. It was something that I had had in my desk for two or three years, and I had no idea that it would 'take' as it has. It came from my heart—and it must be that which has made it seem authentic. I don't know of any one whose approval of what I write gratifies me more than yours does.

I am quite willing that "the boss" should have a chance to decline the next thing of the sort that I write. I send to the *Atlantic* because Mr. Scudder so often asks me for something— and I seem to have become a sort of regular contributor.

But, much as this letter that praises my work pleased and heartened me, Bobby, I believe that other one, written the middle of July, gratified me even more,—because of its confidential speech about yourself, on your thirty-third birth-day. Your confidence is better even than your praise. For my part, I have not the slightest doubt that you *have* built on a broad basis, on which a very noble structure of character and attainment, moreover, has been erected. You are prepared for anything you choose to undertake, and, if you can escape becoming too critical of your own work, I have every confidence in the result. To one who knows you as well as I do, it seems almost absurd that a birth-day should bring to you any dissatisfaction with what has so far been accomplished.

Will John come back this year? I heartily hope so. I need not tell you how distressed I was to hear of your niece's serious illness. I trust it may turn out better than you fear.

It does me good to hear of the fine vacation you had. Although I did not take any, I don't feel the worse for it. I kept steadily at the 'Epoch' all summer, reeling off something over three hundred pages of *mss.*—about two-thirds of the whole. I hope to revise this and write the rest this Winter.

Is it literally true that the volumes of the Scribner series are 'in the press' as advertised?

Warmest regards from Mrs. Wilson and warmest affection from   Your sincere friend,   Woodrow Wilson

ALS (WC, NjP).

EDITORIAL NOTE
WILSON'S TEACHING AT PRINCETON, 1891-92

The Department of Philosophy at Princeton, which embraced all subjects in the humanities except English and oratory, archeology, the history of art, and ancient and modern languages, was reorganized into sections by fields in 1891. Wilson now became a member of the section entitled "History and Political Philosophy." His copy for the catalogue for 1891-92 differs substantially from that in the catalogue for the preceding year[1] and is reproduced as follows:

IV. History and Political Philosophy.

PROFESSORS SLOANE AND WILSON. . . .

6. Political Economy. Elementary course. Junior Required; second term [2]. Professor Wilson. *Walker*: First Lessons in Political Economy. . . .

11. General Jurisprudence, the philosophy of law and of personal rights. Lectures, recitations, collateral reading. Given 1891-92, alternating with 13. Junior and Senior Elective; first term [2]. Professor Wilson. *Holland*: Elements of Jurisprudence.

12. International Law. Lectures, recitations, collateral reading. Given 1891-92, alternating with 14. Junior and Senior Elective; second term [2]. Professor Wilson. *Hall*: A Treatise on International Law, 3d ed., 1890.

13. Public Law, its historical derivation, its practical sanctions, its typical outward forms, its evidence as to the nature of the state and as to the character and scope of political sovereignty. Lectures, recitations, collateral reading. To be given 1892-93, alternating with 11. Junior and Senior Elective; first term [2]. Professor Wilson.

14. American Constitutional Law, state and federal. Lectures, recitations, collateral reading. To be given 1892-93, alternating with 12. Junior and Senior Elective; second term [2]. Professor Wilson. *Cooley*: General Principles of Constitutional Law. . . .

18. Administration. Lectures and collateral reading. Senior Elective; second term [2]. Professor Wilson. *Bryce*: The American Commonwealth.

19. History of Political Economy. Lectures and collateral reading. Senior Elective; first term [2]. Professor Wilson. *Ingram*: A History of Political Economy.[2]

About the courses in administration, elementary political economy,

---

[1] See the Editorial Note, "Wilson's Teaching at Princeton, 1890-91."

[2] *Catalogue of the College of New Jersey at Princeton . . . 1891-92* (Princeton, n.d.), pp. 35-36; brackets are in the original and denote the number of lectures each week.

and history of political economy, which Wilson gave in 1891-92, not much needs to be said here, since he virtually repeated the courses described in the Editorial Note, "Wilson's Teaching at Princeton, 1890-91." The final examinations printed at February 7 and June 2, 1892, furnish last glances at courses in political economy that Wilson would never give again because Princeton added a specialist in this field in 1892.

In his new second-term course on international law, Wilson (as the announcement printed at January 27, 1892, reveals) required his students to read during his absence in Baltimore the first two parts of William Edward Hall's *A Treatise on International Law*, 3rd edition (Oxford, 1890), for coverage of such technical subjects as the laws of war, of military occupation, of blockade, of contraband, of neutrality, etc. Upon his return to the classroom at Princeton in the second week of March, Wilson gave an introductory lecture and then went on to survey the history and development of international law from ancient times to his own day.[3] Frequent references in his letters to his wife during these weeks indicate that Wilson was struggling to stay ahead of his class. Only the notes for his introductory lecture are printed, at March 8, 1892. However, good views of the scope of this course may be obtained from the description of Wilson's notes printed at March 8, 1892, from the final examination printed at May 19, 1892, and from a syllabus printed by undergraduates in the spring of 1892.[4] In addition, there is a good set of notes in the Wilson Papers, Library of Congress, taken in this course in 1894 by Andrew C. Imbrie, '95.

Wilson's Course on Jurisprudence, 1891-94

During 1891-92, Wilson worked hardest on his new first-term course on jurisprudence. This, along with his course on public law, he regarded as the cornerstone of his undergraduate program in the philosophy and history of law because it was intended to give students an introduction to the large dimensions and elementary principles of the science of law.

Wilson's first and main task was to get his bearings for a specialized study of the science of law. Hence he turned to the works of one of the foremost authorities of the day, Adolf Merkel. First, Wilson read and carefully translated Merkel's article on jurisprudence in Holtzendorff's encyclopedia.[5] Obviously much impressed by Merkel's survey, he next turned to the German authority's larger work, *Juristische Encyclopädie* (Berlin and Leipzig, 1885), translating the table of contents and pages 1 through 34, and writing a summary in outline form of pages 81 through 151 of this book.[6] At about the same time, Wilson also read and took notes from Edwin Charles Clark, *Practical Jurisprudence, A Comment on Austin* (Cambridge, 1883),[7]

---

[3] His notes for these lectures were based in part on the body of shorthand notes in WP, DLC, with the WWhw title "History of International Law."

[4] *Syllabus on International Law Taken from the Lectures of Prof. Woodrow Wilson 1892* (Princeton, N. J., n.d.). This syllabus did not cover Wilson's last two lectures on May 16 and 17, 1892.

[5] Wilson's translation is printed at Aug. 1, 1891.

[6] WWhw MSS. (WP, DLC).

[7] WWhw loose pages (WP, DLC). The charge slip still in the Wilson Papers shows that Wilson checked this book out of the Chancellor Green Library on July 10, 1891.

and presumably also from the work that he had chosen as the text-book for his course, Thomas Erskine Holland, *The Elements of Jurisprudence*, 5th edition (Oxford, 1890).

Having thus staked out what he thought were the proper boundaries of the field, Wilson prepared, probably in mid-September, a list of twenty-five topics for lectures in the course that he was beginning to call "Outlines of Jurisprudence."[8] At about this same time he wrote out the elaborate memorandum, *"Derivation of the terms for 'Law,'"* reproduced on pages 306-307. Next he wrote out rather detailed outlines, with guides to authorities, for lectures on twenty topics.[9] Having found his way, he proceeded to type up the notes for his lectures. These notes he considerably revised when he gave the course a second time, in 1893-94. Wilson revised and retyped the 1891-92 notes for many of his topics;[10] however, he was able to use some of his 1891-92 notes without any changes.

Readers may obtain a close view of Wilson's course as he gave it in 1891-92 from the outlines and notes cited above, and particularly from an undergraduate syllabus published in 1892.[11] The examinations printed at February 2 and May 14, 1892, also give a good intimation of the course's coverage and emphasis.

Although based very considerably upon his notes prepared in 1891-92, Wilson's course on jurisprudence in 1893-94 represented his fully matured conception of the field. It was in fact substantially the course that he continued to give at Princeton until 1910, although later he did rearrange some topics and added two new lectures. The reader may obtain an overview of the jurisprudence course of 1893-94 from the description of the lecture notes, printed at September 26, 1891, and from the classroom notes taken in 1893-94 by Andrew C. Imbrie, '95, in the Wilson Papers, Library of Congress. The Editors believe that the notes printed at September 26 and October 20, 1891, suffice to indicate the level and nature of the course.

Wilson's careful annotation of his jurisprudence notes reveals all his sources and authorities. In addition to Merkel, Clark, and Holland, already mentioned, Wilson relied most heavily upon Diodato Lioy, *The Philosophy of Right*, translated by W. Hastie (London, 1891);[12] articles in the *Century Dictionary* (6 vols., New York, 1889-91); Georg Friedrich Puchta, *Cursus der Institutionen* (3 vols., Leipzig, 1841-47); William Markby, *Elements of Law Considered with Reference to Principles of General Jurisprudence*, 4th edition (Oxford, 1889); Rudolph Sohm, *The Institutes of Roman Law*, translated by James C. Ledlie (Oxford, 1892); and John B. Minor, *Institutes of Common and Statute Law* (4 vols., Richmond, 1876-79), Volumes II and IV.

[8] A two-page WWhw MS. entitled "Course I. *Outlines of the Science of Jurisprudence*" (WP, DLC).

[9] WWhw, WWT, and WWsh outlines and notes on half sheets (WP, DLC). The first topic is entitled "I. Place of Law in Political Science (i.e., in the General Theory of Society)."

[10] He followed new topical outlines—WWT MSS. (WP, DLC) dated Sept. 15, 1893, and Jan. 20, 1894.

[11] *Syllabus on Jurisprudence. Taken from Lectures of Prof. Woodrow Wilson. 1891-92* (Princeton, N. J., n.d.).

[12] Wilson's handwritten, typed, and shorthand notes on Lioy are on two loose pages in WP, DLC.

From the Minutes of the Princeton Faculty

3 P.M., Wednesday, Sep. 23rd, 1891.
. . . The following Professors were appointed members of *The Committee on Discipline*[1] as determined by action of Faculty, May 15th, 1891.

The Dean Chairman and Professors Duffield, Packard, Young, Winans[2] & W. Wilson of the Academic Department and Professors Cornwall and Macloskie of the Scientific Department.

[1] This marked the establishment of this committee as a standing committee of the faculty. Heretofore, the President, Dean of the College or Faculty, the faculty, and *ad hoc* committees (appointed, for example, to deal with riots) had dealt with discipline cases. Wilson served as secretary of the Discipline Committee throughout his membership on that body until 1899, when he resigned to become chairman of the Library Committee.

The following minutes of the Discipline Committee kept by Wilson from September 23 through about November 24, 1891, and selected samples of the reports of the Discipline Committee to the Faculty are printed in order to show the kind of work that Wilson and the committee did. Names have been omitted because of the confidential nature of these records.

In addition to the longhand minutes printed below, there are WWsh and WWhw pencil notes on some seventy loose pages (WP, DLC) for meetings of the committee on March 26, 28, and 31, April 2, 5, and 12, June 8, September 23, 26, and 28, and October 8 and 18, 1892; January 16, March 10 and 14, May 2 and 9, September 20 and 22, October 5, 7, 9, and 13, and November 1, 6, and 14, 1893; September 24, 1894; and April 1 and 4, 1895.

[2] Samuel Ross Winans, Professor of Greek and Instructor in Sanskrit.

Wilson's Minutes of the Discipline Committee

[Sept. 23-c. Nov. 24, 1891]

Registrar's Office 23rd. September, 1891
Woodrow Wilson elected Secretary.
The Dean informed the Committee of two cases:

1. That of ——, second year special student, of ——, charged with imposing himself as a room-mate upon Mr. ——, of the entering class, at the Nassau Hotel on the nights of Sept. 18 and 19. Mr. Wilson deputed to take the testimony of Mr. Cook,[1] proprietor of the Hotel.

2. Case of ——, of ——, charged with insulting conduct towards candidate for entrance at the Nassau Hotel on the evening of Sept. 22.

Voted, That Messrs —— and —— be summoned before the Committee for to-morrow, Sept. 24, at 9 A.M. Adjourned till that time.　　　　　　　　　　　　　Woodrow Wilson, Sec'y.

Registrar's Office 9 A.M., 24 September, 1891
Mr. Matthew Goldie[2] appeared and informed the Committee, on

[1] A. D. Cook.
[2] The college proctor.

the testimony of eye-witnesses (a graduate of the College, class of '73, and Mr. Cook, proprietor of the Nassau Hotel) that

On the night of Tuesday, the 22nd. Sept., Mr. ——, of the class of '94, took an active part in "guying" an entering Freshman at the Nassau Hotel; poked him in the stomach, saying to him "You are the damnest fresh Freshman I ever saw"; and was thereupon struck in the face by the Freshman. On a previous evening —— had undertaken to put a Freshman out of the billiard-room of the Hotel.

Examination of Mr. ——: Statement of the charge made to Mr. ——. He deposed: that the facts of the case were stated with substantial correctness; that he was "very, very sorry" for what had happened; had been asked by companions to go to the Hotel; went into the hallway of the Hotel, where he found a crowd talking to a Freshman; joined the crowd; did address to the Freshman the language alleged, but willing to take his oath that he did not *touch* the man. Said that Leggett,[3] the college constable, had told him that 'guying' a Freshman was not hazing, and that the Vice-President of his class had said the same thing. Declared that he was ready to apologize to the man he had insulted. Alleged that the resolution against hazing passed by his class during the college year last past was universally understood to mean only that the more extreme forms of hazing should be avoided, as, e.g., entering the rooms of Freshmen, taking men from their rooms, etc.—that this was understood in the class meeting at which the resolution was passed, having been explicitly stated by the speakers who had advocated the action.

Mr. —— having appeared and made satisfactory explanations with reference to the charges made against him, it was ordered that no record of the circumstances be made.

Voted in the case of Mr. ——, That the Committee recommend to the Faculty that Mr. —— be suspended from College for one term for insulting treatment of a fellow student, his offence being aggravated by the violation of a promise given to the Dean after a solemn warning because of previous similar conduct. This action, it was understood, should be entirely independent of any action to be taken by the Faculty with reference to Mr. ——'s standing in respect of scholarship.

Adjourned.   Woodrow Wilson, Sec'y

Faculty Room, 12 M., Saturday, 10 October, 1891
Case of ——, of ——, and ——, of ——.
Mr. Matthew Goldie's statement, obtained from eye-witnesses, read by the Dean, to the following effect:

[3] William Leggett, night watchman.

On Wednesday evening, 7 October, —— and —— went to the pool-room of the Nassau Hotel, between eight and ten o'clock, under the influence of liquor. —— went up to John Warren,[4] a man of the town, supposing him to be a Freshman, ordered him out of the room, and when he refused to go slapped him in the face. Benham,[5] the man in charge of the pool room, interfering, told —— that he would be 'getting a licking' himself if he kept on at that sort of thing. —— thereupon threw off his coat and a second time attacked Warren, who struck him and knocked him over on one of the tables. —— was then put out of the room.

Mr. —— appeared before the Committee.

Goldie's statement was repeated to him by the Dean

Mr. —— deposed: That, while some of the statement was true, he was not intoxicated; that he did not throw off his coat and that Warren did not strike him. That the day was his birthday and that he had taken a bottle of champagne with a friend, being in the habit of drinking wine with his friends at home. That he did what he did only as a joke: asked the man what he was doing there, and whether he was a freshman; was told in offensive language that it was none of his business; and then struck the man in the face.

Mr. —— appeared and a statement of the circumstances alleged was made to him by the Dean.

Mr. —— deposed: That he was ——'s room mate, and had taken with —— on the evening in question a bottle of champagne. That he went with —— to the pool room but saw nothing of the row that ensued, he himself being at the extreme rear of the room and the row taking place in the front part of the room. That he was not conscious of having been affected by the wine,——was simply conscious of being a little warmed by it, and of 'cutting up' a little, and 'acting funny.' Admitted that the wine had deprived him of his self-command. Said that he was not himself put out of the pool-room, and that he had understood that —— was not put out, but taken out by class-mates.

Voted in the case Mr. ——, that, in view of the nature of his offence, and of his otherwise excellent character and record, he be severely reprimanded simply.

Voted in the case of Mr. —— that it be recommended to the Faculty that he be suspended from College for one term and that, in view of his grave difficiencies in scholarship,

4 Of 18 Pine Street.
5 George M. Benham.

he be obliged, if he should return at the end of that time, to enter the lower class.

Adjourned.   Woodrow Wilson, Sec'y.

Faculty Room, 12 M., Saturday, 17 October, 1891

Mr. Matthew Goldie appeared and made the following statement:

Mr. Lavake,[6] of the town, who keeps a Freshman eating club, stated to him that Sophomores were in the habit of taking Freshmen from his house to a Sophomore eating club at Mrs. Dohm's[7] house, to wait on the table there—that more than forty men had been treated in that manner; and that the principal men concerned were ——— and ———, of the Sophomore class, School of Science, and ———, Special student, S. S.[8] These men came to his house on more than one night this week, but did not then get any Freshmen, being warned away by Mrs. Lavake.[9]

Mr. Goldie stated that the name of the club to which these men belong is the "White Elephant"; that the club was until recently conducted by Mr. ———, but is now under the management of ———, Sophomore, S. S., ——— having gone to the foot-ball training table.

Mr. ——— appeared. The nature of the information against him stated by the Dean. He deposed: That he did not "remember" being concerned in any case of the nature stated; did not "think" that he had ever done anything of the kind—and persisted, upon examination, in couching his denials in that form. Specifically denied having been at Mrs. Lavake's house at any time during the week.

Mr. ——— appeared and, after hearing a statement of the charges, said, in answer to questions:

That the "White Elephant" club took its meals at Mrs. Dohm's; that he would not deny that the club had had Freshmen to wait on the table; that he had been at Mrs. Lavake's house one night this week, but went there simply to see Mr. ——— of the Freshman class, who is from Lawrenceville school, a friend of his, he also having come from that school, and who was expecting to buy some things from him. That he did not "remember" any case of a Freshman being taken to the "White Elephant" club to be made to wait on the table in which he was himself concerned,—had no recollection of having himself been connected with the

6 Thomas William Lavake, jeweler, of 148 Nassau Street.
7 Mrs. M. E. Dohm, of 116 Nassau Street.
8 School of Science.
9 Juliet Stratton (Mrs. T. W.) Lavake.

practice on any occasion. That he regarded the acts charged as hazing.

Being more closely examined touching his visit to Mr. ——, he said: That Mr. —— did not room at Mrs. Lavake's, but on University Place; that he called on Mr. —— at Mrs. Lavake's just before the evening meal hour, and that other Sophomores, members of the White Elephant club, were with him at the time; that he did not know what these other members of his club were there for at that time, but that they were not there for the purpose of taking Mr. —— to wait on their table—he (——) would not have allowed that, for —— was from Lawrenceville, and he always sought to protect Lawrenceville boys from hazing. Mrs. Lavake had warned him, but without justification.

Mr. ——, appeared.

The case having been stated to him, he said, in answer to questions: That he was a member of the White Elephant club. That Mrs. Lavake had both a Freshman and a Sophomore eating club. That he had been at Mrs. Lavake's house on Thursday evening last (Oct. 15), having gone in with a '94 man, who belonged to the Sophomore club taking its meals there. His object in going in was to see the pictures of athletic events contained in an illustrated paper which the Sophomore had. He went, however, into the dining room, not of the Sophomore, but of the Freshman club, where the Sophomore whom he had followed in was showing the paper to some Freshmen. Mrs. Lavake saw him and warned him against molesting the Freshmen. He knew nothing of the other Sophomore's who were at Lavake's on the same evening. This was the only time he had been at Lavake's. He had not been engaged in taking men to his club to wait on the table. Had taken a Freshman there, but as his friend, not to wait on the table. Had been with a crowd of some fifteen or twenty other Sophomores on the platform in front of Mrs. Dohm's, where there are five Sophomore clubs, when Freshmen who were passing were summoned to wait on the table. Had not in any case protested against the practice, but had never been prominently concerned and believed himself as little guilty as any member of his club. Did not think that any of his club disapproved of the practice. Realized that this was a form of hazing, however, and that it subjected men to discipline. Believed, too, that it was in contravention of the resolution against hazing passed by his class last year. He had not himself been present when

that resolution was passed, but had felt bound by it. Freshmen had never, so far as he knew, refused to obey the sum-
mons to wait on Sophomores at table. He had himself been
made to do this when he was a Freshman, but had not regarded it as an indignity—had rather enjoyed the fun of it.
Supposed, however, that it was a form of intimidation.

Mr. —— had not himself been running the club for some
three weeks: Mr. —— his substitute, but only his substitute.
—— still the responsible manager.

Case adjourned till Monday noon.

Woodrow Wilson, Sec'y

Faculty Room 12 m., Monday, 19 October, 1891
Case of the White Elephant Club resumed.
Mr. —— appeared and testified as follows:
That he got up the club, but remained with it only about
two days, at the beginning of the term. That the club is
called the "White Elephant" often, but really has never given
itself a name, only about four of the members of the White
Elephant club of the session 1890-1891 being members of
it. That he was now at the foot-ball training table; but expected to go back to the club after the close of the foot-ball
season. That, though the club was still nominally under his
management, he was not now in fact the responsible head of
it; but that Mr. —— was his responsible substitute. That he
thought he rembered [remembered] one case of a Freshman
being brought to the club to wait on the table during the
two days he was with it; and that on that occasion he had
tried to discourage the practice, having been told by Mr.
Dohm that nothing of the sort should be allowed.

The college laws touching such practices were read to the
witness by the Dean

He said that he did not believe in hazing, and had earnestly tried to discourage what he saw of it at his club.
Even from selfish motives he wanted his club to avoid
dangerous practices. He had at present no pecuniary interest
in the club, ——, taking his place as a free boa[r]der; but
expected to return, and felt that it would be very hard on
him, were the club to be disbanded. Did not believe his club
was any more guilty than the other Sophomore clubs in
this matter.

Mr. —— appeared, and, the case having been stated to him by
the Dean, testified as follows:
That he had temporary charge of the club. He had been

aware that the practice charged was being indulged in by
his club, and had tried to discourage it. Very little of the sort
had taken place in his presence; that such things never
occurred except at dinner, and that he was almost always
late at dinner because it was his practice to run on the track
at the athletic field every afternoon from five to six o'clock.
On one or two occasions he had found Freshmen at the
club, but all the men had left about five minutes after his
entrance, taking the Freshmen with them. One evening he
found a Freshman there whom [he] had seen on the track and
had immediately sent him away, none of the club members
objecting. His only duty as manager was to speak to Mr.
Dohm when there was anything to be complained of. There
were five clubs at Mr. Dohm's, a mixed club, a Senior club,
and three Sophomore clubs.

A correction: —— wished to say, through Mr. Goldie, that it was
Wednesday evening, the 14th, not Thursday, the 15th, that
he visited Mrs. Lavake's.

Voted, That it be recommended to the Faculty that every man
responsible for a club be required to file with the Registrar
a list of the members of his club at the time of its formation,
and to acquaint him promptly with all subsequent changes
in the list.

Voted, That it be recommended to the Faculty that the eating
club formed by Mr. ——, and generally known as the White
Elephant Club, be disbanded.

Adjourned,   Woodrow Wilson, Sec'y

Faculty Room, 12 M., Tuesday, 24 Nov., 1891
Case of Messrs. —— and ——, charged with participation in the
destruction of college property on the evening of Saturday,
Nov. 21st., when a disorderly crowd gathered in front of the
college offices and stones were thrown by which one of the
windows of the Treasurer's office was broken and damage
done within the office. The college watchmen identified
Messrs. —— and —— as having been with the crowd.

Mr. —— was summoned, and the charges stated to him by the
Dean. He deposed, under examination,
That he was coming past the Offices on his way from University Hall, whence he had come alone, and that, seeing the
crowd, he stopped a moment to see what was going on. That
while he stood there one or more stones were thrown at
the windows of the college offices, but that, although he did
not do or say anything to prevent the mischief, he took no

part in it and did not identify himself with the crowd. He asked the men in the crowd what they were doing, but does not remember receiving any answer. Did not think that there were more than two or three men in the group from wh. the stones were thrown. When the glass was broken those concerned ran away; he did not. Does not think that the damage was premeditated, but heard something said about Whig Hall windows. Thought that one stone was thrown before he reached the group; two, perhaps, were thrown after he reached it.

Mr. —— appeared, and the case was stated to him. He deposed That he was not on the college grounds after 9 o'clock on the evening in question,—an hour or two previous to the time at which the damage was said to have been done.

No action taken—Adjourned.

Woodrow Wilson, Sec'y

Faculty Room, 12 M., Nov., 1891

Case of —— and —— resumed.

Leggett, college watchman, appeared and deposed:

That on Saturday night, 21 Nov., at midnight, he was standing with Calhoun,[10] the other night watchman under the gas-light near the north end of West College, when six students came out of West College. Time of night fixed by the fact that the electric lights of the town went out as they stood there. Among the students who came out of West College he identified ——, whom he knew very well, and who spoke to him as he passed. The group of students passed on in the direction of the College Offices and when they reached the front of the offices there was the noise of glass being broken. The students stood just in front of the offices when the glass was broken; did not leave the walk or stop for any length of time. Was sure that the students who came out of West were the same that stopped in front of the offices. He did not see —— after the breaking; but did meet ——, who did not run but came, walking slowly, from the place where the group had stood. Did not know that —— was with the group when it came out of West: he might have come up from the opposite direction, from the street.

Calhoun appeared and testified, That at about a quarter past 12 o'clock on the evening in question five young men came out of West College. Thought that he recognized —— among them. The men went as far as the front of the College

10 Samuel Calhoun, night watchman.

Offices, stood there talking for some time, then broke the glass and ran. One of them walked towards him and was recognized as ——. Had thought that he recognized —— with the men who came out of West by a light coloured corduroy suit of clothes, just such as —— had on when he identified him with certainty a few minutes later. He was standing by Leggitt when Leggitt spoke to —— and heard him speak to him. When the group came out of West they were singing; but when they saw the watchmen they stopped singing. The electric lights were put out between the time when the group of students emerged from West and the time when the stone was thrown by which the glass was broken. It was quite dark in front of the offices when the group was standing there. After the throwing of the stone two men ran away down the campus, two round back of of Reunion Hall. The electric light was burning when Leggitt spoke to ——.

Mr. ——, recalled, deposed, That, on the night in question he was in East College from supper time until about half-past eight, playing whist with —— and others; then went, with ——, to ——'s room in Edwards Hall, and stayed about one-half or three quarters of an hour; then returned, —— accompanying him all the time, to his own room in Reunion Hall, where —— stayed with him until almost twelve o'clock; after which he (——) wrote a letter until, perhaps, one o'clock, when he went to bed. —— and —— board with him.

——, recalled, testified that he heard Leggitt say, "Good evening Mr. ——," as the group from West passed them, and heard the student reply to the salutation. Immediately asked Leggitt who it was he had spoken to (not himself knowing ——) and Leggitt replied that it was ——.

No action taken—Adjourned.   Woodrow Wilson, Sec'y

WWhw minutes entitled "*Minutes of Committee on Discipline   College of New Jersey*," loose pages (WP, DLC); list of names of members of the committee on second page not printed.

From Daniel Collamore Heath

Dear Prof. Wilson,   Boston, Mass.   Sept. 24, 1891.

Yours of the 22d received on my return from ten days' absence in Missouri where I have been to look after state adoption of our Lessons in English.

I hasten to enclose the amount of royalty due you, which

should have been sent the 15th. The apology is due you rather than us.

I also send a copy of Gide's Political Economy,[1] with my compliments and best wishes; don't return it or pay for it. I think you are going to like it well enough to use it by and by, if the reports that come to us from other colleges are true.

The reference to your book in the circular letter which we sent out concerning the Gide, has stirred up some new people on it, and some commendations of the book from others who have been using it. It now seems likely that the letter is to do your book as much good as the Gide. I also send a copy of Mr. Wenzel's little book, which I supposed you had received long ago.

Yours very truly,   D. C. Heath.

TL (WP, DLC). Enc. missing.
    [1] Charles Gide, *Principles of Political Economy*, trans. by Edward Percy Jacobsen (Boston, 1891).

From Jesse Lynch Williams[1]

Reunion Hall [Princeton, N.J.]

Dear Sir: September twenty fifth [1891].

It is my great pleasure to inform you that at a meeting of The Executive Committee held yesterday you were unanimously elected to be a member of The *Graduate Advisory Committee* of The *University Athletic Association.*[2]

This election was ratified at a mass meeting held today.[3]

Sincerely   Jesse L. Williams   Sec't'y Exc Comm.

ALS (WP, DLC).
    [1] Class of 1892.
    [2] The University Athletic Association, which had general responsibility for and supervision over all athletics at Princeton, was governed by a Graduate Advisory Committee and an Executive Committee of undergraduates elected by the various undergraduate athletic associations.
    [3] For a brief news report, see *The Princetonian*, XVI (Sept. 25, 1891), [1].

Notes for a Course in Jurisprudence[1]

[Sept. 26, 1891-Dec. 16, 1895]

Contents:

(a) WWT and WWhw notes for lectures on the following topics, with composition dates when given: "I. *Place of Law in the General Theory of Society*" (Sept. 26, 1891, and Sept. 15, 1893[2]), printed as the next document; "II. *Law: Its Origination and Development*" (Oct. 10, 1891, and Sept. 16, 1893); "II. *Law: Its Character*" (Oct. 20, 1891, and Sept. 18, 1893), printed at Oct. 20, 1891; "III. *Law: Its Natural and Formal Branches*" (Oct. 21, 1891, and Oct. 16, 1893); "V. *Jural Relationships: Their Nature and Incidents*" (Oct. 31, 1891);

"V. *Jural Relationships* (continued) *Their Classification*" (Nov. 2, 1891, and Oct. 17, 1893); "VI. *Jural Relationships: Their Inception and Development*" (Nov. 9, 1891, and Oct. 23, 1893); "*Administration*"[3] (Nov. 21, 1891, "Yale, 10, Harvard, 0"); "VIII. Administration of Law by the Courts" (Nov. 16, 1891); "IX. The Conflict of Laws" (Nov. 24, 1891); "X. Function of Legal Science in the Life of Law" (Nov. 30, 1891); "XI. Public Law. . . . *Criminal Law*" (Dec. 7, 8, and 9, 1891); "XII. Civil Procedure" (Dec. 19, 1891); "XIII. *Private Law*: 1. Personal Relationships not of Contract" (Jan. 25, 1892); "XIV. *Private Law*: 2. *Contract*" (Jan. 25, 1892); "XV. II. *Private Law: 3. Property*" (Jan. 15, 1894); "*Succession*" (Jan. 20, 1894).

(b) WWhw notes for lecture on security for debt, probably composed in 1895.

(c) WWsh notes for a lecture on torts, dated Dec. 16, 1895.

¹ These notes, which Wilson used in his jurisprudence course from 1891 through 1894 and with some rearrangement and a few additions until 1910, were found in the Wilson Papers in a highly disorganized and scattered state. The following reconstruction was possible only because Andrew C. Imbrie's classroom notes, taken in 1893-94 and now in the Wilson Papers, provide a full and clear guide to the order of lectures (and topics) in the course that year. One of the composition dates is out of proper chronological sequence because Wilson slightly rearranged his lectures in 1893-94 while continuing to use notes written in 1891-92.

² The double composition dates indicate notes revised or rewritten at the latter date.

³ In the Imbrie notes, this lecture is entitled "Execution of Law by Administrative Authority."

Notes for a Classroom Lecture

[Sept. 26, 1891]

Outlines of Jurisprudence.
I. *Place of Law in the General Theory of Society.*
1. *Belongs to the general domain of Political Science or Politics.*
   May be *too narrowly conceived,* as a command of individual origination, framed and enforced upon the *arbitrary choice* of rulers.
   Some law does, indeed, wear *this appearance.* There are cases of the imposition of law, for generations together, upon *cowed subject populations* by a minority, established in power by conquest, and maintained in power by armed and organized force. *But even in such cases* the law thus arbitrarily imposed will be found to *penetrate but a very little way* into the daily life of the people,—*unless, indeed,* by degrees and in the long run, an organic habit of submission be established.
2. *For Law is an organic product,* the result of the association of men with each other and the consequent institution of certain definite relationships between them.
   The Family,—Government,—Property,—Contract.

Hence, the importance for the lawyer of a constant study *of* his *national literature,* that he may be penetrated by its authentic spirit. Hence, also, the significance of *Coke's notable dictum,* *"Melior est petere fontes quam sectari rivulos,"* It is better to explore the sources than to tap the streams.

3. *The associated life* out of which the Law springs *produces* many things:—*natural ties,* ties of *habit or affection,* ties of *interest,* a developed set of rules of *social morality*

4. *Law*[1] *takes up whatever is* in this wise *completed, made ready to be reduced to a uniform rule of conduct* and provided with an invariable compulsive standard or sanction.

It is *also itself a modifying force,* in its turn exercising an important disciplinary evolutionary or crystalizing influence.

The view that law is produced by the *general* habit of society must be modified in part because of the economic classification of modern society[.] Laws must now be made for groups and occupations and the habits or practices in which they are rooted proceed from such groups and occupations. There is unquestionably present, besides, thr. all the process, the guiding direction of the *human conscience,* the god-given sense of righteousness and holiness.

5. *It Differs,* e.g.,

(1). *From Ethics and Morality:* W.C.,[2]

(a) *The Individual Ethic:* the instructed distinction between what is right and what is wrong; the rectitude of relationship to God in respect of his revealed command; *absolute* integrity; conscientious pursuit of *essential well-being.*

(b) *The Social Ethic:* which is an Ethic of cause and effect, of ends and the effective means thereto; which is *at bottom utilitarian in the higher sense* of the term, affecting, not the separate action and well-being of the individual man, but the *combined and coöperative action* of men, and social well-being. Morality in the derivative meaning of the word.

Both the individual and the social Ethic *supply rules of action,* but rules which are in most cases neither uniform nor directly enforceable,—as the rules of Law must be.

----

[1] "One of the first and noblest of human sciences,—a science which does more to quicken and invigorate the understanding than all other kinds of learning put together; but it is not apt, except in persons very happily born, to open and to liberalize the mind in exactly the same proportion." *Burke* [WW's note; footnote number supplied]

[2] Wilson's abbreviation for "wherein consider." [Eds.' note]

Derivation of the terms for 'Law'

Jurisprudence. Roman.	Greek.	Teutonic.	Wrong and Right.

Roman.

Jus Indo-Germ root—
{ YU, YUJ in Sansr.,
ZI Gr., JU, Goth.
(ζυγόν, ζεύγνυμι; jugum;
jungo, conjux; yoke)

"Connexion ratio than constraint" = "that which is fitting,"
'orderly'; regular. ("A rule (that which is regular) administered (but not made) by a magistrate" (judex = one who declares the law, i.e. the regular practice).

Lex (legere, λέγειν) root—
meaning, "to pick, or take
things one from another (ἐ—
go, in picked out to serve)
Secundum = was ordo. Leges
publicae = "public or national
law, in all of. Seven the word
declaratia, most probable, read
from a written document."

Greek.

θέμις, θεσμός =
"that which is right, or appointed or ordained by
Heaven" (θεσμοί, the plural form used)

θέμιστες = (1) Principle
of law; (2) Decisions
or Principles (θέμιστες
original) pieces or rights
out by the magistrate.

θεσμοί = (in secondary
Seven) ordinances
"By the Greeks the ordinance of
Heaven (θέμις) was conceived to
come first; then its declaration of
that ordinance by men, whether in
conjunction, judgments, or rules of
law, in all of. Seven this word
θέμιστες Freeun. It is that the
word ... ordonn- Enforcen Declaration confined to the Seven"

Teutonic.

I **Moeso-Goth.:**
Witoth = "that which is
observed or kept" *

II **Anglo-Saxon:**
æ (aewum, aïév,
aïáv, ays)
memorial customs.

Dom (fr. DHA, to Or-
...root from which
θέμις θεσμός...
= judgment...judgment
...Domas
(Dom ready = θέμιστες)
English:

Law (lagu, laga) Root
meaning, that which lie
or rests; in fixed. Im-
ported from the Danish
(lagu) and therefore, be—
Cause foreign, quin a...

Wrong and Right.

I. **Right** (that which
was for law in so many
languages) [RIJU, mean
tur, riht; recht; Root
meaning physical strength
res] That which is straight

Reg. fr. Seven roots and
= Directus.

II **Wrong** from an
original root which sig—
nifies to twist or bend

Similarly
Droit = "that which is
physically straight" or
morally right

Tort (tortus) = tortus tot.

If [judgement] (δικη), [general signification]
= law in general.

that we first come to the
notion of abstract [justice];
but it is a third word,
originally meaning
simply custom or what
is used which survives
the others as the [generic]
al name (νόμος) of
law." (pp. 57, 58)

νόμος = use or
custom /

Common laws (from
folc-riht) = "the
right or less common
to all the people, as
distinguished from those
of particular classes.
(Analogue: jus pub-
licum).

(statute or ordinance)
* αςτιναα = θεσμοί
δεσμος = θεμιστες

(Analogue to law (or
meaning that which is set)
term. θεσις)

*Wilson's table of the derivation of terms for "Law"
used in his course in jurisprudence*

(2). *From Political Economy*, which is not a body of enforce-able rules, not a science of certitude and prediction, but simply *a reasoned exposition of the interaction of forces* of interest, or of whatever other motive, in the production, exchange, distribution and consumption of wealth.

(3). *From Politics*, in the narrower or more specific sense of the term. This is *the discretionary management of current affairs*; is productive, and very directly productive, of Law; but whose rules are manifestly themselves outside the sphere and conception of Law.

All of these contribute, in their several spheres, *to* the ultimate contents of *Law*,—to the rules which are complete and and ready for formulation, general acceptance, and sys-tematic enforcement; *but*, so long as they retain their identity, *they are separate from Law*.

> The *forces of Nature* contribute to make up all chem-ical compounds and elementary physical substances; but they are not themselves the characteristic subjects of the *science of Chemistry*.

6. *Law*, therefore, *is that portion of the established social thought and habit which has gained distinct and formal recognition in the shape of imperative uniform rules backed by the power and authority of Government.*

> Develope here *the distinction of Puchta* between a *person*[3] (that is, a being subject to jural relationships, because capable of them)—and an *individual* (a being subject to an infinite variety of other, and often much more subtle, re-lationships).

The social habit upon which Law is founded *may*, as we have seen, *have been forced* upon a submissive people by a long course of despotism; *or it may have formed itself* gradually through the uncoerced operation of free social forces; *but habit is in any case the necessary basis* and ultimate sanction of all Law. It is not necessary to blink the fact that there are forces of coercion that make for Law, as well as courses of freedom.

9-26-'91
9-15-'93.

WWT and WWhw MS. in body of lecture notes described at Sept. 26, 1891.
[3] Here Wilson inserted a marginal note: *"Puchta's* generalized 'Person.'"

From Robert Bridges

My dear Tommy: New York   Oct 7 1891
    I have never met Mr. Scudder (Horace E.) and I want to write

him about a personal matter within a few days. I should like to be authenticated to him, and would be please[d] to have a note from you to send with my letter. I do not want to approach him through this house or magazine, or I should not trouble you for an introduction.

Eleanor is still very ill, and her recovery is doubtful. Dr. Carr has been down to see her and has done his best. John will not return to college.

Hoping to see you by and bye—

In haste   Yours faithfully   Robert Bridges

ALS (WP, DLC) with WWhw notation on env.: "Ans. Oct. 8/91."

To Horace Elisha Scudder

My dear Mr. Scudder,   Princeton, New Jersey, 7 October, 1891

Could you without trouble send me the name and address of the principal lecture agency in Boston? The lecturing ambition has got hold upon me, and, finding myself this year possessed of two or three written lectures and a free end to each week, because of the concentration of my college work at the other end, I've determined, if possible, to obtain a few engagements in New England. Please do not take any trouble about this, but tell me if you know.

We have started in upon the college year here and the ardour of the work is upon me notwithstanding the fact that the ardour of other work was upon me all Summer. There are new lectures to be prepared this year, as there will be next year and the year after, and ardour is necessary if the thing is to be done.

I sincerely hope that your health is quite re-established now.

With warmest regard,

Most sincerely Yours,   Woodrow Wilson

ALS (in possession of Henry Bartholomew Cox).

To Robert Bridges

My dear Bobby,   Princeton, 8 October, 1891

Here's the introduction to Mr. Scudder;—though, as I say in it, it seems absurd to me that you should need such a thing, I'm mighty glad to be instrumental in bringing two such men together.

Your news about Eleanor makes me sad indeed—and I hope even against hope, for your sake,—for I know how you and your brother love the child. I am sincerely sorry that John is not to come back. I had hoped that his mind might get what discipline could give it—That's all it needed.

Yours in haste and affection,   Woodrow Wilson

ALS (WC, NjP). Enc. missing.

A News Item

[Oct. 10, 1891]

Prof. Woodrow Wilson's elective class in Jurisprudence numbers 180.

Printed in the *Princeton Press*, Oct. 10, 1891.

From Edward Wright Sheldon

My dear Wilson: [New York] October 12th 1891.

Mrs. Stewart,[1] my late partner's wife, is thinking of moving to Princeton next spring or autumn with her four children, and of staying there while the two boys are in college. I am trying to find a house for her now—being warned by the rush for the old town—and having seen Professor West's house[2] yesterday, write to ask if there is any chance of that being available during the coming year. I do not know him, and hearing that he is in the midst of trouble,[3] have chosen this way of getting your opinion on the point. Of course, you will use your discretion about speaking to him, and with equal generosity, I hope, will pardon me for troubling you in the matter.[4]

Sincerely yours,   Edward W. Sheldon

ALS (WP, DLC) with WWhw notation on env.: "Ans. Oct. 15/91."
  [1] Frances Gray (Mrs. William Adams Walker) Stewart.
  [2] At 5 Prospect Avenue.
  [3] West's wife, Lucy Marshall Fitz Randolph West, after the birth of her first child, Randolph, on August 7, 1890, had become the victim of the mental illness that would afflict her for the rest of her life.
  [4] Perhaps Wilson did speak to West about this matter. In any event, West did not rent his house, and Mrs. Stewart did not move to Princeton.

From Francis Fisher Browne

My Dear Sir: Chicago, Oct. 12 1891.

If you could find it agreeable and convenient to make a short review of Sidgwick's "Elements of Politics" for *The Dial*, I should take much pleasure in sending you the book. It seems an uncommonly enticing and presumably important work.[1]

Truly yours,   F. F. Browne

ALS (WP, DLC) with WWhw notation on env.: "Ans. Yes."
  [1] Wilson responded with the letter and review printed at Oct. 24, 1891.

From Joseph Ruggles Wilson

My precious son and dearest friend—   Clarksville, October 13/91

It would of course afford me real pleasure to have letters from you more frequently. But I reflect upon your many time-occupying engagements and feel that my pleasure must yield to your necessity. It is well to have plenty to do—but to overdo may not be so well: and is not one's life overdone when little or no room is left for the indulgences of natural affection? It goes without saying that I am always your devoted father and lover: a devotion which has too deep a rootage to be ever disturbed. But, my dear one, for your own sake do not cease to pull at the latch string which the unlocked door of a faithful heart holds out to your grasp, and which is so responsive to every touch of a hand that has never yet failed in having its warmth met with warmth. I do not suspect for a moment—(the suspicion would kill me—) that there creeps through my darling boy's thoughts the ghost even of a chill when his old father is present to them. This is not it. I have no wish which has not your welfare at its centre—and I seriously think that, in the act of squeezing out the juices of your life, you would do well to water with many of them this age-fading plant—at least with *some* of their big drops. Ah, my son, you have plenty of friends, I am thankful to know, and a deserved abundance of admirers amongst those whose pleasure it is to know you well—yet you have only one parent, the truest of all your friends the intensest of all your admirers:—and if I were you I would cultivate him still even though he may seem to need it not. I am sure that you are incapable of thinking of me as thus a round-about complainer. Your love and mine are not composed of the stuff which enters into the make-up of the common article; and they are able to retain their entire vigor and even to grow stronger were we never again to interchange letters, or never again to stand face to face. Still the closest love however deep its strike into the soil of a well-tried confidence, ought not to be denied certain of its natural joys; &c. &c.

I have just risen from a bed of sickness which threatened to prostrate me by the sheer force of suffering. But it was as short in its duration, I am happy to add, as it was cruel in its tearings for about forty-eight hours. I am now a believer in purgatory. It took me on Friday—a throat inflammation that forbade even the thought of swallowing—and to-day I met my classes as usual: thus not missing an hour of recitation. I have a noble junior class of about twenty of the finest fellows I have ever afflicted with the thorns of theology: and my prayer is to be spared to the end of their course.

Josie is well and doing well in his small way. I do not see much of him, either by day or night and am therefore very solitary nearly all the while—yet not miserable. Love to dear Ellie.

Your loving   Father

ALS (WP, DLC) with WWhw notation on env.: "Ans. 18 Oct., '91."

Notes for a Classroom Lecture

[Oct. 20, 1891]

Outlines of Jurisprudence.
II. Law: Its Character.

1. *Law is*, in one aspect, *a Body of Principles*, a body of Doctrine.

As such, it constitutes *a mirror of prevalent conceptions* as to ethical standards and social relationships.

It is because of this fact that it has often been said that, *if nothing remained of a people but its laws*, the history of its civilization could be accurately extracted from them. (E.g., *Hening's Statutes* of Virginia).

The chief difficulty, in historical inference, that of *obsolescence*.

Two questions must always be *asked of Law as Doctrine*:

1. *As to its Expediency*: Is it suited to its object, to the purposes of its authors? E.g., laws *against public meeting*, freedom of opinion, etc.

2. *As to its Justice*: Does it correspond with actual fact and with moral truth? *In a case of conviction*, e.g., the question is two-fold: (a) Does the act of the accused come within the terms of the Law? (b) Does the punishment denounced accord with true views as to desert and responsibility,—does the punishment suit the crime?

The *relations between Justice and Determinateness*. (Following Precedent).

The causal relationship between Justice and Expediency in the sphere of Law.

Only that is expedient which is just.

But this is *only another way of saying* that only that is expedient which tallies substantially with prevalent standards of judgment as to conduct and its responsibilities. There have been imaginary offences, like witchcraft.

Justice and expediency have, therefore, *shifting boundaries*, —boundaries which shift with ethical conceptions and social developments.

Moral Development, Individual and National: "Moral development takes place in the same manner in the individual man and in the social man. Virtue is always an effort, a habit of making reason triumph over the senses and follow the dictates of the moral law. Politics does not differ essentially from ethics, only the peoples are allowed a greater latitude in the fulfilment of their proper duties as they are not confined within the narrow round of a generation. This may be shown by an example. A courageous man does not hesitate to sacrifice his life to his honour; but a people takes account only of grave offenses, and even dissembles them until its armaments are ready and its alliances concluded. Without denying that the statesman has a greater variety of means, we come to the conclusion that, just as in private life virtue is what is supremely useful, so in politics honesty is the best policy." *Lioy*, *I.*, pp. 110, 111. Diodato Lioy "The Philosophy of Right" trans. W. Hastie, Lond. '91

> *Criticism:* The *standard cannot be the same* for State and Individual because they are not similarly made up. *The State is a complex* of individual forces; must depend upon *average judgments*, and, ∴, follow a *utilitarian Ethic.*

2. *Law is also an Active Force, an expression of Will.* It is not merely a body of opinion, its [it] is also *a body of principles in operation.*

It is *operative in two ways*; for it exercises both an ethical and a physical compulsion. It involves:

1. *An Ought,* in proportion as it is received as just. It is *a source of conviction and motive* in proportion as it is received as true. *This ethical force*, moreover, *is its principal force, its force for the majority*. It is daily influential in moving men to do even what they conceive to be contrary to their individual interests. And this *even when it is unjust in parts*, provided it be deemed sound and just as a whole.

2. A *Must,—for the minority,* who do not yield to its moral force or feel its moral compulsions.

In cases of conquest, like that of the Normans, this Must, this physical compulsion, may be operative for long periods together even against the majority, the law possessing an ethical force only for the conquerors.

The self-evident fact, however, that the ethical force of law is what it must in all normal periods depend upon, is *proof sufficient* of our recurrent proposition, *that Law is* always in the last analysis based upon custom.

3. *The Critical and Uncritical Ages of Legal Conception*:

It is necessary, if we would conceive the history of Law aright, that *we should not conceive* of the *ethical judgments* upon which it rests *as always*, or even often, *conscious and critical* judgments. *The primitive man* was very humble and docile in his acceptance of traditional law. For him it would have been *impiety to question* what had been received from the gods, or, what was for him the same thing, from revered ancestors. He was *dominated by fear and awe. His successors* have been dominated for long ages together *by fear and blind habit,*—by 'never having heard of such a thing in their lives.' The ages have been few and modern in which law has been critically scrutinized and challenged at all points for its reasons. The ages have been still fewer and still more modern in which it has been made in any degree to conform to systems of philosophical thought.

20 Oct., '91.
18 Sept., '93.

WWT and WWhw MS. in body of lecture notes described at Sept. 26, 1891.

From Edwin Oscar Smith[1]

Young Men's Christian Association,

Dear Sir,   Wesleyan University, Oct. 23, 1891.

I write to ask if you can within a month or so deliver a lecture in Middletown; if you have what may be termed a "popular" lecture; and what your terms would be in case you find it possible and agreeable to come.

Prof. Winchester suggested that you might be willing to come back to Middletown on such an errand, and of course your friends in town and in college would be glad to see you.

The proceeds of the lecture would go toward the publishing of the junior annual, the Olla Podrida.

Yours respectfully,   Edwin O. Smith.

ALS (WP, DLC) with WWhw notation on env.: "Ans. Oct. 30/91."
   1 Wesleyan, '93.

From Caleb Thomas Winchester

Middletown, Conn.,

My dear Professor Wilson,   October 24 1891.

I know that I don't deserve to be remembered by any of my friends: for I am the worst correspondent in the world. Your letter of last July confronts me, in the rack on my desk, a dozen times a day, and I've had good intentions enough with reference to that letter to pave a quarter-section of the place not named to ears polite. But I shall only make a bad matter worse if I attempt to varnish my negligence with any excuses, so let me own it up at once, and acknowledge gratefully the remembrance of your last letter as one of my "uncovenanted mercies."

Sometimes I do have vague plans of getting something printed, and the invitation which you kindly transmit from Mr. Bridges, I may some day accept. I don't know, however, whether I shall ever get any MS. actually ready unless I am somehow forced to. I never have anything that seems to me quite worth printing, and unless I am forced into it by some kind of a definite engagement I am doubtful whether I get anything really out of my hands. For the past year I seem to myself to have been more than usually sterile-minded, and this year I am trying to prepare a new course of lectures for my seniors which, thin as they are, take nearly all the time I can spare from my other work.

I read with much interest your paper in a recent Atlantic. What a good English professor and critic was lost when you turned aside to history and political science! And yet not lost either: for you are not in the camp of the philistines, and a deal of the best criticism and general literary work nowadays seems to me to come from the men who are not in any narrow or technical sense literary men. There is your ideal and model—Walter Bagehot; I wish you would tell me how to get, as well as you have, his charm of racy, practical yet suggestive expression.

I'm glad you think to lecture—glad for the lucky hearers, and glad because in moderate doses lecturing, like sherry, is pleasant and probably profitable to the lecturer. Profitable for experience and doctrine I mean; to the pocket, it may also be profitable, but unless you are more lucky than I, only in a moderate degree. As to ways of getting at it, I have never tried to use any bureau or other agency, and I suppose you wouldn't. You wouldn't care to try the "popular lyceum course," exactly I suppose in competition with the itinerant funny man and the itinerant "symphony company." For my part, I fight rather shy of the intelligent popular audience, they only want to be tickled and I'm not successful at that. The gift to speak on broad general topics which every good citizen ought to know something about is a gift to be coveted; and the man who has it can do a great deal of good on the lecture platform, I think, and must get a good deal of satisfaction out of it. But I haven't that gift. Of late I've lectured very little before the general, mixed audience. I really have only two engagements of that sort this year. The rest are before colleges, schools, or some organisation of that sort. But now and then you find an audience that expects *not* primarily to be entertained—that's the blessed kind of audience, *I* go for, provided only they are not *too* wise. There's a course of lectures, for instance, in Norwich, Conn. in which I've spoken every year for six years. The audience are not specially intelligent perhaps, only they don't think of a lecture as a substitute for the theater or a game of whist exactly, and are not indignant if their speaker isn't "so darned funny"—as the man said of Joseph Cook.[1] I'm sure you would like to speak there. I'm afraid it is too late for this year; but I've taken the liberty to mention your name to Dr. Robert P. Kerp, who runs the course and you may sometime hear from him. If I were to draw advice from my own experience I should advise any one looking out for opportunities to lecture to search out some *ladies'* society or club. My own most pleasant and profitable lecturing I think has been done in Hartford before an audience composed, as you remember, largely of elect ladies. Ladies literary clubs invited me, heard me, and paid me—paid me the only *large* honorarium I ever received. And I think that, with the probable exception of the Baltimore people, I've nowhere had so intelligent and appreciative audiences. Would you object to a mention of your name sometime when I see or write to one of the ladies who "managed" me?

What do you think of this University Extension movement? Is there a chance to do good work in that? I've had four letters from the Philadelphia society asking about lectures; but I cannot give any this season unless I can get in three or four on off days while I am absent on my Baltimore trip. The worst of it is, I think, that those people expect to pay but very little—some $20. a lecture and then want six lectures. But perhaps they pay more for lectures from abroad—that is, from outside their own circle or city. My own feeling is that it's not worth while to lecture for less than about $35.00. A smaller figure than that implies that the audience is very small and very indifferent. By the way, the Secretary of the "American Society for the Extension of University Studies" is Willis Boughton, 1602 Chestnut St. Phila— probably you know more about all this than I do: I have no doubt, however, but that if Mr. Boughton knew that you were available he would invite you for some of his courses.

You may be sure that if I can do anything to give people the opportunity of hearing you, I shall.

I am complimented by the return of Mr. Axson to Middletown. I only fear that in our lack of definite provision for graduate instruction, and with so very few graduate students for associates he will feel keenly the want of congenial atmosphere and surroundings, to say nothing of the lack of positive instruction. I am very anxious that he shall not regret his decision to return, and we shall all of us do what we can to make it worth his while. Would there were fifty of him! Only then we of the faculty should need to be multiplied by ten and raised to the nth power.

Things go on in the college about as usual. We are slowly increasing in numbers—263 I think this year. Mr. [W. M.] Daniels your Princeton man who takes Commons' place[2] in pol. economy, seems a very pleasant, attractive fellow and is very well-liked, I hear by the students. Stephenson seems getting on rather better, but I really don't know how well. He has given up his plan of plunging the Sophomore—who, as a rule, doesn't know Queen Anne from Queen Elisabeth—into a course of mediaeval church history, as a propaedeutic for the later historical work. Like enough he may learn some sense here to match the history he learned at the Hopkins.

Mrs. Hazen, as I suppose you have heard, has had a long and trying illness, which at one time was very serious. She is slowly recovering but isn't yet able to sit up. I think Dr. Hazen now wishes he had taken her into the mountains this summer instead of to the sea shore. By the way, I found an almost ideal place this summer. Come and try it next season with Mrs. Wilson and the children. It is Waterville, N. H. A little valley, 1550 feet above the sea, no houses save the hotel and two or three cottages, noble mountains rising all about you, bracing air, water that has a touch of Helicon in it, beautiful walks and climbs, and a company of very sensible and affable folk. One must be a college professor, a D.D. or a public officer to get in, they say. *You're* qualified. If you get a good room you can work there pretty well— save that you're away from libraries.

But it is late. This dilute epistle is too long. I wish you could come up to Middletown for a day or so and bring Mrs. Wilson with you. And a good many people wish that same. Run out of the open end of some one of your weeks—lucky man to *have* an open end!—and come and see us.

Mrs. W. unites with me in hearty regards to you both, and hearty invitations to Middletown, and I am, as ever,

Yours very Sincerely   C. T. Winchester

ALS (WP, DLC).

1 The Rev. Joseph Cook, Congregationalist minister of Boston, renowned for his lectures defending traditional religious beliefs against Darwinism.

2 Commons, who had been let go by Wesleyan on the ground that he was a a failure as a teacher, was in 1891-92 Associate Professor of Political Economy at Oberlin College. See John R. Commons, *Myself* (New York, 1934), pp. 44-45.

To Francis Fisher Browne

My dear Sir,   Princeton, New Jersey, 24 October, 1891
    I had examined Sidgwicks 'Politics' quite thoroughly, in our library copy, before the copy you sent me arrived,—so that I am able to send you my notice at once. I hope it will prove to your mind.   Very sincerely Yours,   Woodrow Wilson

ALS (de Coppet Coll., NjP).

A Book Review

[c. Oct. 24, 1891]

THE ELEMENTS OF POLITICS. By Henry Sidgwick, author of "The Methods of Ethics," and "The Principles of Political Economy." New York: Macmillan & Co.

It is difficult to find a just criterion by which to judge Professor Henry Sidgwick's "The Elements of Politics." It is not historical, not an analysis of the growth of institutions; if it were, one could apply to it the test of insight. It is not constructive; if it were, one could ask whether it was consistent and sufficiently considerate of practical conditions. Its object is to "expound, within a convenient compass, and in as systematic a form as the subject-matter" will "admit, the chief general considerations that enter into the rational discussion of political questions in modern states." It is an attempt to generalize experience in order to frame standards of judgment for the guidance of politics in the future. Professor Sidgwick, as everybody knows, is an adherent of the utilitarian school of philosophy. Standards of experience are, therefore, in his thought, also standards of morality. His method throughout, consequently, is like that of the better writers upon international law. The sanctions of international law are morality and experience. Its principles conform to the general ethical judgments of the world and to the higher laws of expediency. It is a formulation of particular cases and "general considerations": where it does not read like a treaty, it reads like a tract.

    Austin described international law as a body of "positive morality"; Mr. Sidgwick's "Elements of Politics" might be described as a body of positive wisdom—which he would deem much the same thing. His propositions are almost all of them evidently true,—many of them are, indeed, only too obviously true,—as "general considerations"; but that, it seems to me, only makes them the more questionable as standards of political action. For the course of politics is subject in each nation, not to general, but to particular considerations. General considerations are applicable only if you presuppose a uniform development and a uniform experience. They may be useful, as norms, as points of departure, perhaps; but special considerations must always shape policy. Each nation has its own individuality, its own prepossessions, its own enthusiasms and antipathies, its own capacities and incapacities; each nation is in its own stage of development, moreover; its life shapes its character, and its life is made up of a thousand-score events great and small;—and these things command its politics.

The study of politics should not be a study of comparative anatomy,—a State is not a cadaver! It should be a study of the special sources and conditions of life and national character, a study of circumstantial psychology, of incidental development, of eventful heredity. There may be Elements of English Politics, or of American, or of French or Prussian; but the elements of general politics, if cast into general considerations, must either be quite colorless or quite misleading. The considerations urged by Professor Sidgwick are for the most part quite colorless: his cases are entirely hypothetical cases; national institutions and historical events are only illustrations in point.

To stop with this criticism, however, would be to do the book scant justice. Of course the actual experiences of civilized States are the background of its thought,—the hidden data of its hypotheses; and, although it is clearly impossible to extract many general considerations from the infinite variety of political circumstance, and although it is doubtless wiser not to try to do so, but to seek rather to vivify to the conception the life and genius of particular States, setting forth their historical itinerancy, deciphering the causes of their grandeur or decadence; it is, nevertheless, possible to some extent to generalize political experience in such a way as to be profitable for doctrine and for reproof, if not for instruction in the daily conduct of affairs. And Mr. Sidgwick has accomplished this with a reasonable degree of success. If his matter is often lifeless, the fault must be charged to his method and his style.

His chapters afford a rich variety of topics. His procedure is deductive, "based on psychological propositions not universally and absolutely true, but approximately true of civilized men," but his treatment is of course more or less saturated with experience. In the first part of the work he deals with fundamental questions, such as the relation of the State to law, and of individuals to each other under law; with the principles which should obtain in legislation in respect of the extension or contraction of the sphere of free individual action; with questions of property, inheritance, and remedial justice; with the relations of law to morality; and with the principles of "international duty" and "external policy." In the second part he considers the structure of governments, their methods and instruments, their several parts and the relationship of those parts to each other, their local or sectional parts, their relations to voluntary associations, the part of the people in government, the influences of parties and of party government, and the ultimate seat of political power. His main aim he fully accomplishes: he sets forth with admirable impartiality perhaps all the general considerations which his topics can be made to yield touching the question, What ought the constitution and action of government to be? If the reader lays the book down with some disappointment, some feeling of inconclusiveness, he may rest assured that the best has been done that circumstances permitted. Politics is "embedded in matter"; when the attributes of matter are looked at by themselves they must needs look thin.

WOODROW WILSON.

Printed in the Chicago *Dial*, xii (Nov. 1891), 215-16.

From Herbert Baxter Adams

Dear Sir: Baltimore, Md., October 26, 1891.

President Gilman desires to issue in connection with his next Annual Report a complete bibliography of all the published work of Johns Hopkins men, whether members of the academic staff or University graduates, and has charged me with the work of the Historical Department. Will you kindly send me, *as soon as you can conveniently*, a full list of your contributions to science or education, including notable book reviews? In each case the title of the contribution should be given with exact reference to the magazine or periodical in which it appeared, with the date and place of publication.[1]

The following form will serve to indicate the kind of reference desired:

Adams, Herbert Baxter. The Higher Education of the People. An Address delivered before the State Historical Society of Wisconsin, January 28, 1891: (Proceedings of the Thirty-eighth Annual Meeting of the State Historical Society of Wisconsin, Madison, 1891).

Ely, Richard T.   The Labor Movement in America: (New York, T. Y. Crowell & Co., 1886. 8vo pp. 383).

Very truly yours,   H B Adams

TLS (WP, DLC) with WWhw notation "Ans." and WWsh on env.
[1] This seems to have been intended to be part of the collection which later appeared under the title *Bibliographia Hopkinsiensis, 1876-1893* (6 parts in 3

vols., Baltimore, 1892-94). The six parts published covered philology, chemistry, geology, physics, astronomy, and mathematics. It appears that no bibliography of the Department of History, Politics, and Economics at the Johns Hopkins was published before the one which appeared in the memorial volume, *Herbert B. Adams, Tributes of Friends, with a Bibliography of the Department of History, Politics and Economics of the Johns Hopkins University, 1876-1901* (Baltimore, 1902). Wilson's section, pages 155-57, included only his books and major articles.

From Caleb Thomas Winchester

My dear Professor Wilson: Middletown, Ct. Oct. 27th 1891.

This note is not an answer to the very hearty and very welcome letter I received from you this afternoon, but only an attempt to get ahead of your many Middletown friends in saying that I hope you will consent to stay at our house during your lecture visit to Middletown, and that you will, if possible, bring Mrs. Wilson with you. Mrs. Winchester, you may be sure, joins me very heartily in this invitation—both clauses of it. When is it you are to come? I hope not during Thanksgiving week or the Thursday or Friday of the week previous, as on those days I may be absent—taking my Thanksgiving visit to Wells College.

We are all delighted to know that you can come to talk to us, and with us. I believe you may expect a good house full of your old friends, with a plentiful sprinkling of unlucky younger fellows who wish they had been old enough to be of the numbers of your friends.

Hoping that nobody is beforehand with me in this request of this note, I am

Yours very cordially   C. T. Winchester

ALS (WP, DLC) with WWhw notation on env.: "Ans. 30 Oct/91."

From James Monroe Taylor[1]

Dear Sir,   Poughkeepsie, N. Y. Oct. 29, 1891.

Can you give us one or two lectures here,—or a brief course, say three,—at some time after the first week in February, and before the last week in March?[2] I need not assure you of a hearty welcome. We should hope for the privilege of entertaining you in the College, during your stay. May I ask you to state, for my Committee, what compensation you receive for such work?[3] The choice of subjects, and the exact date, or dates, could be left undetermined, now,—but I should be glad to fix my lists for the winter.

I am   Very truly yours,   J. M. Taylor.

ALS (WP, DLC).
[1] President of Vassar College, 1886-1914.
[2] Wilson's reply is missing, but in it he obviously said that he was too busy

to accept any more outside engagements for the academic year 1891-92. President Taylor, in correspondence which is also missing, must have renewed the invitation in the autumn of 1892, for Wilson delivered the address, "Democracy," printed at Dec. 5, 1891, at Vassar on December 9, 1892. See the news report printed at Jan. 1, 1893, Vol. 8.

[3] As revealed by Wilson's list printed at the end of "Democracy," he set the fee at $50.

To Edwin Oscar Smith

My dear Sir,   Princeton, New Jersey, 30 October, 1891

I have delayed answering your letter of Oct. 23 in order that I might make sure of my future times of leisure for such an engagement as you propose.

I should like very much to come to Middletown to lecture and I could do so with perfect convenience about the middle of December, if that will suit your convenience. I could lecture on any evening of the week except Monday and Tuesday. My terms—which for most people would be $50 and expenses—would, for you, be $35 and expenses. My subject would be 'Democracy.'[1]

If this suits you as to time, subject and terms, I will be very glad indeed to come.

                    Very sincerely Yours,   Woodrow Wilson

ALS (photostat in CtW).

[1] Printed at Dec. 5, 1891; see also the news item printed at Jan. 18, 1892.

From the Minutes of the Princeton Faculty

                                    5 5' P.M., Friday, Nov. 6, 1891.

. . . Professors Sloane, Fine & W. Wilson were appointed a Committee to arrange for the restoration of the Billiard Tables in conformity with the Remit from the Board of Trustees.

From Joseph Ruggles Wilson

My precious son—   Clarksville, Tenn., Nov. 7/91

I have just returned from Memphis, where I spent two days in the service of our divinity school here. The Synod of Kentucky, finding that the directors of this institution were utterly opposed to a surrender of the theological department for the sake of a large seminary to be located at Louisville (and which exists only in the clouds of a rose-colored future)—has had the cheek to ignore us altogether, and to appeal to the Synods (our constituents) for co-operation, &c[.] Well, it sent commissioners to the Synod of Nashville, and wheedled a majority into passing what would seem like a sanction of the new departure. The same was repeated at Synod of Arkansas. It was important therefore that the thing should be effectivally stopped, by blocking it, if possible, at the Synod of Memphis. Accordingly Mr. D. N. Kennedy[1] and myself went down last Tuesday (4th)—met the Synod, and in its presence confronted the Kentucky men throughout a four hours' debate[.] The upshot was that we routed them, horse, foot & dragoon.[2] The other Synods were not properly managed, or these delegates of selfishness could have had no more showing than we gave them at Memphis. The next contest will be next week at the Synod of Mississippi, where Dr. Palmer[3] will work the laboring oar. I made a good speech—the papers saying that Tennessee ought to be proud of me, &c. &c—you know the sort of nonsense.

I found your letter awaiting my return, and it afforded me a signal pleasure as you can easily guess. You seem to have enough of company to satisfy any reasonable want in that direction; along with enough work to gratify the incarnate spirit of industry. Maybe, however, one will serve to balance the other in the way of keeping the internal machinery well a-going. Assuredly all toil and no relaxation cannot be best, and for my part, when I was of your years and long afterwards, I delighted in entertaining. We have to become men of the world sometimes in order to keep from being men of the monastery. The stilts of study are not good for *constant* use. I will be greatly pleased to see the articles you are writing for the journals—& to which you refer. I do not doubt as to their prospective excellence, and shall read them with the eye of gigantic love.

Dode[4] & I are rocking along in our double groove, but which not being parallel forbids more than an occasional half hour together. We have of course many things in common; and prominent amongst these is our unswerving love for you and yours (which are also *ours*). Make dear Ellie to think of us now and then as she can spare the time and cause yourself to know that we are such lovers as are not often found in either fatherhood or brotherhood.   Your devoted   Father.

ALS (WP, DLC) with WWhw notation on env.: "Ans. Nov. 17/91."

[1] Of Clarksville, secretary of the Board of Directors of Southwestern Presbyterian University.

[2] The Synod of Kentucky, after refusing to join other synods in supporting Southwestern Presbyterian University, had organized a theological class at Central University in Richmond, Kentucky, in 1891. At the same time, the Synod of Kentucky appealed to the synods supporting Southwestern to join it in establishing a new seminary without any connection with an existing institution. Joseph Bardwell, "The Southwestern Presbyterian University and 'The Proposed Theological Seminary for the Southwest,'" New Orleans *Southwestern Presbyterian*, Nov. 5, 1891.

The overture of the Synod of Kentucky was presented to the Synod of Memphis when it met in the Second Presbyterian Church in Memphis on December 3, 1891. Dr. Wilson and Kennedy opposed the overture. The Synod of Memphis not only rejected the overture but also urged the Synod of Kentucky to abandon its plan for a separate seminary and to support Southwestern Presbyterian University. J. D. Leslie, "Synod of Memphis," *ibid.*, Nov. 19, 1891.

The Synod of Kentucky discontinued its theological class at Central University in 1892 and, joined only by the Synod of Missouri, founded the Louisville Presbyterian Theological Seminary in 1893. Robert Stuart Sanders, *History of Louisville Presbyterian Theological Seminary, 1853-1953* (Louisville, 1953), pp. 29-36.

[3] The Rev. Dr. Benjamin Morgan Palmer.
[4] J. R. Wilson, Jr.

From Joseph R. Wilson, Jr.

My dearest brother: Clarksville, Tenn.   Nov. 7 1891

The fact that I have not written for many weeks does not prove that I do not think of and love you and yours as much as ever, but that I am as busy as a bee. My work keeps me on the go almost constantly, and when my day's duties have been performed I am too tired to think much of letter writing. I do not mind being so busy, I rather like it.

Now there is one matter concerning which I want your advice, and the sooner you can give it me the better will I be pleased. When father is asked his opinion concerning such matters he always says he does not know so I go to you as next best. You know I have engaged myself to Kate. I am now receiving about sixty five or seventy dollars each month. Could I well aford matrimony under the circumstances? This seems one absurdly silly question, I know, but I always was in the habit of thinking aloud to those nearest to me, you know, and I do not care to break myself of that habit. The best board will cost me $35 or $40 per month for two. What do you think? I feel now that I will not be contented until I am married, but I do not want to precipitate matters too much and risk being pinched.

Father has just returned from Memphis where he went to fight representatives of the Kentucky Synod who are striving to take away a portion of the support of the S. W. P. U. and establish a new theological school at Louisville. You will see a brief account of the matter in the Progress and a full act. in the Memphis papers I send you.

Father and I are now in statu quo and write in unbounded love to you & your dear ones. Please write soon.

                              Your aff. bro.   Joseph.

ALS (WP, DLC) with WWhw notation on env.: "Ans. Nov. 17/91."

A Lecture on Sovereignty[1]

Nov. 9, 1891

Political Sovereignty.

The conception of political sovereignty is one of those interest-ing portions of doctrine wh. belong in common to several distinct branches of study. No systematic discussion of any part of the science of politics can advance very far without it. It is even more indispensable to the student of legal systems than to the student of institutions. It is a question central to the life of the states and to the validity of law. And it is rendered the more interesting by the fact that it is a critical question, used by all schools alike as a capital test of orthodoxy. No man who cares a whit about his standing among students of law or of politics can afford to approach it lightly. Whatever he says about it he must need say with a profound sense of responsibility. He must undertake the discussion of it with the same sort of gravity, with the same deep sense of personal risk that the political economist evinces when he ventures an opinion about Value or hazards a theory of Distribution. When once he has committed himself to an opinion concerning it, he may be sure that with a large and influential number of his fellow students he can never there-after pass for a man of undoubted scholarship or unclouded sense.

If it is awkward, under such circumstances, that the con-ception should be so indispensable, it doubtless has the advantage of forcing boldness upon us. If for nothing else than for the sake of a *modus vivendi* we must out with whatever notion it is that we have accepted or invented with reference to the nature and lodgment of Sovereignty. It is on the whole, safer to be explicit than to hedge.

And yet it is not easy to be explicit; for there are no suitable

---

1 Wilson delivered this address, which he soon published in a slightly revised form in *An Old Master and Other Political Essays* (New York, 1893), before the Faculty Philosophical Club at President McCosh's home at 33 Prospect Avenue on about November 9, 1891. The only published report of the affair, in *The Princetonian*, xvi (Nov. 13, 1891), [3], reads: "Prof. Wilson read a paper on 'Political Sovereignty' at a recent meeting held at Dr. McCosh's residence."

The Philosophical Club, organized by McCosh in 1888, was holding monthly meetings by 1890-91, and its membership had been restricted to the professors and fellows of the Philosophy Department.

Wilson had first become intrigued by the problem of sovereignty while writing *The State*, and he had adverted somewhat substantially to the subject in a lecture, "The Development of Law," before the Historical Seminary at the Hopkins. See the Minutes of the Seminary of Historical and Political Science, printed at March 15, 1889, particularly n. 2, Vol. 6. The address, "Political Sovereignty," printed here, was a crystallization and recasting into literary form of the three lectures on sovereignty that Wilson had given in his course on public law at Princeton in late 1890. The notes for these lectures are described at September 15, 1890. [Eds.' note] terms to be explicit with. One no sooner begins to examine the field and the matter of controversy than he begins to suspect that it is all a question of terminology. After being hurried in bewilderment thro' one of Browning's short poems without being permitted to be quite sure at any point of the full meaning, we are led, in our disappointment, to wonder with Mr. Birrell if it can be the *punctuation*.[2] In what we read of Sovereignty we are led to wonder if it can be the *words* that confuse us. It must be evident to everyone who has not been sophisticated by the terms themselves, or committed beyond retrieval by the controversial use of them, that when, e.g., the people of the United States and the Czar of Russia are put together in the same class as sovereigns, language has been forced to a very artificial use, and one term made to cover two radically different things. There is clearly a striking contrast between these two sovereigns, in character, in method, and in power. Doubtless an excellent way by which to enter our subject would be through an examination of this difference. But another way is more direct.

Let us begin with an accepted definition of Sovereignty. It is both decent and convenient to take that of Austin: that celebrated definition which he received through Bentham from Hobbes. Austin conceived a sovereign very concretely, as a person or body of persons existing in an independent political society and accorded the habitual obedience of the bulk of the members of that society, while itself subordinate to no political superior; and law he defined to be the explicit or implicit command of such a person or body of persons addressed to the members of the community, its inferiors or subjects. Supreme political authority he conceived to rest in each independent community in some such determinate sovereign person or body.[3]

Some part of the lineage of this conception is German. Austin had studied in Bonn while it was the residence of such men as Niebuhr, Schlegel, Arndt, Welcher, Mackeldey, and Heffter, and at a period when controversy touching some of the fundamental questions as to the province and method of Jurisprudence

---

[2] Augustine Birrell, "On the Alleged Obscurity of Mr. Browning's Poetry," *Obiter Dicta* (New York, 1885), p. 74. [Eds.' note]

[3] By the very term used to describe it, moreover, this Sovereignty is supremacy,—is subject to no limitation. Every law is a command, the command of a Supreme Authority, and it would be a singular contradiction in terms to speak of this supreme power as limited by law. How can the supreme author of law within a State be himself subject to law: how can the creature bind the creator? How can one refrain from smiling at the logical incapacity of those who speak of limitations to sovereignty, and,—more absurdly still,—of divisions of sovereignty? Is there a hierarchy of supremacies—can there be a coordination of creators? [WW's note. Wilson is here paraphrasing and quoting from John Austin, *Lectures on Jurisprudence, or the Philosophy of Positive Law*, abridged by Robert Campbell (London, 1875), Lecture VI, pp. 82-147.]

Wilson as a young professor at the
College of New Jersey

Ellen Axson Wilson in the 1890's

Jessie Woodrow Wilson
and Margaret Wilson

Eleanor Randolph Wilson

The Wilsons' home at 48 Steadman Street, later Library Place

Nassau Hall

The front campus of the College of New Jersey about 1890

Francis Landey Patton,
President of the College of New Jersey and
Princeton University, 1888-1902

William Milligan Sloane,
Professor of History
at Princeton, 1883-1897

James Ormsbee Murray,
Dean of the Faculty
of Princeton, 1883-1899

was in its keen youth. His thought was mature, indeed, before he went abroad, and Nature had very imperatively commanded of what sort that thought should be by giving him a mind framed for abstract conception and sharp logical processes; but contact with German thought certainly contributed many important elements to his mental equipment, and Thibaut became scarcely less his master than Bentham. It was inevitable that it should be Thibaut rather than Savigny. Savigny was the great leader of the historical school: he believed that all law was rooted in old habit and that legislation could modify law successfully and beneficially only by consenting to the secondary rôle of supplementing, formulating, or at the best guiding custom; and he was at weapons drawn with the school of Thibaut, who proposed to lay legislative hands on the entire body of German law and make a Code which should be common to all the German states and so help to make Germany a national unit. To attempt thus to systematize law where by natural development it was unsystematic seemed to Savigny a deliberate effort to render it artificial. Law, he maintained, did not often grow into a logical system, but was the product of daily accretions of habit and sluggish formations of thought wh. followed no system of philosophy: it was not the business of legal science to force it into logical categories,—it was its function, rather, to give a clear explanation of the principles and order of its life and a satisfactory working analysis of its several parts and conceptions. Thibaut, on the other hand, believed it to be the legitimate function of the jurist to make piece-meal law up into organic wholes, rendering it clear where it had been obscure, correcting its inconsistencies, trimming away its irregularities, reducing the number of its exceptional provisions, discovering and filling in its gaps, running it through with threads of system, giving it elegance of style and completeness of method. He thought it possible to change law from a system of habits into a system of commands. Of course these were the ideas which were most attractive, most natural, to the mind of Austin, who described his intellectual office to be that of 'untying knots,' unravelling confused notions by means of logical analysis.

But, however natural such conceptions may have been to Austin, it must certainly be regarded as singular that, though rejected on the Continent, where sovereignty had throughout the most important formative periods of European history been quite unequivocally lodged in unmistakable sovereigns, they should have been accepted in England, the country where law had been least subject to doctrine, most observant of times and circumstances, most piece-meal in its method of construction, least like a set of commands and most like a set of habits and conventions. Doubtless we are to remember, however, that the feudal theory of law had long been held with perfect confidence by English lawyers in calm despite of fact. Probably it is true that the English mind, with its practical habit, likes nice systems well enough because of their appearance of completeness—has a sense of order which enjoys logic, without having any curiosity or capacity for the examination of premises. The Englishman has always been found ready to accept from those who had the leisure to amuse themselves in that way, interesting explanations of his institutions which did not at all fit the actual facts; and it has caused him no inconvenience: for he has not perceived the lack of adjustment between his actual transactions and the theory he has accepted concerning them. He has of course not troubled himself to alter his institutions to suit his philosophy. That philosophy satisfied his thought and inconvenienced neither Parliament nor the courts. And so he had no doubt Austin was right.

Austin's logic is unrelenting, and the loyalty of his followers unflinching. He will have it that all laws are the command of a determinate person or body of persons, the sovereign authority of an independent political society; and proofs to the contrary have only partially disconcerted his disciples. Sir Henry Maine having shown that throughout the greater part of history the world has been full of independent political societies possessing no such commanding sovereign, and it having become notorious that legislation has everywhere played a late and comparatively subordinate part in the production of law, the latest writers of the Austinian school have reduced Jurisprudence to a merely formal science, professing to care nothing for the actual manner in which law may *originate*, nothing even for most of the motives which induce men to obey law, provided you will but concede that there is, among a great many other imperative motives, one which is universally operative, namely fear of the compulsion of physical force, and that there is at least one sovereign function, namely the application of that physical force in the carrying out of the law. They ask to be allowed to confine themselves to such a definition of positive law as will limit it to "rules which are *enforced* by a political superior in his capacity as such." They take for their province only a systematic description of the forms and method "of the influence of government upon human conduct" through the operation of law. They virtually abandon the attempt to find any universal doctrines respecting the rôle of government as a *maker* of laws. For them government is not a *creative* agent, but only an instrumentality for the effectuation of legal rules, already in existence. So hard is the principle of life to get at that they give over all attempts to find it, and, turning away from the larger topics of the biology, restrict themselves to the morphology of law.

When it came to pointing out the body of persons with which sovereignty was lodged in particular states of complex constitutional structure, Austin was sometimes very unsatisfactory. Sovereignty is lodged in England, he says, in the King, the peers, and—*not* the House of Commons, but the *electorate*: for he holds the House of Commons to be merely a trustee of the electors, notwithstanding the fact that the electors exercise their right of franchise under laws which Parliament itself enacted and may change. In the United States he 'believes' it to be lodged "in the States' governments, as forming one aggregate body"; and he explains that by the government of a State he does not mean its "ordinary legislature, but the body of its citizens which appoints its ordinary legislature, and which, the union apart, is properly sovereign therein." Apparently he is led thus to go back of the House of Commons and the legislatures of our States to the electorates by which they are chosen because of his conception of sovereignty as *unlimited*: if he stopped short of the electors some part of his sovereign body would be subject to political superiors. If he were to go beyond the electors to the larger body of the people—to the women and the men who cannot vote—he would come upon, not a 'determinate,' but an indeterminate body of persons. Our own writers, however, having made bold to embrace the dogma of popular sovereignty with a certain fervor of patriotism, have had no hesitation about taking the additional step. They maintain, with Lieber, that, "according to the views of free men" sovereignty "can dwell with *society*, the *nation*, only."[4] Writers like the late Judge Jameson, of Chicago, declare that they have very definite ideas of what this means. They think that Mr. Bryce expounded the doctrine when he wrote his Chapter on Government by Public Opinion. "When the true sovereign has spoken," says Judge Jameson,—"at public meetings, by the press, or by personal argument or solicitation,—the electorate, when it acts, either registers the behests of the people or ceases betimes further to represent them." "The pressure of public opinion consciously brought to bear upon the electorate," he declares to be, even when 'inarticulate' (whatever inarticulate

---

[4] Francis Lieber, *On Civil Liberty and Self-Government*, 3rd edn. (Philadelphia, 1874), p. 152. [Eds.' note]

pressure may be) "a clear and legitimate exercise of sovereign power";[5] and he thinks that Mr. Herbert Spencer meant the same thing when he declared that "that which, from hour to hour, in every country, governed despotically or otherwise, produces the obedience making political action possible, is the accumulated and organized sentiment felt towards inherited institutions made sacred by tradition," inasmuch as Mr. S. proceeds to say with all plainness, "Hence it is undeniable that, taken in its widest acceptation, the feeling of the community is the sole source of political power; in those communities, at least, wh. are not under foreign domination. It is so at the outset of social life, and it still continues substantially so."[6] And yet, if Mr. Spencer means the same thing that Judge Jameson means, what are we to think of the present fraternization of France and Russia? If the people be sovereign in France and the Czar sovereign in Russia, it is perhaps quite conceivable that one sovereign should love another; but, if it be true, as Judge Jameson makes Mr. Spencer say, that it is the people, even in Russia, who are after all sovereign, what are we to think of the fondness of the French sovereign for a government which is holding the Russian sovereign in subjection? If this be correct thinking it puts us into awkward quandaries, troubling our logic, as well as condemning our lives.

Apply this doctrine of our masters in American law to our actual political conditions, and see how far it simplifies the matter. In the United States, so runs the orthodox creed, the People is sovereign—the verb is singular because the people under this doctrine constitute a unit. And yet it is notorious that they never have acted as a unit, nor ever can act, under our existing constitution. They have always acted, and must always act, in state groups. And in state groups what action do they take? They assent to constitutional provisions, or decline to assent to them; and they select certain persons to act as law-makers, as judges, or as executive officers of government. Do they choose policies? No. Do they frame constitutional provisions? No: they only accept or reject them. In the only case in which they speak directly concerning specific provisions of law, they neither command nor originate. They receive or decline what is offered them. They must wait until they are asked. They have neither initiative nor opportunity to construct. They must be consulted concerning government, but they do not conduct it.

Nor is it otherwise, upon last analysis, in Switzerland, where

[5] John Alexander Jameson, "National Sovereignty," *Political Science Quarterly*, v (June 1890), 200. [Eds.' note]
[6] Herbert Spencer, *The Principles of Sociology* (3 vols., London, 1876-96), II, 327. [Eds.' note]

the *Referendum* exists—where, i.e., the people vote upon specific measures of ordinary legislation not only, but where they are also provided with means of imperative initiative. By petitions bearing a certain large number of signatures they can propose definite legislation, compel action upon the proposals by their legislatures, and an ultimate submission of the question to popular vote. But see what this is when examined. The eyes of the community, the men of information and progress get up a petition: i.e., an indeterminate body and a minority demand that certain laws be formulated and put to the vote. The thing is done; but the measure defeated, let us say, at the polls. The eyes of the community have desired certain things, have offered them to the slow digestive organs—and they have been rejected. Are the digestive organs, then, sovereign, and not the initiative parts, the eyes and the reason? Is it sovereign to stomach a thing and not sovereign to *do* a thing?

But turn the chase in another direction, if peradventure we may yet run this sovereign people to cover. The more absolute democratic theorists, it is true, decline to restrict the sovereign body to the electorate, to those who have votes. The voters are simply the agents of the community, they say. The press and the pulpit, the private argument and the curtain lecture command—voters, if they are faithful, obey. Others, however, no less democratic, no less desirous of holding ideas which may be reckoned suitable for free men, seek for a more determinate body, content themselves with the qualified voters, and think with relief that all difficulties are removed. The *electorate* is sovereign.

But is the electorate a more determinate body than the population? Does registration afford us any more certain results than the census yields? Do the electors act in determinate numbers? Is there a quorum? Have they any choice but to act under the forms and within the limits assigned by law? Can they command without invitation, or assent without suggestion? Are not the agencies which Judge Jameson fixes upon as sovereign after all more active, more self-directed, freer to criticize, to suggest, to insist. The press, the pulpits, the mass-meetings, the urgent friends, the restless, ambitious wives, the pert and forward children can at any rate keep on talking in the intervals, when the electors are reduced to silence, patiently a-waiting an opportunity to vote. Moreover, if we are right in accepting this miscellaneous sovereign of men, women, and children, and in understanding Mr. Spencer to mean that always and everywhere the sentiments and conclusions of this body have had the validity and imperativeness of sovereign determinations, the history of Sovereignty is manifestly greatly simplified for us. Our determinate body of persons, the free population, is always present and has always been present, under all constitutions: all that we have to inquire is, What means had they for the expression of their will; How were their dispositions and judgment made to tell effectually upon the consciousness of those who framed the laws? True this sovereign body has its points of resemblance to the god, Baal. Those who call upon it call in vain if it be not the season fixed by law for voting: there is no voice, nor any that answer nor any that regardeth. No fire proceeds from it to consume the sacrifice. It may safely be mocked, sovereign though it be. Perhaps it is talking, or it is pursuing, or it is in a journey, or peradventure it sleepeth, and must be awaked. Oftentimes it is cowed also, and, if it speaks, it speaks but in mutterings. But at least it has no regular periodicity of incapacity such as is suffered by the body of electors. If we are to choose, in making selection of our sovereign, between the population and the electorate, it is evidently a choice between confused voices and a voice that cannot select either its time of speaking or the subject upon which it is to speak.

This is a singular pursuit, this diligent search for a sovereign amid the obvious phenomena of politics. If laws be indeed commands, and not only commands but the commands of a *determinate* person or body of persons, it ought surely to be possible to find this determinate source of authority. And yet it would seem that it can be discovered only by much ingenious analysis. We find Mr. Sidgwick in his Elements of Politics[7] going about most uneasily in his last chapter, to find the thing which he would have us call Supreme Political Power rather than Sovereignty. He has been looking forward, not without nervousness, to this inquiry throughout the chapters which precede, for the matter puzzles him a little. Political power is exercised, he perceives, through some organ of government; but he cannot conceive that the power of this organ is its own power: he is engaged in a study of dynamics. What moves this organ, whence does it derive its power? How is it influenced? Is it itself commanded, overawed, constrained from any quarter? And so he runs into the metaphysics of government. Taking a prince as a simple and normal organ of government, he analyses the subjection of princes to their ministers, to priests, to mistresses, to the violent protests of an insubordinate people. Then he weighs the will and the independence of the prince, and con-

---

[7] See Wilson's review of this volume printed at Oct. 24, 1891. [Eds.' note]

cludes that no influence that he can throw off without losing his own authority is a sovereign influence; but that any influence which can threaten his power if he resist is a sovereign influence, the true depository of ultimate, supreme political power. Sovereignty thus becomes a catalogue of influences, a scheme of public action in all its phases.

Can we accept these singular processes? If a physicist were to discard all the separate laws, all the differential analysis of his science and reduce its entire body of principles to some general statement of the correlation of forces, he would hardly be conceived to have done physics a service; if in our study of anatomy we should turn away from structural adjustment and functional force to take account of the thousand and one influences which in individual cases affect the organs from without, we should obviously be abandoning the science itself. It seems to me that we do a very like thing if, in studying the structural forces and organic actions of society, its organs of command, its organs of execution, its superior and its subordinate authorities, its habitual modes of structural life, we abandon all attempt at differentiation, throw all analysis into hotch-potch, and reduce everything to terms of the general forces which mould and govern society as a whole. We confuse our thought in our effort to simpl[i]fy it. We lose, we do not gain, by putting powers of different sorts together into the same categories, driving them abreast, as if they pulled together, in the same propositions.

A very different method, and even a different set of conceptions, seem to me necessary. We have been mistaken in looking for any unlimited power. There is no unlimited power except the sum of all powers; and our legal theorists have sought some unlimited sovereign by the process of summation—by making it consist in the combined powers of the community. Sovereignty, if it be a definite and separable thing at all, is not unlimited—is not identical with the power of the community. It is not the general vitality of the organism, but the specific originative power of certain organs. Sovereigns have always been subject in greater or less degree to the community—have always been organs of the State, and never the State itself: but they have been sovereigns none the less: they, and not the State itself.

I shall insist, ∴, at all stages of the discussion, upon distinguishing clearly these two quite different things: the powers and processes of governing, viz., and the relations of the people to those powers and processes. Those relations are relations of assent and obedience,—and the degree of assent and obedience mark the limits,—the sphere—of Sovereignty. Sovereignty is the daily operative power of making and giving *efficacy* to laws. It is the substantive, living, *governing* power. It is daily in command of affairs. It lives; it plans; it originates, it executes. It is the organic origination by the State of its law and policy. The Sovereign Power is the highest originative organ of the State. That free populations themselves elect the sovereign body by the selection of its members, does not make those populations that sovereign body. That that sovereign, originative body must prudently regard the state of opinion among those populations, does not make them any less sovereign than kings have been who reigned by hereditary right and yet found it needful to please their subjects. The obedience of the subject has always limited the power of the sovereign. (Burke)[8] This is the covert admission of the Austinian definition itself, though not many of the orthodox have called attention to the fact. The sovereign power is that to which "the bulk of the community is habitually obedient,"—the acquiescence and coöperation of the community has always been indispensable to its exercise of authority. When we are discussing the influences which tell upon the action of the chief originative organ of the State, we are discussing, not sovereignty, not the function of origination, command, and guidance, but the natural and universal limitations of sovereignty, the conditions of acquiescence, cooperation, obedience on the part of the people; the natural laws, the structural checks and balances of the organism. There is no hope for theory if it is to neglect these obvious distinctions.

Fortunately there is no serious dispute about the facts of the case: the materials for generalization, at any rate, are not doubtful. At all times and under all systems there have been two sets of phenomena visible in government: the phenomena of command and the phenomena of obedience, the phenomena of governing and the phenomena of being governed. Obedience, moreover, is not always an automatic, unconscious thing: it is a submission of the will, an acquiescence, the product either of choice or of habit. This has been observed from the first. Bodin, from whom we get our word sovereignty, and much of our conception of the thing, sovereignty, conceived the facts of the case very practically. He drew his conception, of course, from the existing French state of his time,—1530-1596, the time

---

[8] "The Eastern politicians never do anything without the opinion of the astrologers on the fortunate moment. . . . Statesmen of a more judicious prescience look for the moment too; but they seek it, not in the conjunctions and oppositions of planets, but in the conjunctions and oppositions of men and things."—Burke, To a Member of the National Assembly, 1791. [WW's note. See *The Works of the Right Honorable Edmund Burke*, 5th edn. (12 vols., Boston, 1877), IV, 44.]

of Francis I, Charles IX, and the Huguenot wars,—after France had felt the power of Louis XI, after the disintegrate order of the feudal system had been replaced by a compact and centralized monarchy. During the Middle Ages sovereignty had been 'in commission,' had been ascribed to all powers from which there was no appeal. Sovereign powers and the irresponsibility of supreme authority had habitually been associated with feudal immunities of all sorts,—at least of all the greater sorts,—having become as it were attributes of ownership. In France, however, the royal power had absorbed all the greater immunities and had thus become supreme. The great holdings in the hands of the feudal lords were divested of their old-time attribute of political supremacy, and the occupant of the throne became the only sovereign. It was in this stage of sovereignty that Bodin undertook his analysis. The sovereign, he said, was supreme over the laws, but was bound, nevertheless, by contract, by private law, and by vested interests, i.e. by certain conditions of acquiescence on the part of the governed. The feudal Estates, stood under the existing order, as he analyzed it, for vested interests, for sacred property rights: and taxes, which came out of property, could be taken only with the assent of those who possessed property. In short, the supremacy of the sovereign was in fact limited, the frontiers of sovereignty being marked by certain antecedent rights, by certain established prerogatives of property and vested privilege,—not a scientific but a natural frontier, lying along the old mountains of habit, the well known rivers of precedent. In other words the jurisdiction of sovereignty is a jurisdiction secured by the assent of the governed—by accommodation rather than by an absolute exercise of power.

We know that the history of politics has been the history of liberty, that is, the history of the enlargement of the sphere of independent individual action at the expense of the sphere of dictatorial authority. It has revealed a process of differentiation. Certain freedoms of opinion and utterance, of choice of occupation and of allegiance, of fair trial and equitable condemnation, have been blocked out as inviolable territories, lying quite beyond the jurisdiction of political sovereignty. Beginning with that singular and interesting order of the classical states of the ancient world, under which the individual was merged in the community and liberty became identical with a share in the exercise of the public power, we witness something like a gradual disintegration, a resolution of the state into its constituent elements; until at length those who govern and those who are governed are no longer one and the same, but stand face to face treating with one another, agreeing upon terms of command and obedience, as at Runnymede. Conditions of submission have been contested, and, as liberty has gained upon authority, have been formulated; the procedure and the limitations of authority have been agreed upon, liberty has encroached upon sovereignty and set bounds to it. All of which is but another way of saying that both the measure and the forms of political authority, on the one hand, and the extent and standard of obedience, on the other hand, have, as time has advanced, been given more and more definite and explicit statement. The process is old: only some of the results are new. What both political philosophers and political revolutionists have sought for time out of mind [h]as been a final definition for that part of the Austinian conception which concerns the habitual obedience of the community. These definitions, these balancings of liberty and privilege against authority, we now call *constitutions*. At last peoples have become *conscious* of their relations to the highest powers in the state, and have sought to give certainty and permanence to those relations, defining, either by means of stubborn practice or solemn covenants contained in written documents, the extent and the conditions of their subordination. A constitution government has always had; but not until this latest age these conscious formulations of practice and of principle which determine the whole organization and action of the State, the domain of authority, the neutral territory of liberty, the postulates of obedience. Law is not a creative agency at all, except to a very limited extent. It has really never been a command in the full sense of that word. It has originated *forms* and *means* rather than substantive conditions. Its function is regulative, formulative. It takes up the completed tendencies of the community and turns them into formal rights and duties: it transforms practices into legal institutions. But tendencies and practices are matters of evolution, not of creation out of hand. And it is thus with the highest forms of law, as well as with all others. Constitutions also are definitive rather than creative. They sum up experiences: they register consents. Certainly Mr. Spencer is right when he declares that that which in every country, under whatever system governed, "produces the obedience making political action possible, is the accumulated and organized sentiment felt towards inherited institutions," and that "the feeling of the community is the sole source of political power." But this does not mean what Judge Jameson reads into it, that sovereignty and the feeling of the community are one and the same thing; that the *basis* of sovereignty and the *exercise* of sovereignty are identical;

that the origination of a command and the obedience yielded to it are indistinguishable: that there is no difference between law-making and the choice of law-makers. Sovereignty has at all times and under all systems of government been dependent upon the temper and disposition of the people: to make this temper and disposition sovereign is to miss all analysis of government. Authority and the exercise of it there always has been and always must be in every State: government there must be, law-givers and subjects, under whatever constitution. There is else no organization. Authority, too, must always be lodged with some definite organ or organs of the State, must be determinate in character, exercise, and lodgment.

Sovereignty is an active principle, a principle of command and guidance, and not merely of superintendence. The will of the community, the disposition and desires of the organic State as a whole, are indeed, in the last analysis, the foundation, as they are also in many instances the direct and immediate source, of law. But that will is exercised by way of approval or dis-approval, acquiescence or resistance, it is not an agency of initial choice. The sanctioning judgments of a people are passive, dor-mant, waiting to have things put to them, unable themselves to suggest anything, because without organs of utterance or sug-gestion. I cannot predicate sovereignty of my physical parts, but must ascribe it to my will, notwithstanding the fact that my physi-cal parts must assent to the purpose of my will, and that my will is dependent upon their obedience. The organism unquestionably dominates the organs; but there are, nevertheless, organs & organs of origination which command and rule.

A written constitution adopted by popular vote affords per-haps, some of the nicest tests of theory. Here we have the most specific form of popular assent. In a written constitution the powers of the government are definitely set forth and specificaly lodged, and the means by which they may be differently consti-tuted or bestowed are definitively determined. Now, we know that these documents are the result of experience, the outcome of a contest of forces, the fruits of struggle. Nations have taken knowledge of despotism. They have seen authority abused and have refused to submit; have perceived justice to be arbitrary and hidden away in secret courts, and have insisted that it be uniform and open; have seen ministers chosen from among favorites, and have demanded that they be taken from among representatives of the people; have found legislation regardful of classes, and have clamoured to have laws made by men se-lected by all classes; have found obedience irksome because government was disordered in form and confused in respect of responsibility, and have insisted that responsibility be fixed and forms of order and publicity be observed. Sometimes only a steady practice has accomplished all this: sometimes documentary securities have been demanded. These documentary securities are our written constitutions. In them are set forth the terms of command, the conditions of obedience.

All this is plain enough in the case of written constitutions which are not submitted to the pe[o]ple for adoption,—in the case of a Charter wrung from some stubborn prince by the leaders of a nation, or in the case of a French constitution made valid by the action of a constituent assembly. When such documents are submitted formally and of course to the popular scrutiny and assent, to be accepted or rejected by the regular electorate, their character *seems* different. It cannot of course be pretended that they are in any real sense originated by the electors, who exercise, evidently, a control merely, not a sovereign initiative; but the part played by the electors in the adoption of these instruments is so normal, they act so clearly as an organic part of the State, that it is not unnatural, it is even figuratively suggestive and politically wholesome, to speak of them as the ultimate sovereign power. For when this constitutional law is once made by this process, it is elevated above all other law; it commands the action of all organs of the State; it becomes the supreme rule of state life. It is easy, as it is impressive, to believe that it proceeds from the people, and constitutes their sovereign behest concerning government. But of course it does not. It proceeds from some special or some regular organ of the State; its provisions are fixed upon by the debated determinations of a comparatively small deliberative body, acting usually under some form of legal commission, and are accepted as a whole and without discrimination by the diffused, undeliberative body of voters.

What confuses our view is the fact that these formal documentary statements of the forms and degrees of obedience to which the people assent, the methods of power to which they submit, the sort of responsibility upon which they insist, have become, from the very necessity of their nature, a distinct and superior sort of *formal* law, and we seek the sovereign who utters them. But they are not the utterances of a sovereign, they are the covenants of a community; and time out of mind the community has, whether formally or only virtually, made such covenants with the sovereign. Always and everywhere sovereigns have been obliged to be regardful of the sentiments of the community in respect to the exercise of authority, sensitive to its censure, fearful of its insubordination. When despotism in France was "tempered by epigram," the sharp tongues of the wits spoke, after a sort, the constitution of the country,—a positive law whose sanction was ridicule; but the wits were not sovereigns: the *salons* did not conduct government. Our written constitutions are only more formal statements of the standards to which the people, upon whom government depends for obedience, will hold those who exercise the sovereign power.

I say nothing, of course, against the power of the people. Ultimately they control the action of those who govern, and it is salutary that it should be so. It is wise, also, if it be not indispensable, that the extent and manner of their control should be explicitly set forth and definitely agreed upon in documents of unmistakable tenour. But such control is no new thing; it is only this formulation of it that is new. We are doing nothing to its detriment, if we conceive Sovereignty to be the active, originative principle in government, if we accept the habit of the community in respect of obedience as the measure of the existence and efficacy of soverereignty, and recognize written constitutions as the formulations of that habit of obedience.

It seems to be, after all, a question of words; and yet, upon examination, it is more than that. Mr. Ritchie, of Oxford University, in an able article on The Conception of Sovereignty contributed to The Annals of the American Academy of Political and Social Science, (Jan., 1891),[9] perceiving vaguely some part of the distinctions which I have pointed out, and wishing to realize them in his thought proposes to distinguish *three several kinds of sovereigns*: viz. a *nominal* sovereign, the English queen, for example; a *legal* sovereign, that is, the law-making body; and a *political* sovereign, that is the voters, whom we might call the sovereign of appeal. But why not confine ourselves to substantives, if we may, and avoid the quick-sands of adjectives. Sovereignty is something quite definite; so also is power; so also is control. Sovereignty is the highest political power of a State lodged in active organs of the State for the purposes of governing. Power is a positive thing; control, a negative thing. Power belongs to government, is lodged in governing organs; control belongs to the community, is lodged with the people. To call these two things by the same name, Sovereignty, is simply to impoverish language by making one word serve for a variety of meanings

Even this amendment of theory, however, does not make it

[9] David G. Ritchie, "On the Conception of Sovereignty," *Annals of the American Academy of Political and Social Science*, 1 (Jan. 1891), 385-411. [Eds.' note]

easy to point out in each particular government the organs in which sovereignty is lodged. On the whole, however, it is safe to ascribe sovereignty to the highest originative or law-making body of the State,—the body by whose determinations both the tasks to be carried out by the Administration and the rules to be applied by the courts are fixed and warranted. Even where the courts utter authoritative interpretations of what we call the fundamental law, that is, the law embodied in constitutions, they are rather the organs through which the *limitations* of sovereignty are determined than organs of sovereignty itself. They then declare the principles of that higher, constituent law which is set above sovereignty and which expresses the limitations upon sovereignty operative in all States but given definite formulation only in some. As for the Executive, it is the agent, not the organ, of Sovereignty.

But, even if it be comparatively easy, thus to fix upon the organs of Sovereignty in a unitary State, what shall we say of the federal state? How apply our analysis to that? One is tempted to say, with Dr. Merkel, of Strassburg, that federal states give direct contradiction of fact to prevailing theories respecting the necessity for unity of power, indivisibility of Sovereignty. Here, as he says, we have organs and authorities in possession of powers exclusively their own for the furtherance of functions necessary to the ends of the State as a whole existing side by side with organs also in full possession of powers exclusively their own for the futherance of the local and special functions of the member States. We know, moreover, that these two sets of organs are in fact coördinate; that the powers of the States were not derived from the federal authority,—are even antecedent to the powers of the federal government, and historically quite independent of them.

And yet no one who ponders either the life or the formal structure of federal states can fail to perceive that there is, after all is said, an essential unity in both, a virtual creation of a central sovereignty. The constituent act can, I conceive, have nothing to do with our analysis in this matter. The way in which the federal state came into existence is immaterial to the question of sovereignty. Originative life and action, the attributes of sovereignty, come after this. Character and choice are postponed to birth, sovereignty to the creation of the organism. A supreme directing organ is characteristic of organic political structure, not of the organizing act. The constituent act simply creates a thing capable of exercising sovereignty, of having sovereign organs. After the organic law has come into existence, by whatever process, then the processes of independent life begin. Thereafter, in all federal states, the amendment of the fundamental law is an organic act, depending, practically without exception, upon the initiative of the chief originative organ of the federal state. Confederations are here out of the question: they are, of course, associations of sovereigns. In the *federal* state, however, self-determination with respect of its law as a whole has been lost by the member-states[.] They cannot extend, they cannot even determine, their own powers without appeal to the federal authorities. They are unquestionably subject to a political superior. They are fused, subordinated, dominated. Though they do not exercise their powers by virtue of delegation; though their powers are indeed inherent and in a very important sense independent; they are yet inferior to a body whose powers are in reality self-determined, however much that self-determination may be hedged about and clogged by the forms of the fundamental federal law. They are still states because their political rights are not also legal duties, and because they can apply to their commands the full sanctions of law. But their sphere is limited by the presiding, the sovereign powers of a State, superordinated to them, whose own powers are determined, under constitutional forms and guarantees, by itself. They have dominion; the federal state has sovereignty. For with the federal state lie the highest powers of originative legal determination, the ultimate authority to warrant change and sanction jurisdiction.

Let us return for a moment, in closing, to Judge Jameson, for a proof text. "Obviously," he says, "if there is a vast body of influences, no matter of what kind, moral or physical, at work back of the Austinian aggregate, . . . the source of those influences must be sovereign." "Without the people, to teach, to stimulate, to guide, to correct, and to punish, this complex machine of government would have gone to ruin a hundred years ago."[10] How evident the confusion is! The *springs of political action* are hopelessly confused with the governing power. And those who see this, and fall back upon the qualified electors, have not retreated far enough to escape the fallacy. Those who choose the governors are not themselves the government.[11]

WWT and WWhw MS. (WP, DLC).

[10] Jameson, *op. cit.*, pp. 210-11. [Eds.' note]

[11] At the end of this lecture, Dr. McCosh is alleged to have said, "Umph! I have always held that sovereignty rests with God." It is said that Wilson replied, "So it does, Dr. McCosh, but I did not go quite so far back in my discussion." Ray Stannard Baker, *Woodrow Wilson: Life and Letters* (8 vols., Garden City, N. Y., 1927-39), II, 18-19. [Eds.' note]

From Charles Bertram Newton[1]

Dear Sir, [Princeton, N.J.] Nov. 9, '91

I have the honor to inform you that you have been unanimously elected an Honorary Member of the Cap and Gown Club of Princeton University. Respectfully C. B. Newton Sec.

ALS (WP, DLC) with WWhw notation on env.: "Ans. 11 Nov./91."
[1] Class of 1893.

To Edwin Oscar Smith

My dear Sir, Princeton, New Jersey, 11 November, 1891

In answer to your letter of the 9th, I would say that the 10th of December will suit me very well indeed as the date for my lecture. Unless I hear from you to the contrary, therefore, I shall consider that date as fixed upon.

Very Sincerely Yours, Woodrow Wilson

ALS (photostat in CtW).

From the Minutes of the Princeton Faculty

5 5′ P.M., Friday, Nov. 20th, 1891.

. . . *Resolved* That a Committee be appointed to consider the question of appointing monitors for the large classes.

Profs. Hunt, Duffield & Wilson were appointed the Committee.[1]

[1] This committee submitted its first report on January 8, 1892. For its final report as amended and approved by the faculty and which established a monitorial system for large classes, see the Princeton Faculty Minutes, June 8, 1892.

A News Report

[Dec. 2, 1891]

SOUTHERN CLUB BANQUET.

The Southern Club[1] held its first banquet at Clark's in New York on Wednesday evening before Thanksgiving. The dinner was served in excellent style to forty men, among whom were representatives from other of the sectional clubs. Prof. Woodrow Wilson was introduced by Mr. Phinizy,[2] toast master, and president of the Southern Club; he responded to the toast "Literature and Life of the South."

J. M. Huston,[3] president of the Phildelphia Club[4] spoke on "Princeton Men in Public Life." Among the other speakers were: J. M. Brennan '92, G. T. Dunlop '92, J. H. Hanna '92, W. A.

Guild '93, J. M. Broadnax '94, Richardson '93, Fentriss '94 and Fentriss '95.[5]

Printed in *The Princetonian*, xvi (Dec. 2, 1891), [1].
[1] A newly formed organization of Princeton undergraduates. They met on November 25, 1891, before the Princeton-Yale game in New York on the following day.
[2] Bowdre Phinizy, '92, from Augusta, Ga.
[3] Joseph Miller Huston, '92.
[4] Another undergraduate club.
[5] John Menifee Brennan, '92, from Paris, Ky.; George Thomas Dunlop, Jr., '92, from Washington, D. C.; John Hunter Hanna, '92, from Henderson, Ky.; William Alexander Guild, '93, from Gallatin, Tenn.; James Maclin Brodnax, '94, from Mason, Tenn.; Hugh Richardson, Special, from Vicksburg, Miss.; James Fentress, Jr., '94, from Chicago; and David Fentress, Special, from Chicago.

From James Bryce

Dear Mr. Wilson   London, Dec. 2/91

It is so difficult for a European, however interested he may be in American affairs, to follow the course of events in your country, that I am tempted to ask you whether you would do me the favour of informing me if any changes have happened since 1885 which have made the description you then gave of Congressional methods and their results no longer correct, or have affected your own views upon the subject. I am revising my book for another edition: and in the chapters on Congress (chapters X-XX) find some things to retrench as superfluous, and one passage, relating to the tariff and surpluses, in which the Pensions Act of 1890 and the McKinley tariff make slight alterations necessary. On the whole, however, it seems to me that the views set forth in those chapters, which generally coincided with, and whose formation was sensibly affected by, the views of your "Congressional Government," are well founded and still in point. But I may have missed facts that ought to be modify [modified by] them: and should be grateful for your opinion, if you can find time to let me have it.

I have been re-reading your notice of my book in Pol. Sc. Quarterly for 1889;[1] and must thank you, not merely for the good opinion you express, but for that (which an author, as you probably know, values most) exercise of thought upon the subject and the book which has enabled you to understand the author's attitude, his effort, the reasons why he has in some directions come short. I agree with a great deal, indeed perhaps with most, of your very instructive criticism, but doubt whether I could, without recasting the book (for which time fails) attempt to remedy the chief defect you signalize. To treat of either the institutions or the national character of your country historically would involve much new matter, and might distract the average reader from the actualities of the State and people as they now stand. Perhaps however you and some other critics who have taken the same view rather mean that in dealing with particular phenonema of institutions or character some paragraphs ought to be given to the illustration of the present by the past. I feel how much more light might so be thrown, were the book to write over again. Believe me   Very truly yours   J Bryce.

ALS (WP, DLC) with WWhw notation on env.: "Ans. 18 Dec., '91" and WWhw and WWsh notes for reply on loose slip of paper.
¹ It is printed at Jan. 31, 1889, Vol. 6.

EDITORIAL NOTE
"DEMOCRACY"

Wilson used the address "Democracy," printed below, more frequently before general audiences in the 1890's than any other, even more often than "Leaders of Men,"¹ and one is tempted to believe that it was his favorite public speech of the decade. However that may have been, it is true that "Democracy" embodied most comprehensively and succinctly Wilson's thinking during this period about the development, character, and functioning of modern democracy, as well as about the role that enlightened and responsible leadership should play in a democratic polity. One who has read all of Wilson's lectures and writings to this point will at once see in "Democracy" ideas and themes that had preoccupied Wilson since his undergraduate days. This reader will, more specifically, recognize in "Democracy" digested and revised versions of passages from "Government by Debate" (1882), "The Modern Democratic State" (1885), "The Functions of Government" (1888), "Character of Democracy in the United States" (1889), "Leaders of Men" (1889-90), "The Evils of Democracy" (1890), and "Political Sovereignty" (1891).

The correspondence between Edwin Oscar Smith and Wilson, printed in preceding pages, well documents the invitation that prompted Wilson to compose "Democracy." Moreover, Wilson's letter to Smith of October 30, 1891, indicates that Wilson by this date had at least chosen the topic of his lecture and probably had begun preliminary work on it. Stockton Axson to Ellen Wilson, December 17, 1891, and the news item printed at January 18, 1892, are the only extant contemporary reports of Wilson's first delivery, on December 10, 1891, of "Democracy" in the Russell Library Hall in Middletown, Connecticut.

Wilson's well-worn typescript bears the evidences of numerous changes, some of which he undoubtedly made from time to time as he used the manuscript. These changes have been incorporated into the text reproduced below. On the last page of the typescript, Wilson kept a record of the occasions on which he used this address and a

¹ Printed at June 17, 1890, Vol. 6.

partial record of the honoraria he received. This list is printed as part of the text.

Insofar as is known, Wilson permitted publication of "Democracy" only once, and then in the student monthly of a girls' college,[2] which he knew would not have wide circulation. The story of Wilson's unfulfilled plan to publish "Democracy," along with "Leaders of Men" and other addresses, in about 1902 will be told in a future volume. Accompanying the typescript of "Democracy" in the Wilson Papers is a two-page outline of the address.

[2] The Elmira, N. Y., *Sibyl*, xxii (July 1893), 174-94. *The Sibyl* was the monthly of Elmira College.

A Lecture

5 December, 1891

Democracy.

Nothing has ever come so near making poets of certain of our duller historians as thought of those little democracies that lie snug about quiet Luzern, on the northern slopes of the Alps, in that rugged Switzerland where liberty and valour have grown old together. A delicate bloom appears upon the surface of their arid style as it approaches the history of those old and staunch confederates in freedom. Their adjectives begin to glow with a rich, unwonted colour, their verbs quicken into a sudden life. They speak always with a certain warmth and fervor of those quiet self-respecting yeomen of the mountains, time out of mind self-governed and self-defended. Be their political principles what they may for *other* times and places, they are democrats in Switzerland. Even German sentences soften and succumb to this charm of rural liberty. They cannot resist the attractions of gatherings of freemen in political assembly "under God's free heaven upon a Springtide Sabbath-day."[1] 'Without the circle stand the wives and children and those who cannot take part. The magistrates sit upon the Tribune. The proceedings open with prayer and song

[1] Wilson is freely translating the following passage from Alois von Orelli, *Das Staatsrecht der schweizerischen Eidgenossenschaft*, in H. Marquardsen (ed.), *Handbuch des Oeffentlichen Rechts*, iv, 107: "Unter Gottes freiem Himmel versammelt sich an einem Frühli[n]gssonntag die stimmfähige Bürgerschaft mit der Obrigkeit an der Spitze, letztere auf einer Tribüne. Ausserhalb des Ringes stehen Frauen, Kinder, unbetheiligte Zuschauer. Die Eröffnung geschieht meist durch Gebet und Gesang und mit einer feierlichen Ansprache durch den Landammann, dann folgen die Wahlen der Landesbeamten und die Beschlüsse über die gesetzgeberischen Vorlagen. Die Abstimmung erfolgt durch Aufheben der Hände. Abzahlung findet selten statt. Das Mehr wird ermittelt durch Abschätzung von der Tribüne herab. In zweifelhaften Fällen wird die Abmehrung wiederholt, oder die Annehmenden und die Verwerfenden haben sich je auf eine Seite zu stellen. Den Schluss der Verhandlungen bildet die feierliche Beeidigung erst der Beamten, dann der sämmtlichen Landleute nach einer alten Eidesformel, die vom Landschreiber verlesen wird. Nachher geht alles Volk ruhig auseinander." [All notes Eds.']

and a quiet, solemn address by the presiding magistrate. After that the officers of the year are elected and the legislative proposals voted upon,—all with a simple show of hands, seldom formally counted,—merely reckoned from the Tribune. And then the proceedings close, devoutly as they opened, with a covenant read by the clerk and taken, in accordance with hallowed ancient forms, first by the magistrates and then by all the people. This done, the assembly quietly breaks up,—and every one goes his own way.' So comely is freedom when you behold its features thus decked in simplicity and demeaned with quietness!

Much the same thing has happened to those who have written of our American town-meeting. We have discovered a most interesting pedigree for it, and that pedigree has greatly excited our fancy. We look in at the doors of some unpretentious town-hall one day in the Spring upon tradesmen and farmers, hard, weather-stained faces, and faces carved bargainwise by traffic;— the doctor with his sanitary notions, and the parson with his plans of reform,—note the self-important dignity of the Moderator, and the wise glasses upon the nose of the clerk; hear the report of the Selectmen made and pricked with comments; unconsciously get warmed by the shrewd rigour of the debate that springs up about taxes and town improvements; watch the elections to their close; and then,—even as we stand there,—all the long lineage of this business steals into our thoughts. Our historians stand at our ear with their Tacitus in hand,—and lo! the whole scene changes! Instead of being in a close, bare room surrounded by the homely figures of our rustic neighbours, instead of the town-hall and its group of farmers and tradesmen,—we stand among a sturdy host of freemen gathered about their tribal chiefs in the glades of a primal forest, clamourously making known their will in the selection of magistrates and in the declaration of the laws and customs to which they will be obedient. We are in the Germanic folk-moot, mother of town-meeting and cantonal assembly! That rustic gathering in the town-hall has become as poetical as that other Springtide assembly under God's free heaven in the Alpine valley!

There is, indeed, a certain difficulty for us about this apotheosis of the town-meeting: for we know the men of whom it is made up, and we are not deceived as to their character. Good fellows though they be, in the main, and shrewd; interested in the business of the town, and attentive to it in season and out of season, they do not often have large views about things; they are niggardly quite as often as they are public-spirited; they are,—well, we know what they are: they are small enough fellows, many of them. And when our skeptical mood is on us, analogies tempt us, likelihoods beckon us on. We wonder whether the make-up of the Swiss cantonal assemblies, for all they are lifted so near heaven in so divine an air, would bear close examination any better.

But it does not do to inquire too curiously about such matters. *Group* men how we may, we know that they remain men, and that grouping does not materially improve their natures. But the beauty of cantonal assembly and town-meeting is not the beauty of wisdom. It is the beauty of self-control, the dignity of self-government. It is the fine schooling in the formation of opinions about things that affect the general welfare, be those opinions wide or narrow, that we admire. It is the drill in stating general views, and then submitting to the majority, if you cannot vote with it. There is more contentment a thousand-fold to be got from this participation in a rugged self-government, and more growth too, than from the wisest system of tutelage and subjection that imperialists ever invented. The poets are right when they forget the homely ways of Liberty, and sing to it as to a *spirit* that makes brave, that provokes to virtue, that elevates with hope and with a sanctifying ardour for high things. A cantonal assembly is as dignified as a Parliament: a town-meeting is the epitome of a long history of freedom.

There has been no debate about these things among wise men these thousand years and more. Demosthenes addressed a town-meeting; the *Roman* cantonal assembly governed the world. The democracy of the local assembly is not modern: it is as ancient, probably, as Aryan states, and now needs neither explanation nor vindication. It is not of this democracy that I would speak, but of quite another: that *modern* democracy in which the people who are said to govern are not the people of a commune or a township, but all the people of a great nation, a vast population which never musters into any single assembly, whose members never see each others' faces or hear each others' voices, but live, millions strong, up and down the reaches of continents; building scores of great cities throughout fair provinces that would in other days have been separate kingdoms; following all callings under all climes; and yet not *separate*, but standing fast in a vital union of thought and of institutions, conceiving themselves a corporate whole: acting so, and so accepted by the world. There is no simplicity here! The new democracy is manifold, intense, dramatic, thrilled through and through with a new life, facing a new destiny,—with many questionings, but also with high and confident hope. We must needs look long and earnestly both into the past and into the present to understand *it*.

Of course we think first of our own great nation, with its variety within unity; and it is our natural disposition to take it as our standard *type* of *democracy on the grand scale*. This, indeed, is also the disposition of the world at large. For our polity is in every way a child of the modern world. Here, upon a new continent, in an open and free arena, have the forces of the modern world deployed, manoeuvred, contested, won victories and suffered defeats; and the older nations, looking anxiously on, have sought to read their own fates in the moving features of the great spectacle.

Long ago, in the sanguine youth of political philosophy, it used to be easy to explain systems of government and understand complex societies; but our first confidence of speculation about these matters has been dissipated. A more careful study of history than we were once prone to be satisfied with has convinced us that the stuff we handle when we examine institutions is infinitely more complex than we had any thought of. Every fibre of it is interlaced with countless other fibres, and the life that trembles and thrills in these fibres has come out of the old past: still answers to old impressions, still hides old habits and responds to old suggestions. Every piece of the structure is old, though its youth is ever renewed.

And yet the new life is so much broader than the old, and so much richer! It grows, too, so much more unified in character. The old world of the Chaldee and the Mede and the Persian, of the Jew, the Greek, and the Roman, was a world quicked, alarmed, made various by *national* forces. Nation was *contrasted* with nation by features of sharp individuality. Each stood for a separate and characteristic influence. But in us these old forces once distinguishable are all *combined and made universal*: the old differentiation is gone. Ours is a day, not of national so much as of *international* and common forces. There is everywhere a free interchange of ideas, a wide community of intellectual and moral standards; there are common means of knowledge; there is quick intercourse and a general familiarity with the ends of the earth. No nation any longer lives apart; it is sharp give and take between the peoples of the world. Each contributes to the others' cultures; each shares the science and the civilization of all the rest. Their laws, their philosophy, their comforts, their education, their armaments and discipline, their manners even, and their sports, they have in common. How greatly do the correspondences now outnumber the contrasts in the lives of nations. If it were not for the costumes still to be seen here and there in the picturesque corners of the old continent, if it were not for the transparent disguises of language and the petty varieties of etiquette, how easy it would be to feel at home *anywhere in the civilized world*! If we are to explain this great democracy of ours, we must explain, not only everything which is its own, but also everything in it which was once the property of others: not only what it has derived from its own immediate and legitimate English ancestors, but also everything which it has received by gift or seized upon that was once part of alien polities. This Spirit of the Age is an infinitely more difficult thing to trace and analyze than all the clauses of all statutes. We know the pedigree of the little cantonal assembly and of the familiar town-meeting; but how shall we trace the lineage of this vast democratic *nation*, full, as it is, of *all* modern impulses, child and heir, as it is, of all the modern world? Who shall teach us the secret of this new world, hot with steam, tremulous with electricity, eager, restless, tireless in its pursuit of things both new and old?

> "The Spirit of the World hath told the tale,
> And tells it: and 't is very wise and old.
> But o'er the page there is a mist and veil:
> We do not know the tongue in which 't is told"
> E. R. Sill, *The Book of Hours.*

And yet, if you will but think of it a moment, the past, which is finished, and which lies open before us to be examined, is much longer, than the present, which confuses us,—much vaster and more dominant every way. *Government* is *old*, and we know its history. It is full of familiar lessons and oft learned tales of struggle. It is as old as love and loyalty and intrigue. It does not change its nature underneath the masquerades of this many-costumed, stage-like world of ours. The old features are there, for those to see who look directly, with undazzled eyes.

A farmer sat wonderingly beside the ring in a great circus, gaping at everything that his astonished eye saw, until the trained horses were brought in, and then a look of quiet sagacity settled upon his countenance, and he seemed at home. He watched each docile manoeuvre to its close, and then he turned to a stranger at his elbow and said wisely, "Them thar horses aint had no oats *this* day." "How do you know?" replied the man addressed. "Say, mister," said the farmer, "you don't s'pose them thar's the *fust* horses I ever seed, do you?" *A queen* seeking pleasure one day in the forest with her daughters and a gay company from the court, conversed in kindly courtesy with an humble peasant woman as they loitered by the way; and the woman was drawn on to be bold. "I fear my lady the princess is not well the day," she said, as her eyes scanned the features of one of the royal damsels. "How dost thou know it is not well with her?" asked the queen quickly. "Ah, my lady," said the woman, "Your Majesty maun ken I ha' e'en had lassies o' my ain." Horses have had their character time out of mind; and princesses pine for love just as other maidens do.

Government also is singularly steadfast and old in its ways. Invent as fast as we may in other fields, we do not invent many new things in the sphere of politics. Since the Germanic tribes added representation to the old Roman machinery of rule, what novelty has been introduced, that was not merely a novelty of form? What Aristotle himself wrote about politics still seems astonishingly modern: it can hardly have been written two thousand two hundred and some odd years ago: for how sound and fresh it keeps! We have shifted our *point of view* a score of times; have looked at government now from this side and again from that; have woven theories, caught ideals, conceived pro-grammes of reform; but all the while *the great underlying facts of government* have remained the same.

Look for a moment at what we have ourselves attempted: at what we have, and what we have not, accomplished. Those who framed our federal government had planned no *revolution*: they did not mean to invent an American government, but only to Americanize the English government, which they *knew*, and knew to be a government fit for free men to live under, if only narrow monarchical notions could be got out of it and its spirit liberalized. They thought (what Sydney and Locke had thought before them), that, in order to be pure and efficient, government ought to exist for the people, ought to serve their determinate purposes and all their permanent interests. But they thought also that it ought to be *guarded* against the heats and the hastes, the passions and the thoughtless impulses of *the people*, no less than against selfish *dynasties* and hurtful *class intrigues*. Accordingly they made it only in part a directly democratic government. They carefully sought to break the force of *sudden majorities*. They made only one Chamber the direct choice of the people, and only to that one Chamber did they assign a short term of tenure. The choice of the other Chamber they made to depend only in-directly upon the preferences of the people; and they extended the terms of *its* membership much beyond that of the popular House. They arranged that the *Presidential* term also should span twice the life of the people's chamber. And, above all, crown-ing and steadying the whole structure, they placed *the Supreme Court*, with its *life* tenure,—made independent of parties, pledged only to preserve the fundamental law in its integrity. They meant the government they were building to stand firm, whatever storms of passion, whatever sudden tumults of party, whatever keen ardours of too sanguine reform might for a time prevail.

We have in a measure *undone* their work. A century has led us very far along upon the road of change. Year by year we have sought to bring government nearer to the people, despite the original plan. We nominate the President now in popular convention: we seek to determine at the ballot box who our federal Senators shall be when our state legislators shall have met to register our preferences; and we warn the Senators, when once they are fairly chosen, not to brave *too* rashly the displeasure of the triumphant majority which the people have sent to the lower House. We grow daily more and more uneasy because a man may be made President who has not received a popular majority in the vote for electors. We declare, and most of us believe, *that the people are sovereign*, and we diligently endeavour to make their sovereignty real and operative in all things.

The most solemn thing about it all (for some of us) is that we have to read *learned and elaborate treatises*, grave scientific dissertations concerning the matter, from gentlemen who are very sure that they know what they mean when they speak of the sovereignty of the people. "According to the views of free men," says Dr. Lieber, with patriotic fervour, "sovereignty can dwell with *society*, the *nation*, only."[2] And the late Judge Jameson tells us specifically what this means. This sovereignty may be heard to speak, he declares, "at public meetings, in the press or in personal argument or solicitation":[3] its exercise is the pressure of public opinion,—and of *private* opinion, too. The newspaper, the pulpit, the friendly disputation, the curtain lecture, command what shall be done: the voters, if they be faithful, do what is commanded. Surely one would need the moral facility of the *Vicar of Bray* to stand the strain of conforming to *all* the dictates of *such* a sovereign power! If we be democrats of this measure, we *must*

"old principles revoke,
Set conscience at a distance."

But, after all is said, what new thing have we in fact discovered? Even if ours *be* the first government in which public opinion was ever *enthroned* and *openly hailed* sovereign, we did not originate its sovereignty: we only extended it and made it a

[2] Francis Lieber, *On Civil Liberty and Self-Government*, 3rd edn. (Philadelphia, 1874), p. 152. Wilson slightly altered the word order.
[3] John Alexander Jameson, "National Sovereignty," *Political Science Quarterly*, v (June 1890), 200.

little more definite. We are not the fortunate discoverers of the wisdom of being heedful whether those who are subject to government will obey when acts of government are attempted. Sir Henry Maine tells us that there has never in the world been any absolute power of wilful and and [*sic*] arbitrary command in the making of laws. *The feeling of the community* Mr Herbert Spencer declares to have been "the sole source of political power" from the very "outset of social life" until now. "In every country," he asserts, "whether it be governed despotically or otherwise," "that which, from hour to hour, produces the obedience" which alone can make "political action possible, is the accumulated and organized sentiment felt towards institutions made sacred by tradition."[4] And no one who has studied the history of political society can doubt this for a moment. "The Eastern politicians," says Burke, "never do anything without the opinion of the astrologers on the fortunate moment. . . . Statesmen of a more judicious prescience look for the fortunate moment too; but they seek it, not in the conjunctions and oppositions of *planets*, but in the conjunctions and oppositions of *men* and *things*."[5] The tyrant has always been most wise when he was most prudent, when most diligent in endearing himself to his people. We know that in France tyranny was even "tempered by epigram"; found it well to be upon its guard against stinging comment; felt weakened by the laugh of the *salon*. We know that Sir Philip Sydney and Locke and Hooker talked long ago of the people as the source of all authority.

But the pleasure of the people, though it be the *source* of authority, is not therefore *authority itself*, according to any logic I have yet heard of. The soil and its kindly powers are the source of the farmer's crops; and yet he chooses what to sow and what to reap. The law is the source of my liberty, and those who made the law the authors of it; but my liberty is my own: I exercise it. The power of the President of the United States is, indeed, derived from laws to which we, or our fathers for us, have assented: but *he exercises* the power, and *we obey*. We are consulted about laws, but we do not originate them; neither do we carry them into execution. Our wishes are generally regarded, so far as they are known, in the conduct of government; *but we do not govern*. All that we have effected (in what we call our democratic arrangements) is comprehended in new and convenient ways of keeping those who govern and those who are governed

[4] Herbert Spencer, *The Principles of Sociology* (3 vols., London, 1876-96), II, 327.
[5] From "A Letter to a Member of the National Assembly," *The Works of the Right Honorable Edmund Burke*, 5th edn. (12 vols., Boston, 1877), IV, 44.

in relations of sympathy and mutual confidence: we have not turned the governed into governors. That were impossible. There must be rule, under whatever polity, and there must be rulers: command and obedience, authority and submission to authority: we shall not escape being governed by arranging that the government be mild and beneficent, willing to regard our interests, and even our wishes upon fit occasion. We must always have a system of laws: and we must always have those laws put into execution. The people may be represented in the federal House and in the State legislatures,—I hope that they are; but they cannot themselves be present there and vote. They have set these men over them in authority: they must consent to be governed, whether they choose the governors or not.

Consider for a moment, then, what it is that we *mean* when we say that we have here in America *a sovereign people*, a nation *governed by itself*. You remember the story that Mr. Birrell tells (what good story does Mr. Birrell *not* tell?). " 'Napoleon is not a man, but a system,' once said, in her most impressive tones, Madame de Staël to Sir James Mackintosh, across a dinner table. 'Magnificent,' murmured Sir James. 'But what does she mean?' whispered one of those hopelessly commonplace creatures who go about spoiling everything. 'Mass! I cannot tell!' was the frank acknowledgment and apt Shakspearian quotation of Mackintosh."[6] We cannot mean that the people themselves *originate measures* and *shape policies*, as those little groups do that meet from season to season in town-halls and in Swiss market places, seeing questions singly and at the same time, debating them face to face, making deliberate resolution, and instructing officers what to do. We know, of course, that nothing like this can happen. We know that even when they exercise the highest functions given them by any constitution,—even when they vote upon constitutions themselves,—the people have no *originative* part in government. They have not even *an alternative choice*. They can but accept or reject what conventions or legislatures offer them: and, if they reject, they can propose nothing in substitution for what they decline. They are oftentimes consulted; but they can never act for themselves. There are seasons when they are *like the god, Baal*. Those who call upon them call in vain, if it be not the year or month for voting:—there is no voice, nor any that answer, nor any that regardeth. No fire comes down, offer what tempting sacrifice you will. Upon occasion they may safely be mocked, sovereign though they be. Perhaps they are talking, or they are

6 Augustine Birrell, *Obiter Dicta, Second Series* (New York, 1887), p. 246.

pursuing, or they are in a journey, or peradventure they sleep, and must be awaked.

It is, after all, better to understand our government as what it really is, than to speak of it in vague phrases which represent it to be what it is not. We neither dishonour nor alter it by seeking to comprehend its real character. As an exercise of patriotism, —and perhaps also of patience,—let us examine one or two of the assumptions upon which we have built our theory of government hitherto.

We hold that the people are sovereign, that voting is a *governing* act, not a *consenting* act, merely: that majorities speak, and that majorities effectuate, *purposes of their own.* In order to hold this view intelligently we must assume, in the first place, that there always comes into existence *one prevalent opinion* upon each question that arises: a prepared judgment which the people can confidently be called upon to express whenever there is occasion or desire to appeal to them. Now the moment we state this we know that it is ridiculous: that it is even particularly ridiculous when applied to this age of ours. For this is preëminently an age of absorbing labour, "and the necessary effect of all this labour," to quote Mr. Bagehot, "is, that those subject to it have no opinions. It requires a great deal of time," he adds, "to have opinions. . . . If you chain a man's head to a ledger, and keep him constantly adding up, and take something off his salary whenever he stops, you cannot expect him to have a sound conviction"[7] on the silver question, substantial views on the Behring Sea controversy, or original ideas upon the situation in Brazil. We know that the making and the modification of laws is fit matter for study; that questions of policy, whether domestic or foreign, are full of intricacy: we know that there is almost no subject upon which there can be said to be in any community a *single* prevalent opinion, at once diffused and intelligent: and yet we assume that the people are constantly getting definite convictions ready for the measurement of each question of government!

If we do *not* assume *this*, we are driven to other assumptions no less remarkable, and no less awkward to defend. Since we cannot believe that the complicated questions which arise in connection with the conduct of the affairs of a great nation are always intelligible, or often generally understood: if we know that they are very difficult questions, many of them, and demand a certain mastery of details for their comprehension; we are

[7] "The Character of Sir Robert Peel," *The Works of Walter Bagehot*, ed. by Forrest Morgan (5 vols., Hartford, Conn., 1889), III, 20-21.

forced to assume that there is, at any rate, *an average judgment* which is to be trusted, an unstudied and instinctive opinion touching the larger bearings of the more general questions of politics which is a good and even final opinion. We take leave to assume that when such matters are put *in a broad and general way*, in the newspapers and on the stump, there will be a sort of average impression produced concerning them which will prove to be a safe enough impression in the long run: that a species of instinctive common sense on the part of ordinary people will perceive the points at issue in their just proportions; and that the politicians will, as a consequence, get a safe mandate from the vote. Do we indeed know the facts of party division and party action: the old prejudices that hold parties together; the persistent sympathies and antipathies that stiffen their separate organization; the *personal* forces that are at work within them; the interlaced jealousies and cupidities that knit them into wholes: and do we, nevertheless, believe that the political action of majorities embodies an *independent average conviction* upon questions *considered in some sort upon their merits*? It seems incredible! And yet we talk as if we *did*!

To reason thus brings us into view of another assumption, still more curious when subjected to analysis. It is, that the will of majorities,—or, rather, the concurrence of a maj[or]ity in a vote,—is the same as the *general* will. We look back to that singular Revolution of 1688 in England, and to the anxious period which followed, when the Catholic family which had been thrust out was trying, whether by intrigue or by force, to dispossess the Protestant family which had been put in. We remember how steady the Whig success was, in the main: how even the Tories, when they came into power, had first to conceal and then to abandon all designs for a second restoration when Anne should be dead, dominated in spite of themselves by the Whig programme which had guided the Revolution; and then, with all this in mind, we turn to the pages of grave, careful, truth loving Mr. Hallam, and read with amazement that during all that time it is certain that in that same kingdom of Britain those who were either Catholics themselves or sympathizers with the plans for a Catholic restoration were considerably in the majority, —and were influential people, at that! What does it mean? It means that the will of majorities is *not* the same as the general will: that a nation is an *organic* thing, and that its will dwells with those who do the *practical* thinking and organize *the best concert of action*: those who hit upon opinions *fit to be made prevalent*, and have *the capacity to make them so*.

"For just experience tells, in every soil,
That those that think must govern those that toil";[8]

must govern all *who do not do like effectual thinking.*

What, then? Am I a political pessimist? Do I distrust the foundations, question the most essential conceptions, of the government under which we live? Do I suspect the people of blindness and all their leaders of charlatanry, and hold up popular government to be laughed at as a farce? By no means. I simply take the liberty of believing in democratic institutions *as I understand them.* I *believe* in the people: in their *honesty* and *sincerity* and *sagacity*; but I do not believe in them *as my governors.* I believe in them, rather, as the wholesome stuff out of which the fabric of government, wherever and whenever constructed, is woven, in homely, but also in most useful and beneficent wise. Let me give you at once an example that will illuminate my meaning. I believe, as I feel sure you also believe, that that reform of the civil service for which we have so long been struggling, with varying degrees of success, is imperatively necessary, and that it embodies eminently wise principles of government. *But it is not democratic in idea*: by which I mean that it is not consistent with those *modern assumptions* touching the nature of democratic government which we have just been discussing. It rejects the average man and the average training: it rejects the idea of constantly renewing the official *personnel* of the government from out the general body of the people. It seeks to substitute for the person whom we call "the man of the people," so far as possible, *the men of the schools*, the trained, instructed, *fitted* men: the men who will study their duties and master the principles of the business of their Departments. The ordinary politician is *right* when he says that this is not democratic. It is *not* democratic in the sense in which we have taught our politicians wrongly to understand democracy. It *is*, nevertheless, *eminently democratic*, if we understand democracy as history has given it to us. It is democratic in this sense, *that it draws all the governing material from the people*,—from such *part* of the people as will fit themselves for the function. It thus plans to renew from generation to generation the youth and the variety and the integrity of the administrative capacity employed in the public service. It avoids the narrowness of aristocracy, and the degeneracy of the monarchical polity, by selecting its instruments from the widest, richest, most perennial sources. It is *but another process of representation.*

8 From Goldsmith's "The Traveller."

What we really mean when we say that the people govern is that they freely consent to be governed, on condition that *a certain part* of them *do* the governing,—that part which shall, by one process or another, be selected out of the mass and elevated to places of rule:—and *that is the best democratic government* in which the processes of this selection are best: where *self*-selection for leadership and influence is most encouraged: virtue provoked to exhibit itself and excite emulation; strength and originality heartened to display themselves and compete for the best prizes; knowledge invited to speak and approve itself useful: where the texts of patriotism read after the manner of that noble sentence of Milton's: "I cannot praise a fugitive and cloistered virtue, unexercised and unbreathed, that never sallies out and seeks her adversary, but slinks out of the race, where that immortal garland is to be run for not without dust and heat." A self-instructed, self-mastered, self-elevated man, *like Lincoln,* is no more a man of the people than Washington was. He has *come out* from the people; has separated himself from the indistinguishable mass of unknown men by reason of excellency and knowledge; has *raised himself above* the common level of others and constituted himself a master-spirit among men, holding credentials of rulership which they can never show unless they *likewise strive* as he strove.

That this is a much higher conception, and a much nobler, than the other, I need not claim. The people do indeed govern. They govern just in proportion as they produce the stuff out of which governors and kings are made; just so far as they show the discrimination to choose such when they are made manifest. The advantage of democracy over aristocracy and monarchy is not an advantage of structure, of nice adjustments of balance and successful regulations of force: in these points aristocracies and monarchies have often proved superior to democracy. *They* have a quickness and certainty of resolution and movement which democracy can hardly hope to acquire. Democracy's advantage, rather, is its variety and symmetry of development, its fulness of opportunity and richness of material. In it, not a few men of privileged blood only, but all men of original force are quickened to make the most of themselves. *Self-preparation* is the stimulating law of success for every man. Even though it conduct through ways of struggle and sacrifice, where one must scorn delight and live labourious days,—even though it cost nights racked with every aching pain of study, *it must be accomplished.*

> "A people is but the attempt of many
> To rise to the completer life of one.

And those who live as models for the mass
Are singly of more value than they all."[9]

It is the freedom to attempt the great rôle of *living thus as models for the mass* that fills a democracy with an inextinguishable life, an unconquerable energy, that heartens it with an undismayed confidence, an unfaltering hope. "Methinks I see in my mind a noble and puissant nation rousing herself like a strong man after sleep, and shaking her invincible locks; methinks I see her as an eagle mewing her mighty youth, and kindling her undazzled eyes at the full mid-day beam."[10] Such a vision is even more real to the mind's eye in our own day than it was in Milton's.

Democratic nations are not made in a day; and they have never been made at all save in Switzerland, in England, and in the United States. France, possibly, will become one, bye and bye, after she shall have had still other discipline, a few more hard lessons in self-control. Even in England there are some rebellious pulses, beating still from old days of discord and insubordination: the drill of liberty has not extended to all classes. But it was her drilled classes that she sent to America: and that first blood has so far kept its advantage. We have many things to fear; but we have, nevertheless, *a mighty fund of unsurpassed civil capacity*: we can impart it to the best of those who come to us with other blood in their veins. Think what it is that you have in a democratic nation, made as ours has been. You have an adult, disciplined, self-possessed nation,—with a self-possession born of long experience. Other polities belong to *the long days of preparation* for freedom:—freedom to choose what causes and what leaders the people will. The strict, severe forms of monarchical authority belong to the season of schooling: *all* hereditary systems of rulership, to seasons of immaturity or of unstable, wayward choice. These sterner and more disciplinary systems belong also to those parts of the world where nations are pressed against nations, and there is friction and hazardous rivalry: where, accordingly, peoples must have the union, the organization, and the promptitude of armies. When days of tutelage and of discipline are passed: when a nation has been kept from rash excesses, though not from all exercises of liberty, until its sinews are firm and it has learned conduct, then it may be trusted to make its own choices, to live its own life.

True, its very freedom may turn out to be its danger: but not so long as it retains that love of order, and that consciousness of

9 From Browning's *Luria: A Tragedy.*
10 From Milton's *Areopagitica.*

the need for law, in which it has been bred in its youth: its ineradicable feeling for institutions is its equipoise: *and with that equipoise it has attained its sovereignty.* This is the sovereignty over itself, the sovereignty of self-respect and self-control; which is a power over self, not only, but over others as well. The good-natured but earnest audience, that sits in the seats and boxes and hears the play, is sovereign: makes sovereign disposition of its favours: damns play and author, or else gives them vogue and success. Our nation is not our audience: for what we do is not a play in its eyes, but part of its own life, significant for its fortunes. It must and does have a care in its applause: it is sovereign in its condemnation, even though it condemn by silence or by inattention.

The freedom of the democratic nation consists, let me repeat, not in governing itself: for that it cannot do; but in making undictated choice of the things it will accept and of the men it will follow. It need no longer always accept and always like the things it is told to like. It makes adult choice. Conceive it mechanically, and it is a great, sensitive registering machine: we may study to play upon it,—we *must,—study to play upon it,* and make it register our best suggestions. This, it seems to me, is an infinitely more vital, animating way to conceive democracy than to imagine the people what they are not, our masters. If they are indeed sovereign, in the sense of that other, clumsy, invention of our Rousseauite philosophy, why then we must conform in all things; must be patient and humble under the tyranny of our next door neighbour; must suppress our individuality, endeavour to catch the common thought, the cant phrases, and repeat them continually. But if we live in a nation that waits to be led, and which has sovereign liberty *to follow even us,* if we can convince or move it, what an incentive have we to be *ourselves* in all sincerity, press our claims, fit our thought to effect its purpose betimes, *mend our lives* to suit the station we would achieve!

How we *cheat* ourselves by living in subjection to public opinion when we *might make it!*

> "The spirit of a single mind
> Makes that of multutudes take one direction."

It is singular how we obstinately miss the point of so many obvious lessons. I can imagine how a reformer might lose heart where divinity did hedge kings and classes and all ancient wrongs high about on every side, and it were impiety to touch the least abuse. But where every man is free to speak, and to speak his own mind, because those who listen *are old enough to hear,* I can see nothing but matchless opportunity. There a man may be a poet indeed! All minds are free to hear him, all ears open to take his music. There a man may work his will upon speech and action, *if he have but will enough*. It is a question of strength and courage, not of tolerance or opportunity. He may fare roughly at first: may have to fight for his ground; but what *man* would wish else? There are heat and dust in the arena; but he counted upon these: and he will not fare *unjustly*. Let him but see to it that his words tell, that his knowledge and his control of his materials increase with the attention he attracts, that his mastery grows with his endeavour, *and he will win. A free nation loves a bold man*. It uses slaves only for lack of better men: because the work *must somehow be done*.

When I take this view of the life of a free nation,—a people, not self-directed, but directed by its boldest, most prevalent minds,—I can justify my tolerance of *parties*, and my impatience with those that scorn them and make as if they could do without them. Parties preserve impulses, which would otherwise be diffused and lost. They are the whippers-in for those who plan and originate, and render the impression which these make upon their generation permanent. They perpetuate approved opinions, energize accepted convictions. They must be forgiven much of their worship of "dead issues": for they can keep their corporate feeling, their sense of *identity*, only by remembering old struggles, maintaining old comradeships; only by a keen pride in what they *have* done. It is thus that continuity of consciousness is preserved in a nation *in respect of the abstract things of its life*, the invisible things that are eternal, the principles which are the secret springs of action. They prove, at the same time that they make possible, the organic operation of state life.

Of course parties are often blind and intractable: and they almost always take ideas slowly and reluctantly; but inasmuch as they accept convictions for the organism as a whole, whose active life they embody, it is just as well that they *should* accept them slowly. Close knit fibres and a certain stubbornness of structure hold a nation together, as they do every other organism. When we come on the field it is already occupied. Habit, prejudice, established conventions, fixed systems of thought are in possession, and it will be fighting work to dislodge them. Else, society would not long endure. It cannot get along without institutions and steadfast beliefs. But I think that you will agree with me that this only makes it the more certain that we shall have vigour in our growth, and consistency in our reforms. *Mr.*

Mill complains[11] of the intolerance of society towards heretical ideas, whether in the field of religion or in the field of politics, and believes that society suffers detriment because of their undue suppression. They may "never blaze out far and wide," he says, "but continue to smoulder in the narrow circles of thinking and studious persons among whom they originate without ever lighting up the general affairs of mankind with either a true or a deceptive light. . . . A convenient plan for having peace in the intellectual world," he admits; but he declares that "the price paid for this sort of intellectual pacification is the sacrifice of the entire moral courage of the human mind." It seems to me, however, that Mr. Justice Stephen makes the right reply, and adorns it with the proper tale. "An old ballad tells how a man, losing his way on a hill-side, strayed into a chamber full of enchanted knights, each lying motionless in complete armour" beside his war horse, standing still as he. Upon a däis lay a sword and a horn, and a voice, proceeding from some invisible source, bade the intruder, if he would lead this goodly company, choose between them. He seized the horn, and winded a lusty blast upon it: whereupon, instantly, in the twinkling of an eye, knights, horses, chamber,—all vanished out of sight, and the same voice as before rang out with this keen rebuke:

> "Cursed be the coward that ever he was born
> Who did not draw the sword before he blew the horn."[12]

The moral is both plain and wholesome. We do not wish a world or a community setting up alters *to Unknown Gods*, spending its time "in nothing else, but either to tell, or to hear some new thing." The disturbing of old convictions is a deeply serious thing: we would not have it *lightly* done. Let every man be responsible for what he thinks and says; *but let him fight,—make* him fight,— for it. If he will not fight, if he have not the courage of his thought, if he hold not his intentions in fighting earnest, he is not the kind of man by whom we wish to be conquered. We do not care to be swayed by mild doubters: we cannot base a polity or live a national life on skeptical 'ifs.' But, while we are thus general challengers, let us accord every knightly courtesy to those who come into the lists against us. It is thus that we shall renew the heroic age. It is thus that we shall follow the dictates of that true, wise Freedom,

> "Who, like great Nature, would not mar
> By changes all to [too] fierce and fast

---

[11] In *On Liberty*.
[12] James Fitzjames Stephen, *Liberty, Equality, Fraternity* (London and New York, 1873), p. 78.

This order of our Human Star,
This heritage of the past."[13]

"Love not pleasure, love God; this is the everlasting Yea."[14]
Carlyle himself furnishes us with an instance of this free spirit
of combat,—the aggressive new things against the intrenched old
things. In the year 1819 Scotland fell upon *troublous times in
politics*. Armed political disturbance was feared, and good citizens
of the conservative sort began diligently to acquire the military
habit. Carlyle tells us how he one day met a friend hurrying
with his musket to the drill. " 'You should have the like of this,'
said he cheerily, patting his gun. 'Yes,' was the reply, *'but I have
not yet quite settled on which side.'*["]][15] Democracy, it seems to
me, is the privilege of settling *on which side* you will shoulder
gun and jeopard life. We remember, with Mr. Birrell, Sir David
Ramsay's reply to Lord Rea. "Then said his lordship: 'Well, God
mend all.' *'Nay, by God, Donald, we must help him to mend it.'* "[16]
Such is the strong meat upon which free men must be nurtured.

> "We know the arduous strife, the eternal laws
> To which the triumph of all good is given,
> High sacrifice, and labour without pause,
> Even to the death:—else wherefore should the eye
> Of man converse with immortality?"[17]

Some impressions there are, indeed, as we all know, which no
society will take willingly or at once. Some thoughts there are
which their authors shall never live to see acknowledged to be
immortal. Some power there is which is not immediate, but
cumulative. Some notes which ears now dull will only slowly
be quickened to hear,—beguiled to love. It is not *nice adjustments
of thought* that this great lusty organism is fitted to register.
Though impressed easily by the literature of action, as by any
dramatic force, it is rather thick-skinned to *the subtler forms of
sentiment*. It contains *circles* that will greet the minor poet, the
quiet writer of out-of-the-way thoughts, and give him good cheer,
—that *best of cheer* which consists in the assurance that his works
have been read: and it will be tolerant towards these circles of
enthusiasts, so far as it knows about them, even if it be a little
contemptuous for a time. The merit that impresses it at once must
in some sense be *public merit*: it will simply let private merit

---

13 From Tennyson's "Freedom."
14 From Carlyle's *Sartor Resartus*.
15 As quoted in Augustine Birrell, *Obiter Dicta* (New York, 1885), p. 35.
16 *ibid.*, p. 42.
17 From Wordsworth's sonnet, "O'er the wide earth, on mountain and on
plain."

alone, to enjoy its friends and exercise its virtues in obscurity. So many people are talking that it will hear only the louder and clearer vioces [voices]. It will oftentimes allow itself to listen for a season to those who are *merely* loud and insistent.

But in these respects it is not different from the rest of the world. Indeed, democracy is in almost all respects simply *a large epitome of the rest of the world*: its peculiarity lies in its *free combination* of the *elements* of the rest of the world. To point this out is to make no great discovery; but to understand it thoroughly, and to put it in the place of the Rousseauite theories is as *good* as a great discovery. It secures attention for the only law of political progress that Providence has yet fully unfolded. *The law of liberty* is a *law of character*, of *discipline,* and *not* of forms of government. Progress in politics is progress in social justice. The object of forms of government is clear: it is, to repose confidence wisely, or to fix responsibility distinctly. The *test of excellence* for forms of government is the character of the order and of the individual service which they secure. There must be character on the part of the people to judge character on the part of the official. That is the condition precedent to democracy. If there be not popular capacity, why then Nature must herself cast the parts of ruler and subject: they must be determined by blood and inheritance. A polity of free popular choice, like our own, depends for its success upon the permanency of a certain character on the part of the people. Without a firm love for order on their part, a sagacious insight into the character of men, and a steady preference for openness and honesty in the conduct of affairs, the whole structure would go presently to pieces. This law of liberty is not enough studied among us. It is not the law of doing what we please, but the law of *pleasing to do what is right.* It is a sort of sublimated principle of expediency.

We have fallen into the habit of identifying it with a large *freedom of individual action,* and that side of it unquestionably deserves the emphasis which it has received. Liberty, nevertheless, is not identical with individual privilege. It is a thing of *social organization.* A man's freedom is lost the moment he is cut off from society and thrown upon his own resources, to do everything for himself. Instantly he becomes a slave to Nature. His strength lies of course in coöperation, in combined and regulated social effort. It is not in being let alone by government that my liberty consists, but in being assisted by government to maintain *my equal place* among my fellows. Some power stronger than I am must define my rights; else they are measured by my might and not by my right: I must depend upon my own wits in a general struggle. Liberty is like steam, effective only when confined. It is the order of society that makes me free, just as it is the order of nature that keeps me alive. The one keeps my organs in their places and at their functions, without pause or miscarriage, holds my house erect about me, entitles me to call what damage I suffer *accident*. The other enables me to count upon what *you will do*, to get help upon the terms of giving it, to make reasonable reckonings and confident plans. If I make breach of this order, I lose my liberty. I break bounds, and am an outlaw; I forfeit bond and must yield myself up. "Law is the *external organism of human freedom.*"

Look, then, what a nice equipoise things are in where order is steadied and maintained, not by armies, not by the arrogant force of a few who are habituated to the exercise of a proud mastery and overlordship; but simply by a pervasive, dominant sentiment, by a diffused, universal law-abiding sense and sentiment of duty. Do you not see at once the beauty and the delicacy of such a society? In it, we are obedient to *what*? *To standards of character*. Our liberty is measured by our assent to the general virtue, our participation in the general *steadfastness of spirit*.

There is a passage of Ruskin's so apposite here that I venture to quote it, even at the inevitable cost of paling my own rhetoric. "How false is the conception," he exclaims, "how frantic the pursuit, of that treacherous phantom which men call Liberty! There is no such thing in the universe. There can never be. The stars have it not; the earth has it not; the sea has it not; and we men have the mockery and semblance of it only for our heaviest punishment. The enthusiast would reply that by Liberty he meant the Law of Liberty. Then why use the single and misunderstood word? If by liberty you mean chastisement of the passions, discipline of the intellect, subjection of the will; if you mean the fear of inflicting, the shame of committing a wrong; if you mean respect for all who are in authority, and consideration for all who are in dependence; veneration for the good, mercy to the evil, sympathy with the weak;—if you mean, in a word, that Service which is defined in the liturgy of the English church to be 'perfect Freedom,' why do you name this by the same word by which the luxurious mean license, and the reckless mean change;—by which the rogue means rapine, and the fool, equality; by which the proud mean anarchy, and the malignant mean violence? Call it by any name rather than this, but its best and truest is, Obedience."[18]

---

[18] From Ruskin's *Seven Lamps of Architecture*, Chap. 7, Sects. 1 and 2, which Wilson had copied into his Confidential Journal on December 29, 1889. See the entry at this date in Vol. 6.

Our obedience to our law of liberty, which is *the law of service and of order*, involves, however, even more than this. It sets us also a law of *endeavour*. In such a community no man dare be wholly a private man. We dare not be neutral as between respect for law and defiance of it. We dare not be timid about speaking out when principles of justice or of integrity are drawn in question. We dare not keep our thoughts at home if we have conceived anything that might contribute to the general enlightenment. We are among the trustees of this ordered liberty; and as questions arise which affect it we dare not decline to study them. We help to chose those who shall lead: we dare not neglect to scrutinize their characters and their purposes. Ours is part of the general consciousness: we must see to it that that part is pure, and penetrated with just thought.

You may say that these are lessons in conservatism read to a generation of progress. Well, a little emphasis put just now upon conservatism would not harm us: for it is radicalism which receives most of the emphasis in what we say nowadays in our discourses. When old structures are being remodelled on all hands, there is something reassuring in uncovering the foundations and finding that they, at any rate, are so far undisturbed: that the reforms proposed are *structural* rather than fundamental, and that those which are *proposed* vastly outnumber those that are executed. But I have not confined myself to conservative doctrine this evening; and the conservatism which commends itself to me is not the conservatism of inaction. I believe that the law of liberty which I have just now been enlarging upon is also *a law of progress.* Indeed I could not imagine liberty in a world in which there was no progress. But *progress is a march, not a scamper.* It is achieved by advance *in hosts and under discipline,* not by the running hither and thither of inquisitive crowds. It is a slow thing, of *movement together* and in united masses, a movement of *states,* not an elegant intellectual diversion of dreaming dreams and then forming societies to carry them out. It is the advancement of the race, not the publication of theses.

You *accomplish* it by imparting the solid portions of an education to as large a part of the people as possible; by yourself stirring as large a circle of thought as you can; by being yourself hospitable to all moderate propositions of reform; by helping to make propaganda of the best ideal of civil order; by doing your part to set the fashion in that sort of liberal minded moderation which is fearless in *examining* the foundations of things, but fearful of *disturbing* them too rashly. In the words of Burke, "Duty demands and requires, that what is right should not only be made known, but made prevalent; that what is evil should not only be detected, but defeated."[19] There are *wise* ways in which this may be done, and there are *unwise* ways. *Spasmodic* ways, and instrumentalities that have little permanency, *are unwise*: and that is the reason why we should look closely to our forms of government. Here, fortunately, we can quote Burke again. "The due arrangement of men in the active part of the state, far from being foreign to the purposes of wise government, ought to be among its very first and dearest objects,"[20]—just in order that what is shown to be right may presently be made prevalent also. In a democratic nation *we may help to make up the general mind*, to form it to the right ideals and purposes; and when it is made up, the governing power ought to respond, and cast its judgments into measures. Pope was seldom quite so far from the truth as when he wrote those familiar lines,

> "Of forms of government let fools contest;
> Whate'er is best administered is best."

The best administered tyranny, the most nicely executed injustice the world ever saw, did not compare in excellence of result with the clumsiest system of self-government. For what you want to produce is *not administrative acts*, but *happy and prosperous populations*. Government is the art of producing high averages in independence and happiness.

Observe that my ideal *reverses the order of the socialist*. He wants *first* a new constitution for society, new orders of authority and adjustments of organization, in order that thereby a new nature *may be wrought out* for society. I believe that the work must be carried on in the opposite direction. It must begin, not at the end of organization, but at that of *character. Organization is a product of character*, not an antecedent and cause of character. The body is not the cause, but the instrument, of the spirit. Let no one make the mistake of supposing that the cultivated and thinking class in any community, the class that squares its beliefs and its conduct by rational standards, is in any practical sense the directing and determinant portion of the community, *a commission to administer its mind* and *regulate the courses of its life*. Political ideas do not become practicable until they become virtually universal. The process of life for them is a process of *permeation*. That is the reason that ideas, *fit* from the *first* to reform abuses, have never reformed them speedily or at once. They have had to penetrate so many unprepared minds in their progress to-

---

[19] "Thoughts on the Cause of the Present Discontents," *op.cit.*, I, 526.
[20] *ibid.*, p. 470.

wards general acceptance, have had to be put in so many different ways to so many different men, have had to be rubbed over so often with old phrases so as to remove their suspicious appearance of newness, have had to be kneaded so labouriously into the general mass of common thought.

And so every man who writes a book meant to give currency to new ideas, meant to furnish formulae for action, ought to fit it for common use by employing familiar words and accepted phrases, by a liberal ad-mixture of old doctrine with the new, so as to prove that the two *will mix*. And he ought to pray that as speedily as possible it may come to be regarded as, authoritative, indeed, but *commonplace*. You will find that all the classical, standard works in politics have become very commonplace reading. You shall not be startled by anything that Aristotle says: it all seems matter of course. You shall have no sensation of novelty in turning the pages of Montesquieu: you shall seem to have heard it all before. And you have. It has been worked over a thousand times since his day, well, ill, indifferently, *by everybody*, and has become common property. *That is its immortality.* Again and again in reading the *Federalist* you are moved to say, Buzz, buzz! we have been convinced a century on these points! We have forgotten how bitter a dose it all was to scores of sensible and influential people only three or four generations ago. It seemed *revolutionary* to them; to us it seems *tedious*: too evident by half to have needed exposition. How superfluous seem to us now Milton's fervid arguments for freedom of the press; how melodramatic those old purturbations about the establishment of kingly tyranny in this country! We can hardly take our colonial ancestors seriously enough, after that interesting period of our lives when we used Otis and Henry for school declamations. We wonder how they could possibly get so excited over the actions of so unheroic a creature as George III., whom we regard, or rather *dis*regard, as a fat mediocrity. But such is the cost of success in moving masses of men; and you must conform to the necessities of the case. Try to write books fit to *become* commonplace, but *not commonplace to begin with*: books which will some day come to be praised by everybody as classical, accepted by everybody as authoritative, but read only by those who must say that they have read them. Make *literature* out of them if you can: you may get them read for generations in *that* way; but do not try to make them permanent engines of reform. Be insinuating and suggestive: do not be *impossible*.

But I have drawn my thesis out long enough: I have sufficiently extended and manifolded the effort to make the thoughts of this essay at exposition prevail by making them commonplace. Summed up, it is simply a lesson in duty. I maintain only that it is a more serious matter for the individual to belong to a great democratic nation than to live under any other polity. *He is put upon his honour*; he is challenged to use his strength; he is thrown into the midst of solemn opportunities, *and trusted to use them*; he is given leave to create great occasions. He is the more exalted sort of citizen, being bidden think upon the public weal and make others think with him. Sovereign powers are almost within his choice. If he live idly and ignobly he shall suffer the greater condemnation. He has the great Germanic heritage of liberty to preserve and to transmit. It is with us as it is with the countrymen of the iron Duke, the great Wellington:

> "Not once or twice in that rough island-story
> The path of duty was the way to glory:
> He that walks it, only thirsting
> For the right, and learns to deaden
> Love of self, before his journey closes,
> He shall find the stubborn thistle bursting
> Into glossy purples, which outredden
> All voluptuous garden-roses.
> Not once or twice in that fair island-story,
> The path of duty was the way to glory:
> He, that ever following her commands,
> On with toil of heart and knees and hands,
> Thro' the long gorge to the far light has won
> His path upward, and prevailed,
> Shall find the toppling crags of Duty scaled
> Are close upon the shining table-lands
> To which our God Himself is moon and sun.
> Such was he: his work is done.
> But while the races of mankind endure,
> Let his great example stand
> Colossal, seen of every land,
> And keep the soldier firm, the statesman pure:
> Till in all lands and thro' all human story
> The path of duty be the way to glory."[21]

Read in Middletown, Ct., December, 1891. (Opera House).
Read at Vassar College   50
   "   " Elmira Female College—At Durham (Trinity College), N. C.[22]   100

---

[21] From Tennyson's "Ode on the Death of the Duke of Wellington."
[22] Wilson ran two separate deliveries together here.

" " Johns Hopkins (in Historical Seminary) —
" " Princeton (Ladies' Club) —
" " Philadelphia ("Summer Meeting"), 29 June, 1895. 100
" " Brooklyn (Institute), 14 Oct., 1896 100
" " Pittsburgh, 28 Oct., 1897. 100
" " Oberlin, Ohio, 14 January, 1898. 100
" " Mt. Holyoke College, S. Hadley, Mass.,
9 Mar., 1898. 100
" " Stamford, Conn., 17 Mar., 1898, 100
" " Nashville, Tenn. (Vanderbilt University)
14 June, 1898 100
" " Hartford, Conn., (Theol. Sem.) 5 April, 1899 50

WWT MS. with WWhw emendations (WP, DLC).

Stockton Axson to Ellen Axson Wilson

[Middletown, Conn.]
My dear Sister: Thursday night [Dec. 17, 1891]
I write just a word to tell you about my plans for the holidays. I shall, I fear, have to spend the most of my time in Middletown but I must get down to Princeton for a few days. I will leave Middletown Wednesday morning and spend the day in New York. . . .

Brother Woodrow's lecture was one of the finest things I have ever heard. As I listened to his noble sentiments clothed in their faultless language and delivered in tones rich as fine music I was impressed with the power which high thinking on *any* subject has over us, especially when such thinking is enriched by a poetic imagination. That lecture fulfilled one of the prime conditions of poetry, for it made the hearer "live more," inspired him with loftier ideals and gave him broader views of the fair expanse which lies beyond the range of common-place which ordinarily presses so narrowly about him.

He doubtless told you of the pretty reception which the boys gave him, when as he stepped on the platform they rose and made the house ring with the college yell.[1] That was better testimony of appreciation than innumerable fine speeches. . . .

Affectionately yours Stockton Axson

ALS (WP, DLC).
[1] See the news report printed at Jan. 18, 1892.

To James Bryce

My dear Mr. Bryce,   Princeton, New Jersey, 18 December, 1891

It gives me sincere pleasure to answer your letter of Dec. 2, which reached me last week, both because it affords me an opportunity to be of some small assistance to you, and because it enables me to express to you directly my very sincere admiration for the great work which every intelligent man among us on this side the sea would now feel it a distinct discredit not to have read.

Nothing has happened since 1885 which seemed to me to invalidate any essential part of the criticism of our system which is contained in "Congressional Government"; but some changes have been effected in the committee organization of the House of Representatives which affect the detail of a portion of my description of the legislative machinery; and the rules adopted by the last, the Fifty-first, Congress, over which Mr. Reed presided, certainly contained some rather startling suggestions as to what *might* be done with the Speaker's office. You have yourself discussed these rules in one of our Reviews,[1] and I need not speak of them further than to call your attention to an article to which they gave rise which you may not have noticed. It was written by Prof. A. B. Hart, of Harvard, for the March number (1891) of the *Atlantic Monthly*, and was entitled "The Speaker as Premier." In substance, it advocated the formal investiture of the Speaker of the House with such complete leadership and responsibility in respect of legislation as would make him a sort of Premier, so far as that branch of Congress was concerned. When Prof. Hart asked my opinion upon the article, I of course said that there could be no analogy between any official, however powerful, who was merely an officer of one (or of both) of the Houses of the Legislature, and an English or Continental premier, who was also the leading member of the *executive* branch of the government: that the significance of the premier's office was that in him, and his colleagues, an integration was effected between the legislature which sanctioned measures and the Executive which had to make them workable or take the consequences of failure. He replied that the point was *new* to him, but had great weight.[2] So difficult is it for the most intelligent of Americans to see the essential point of the difference between our own system and other systems! They think that what we need is concentration of power, and consequent concentration of responsibility, in the Houses merely; when what we need is the marriage of legislation and practical statesmanship—a responsible direction of those who make the laws by those who must carry them out and approve or damn themselves in the process.

The change in committee organization to which I referred was made by the 49th Congress in 1886. It consisted in taking away from the Appropriations Committee of the House about one half of its work (and power). The Consular and Diplomatic (appropriation) Bill was assigned to the Committee on Foreign Affairs; the Army and Military Academy Bills were assigned to the Comm. on Military Affairs; the Naval Bill, to the Comm. on Naval Affairs; the Post-Office Bill to the Comm. on Post-Offices and Post Roads; and the Indian Bill to the Comm. on Indian Affairs; leaving to the Appropriations Comm. the Legislative, Executive, and Judicial, the Sundry Civil, the Deficiency, the Fortification, the pension, and the District of Columbia Bills,—a little more than one-half the appropriations for carrying on the government. This is, of course, the disintegrating committee division carried some steps further. Its inevitable tendency is to increase and diversify (and confuse) expenditure.

I am glad that what I wrote of your book in the Political Science Quarterly seemed to you as appreciative of the 'attitude and effort' of its author as it was meant to be. Because the criticism had, in the nature of the case, to be much more elaborated than the appreciative portion of the *Review*, I was afraid that my very great admiration for the book might be unduly obscured. My emphasizing of the historical view doubtless grew out of my own intense engagement on that side of the study,—and my own intense conviction that leadership, and not *bossism*, is of the essence of our institutions; bossism being one of the crude things we have not yet thrown off.

I wish I might some day have the pleasure of *talking* these points over with you! With much regard,

Very sincerely Yours,   Woodrow Wilson

ALS (Bryce Papers, Bodleian Library).
1 James Bryce, "A Word as to the Speakership," *North American Review*, CLI (Oct. 1890), 385-98.
2 See A. B. Hart to WW, March 12, 1891; WW to A. B. Hart, May 19, 1891; and A. B. Hart to WW, May 24, 1891.

To John Franklin Jameson

My dear Jameson,   Princeton, N. J., 1 January, 1892.

A happy New Year from both of us! I am not writing on the first day of the year to signalize the beginning of a new period of good resolutions. It does not require a good resolution to write to you, but only an accommodating conscience which will permit one to lay aside all the things he *ought* to do and indulge himself in the things he *likes* to do. I mean to keep out of the lunatic asylum, to which you so feelingly refer,[1] by encouraging this accommodating humour on the part of my conscience, and I commend the same course to you. It is the most attractive sort of hygiene you can imagine; and it must rest upon the right principle, for it is so evidently in accordance with nature. I find I have practiced it more or less all my life,—but quite unconsciously and therefore quite unscientifically. It is only of recent years that I have cultivated it as a rational system of rest.

I am just recovering from an attack of the grip; and, while confined to the house and kept away from my tasks by it, I have had abundant time to think over such things. Certainly I must do *something* to keep me out of the asylum; for my work, instead of decreasing, is increasing. I have just contracted to deliver ten lectures on constitutional law at the New York Law School[2] (the Columbia secessionists)[3] after my return from the Hopkins.

When do your own lectures come at the Hopkins? I wish they came at the same time that mine do (in February) so that we might see a great deal of each other.

I have been very much interested indeed in the lecture programmes of your Association,[4] which you were thoughtful enough to send me. You are especially to be congratulated, it seems to me, upon getting Winchester of Wesleyan. He is one of the most interesting and admirable of lecturers. I can never hear him too much. He is the man who ought to be Donovan professor of English Literature in Baltimore.

I know Miss Louise Arnold, of whom you speak with so much pleasure—and it is my judgment that she ought to stay at home, and not go about disturbing the hearts of young professors all over the country. She has an aunt living here,[5] with whom she spent several months during the last college year—and she simply played the mischief among the younger men of the Faculty! She is certainly a beautiful and charming young woman. Her mother— only seventeen years her senior—is scarcely less attractive, we think.

With warmest regards to the Gardners[6] and all cordial messages for yourself from us both.

Most faithfully Yours   Woodrow Wilson

ALS (J. F. Jameson Papers, DLC).
  [1] The letter to which Wilson is referring is missing.
  [2] See the Editorial Note, "Wilson's Lectures at the New York Law School."
  [3] Controversy disrupted the Columbia Law School in 1891 when President Seth Low and the Trustees of Columbia College decided to reorganize the Law School and integrate it more fully into the university. The aged Warden, Theodore William Dwight, decided to retire, and his disciples and colleagues, Professors George Chase and Robert Davison Petty, resigned. Dwight died in June

1892, but Chase and Petty, together with a group of Columbia Law School graduates who banded together as the "Dwight Alumni Association," determined to perpetuate Dwight's ideals and methods of instruction by forming a new law school. Chartered as the "New York Law School," the institution opened on October 1, 1891, on the eighth floor of the Equitable Building at 120 Broadway. Chase was the Dean, and Petty and Albert G. Reeves (a former instructor at Columbia) were part-time professors. Instruction at the New York Law School strictly followed the "Dwight method," that is, the study of textbook commentaries on law and cases. Enrollment at the Columbia Law School fell off badly for a time, and the New York Law School was, in its first year, the second largest law school in the country and, by 1904-1905, the largest. For an extensive discussion, see Julius Goebel, Jr., et al., A History of the School of Law, Columbia University (New York, 1955), pp. 113-52, 446, n. 82.

4 The Historical and Economic Association of Brown University.
5 Mrs. Richard J. Arnold, of 31 Nassau Street.
6 That is, the Henry Brayton Gardners.

From the Minutes of the Princeton Faculty

5 5' P.M., Friday, Jany. 8, 1892.
. . . The Report on the *Monitorial System*[1] was read, discussed and adopted in part (Sections 1. & 2.), and was then recommitted to the Committee for further inquiries as to certain points.

1 See the extract from the Princeton Faculty Minutes, Nov. 20, 1891.

To the Editors of *The Princetonian*

Dear Sirs: Princeton, January 8 [1892].

When the plan of reviving boating at Princeton[1] was first mentioned to me my judgment was in a balance between two conclusions; I am sorry to say that it is still in the same uncomfortable position. My sympathy with all forms of athletics is so great, and my admiration for boating, in particular, as a manly sport, so sincere, that I find it impossible to exclude from my thought the hope that some practicable way of reviving boating among us may be hit upon. And yet my practical judgment experiences many difficulties about the matter.

We had boating here when I was in college, and I know from personal observation how very unsatisfactory it is to row on the canal.[2] I know, too, how difficult it is to train a crew there. The water is too sluggish, the obs[t]ructions are too many, the management of the boat is too difficult. It would be necessary to supplement practice there with practice on some better course. But there is no better course nearer than Trenton or Philadelphia, and it would not be possible to go so far more than once a week; and every week there would be a change of boats and a change of water, with no good chance of getting fully accustomed to either.

To carry on so elaborate and fatiguing a method of practices would require a very great expenditure of three very valuable things: enthusiasm, time, and money. Could we get enough of these three things to conduct boating through its first inevitable stage of non-success; could we spare enough of these three things from our other athletic undertakings? Unquestionably foot-ball, base-ball, and athletics in general would be benefitted by boating, provided it did not require so great an expenditure of but partially repaid effort as really to subtract from the sum total of our energy, rather than add to it, and that, it must be allowed, is a significant proviso. It contains, indeed, the whole question of advisability.

If I must sum up my views, I am afraid that I must pronounce against the feasibility of the plan. On the one side is the very sincere wish that we might have boating. But, on the other hand, my practical judgment is given pause by the question, How?

Very sincerely yours,   Woodrow Wilson '79.

Printed in *The Princetonian*, xvi (Jan. 19, 1892), [3–4].
  [1] *The Princetonian*, December 14, 1891, announced that during the next few weeks it would publish "communications from prominent alumni on the subject of the reorganization of the crew." Noting that the matter had been the subject of much recent campus discussion, the editorial continued: "It is our earnest hope that something besides mere words may come of this agitation. We have yet to hear the first adverse opinion on the question—a fact which seems to point to Princeton's once more seeking athletic honors on the water." On December 21, just before the Christmas recess, *The Princetonian* sent a form letter to "about twenty of the alumni" soliciting their opinions upon the revival of the crew. The editors, in their issue of January 13, 1892, admitted that the tenor of the replies had been "disappointing in their lack of enthusiasm."
  A special issue of *The Princetonian*, dated January 19, 1892, was devoted to printing ten of the replies to the form letter, together with a brief history of Princeton's unsuccessful attempts between 1872 and 1883 to establish a crew. In addition to Wilson's letter printed above, the special issue published communications from such prominent alumni as James W. Alexander, '60, Henry B. Thompson, '77, and Edgar Allan Poe, '91. Seven of the ten replies were distinctly pessimistic about the prospects for a crew at Princeton. The chief obstacle cited was the fact that there was simply no adequate body of water near the campus on which to row. Interestingly, one or two of the replies mentioned the possibility of forming an artificial lake in the lowlands near Princeton. This would not happen until 1906, when Wilson was President of Princeton University, with the creation of Lake Carnegie.
  [2] See Wilson's editorial in *The Princetonian*, iii (Jan. 16, 1879), 136, printed in Vol. 1, p. 445.

A News Report

[Jan. 18, 1892]

Professor Woodrow Wilson, of Princeton, lectured, Dec. 10th, in Russell Library Hall, under the auspices of the *Olla Podrida* Board, upon the subject, "Democracy." Upon the appearance of the speaker, a rousing Wesleyan yell was given by the college students in the gallery. The Professor began with a comparison between our present government and the Roman and Swiss republics and the early German cantonal gatherings. He then discussed the relation of the opinion of the majority to political action, the nature of liberty and law, and certain false assumptions that underlie popular notions concerning self-government. The striking thought of the address was the conclusion that the people do not govern themselves after all, but freely consent to be governed by those who prove themselves most capable of exercising governing power. The lecture was thoroughly enjoyed by all who were present. After the lecture the Professor was tendered a reception in the parlors of the Eclectic Club-house, which was largely attended by his friends in the city and college.

Printed in the Middletown, Conn., *Wesleyan Argus*, xxv (Jan. 18, 1892), 61.

To Albert Bushnell Hart

Dear Professor Hart,   Princeton, New Jersey, 20 January, 1892.

I feel pretty sure that I can have my MSS. ready for the publishers by the time that your volume is ready for distribution.[1] My hope of finding time during term in which to work at the task has not been justified by the event, and I shall be obliged to devote the greater part of another summer vacation to it.

I enclose a copy of the chapter and section headings of my volume, as I have planned and in part executed it; and I should like to have your opinion of it. The red line indicates the point up to which I wrote last summer. I shall devote less space to the topics which follow than to those I have gone over, because most of what is to come has its explanations back in what I have written.

You will see that I have already written such an introduction as you suggest. Let me say that if there is any part of my manuscript that you would like to see, I will send it to you with pleasure. Of course I shall rely upon you for the freest sort of criticism; for as you know I am not a professional student of American history, and I naturally feel a little uneasiness about the details. My MSS. as it now stands is of course not in its final shape; but it shows my method of treatment distinctly enough.

I had an interview with the Mr. Reiley of whom you speak, and must say that I was very much impressed by the fellow. You surprise me by what you say about his not having had any training. I think that you must have misunderstood him. He told me that he was a son of the Professor of Latin at Rutgers College[2] (whose faculty contains some very scholarly men indeed), that he had had the usual college drill there, and had spent some time in special preparation for this work abroad. He brought the most cordial sort of recommendation from President Austin Scott, who said that he knew all about him, and believed in him. It would indeed be incredible that a man without training could accomplish any part of what he is attempting. Without having any right to a critical judgment about such matters, I was impressed in spite of myself by the man and by his interesting sketches.

Very sincerely Yours,   Woodrow Wilson

TCL (RSB Coll., DLC).

  [1] Hart's letter to which this is a reply is missing.

  [2] The Rev. DeWitt Ten Broeck Reiley, Professor of Latin Language and Literature at Rutgers from 1860 to 1885.

From James Burton Pond[1]

Dear Sir: New York, Jan. 21st, 1892

  Mr. H. T. Thomas, of the firm of Scribner & Sons, called on me a few days ago and gave me a syllabus of several of your lectures and asked me to communicate with you.[2] I know considerable about you and your work. It requires a pretty big name to bring the public to a scientific lecture. I have tried for sometime past to get Prof. Bryce, as his "American Commonwealth" has made his name almost a household word—and have been unsuccessful. You see the general public want people that are very well known. It is very difficult getting a new lecturer before the public nowadays, as there are so many Agencies that have used their persuasive powers with Lecture Committees to that extent that it has impoverished them, and it is the name now that draws.

  I think with the machinery I have, I am able to get as near the public as anybody, but I cannot make a success of all I undertake. I wish I could. There is a place for your lectures in the best Courses in the country I think, if the Managers can be convinced of the fact. Of course, it is necessary for me to hear you before I would place your name on my list. This I would gladly do whenever there is an opportunity in the city or near by. If it would be convenient for you to call sometime when you are in New York, I would be glad to see you.

Yours Very Truly,   J. B. Pond

TLS (WP, DLC) with WWhw notation on env.: "Ans. 29 Jan'y, '92."

  [1] One of the leading agents for lecturers and performers in the United States at this time. Pond managed lecture tours for, among many others, Henry Ward Beecher, Henry M. Stanley, Arthur Conan Doyle, and Mark Twain. The absence of any additional letters to Wilson from Pond indicates that Wilson never lectured under his auspices.

  [2] It seems likely that Robert Bridges had visited the Wilsons during the Christmas vacation; that Wilson had given him the "syllabus" and asked him

to get in touch with Pond; and that Bridges had sent Thomas to Pond's office with Wilson's "syllabus" and a letter about Wilson.

From Philippus William Miller

Dear Tommy   Philadelphia, Jany 23 1892
Yesterday we held a meeting of the Executive Committee of the Phila. Alumni of Princeton, relative to our annual dinner. When the question of who should speak came up they all turned to me and asked for you again. You made a great hit last winter and committee and alumni were much pleased.[1] So I promised I would write you. The dinner this year will be on Feby 19th which is Friday. If you can accept, please do. We all earnestly desire it, and we will make the same arrangements as last year for your comfort. You will let me know of course as soon as you conveniently can. You may choose your own subject.[2]
Yours affectly   Philippus W. Miller

ALS (WP, DLC) with WWhw notation on env.: "Ans. 29 Jan'y, '92."
[1] See Wilson's notes for this address, printed at Jan. 30, 1891, and the news item printed at Jan. 31, 1891.
[2] See the report of this affair printed at Feb. 22, 1892.

From Albert Bushnell Hart

Dear Prof. Wilson: Cambridge, Mass.   Jan. 24, 1892.
Yours of the 20th is at hand, and gives a gratifying prospect for your MS.
Your subdivision seems full and excellent; but for the purposes of the series I would suggest a more minute analysis. Thwaites has fourteen chapters. I shall have thirteen. The object is to make the book convenient for class use, for assigning lessons and topics. I think we had better follow that principle all the way through
The division into numerous successive paragraphs is even more important, for similar reasons. Thwaites made 130; I shall have at least 120; and the value of the series will be increased if your volume is about the same.
The reviews have highly commended the system of maps and of bibliographies under each chapter. Your maps are all ready (and printed) and your suggestions have been duly observed.
As for Mr. Reiley, the boy seems entirely candid and straightforward, and answered my questions promptly and manfully; but it appeared that he had never taken a degree (nor, so far as I could understand, attended a college)[.] He says he considers himself educated because he "has read all the college text-books." He does not claim to read either German or Latin (!) readily, and

knows no Greek. He has never had any systematic study under any historian or geographer. He does not know some of the most common secondary books on historical geography, and makes no pretence to have used sources. Nothing short of a miracle could produce a valuable work with such preparation. In fact the best thing in his favor was a very flattering letter from Prof. Sloan, who of course is an expert and has confidence in his results.

In working out your Epoch volume I should like to make the same request that the Vicar's wife made to the painter: "not to be sparing of his diamonds in her stomacher." I hope you will introduce lots of snappy brief quotations. I could not get Thwaites to do it but I mean to do it myself—not extracts, but phrases quoted in the text

Is Princeton to be in working order between Feb. 4 and 18?[1]
Sincerely yours,   Albert Bushnell Hart

ALS (WP, DLC) with WWhw notation on env.: "Ans. 29 Jan'y, 1892."
[1] Hart was presumably referring to what he thought was the examination period. Actually, it fell between January 29 and February 10, 1892.

From James Bayard Henry[1]

Dear sir: Philadelphia, Pa.   January 25, 1892
Our annual Alumni Dinner comes off on the 19th of February at the Bellevue, due notice of which will be sent later on. The Executive Committee are most desirous that you should be present on that occasion as one of the representatives of Princeton, and I trust nothing will prevent. We are endeavoring to make this the greatest dinner ever given by any College Alumni Association in Philadelphia, and trust you will be with us on this occasion, and ready to say a few words in relation to the progress and future of our dear old College.

With kindest regards, and hoping that nothing will prevent your being present,
I am   Yours truly,   J. Bayard Henry

TLS (WP, DLC) with WWhw notation on env.: "Ans. 29 Jan'y, '92."
[1] (James) Bayard Henry, born Philadelphia, Jan. 15, 1857. A.B., College of New Jersey, 1876. Studied law in Philadelphia and practiced there throughout his active career. Director of many corporations and active in Philadelphia religious and civic groups. Member, Pennsylvania State Senate, 1898-1902, and of the Select Council of Philadelphia, 1908-11. Life Trustee of Princeton, 1896-1926. Died Sept. 17, 1926.

An Announcement

[Jan. 27, 1892]

PROF. WILSON'S CLASSES FOR THE SECOND TERM.

Prof. Wilson expects to be absent in Baltimore until the close of the week ending March 5.[1] Within a week after his return he will examine his second term classes as follows:

The class in Political Eeconomy (Junior required) in the whole of Walker's First Lessons in Political Economy, (published by H. Holt).

The Senior elective class in Administration in Bryce's American Commonwealth, Part II ("The State Governments").

The Junior-Senior elective class in International Law, in W. E. Hall's International Law (Oxford Press), Parts I, ("General Principles"[)] and II, ("The Law Governing States in their Normal Relations").   WOODROW WILSON

Printed in *The Princetonian*, XVI (Jan. 27, 1892), [1].
[1] See the Editorial Note, "Wilson's Lectures on Administration at the Johns Hopkins, 1892."

From Cyrus Hall McCormick

My Dear Wilson: [Chicago]   Jany 28, 1892

I am glad to have your letter of the 24th.[1] It is clear and concise, and upon a most important subject. It is not a letter, however, that can be answered without considerable thought, but the subject will have due attention and I shall advise you later on as to how the matter shapes itself in my mind.[2]

I regret that you will not be at Princeton when I attend the Trustees Meeting. Yours sincerely,   Cyrus H. McCormick

TLS (C. H. McCormick Letterpress Books, WHi).
[1] Wilson's letter to McCormick, his classmate and a Princeton trustee, is missing, but subsequent documents (particularly EAW to WW, March 15, 1892; and WW to EAW, March 17 and 30 and May 5, 1892) indicate both Wilson's reasons for writing the letter and its contents. Professor Richard T. Ely of the Johns Hopkins had probably informed the university authorities in early January that he intended to resign in order to accept a professorship at the University of Wisconsin; and President Gilman or Professor Adams may have written to Wilson about the possibility of his coming to the Hopkins. (For a note about the public announcement of Ely's resignation and the rumor that Wilson might be invited to the Hopkins, see EAW to WW, March 15, 1892, n. 4.) Thus Wilson, in his letter to McCormick of January 24, may well have suggested that the invitation from the Johns Hopkins, if it should come, would create a good opportunity for McCormick to press the matter of the establishment of a School of Law at Princeton among the trustees. In any event, Wilson's letter to his wife of March 30 makes it clear that Wilson had expressed considerable dissatisfaction about his salary in his letter to McCormick of January 24. And Wilson's letter to his wife of May 5, 1892, reveals that he had described his plans for a law school in some detail in the same letter to McCormick.
[2] Actually, McCormick does not seem to have written again until May 4, 1892, and then in reply to another letter from Wilson.

From Joseph R. Wilson, Jr.

My precious brother: Clarksville, Tenn.   Jany. 28/'92.

The reason why father has not replied to your last letter is that ever since two weeks ago last Sunday he has been very sick, most of the time being spent in bed. The cause of his sickness is a swelling of the prostate gland and a consequent inability to pass water from the bladder. The trouble came upon him suddenly & a doctor was summoned who had to introduce a catheter to draw off the water. This *I* now do three times a day, a rubber tube being used. The operation is a simple one and I give father but little pain. I never saw such suffering as father had to endure during the first twelve days of his illness. The doctors were very anxious about him and I felt very helpless here alone although faculty & students were very kind, one or more of the boys staying each night and most of the day. The sick one is alright now, the doctor says. He is recovering strength and says he will attend his classes next week. He sits up now a greater part of each day and has a good appetite. I did not tell you of father's illness because I knew it would make you uneasy. If, however there had been immediate danger I would have sent for you without delay.

Father's trouble is not an unusual one with an aged man, the doctors say, and there is now no cause for anxiety concerning his condition. If I do not write again at once take *no* news as *good* news. If, however, you should happen to get another letter in a very few days do not think upon its receipt that father is worse.

Father joins me in great love to you & Sister E. Excuse pencil & haste.   Your aff. bro.   Joseph.

ALS (WP, DLC) with WWhw notation on env.: "Ans."

From William Royal Wilder

My Dear Wilson: New York, January 29th, 1892

I forgot whether I have acknwoledged [acknowledged] receipt of your cheque for the sum of $20[1] or not. The same has this day been forwarded to Bridges and herewith you will find our joint and several thanks.

Cordially yours,   Wm R Wilder

TLS (WP, DLC) with WWhw notation on env.: "Recp't—(Isham cup)."

[1] Wilson's contribution toward the purchase of a large silver punch bowl and ladle, which was made to order by the Gorham Company and displayed by that firm at the World's Columbian Exposition in Chicago in 1893. Wilson and other members of the Class of 1879, who had long benefited from Isham's lavish hospitality, presented the bowl and ladle on the occasion of the fourteenth "Isham dinner" on May 26, 1892. See Alexander J. Kerr, "The Isham Dinners," *Fifty Years of the Class of 'Seventy-Nine Princeton* (Princeton, N.J., 1931), p. 200.

From Philippus William Miller

My dear Tommy,   Philadelphia, Jany 30 1892
I have just received your letter accepting the invitation of our committee to speak and eat on Feby 19th[.] I am delighted, and so will the committee be, when I report at our next meeting. I will give you ample notice as to accommodations &c in the mean time let me know what your "toast" is to be.

Affectly yours   Philippus W. Miller.

Or shall we select it?—as you please   P.

ALS (WP, DLC) with WWhw notation on env.: "Ans."

EDITORIAL NOTE

WILSON'S LECTURES ON ADMINISTRATION AT THE JOHNS HOPKINS, 1892

This particular note supplements the more general Editorial Note, "Wilson's Lectures on Administration at the Johns Hopkins, 1891-93," printed earlier in this volume.

The Wilsons went to Baltimore on January 30, 1892, and lived at 1002 Cathedral Avenue. Wilson lectured four times a week for the next six weeks, from about February 1 through March 4, and his notes for these lectures are printed all together at their first delivery date, not at their composition dates.

As these composition dates reveal, Wilson went to Baltimore in 1892 with notes in hand for only the first two topics, "Administrative Functions: Resumé of First Course" and "*Division and Coördination of Powers and Functions.*" His composition dates for the following notes show that he worked them up, as it were, from day to day, staying not too far ahead of his class.

Wilson made fairly detailed shorthand outlines for portions of his 1892 notes on central administration in France and Prussia. These outlines, entitled "*France: Central Admin.*" and "*Prussia.* Central Administration," are on loose pages in the Wilson Papers, Library of Congress.

Notes for the final topic, "Sovereignty," with the composition date of February 27, 1895, were added when Wilson repeated the second series in that year.

Notes for Lectures at the Johns Hopkins

Second Year Course).   [c. Feb. 1, 1892–Feb. 27, 1895]

ADMINISTRATION.

I. Administrative Functions: Resumé of First Course.

1. *Definition* of Administration: "*The continuous and systematic carrying out in practice of all the tasks which devolve upon*

the State. These the State has had laid upon it *by reason of its history, through Law*, which is the product of its history, embodying what it has learned regarding liberty and authority, right and obligation.["]¹

2. *Differs from Legislation* as *origination* differs from *discretion*, as the *determination of policy and* of *general rules* differs from the *adaptation of means* to ends.

   Its field is the *field of organization*, the adaptation of means to ends; its questions are *questions of adjustment*. Its frontiers are the frontiers of state interference.

3. *The Question of Function* one upon which the study of Administration throws great light. *In one sense* and to a certain extent the *functions* of government are *determined by the conscious and deliberate choice* of constituent law,—of legislation; *but* looked at from another point of view, they are *in a very real sense independent of legislation*, of choice, because as old as government, and *inherent in its very nature.* Administration cannot always wait upon legislation, *but must be given leave*, or take it, *to* proceed without specific warrant in giving *effect* to *the characteristic life of the State.* Administration rests upon customary, and so to say essential, law as well as upon legislation.

4. *The Real Nature of the (historical) State*: Every state is *the historical form of the organic common life of a particular people*, some form of organic political life being commanded by the very nature of man. The State is *an abiding natural relationship*; the *eternal, natural embodiment and expression of a higher form of life than the individual*, namely that common life which gives leave and full opportunity to the individual life,—makes it possible and makes it complete.

   Each nation has its own State, i.e., *its own form of organic life*, its own functional characteristics, produced by its own development.

5. *The Theories of State-life*: (a) the *Weal* (or *police*) *State*; (b) the *Law-State*; (c) the *Constitutional State* (adult, self-directed).

   Administration, in the constitutional state, *includes* within its scope *all the necessary and characteristic functions of the state*, largely defined and always limited by law, to which it is of course subject, but serving the State, not the law-making body of the State,—possessing a life not resident in statutes.

¹ Here Wilson is quoting, with minor changes, from the definition given at the beginning of his first Hopkins lecture on administration in 1891, printed at Jan. 26, 1891. [Eds.' note]

6. *The Theoretical vs. the Actual division of Functions*:
   The theory really predicates *a division of organs*, based upon a difference of a radical sort in the functions: and there is of course a real *distinction between Legislation and Administration*; between *Legislation and Adjudication*; and between *Adjudication and Administration*.

   But in practice there has been no sharp differentiation of organs to correspond to the full with these differences of function. The argument for such a division of organs simply *an argument from convenience*, in the highest sense of the term. *The object* of actual developments, not a system of mechanical checks and balances, but simply *organic differentiation, with its accompanying diffusion of vitality and accession of vigour*: no part overworked, but each skilled and instructed by specialization; each part coördinated with and assisted by all the others; each part an organ, not to serve a separate interest, but to serve the whole.

7. *Administrative Law,—what*?
   "The sum of the legal rules obtaining in a State in respect of the public administration" (Sarwey),[2] i.e., *the whole body of rules, however derived, which determine the powers and the modes of action of administrative authorities*, on the one hand, *and*, on the other, *the obedience or submission of individuals to administrative action*.

   ("*With* the organic separation of legislation and administration, *the point of departure of the constitutional state*, the *germ of* the development is created whose product is *administrative law*."—Sarwey, p. 33).

8. *Relationship of Administrative Acts to the Laws*:
   A *question to be answered for each government separ'tely* (*E.g., in our own case* upon the theory of the law-state; *in England*, upon such theory as we may adopt concerning Prerogative; *in the case of the governments of the continent*, upon the knowledge of the fact that the police state stands back of the present constitutional state).

   But, in the case of *every historically normal government*, we may, perhaps, say that, in the absence of specific legal developments to the contrary, *the presumption* is in favour of the principle, that *the sphere of administrative activity is as wide as the sphere in which it may move without infringing the laws* (statutory or customary, in their letter or in their reasonable inferential meaning).

---

2 See the Editorial Note, "Wilson's Lectures on Administration at the Johns Hopkins, 1891-93," for an explanation of the treatment of Wilson's notes and references. [Eds.' note]

9. *Relation of Administrative Action to Personal Rights: Bills of Rights. How far does the mere statement* or enumeration of individual rights in a constitution avail to *make* them *positive rights?* When stated in their most abstract and general terms (e.g., *Inviolability of person,* etc.) they constitute no absolute check upon administrative action. *Their validity depends upon the admission and definition of exceptions,* upon the running of clear lines of positive law between those invasions of individual right by executive power which are necessary to the order and energy of the State and those which are unnecessary, arbitrary, and tyrannical. *Positive law must make* all *invasions regular* (i.e., deliberate and *just in process*) and must confine them strictly to *necessary cases.*

Note the specific (and generally negative) *form of the items of our constitutional Bills of Rights,*—their tendency to take the shape of *particularized administrative provisions:* 'No quartering of soldiers in time of peace, *except in a manner prescribed by law;* no unreasonable seizures or searches of persons or premises *except upon warrant* issued upon probable cause, supported by oath or affirmation, designating a particular person, place, etc; no criminal prosecution *except under certain safeguards,*' etc., etc.

31 Dec. '91.

I. *Division and Coördination of Powers and Functions.*

1. *Two distinct parts* to this topic, which should be sharply separated: (1) Division and Coördination as *between central and local* authorities, and (2) Division and Coördination *among the central* authorities.

I.

Between Central and Local Authorities:

2. *What is to be the Standard* or Basis of Differentiation? *Nature of the Problem:*
Evidently one of the widest and most important, and at the same time one of the most complex and difficult, questions connected with the study of government. It is not a single, but a double, question, concerning

   (a) *The life of the State* as a whole, as a political unit, and

   (b) *Individual initiative and the vitality of local government,* coming very near indeed to questions of liberty, and the diffusion of political capacity.

3. *General Considerations*:

Supervision there must be: but in what matters and upon what basis? *Upon the principle* that local autonomy and variety are to be given full leave up to the point at which they clearly come into collision with the interests of the State as a whole, by weakening it or threatening its integrity.

A supervision, this, *which is not interference or direction, nor* the *guidance* of local affairs; which is not even presidential; *but prudential*, and in the interest of the State rather than (directly) of the local unit:—whose object, i.e., is, not to take care of the local unit (tutelage), but to take care of the national unit, of the honour and prosperity of the State as a whole.

The units of local government *ought* unquestionably *to be homogeneous in make-up* and interest (not city *plus* country districts, e.g., or mining district *plus* agricultural); and then each should be left absolutely free in the management of those concerns which have a virtual *permanent limitation* to the locality.

Highways are not so limited that their several parts may be differently kept. *Contagious diseases* are not so limited. Neither is *Bankruptcy*; Nor *pauperism*.

This is *simply the principle of individual liberty extended*.

It happens to coincide with the distinction (presently to be discussed) between intensive and extensive economic administration, and also with the distinction between economic and political, to a certain extent; but these do not hit the same principle exactly. It is *a principle of functional self-determination*, which issues in *a difference of kind*: local vs. general—communal vs. national.

Logically it requires, besides, *divisions intermediate in size* between the commune or township and the State; and a corresponding set of *intermediate officials*: inasmuch as there are local interests not quite so narrowly localized as those of the commune or township (e.g., neighbourhood roads), nor yet so widely extended and universal as to be of national concernment.

3. [4.] *Various Solutions of the Question*:

A. *The French Answer*, an argument for complete national unity, and for uniformity both in the provisions of law and in their application. *M. Aucoc* typical in this respect. His argument for centralization is, that the *national solidarity and glory* of France, the general good and the united vigour of the country, can be maintained only when there is a strong and uniform administration throughout her territory. *Liberty,* he says (with charming *naiveté*) is no doubt a *very precious* thing; *but* the other good things which society can procure for us must not be sacrificed for it.[3]

Aucoc emphasizes three faults on the part of local authorities which he conceives it to be the duty of the central authorities to correct:

> *Violations of the general principle of liberty and equality* before the laws;
>
> *Negligence* in function;
>
> *Extravagance*
>
> He would practically leave no field for local spirit or conscience in the conduct of affairs.

Napoleon's dictum: "The personal proprietary interest is ceaselessly on the watch, bears fruit continually; on the contrary, the interest of the community is by nature somnolent and sterile: personal interest needs nothing but its instinct; the interest of the community requ[i]res virtue, and that is rare." (From memorandum dictated to Ministry of the Interior in 1800). *Therefore* the central authority must itself furnish the virtue necessary for the conduct of local affairs?

Aucoc urges a stronger reason when he suggests the necessity for some *defence of local minorities.*

But the whole of this French argument misses *the principle of life,* which is, *not uniformity, but variety.*

Professor Simon Patten's answer to this argument for uniformity would be,[4] *the impracticability of making and applying uniform laws* (particularly with regard to the economic interests of society) which will adapt themselves to the almost infinite variety among the social and economic conditions of the several communities that make up a State.[5]

---

[3] *Without liberty,* these other things will not for very long continue to be obtained. When the individual becomes helpless (initiativeless) and submissive there will be a steady degeneration to the *Weal State.*

[4] "Decay of Local Government in America," in Annals of Am. Acad. of Pol. and Soc. Sci., I., p. 26.

[5] Points of Patten's paper:

States and townships created in this country by the Surveyor, without regard to diversities of soil, physical features, or climate.

P. 33, Illustration by diversities in Illinois. Question of local option in other matters than the liquor traffic.

Imitation in law-making among our States, instead of a regard for local needs and peculiarities of condition.

Separation of cities from States, and their erection into separate commonwealths, after the kind of the German free cities (?).

His arguments, however, unfortunately *prove too much.* They would preclude uniform legislation upon some subjects of the greatest importance in the cases of the majority of modern national governments; and would logically lead to putting legislation into commission, among the several constituent communities of each large State. It is now apparently, *too late to cut out economic units* to serve as States.

B. *Divisions* of function *according to Kind* vs. divisions *according to Locality* of the tasks involved.

Might solve a certain part of Patten's difficultu [difficulty], inasmuch as districts with special interests or under pecul[i]ar conditions might be put *under special Bureaux* possessed of special functions under appropriate legislation.

Tried in Prussia and elsewhere, but found wanting because of the absence in most cases of any such sharp and mutually exclusive distinctions between district and district as it presupposes.

Besides being impracticable, it does not solve the difficulty of principle or theory.

C. *Experimental Classification,*—according to the *breadth or universality of interests*, as revealed by experience.

Trial lists of functions appropriate for uniform direction from the centre. E.g. this, *from Aucoc:*[6] National roads; the greater railways; navigable rivers; canals; ports; lighthouses; post and telegraph; part of public education; certain matters concerning public worship; and much of administrative police, (including sanitation, I suppose).

Noteworthy that with regard to almost every one of these matters *differences of national development and differences of legislative practice* (differences, i.e., of history and of judgment) may govern, and have governed. All turns upon an interpretation of what shall be included under the term "general interest" or "national concern."

Such classifications may be practically correct, and yet not be successful general statements. They *lack vitality.* We approach a criterion of Kind; but it does not become either clear or precise. Convenience is a policy rather than a principle.

D. *'Political'* distinguished from *'Economic'* interests. Cannot

6 P. 104.

this serve as a basis for a division of Kind between central and local administrative functions?

Meier suggests this in his distinction between '*magisterial*' functions and '*economic.*' At any rate, he conceives the economic functions of local authorities to be much more characteristic and much more intensive than the economic functions of central authorities. *The budget*, he points out, is *much more central to local than to imperial administration.*

[(]It is on this ground that he *justifies the three-class system of voting* in local elections, while questioning its justice when applied to national affairs).

Sarwey embodies a similar idea in his suggestion, that, for the sake of unity in administration, and for the sake of definiteness of responsibility to the representatives of the people in their national body, *each branch of administration should have at its summit some central organ*, in which 'government' and 'administration' are united.

(The word '*Government*' is here used to mean those central organs (or that central organ) of the State by which the State's unity is represented, as over against foreign powers, or as over against the representatives of the people: The 'responsible' Executive, in the technical sense of the word; in whose hands the Administration is an instrument.)[7]

This distinction is only partially true, only a suggestive commentary, but it comes nearer than any other yet mentioned to furnishing a general principle.

Summary of these Suggestions:

They may be summed up under three heads:

(1) *Solidarity*: a uniform will, for the purpose of realizing national unity and power.

(2) *Size of the function*, and consequent relalations [relations] to the general convenience.

(3) *House-keeping vs. supervision* and the determination of policy.

In each case the proper terms are missed. It is *not a question of convenience*, or glory, or management, but *a question of life*.

---

[7] *The French* have an almost identical distinction: '*Gouvernement*,' "the direction of those affairs for which the name political is reserved, that is to say, the relations of the head of the State with the 'great bodies' of the State"; *Administration* something "altogether different*," viz., the power which acts for the "collective needs of the citizens," where individual or private corporative initiative does not suffice.—Aucoc, I., 94, 95.

1. *We are dealing*, on the one hand, *with a general life*, with its questions of *commerce*, health, general intercourse, *common order*, uniform *civil law* and *political privilege*: its common means, facilities, securities.

2. *We are dealing*, on the other hand, *with communal life, local life*, with its local resources, business, natural situation and environment, *tastes, pleasures*, needs for order and needs for development.

It is these two things that we are to distinguish and harmonize, without sacrificing either to the other.

4. [5.] *Distinction* between *Centralization* and *Concentration* in Administration.

This distinction is part of the clue to the difference between French and German systems of administration.

By Centralization is meant the *direct dependence* of officers of all grades and functions upon the central authorities: because appointed and subject to removal by those authorities.

Concentration, on the other hand, although it indicates *an equal integration* of the service, an equally systematic and unified organization, means also (when employed for the purposes of the present distinction) a certain independence of tenure on the part of local officers; admits of their local election, and of their exemption from removal by the central authorities. They are *subject to its oversight*, but they are not its creatures.

The predominant feature of *the French* administrative system is *Centralization*; but in *Germany* administration is *concentrated*, rather than centralized.

The question with the freer governments is one of concentration of authority rather than of centralization of organization. An interesting and important distinction to keep in mind in the case of England.

5. [6.] *Differences between Legislation, Adjudication, & Administration in the matter* of centralization (or concentration), both historically and essentially.

1. *In legislation* the *centralization* of authority is *modern*. It was characteristic neither of the ancient nor of the mediaeval State, but is the product of modern universalizing & unifying tendencies.

2. *In adjudication* it is *more ancient*; though in this field too it was almost unknown to the mediaeval world. It has *sprung from the growth of the monarchical power* in our modern states.

3. *In administration*, though not more recent than in the

other fields of government, its justification (if it have any) must be otherwise argued. For, while uniformity in private rights and in the major principles of public law and constitutional structure may be desirable, and certainty and uniformity in the application of those rights and principles by the courts of law indispensable for fixing the legal habit and facilitating the legal life (as well as for promoting a common national consciousness and a common liberty), it by no means follows that uniformity is the best rule in Administration, which is the detailed carrying out of all public functions in behoof of all sorts of localities and amongst all varieties of social and economic condition.

It is most noteworthy in this connection *that Unity* (both national and international) *is a characteristic mark of the modern time*: a result of the modern cheapness, ease, and speed of intercommunication, which produce in many spheres an almost universal community of interests, conditions, and ideas.

Such tendencies seem permanent, and we would not resist them if we could; but they increase the difficulty of *our problem*, which *is*,

7. *Local variety and vitality without loss of vital integration.*

Local authorities must be allowed, if they are not to be smothered, to move freely within liberal limits of law, not under direction, but only under a limiting supervision.

For the purpose of illustrating the practical *solutions* of this problem, we shall *study three types*, partially first, by means of an examination of them on the side of central organization, and more intimately, in the second place, by means of an examination of their characteristics of local administrative differentiation.

These three types are the following:

1. *The German*, under which elected local authorities are kept within the bounds of their jurisdiction by the supervision of officials who are themselves in a sense independent, inasmuch as they are subject to removal only by judicial process.

2. *The French*, under which there is virtual centralization. Neither the local nor the central officials are independent. All the more important of them are appointed, and almost without exception removable at the pleasure of the central authorities. The local bodies are under tutelage rather than under supervision. (von Sarwey, 105, 2, 3.).

3. *The English-American*, wh. is a statutory mélange, neither centralized nor concentrated, without system.

23 Jan'y, 1892.
Re-written and re-arranged, 22-23 Dec., 1892.

II. *A Professional or a Non-professional Service?*

1. *What constitutes a professional service?*
   (1). A *technical training* in the specific tasks of the several branches of administration.
   (2). *Competitive tests* for appointment to office.
   (3). *Permanent tenure.*

   We have had all the *arguments for* appointment by *competitive tests in* connexion with the agitation for *civil service reform*; we have seen that a *complete reform* of the service *involves*, too, *permanency of tenure*; but we have failed to see how far it necessitates technical training of a systematic and extended sort.

2. *Arguments for Technical Training* with a direct view to competitive tests and a permanent tenure.

   Consider, e.g., *the* financial *knowledge necessary* for the proper administration of the *Treasury Dept*: its supervision and control of *national banks* and the *currency*; the technical niceties of the *coinage*; the legal knowledge necessary for the decision of qus. touching *claims* and *the tariff*; the complexities of expert accounting; the proper use of *reports of consuls*[;] the management of the *Bureau of Printing and Engraving*; etc. — *Treasury.*

   In the *Dept. of State*, the knowledge of foreign *countries*, usages, and *languages*; diplomatic *etiquette and usage*; the compilation of *instructions* comportable with *International Law*, and knowledge of all matters affecting that Law in all its branches, etc., etc. — *State.*

   In the *Army and Navy Depts.*, qus. of *equipment, ordnance*, new *weapons* and new means of defence; *construction* (of armoured vessels, e.g.)—all of which must have its civil side of *personnel*. — *Army & Navy. West Point Annapolis*

   The *Post Office Dept.*, with its own complex technical details. — *P. O.*

   The Dept. of the Interior: collection of the *census*; administration of the *public lands*, including *forests* (about wh. a whole science has grown up); *patents; educational statistics*, etc. — *Interior.*

   Dept. of Agriculture with its purely scientific tasks. — *Agriculture.*
   Labour — *Labour.*

Internal Improvements entrusted either to engineering bureau of the War Dept. or to private contractors.

For Example of what a *thorough technical education* involves, *note* the ground covered by *M. Aucoc* in his lectures on Administration in the *School of Roads and Bridges*:[8] *Vol. I*: The Organization and Functions of Public Authorities; *Vol. II*: General Rules for the Execution of Public Works; *Vol. III*: National and Departmental *Routes—Bridges and Ferries— Roads of General* and Roads of *Local* Interest—*Tramways. Vol. IV*: Rural and Urban Public Ways—*Waters.*

In Vol. I. minute and detailed discussion of the organization and particular functions of the authorities entrusted with the direction of public works.

*Outlines of the laws of property—*Financial aspects of the administration of public works—Relation of the public authorities to contractors. *Relations of public works to private property* (condemnation, damages, etc.)—*Rights* and responsibilities of *ripuarian* [riparian] *owners.* Railways, etc., etc.

In short, the whole *governmental detail and legal environment* of public works. Other depts. of the same School of course give minute instruction in the sciences and mechanic arts necessary to the execution of the duties of the Dept. of Public Works.

Government Schools and *bureaux of instruction in connexion with the various branches* of the public service necessary if technical training is to be made effectual, uniform, complete. (Instance of the *Prussian Statistical Bureau.*).

3. *Argument for Permanent Tenure,* simply that the service *cannot be made professional without* such security—*cannot attract* the best talent or provoke to the acquirement of the best training.

Involves: judicial or semi-judicial removal from office. *Removal 'for cause'* is not secured when cause can be merely alleged by the removing authority: is *secured only when cause is proved* under strict (judicial) safeguards, permitting the hearing of both sides.

4. *A Professional Service* chosen by competitive examination *democratic,* because

(1) *It opens the service* to the talent and perseverence of the nation: to all who will qualify themselves in a superior degree;[9]

---

[8] Wilson refers to the work by L. Aucoc, already cited, the fourth volume of which, although announced, had not yet been issued. [Eds.' note]
[9] The *Roman Catholic Church* in the Middle Ages.

(2) *Security of tenure ensures legality* in administration, constitutes a safeguard *vs. arbitrary or partisan measures*—by putting officials under judicial supervision, and securing their tenure upon condition of legal good behaviour. (*Arbitrary government,* that has selfish purposes, its insensitive exercise of government, its choice of tools rather than of competent officers, etc., etc.)

5. *Gneists Objections considered*:[10]

Gneist objects that *executive public administration* can be carried on only through *a removable service*; that all constitutional *ministerial government* is unalterably and *inevitably party govt.*; and that constitutional party govt. *requires strict subordination* on the part of officials, entire submission to *the effectuation of party purposes*; at the same time that the compulsive powers of the State and all *magisterial functions* of the public service must be exercised *without party bias.* In short, administrative officers must be at the disposal of party chiefs, but must themselves be unpartisan in the discharge of their official duties. *A professional service must either be the master of society or it must be its servant* and observe changing party directions. *If it be not professional,* it must itself be partisan, and there is the tremendous burden of the *patronage.* You can have appointment *without patronage* only by having an *unpaid (honour) service* in local govt: appointment but no salary.

Criticisms: Exaggerates the necessities of party govt. Given a certain number of *political officers* changing (at the top and upon the surface of the Service) with changes of party, there is no reason why *the rest* of the Service should not be *professional in the strictest sense* of the term. It is *only to carry elections that partisan use can be made of the rank and file—as outside workers, not as officials.* There is a distinction between political and administrative officers wh. solves the only difficulty that exists. All legal instructions the official must in any case obey; illegal instructions no official may in any case obey.

6. *Nature of Self-government* (or *Self-administration*).

A qu. of local govt. most of all, perhaps; but also a qu. of administration in general.—"*Honour offices*"?—*Election? Here, again*, we must make the *distinction between offices of policy and control* and *offices of administration proper*: the distinction between policy and administrative instrumentalities. Let elected officers (who are non-professional within our present

---

[10] "*Der Rechtsstaat,*" 2nd. ed., ('79), pp. 284, 285.

meaning) have at their service a full corps of professionally trained experts. *The political atmosphere will determine all the rest.*

1 February, 1892

Return to Topic I., Division,[11]

II.

Division and Coördination of Functions among Central Authorities.

Division a *comparatively simple* qu., of logical classification of main sorts of business with those practically ancillary to them—a special Dept. (Interior) being provided to take all branches not important enough to be erected into separate Depts.

Coördination much less simple: Involves *two qus.*

(1) *Authority of the Head of State* over administration as a whole;

(2) The *organic* (*collegiate*) *union* of the several *depts.* and their *subjection to* a superintending (*judicial*) *council—one or both.*

It is *in* respect of *coördination* that *modern governments differ* most characteristically, and that *the principal qus. of organization arise.*

III. *Central Administrative Organization, its conditions, principles, and* (*historical*) *development.*

The study of administrative organization, *not* a mere study *of forms, but* a study *of the intimate principles* of state life, of the minute tissue, the muscular and nervous system, *of govt.*

Historical.

1. *Common Derivation* (from the *patrimonial State*) *of the public services of most of the modern European states.* This true even of the local govt. of these states; but the development of the central govt. exhibits more uniform results. *In England,* e.g., there is substantially the same process of development in the central organization as is to be seen on the Continent; but Eng. *local govt. came out* of the Middle Ages *with peculiar features of its own.*

2. *Other Sources*: Present states of Europe not simple and immediate evolutions from the patrimonial state of the Middle

[11] Having omitted point "(2)" in "Topic I" [see p. 384], Wilson presents it here. [Eds.' note]

Ages. *The modern state (the* centralized state in wh. power
is *political* and *not possessory*, office a public trust and not
a private perquisite,—a society, not a set of proprietary relationships) *was grafted on the patrimonial*, the old growth
as often giving place to the new as controlling and giving
shape to it. *The graft*, indeed, has dominated the whole later
growth, *absorbed all the sap*, created the species.

3. *Growth, first by Absorption* (centralization) *of local* (diffused) *powers* and Functions—and *then by extension*, multiplication of central functions. (*a*) *A single organism created,*
(*b*) that *organism* itself *expanded*, made various *in its powers
& activities.*[12]

Consequent *early prominence of the admin. of Justice* in
the process of centralization—to effect a general admission of,
and submission to, royal authority. Centralization *immediately followed in Finance and in* the administration of *the
military power*—the two sinews of authority.

Example: the growth in importance of the *office of Con-*
troleur Général in France—the transition from (a) to (b)
occurring circ. 1661 (Colbert's accession): (*a*) Office created,
1547, after the breakdown of the old patrimonial (household)
organization. Until 1554 there were two *Cont. Général*; after
that date, only one. (*b*) 1661, *Colbert and mercantilism*:   *Local nobility* (provin-
cial) *at same
time ab-
oorbod (Louis
XIV)*
state *subsidies* wh. gradually drew to the central govt, the
superintendence of almost all industry—almost the whole of
the economic life of France. *1661-1789, the Cont. Gén. had
charge*[13] of all subsidies or imports in respect of the clergy,
interior or foreign commerce, the India Company, agriculture, manufactures, the victualling of the troops, manufacture of powder and saltpeter, the post, the public domain, the
revenues of the *pays d'etats*, money, the parliaments and
other superior courts, roads & bridges, etc.

Why did not a similar development take place in England?
Because of the *vitality of local govt.*, but more especially because of the *attitude of Parliament* towards extensions of the
central power. Besides the *pride and independence of the
provincial governing class* (lieutenants general + Justices of
the Peace) in local govt.—not so swallowed up as in France.

12 In Eng. the first process not complete; therefore the second process did not
go the length of centralization. On the continent, on the contrary, the centralization was so complete that the difficulty has been to revitalize the local communities.
13 *See Chéruel*, "Dictionnaire Historique des Institutions, Moeurs, et Coutumes
de la France," Art. 'Controleur Général.'

4. *Organization largely determined by historical circumstance,* under *two main tendencies*:

 (1). *Monarchical centralization*: generally characterized by the closest *administrative* (i.e. organic, systematic) *integration*, under such bodies as a Council of State. (The close technical integration in *French administration* unquestionably *derived from her monarchical history*—another feature added under —)

 (2). *Democratic oversight and control*: normally characterized by *ministerial responsibility*—which effects *integration in* respect of *all administrative matters wh. attract public attention.* Somewhat *haphazard, accidental,—unsystematic* in high degree.[14]

5. *Political (i.e. responsible ministerial) vs. Administrative Integration. The former* best *for keeping a professional service from playing the master* of society. The *latter* necessary for *administrative efficiency and consistency.*

Regierung vs. *Verwaltung*—*Gouvernement* vs. *Administration*

 In the one case, we are regarding the political life and choice of society as an organic whole. *In the other,* we are studying Administration as a business: *Two separate* (and yet united) *phases* of govt. (wh. *Mr. Stickney*[15] *et id omne genus* do not distinguish). *Government is not "merely a business."*

6. *Relations between the two sides in an ideal System:* The *political offices* merely *presidential* and devoted exclusively to the *origination and adaptation of policy* in every stage—imperative as regards the *purposes* which Administration is to have in view, and *dealing directly with all qus. of legislation;* but *guided,* in ways and means—*in all* the *business* of administration—*by the officials of the permanent technical service.* The *latter brought into some formal organization* of control in matters purely administrative *like the Council of State. The Administration an instrument,* but an instrument *with an independent intelligence* of its own.

7. *Division of Business by Legislation vs. by Decree.* Here, *again,*

Control thr. the *Budget*.

we come upon the *distinction between the political and the administrative* sides of govt.—the side of choice and the side of business. At least we *ought* to come upon it. *The determination of the functions that are to be undertaken and of the relations wh. functionaries are to bear to the controlling*

---

[14] *Note the English* rule, in the making up of Cabinets, of having *every* prominent interest (e.g. of late Irish affairs) *represented in the House of Commons* by a responsible ministerial spokesman.

[15] See Wilson's comments on Albert Stickney's *A True Republic*, in Vol. 1, pp. 546-48, and in WW to A. Shaw, June 8, 1885, Vol. 4, pp. 692-93. [Eds.' note]

political bodies—these are proper (so far as they are possible i.e. practicable) *matters for legislation*. But *interior divisions* and *adjustments of admin. work* are surely, not matters for enactment, but *matters for decree*. (Even to *the erection of new Executive Depts?*)

8. *Double (non-political) Function of Central Authorities*:
   (1) *Actual administration*: i.e. actual detailed execution of law, actual performance of the business of the State. This the *most prominent*, most intricate, of course, (and, so to say, *most historical*) part of Administration.
   (2) *Supervision*—oversight or assistance, directed either towards *individuals or* towards the *local (or minor) bodies* of the State.
   This supervision of *two grades*:
   (α) *Authoritative*: Keeping minor authorities within their jurisdiction; sanctioning certain of their undertakings; commanding them, upon occasion, to the exercise of their functions;—*as towards individuals*, inspecting certain wares, e.g., buildings, &c., sanitary police, etc., etc.
   (β) *Suggestive*: systematic *information*—scientific and technical *skill*—expert *advice*. (Comparatively *modern*). *Differs* in this whole range of supervisory activity *from local govt.* wh. does not exercise it in either grade mentioned.

9. *Double Organization to correspond*—with different degrees of dependence upon the political authorities of government. *Only administrative activities* proper *need* a system of administrative *integration*.

   The greater the independence of the suggestive (so to say, *scientific*) *organs the better* (science being thus integrant), provided they be adequately manned and equipped. *Their choice of personnel* probably a whit more *delicate* and *difficult* than that of any other part of the public service

   Authoritative supervision, doubtless, *needs administrative integration* almost, if not quite, as much as administration proper. *It is hardly less necessary to the general life* of the State.

2 February, 1892

IV. *Central Administrative Organization in England.*

1. *Nature and Derivation of the English State*:
   Its *constitutional character* apt to obscure for us *its administrative character*. That *latter began* to take shape under the

Norman and Angevin kings (esp. Wm the Conqueror and Henry II.)—had, indeed become *finally fixed before the constitutional history* (i.e. to say, before the system of national, parliamentary, control) *began.*

Before any other European country, it became a feudal state with *administrative concentration.* This chiefly *the work of Henry II.,* who curtailed privileges on all hands; himself went, and sent his judges, on circuit, looking into all things; unified and systematized judicial administration (*Assize of Clarendon,* 1166); and brought all officials into subjection to himself. (E.g., *removal of sheriffs,* 1170,—an act wh. Stubbs pronounces without "example in the history of Europe since the time of the Roman Empire, except possibly in the power wielded by Charles the Great."). *Established uniformity and legality without destroying customary law*—wh. was now declared before the king's judges and under the king's rules of procedure, instead of before sheriff or baron.

The Curia Regis—Exchequer: (a) accounts, (b) fines and taxation, (c) all king's causes[16]

Character: royal power overseen by national parliament—custom of the realm administered by royal judges—local government (including collection of taxes) by royal officers (sheriffs, justices, etc.) who were, nevertheless, in a real sense local representatives.

Moulded as a province before it acquired character as a kingdom.

Ministerial system largely the *product of parliamentary government.*

2. *Historical Development of the Central Bodies*: (α) In respect of *administrative action,* and (β) in respect of *counsel*—Privy Council, Cabinet, etc.

The *latter has obscured the former in written history*—except in Gneist. (*Hallam* a notable example).

---

[16] It was Henry II. under whose rule "the races of conquerors and conquered in England first learnt to feel that they were one. . . . It was he who abolished feudalism as a system of government, and left it little more than a system of land tenure. It was he who defined the relations established between Church and State, and decreed that in England churchman as well as baron was to be held under the Common law. It was he who preserved the traditions of self-government which had been handed down in borough and shire-moot from the earliest times of English history. His reforms established the judicial system whose main lines have been preserved to our own day. It was through his 'Constitutions' and his 'Assizes' that it came to pass that over all the world the English-speaking races are governed by English and not by Roman law. It was by his genius for government that the servants of the royal household became transformed into Ministers of State. It was he who gave England a foreign policy"—etc. (*Henry II*—Twelve English Statesmen Series—by *Mrs. J. R. Green,* pp. 1, 2.).

In both divisions of the inquiry it is evident that *practical exigency has played a greater part than theory.*

(α) *In respect of administrative action*:

Patrimonial state and *Household Officers*: England apparently from the first more national—less patrimonial—in structure than other European states. *No special royal fief, but a royal domain* wh. had been folc[folk]-land. Feudal household officers less prominent, ∴., as first ministers of state.

Justiciarius totius Angliae—Seneschallus totius Angliae (*Lord High Steward*)—*Lord Great Chamberlain*—Constabularius totius Angliae (*Lord High Constable*)—Marescallus Angliae—Cancellarius Regis (*Chancellor*)—Treasurer (*Lord High Treasurer*). *Such* of these officers as *became hereditary* holders of household officers [offices] (e.g. the Steward, Chamberlain, Constable, Butler, and Marshall) *declined* to merely honorary duties—e.g., in the Exchequer—and tended to disappear. *Those*, on the contrary, (like the Justicias, Chancellor, and Treasurer—tho.' the first-mentioned disappeared after *temp.* Henry III) *wh. were more general (national) in function and* constituted *revocable trusts, became instruments for subsequent* admin. *development.*

Development of the Treasury: Lord High Treasurer (usually occupying also the post of Treasurer of the Exchequer) at the head of the old Exchequer system. 18 Henry III, office of Chancellor of Exchequer created, to "reside at the Exchequer of Receipt, and to have a counter-roll of all things pertaining to the said receipt"—assistant and check upon Ld. H. Treas. Then member of Treasury Commission (temp. accession Geo. I.)—Finally working head of Treas'y.

Home, Foreign, Colonial, War, and India Offices, all developed out of direct secretarial service of the Sovereign.

Admiralty: Lord High Admiral, first app., 1385: after 1405 a regular succession. Commission, first 1636: again after 1688. Present *status* under Act of 1690. Original office occasionally revived—last time in 1827, for Duke of Clarence.

Board of Trade (1786—succeeding Commissions and informal committees) *and Local Government Board* (1834, Poor Law Board—1871 present arrangement) both in form Committees of Council.

Board of Agriculture (1889) ditto.

Other Committees of Council (E.g. *Education Dept.*, 1853).

(β) *In respect of counsel*: The *Permanent Council—*the *Privy Council—*the *Cabinet.*

3. *The Several existing Departments*: their development and Functions. Instead of a detailed account (for which see, among other authorities, Traill *Central Government*) *take several typical cases* for closer examination:

(1) *The Home Office.* In some sense derived from *a household office*, that of *King's Clerk* (so called till Henry III.), *a personal servant of the sovereign—*afterwards King's Secretary—*temp.* Elizabeth "Our Principal Secretary of Estate" (Sir Robt. Cecil, also called 'Our Principal Secretary.') *Temp.* Henry VIII. *office becomes invariably associated with membership of the Privy Council* (i.e. ceases to be merely personal service of the sovereign) and is divided. Declined somewhat under James I. to rise steadily thereafter—especially after 1688: that date wh. marks the (so to say) *publicization* of the admin.

Traces of origin: needs no patent (tho'. one is now generally given) but only the delivery of the seals,—a Secretary of State the only channel for the communication of the sovereign's will in any matter—his *countersignature* necessary to the validity of the sign-manual— the five Principal Secretaries of State duplicates of each other in function and privilege: one always attends the Sovereign[,] one always remains in London, etc. etc.

Traill, 61-67.

Functions: (1) *Chief of constabulary*: maintenance of order, protection of life and property. Discipline, equipment, in part payment, of constabulary. 'Home Secretary' has himself, under certain circumstances, the powers of a magistrate. Qus. of extradition. (2) *Superintendence of the local magistracy—*power to reverse or modify decisions wh. threaten manifest injustice. (3) "*Post-judicial administration of the criminal law*" (prisons, prison discipline, etc.). (4) *Advice in matters of pardon—*wh. involves, often, the re-opening or reviewing of criminal cases (because of discovery of new material evidence)—the English criminal law allowing no appeal on the facts. Secretary generally in such cases consults the judge who presided. (5) *Regulation of labour in factories* and *mines, inspection of coal mines*, regulation of *schools of anatomy*, licensing of *vivisec-*

tion. Improvement of *lunatic asylums* and protection of *pauper lunatics. Registration of aliens.* "Empowered to grant *certificates of naturalization* conferring civil rights as Eng. subjects upon foreigners of good repute" who can prove continued residence and the purpose of continued residence.

(2) *The Board of Trade: History—Cromwell* attempts a commission, *1665. 1660* (Chas. II.) two commissions created, a Council of Trade and a Council of Foreign Plantations. United *1672* (Council for Trade and Plantations). *1768,* a Sec'y of State (the third) for the "American Dept.," the Council, however, still continuing in existence till reorganization of *1782* (*Burke's motion*) when the Secretaryship was abolished, together with the Council. *1782-1786,* an informal committee of the Privy Council. *1786* Committee of Council for Trade, advising the several Departments upon commercial matters and preparing Orders in Council. Negotiation of commercial treaties given (*1872*) to Foreign Office. *Traill, 123-132*

Members: a President, the First Lord of the Treasury, the Chancellor of the Exchequer, the 5 Principal Secretaries of State, the Speaker of the House of Commons, and the Archbishop of Canterbury. Really, the President and his permanent official staff. (Persistent conservatism as illustrated in the recent construction—1889—of the *Board of Agriculture*)[17]

Functions: (1) *Statis[t]ical and Commercial Dept.—* supervision and collation of the monthly and annual trade accounts; statistics of railways, agriculture, cotton, emigration. Advice upon commercial matters to other Depts., when asked.

(2) *Railway Dept* (1840)—*Inspection* before opening to the public; inquiry into *accidents.* Reports to Parl. on *railway rates,* and on '*level crossings.*' Examines and approves *bye-laws*; appoints *arbitrators,* umpires, etc.; grants use of eminent domain. Substantially same over-

---

[17] *Act of 1889* "provides for the establishment of a Board of Agriculture consisting of the Lord President of the Council, Her Majesty's Principal Secretaries of State, the First Commissioner of Her Majesty's Treasury, the Chancellor of Her Majesty's Exchequer, the Chancellor of the Duchy of Lancaster, and the Secretary for Scotland, and such other persons, (if any) as Her Majesty the Queen may from time to time think fit to appoint during Her Majesty's pleasure: Provided that the Board shall not be entitled to act *unless the President* or one of the officers of State above mentioned is present. *It shall be lawful for Her Majesty the Queen from time to time to appoint any member of the Privy Council to be President of the Board during Her Majesty's pleasure.*" Notice the *net-work of fictions* in this Act.

sight, also, of *tramways*. A certain oversight over the *metropolitan gas companies*. Registration of *joint-stock* companies—and the granting of *commercial charters*.

Railway Commissioners Court established in *1873*.

(3) *Marine Dept.* (1850) "The health, discipline, and proper treatment of ships' crews, the professional competency, care, and conduct of those in command of them, and the condition, equipment, and management of their ships" (p. 130).

(4) *Harbour Dept.* Light houses, pilotage, harbours. Weights and measures, with local inspection. Standards of *purity and weight of* gold and silver *coin* for the Mint and Assay Office. Standards for the *measurement of gas. Tests of petroleum.*

(5) *Financial Dept.* General accounting of the Board and control of receipts and expenditures. "Receives, examines, and presents to Parliament the *accounts of Life Assurance Companies.*["]

The President of the Board of Trade invariably *a member of the Cabinet since 1864.*

Traill, 133, 139.
(3) *Local Government Board. History*: Poor Law Board *1834*, upon enactment of new system of poor relief,—reporting periodically to Home Office, but not strictly an executive body at all. *1847-'8* made a branch of the admin. service and given responsible representation in Parliament (a President and four Cabinet ministers, after fashion of Board of Trade). *1871* abolished and replaced by Local Govt. Board, with much wider range of functions. (*Usual gathering together of miscellaneous powers hitherto distributed.*). *Members*: a President, the Lord President of the Council, the 5 Principal Secretaries of State, the Lord Privy Seal, and the Chancellor of Exchequer. Like the Board of Trade, "*a Board only in name.*"

Functions: In general, "supervision of the laws relating to the public health, the relief of the poor, and local government." *In particular*: (1) *Initiatory*, ('Actual Administration' + 'authoritative supervision' under our own analysis): E.g. commanding local authorities to their duties in caring for the public health; and establishing, of its own motion, sanitary regulations, for the prevention of the spread of contagious diseases. (2) *Remedial*, to make good, on complaint, the neglect of local authorities either by direct admin. action or by an order to the local authority to fulfil its duty in the premises within a certain time,—the costs falling upon the local authority. (3) *Supervisory, sanitary inspection, audit* (exc. boroughs), warranting of *local loans* for expenditures on public works, etc., and of *changes of boundaries* of local areas.

Its President not always a member of the Cabinet, but always of Parliament, and, by custom, of the House of Commons.

In this Dept., more, perhaps, than in any other, is *the tendency towards the 'concentration' of administration shown* in England.

4. *Integration:* (1) *The Head of the State:* Master, chief minister, or formal chief figure merely?

(2) *The Cabinet:* ministerial consultation (confined for the most part to political qus.); the *supervision of the Treasury;* the *solidarity and political responsibility* of the Cabinet as a whole.

No staatsministerium nor Council of State (since the abeyance of the Privy Council); *no Court of Conflicts.* The whole *integration personal and political, not administrative.*

9 February, 1892

V. Central Administrative Organization in France.

1. *Derivation and Character of the French State:*

A singularly *logical feudal derivation,* and a remarkably *steady* and *rapid development,* resulting in the *absorption of authority and consideration by the royal power.* Resulting simplification of society: *the Court—the People;* and of Administration: *the royal will—the agents* of the royal will. (*M. Aucoc* still emphasizes agents (and auxiliary agents), councils, and tribunals as the constituent elements of Administration).

Aucoc, I., 91-167

Ducrocq, I., 56-89

Lebon, (in Marquardsen)

Present character: administration of all affairs (except the few, strictly local, matters wh. are left to the communes) *by agents of the central authority* (an agent being defined as one who comes into direct contact with the citizens in the conduct of govt.), *either directly or through auxiliary agents,* (who act under orders fr. the agents)—who are *advised by* elected (or partly elected) *councils, but* who act, nevertheless, upon their own responsibility,—*under the restraint of tribunals* wh., although judicial in function, are *administrative in make-up. Add* to this an ordinary *judicial administration* altogether *centralized,* and the picture is complete.

2. *History of Administrative Development*:

Centralization in France "the *product of the struggle* of the royal power *with the feudal* system"—of the building together of that royal power wh. at the Revolution became the national power. "*Administrative unity* developed along with *national unity*, and in order to facilitate it."

A. Administrative unification *began in the field of Justice*— in wh. the royal power set about establishing its supreme jurisdiction *as early as the 12th century*, when the absorption of the great provinces and feudal estates had fairly begun. *Beginning with* the merely feudal jurisdiction of the *Parliament of Paris*, the centralization of the admin. of justice advanced by almost insensible stages, and with occasional set-backs, until *completed in the celebrated Ordinance of Blois, 1499* (affecting the entire admin.—by Louis XII. with assistance of his "Great Council," wh. had been set up as an admin. check upon the Parliament of Paris. In preparation, Louis read Cicero's "Books of Offices."). *Parliament of Paris supplemented by* various *provincial parliaments* in the course of this development.

The part played by *practical exigency* and the part played by (*Roman legal*) *theory*.

B. From *the 12th century also* dates the beginning (Philip Augustus) of the state's *control of* all the higher forms of *education*. *First* step, foundation of the *University of Paris by Philip Augustus*. Although most of the pupils of the higher institutions of learning were candidates for the priestly office, the education they obtained was directed and controlled by lay officers of the Crown.

C. At the *close of the 13th century* similar centralization began to be effected in respect of the administration of *Finance*. Until that time the only income of the state was the feudal income from the domains of the crown. With the acquisition of new provinces and of *royal control* over *justice* and *education* came *taxes* and their ordered administration. The establishment of *places for the receipt of customs* duties, and of *cours des comptes* dates from the first years of the 14th century.

D. *A standing army* came into existence under *Charles VII.* in the *15th century*, being reformed and perfected in organization by Louis XII. at the close of the century.

A war marine was first created in the *17th century*.

(α) *Beginning with 16th* century, we find, alongside the old (typical) *Chancellor, Chief Justice, Constable, Chief of Military* affairs, and *Superintendent of finances,* (derived, directly or indirectly, from the *household offices* of the feudal régime) *a number of Secretaries of State* (*Cf. Eng. admin.* development), whose function it is to note and execute the purposes of the monarch—and a tendency to put the old functions of the Chancellor into commission. Except in cases of Justice and Finance, *little insistence upon strict divisions* of business. Division of *functions among* the (4) *Secretaries* of State, *territorial*—for carrying out decrees of the king in council. (True in middle of century, 1547; but change about to set in). Development of Machinery Aucoc: I., 131 et seq.

(β) More distinct *differentiation attempted.* 1567, a Minister of the *Royal Household* (a sort of clerk of patronage) created; 1589, a Minister of *Foreign Affs.* (including functions of the later War Dept.) 1626, division of maritime affs. bet. Depts. of For. Affs. and of War.

(γ) *Work of concentration* continued (tho'. not wholly completed) by *Louis XIV. and Colbert*—latter uniting with his control of finances the direction also of all royal buildings, of roads and bridges, of commerce and manufactures, etc. Services not classified remained with the Secretaries of State, still on the basis of a territorial division of functions, being altered only according to the practical conveniences of the case. *Louvois* brought under his own dept (of War) such services as were necessary for the accomplishment of military operations.

(δ) *Reaction* (*on part of the nobles*) under the *Regent* vs. the admin. centralization of Louis XIV. *Commissions* substituted for ministers—worked badly—abandoned by the Regent, 1718.

(ε) *1789 six ministries in the modern sense*: 1. Keeper of the Seals, President of the Council, and Chief Justice (office of Chancellor and of Keeper of the Seals sometimes separated, sometimes united); 2. Controller-General (as developed by Colbert); 3. Secretary of State for Foreign Affs.; 4. Sec'y of State for War; 5. Do. for Naval Affs.; 6. Sec'y of State of the Royal Household—whose functions included ecclesiastical Affs., both Catholic and Protestant.

Still traces of territorial divisions of function: *E.g.,*
police in the frontier provinces under Dept. of War,
in others under Minister of Royal Household, who
has his analogies of the English Home Secretary.

(ζ) *With the Revolution entered logic.* Commissions for a
time under Terrorists and Directory—soon abandoned
for logical, and more and more minute, divisions of
function among distinct ministries.

Lebon again.   E. "*Under Louis XIV.* the central administration was almost
in all points organized as it remained until the Revolu-
tion." (L). There was associated with the king a *Council
of State* divided into five sections; and seven ministers, at
the head of as many depts. of admin. *The Council* had
only *advisory* powers, the king of course not being bound
by its conclusions; but its advice extended over the whole
field of govt.—*over legislation as well as over administration*, as wide as the domain of the royal power.

F. *The service of the Revolution and of the first Empire* was,
that they brought *order and method* into the division and
admin. of govt. powers. The object of the revolutionary
reforms was *in no sense* to *energize* the *local* organs of
govt. or to give them independent life and self-direction;
it was, rather, to *stamp out* what remained of *particular-
istic tendencies* from the *ancien régime*, and bring all
things under a single national authority wh., in Assembly
and Convention, had supplanted the royal authority. Unity
and system, their object. Consulate and Empire confirmed
these tendencies—and *Napoleon's genius supplied the appropriate organization*, that indicated above.

G. There came in *with the Revolution, also*, that *absolute-
ness of theory* wh. commanded, among other things, *the
French division of powers*, with its separate administrative courts—sundering the several parts of judicial authority.

3. *The Existing Departments of the Central Administration:
Their Organization and (characteristic) Functions:*
Present Ministries: 1. Justice; 2. Foreign Affairs; 3. Interior;
4. Finance; 5. War; 6. Marine and the Colonies; 7. Public
Education, Religion, and the Fine Arts; 8. Public Works; 9.
Agriculture; 10. Trade and Industry; 11. Posts and Tele-
graphs.

Common Features of Organization: At the head of each
Dept., *a Minister* often assisted either by an *Under Sec'y of
State* (who is chosen from among the members of the Cham-

ber of Deputies and whose duties are parliamentary) or by a *General Sec'y*, who is usually an ordinary official whose duties are wholly departmental, not parliamentary. An Under Sec'y of State is not necessarily an admin. officer; and the office is created or abolished according to circumstances, upon changes of ministry. Neither is the post of General Sec'y always maintained: its maintenance, also, is a qu. of convenience. Whether the Minister have such associates or not, his decisions are independent, he alone has a seat in the Council of Ministers; and he alone is responsible for acts done under his authority.

The Cabinet of the Minister in each Dept. is *his confidential council*. Its membership is not fixed, changing with a change of Ministers: it consists of departmental officials specially in the Minister's confidence. It receives, opens, distributes all *correspondence*; all matters which come before the Minister for his *approval or signature* pass thr. its hands. It prepares all *legislative matter* and all business touching the relations of the Minister to *the Chamber* or to *the President*. It handles all *qus. that personally affect the Minister*. Certain divisions of the Dept. are directly subject to it: e.g., the bureau for the arrangement and registration of correspondence, *the archives, the library*, etc.

Two-fold function of a Minister: a *direct agent* in the detailed execution of the tasks of the State *and* (in the first instance) *a judge* of the meaning of the laws with regard to administrative action, of the validity of the acts of his subordinates, and of their responsibility for their acts, of compensation to injured persons, etc.

Interior organization of each Dept. determined *by decree* passed *in the Council of State*.

Two Departments may serve as types of the rest.

1) *The Ministry of the Interior*: Of the usual 'omnium gatherum' style of depts. of the Interior—though the most notable and important of the Depts., perhaps. *The name* 'Ministry of the Interior['] new (*since 1790*)—*formerly* the field of the *Minister of the Royal Household*.

It falls into:

1. *The Cabinet*, with the following sub-divisions: bureau for general or political correspondence; bureau for *personnel* (nominations in the prefectural administration); press bureau; bureau for Algeria; and bureau for labour associations, whether of employers or of employees.

2. *The Directory of Secretaryship and Accounts*, wh., outside the section of accounts, considers qus. affecting mutual associations and public charitable institutions.

3. *The Directory for Departments and Communes*, whose two sub-sections handle all matters concerning either Depts or Communes over wh. the State has control. These include, e.g., elections, pensions, loans, law-suits; railways of local importance and departmental roads; insanity, pauper children, begging; communal streets and ways; communal hospitals, charitable institutions, and pawn-shops.

4. *The Directory for Prisons*—including the administration of houses of reform, agricultural penal institutions, private as well as public, and protective associations for released prisoners.

5. *The Directory for the Public Safety*, wh. has supervision of all police except that of Paris—"especially the political police"—oversight of political or other associations, of railways, of public places, of printing and book-selling, of passes, of the relations of the police force to the Minister of the Int., etc. This bureau is, of course, the special assistant of the Dept. of Justice.

There is under this Dept., of course, *a corps of inspectors*, of prisons, charitable institutions, etc.

"*Under the Ministry* of the Interior, as under most of the Ministries, there exist a certain number of *committees, commissions*, and *councils* with consultative and advisory functions, which are constituted in part of officials and in part of persons not connected with the Administration: I mention here only the Higher Prison Council and the Committee on the Protection of Little Children." (*Lebon*).

2) *Ministry of Public Instruction, Religion, and the Fine Arts*: (Handling matters wh., *before the Revolution*, fell to the *Minister of the Royal Household*) really constitutes a *three-fold ministry*, bound together only by the presidency of the Minister:

A. *Public Instruction*:

1. *The Directory for University Instruction* (*l'enseignement supérieur*), under wh. are placed the faculties of professional instruction, of law, of medicine, of protestant theology, the higher apothecary schools, and the schools and preparatory institutions for the

higher education. To it are submitted all *qus. concerning the granting of degrees, scientific and literary institutions* (Collège de France, museum, technical schools for the higher studies—*école pratique de hautes études*—schools of cartography, of living oriental languages, schools at Athens and Rome, observatories, *école normale supérieur*, etc.) *and the administration of academies* in the Depts.

(*The word 'university'* is used *in France* to include all public educational institutions. "Even when, in some city, several faculties for academic instruction are united, they are sometimes called by the name, University")

2. *The Directory for Secondary Instruction*, for *lycee* and higher boys' and girls' schools with classical and (or) special instruction.

3. *The Directory for Primary Schools*: management and educational plans of schools for small children, popular schools, trade schools and schools of manual training; normal schools and professional, including the qu. of their establishment.

4. *The Directory for the Secretaryship* (*du sécrétariat*) under wh. are placed *learned societies*, the Institute of France, the great public *libraries*, the popular libraries, *scientific undertakings* and voyages, state and Departmental *archives*, etc.

5. *The Directory for General Accounting*—common to this section (*A*) and to B., The Fine Arts.

Various inspectors, councils, and *advisory committees*, notably the *Conseil supérieur de l'instruction publique*, wh., besides advisory functions with reference to qus. of organization and plans of instruction, has the function of final decision in cases of discipline

B. *Religion*: storm centre of persistent qus. of great agitation, the Catholic party on the one side, the radical party, on the other.

5 *communions recognized* by the State: the Roman Catholic, the Reformed or Calvinistic, the Lutheran, the Jewish, and (in Algeria) the Mohammedan.

1. *The Cabinet Directory* of this branch *nominates bishops*, applies political discipline to the clergy, adjudicates conflicts with the spiritual authorities, considers appeals to the Council of State on the

ground of misuse of office, contests bet. communal authorities and the bodies wh. administer parish property—*all contested points bet. church and state.*

2. Besides the Cabinet, there are a *Division for the affs. of the R. Catholic communion,* and a 3. *Division for the affs. of the non-Catholic communions.* To the first go qus. of clerical *personnel,* administration of church property, administration of diocesan institutions, gifts and bequests, etc.

4. *A third division* attends to all matters *of accounting.*

C. *The Fine Arts*:

  1. *Administration of the Fine Arts proper: purchase* of works of art for public buildings; *art instruction* in the art schools of Paris and Rome and in the Depts, and instruction in drawing; *museums* and *exhibitions; historical monuments; subsidized theatres* and the *dramatic censorship; musical* conservatories and *schools*; state *manufacture of Sévres ware* and of *Gobelin and Beauvais stuffs*—etc.

  2. *Directory for Public Buildings*: (transferred from Min. of Public Works, 1881). Erection and maintenance of all public structures not specially devoted to the use of other ministries—esp. the state palaces.

    A very *large number of consultative bodies* is associated with this Section.

4. *Integration*:

  I. *The Head of the State*: the President of the Republic: The *formal centre* of all administration—*hardly* as yet established in any *such ministerial influence as that of the English sovereign.*

    Exercises *the appointing power, but* subject to the counter-signature of the Minister in whose Dept. the app. is made—and in compliance with his nomination.

    Exercises *the ordinance-making power—but*, again, subject to the counter-signature of the minister whose Dept. is affected, and always upon the proposition of that Minister.

    Sanctions supplementary extraordinary credits, when the Chambers are not sitting; declares certain works of public interest; sanctions *grants of eminent domain* in the execution of public works; grants *concessions* to railways, mining and drainage enterprises, etc.—at the suggestion of the various Ministries. *The supplementary credits* he is obliged to sanction when the Council of Ministers command. Do. with reference to *nomination of members of the Council of State.*

An appeal lies vs. executive decrees to the Council of State on the ground of excess of power or invasion of essential right; *to the Minister* also in whose proposals the decree originated, upon other grounds, for relief or modification.

II. *The Ministers* as *Cabinet* (political integration) and *as Council* (administrative oversight). Here again the distinction bet. *Government* and *Administration.* (*Ducrocq*—§§21-31, 38, 39, 47-51—attempts *enumeration of matters distinctively governmental*: Promulgation of laws; composition of the executive power, its duration and transmission, constitutional conditions of its functions; ministerial responsibility and the interrelationships of executive and legislature; revision of the constitution; process of law-making (and the participation of the executive therein); mode of election of the President; *etc.*).

III. *The Council of State (Conseil d'État)*:

    1. *History and General Character*: Originated, like most such bodies, in the *feudal court.* The constant growth and abiding power of the Crown; and the absence of a parliamentary development such as England's kept it vital and in some sort whole. But, *while it did not disintegrate, it did differentiate.* The creation of the *Parliament of Paris* (13th century) was, so far forth, its dismemberment. *Chamber of Accounts*, also, split off.

    Still, *3rd. to 16th centuries*, the king in council a real integrating and controlling power.

    15th century experiment of *Great Council* with part of the judicial functions of the Council of State—but this reabsorbed.

    16th century legislation, finance, administration—all qus. wh. interested the sovereign, came within cognizance of C. of State.

    Sections of course, for various classes of function: after Louis XIV., five: (*a*) Council of State proper—or chief branch—(foreign & political qus.); (*b*) *Correspondence* (qus. of interior admin.); (*c*) Royal Council of Finance (domains & aids, duties, taxes); (*d*) Royal Council of Commerce; (*e*) Privy Council (court of conflicts and of cassation).

    These did not tend to become ministries—as in Prussia. *Functions of of* [sic] *Sections* (*b*)-(*d*) inclusive were, in effect legislative, as well as judicial and administrative.

Membership: Chancellor or Privy Seal, as president; Secretaries of State; Ministers of State; and maîtres des requêtes.

Replaced under Constituent Ass., by Council of Ministers and Court of Cassation; *revived* and worked hard *by Napoleon; insignificant under Restoration; used by the govt. of July* in the preparation of admin. law; *after '48 as an instrument in the hands of the Ass.* to control the govt.; 1852 made *a masterful pro-bouleutic body.*

Has *preserved throughout a certain integrity of function*: the chief guiding organ in the conduct of admin. affairs.

2. *Functions*: Merely an administrative organ, though of course legislative proposals may be submitted to it, as to any other commission. *Its determinations final only in the decision of appeals upon contested ques. of admin. law.* In all other matters, even those wh. *must* be referred to it, its conclusions are merely advisory.

(α) *Judicial*: conflicts of jurisdiction between the lower admin. courts; all complaints on the ground of lack or insufficiency of authority on the part of officials of any grade; appeals to quash judgments of the Court of Accounts and decisions of revisional councils, on the ground of irregularities of form or breaches of law; appeals fr. the lower admin. courts; a court both of first and of last resort for determination of admin. acts or in affairs specially determined by enactment (election to Gen. Councils, acts subject to appeal of Prefect or Minister, etc.) *Prize Court also*, in time of War.

The Council of State is *the supreme court of appeal upon (legal) admin. qus.* not only fr. special admin. courts of first instance, but also fr. the ordinary courts

(β) *Advisory*: (a) *Upon administrative affairs.* The regulative power of the Ministers is very wide, under general administrative ordinances or under laws specifically granting powers. Thus a public admin. decree (i.e. a decree passed in the Council of State) of Nov. 15, 1846, gives to the Minister of Public Works the power to regulate the number of cars that shall make up a R. R. train, the number of brakes wh. a train must have, and the conditions under wh. explosives may be transported. Another, 10 Aug., '52, authorizes the same Minister and the Min. of the Int. to regulate the passage of trains over suspension bridges. The courts have upheld these ordinances.

Rule as to submission of admin. qus. to the Council. In theory, the President, the ordinance-making power (with counter-signature of Minister); but some ordinances must be submitted to the Council. Which? A *law of 24 May, 1872,* enacts that the Council must be called upon to give its advice upon all 'ordinances of public administration' (*d'administration publique*). What does this phrase include?

The practice: Ministers in the habit of consulting it with regard to all important ordinances, or decrees issued in the form of ordinances; with regard to most qus. of law arising in connexion with administration; with regard to disputed qus. and all qus. of a delicate nature.[18]

Appeal may be taken to the Council fr. executive decrees on the ground of excess of authority or invasion of essential right. I.e. in cases not submitted to the Council beforehand.

(b) *Upon qus. of legislation*: In the preparation of laws the functions (of advice and assistance) exercised by the Council are in no degree obligatory. They are wholly facultative. Indeed *a law of 1875* permits the Ministers to have the assistance of special commissioners, appointed by the President, in the preparation of legislation. The Council is, nevertheless, frequently consulted. *Legislative* qus. are *referred* to it for examination *by the Senate and by the Chamber*, and *bills* prepared by the Govt. are submitted to it *by special decree*, as an expert commission of advice.

3. *Membership and Organization*: First, as to membership,
    1. *Keeper of the Seals and Minister of Justice,* who pre-

---

[18] E.g., Religious qus., the administration of public property, the control exercised by the Head of the State of the Departments or Communes, the preparation of "a large number of acts wh. concern the service of public works," granting of privileges for such undertakings as canals, railways, river improvements, etc., Its advice not necessary in the case of public works sanctioned by the Assembly itself. It *revises pensions,* also.

The number of administrative matters passed upon by the Council, 1871-1879, was 139,058 (17,382 1/4).

The qus. *submitted* to it are said to be "almost *exclusively questions of law.*"

sides over judicial sessions, where he has no vote; who may preside over the full Council or over any of its several sections, and there vote, in his ministerial capacity, as Keeper of the Seals.

The other ministers have seats in the Council and may vote upon qus. affecting their own Depts. Upon other matters they have only a consultative voice.

2. *Vice President*	Appointed or removed by the Pres. in the Council of Ministers—fr. French citizens 30 yrs. of age. Salaried.
3. *Four chairmen of Sections*	

4. *Twenty-six councillors in ordinary service, eighteen in extraordinary service.* Appointed by the Pres. in Council—those in extraordinary service from among high admin. officials in active service: who, after being appointed receive no special salary as councillors, and who lose their seats upon their exit fr. admin. office. They have votes in the Council only upon qus. wh. affect the Depts. to wh. they belong.

5. *Thirty maîtres des requêtes (reporters* upon proposals) and a general secretary of like rank. Must be at least 27 yrs. of age. Appointed or removed by decree upon the nomination of the Vice President and the sectional chairmen. One-third of the appointments to this grade made from class 6, of Auditors. *Salaried*

6. *Thirty-six Auditors*—of whom *12 are of the first class*. Auditors of the second class are appointed, upon *competitive examination*, for 4 yrs. Must be at least 21, but not more than 25 yrs. of age. Auditors of first class chosen fr. those of the second by nomination of the Vice President and the sectional chairmen—and should not have passed their 30th year. May be removed as *maîtres des requêtes* are. *Salaried.*

7. *A special divisional Secretary for contested administrative cases.* Same qualifications and method of appointment as *maîtres des requêtes.*

Office of councillor in ordinary service, of *maître des requêtes, and of Auditor incompatible with* any other office, parliamentary or administrative (except the superior offices of army and navy, office of marine inspector or inspector of waterways, roads, or mines, the office of engineer, and that of university professor). *Also incompatible with* any office under an association wh. receives any concession, grant, or benefit fr. the State

After a service of 3 yrs. in the Council, however, councillors, *maîtres*, and auditors may be employed (for a period of not more than 3 yrs.) in active admin. service without loss of their seats. They cannot, however, receive any additional salary for such services.

Organization and Procedure: Although the decisions of the C. are final only when they concern contested qus. of admin. law, four of its five sections are set apart for the consideration of admin. qus. of the ordinary sort. These four are:

1. The Section for legislation, justice, and foreign affairs.
2. The Section for the Interior, Religion, Education, and the Fine Arts.
3. The Section for finances, posts and telegraphs, war, marine and the colonies.
4. The Section for public works, agriculture, and commerce.

Distribution of the members of the Council among its several Sections affected by decree as regards councillors in ordinary service, and by ministerial resolution as regards all the rest.

Maîtres des requêtes have votes upon all matters referred to them for report either in the sections or in the general council. Upon other matters they have only a consultative voice. *Same true of auditors, except* that they have no votes in the general Council.

Qus. go first to the several *Sections* and, after being prepared by them, go *to the general Council, if* they fall within the terms of the law of 1872 (and '79?)—if, i.e., they are *ordinances d'administration publique.*

Quorum: In Sections, 3 ord. councillors of the Section; in full Council, 16 ord. councillors.

Judicial Jurisdiction: exercised thr. two agencies:

1. *Section du contentieux*, to wh. are submitted *all qus.* concerning wh. any special motion has been made by a commissioner of the govt. or a councillor, but *wh. do not require any oral proceedings* (E.g. direct taxes, elections, the carrying trade, appeals on ground of lack of authority or excess, penalties inflicted by the prefectural council, etc.).

2. *Assemblée spéciale du Conseil d'État délibérant au contentieux*, composed of the members of the *Section du contentieux* and two members fr. each of the other sections of the Council, presided over by the Vice President. In the deliberations of this body (the supreme administrative court) the Ministers cannot take part. *Four maîtres des requêtes represent the govt.* (as commissioners) in this body.

IV. *The Court of Conflicts*, consisting of the Privy Seal as President, 3 councillors chosen by their colleagues, and 3 members of the Court of Cassation chosen by their fellow judges, besides two members chosen by those already mentioned, and two substitutes, *stands and mediates bet. the administrative and the ordinary judicial jurisdiction*, determining in cases of dispute to wh. forum particular cases or causes belong. *Term* of office, *3 yrs.* The ordinary jurisdiction represented before the Court by states-attorney app. for two yrs. by the Court of Cassation, the administrative, by *a maître des requêtes* app. by the Council of State for the same term.

This the only concession contrary to the strict theory of the absolute division of powers.

24 February, 1892

VI. Central Administrative Organization in Prussia

1. *Derivation and (historical) Character of the Prussian State.*[19] Like, and yet *unlike*, the derivation and development of the *French State. No complete feudal process* of amalgamation, because no complete feudal structure.

Brandenburg not a central piece of territory like the Duchy of France, surrounded by like domains, but *a frontier province of the Empire* wrung from the Wends and *colonized* as extended. *Added to*, not out of feudal pieces of same kingdom absorbed, but *by various conquests and acquisitions of foreign territory*: a *Lithuanian* district colonized by the Teutonic knights and become a fief of Poland; *Pomerania* obtained fr. Sweden, and *Silesia* snatched fr. Austria; pieces of dismembered *Poland*, etc., etc. Absolutism in the original Mark,

[19] For a very admirable *sketch of Prussian history*, showing with clearness the genesis of the state, see the *Encyclopaedia Britannica.* Cf. *Bornhak*, II, 369-397. *Sarwey*, p. 105, '3,' (fine print). *Schulze*, (in Marquardsen) p. 61.

greater or less mastery over the (largely feudalized) conquered territories.

Administration developed according to the most varied exigencies and conveniences, and for a long time with a view to commanding the resources, rather than with a view to conducting the ordinary govt., of the various portions of the kingdom. *A makeshift machinery of Boards* wh., unlike the French councils, were *executive*, and not merely advisory bodies—and whose *jurisdiction* was *often territorial* in its limits, *rather than essential*, because of the great and persistent variety in the character of the several provinces of the kingdom and in the degree of control exercised over their administration by the central govt.

Characteristic marks: (*a*) the most bewildering variety in local govt., (*b*) Administrative action thr. Boards, (*c*) Lack of systematic division or coördination of administrative functions: *The king the only integrant*—administering thr. commissions.

2. *History of Prussian Administrative Development*:

   1. *The 'Patrimonial State' administering its domains* thr. officers of the Household or Court. Only over his own immediate domains could the prince exercise complete sovereign powers—tho. the authority of the early Markgrafs was uncommonly great. Whenever *authority* was to be *exercised outside* his own immediate domains it was necessary to act thr. *the instrumentality of the local authorities*, whether urban or rural. The Council of Estates.

   2. With *the widening of territory* came, as usual, the need for new administrative machinery. This first resulted in the *creation of a Privy Council*. Such a Council was created for Brandenburg in 1604, when nine persons were constituted a council for the admin. of all affairs except those of justice and the church. *In 1651*, with the growth of Prussian power, this Council became the chief admin. organ, not only for the Mark, but also for all dependent territories. ('*Prussia*' acquired, 1618, as a duchy).

   3. *No very close integration* of administration *proved possible* under this organization, and *after 1651*, when the leasing or farming system was introduced into the administration of the revenues, *a central bureau for the superintendence of domains and royal dues was formed*, consisting of four so-called *Staatskammerräthen*, placed immediately above local domains chambers set up in the several provinces. *In 1689 an Exchequer Court was established* as

the central administrative organ in these matters. *Ten years later* there was put above this Exchequer Court, at the summit of financial administration, *a Supreme Directory for Domains.*

Experimentation.

At the same time the military intendants and commisaries, who had by degrees gotten into their hands almost the whole of tax collection and police, represented an administration wh. sadly needed integration. *A General Military Commisariat* was accordingly constituted (1655). In 1712 this body, wh. was collegiate in its action, was placed as a central board over all the provincial commisariats.

Meantime the Great Elector (1640-1688) had begun to *consider foreign affs.,* no longer in the Privy Council, but *in a select committee* of Counsellors wh. never gained formal constitution.

4. *By this time the Privy Council had fallen into the background*—killed by subtraction—and *a new integration had become necessary.* The Council had acquired a supreme judicial jurisdiction, and it still represented certain minor prerogatives of supremacy and grace; but it had practically lost its administrative position.

The custom grew up, therefore, *of treating the chairmen of the new central boards and the presidents of the higher courts as members of the Council* for consultation upon affairs of common interest—and the Council acquired *a mixed character,* being in part a special board, and in part a sort of *Staatsministerium.*

5. *Friedrich Wilhelm I.* (1713-1740) erected a General Financial Directory *and* a General Directory for War, ten years later consolidated, as a General Supreme Financial Directory for War and Domains, under the presidency of the king himself, but *subdivided into 5 committees* among wh. the work was parcelled out. He also instituted (1714) *a General Chamber of Accounts,* divided into sections for war and domains.

Foreign affairs, meantime, had acquired a separate formal board of its own, a special *Kabinettsministerium.*

6. *1737 witnessed,* upon the appointment of Sam'l of Cocceji as chief justice, *the erection of a Supreme Ministry of Justice* wh. robbed the Privy Council of the greater part of the few functions which remained to it. *There were now 3 separate depts.* of internal administration besides the Privy Council (of wh. the chiefs of these depts. were

members). This Council had now become predominantly a council of ministers under the interchangeable names *Geheimer Staatsrath, Geheimes Staatsministerium.*

7. *Then a fresh disintegration: Frederic the Great* created several *new depts.—and upon a new method.* The committees of the General Directories had divided this work partly upon a geographical basis, partly upon a division of business according to kind; the new depts. were erected solely for specific kinds of business. As business increased, moreover, it ceased to be possible to consider all matters *in Plenum* and *the several committees* were left to *act independently,* as if separate depts., under the several ministers. *The General Directory was going to pieces* as the Privy Council had done. *Silesia* from the first had a separate Ministry of her own at Breslau. *South Prussia* was under the *Kabinettsministerium* (of foreign affs.). Frederic added still further to the confusion by creating, upon a French model, a *special body for the administration of indirect taxes and of certain royal dues* in the provinces this side the Weser!

He added to the Dept. of Justice oversight of ecclesiastical and educational affs.

8. *Then partial re-integration.* In 1787, the year after the death of Frederic the Great, the special excise and its administration were restored to the General Directory. 1798-'99 saw all *the separately administered provinces* (except Silesia) *brought within the general system.* But the variety of business was too great for further integration of that sort.

   Meantime the *Kabinettsministerium* (without undergoing any essential change of function) *lost its collegiate action*; as did *also the Dept. of Justice,* to wh. additional business was assigned (e.g. ecclesiastical and educational oversight, by Fred. Great), and whose several members came, by degrees to act separately in the prosecution of its various classes of business.

   In 1787 also *a Supreme Military College* (Board) *and a Supreme School Commission* were added to the general variety. The Privy Council could of course effect no real unity in this miscellaneous mass.

9. *Then appeared the 'Cabinet'* (to be carefully discriminated fr. the *Kabinettsministerium*). The ministers ordinarily communicated with the king, not orally, but in writing only: the king of course needed assistance in the handling and consideration of their voluminous communications— and *a 'Cabinet-secretary'* became the intermediary for that

purpose. Cabinet-secretaries came presently to be called *privy-cabinet-councillors*. All business passed thr. their hands and was given shape by them; *they alone had access to the king*; in them alone was the administration unified. In fact, tho. not in legal theory, they tended to become *intermediate powers* bet. sovereign and ministers.

1808-1810.

10. *This tendency, however, never completed itself*. December *1808-'10* (substantially upon *a plan of Stein's*) the reform came wh. was to create the Prussian administration of to-day. Took shape in *the Ordinance of 27 Oct., 1810. wh. emanated fr. Hardenberg*. Stein's plan for a veritable *Staatsrath* was put aside; but *ministeries for Foreign Affs., Int., Finance, Justice, and War were created*, supplanting the old organization of Directories altogether. *The 'Cabinet' was continued*, the ministers still having no personal access to the king; *but the office of Chancellor of State was created* and the Chancellor was given direct access to the king, together with a virtual oversight over all branches of administration, and in him unity was effected. (The Chancellor was not the *legal* superior of the ministers, but his personal access to the king made him practically prime minister). *This great office lapsed with the death of Hardenberg in 1822.*

11. *On the 3rd. of June, 1814*, the *Staatsministerium* was formed, under the presidency of the Chancellor; and in *1817 the Staatsrath was partially revived*. (See *post*.).

It is evident that *the part played by practical exigency* in this development was incalculably greater than *that played by theory. Stein a veritable student of affairs.*

3. *The Existing Departments of Central Administration: their Organization and Functions*:

I. *Common Features*: The organization *bureaucratic in* every instance; *but the Minister* is in all cases *responsible* for the decisions taken. *Central personnel*, the Minister, often an Under-Secretary, fr. one to five Directors, and from 5 to 38 Executive Councillors.

Where the Dept. is divided into sections, special classes of affs. may be left to the decision of these sections, each of wh. is presided over by a Director, who has only a casting vote. *The Minister calls the Councillors of the Dept.* together *into a Plenum*. He can also assign executive duties to the councillors severally.

The Minister issues all general orders wh. are merely regulative of the conduct of the business of the Dept. He *acts, too, in a semi-judicial capacity* in interpreting the duties of the several officers and sections of the Dept. and in dividing the work of the Dept. among them. His interpretations of law are, however, of course *not conclusive as against the higher* councils of state or the higher judicial *bodies.*

II. *The Several Departments: Nine in number:*

1. *Foreign Affairs* (est. 1810) is *now an executive dept. of the Empire; but* it still *acts as a Prussian dept.* in the direction of those relations of Prussia with the other German states wh. do not fall under imperial law, as well as the relations of Prussia and the Papacy. The ministers sent by Prussia to the other German courts and to the Vatican are under this Dept.[20]

2. *Interior: Personnel:* the Minister, an Under-Secretary, one Director, and eleven executive councillors. *Competence:* all matters of internal administration not specially assigned to other Depts. The immediate and most direct superior of the several bodies of local govt.

It has *under it the following special bureaux* and commissions: (1) The Berlin Presidency of Police and *Bezirksausschuss;* (2) The Central Statistical Commission; (3) The Statistical Bureau; (4) The Cathedral Chapter of Brandenburg; (5) *Die ritterschaftlichen Kreditsverein.*

3. *Ecclesiastical, Educational, and Sanitary Affs.* (set off from Interior in 1817, Nov. 3). *Personnel:* the Minister, as Under-Secretary, three Directors, and 30 executive councillors. Divided into *four sections: (Formerly:* For Lutheran church affs.—For Roman Catholic church affs.—For educational affs.—For Sanitary affs.) *Now:*

1. *For Ecclesiastical Affairs*—exercising a general oversight simply.

2. *For Higher Education*

3. *For Primary Education*

Including technical education till '84 when *professional industrial schools,* including industrial art schools and the administration of porcelain manufacture, were *transferred to the Ministry of Trade and Industry.*

Placed over the Universities, the provincial colleges, including the medical colleges, etc., etc.

4. *Medical and Sanitary Police.* Whenever the regulations

---

[20] Prussia pays a certain sum into the Imperial treasury on account of her separate use of this Dept.

required in connexion with this police function affect other Depts., however, they must be agreed upon by consultation with the Ministers whose Depts. are affected.

4. *Trade and Industry* (est. 1848, and until 1878 including Public Works). *Personnel*: the Minister, an under-sec'y, and five executive councillors. *Controls* all administration either directly or indirectly affecting trade and industry. *E.g.*, shipping, the fitting out of ships, pilotage, schools of seamanship, trade and industrial schools; private banks; trade, professional, and industrial corporations and societies; stock companies; insurance companies.

5. *Agriculture, Domains, and Forests*: (1848, 1879). *Personnel*: the Minister, an Under-Sec'y., two Directors, 19 executive councillors. *Three Sections*:

   1. *For agricultural affs. and studs*;
   2. *For Domains*;
   3. *For Forests and Game.*

   Has *under it the following agencies*: The College of Agricultural Economy (*Landesökonomickollegium*), *Das Oberlandeskulturgericht*, The Agricultural Credit Institutions, The Technical Commission on Veterinary Affs., The Central Marsh Commission, The higher agricultural schools (*Lehranstalten*), The veterinary schools, The Horticultural Institute of Potsdam, The forest academies, The Examining Commissions for forest assessors and over-foresters, and the public and local studs.

6. *Public Works* (set off fr. Trade and Industry, 7 Aug, 1878.) *Personnel*: the Minister, 5 Directors, 38 executive councillors. *Four sections*:

   1. *For mining, smelting, and salt works.* Includes oversight of the Geological Institute, the Berlin Academy of Mines, and the Examining Commission for technical mining officials.
   2. *For Railway Administration.* Management of the affs. of the roads being built by the State or in operation under its control.
   3. *For Buildings.* All the interests and outlays of the State in respect of buildings; sanctioning of plans and estimates; building police, etc.
   4. *For Private Railways.* Acts thr. various commissions.

7. *Finance.* (1810). *Formerly included Domains and Forests* (a reminiscence, evidently, of the old régime, with its General Financial Directory for Domains). *Personnel*: the

Minister, an Under-Sec'y., two Directors, 22 executive councillors. *Three Sections*: (1). *Of Accounts and the Treasury*; (2) *For Direct Taxes*; (3) *For Indirect taxes.*

Has *under it the following agencies*: The General Directory for Lotteries, the Mints, the General Directory of Widows' Institutes, the Directory for the Administration of the Direct Taxes in Berlin, the Provincial Tax Directories, the administration of the state debt,

8. *Justice* (1810). *Personnel*: the Minister, an Under-Sec'y, one Director, 14 executive councillors. *Oversees whole administration of civil and criminal justice, judicial appointments* and the conduct of those appointed; *preparation of laws* affecting the Dept.; and the pawning business.

Under it are the Superior Courts and the Examining Commission for the Dept.

9. *War* (1809, 1816, 1851). *Seven Sections*: (1) The Central Section; (2) The General War Dept.; (3) Section for *personnel*; (4) Dept. of Military Economy; (5) Invalid dept.; (6) Dept. for the sick; (7) Medical section.

Note the absence of a Navy Department.

4. *Integration*:

I. *The Head of the State*: the king. If now less than master, he is *more than a minister* (with the permanency and intimate knowledge of affairs possessed by the Eng. sovereign). *In power*, as well as in influence, he may be said to be *permanent chief minister*, the real directing head of the government. In his case, as in that of the French President, it is *required by law that almost all his acts shall be dependent* for their validity *upon the countersignature of a Minister; but*, both by tradition and by personal, Hohenzollern force—as well as by reason of the absence of parliamentary responsibility on the part of the ministers—*he is potential master always*—always in a position to render countersignature a mere formality.

His assent is necessary:

1. To all additions to or changes in *enactments, ordinances, or constitutional rules.*

2. To all *principal accounts or plans.*

3. To the *application of all regulated funds in the following cases*: (*a*) important readjustments of salary or service, (*b*) new or exceptional assignments of pensions, (*c*) exceptional grants or aids, exceeding the funds devoted to the purpose, (*d*) new outlays of any sort.

4. To *irregular administrative expenses.*

5. To *nominations of councillors of all the Depts.* and of provincial colleges, etc., *together with* many the sanction of whose appointment has been specifically reserved by the king.

6. The *bestowal of all titles* derived fr. the position of councillor.

7. For *the more important acts of clemency (Gnadenbewilligungen).*

Every minister and every departmental chief must report to the king the chief estimates for the fiscal year, and must submit to him a biennial financial abstract and summary of his administration. The Minister of Finance must submit such a statement every month.

There is a special Ministry of the Royal Household wh. is a sort of commission to administer some of the duties immediately connected with the sovereign wh. were once performed by the Chancellor of State (Hardenberg).

II. *Das Staatsministerium: Collegiate ministerial superintendence: Consists of* the Ministers of the eight Depts. of the Administration (the Dept. of Foreign Affs. being regarded as an Imperial, not a Prussian office), together with certain ministers with (at any rate, without *Prussian*) portfolios—generally heads of branches of the Imperial administration (E.g., the Foreign Office, the Interior, etc.)

May sometimes be presided over by the king (when it is the 'Kronrath';) but is *generally presided over by a president*, who has no special prerogative save this of presiding during sittings of the body. He may be chosen outside the body of ministers; but in that case he has no vote.

Besides the regular members, there are one Under-Sec'y and 3 executive councillors, who act as *a secretarial commission*, and are present at sittings, without a vote, but with a consultative voice.

Meets once a week, oftener if necessary, to consider general subjects of administration, or such subjects as overlap fr. one Dept. to another.

Functions: In general, to effect unity in administration, representing the will of the state as a whole, wh. would otherwise be represented by the king alone, in whose day there are only twenty-four hours.

In particular, individual ministers must bring before the body general reviews of the work of their Depts.—*particularly*

1. *All proposals*, without exception, of additions to, or changes in, existing law, statutory or constitutional, as well as of ordinances of general interest.
2. The *administrative acts of the Superior Presidents* (of the Provinces) for the current year.
3. *Administrative plans* for the coming year.
4. The *monthly* so-called *Zeitungsberichte* of the (local) 'Administrations.'
5. *Periodical reviews* of the condition of the general funds.
6. *The accounts of the principal general and provincial funds*, so far as they affect the current management.
7. *Divergent views* between ministers of different Departments.
8. *Military arrangements*, so far as they affect Prussia (and may become *the subject of instructions to the Prussian members of the Imperial Bundesrath*).
9. Proposals for *the appointment of Superior Presidents, Presidents of 'Administrations,'* the *higher officers of justice*, directors, superior forest-masters, and those of like rank or importance.
10. *General rules and provisions concerning stock studs*—or changes in such rules and and provisions.

Special Functions (wh. give it some similarity to the French *Conseil d'État*): participation in the *establishment of a regency*; thc promulgation of ordinances *having the effect of law* (enactments); declarations of the *'state of seige'*; the *suspension of certain articles of the constitution*; the *summoning and dissolution of communal representatives* (thr. the king); the *discipline of non-judicial officials.*

Under the Staatsministerium are: 1. The Central Survey Commission of Prussia; 2. The Court of Conflicts; 3. The Court of Discipline for Non-Judicial officers; 4. The Supreme Administrative Court; 5. The Examining Board for higher admin. offices; 6. The Colonization Board for West Prussia and Posen; 7. The Literary Bureau for the *Staatsministerium*; 8. Imperial and Royal Prussian Gazette; 9. The editing of the Prussian collection of laws. (*Gesetzsammlung*).

III. *The 'Cabinet'* (See 9 & 10 under Historical Development) Once the influential intermediary bet. ministers and king, and wh. subsequently (*temp.* Hardenberg) consisted of the Chancellor of State, a privy councillor, and certain selected military advisers, *has now lost its significance* because of the direct access of all the ministers to the king and the necessity for their counter-signatures to the validation of his acts. Its function is now scarcely more than formal.

It acts in two sections—the one civil, the other military—the civil section consisting of privy councillors, the military being identical with the section for *personnel* in the Dept. of War. *Written documents and petitions* wh. are to go fr. the king to the ministers, or wh. come fr. outside officials or persons to the king, pass thr. the hands of these sections. *The only influence* that the Cabinet can exercise *must touch those acts of military administration wh.* the king may perform without the intervention or counter-signature of a Minister.

IV. *The Council of State (der Staatsrath),*[21] as reconstituted in *1817. (Since 1848 it has been moribund.* For a few years after 1848, a smaller circle of the body absorbed its functions). *This is the Privy Council,* whose history we have already traced in its main features.

Membership: (*1*) Princes of the blood royal of more than 18 yrs. of age; (*2*) *Ex officio,* a President, the field marshalls, ministers of State actually engaged in the conduct of administration, the Sec'y of State, the first President of the Supreme Chamber of Accounts, the Privy Cabinet-councillor, the military officer in attendance upon the king (when present in Berlin), the commanding generals, and the Superior Presidents; (*3*) public servants upon whom the king confers a seat and vote in token of special confidence.

Nominal Functions: In theory it is *the highest consultative body for the king,* though it has *no direct part in administration.* It is competent to consider, *1.* All proposals of laws or ordinances concerning wh. the king chooses to consult it. *2.* Such subjects as are specially referred to it by law (there are none such now). *3.* All matters wh. the king, in particular cases, may refer to it.

V. *The Supreme Chamber of Accounts (Oberrechnungskammer):*
Created in *1714 by Friedrich Wilhelm I.;* passed thr. various vicissitudes during the century, sometimes directly under the king, and sometimes a sort of bureau of the

---

[21] Following the page of the manuscript on which this topic is discussed are two loose pages of WWhw and WWsh notes concerning the Council of State. Undoubtedly written in 1892 or after, they were taken from Léon Dupriez, *Les Ministres dans les principaux pays d'Europe et d'Amérique* (2 vols., Paris, 1892-1893). [Eds.' note]

General Directory. Only incidentally mentioned in the reforms of 1808-10. In 1817 placed directly under the Chancellor of State and made a universal instrument of financial control. Further invigorated 1824, 1872.

Constitution: that of a court, its members having the tenure and responsibility of judges. Constitutes *a distinct branch of the govt.*, directly subordinate to the king, and *independent of the ministers*. Important qus. decided in full session, subordinate in sections of the Court.

Functions: Oversees the finances (and the management of state property) *not only of all the Depts. of State, but also the transactions of all institutions in whose behalf the credit of the State, or its aid in any form, is pledged.* The *budget* is examined by it before being presented to the *Landtag*, and *goes to the Landtag with its comments*. The comments verify the statements of the budget, point out the proposals wh. involve changes in existing law or new taxation, etc.

VI. *The Supreme Administrative Court*: the Prussian organization *differing from the French in making the supreme admin. tribunal a distinct body*—not a judicial committee of the Council.

Established by a law of *3 July, 1875* (amended 2 August, 1880).

Membership: made up altogether of qualified professional civil servants (and thus *contrasted in constitution with the lower administrative courts*, in each of wh. a majority of the members are chosen by election of the local representative bodies). *Consists of* a President, sectional chairmen and "the necessary number of councillors." All its members must have completed 30 yrs. in age, and must be qualified, one half for judicial, one-half for high administrative service. They are appointed by the king, for life, upon the nomination of the *Staatsministerium*: and may hold no other offices except such as the law leaves open to judges.[22]

VII. *The Court of Conflicts (Gerichtshof für Kompetenz-konflikte)*:

Dates back to a law of 8 April, *1847*, which was in part an *adaptation of French models*—connecting Prussian practice with the old French principle of *evocation*,—the interference, in other words, of the Administration with the

[22] *For the history, nature, organization,* and *procedure* of administrative adjudication, See *Bornhak*, II., 397 *et seq.*

ordinary jurisdiction and the appropriation of such cases as interested or affected the central authorities. (*See Bornhak*, II., pp. 479 *et seq.* esp. pp. 487-489.) *Not a definite, positive law* of administrative jurisdiction, *but an unlimited negation* on the courts—an unlimited right to interfere.

The law of 1847 (wh. is still in force) *made up* the Court *from the Privy Council (Staatsrath)*. It is to consist of the President of the Council, a Secretary of State, and nine members of the Council (of course any one can be sworn into its membership, See *ante* IV, (3)) of whom *five* must be *judicial* and *four admin.* officials. *Bornhak criticises this organization* on these grounds: (*a*) it does not give the tribunal a sufficiently independent standing, (*b*) cases are made up, under the law of '47, upon the initiative of the administrative authorities exclusively (*evocing* [evoking] pending cases from the ordinary courts upon the French model)—*cannot be raised by the courts* concerning the jurisdiction wh. the Administration arrogates to itself (p. 488).

Appointment is for life (or for the term of the highest administrative office held by the appointee).

The Government and The Administration.

Taken, in . . . substance, fr. lectures on public Law[23]

The distinction bet. the Government and the Administration, made by both French and German writers upon Administration, may be made the vehicle of a most instructive analysis.

When we analyze the political activities of modern communities, we find that

The daily life of the State is expressed in the action and the minor choices of Administration; that

Its greater choices and its means of modification are exercised in Law-making; and that

Its means of adjusting the action of government to the life of individuals, the law to private right, is found in the Courts.

All these functions were once, at least theoretically, combined in the Head of the State. The history and significance of their differentiation may be studied best by means of an examination of the present status of the Head of the State. He is not any longer, if he ever was, the Actual Administration. He is no longer the actual Law-giver. He is no longer the actual Judge. But in most States he still, in form if not in fact,

[23] Notes for these lectures are described at Sept. 15, 1890. [Eds.' note]

presides over Administration, sanctions Legislation, appoints and sustains Judges. He is still in some sort the representative of the unity, the personality of the State: of its majesty and sovereignty. There are traces everywhere of the idea that he is at least the typical sovereign and source of authority: the action of the other organs of the State simply a function of substitution. This illustrated in

I. The Possession of the Initiative in Legislation by the Head of the State, in almost all modern States, of whatever type, as well as of a wide sphere of origination not only, but also of independent action, in foreign affairs.

The Prussian constitution, with its stiff maintenance of the sovereignty of the king in the face of popular representation, is the plainest example of this principle amongst modern gov'ts.

II. The Inviolability of the Head of the State, his personal irresponsibility, under most modern consts., and exemption fr. the usual sanctions of the law.

The Head of the State still stands, in short, for the unit, Government, acting alike through Legislation, Administration, and Justice. The State is whole in him: and its differentiation is displayed, in each instance, by the

Several Types of Headship, as regards the relationship borne by those who exercise the highest executive functions to the laws: Three classes:

(1) Autocratic: where there is no constitutional means of controlling the acts of the Head of the State. E.g. Russia, Turkey, Persia, (Venice).

(2) Constitutional: where there are means of controlling the public acts of the Head of the State, at the same time that there is no personal liability on his part to arrest or other punishment. E.g., England, Spain, Italy, Prussia (?), Bavaria.

(3) Republican. So far as the Head of the State is concerned, a Republic may be defined, generically, as a form of gov't. under wh. the Head of the State is made subject to a complete subordination to the laws, and is, besides, laid under a personal responsibility for his observance of them. E.g., United States, France, Switzerland, (Rome, the *imperium*, even of the Dictator, shielding for only a brief term.). *Comp. Gareis, "Allgemeines Staatsrecht," in Marquardsen, I., 38-40.*

Even in the most archaic monarchies the power of the single monarch or chief was limited very sharply by custom,— a custom backed by the imperative sanctions of religion, and thus, to all intents and purposes, by positive law. *History:*

In subsequent monarchies the power of the monarch has been limited by

(a) Physical restraints (the danger of revolution); and by

(b) Moral restraints: the attrition of criticism (the opinions of the monarch himself, shared with his subjects,—and the opinion, pointed by jest and epigram, of observant men of the people).

The final stage of restraint is reached

(1) In its first phase when the corporate privileges of the people (Estates, feudal councils, Representations of Taxes, &c.) stand stiff in the way of the monarch's will as tough, concrete *institutions*; and

(2) In its second phase when the habitual ('conventional') attitude of the representative body towards the monarch or his representatives has taken the definite shape of constitutional rules.

All this means, simply, (a) a coming into consciousness of power on the part of the people, and (b) an effectuation of the power through concrete institutions. Time out of mind European monarchs have been bound by coronation oaths: now those oaths have been given a definite content thr. representative institutions. The Sovereign is such now, ∴ , only representatively.

Present Legal Status of the Head of the State:

(1) In the Unitary State, he occupies a position of presidential participation in the origination of law and policy, enjoying, at least nominally, the important prerogative of initiative in legislation.

(2) In the Dual State, he occupies this position towards the law and policy of two States at once. In such a case as that of Sweden-Norway, he presides over States wh. are reckoned One only in respect of foreign affairs; while, in such a State as Austria-Hungary, the gov't. over wh. he presides is reckoned that of a single state also in the administration of a joint budget, and in coöperation in matters of common concern thr. a Joint Committee of the Legislatures of the two countries.

(3) In the Federal State, he is either

(a) the executive agent of the central gov't. in the carrying out of the laws; its representative in all dealings with foreign powers; and (veto-wise) a participant in the law-making function (as in the United States); or

(b) All this, with the exception of the Veto, but with the

important addition of an initiative in legislation (as in Switzerland); or

(c) A member of the Sovereign Body as Head of the presiding member State (as in Germany)

In all three cases the Head of the State is strictly subject to the laws, to const. rule and procedure; though in two cases the responsibility is direct and personal, while in the other case it is only through ministerial proxy.

Sovereignty: Its Nature and Lodgment

From Lectures on Public Law[24]

Authority there must be, and always has been, in every State. There is no organization without it.

This Authority must be, and always has been, lodged in some definite organ or organs of the State. It must be determinate both in character and in lodgment.

Hence the conception of Sovereignty: of the lodgment in every State of a supreme authority or power in the hands of some particular person or body of persons; and the habitual association of this idea of vested authority with the idea of the State itself. The concepts 'Sovereignty' and 'Sovereign' always go together, as if inseparable in thought.

Fundamental Ideas:

I. Sovereignty is an active principle, a principle of action and origination, and not merely of superintendence. The will of the Community, of the organic State as a whole, is, in the last analysis, the foundation, and in many cases the source also, of Law.

> "The sovereign State can designate as its interest and raise to be a subject of law whatever interest it will, and can in the pursuit of that interest adopt what means it will,— this is Sovereignty, an essential property of the State, as the Sovereign Community"—*Gareis*, 29, III.

Sovereignty is Authority equipped for supreme guidance and command.

A test case: the dogma of popular sovereignty: the sovereignty of the electoral body. This, if Sovereignty at all, is dormant Sov.—waiting to have things put to it, and without organs of suggestion, or origination.

Take the case of a written constitution in which the process of amendment is made to involve the action of much more than a mere majority of the electors. The Sovereign is bound.

---

[24] Here Wilson refers to notes for his course on public law prepared in 1894-95. They are printed at Sept. 22, 1894, Vol. 9. [Eds.' note]

Was he Sov., then, only in his original assent to limitation? After that, who is Sovereign?

II. Sovereignty must, surely, to possess any substance or virility, be conceived of as the daily operative force of Gov't., and not simply the ultimate consent of the governed.

Attributes of Sovereignty (selected fr. Bluntschli's *Staatslehre*, 363, 364)

(1) By its very nature, the highest power in the State.

(2) Subordinate to no superior political authority.

(3) Its authority central and general, not local or partial (of a part.)

Bluntschli adds

(4) Unity, because the State is organic, and unity of structural power is necessary to its welfare.

Definition of Sovereignty: Sovereignty is the organic self-determination by the State of its law and policy: and the sovereign power in any State is the highest constituted and organized power therein entrusted with the choice of law and policy.

The scope of Sovereignty does not necessarily include the constituent act. That is a matter of constitution: i.e. of the *limitation* of sovereignty.

Fundamental Questions:

1. Is Sovereignty susceptible of Limitation?

Certainly of limitations *de facto*. Susceptible also of limitations *de jure*. Law, of course, receives its explicit formulation and specific sanction fr. the law-making power in the State; but its ultimate sanction is Obedience,—and that is a sanction outside itself: i.e. a Limitation. If the *terms* of this Obedience be set forth in a distinctly formulated constitution, it becomes a limitation *de jure*.

We thus relieve Sovereignty of its imprisonment in the constituent act, and set it free for a daily operation such as it must in fact possess. Else we sh. have no Sovereignty wherewith to make Statutes.

2. *Is Sovereignty Divisible?* Are sovereign powers distributable? In a unitary State, a question of "checks and balances." With regard to dual and federal states to be considered presently.

Legislative, Executive, and Judicial powers may be characterized as originative, administrative, and interpretative.

The Courts, even when given the power of authoritative interpretation of fundamental law, do not *exercise* Sovereignty: they declare its limitations, enforce the covenants of the community. When they do not possess that power they are, of course, mere interpreters of the sovereign will.

The Administration acts under the laws, and in obedience to them. It is the agent, the chief and most active agent, but it is not an originative organ.

The Legislature alone, in the modern constitutional State, is the organ of origination and command (i.e. of Sovereignty) and it is limited, offset, balanced only by the organic habit of the community in respect of Obedience: a habit wh. may be expressed either in mere 'conventions' or in written constitutions.

"Government," ∴ , has to do with sovereign determinations, and, in so far as the Head of the State or the Ministers of State are associated with the Legislature in the origination of law or policy, in so far as it is given to them to take part in shaping the course of the State, they are a part of the Sovereign Power: integrated, and, so far forth, *incorporated* with it.

"Administration," on the other hand, has no direct part in the exercise of Sovereignty, is merely the trusted agency thr. which the sovereign will is carried into detailed execution. Its very position of confidence, however, the very fact that it must be trusted by the Sovereign to execute its purpose, makes it necessary in every well constituted gov't. that "Government" and "Administration," choice and execution, will and performance, should be closely, and even intimately, associated.

3. Is Sovereignty Necessary to Statehood?

This brings us to the qu. of associated States, dual or federal gov'ts., and makes a preliminary discussion necessary.

Take the German Empire and the United States as Types:
(1) Origins of the two constitutions:

The North German States, drawn into treaty relations with each other by the circumstances of 1866, agreed to the assembling of a Nat. Diet, to consider a federal const. This Diet was composed of representatives elected under similar election laws, adopted severally and independently by the States (by agreement). It considered a draft const., amended, and adopted it. This const. was accepted by the Allied Powers, and created the N. German Confed., 1867. The S. German States afterwards entered this Confederation, by treaty (1870-'71) and it became the German Empire.

Our own fed. const. was adopted by representative assemblies separately elected in the several States for the purpose.
(2) Scope of Federal Powers:

In Germany, until Dec. 20, 1875, the usual fed. powers, with the addition of a right to legislate touching obligations and notes, criminal law, and commercial law. Since 1873, the whole field of civil and criminal law, including procedure.

In the case of our own Gov't., the familiar list.

(3) Amendment. In Germany, ordinary legislative procedure, except that 14 negative votes in the *Bundesrath* defeat. In our own Gov't., ⅔ of Congress and ¾ of the States, acting either thr. their legislatures or thr. special representative conventions.

(4) Character of the Whole. In Germany Sovereignty is held to belong to the princes of the associated States and the Senates of the free cities, and to be representatively exercised by the *Bundesrath*.

In the United States there is no such special fed. organ. The fed. gov't. is a corporate whole. We have rejected the idea of the separate Sovereignty of the several States or their gov'ts. Even in the Senate, not the States as gov'ts., but the States as electoral units, are represented.

(5) Derivation of the rights of the member States. In neither case derived: in both cases original and inherent. Limited by the powers and the superintending authority of the fed. State, but not thence supplied with their own authority or jurisdiction.

(6) Scope and Nature of State Rights: Powers of independent right, not powers of duty: powers supplying the fullest sanctions of law. Limited, as a general rule, only by the powers *actually exercised* by the fed. gov't.

Singular position of the German States under the arrangements of 1873.

(7) Relation of the Federal Government to the Member States. In what sense their political superior?

Only in the sense of being able to set bounds to them; or, in the case of the German Empire, to occupy at will more and more of a specified field of law, and so draw the bounds closer and closer about the States.

Is Such a Distribution of Sovereign Powers Susceptible of being Squared with any Definition of Sovereignty that will bear Examination?

Evidently our own Definition postpones Sovereignty to the creation of an Organism: postpones life and action to birth.

First there must be an organic State: as there was not in this country in 1787-'8 or in Germany in 1867. The organizing or constituent act creates a Thing capable of exercising Sovereignty, and of having sovereign organs.

After that, amendment is organic, and upon the initiative

of the sovereign organ. To exercise any other than the constituted powers, in accordance with constitutional method, is to
destroy (or, at any rate, suspend) the organic life, and induce
revolution, wh. may produce a different organism.

Again the Question:

Is Sovereignty Necessary to Statehood? Are the member communities of a fed. State themselves States? Yes, to the latter, No, to the former, Qu.

Comp. La-
band, I., 52-
80 (2 ed.) &
Jellinek, 201,
203.

Any body politic whose powers are not derivative, but original and inherent; whose political rights are not also legal
duties; and wh. can apply to its commands the full sanctions
of law, is a State, even tho. its sphere be limited by the presiding and sov. powers of a State, superordinated to it, whose
powers are determined, under constitutional understandings
and safeguards, by itself.

Sovereignty *vs.* Dominion

Sovereignty is political choice and law-giving subject to no
superior.

Dominion is political choice and law-giving, independent,
indeed, in the exercise of a full freedom in the selection of
means, and with unqualified power to apply the sanctions of
law, but within a subordinate sphere: subordinate because
limited by the sphere of a superordinated State.

Sovereignty and Constitution (again): Here, again, in this
complex State, with its nice divisions of sphere and adjustments of function, the Constitution expresses the limitations
of Sovereignty, the conditions of obedience on the part of the
Community.

What of the Dual State?

Austria-Hungary a plain case. Austria and Hungary severally exercise Dominion; Sovereignty belongs to the Delegations
and Joint Ministries.

Apparently Sweden and Norway retain their Sovereignty;
and yet in foreign affs Norway is dictated to by Sweden; and
in administrative matters affecting both kingdoms there is a
system of Joint Councils wh. seems to supply common organs
of sovereign determination.

What is the character, in respect of Sovereignty, of a mere
personal union of two kingdoms?[25]

Austin's Conception of Sovereignty

Austin conceived a Sovereign very concretely, as a person

Taken fr.
lectures on
Public Law.

[25] Comp. *"An Old Master."* [He refers to his essay, "Political Sovereignty,"
in *An Old Master.* An early version of this essay is printed at Nov. 9, 1891.
Eds.' note]

or body of persons existing in an independent political society and accorded the habitual obedience of the bulk of the members of that society, while itself subject to no political superior. This person or body of persons he conceived of as exercising the full political power of the Community.

Law he conceived to be the explicit or implicit command of such a person or determinate body of persons, addressed to the members of the Community, its habitual inferiors or subjects.

It is, of course, a Question of Fact whether there is in every independent body politic such a sov. person or body of persons, exercising the full political power of the Community[.] History alone can answer the qu. It, when interrogated, discloses, that.

(1) Bodin, who originated the word (*la souveraineté*) and formulated the idea conceived Sov. as limited (a) by contract, (b) by all private vested interests.

(2) That there never has been any power of absolute command, under any form of gov't. (Sovereignty was predicated in the Middle Ages of any power from wh. there was no appeal.

(3) That the history of progressive gov'ts has been the history of progressive limitations to the sov. power of origination & command.

(4) That constitutions have served, not to originate, but merely to formulate and render definite these limitations.

(5) That the election of representatives is, not a method of exercising Sovereignty, but a method of constituting the sov. organ of legislative choice.

27 Feb'y, 1895

WWT and WWhw notes, with WWsh additions (WP, DLC).

An Examination

February 2, 1892.

EXAMINATION IN THE
OUTLINES OF JURISPRUDENCE.

Answer concisely, leaving out all irrelevant matter.

1. What part does Law play in the organic life of society? Distinguish its function from that of Ethics, that of Political Economy, and that of Politics. Define Law, in view of these distinctions.

2. Give, in outline, the main points of Puchta's distinction between a Person (in the juristic sense) and an individual, and show what bearing it has upon the definition of Law under question one, above. What connections has this with questions of *Status*?

3. What were the several historical stages in the growth of Law?

4. Analyze the ethical force of Law, showing upon what it is based and how it is related to the physical force which is the ultimate sanction of Law.

5. Distinguish (a) rights *in rem* and rights *in personam*, and (b) rights antecedent and rights remedial.

6. What jural relationships arise by the mere operation of natural causes, or the mere absence of action? In what other ways do jural relationships arise? What, in general, are the jural consequences of illegal acts?

7. What are the several sorts of legal interpretation by the courts? What is the difference between interpretation and "constructive inference"?

8. What is the function of Legal Science in the life of Law? How does this function differ from that of the courts?

9. What, in Puchta's conception, are the nature and limits of Freedom; and how does jural differ from moral freedom?

10. How does Puchta, in his discussion of "Public Right," bring out the difference which the lawyer must observe between the natural union of a People into a nation, and their jural relations as members of a State?

Printed examination (WP, DLC). Att.: WWhw list of students and their grades.

From John Howell Westcott[1]

Dear Wilson: [Princeton, N. J.] Feb 2. 1892

I do not want to be a nuisance to you—but I am driven by stress of circumstances to seriously reopen the question we discussed rather offhand the other day—about your land behind West's.[2]

We have got to leave our house Oct 1st—we can find nothing fit to live in at any price—not to speak of a reasonable price. It seems we must build a house or move away from Princeton. We have looked at pretty much all the building lots in the place and there is some objection to all of them.

Now is there any part of your land you are willing to sell at once? I am in some hurry because I have my passage to

Europe engaged for Apr. 14. & want to have the question of our future decided before I go. We would rather have the top of the hill of course—which you probably want to keep. We though[t] you might let us have a narrow drive along West's back fence & cut off a strip at the rear of your lot running clear down the hill, say 65 ft wide, leaving you a depth of 200 ft. Or you might sell us a piece at the foot of the hill running along the lane. Our predicament is my excuse for bringing the subject up again. But of course we don't wish to ask any favors. If you mean to sell, however, we should rather it would be to us, and now. Can you fall in with any of these suggestions & name a price—for any part, large or small, that you are willing to sell.

Very truly yours   J. H. Westcott.

This will explain my second suggestion[.][3] If you would sell a lot fronting on Washington St we should be satisfied with 80 ft, leaving I think 300.

ALS (WP, DLC) with WWhw notation on env.: "Ans. 4 Feb'y, '92."
   [1] Born Philadelphia, Aug. 3, 1858. A.B., College of New Jersey, 1877; A.M., 1880; Ph.D., 1887. Attended the University of Pennsylvania Law School, 1879-81, and practiced law in Philadelphia, 1881-85. Spent his entire academic career at Princeton as Tutor of Latin, 1885-87; Instructor in French, 1887-88; Assistant Professor of French, 1888-89; Professor of Latin, 1889-92; Musgrave Professor of Latin and Tutor in Roman Law, 1892-1925. Editor and translator of many Latin works. Died May 19, 1942.
   [2] See JRW to WW, May 11, 1891, n. 2.
   [3] Here Westcott drew a sketch of the boundaries of the lot that he wanted to purchase from Wilson.

From Albert Bushnell Hart

Dear Prof. Wilson: Cambridge, Mass. Feb. 4, 1892.
   Your cordial letter has been received. I leave tomorrow for the University of North Carolina, where I give some lectures, and shall return via Baltimore in about ten days. If you will be so good as to let me know at Chapel Hill N. C. what your lecture hours are, I should like very much to hit one, and in any event will stop over to see you.

Sincerely yours,   Albert Bushnell Hart

ALS (WP, DLC) with WWhw notation on env.: "Ans. 5 Feb'y, '92."

An Examination

February 9 [7],[1] 1892.

EXAMINATION IN THE
HISTORY OF POLITICAL ECONOMY.

Answer concisely, leaving out all irrelevant matter.

1. What does the history of Political Economy prove with regard to the nature of the science? Why should it have received so great a development in our own century?

2. What is the "Law of Nature" or "Natural Law" of which the Physiocrats had so much to say? Whence was the notion derived, and to what economic doctrines did it give rise?

3. Characterize Adam Smith as a man and as a professor; outline the work of his chair as a whole, as he planned and in part carried it out; indicate the place occupied in it by his work on "The Wealth of Nations"; point out the negative and the constructive sides of that work; and give Hildebrand's six points of criticism upon "Smithianism."

4. State the characteristic doctrines of Malthus and give some account of the origin of his work on Population.

5. What position in the history of Political Economy should be assigned to Richard Jones, and what were his specific contributions to its thought? What were the characteristic views of Henry C. Carey?

6. Why was there an "historical school" created by reaction from the views of the "orthodox" writers? State the several points of contrast between the two schools.

7. What is the nature and what the object of modern Socialism? What conditions give rise to it; what feature of the present industrial system does it chiefly attack; and what conditions create opportunities for its propaganda?

8. Contrast St. Simon and Louis Blanc in theory and in practical programme, and indicate the relationship of St. Simon to the Socialistic movement as a whole.

9. Set forth the points of difference between French and German socialistic writers. From what class of writers does the active socialism of to-day draw its inspiration, and why?

10. Give in full the theoretical views of Marx and Lassalle; show how far Lassalle's views coincide with those of Marx; give the practical programme of Lassalle; and criticize both writers by means of a discussion of Labour and Value.

Printed examination (WP, DLC). Att.: WWhw list of students and their grades.
[1] This examination was actually given on February 7, if not a day or so before, as the following letter from A. P. Dennis discloses.

From Alfred Pearce Dennis

My dear Professor Wilson: Princeton, N. J.   Febry. 7. 1892
    The Examinations in Jurisprudence and Pol. Econ. passed off
smoothly under the "vicariate" of Mr. Coney[1] and myself. By
reference to the lists ("*Lame-duck*" as Professor Sloane calls
them) I have culled out the papers of 15 or 20 men whose standing though regular is not good in the community. Today's work in
Hist. of Pol. Econ. of these inveterate backsliders in the academic
fold I send down by express.
    If I can in any way be of possible assistance to you during
your absence & upon your return, it will give me pleasure to
have you call upon me for such service. Wishing you a pleasant
stay in Balto. and an early return.
                        Yrs. Sincerely   Alfred P. Dennis.

ALS (WP, DLC). Enc.: "Memorandum of Absentees in History of Pol. Economy
Exam."
    [1] John Haughton Coney, Fellow in Social Science.

From Henry Nevius Van Dyke

Dear Dr. Wilson: Princeton, N. J. Feb. 9, 1892.
    President Patton has received your letter of Feb. 4th.[1] He is
quite unwell at present & cannot give the matter attention; but
he will do so as soon as possible.
    Very truly yours,   H. N. Van Dyke   President's Secr.

ALS (WP, DLC).
    [1] In his letter, which is missing, Wilson apparently requested President Patton
to give him some idea of the remarks that he intended to make to the Philadelphia alumni on February 19.

From Francis Fisher Browne

My Dear Sir: [Chicago] Feb. 10, 1892.
    Would the work named on this slip—just published by Mac-
millan—be likely to interest you as material for a *Dial* review?[1]
If so, I should take much pleasure in sending you the volumes.
There would be no pressing haste for the notice.
                        Very truly yours,   F. F. Browne

ALS (WP, DLC) with WWhw notation on env.: "Ans. 23 Feby. '92." Enc.
missing.
    [1] Wilson's review of this work, Henry Jephson, *The Platform: Its Rise and
Progress*, is printed at Oct. 1, 1892, Vol. 8.

From John Frelinghuysen Hageman, Jr.[1]

My dear Prof. Wilson,   Princeton, N. J., Feb 11th 1892

Your letter should have been answered before, but, like your-self, I am so busy that it is impossible to keep up with my work.

It will give me great pleasure to do all in my power to make a sale of your land, either in whole or part.

As you know Westcott is thinking of buying somewhere. If you fail in making a sale to him it ought to be possible to succeed elsewhere. I will write to you again.

Will you remember us to Mrs. Wilson. And believe me

Most sincerely yours,   John F. Hageman, Jr.

ALS (WP, DLC).
[1] A Princeton lawyer and real estate agent and the son of the historian of the Borough of Princeton.

From Ethelbert Dudley Warfield[1]

Easton, Pennsylvania.
My Dear Doctor Wilson: February 13th, 1892.

We want an additional lecture in our Y.M.C.A. course to take the place of one which had been originally scheduled for Thomas Nelson Page,[2] and I write to ask if you could come to us and give us a lecture, which I would be very glad to have of a sub-stantial nature, at some time between the 10th and the 30th of April. The dates which would be most satisfactory are the 14th or the 15th. Please write me if you can come, and if so, upon what terms.[3]

With Warmest regards for Mrs. Wilson

Very truly,   Yours,   E. D. Warfield

After my talk with you in Princeton in June I decided to try your "State" with an elective class, & I am using it with increasing satisfaction.

TLS (WP, DLC) with WWhw notation on env.: "Ans. 23 Feby. '92."
[1] President of Lafayette College.
[2] A popular writer of short stories, essays, and verse. Page was Ambassador to Italy, 1913-19.
[3] Wilson's reply of February 23, 1892, is missing. He must have declined, for the student publication, *The Lafayette*, contains no notice or report of any address by Wilson during the winter and spring of 1892.

From Joseph R. Wilson, Jr.

My dearest brother: Clarksville, Tenn., Feb. 15/'92.

I have been intending to write ever since I recd. your last letter, but first one thing and then another has prevented. Father has been attending his classes for the past two weeks, but he has not regained his strength by any means and is far from as strong as I would wish. He still uses the catheter for drawing water from his bladder but this gives him hardly any pain now. Father is getting slowly stronger, but the great fatigue of lecturing twice each day, makes the regaining of strength a very difficult job, indeed. He keeps up well, however, and remains cheerful. This is half the battle.

Now I must tell you something about myself. There is nothing certain as yet, but I am contemplating marriage in June. Kate has a great many relatives in and about Cincinnati, and expects to go to visit them about April 1. Our much talked of plan is for me to go to Cin. early in June and bring home my bride. I will go about the time father goes north so he can stop over and marry us. How does this plan strike you? I have one great objection to this, however, and that is I fear you and sister Annie as well as sister E., cannot come to see me married. If I have the wedding in Clarksville would you come? I *must* have you if at all possible. Now, as I have said, our plans are not certain, so please do not mention them except to sister Ellie. I will let you know when all is settled.

It is hard to realize that I contemplate matrimony. The other day I said to myself, "Is Josie Wilson going to get married?" Somehow I think of myself as a youngster and cannot realize that I will soon, in all probability, assume the responsibilities of a married man.

I have written a long letter for me, and must close and write the news to sister Annie. Please write soon. With unbounded love from us both to you, sister E. & the little folks,

Your aff. bro.   Joseph.

ALS (WP, DLC).

From John Franklin Jameson

My dear Wilson,   Providence, R. I. Feb. 16, 1892.

This is what writer's cramp brings me to.[1] But I have no time for lamentations, writing hastily to inquire for some information from you respecting a matter of college policy. We spoke briefly of the expediency or inexpediency of admitting women to full participation in the privileges of New England colleges. Your opinion, based upon Middletown experience, was, if I remember, decidedly adverse, but I did not, as I should have done, ask you to go into details respecting your reasons. The question is likely to come up at our next faculty meeting, next Tuesday.

If it is not too much trouble to you, I wish you would write me the objections which your experience has suggested, especially dwelling upon thos[e] which seem equally applicable to the conditions of instruction in a college situated in Providence.

I hope that all goes well with your lectures, and with the Hopkins, that the children are well, and that Mrs. Wilson's attack of the grippe proved to be neither long-continued nor severe. Believe me, under all the cold regularity of type, as ever

Sincerely yours,   J. F. Jameson.

TL (WP, DLC) with WWhw notation on env.: "Ans. 21 Feby. '92."
1 This letter was dictated and bore a typed signature.

From William Milligan Sloane

My dear Wilson: Princeton, N. J. [c. Feb. 16, 1892]
This letter explains itself. Don't you fail us for your life's sake. Patton is still in bed and you & I have to do the job.

All well here. Kind regard to you and yours

Ever faithfully   Wm M. Sloane

ALS (WP, DLC) with Sloane's handwritten notation on env.: "The dinner is Friday, Feb. 19." Enc.: Bayard Henry to F. L. Patton, Feb. 13, 1892, TLS (WP, DLC), emphasizing the importance of the coming meeting on account of Yale's increasing success in recruiting students from the Philadelphia area, with a note on the face of this letter from Dr. Patton saying that he was too ill to attend the affair and was confident that Sloane and Wilson would represent the faculty "in a way to meet all expectations."

A Newspaper Report of a Meeting of the Baltimore Alumni

[Feb. 19, 1892]

The Princeton Alumni of Maryland.

The orange and black of Princeton was flaunted and the many virtues of the old New Jersey university were estolled [extolled] by eloquent speakers at the Lyceum Theatre parlors last night, when the seventh annual dinner of the Princeton Alumni Association of Maryland was held. . . .

In responding to his toast to Princeton, Prof. Woodrow Wilson said, in part: "What constitutes a college—the men who have gone out from her, or the men who are in it? It is from both of these we must judge. When a man has gone out from Princeton he stands for all that means business and nothing which means foolishness. Princeton is growing marvellously and means to continue to do so, and in the near future to open a law department." . . .

Printed in the Baltimore *Sun*, Feb. 19, 1892.

To John Franklin Jameson

My dear Jameson,   Balto., Md., 21 Feb'y, 1892

Your letter reached me just as I was about to start out on a tour of alumni dinners and I just got back (from Phila.) late last evening, so that it has been impossible for me to answer sooner.

I don't believe that the chief objections to coeducation that made themselves prominent at Wesleyan *would* apply against admitting Providence women—or any women who would live away from the college—to Brown. My *general* ground of objection is this: The first, *experimental* stage of college training for women is passed. We now come—or, at any rate, shall presently come —to a generation of young women who go to college of *course*, as young men have long done; who go, i. e., not because of a special desire or earnestness or fitness or (professional) need to study but for the contacts, experiences, routine, enjoyment, and incidental profit of college *life*—inside the class-room and out. We are *entering* the period of danger; we can judge little from past experience, for that was experience of women who were pioneers, examples, missionary adventurers, not easy going and sociable students. You can judge how much of this will apply to *all* colleges alike.

I am sincerely sorry to learn of your writer's cramp. Here's good fortune to you in getting over it speedily! Mrs. Wilson joins me in warmest regards.

Cordially Yours,   Woodrow Wilson

ALS (J. F. Jameson Papers, DLC).

A News Report

[Feb. 22, 1892]

PHILADELPHIA ALUMNI BANQUET.

The Princeton alumni of Philadelphia held a banquet at the Bellevue Friday evening [February 19]. Dr. Patton had been announced as one of the speakers but was unable to be present on account of sickness.

Prof. Sloane was present, and told of Princeton's material and intellectual prosperity during the past few years.

Yale was represented by Mr. Robert N. Wilson, who spoke of the conservative spirit of literary institutions.

Mr. Charles P. McMichael represented Harvard in an able talk upon Harvard's advantages.

Among the other speakers were Prof. Woodrow Wilson on the

"Future of Princeton"; Judge Calvin Reyburn on the friendly feeling toward Princeton west of the Alleghenies; J. M. Huston '92 on "Princeton of the present."

Among those present were Hon. Craig Biddle, Hon. Calvin Reyburn, Rev. E. R. Craven, D.D., Hon. John Biggs, J. Bayard Henry, T. B. Wannamaker, Rev. W. C. Rockmell [Rommel], Rodman Wanamaker, Dr. T. Morrel, H. B. Thompson, Dr. [William M.] Paxton, Professors Sloane and Wilson.

Printed in *The Princetonian*, XVI (Feb. 22, 1892), [1].

Two Announcements

[Feb. 24, 1892]

All students unexamined or conditioned in Jurisprudence will be examined in the English room on Saturday evening, March 12, at 8 o'clock.

All unexamined in the History of Political Economy will be examined in the English room on Monday evening, March 14, at 7:30 p. m.   WOODROW WILSON.

Printed in *The Princetonian*, XVI (Feb. 24, 1892), [3].

❖

[March 2, 1892]

Prof. Woodrow Wilson expects to meet his classes on Monday and Tuesday, March 7 and 8. The classes in Political Economy and International Law in the Old Chapel; the class in Administration in the English room.   WOODROW WILSON.

Printed in *The Princetonian*, XVI (March 2, 1892), [1].

To Ellen Axson Wilson

My precious, precious darling,   Princeton, Saturday 5 March '92

I arrived here at two o'clock to-day[,] read and was reassured by your telegram (or, rather, uncle R's—for which I thank him very much),[1] and am now settling down in Room 18, Nassau Hotel. I did not write from Baltimore because of packing and last errands and calls. Between five o'clock Thursday and 8 o'clock, Friday, I made 19 calls, saw about your photos., got the scraps from Miss Hurt, and did I know not what other odd jobs. Then I packed till midnight—for it was a job, I can tell you! I left Balto., on the 10:08 train,—the one Maggie[2] came on. I am too tired to be philosophical; but I am bearing the terrible loneliness of this return as best I can. My heart aches to breaking with love and longing: I dare not trust myself to write you a love letter to-day—Wait till to-morrow. In the meantime re-member that I love you so intensely, constantly, absorbingly that *my life is with you*—far away.

I come back to learn sad news. Julia Murray[3] died on Sunday last, and Mrs. Murray looks almost broken.

I am well, if tired. Those words, 'after a delightful journey,' in uncle R's telegram are comforting me, oh so much! I could hardly make my calls for thought of you—and of your face as I saw it last—with the pain of parting on it. But I must not begin that: I can't afford to strain my heart with a lecture to write to-night. I must simply beg you to kiss Margaret and Jessie and Nellie as you know I should want to kiss them, and keep for yourself a hundred kisses full almost to agony of love and tenderness.   In all things,   Your own,   Woodrow

ALS (WC, NjP).
  [1] Randolph Axson of Savannah, whose telegram is missing. Mrs. Wilson had taken the children to Savannah for what was to turn into an extensive visit to relatives in Georgia.
  [2] A servant who had gone with the Wilsons to Baltimore. Numerous "Maggies" worked for the Wilsons at one time or another, and it is impossible to identify this Maggie.
  [3] Daughter of Dean Murray.

From Ellen Axson Wilson

My own darling   [Savannah, March 5, 1892]
  I shall send you just a hasty note this morning to tell you how we are, & as I cannot very gracefully absent myself for a long time so soon, wait until tomorrow to tell you all about every-thing.

We had a *perfectly* safe and easy trip, the children gave not a particle of trouble and slept finely. They were delighted with their beds. I could lean over from above and speak to them and even hold their hands, so they were quite reassured as to being alone. Nellie of course was with me. They were as good as gold from first to last;—as [a] gentleman told me as we were leaving that they were the best children he had ever seen. One old gentleman seemed to think they were all safer for having them the children aboard, "because," he said, he knew the car was full of angels hovering around to take care of them. Nellie seems to be *quite* free from her cough & she was put to rather a severe test too, for the car was *intensely* hot—that was the one discomfort of our trip—and this house of course is cooler than they are accus-tomed to[,] being unheated except in the dining room, & our room; so that I was a little anxious about them. But they are all perfectly well. The weather is *glorious*—quite as warm as with us in May. The children have been out all morning without their cloaks, & the garden is full of flowers.

Interrupted. Have only a second to say I love you, my own husband oh so passionately   Your own   Ellie.

ALS (WC, NjP).

To Ellen Axson Wilson

My own darling,   Princeton, 6 March, 1892

I am certainly in better trim for writing to-day than I was yesterday. After ten hours sleep, my body at any rate is measurably rested: the trouble is with my heart. It is not rested. It is weighted down with an unspeakable sadness from which it seems impossible to escape. I am not *unhappy*—that is not it. I am calm and as full of quiet, untroubled purpose as ever; but there's no heart in the purpose—nothing seems worth while without you—nothing seems to promise anything in the midst of this drear loneliness. I shall do better presently; but for the time I do not *care*, somehow, to feel differently. There seems a sort of dignity and sacredness and elevation in loving you in this way. It somehow seems appropriate that I should be in the possession of such feelings while my home life is dead—my dear one gone, with her three-fold glory of little ones. It's like living a sort of life of worship, made solemn by reason of sheer intensity of devotion. My love for you at such times seems a sort of principle of life—a sort of ideal thing which reminds me in some way constantly of the shortness of life, and of how much there is to do, ere it runs out, if that love is to make itself a name in worthy things done because of it. The strain of such periods would seem to be the strain of growth. Courage must look to itself, purpose must straighten its ways, life must be cleansed and quickened, so that love may be glorified. The pain of separation assuredly blesses us in the long run. It teaches us how strong and how tender the ties are that bind us to each other, how intimately our lives are connected—united.

I suppose, darling, that I have told you all these things a score of times before, in some form or other; but they seem to grow sweeter and more comforting by repetition. They grow *truer*,—that's the secret.

The more I think over your plans the more unwilling do I feel to have you leave Savannah so soon—leave its comfort and climate, which must do both you and the children so much good, and go to Rome, where the discomfort and the bad climate may do you all some harm. Even if what we fear should turn out to

have happened,[1] why could you not go at once to Gainesville,—
say about the first of April,—and postpone your visit to Rome
till *after* the nausea, (since you are to stay South till then
anyhow) when cousin Mary[2] will also be at home, to welcome
and help you? Please, darling give this plan full consideration,
for I am exceedingly anxious to have you stay in Savannah as
long as possible.

I went into the house yesterday, after some books and papers.
Everything seemed all right; but it was a dreadfully dreary experience. It did not chill my body as much as I had expected,
but it chilled my heart through and through. Don't think me
weak, my pet. I am not. I do not *yield* to this loneliness—this
homelessness. I shall keep my spirits up. But my love for you is
tragic in quality—in intensity, and it must have some tragical
accompaniments.

Kiss the children to suffocation—give heartfelt love to the rest,—
and remember yourself as the most loved of wives—loved by

Your own Woodrow

ALS (WC, NjP).
   [1] That is, that Ellen had conceived.
   [2] Mary Eloise Hoyt.

From Ellen Axson Wilson

My own darling   [Savannah] Sunday, Mar 6 [1892]
I had especially bad fortune yesterday in my efforts to get a
letter written & I fear you were very much disgusted with the
disjointed broken-off scrawl that I sent you. But now that I have
a nurse and that things have settled down a little, I hope to do
better. The nurse promises quite well. She is the genuine African
article—very black & very unsophisticated, but apparently kind-
hearted & faithful, with no nonsense about her. The children,
including Nellie, have taken quite a fancy to her. I wish you
could see the children now! They look so much better that they
really seem like different children. Both Nellie and Jessie have a
lovely colour & Jessie's face seems to have gotten round again:—
it is really like magic. I dont think I ever saw Nellie look so
pretty as she did today. Everybody raves over her. Aunt Ella[1]
says they are the *very* sweetest children she ever saw. Nellie is
so sweet and loving with them all,—not at all shy now. She did
an odd thing yesterday, by the way. Leila[2] and I had them in
the Park, where we met Mr. Warren's[3] lame daughter and stopped
to talk. When she left she asked Nellie if she would go home

with her; and the child immediately said "yes," and put her hand in hers. We said "goodbye then"; Nellie responded and actually walked off with her. We thought she would back out in a moment but she went on and finally I had to do the 'backing out.' In the meantime the other children were in great distress about losing Nellie,—Jessie really crying! We asked Nellie afterwards if she was going home with the lady and she said "yes, 'cause thats *my* yady"

I find dear Aunt Ella just the same in both manner and appearance;—to my relief *not* old and haggard like that horrible picture of her that Leila had. Carrie Belle is a sweet, lovely, pretty little thing, with the most *beautiful* eyes. In some respects she is really sweeter than Ellen now because she is more unspoiled and less self-indulgent. Ellen's accident really has been in some respects a serious misfortune as regards the development of her character. But she is perfectly charming.

I of course saw the beautiful new church today. It is a wonderfully perfect reproduction.[4] I don't see how the architect managed it. The inside is much prettier than before however,—softer and more harmonious in colour, and with beautiful mahogany pews instead of the painted white. I saw a number of my old friends after church and had a delightful time. By the way they all think I look *better* than when I was married and "not a day older." I seem to be regarded as quite a phenomenon! It was communion Sunday and part of the programme was the ordination of Charlie Gilbert[5] as elder. I saw the Lawtons,[6]— Mrs. Lawton looks dreadfully—a perfect wreck. You should see Mrs. Dugan[7]—a mountain of fat!—and Charlie Gilberts wife is *thin* in the same degree and looks dreadfully old. He looks just the same and giggles as much as ever. The house here[8] is really delightful—such large, bright rooms and so nicely furnished!— nearly everything new and handsome. It all is singularly convenient too.

But it grows late & I must close. I wonder what my darling is doing now and if he is missing us much. I hope not! But oh, Love, tongue cannot tell how I long to see *you* tonight! My heart seems to fairly melt within me, dearest, at every thought of you with love and tenderness. My own, *own* love! my Woodrow, my husband! I wonder if you *can* know how passionately I love you. Oh me, how it makes my heart ache to think of you there alone! I don't see how I ever made up my mind to leave you! Well, it is the first time and it is going to be the last! *You* will have to do the leaving hereafter!

Goodnight, my love, may God bless you and keep you from all harm is the constant prayer of

Your own   Ellie.

I hope you can read this[.] I have nothing but that horrid "writing fluid" with which I can't write.

ALS (WC, NjP).

¹ Mrs. Randolph Axson.

² Leila and Carrie Belle and Ellen, soon to be mentioned, were all daughters of Randolph Axson and Ellen Wilson's first cousins.

³ J. L. Warren, Randolph Axson's partner in the firm of Warren and Axson, cotton factors and commission merchants.

⁴ Fire had destroyed the Independent Presbyterian Church on April 6, 1889. The church was restored insofar as possible to its former state, and the first service in the new sanctuary was held on June 14, 1891.

⁵ Charles M. Gilbert of 137 Gordon Street, an importer, long active in the affairs of the Independent Presbyterian Church and in the civic and philanthropic life of Savannah.

⁶ General and Mrs. Alexander Robert Lawton.

⁷ Elizabeth Mills (Mrs. Peter) Dougan.

⁸ Randolph Axson's new house at 166 Hall Street.

To Ellen Axson Wilson

My own darling,   Princeton, 7 March, 1892

This is Monday, three lecture day, and the third lecture (for four o'clock) is not ready. I write only to relieve a little the impression my letter of yesterday may have made upon you. Whatever I say, understand, my sweet darling, that your love is a wonderful, an inexhaustible well of pure happiness for me: that I *am* happy—and strong—and reasonable. Whatever betide, I have in your love more than I deserve, and more than enough to make and keep me happy. I am quite well—have just received and am rejoicing in your first letter—and love you passionately—*madly*, my matchless darling. Love to all—and for yourself the whole heart of   Your own Woodrow

ALS (WC, NjP).

From Ellen Axson Wilson, with Enclosure

My own darling,   Savannah Mar. 7 [1892]

I enclose Aunt Lou's letter received today. You may imagine my surprise at this proposed move, and my *delight* too, for Maggie's¹ sake. It is just what Stock² has been constantly longing for, and gives the child the best opportunity possible for her, while under Aunt Lou's care, to be brought up with the associations &c. suitable to her parentage. It will make a *vast* difference in her immediate future. I am so glad I don't know what to do! This letter though has knocked *my* plans into a thousand

bits! Of course I can't go to Aunt Lou when she is "breaking up"
& half sick & without a cook. And I came south expressly to see
Maggie! It is too bad; I should have gotten my bearings more
carefully before I started out on this trip. But it is the first time
in my experience of Aunt Lou that she has not been ready and
willing to have *all* her relatives with her at once if need be; and
this is the last thing I would have anticipated. How very suddenly
all this must have been determined upon, for I heard from her,
you know, when Uncle Tom[3] was last with us & she spoke then
of my spending next summer with her in Gainesville. Now I
shall have to go there and board for a few days and then if I
am sick go home. What do you think of my bringing the nurse
Maggie[4] with me? It strikes me quite favourably,—especially if
I should be sick. It would save your coming for me too. Well
darling the chances are that I will see you a great deal sooner
in consequence of all this!—so you see I can't be very sorry.
Uncle R. brought me your dear letter at dinner time. Please direct
to "166 Hall St." & I will get them sooner. My poor darling,
you must have almost killed yourself that last day in Balt. I am
anxious to hear again and be assured that you are really well
and *rested*. And the conclusion of it all, "a lecture to write to-
night,"—after all that fatigue—seems to cap the climax. I am so
anxious about you my precious one,—and oh how I love you! I
love you 'till it hurts almost past endurance. This is the last
time I shall ever leave you of my own free will! My word upon
that! I have much more to say but it is after eleven and I *must*
stop.

　　With my whole heart and life　　　Your own　　Eileen.

ALS (WC, NjP).
　[1] Her sister, Margaret Axson.
　[2] Stockton Axson.
　[3] The Rev. Dr. Thomas A. Hoyt.
　[4] Identified in Mrs. Brown's letter, printed below.

ENCLOSURE

From Louisa Cunningham Hoyt Brown to Ellen Axson Wilson

Dear Ellie Lou,　　　　　　　Gainesville, Ga.　Mar. 5th/92.
　I sent for Maggie Hulsey,[1] as soon as possible after I rec' yr
letter to ask her if she could nurse for you. She is *anxious* to go
to Sav & to travel around with you & to go North also; she seems
to be much attached to you & little M—[2] also; but her sister with
whom she makes her home since her mother's death is expecting hourly to be confined & she can't get any one to nurse her

sister during her sickness; her sister wants M— to go too & says that M— can go when her babe is two weeks old, that she can do without her then.

Can't you get a nurse while in Sav & let M— meet you in Atlanta & make yr visit here first before going to Columbia, or if you can't come here first Maggie can go on to Sav— when you get ready to start to C—. I make these suggestions. I don't think you can get a better, kinder nurse for yr little ones; and now that her mother & both of her brothers have died & she has to live with her married sister among a crowd of children I think she will do her best to please you & the little folks.

Dear little Margaret[3] is delighted at the idea of seeing you & the little ones, & so we all are. I hope you will have a safe & pleasant trip South.

You said that I must speak frankly about my being well enough to have you visit us; so I will tell you how I am situated at this time; my cook Lucy Vandiner, who came to me when you were confined here nearly six years ago has been sick in bed two weeks with no prospect of a speedy recovery & if I can get another cook I can entertain you & will be happy to have you & your sweet children with my darling M—. Loula[4] would offer to entertain you if she was well enough, but her health seems to be declining again; the dear child looks so pale & feeble; she wants to see you very much. I will begin on Monday to hunt for a cook. My health is much better than it was a month ago, but the Jaundice has left me with a weak back so that I can't walk or work much without suffering. Mr. Brown[5] has decided to move to Athens to live; he has met with a great loss in an investment he made here in G—, so Eddie[6] wants us to live in A— as he thinks his father can make a better living there than here. Eddie is a dear good son[;] he wants his parents near him in their old age so he [can] minister to us in our declining years.

It is dreadful to think of being separated from Loula & her sweet babies[7] but it is to our interest to go. Mr. B— is there now at work and I am here "holding the fort" until he has a cottage erected for us to live in. We expect to break up here about the last of April or early in May. Our lovely (to me) home is offered for sale[.] The move to Athens will be to Margaret's advantage as she will be near such good schools; she begs to study drawing.

We never heard from Ed—[8] until this week & wondered where the bed clothes went to.

Give my love to yr uncle R— & family. It is night & M— is asleep or she would have messages for you all. Kiss the dear little ones for me.   Lovingly,   Aunt Lou.

The reason that I did not [write] the next day after yr letter came I was waiting for M— to decide what to do. She would have gone at once if her sister could have found a nurse.   L. H. B.

ALS (WP, DLC).

1 Who had nursed Ellen during her second confinement in Gainesville in 1887.
2 Margaret Wilson.
8 Margaret Axson.
4 Mrs. Brown's daughter, Loula Brown (Mrs. James Phillip) Evans, of Gainesville.
5 Her husband, Warren A. Brown.
6 Her son, Edward Thomas Brown, then practicing law in Athens.
7 Hoyt Brown, Kathleen, and Jeannette Evans.
8 Edward Axson.

Notes for a Course in International Law

[March 8, 1892-May 1, 1894]

Contents:
WWhw, WWT, and WWsh notes with general heading "*International Law*" and on the following topics, with composition dates when given: "*Plan and Purpose of the Course*" (March 8, 1892); "*History*" (March 15, 1892); "*Its Genesis (continued)*" (March 21 and 26, 1892); "HUGO GROTIUS:—(1583-1645, 29 Aug.)" (April 5, 1892); "JOHN SELDEN, (1584-1654)"; "*Samuel Puffendorf, (1632-1694)*" (April 12, 1892); "RICHARD ZOUCH, (1590-1661) . . . LEIBNITZ, Gottfried Wilhelm, (1646-1716)" (April 19, 1892); "BYNKERSHOEK, *Cornelius van* . . . VATTEL, *Emmerich*" (May 2, 1892); and GREAT INTERNATIONAL CONVENTIONS (*Beginning with Westphalia*, 1648) . . . (1701-1714) *Wars of the Spanish Succession* . . . *The Austrian Succession* . . . *Armed Neutrality at Sea, 1780* . . . *The Napoleonic Wars, 1796-1814* . . . *1830*, disruption of Holland and Belgium . . . *Congress of Berlin*, 1878 ("Added to, 1 May, 1894"). Some emendations and additions made later.

Loose sheets (WP, DLC).

Notes for a Classroom Lecture

[March 8, 1892]
International Law.
Plan and Purpose of the Course:
    Shall depend upon the text-book for the doctrinal body of the Science.
    Lectures will concern the more general topics of the study— those which set it in its proper relations with the other depts. [fields] of Law and Political Science in general
    Among the topics discussed will be the following:
    I. *History of International Law.*
    II. *Some of The Great International Conventions* and the *Principles established by them.*

III. *Influence of the Internal Structure of a State* upon Questions of International Law.

IV. *Some Unsettled questions* of International Law.

But first let us consider what are

The Nature and Scope of the Study:

Definitions: I. *Dr. Bluntschli's*: "The law of nations is that recognized *Law of Nature* which binds different States together in a humane jural society, and which also secures to the citizens of different States a common protection of law for their general human and international rights." *Völkerrecht*, §I.

II. *Dr. Bulmerincq's*:[1] "The aggregate of those rules and institutions which have developed themselves touching the relations of States to one another."

III. *Hall*:[2] "International law consists in certain rules of conduct which modern civilized states regard as being binding on them in their relations with one another with a force comparable in nature and degree to that binding the conscientious person to obey the laws of his country, and which they also regard as being enforceable by appropriate means in case of infringement."

IV. *Maine*: "The Law of Nations is a complex system, composed of various ingredients. It consists of general principles of right and justice, equally suitable to the government of individuals in a state of natural equality, and to the relations and conduct of nations; of a collection of usages, customs, and opinions, the growth of civilization and commerce; and of a code of positive law." International Law, p. 33.[3]

Comment upon these definitions, in the language of Maine (p. 32): "There has been a difference of opinion among writers concerning the foundation of the Law of Nations. It has been considered by some as a mere system of positive institutions, founded upon consent and usage; while others have insisted that it was essentially the same as the Law of Nature, applied to the conduct of nations, in

[1] August von Bulmerincq, *Völkerrecht oder Internationales Recht*, in Marquardsen, *Handbuch*, Vol. I. [Eds.' note]

[2] That is, the textbook for the course, William Edward Hall, *A Treatise on International Law*. [Eds.' note]

[3] "International Law consists in certain rules of conduct which the progress of civilization teaches one portion of mankind to observe in their mutual dealings as members of different states," P. 3. "*Municipal Laws* are rules of conduct observed by men, or by men recognized as binding, towards each other as members of the same State.

["]*International Laws* are rules of conduct observed by men towards each other as members of different States, *though members of the same International Circle.*" P. 44.–*T. A. Walker*, "The Science of International Law." (Lond. C. J. Clay & Sons, 1893). [WW's note]

the character of moral persons, susceptible of obligations and laws. We are not to accept either of these theories as exclusively true."

Is it Law? Austin denies its claim to the title according to any strict signification because of the absence of a sanction,—*because it rests wholly upon opinion,*—as morals do.

"*What we have to notice is, that* the founders of International Law, *though* they did *not* create *a sanction*, created *a law-abiding sentiment*" (Maine, p. 51) and thus *created law under an old* (*the original*) *process*, if not in the full modern significance (of Austin's definition).

The older births of law—through the opinion of the leading classes (literate or priestly) and the acquiescence of the rest of the community—the truly organic process. This *certainly satisfies Prof. Clark's*[4] *generalized definition* of law (with human displeasure as its sanction).

But do the nations constitute a community? "There is," said *Cicero* (quoted, Wheaton, *Hist'y Law of Nations*, pp. 26, 27) "a society which includes all mankind. Within this general society is included another composed of men of the same race; and within that, another still, consisting of the inhabitants of the same state. Thus our ancestors distinguished between the law of nations and the civil law. The civil law is not always the law of nations; but the law of nations ought always to be the civil law." The *generous dream of a philosopher*. Not the fact of the ancient world—*only in part the fact of the modern world. The forces of community*: *Christianity*, the *Roman Law*, *Commerce* (both in goods and in ideas.).

The Christian states of Europe Maine declares (p. 34) to form "a community of nations united by religion, manners, morals, humanity, and science, and united also by the mutual advantages of commercial intercourse, by the habit of forming alliances and treaties with each other, of interchanging ambassadors, and of studying and recognising the same writers and systems of public law." *Note, however, the inorganic character of this community*; how sluggishly public opinion in one nation tells upon the policy of another (case of Russian barbarity).

The history of International Law is, largely, the history of the formation of this community, so far as it may be said to have been formed—*the building up of common opinions* upon

4 Edwin Charles Clark, *Practical Jurisprudence, A Comment on Austin.* [Eds.' note]

common practices and the writings of commonly accepted commentators.

Is it, predominantly, a law of War or a law of Peace—to govern the armed conflicts of states, or their peaceful relations.?

When Hall speaks (title to Part II.) of states "in their *normal relations*" in contradistinction of the "relation of war" (Part III) and the "relation of neutrality" (Part IV), *it is to be remembered that*, throughout the greater part of history *war* has been their normal relation.

"*War*," says Maine, "*appears to be as old as mankind, but peace is a modern invention*,"—and the supposition of the earlier writers upon international law, *that man emerged from an original state of peace*, is *quite erroneous*.

It is both a law of war and a law of peace; but it was *first* of all *a law of war*: *peace* was *its object*, tardily and, even yet, but partially effected. *Its object* was to substitute *for barbarity, humanity*: to substitute *ordered relationships and recognized obligations* for the license, disorder, and invasions of right which provoked war—in short, *to create a moral sense and a community among States. Its law of war* is *humanity*; its *law of peace*, the *moral personality and equality of States*. "Let therefore," *says Grotius*, "the laws be silent in the midst of arms; but those laws only which belong to peace, the laws of civil life and courts of justice, not such as are eternal and fitted for all seasons, such as nature dictates and the consent of nations establishes as applicable . . . to a pure and holy war." (Quoted, Wheaton, p. 56.).

A field for the Study of Law in its essence (its essence not being sanction, but opinion, acquiescence, habit)—*the field*, so to say, *of the General Science of Law—the modern Jus Gentium*, or law acquiesced in, common to, all nations—the modern community of thought in respect of moral and legal obligation.

Position of the courts of the U. S. with regard to International Law: they regard it as part of the general law of the land, except in so far as expressly abrogated or denied by constitution or statute. "The law of the United States" they declare "ought not, if it be avoidable, so to be construed as to infringe on the common principles and usages of nations and the general doctrines of International Law." "*They look upon its rules as a main part of of* [sic] *the conditions on which a State is originally received into the family of civilized nations.* This view, though not quite explicitly set forth, does not really differ from that set forth by the founders of International Law, and it is practically that submitted to, and assumed to be a sufficiently solid basis for further inferences, by Governments and lawyers of the civilized sovereign communities of our day. If they put it in another way it would probably be that the State which disclaims the authority of International Law places herself outside the circle of civilized nations." (*Maine*, p. 38). *Has such a body of principles*, so recognized and so elevated above the heads of sovereigns, *no sanction*, then?

Subject-matter of the Study, States as moral persons, their *normal and* their *abnormal relationships* to one another, *common* (international) *opinion, usage, enactment, coöperation*. (*See Maine's definition* again).

Method of Study:

Historical, in so far as it is the study of *the formation, development, diffusion, acceptance of certain conceptions* as to what is universal, and therefore superior to political divisions, in human relationships. This partly a history of (Roman) law, partly a history of morals.

Analytical of certain *fundamental conceptions of state existence* and action, like the conception of Sovereignty, and of certain general moral conceptions.

Critical of evidences as to the establishment, the existence (by acquiescence, etc.) of international usages, etc. (like the function of the courts in examining evidence as to the existence of a custom in private law.)

Digestive of codes with their (occasional) content of international principles of justice or comity.

8 March, 1892

WWhw MS. in body of lecture notes described at March 8, 1892.

To Ellen Axson Wilson

My own darling,   Princeton, 8 March (Tuesday), 1892.

This is another "three-lecture day," but my notes for the afternoon hour are ready and I have a little more time than I had yesterday to devote to letter-writing. That second letter of yours, which was to contain "all about everything" has not yet come, but my heart is expecting it with a sort of sweet assurance of hope. I hope that you *will* give me every possible detail about your life while you are away, with *my* life in your keeping: it will so help and delight my imagination. Thoughts of you and of our precious little ones are almost my only companions now—they are the only companions I want—and any details that you can give me of what you do and say and hear will make them all the livelier companions. Tell me *everything*: even of the pretty women you see and in what respects they are pretty—of all the compliments that are paid you, my own little beauty—I alone know *how* pretty you are—all your impressions, all your thoughts.

I am willing to do the same; but as yet I have nothing of the kind to tell. I have seen nobody outside my classes, except Dr. Murray and one or two of the men (like Prof. Orris)[1] who take their meals here at the hotel—because I have been at work almost incessantly ever since my return on Saturday. I was so engaged until the last moment in Baltimore that I reached here wholly unprepared to lecture on International Law (my new subject for this term). I had not so much as been able to make up my mind how I was going to treat it: and I did not know what materials I could command on the few topics I had thought of. The consequence was that I had to work hastily, desperately, feverishly: I had even to appropriate part of Sunday afternoon and all of Sunday evening for the purpose, and the lecture was not ready before it was time to go and meet the class (Monday afternoon at 4 o'clock). This afternoon's notes—continuing those of yesterday—I completed this morning between my second lecture hour (10:30-11:30) and one o'clock dinner. I need not tell you, therefore, how out of breath I feel—and how anxious to hear the five o'clock bell, that will end my miseries for the week!

The only *experience* I have had was in connexion with Julia Murray's death. I of course had not heard a word about it, and, meeting Dr. and Mrs. Murray near their gate, returning apparently from a walk, about an hour after my arrival, I stopped *and asked them "how their daughter was"*—when she had been burried four days! Wasn't that dreadful. Of course they understood how it was, and I am sure they did not blame me—but it was none the less dreadful for all concerned! When I came up to the athletic committee meeting I saw Dr. Murray and he then told me that Julia was on the mend—they thought the period of doubt past.

How I love that old gentleman who made the pretty speech about angels watching over your car so long as the children were on it! Did you make any pleasant acquaintances or have any interesting experiences on the journey? Please, ma'am, tell me all about *that*, too. I love everything that has any part in the life of my queen, my own precious little wife, the ornament and glory and *argument* of my life. I am wholly, unreservedly,

Your own   Woodrow.

Much love to all—scores of kisses for the babies—unnumbered kisses for yourself.   W. W.

ALS (WC, NjP).

1 S. Stanhope Orris, Ewing Professor of Greek Language and Literature.

Two Letters from Ellen Axson Wilson

My own darling,   Savannah, Mar. 8 [1892]

I shall write this morning, though I have not yet received your letter, so as to avoid sitting up late to do so!

I have been to see Daisy Anderson,—Mrs. King,[1]—took all the children,—she lives quite near,—and heard all about Rose[2] and the rest. Rose has been very ill for months; they have been most uneasy about her; but it is all right now. She has a fine boy two weeks old and is doing nicely. I had not heard a rumour of all this and was of course much surprised. On account of Rose's health Daisy has Julies little orphan babies[3] this winter,— the two youngest. They are *perfect* beauties, brilliant brunettes, with lovely features, beautiful brown eyes & the most exquisite long bronze brown curls;—and *so* sweet and bright,—poor little things! I heard for the first time the cause of Julie's death. It was due entirely to that awful nausea. It was one of the saddest, most terrible deaths I ever heard of. So intense was her suffering for three months that she was inexpressibly eager to die in spite of her passionate love for her babies. She could retain nothing whatever and was so nervous that the striking of a match would almost throw her into convulsions; and she could not bear, poor girl, to have her husband come in the room because he was heavy and made it shake. She was in the most brilliant health when it began, looking unusually beautiful and full of life and happiness, and she became emaciated beyond recognition. It seems she always suffered terribly in that way; they thought she would die when this dear little "Carol" was coming. But it is a *shame* to fill my letter with so sad a subject,—it is so natural though to speak to you of what my own heart is full of;—and after all since you don't know any of them, it ought to relieve me without saddening you.

The children are still getting on nicely and are perfectly well. M. & J sleep together on a low trundle bed and many are the fights they have about cover and places! As soon as they go to sleep they curl around each other like sleeping kittens. Still they seem to sleep well. I can't separate them with a pillow because the bed is too narrow.

Yesterday when I came up to bed I found Jessie lying flat

on her back in the middle of the floor; she was not even *near* the bed! They never stay covered of course; but the weather is so warm and their nightclothes so thick that there seems no danger. Nellie is my dear little bed-fellow and a very quiet one.

I hope darling that you have a comfortable and *warm* room at the hotel and are not in that cold extension;—and are well—and happy—and not too lonely! How I wish I could see you and know what you are doing and how you are feeling every moment! Oh for that magic glass of the fairy tale! Ah darling my life is so bound up in yours that I do not truly *live* when we are apart. I seem to be separated from myself; there is something unnatural, unreal, phantasmagorical about the whole which reminds one strangely of the classical descriptions of the land of the "shades";—you remember how those disembodied spirits are always wandering drearily about!

But you must not think, dear, that I am not enjoying myself! I am delighted to see everyone and to have them see the children and *rave* over them! I shall always be glad I came,—after I get home! I hope, my precious one, you are going for my sake to have a real "good time"—in New York especially,[4] and will not overwork and get nervous and sick. I am *so* anxious about you sometimes, love, because you have so much to do. You *will* take care of yourself darling,—will you not? Do *no* more study than is good for you and let the rest go without *worry*! I know that last is a hard saying, but you will try? With a heart full almost to breaking with love,   Your own wife,   Ellie

[1] Mrs. Clarence King.
[2] Rosalie Anderson (Mrs. McNeely) Dubose. Dubose was at this time rector of Trinity Episcopal Church in Asheville, N. C.
[3] Julie Anderson McRae, widow of Jack McRae and sister of Rosalie. Julie's children were Carol and Alexander. See EAW to WW, March 10, 1892.
[4] Wilson was about to begin his lectures at the New York Law School.

My own darling,   Savannah, Mar. 9/92.

I am trying hard in the midst of endless interruptions, calls &c. to get a few letters written to others beside yourself—letters that really *must* be written. So I must *try* and write a short letter to you today. I had no letter from you yesterday—will get two today instead I am sure. We are all well and happy and the weather, which has been dull & threatening is magnificent again. We have just been out to "Laurel Grove" the beautiful cemetary,—took all the children, it was exquisite out there in this soft air and sunshine, and they enjoyed it immensely. The poor little things have not an idea what a grave is, and their artless talk about the pretty white "tables and beds" was most touching. Of course

I saw my dear Grandparents graves. The inscription he has placed on hers is beautiful; "Sacred to the memory of Rebecca, fellow pilgrim and life-long helper of I. S. K. Axson"

I wish darling you would send me Stockton's picture as soon as possible and also one of your own[1] as soon as you can get it. I am not *sure* that there are more left,—on the table or in the album; will you please look? I think though we sent the last one to the "Chatauquan."[2] But Pach probably has them printed and ready for sale. Please send *two*, for they have none here,—to my surprise for I thought I had sent them one.

But it is dinner time so goodbye for today my own darling. I love you,—we *all* love you with our whole hearts. Nellie talks a great deal about her "own Papa."

Ever fondly, devotedly, passionately yours,   Ellie.

ALS (WC, NjP).

[1] The photograph taken by Pach Brothers in Middletown in September 1889, reproduced in Vol. 6.

[2] Which did not print it when it ran Wilson's series on the English Constitution.

To Ellen Axson Wilson

My own darling,   Princeton, 9 March, 1892

The two three-lecture days of this week are past and I am tired out, but 'up and taking a little nourishment,' not too tired by any means to feel to the full the delights of that Sunday letter of yours, which reached me this morning. I don't know how often I have read it, or shall read it, if its successor tarries and leaves me without a letter to-morrow, as I was yesterday. All this about the children's health and sweetness, your own youthfulness and beauty (I am interpreting the compliments) the things and the dear ones you have seen and enjoyed, are sweeter to me than anything except your love. That precious tender love passage at the end of the letter I know by heart and have kissed as often as I have read! You cannot give me words enough of love now, my little queen. I do not have your presence to make me conscious of your sweet tenderness and devotion; I cannot see your eyes, to read it all there, and I am heart-hungry—hungry almost to desperation. You wonder whether I am thinking of you (!). I do nothing else! I almost break my heart thinking of you. For my longings are intolerable! And yet I am happy—what a contradiction it all is!—because I know that you love me—that you are the sweetest, loveliest woman in the world, the woman of all others that a man with a soul and mind and a wild passion of tender love like my own would most ardently desire to possess, and that I have possessed you, shall, God being merciful, possess you again—that I do possess now all your love, if not your person and your charming presence. But oh, the difference, my darling! If it were not for the certain joy of the sweet future, when you will be in my arms again, I could not stand it. Either you would have to come back to me or I should have to go to you. Last night at bed-time I suffered simple torment. Every faculty of heart and mind and body yearned for you in a way that was little less than frightful. My eyes grew dim because they could not see you, my ears longed for the sound of your voice, my mind and heart were desolately lonely. I could not tell you in writing all the yearning that I felt—sweet, devoted, unaffected little wife that you are, you would scold me were I to write such things down as you will scarcely let me say to you. Oh, what shall I do for my darling! I could almost make up my mind to drown my thoughts in some sort of reckless pleasure! But, forgive me, darling, forgive me! I must be tearing *your* heart by writing in this wild strain. It is cruel: it will torture you as I would not for the world torture my sweet pet. Remember, darling, that I write with perfect abandonment when I write of my love to you: my whole nature seems concentrated in an intense ardor and un-restraint of expression which carry me beyond all bounds. The very love itself tries to struggle out upon the paper! When I am not writing I can exercise self-control; I can keep my heart within bounds. I do not often call you[r] name out aloud or tremble with the force of my unbounded passion for you. I can be happy and equable—and of course I am so almost all the time. 'Tis when I write that the flood breaks forth and my love must cry out to you across the distance that separates me from you, that lies between you and   Your own Woodrow.

Much love to all (a kiss on the throat for that monkey, Ellen) and kisses all over for the children.

Your   W.

ALS (WC, NjP).

Translation of a Boudoir Scene[1]

[c. March 9, 1892]

D'Albert, singularly moved by the sweet and solemn tone in which she uttered the whole of this speech, seized her hands

[1] Of Théophile Gautier, *Mademoiselle de Maupin* (2 vols., Paris, 1835-36 *et seq.*), Chapter XVI. That this was Wilson's own translation is evidenced by the style, which has a clear Wilsonian tone, and by the numerous emendations of wording in the manuscript. This conclusion has been confirmed by an ex-

and kissed all the fingers, one after the other—then he very gently broke the laces of her robe, so that the corsage opened and the two white treasures appeared in all their lustre: beneath that breast, sparkling and bright as silver, bloomed the two lovely roses of paradise. He lightly pressed the vermillion points with his mouth and passed also over all the contour. Rosalind permitted him to do so with an inexhaustible complaisance, and tried to return his caresses as exactly as possible.

"You must find me very awkward and very cold, my poor D'Albert; but I do not know very well how one should take it;— you will have a great deal to teach me, and really I have imposed a very painful task upon you."

D'Albert made a very simple response—he did not respond at all—and, pressing her in his arms with a new passion, he covered her shoulders and her bare bosom with kisses. The locks of the infanta, half undone, came down, and her robe fell about her feet as if by magic. She stood upright like a white apparition, with a simple chemise of quite transparent muslin. The happy lover fell upon his knees and soon had thrown, each to an opposite corner of the apartment, the two pretty little shoes with red heels—the stockings with embroidered clocks followed them straight.

The chemise, endowed with a happy spirit of emulation, did not lag behind the robe: it slipped from the shoulders, which did not dream of retaining it; then, profiting by a moment when the arms were perpendicular, it proceeded with admirable address and rested upon the hips just where the undulating contour reaches its middle course. Rosalind perceived at that moment the treachery of her last garment and lifted her knee a little to prevent its falling altogether. Thus posed, she resembled exactly those marble statues of goddesses, upon which the intelligent drapery, grieved to cover over so many charms, covers with regret the beautiful thighs, and with a happy perfidy stops just above the spot it is intended to conceal. But, since the chemise was not of marble, and since its folds did not sustain it, it continued its triumphant descent, rested entirely upon the robe, and lay round about the feet of its mistress like a great white greyhound.

It would certainly have been a very simple means of preventing all the disorder for her to retain the fugitive with her hand:

amination of all English translations in print to this date. The date assigned to this translation is somewhat conjectural. However, Wilson did begin to use the lined graph paper on which it was written in early 1892. Since this book was not in his library, Wilson probably used the Paris edition of 1882, which was in the Chancellor Green Library of the College of New Jersey in 1892.

that idea, however natural it may have been, did not occur to our modest heroine.

She stood, therefore, without any linen, her fallen garments making a sort of socket, amidst all the diaphanous brilliancy of her beautiful nakedness, for the sweet rays of the alabaster lamp which illumed D'Albert.

D'Albert, dazzled, contemplated her with ravishment.

"I am cold," she said, crossing her hands upon her shoulders. "Oh, please, one minute more!"

Rosalind uncrossed her hands, pressed the tip of her finger upon the back of an armchair and held it there without moving: she elevated her hip slightly in such a way as to set off all the richness of the undulating line;—she did not appear at all embarrassed, and the imperceptible rose of her cheeks did not have a shade too much: only the slightly quickened beating of her heart made the outline of her left breast tremble a little.

The young enthusiast for beauty could not satiate his eyes with such a spectacle: we ought to say, to the great praise of Rosalind, that this time the reality was beyond his dream, and that he had not experienced the least deception.

Everything was united in the beautiful body which posed before him:—delicacy and force, form and colour, the lines of a Greek statue of the better times and the tone of a Titian. He saw there, palpable and concrete, the cloudy chimera which he had so often sought to detain in its flight:—he was not obliged, as he had complained so piteously to his friend Silvio, to confine his attention to a certain part pretty well made and pass over another for fear of seeing something displeasing, and his amourous gaze descended from the head to the feet and remounted from the feet to the head, always sweetly caressed by a form harmonious and correct.

The knees were admirably clean-cut, the ankles elegant and refined, the legs and thighs of a proud, superb shape, the belly glossy as an agate, the hips supple and strong, the throat the gods would descend from heaven to kiss, the arms and shoulders of a magnificent sort;—a torrent of lovely brown hair, slightly waving, as one sees it on the heads of the old masters, descended in little billows along a back of ivory whose whiteness it marvelously heightened.

The painter satisfied, the lover reasserted himself; for, whatever love one professes for art, it is one of the things one does not long rest content to look upon.

He lifted the beauty in his arms and carried her to the bed;

as if by sleight of hand he was himself undressed and sprang to her side.

The child pressed herself against him and clasped him closely, for her two breasts were as cold as the snow whose colour they had. This freshness of skin made D'Albert all the more ardent and excited him to a very high degree. Presently the fair lady was quite as warm as he. He bestowed upon her the most wanton and ardent caresses. It was the throat, the shoulders, the neck, the mouth, the arms, the feet; he would have covered with a single kiss the whole of that beautiful body which rested almost within his own, so intimate was their embrace. Amidst that profusion of charming treasures, he did not know upon which to fasten.

They no longer separated their kisses, and the fragrant lips of Rosalind made but one mouth with that of D'Albert;—their breasts heaved, their eyes were half closed;—their arms, weak with voluptuousness, no longer had the power to press their bodies. The lover lay in his yearning full upon the fair body of his enchanting bed-fellow: a last obstacle was overcome, his quick and eager movements caused his sweet mistress first a keen pang of pain and then still keener thrills of pleasure. The divine moment approached:—quicker and still more eager were the movements,—and then a supreme throe convulsively agitated the lovers, and inquisitive Rosalind was as much as possible enlightened upon the obscure point about which she had been so curious.

Nevertheless, since one lesson, however intelligent one be, is not enough, D'Albert gave her a second, then a third—Out of regard for the reader, whom we do not wish to humiliate or make desperate, we will not carry our narrative much further.

Rosalind had prodigious aptitude, and made in that one night enormous progress.—That artlessness of body wondered at by all and that cheat of spirit at which no one wondered constituted a most piquant and adorable contrast. D'Albert was ravished, beside himself, transported, and could have wished that that night might last forty-eight hours, so that he might emulate Hercules. Nevertheless, towards morning, in spite of an infinity of kisses, of caresses, of the most amourous fondlings in the world, well calculated to keep awake, after a superhuman effort, he was obliged to take a little repose. A sweet and voluptuous sleep touched him upon the eyes with its pinion, his head sank, and he was asleep between the breasts of his lovely mistress. Whereupon she regarded him some time with an air of melancholy and profound reflection; then, as the dawn cast its pale rays across the curtains, she lifted him gently, laid him beside her, rose, and passed lightly over his body.

She went to her clothes and hastily resumed them, then returned to the bed, bent over D'Albert, who still slept, and kissed both his eyes upon their long and silken lashes. That done, she retired backwards, all the while gazing upon him.

WWhw MS. (WP, DLC).

From Ellen Axson Wilson

My own darling,   Savannah Mar. 10/92

Your two sweet, sweet letters came to hand as I thought they would yesterday. My love, my life! my Woodrow! Such letters make my heart almost break with love, and longing to be in your arms. And yet how happy too! The human heart is truly a strange thing! It is capable of being *at once* so happy and so miserable, and both from the same cause. But the happiness conquers in the struggle, my darling. I am *always* happy in your love; I do not believe there are any circumstances in which I would not be. The sorrows when they come simply overlay but do not displace or drive away that deep heart joy—the jewel of all my life.

I have been called away twice by visitors since beginning this short letter and now it is dinner time and I must stop. It is getting increasingly hard to find time for letter-writing. We are still perfectly well and the weather is still perfectly splendid. Little Carol & Aleck, Julie's children, & Daisy's two little girls have been to see ours and they have all had a fine time in the park,— which you know is almost at our door. Daisy's children are nine and ten years old & *such* sweet, gentle little *ladies*. They look as dainty and pure as their mother and Rose always were. Carol is so much like her mother that it is really startling, and she is the same spirited mischievous fascinating little gypsy. But I *must* go down stairs! With all my heart I am, dearest.

Your own Wife   Ellie.

ALS (WC, NjP).

To Ellen Axson Wilson

My own darling,   Princeton, 10 March, 1892

That is indeed a surprise about Aunt Lou's expected move to Athens. I of course sympathize most heartily with you in your satisfaction at seeing dear little Maggie transplanted to a place where she may bloom according to her extraordinary promise; and yet there is with me an element of doubt and fear. I must confess that I fear to see so beautiful and charming a child taken to a Southern college town—where the restraints upon the intercourse of the two sexes are at a minimum. And you know what Stock has told us about the young scapegraces that go to college in Athens; you know, too, how little Aunt Lou knew of the relations of her own daughters to the men with whom they were acquainted, how little she had to do with their choice of associates and intimates; and you know how much more beautiful Maggie is than they were. My heart sinks within me when I think of these things. It must be the riotous elements in my own blood that make me fear so keenly what even the most honorable young fellows might be tempted by mere beauty to do, where there was no restraint. Of course I exaggerate these dangers inordinately; but dangers there are, if only of premature and foolish marriage. Such an exquisite flower is safest, for a long time—during all the period of immaturity—in seclusion. However, all this is only the 'but' to my heartfelt satisfaction that Maggie is, after all, to "be brought up with the associations &c. suitable to her parentage"—and, then, of course she may come before the time of real danger arrives under our own supremely wise care! What self-sufficient 'fools we mortals be' (I really believe that this generalization covers *every*body except *you*, who are both modest and trusting, my lovely little woman!)

I think I should not hesitate at all to bring Maggie, the nurse, home with you. She would seem to be really attached to you, and her present situation, as regards a home, etc., ought to make her content to stay by us very faithfully. I am thankful for the good fortune of being able to get her.

I don't know what to advise in the way of a change of plans. Probably we had better wait till you learn whether Aunt Lou has succeeded in getting a cook, and then form our plans. At any rate, I shall take a little time to think the matter over.

I am not sure that I can write to-morrow, but I will try to write, of course,—as I need not tell you. It is almost the only comfort of my present life, writing to you. To-morrow, you know, is my first lecture day in New York at the Law School and I shall probably have to consume the whole day going and coming. I am to come back in the evening and dine with Miss Clarke of Middletown at the Arnold's.[1] Mrs. A. is improving very rapidly, I am glad to find.

Oh, how sweet the love passages in your letters are, my precious one—how I dwell, how I *live* on them. They seem, somehow, tangible physical proofs, evidences of your devotion. I must needs substitute them for those embraces of yours, *one* of which, it now seems to me, would give me more joy than I could stand. I am *possessed* by love for you and am in all things

Your own Woodrow.

Please administer as you please my love and kisses, to all the dear ones.

ALS (WC, NjP).

[1] Richard J. and Minnie S. Clarke Arnold, formerly of Providence, at this time living at 31 Nassau Street in Princeton. Their son, Carrington Gindrat Arnold, was a member of the Class of 1895, and his parents had moved to Princeton to be near him during his undergraduate years. "Miss Clarke of Middletown" was apparently Susan C. Clarke, probably Mrs. Arnold's niece.

From Ellen Axson Wilson, with Enclosure

My own darling   Sav. March 11/92.

Your sweet letter of the 8th came yesterday soon after I had finished my note to you. It made me happy, but at the same time *blue* over all that terrible work. Oh my darling, it *frightens* me! The thought of all you have undertaken;—those New York lectures and all—fairly haunts me with the dread of your getting sick or even out of sorts with me so far away. You *will* be prudent, darling, will you not?—and *amuse* yourself! in some ways? Play billiards, join the club.[1] If you don't want to be a permanent member, tell them they must compliment you with "the freedom of the club" for a month after the manner of those Baltimore clubs.

I have just been out calling on some of the old ladies, old friends of the family; we are going this afternoon to a sale of "aprons & bags" at the Church exchange; & tonight we take tea at the Dripps.[2] So you see our pursuits are not exciting and there is nothing much to write about them! Yesterday was prayer-meeting afternoon, and I took the children. They were *very* good,—and very much mystified. But Margaret said she wanted to go again, she "liked that noise"! They are *very* good all the time,—people are so delighted with their friendliness and cuteness. Even Nellie is "kind" to everyone;—tells them that she is "Nennie rite my toter hope" and about the birds that "tried." This morning in bed I asked her if she wanted to see you and she said "yes, because *that* is my *own* Papa, and *this* is my *own* Mama." She is just heavenly sweet all the time and prettier than ever. I am *so* glad people are to see her at this age. I had a lovely letter from Florence Hoyt yesterday,—I think I will enclose it. Your suggestion as to going to Gainesville from here was answered of course before it reached me by Aunt Lou's change of plans. And I don't think I had best stay here much longer than two weeks. I might stay until the first of week after next. You ask about pretty girls; do you know I have not seen *one* since I came except Louise Arnold, who called the other day; so you see my pages will not be able to glow with descriptions of their charms! I am very sorry to disappoint you,—will have to describe the children instead. They really are pretty. Everyone in the house sends love,—the children lots of kisses. I shall have to *keep* my love for my darling for all the post-bags in the country would not hold it. I love you with all my heart and *head* and life! I love you with a tenderness and a passion impossible to express. I am *altogether,*

Your own   Eileen

ALS (WC, NjP).
  1 She undoubtedly refers to the University Club of New York.
  2 The Rev. Dr. and Mrs. Joseph Frederic Dripps. Dripps was pastor of the Independent Presbyterian Church.

ENCLOSURE

From Florence Stevens Hoyt to Ellen Axson Wilson

My dear, dear cousin Ellen,   Rome, Ga. Mar. 8, 1892
    How perfectly delightful that you are really and truly south again. The entire family gave an exclamation of delight when your letter came. Of course it will be perfectly convenient to have you at any time and it seems absurd to speak of it as an imposition when we are so very anxious to have you. Mother[1] joins me in asking you to please give us just as much of your time as you possibly can. Since your letter came I have been in such an excited state that I had to put up my books in despair. How lovely that we are to see the children while they are at such sweet ages! Oh I can scarcely wait. It is a good thing that I have not very long to wait. And to see you again—well there is no use trying to tell you how glad we are. We can do it better when we see you.
    You know Martha[2] is with us now and she was very much delighted to hear that you are coming. She wants you to take one of her nieces as nurse. She says you can get either Ella or Rosa. I suppose they will do as well as any negro. They seem nice. We shall want the children so much ourselves, that it will not so much matter. Of course, though, we shall be away all the mornings. I hope there will be a great many Saturdays and Sun-

days in your visit. Let us know in what train to expect you and you will find some happy people meeting you.

Very lovingly,   Florence Hoyt

Mother would write if she could. Her eyes are acting heathenishly.

ALS (WP, DLC).
  ¹ Mrs. William Dearing Hoyt, Ellen's Aunt Florence.
  ² A servant or nurse, whom Ellen had known in Rome.

To Ellen Axson Wilson

My own darling,   N. Y. 11 March, 1892.
    I am writing at the Astor House, just before going still further down town to deliver my first law-school lecture. I feel a little nervous, of course. I never get used to lecturing—but I am in very fair shape, considering. I write before, rather than after, lecturing because I am surer both of the mails and of my own time.
    I got your letter just before leaving Princeton, at 9:08 this morning. I don't know how I could have come off without it. It was a dear sweet letter—in spite of the dreadful story it had to tell about 'Julie's' death (which was simply heart-rending—surely in such cases there ought to be an operation!) it gave me the keenest pleasure. How wonderfully well you hit my own sensations when speaking of how *unreal* you feel while away from me! Bless your heart! You have crept into and taken possession of my life, my existence, in exactly the same way! What a delight to feel that I *am* an indispensable part of your life, my sweet one. Oh, how proud and happy it makes me! I am not alive without you, my own little wife, my queen. Heart and soul I am   Your own Woodrow

ALS (WC, NjP).

EDITORIAL NOTE
WILSON'S LECTURES AT THE NEW YORK LAW SCHOOL

Wilson's letter to John Franklin Jameson of January 1, 1892, reveals that Wilson had very recently agreed to deliver ten lectures on constitutional law at the newly founded New York Law School¹ in March and April 1892. At about the time that he wrote this letter to Jameson, Wilson probably typed out the list of topics that survives in his papers.² He seems at the same time to have contemplated preparing his notes for the lectures, for he also typed out a title page as follows: "CONSTITUTIONAL LAW. Lectures delivered in the New York Law School March-April, 1892."³

  ¹ About this institution, see WW to J. F. Jameson, Jan. 1, 1892, n. 3.
  ² A one-page typed MS. with handwritten emendations, entitled "Memorandum: Topics for a course of ten lectures at the New York Law School."
  ³ A one-page WWT MS. (WP, DLC).

However, Wilson was so busy during the last weeks of the Princeton term and during his six-week stay at the Hopkins that he was unable to do any work at all on his New York Law School lectures during January and February of 1892. His letters to his wife, just printed, reveal that, if anything, he was under even greater pressure after his return to Princeton in early March because of the need to prepare notes for his new undergraduate course on international law.

The days rushed by, and the date for the first lecture in New York, March 11, was upon Wilson scarcely before he knew it. Still unprepared for the New York series, he used the notes for the course on American constitutional law that he had given at Princeton in the spring term of 1891[4] for the first three lectures in New York on the general nature of constitutional law (March 11), the genesis of American state and federal constitutions (March 16), and the history and legal character of bills of rights (March 18). Having exhausted the usable notes from his Princeton course, Wilson, in his next lecture, on March 23, presented the paper on political sovereignty that he had read before the Faculty Philosophical Club in Princeton on about November 9, 1891.[5]

Wilson's first three New York lectures were elementary, rambling, and filled with historical inaccuracies. It is clear from his letters to his wife that they were not notably successful. The lecture on sovereignty was presumably better received, although it was at best peripheral to his subject.

As Wilson's letter to Ellen Wilson of March 23, 1892, reveals, Wilson realized that he had some hard work ahead if he was going to last for six more lectures. He decided to devote them to great issues in American constitutional law as they had been interpreted by decisions of the United States Supreme Court. Hence he spent March 23 and his following lecture days in New York reading decisions and taking notes on them.[6] These notes he organized into outlines[7] for lectures on sovereignty and the nature of government, according to the decisions of the Supreme Court (March 25), the relative places of the executive, legislature, and courts in the American constitutional system (April 1), constitutional functions of the courts (April 8), the constitutional relations of the courts and legislatures (April 14), the executive and the courts (April 20), and the states and the Union (April 22). Wilson's letters to his wife after March 23 indicate that both he and his students thought that his last six lectures were considerably meatier than his first four. However that might have been, Wilson was invited to repeat his lectures in 1893; and at the end of that series he was appointed a "Special Lecturer on Constitutional Law" at the New York Law School, a position he held through 1897.[8]

[4] Described at March 10, 1891.
[5] Printed at this date.
[6] These notes, which vividly reveal the pressure under which Wilson was working, are on loose pages in WP, DLC. Wilson also took some notes on the backs of envelopes of letters from his wife.
[7] See the body of typed and handwritten lecture notes with the general title "Constitutional Law" and bearing the composition dates for the several parts of March 25 and 31 and April 7 (written in New York), 14, 19, and 21, 1892 (WP, DLC).
[8] See WW to H. E. Scudder, March 27, 1893, n. 2, Vol. 8.

The strictly Wilsonian documentary record of Wilson's lectures in 1892 are his notes for his Princeton course on American constitutional law, the manuscript of "Political Sovereignty," Wilson's notes for and outlines of the last six lectures, and his letters to Ellen Wilson during the course of the lectures in New York. In addition, we have the transcript of a stenographic record of the first five lectures made by two students in Wilson's class, Thomas R. Hart and Willis D. Shafer.[9] This transcript (except for the section reproducing the lecture on political sovereignty, which was obviously a copy made from Wilson's own text) is exceedingly imperfect, in part undoubtedly because Wilson was lecturing poorly and the reporters had difficulty in knowing where his sentences began and ended.

The Editors have restored the text of this transcript to the form in which they believe that Wilson delivered it,[10] and they print their edited versions of Wilson's opening lecture and of the one on the Supreme Court's interpretation of sovereignty below, at their delivery dates of March 11 and March 25, 1892. These two samples, the Editors believe, suffice to indicate the character and quality of the entire series.

[9] A thirty-six-page mimeographed document entitled "New York Law School April 2, 1892. Prof. Woodrow Wilson's Lectures on CONSTITUTIONAL LAW" (WP, DLC).
[10] That is, both by literary editing and by checking the students' transcript against the notes that Wilson used for these lectures.

Report of a Lecture at the New York Law School[1]

[March 11, 1892]

General Nature

The subject upon which I am to speak is the general principles of constitutional law and of our own constitutional law in particular. No one who has been studious of recent years upon this subject can fail to perceive that it is surrounded by a new atmosphere. It is part of the ordinary and general law of the land, not part of the law belonging to politics, not part of the law governing Dred Scott decisions and the like, but part of the general law of the land, that we can regard without emotion, and more in a scientific temperament.

Constitutional law has not as permanent and important a place in our studies as it should have. Nor have we as much concern about its correct interpretation as we should have. Congress is not concerning itself about the questions whether a law is constitutional or not. Are we enough careful of the strict interpretation of the Constitution?—for, as lawyers and citizens, we are responsible for whatever takes place. The interpretation of the Constitution must make the interpretation of all statutes. What-

[1] For the provenance of this document, see the preceding Editorial Note.

ever interpretation is put upon the Constitution is put under our presidency and guidance. The bar must determine the attitude of courts towards these questions, and the courts towards the question of constitutional interpretation. We should guide it if right, and if wrong prevent it.

We as American lawyers have a special idea of constitutional law. When we speak of a constitution we think of a written document which has been framed by a special constitutional convention and submitted to the people and received the sanction of their votes, and it can be changed only by a peculiar process and with an exceptional sanction. When we speak of a constitution, we mean our own, commanding the development of our own law on all sides. But these are not the essential characteristics of constitutional law. It is not essential to a constitution that it should have the characteristics of the Constitution of the United States. We have not got at the elements when we have analyzed that instrument of ours; we must seek further for the general principles of constitutional law. We have to determine what it is that makes the modern idea of a constitution.

The question is not what is the Constitution of the United States, but what is a constitution; when, how, and where did the idea arise that there is a body of law superior to the ordinary law, distinct from it and elevated above it, underlying its principles and interpretation? When did that idea arise? Dicey in his *Constitutional Law of England* does not address himself to this question. The question which Prof. Dicey proposes is this,—what part of these principles and conceptions, which we call the English Constitution, is made up of rules of law which a court will enforce? And what part is made up, not of rules of law of which a court will take notice, but of conventions—for instance, that requirement that Ministers must resign when defeated? The courts will not take any notice of that at all. Should the ministry decline to resign they could not be put out by the courts. We cannot stop at the Constitution of the United States or the constitutions of the several states, for then we would have to examine all the statutes of the states affecting the franchises, and we should have to examine all the statutes which erected the executive departments of the Federal Government. We should have to examine the Judiciary Acts, and examine every part of the statute laws, every clause of the Constitution, before we make up the body of legal principles, affecting the public power. We are trying to determine what does a constitutional lawyer mean when he speaks of the constitution of his country.

The Constitution of Prussia is a Royal ordinance issued by

the King, the gift out of the grace of the crown. It was erected by the King himself, in the presence of a revolution just after the stormy times of 1848 when the King thought something must be yielded to the people. France called a representative body together to conclude a treaty of peace with Prussia. It did that and then usurped powers to frame a constitution and a set of rules governing in the main the chief arrangements of the government. This was never submitted to the people of France, yet the people have since added other principles to that constitution. The English Constitution is made up of the Magna Charta, and the Bill of Rights. These have on the formal side no correspondence with each other at all. They originated in the circumstances of the time. The Continental lawyer means by the constitution, rules which have by historical circumstances a double sanction underneath the ordinary sanction of law and the exceptional sanction of public opinion. The King of Prussia cannot change the constitution made by him; it is held fast in its place by the feeling that it would be unsafe to play with it. Once given forth it cannot be withdrawn. Nor can the legislators of France play with established principles, which have grown into the habits of the French people. They are not at liberty to go at ordinary pace, of legislators, nor to take ordinary means of changing, when they undertake to change the constitutional law. The Continental lawyer means by constitution that he recognizes in the general body of the law a certain set of principles, differentiating from the remainder. He also must recognize that they occupy an exceptional position, having a double foundation of enactment and public opinion.

Modern constitutions represent the result of a struggle between hereditary dynasties and the people in the several states. In every instance constitutional law is an effort in the interest of some one of the several classes of the community or an effort in the interest of the people at large. It is an effort to establish a balance between opposing parties—old privileges on the one hand and new liberty on the other. It represents the movements of a body outside of government. Every part of the recognized portions of the older constitutions of the European states represents the movement of a body free from the government and antagonistic to it, coming to the established territory and privileges for itself, and pushing back the frontiers of authority. That is the key to the constitutional struggles of Europe.

Prof. Burgess of Columbia College notices these distinctions which were before noted by German writers between the state government and the Constitution. The President, Congress, and judges of the United States and the administrative officers do not constitute the United States; they are only instrumentalities in the hands of another power. There is a United States not summoned up but only expressed in these authorities; in other words a public officer himself does not contain the essentials of his state. He simply represents something higher and stronger. There is something back of a public officer, which is the public organism. The United States is singular and not plural. This makes it a united country. If it could be conceived that we should ever strip off this government, we could still stand as firm as ever, ready to make new governments and constitutions. Our political life is not held in the Constitution of the United States, as in a vessel, which if broken the life of it would be dissipated.

The state is a different thing from the government which expresses its purposes and characterizes its life. This is a power outside of the government. Although our state is distinct from the government it is no more distinct than the states on the continent of Europe. All governments have a special body of laws superior to the rest. The only difference between our government and others is the way in which we have embodied that law. It is not so very peculiar. We are not the only people in the world having written constitutions. We set the fashion. Look into the matter and you will see that other countries have not merely copied our Constitution. Nor did we ourselves invent constitutions, for if we had we should have failed. We selected principles and embodied them in a written document. The French did this also. They did not borrow anything from us except mechanical detail, and so in the Prussian Constitution. The language of our Constitution would not be acceptable to the Prussians. We took England's experience and our own colonial experience. England has now framed one document and now another, living as it were from hand to mouth in constitutional law, doing nothing more than was necessary to suffice for the moment. But there can be no retrogression. The movement is forward towards more definite formation of the law of the land in which they live. A written constitution is simply a means of making the laws of a state not more real but more distinct; bringing it within the cognizance of an ordinary man that can read. The English Constitution must be explained to an Englishman. I once had the novel experience of explaining the English Constitution to an Englishman, because the ordinary Englishman knows what he sees, and he doesn't know what he does not see. The American Constitution is plain to an American student, at least to some of them. If an American student should read our Constitution he could understand it. The advantage of the written constitution is in distinctness. The Constitution of England is no more easily amended than the Constitution of the United States because the habit of the English race is peculiar to it. Were a change to be attempted the English would say I never heard of such a thing and therefore it is impossible, which to their minds would be *reductio ad absurdum*. This is the position of the English with reference to their Constitution. If Parliament should attempt something unheard of, it would be regarded as an impossibility. Americans simply know what their Constitution is. They have a more certain law than the rest.

A federal government needs a written constitution. It needs a definite, well-understood constitution more than any other government. A federal arrangement is a nice arrangement of somewhat delicate division of power. It is an arrangement likely to get out of order and likely to cause quarrels. A legislature with limited powers is the very essence of federal arrangement. You must adjust the weights; you must determine the mechanism, or it will be wrecked. If history be looked to, there is reason to suspect that a federal body of law is in a transitional position. It is so complex that it is made up of a great number of pieces. Brazil made a mistake in dividing up into several states and substituting an artificial arrangement for one that was very simple.

The only historical reason for the existence of a federal arrangement is that there are peculiar historical circumstances back of them making the several pieces jealous of one another. Germany and Switzerland are made up of warring states, yet they are drawn together into a common society by their constitutions. If you look into the interpretation of the German law or to the legislation of the Swiss authorities, you will find something taking place there which has taken place in this country. The national constitution is going forward, and the centralization of authority and power is being completed, in those countries as in this country. The object of federal law is to furnish a vehicle for nationalization to hold the separate particles in crystalization until they are ready to coalesce.

I am free to say that I do not wish to see our government completely nationalized if it is too complex, but I do say that we must face the fact that every federal government has had that history so far. It seems to be irresistible. The laws of politics constantly tend to straighten out lines that were crooked. What young man of the present rising generation has the same ideas about the constitutional law of this country that his father had?

What father has the same ideas that his grandfather had? You can trace the steps like geological strata. Once a set of men thought the only principle was state government, and that the federal government is to keep this in harmony. And the other set thought the principal thing was the national government, and then we had war. Now nobody denies that the principal portion of our law is the Constitution of the United States, and that the constitutions of the several states are merely arrangements under it. It was once considered a destructible union. It is now considered an indestructible union—that is, a nation. By indestructible we mean that each state has no separate will of its own, that the forces of law are national and not local.

One of the most useful exercises that a young lawyer can undertake is to note some of the peculiarities of the decisions of Chief Justice Marshall. He very seldom quotes a precedent. He determines the decisions which he strives for by process of reasoning, independent of the technical rules of law, depending upon the history of our institutions. He realizes that in the life of the state there is something necessary and not something mechanical. His whole reasoning depends upon the essential requisites of the government. This depends upon who we are and where we came from. It is an historical question and not merely a question of the interpretation of documents.

In the Constitution of the United States you have a collection of words which are not found in the dictionary but embedded in English history. Every word carries on it some portion of the history of English liberty. Every word is thumb-pointed toward the legislators and judiciary of the colonies. Men do not begin their vocabulary with the Constitution's words according to the meaning they received when it was written. This meaning was received from preceding history. The Constitution takes principles from the history of England and puts them into a definite statement to afterwards be interpreted. The document is an utterance of a long line of historical development.

The characteristics of the modern constitutional states seem to have four essentials, belonging not only to our own government, but belonging to every government, and which assist us in picking out the portion of the ordinary law of the land having this peculiar sanction because inherent in the institutions of liberty, because it is the outcome of antagonistic questions, old authority and new liberty.

The people have some mode of representation. It does not make any difference what the representation is, so long as it be broad enough. For example, the clause in the Constitution guar-

anteeing to the several states a republican form of government
has to be construed by the light of what constituted a republican
form of government. When the Constitution was an adequate
representation of the nation as a whole, in the law-making body,
it was principally made up of the idea that the government
ought to be conducted not in the interests of a class or a small
number of classes, but in the interests of the entire community.
They did not undertake to say what the property qualifications
should be; they said this is an incident and not an essential.
By some process or other we must get a real representation of
the people. It must not be a class government nor an anarchy:
then it will fulfill one of the first conditions of republican institutions.

The next characteristic of the constitution is that the administration should be at all points subject to the law, having no will
apart from the law, no will in contradiction to the law. In expressing the division of powers we use the word Executive, and
we are apt to give it a scientific meaning, the business of carrying out the law. What student has ever contemplated all the
cases that should arise under it? What one has ever been carried
out? Do we get all the criminals? Do we find all the evidence,
and do we always convict all our criminals? How many go loose,
failing conviction for lack of evidence! How many crawl through
some hole that the legislators have left in their enactments! Does
the prosecuting attorney carry out the law? Does not Mr. Delancey Nicoll[2] often say that he shall not prosecute a certain
case any more, often say that he has not a good enough case to
go on with it and suffer a nonsuit? This means that it is impossible to carry out the laws as they are framed. It is impossible
not only to do that but it is impossible to leave chasms. The executive officers of the government often have to deal with cases
not previously cared for. In these cases the courts proceed by
constructive inference to draw the law over the cases and to make
some principle that will suit. The principle of the law depends
upon the spirit of the man. Although the administration is subject to the law, it is not at every point energized by it to do things
which it does. There are cases in which it acts in the spirit of the
laws and not in obedience of any plainly implied command.
The range of any government is just as wide as the law.

The judiciary is given certain independence of action and a
very wide range of independent power in the interpretation of
the law. This is one of the essentials of a constitutional state. And

2 College of New Jersey, 1874; at this time District Attorney of New York
County.

insofar as we give judges short terms, we entrench upon this characteristic of federal government, because when we do this we take away the characteristics of a constitutional state. We are not only not peculiar in having a constitution, but we are not peculiar in having our Constitution interpreted by the courts. In every government the administration should be brought to book by the action of the judicial authorities. If the judicial authorities had the same term, subject to the same electors, subject to the same passing influence, they would constitute no check at all upon the administration, and therefore one of the essentials of a constitutional state is jeopardized. You must have a judiciary with independence of will in order to keep the administration within bounds. It is one of the essentials of a constitutional state that a government should be restrained by the courts.

It is characteristic of a modern constitutional state that it should have a more or less complete and exhaustive statement of the rights which the people regard as essential to liberty. It must have a bill of rights and expression of the fundamental bill of liberty contained in it. In the *Federalist*, the writers do not regard this as an essential. The attitude of Hamilton on the objection that it [the Constitution] did not contain a bill of rights and therefore not a complete bulwark against usurpation, was that it was not necessary, that this is a government by every portion of the people, that its powers are limited to those specified, and if you specify no power which can be usurped it is unnecessary to say anything about it. We have given eighteen powers to the general government, and we have made specific statement of what the government cannot do. And these powers nowhere entrench upon individual liberty, and therefore it is unnecessary to build up individual liberty. We have built a machine to do a certain thing of which it is incapable. But this reasoning has no historical validity. The English race has been careful to embody these principles in definite statement. So all European nations have put in their constitutions some specific statement of individual rights. We do not state our rights in the same way as other governments do. We state them as though we had always been used to exercising them.

These characteristics above stated belong alike to every constitutional government. When we study them as a whole we will lay the only broad foundation for the study of our own specific body of constitutional law.

To Ellen Axson Wilson

My own darling,   Princeton, 12 March, 1892

I am sad on Saturdays because I shall receive no letter next day from my love. I think I shall take all the letters I have received from you yet (5) to-morrow and copy all the love passages in them, making them into one long passage that will ravish my heart. Then as other letters come I can add pearls to the string to my heart's (deep) content. The love passages in these letters, darling, seem to me particularly precious. Your words of love are always tender, and infinitely sweet, but this time they are so *impassioned*, so like eager, breathless caresses—so like those clinging ecstacies of love with which you sometimes (times impossible to forget!) overwhelm me. Bless you, my matchless sweetheart. Perhaps these separations help to teach us how much we love each other.

You should have heard Mr. Arnold praising you, your beauty, your accomplishments, your charm, your cultivation and *learning*, after dinner last night when we were in his smoking room together! It delighted me beyond all measure; and I joined in with all my heart and vocabulary. It would have made you burn up with blushes of sheer pleasure if you could have heard us! He says that Mrs. Brenton Green[1] thinks you one of the most remarkable—one of the "smartest" women she ever knew. I enjoyed the evening very much indeed—as you may imagine from the specimen of the entertainment which I have just given you. Miss Clarke was as genial as possible, Miss Susie [Arnold] looked very sweet and pretty with her lovely neck and—&c. charmingly displayed[.] Mrs. Arnold sent the most cordial messages down to me from her sick room—'her love to you and the children—the children were the most charming she ever saw' (for I took the photographs over to show off)—and everything that was pleasant and even affectionate. I feel sure that I can spend some very pleasant hours with them, to break my loneliness. Miss Clarke left this morning.

The dinner carries me *back* to the law school lecture. It was hard work, very hard work: a room full of critical fellows, members of the faculty included, and your poor boy very keenly embarrassed. But I do not think that I showed my embarrassment: I am sure that I spoke with my full force and with almost as much facility as at any time (for I took myself strongly in hand), and I believe that the lecture was very much appreciated—little as the classes said; but I came home a sadly tired chap, and could not have enjoyed the evening, had not my host and hostesses made me feel so much at ease and at home by their cordiality. Smith[2] was the only other guest of the evening, so we had a very cosey party. I go to New York again Wednesday and Friday of next week.

Ah, my darling, if I could only once a week, when my heart particularly fails me, have just one moment with you—just long enough for one long look into your sweet eyes, one long embrace, straining your sweet body close, close to mine, pressing your lips with a passionate kiss, like an interchange of life, a mixture and union of identities—I could stand this empty room and this empty bed; I could store up happiness enough in that moment to keep me alive!   Your own Woodrow.

Kiss those precious babies again and again and make them talk about me! Much love to all.

ALS (WC, NjP).
  [1] Katharine Porter Greene, wife of the Rev. William Brenton Greene, Jr., pastor of the Tenth Presbyterian Church of Philadelphia, who became Stuart Professor of the Relations of Philosophy and Science to the Christian Religion at Princeton Theological Seminary in 1893.
  [2] Probably Charles Sidney Smith, Instructor in Latin.

From Ellen Axson Wilson

My own darling,   Savannah, Sunday [March 13, 1892]
    Yesterday I failed for the first time to write at all; but I knew that the letter would not reach you any sooner than one written today owing to the Sunday delay. I of course mailed one as usual yesterday *morning*. We were making calls all morning,—made eight,—all over town. Immediately after dinner Uncle Randolph took us driving and we were out until night, and then I found that the wind and dust and sun had so affected my eyes that I dared not use them until I had slept it off. We had a *lovely* drive to Bonaventura and Thunderbolt.[1] They are so uniquely beautiful. How I wish you could see them, and how I regret that you did not when you were here! We went to the old parsonage Friday to take tea with the Dripps,—had a very pleasant evening. Mrs. Dripps is a very interesting woman, and Dr. Dripps was pleasant too and played the devoted to me at a great rate! I am informed that he "raves" over me anyhow! It was both sad and strange though to be in the dear old house under such new circumstances. Mrs. Dripps took me all over the house;—it looks lovely—much prettier I must confess than in the old days. Dr. Dripps has grandfather's study and Rob[2] has my room. I felt especially queer in the parlours though for you know the very last time I was in them was when I was married! It would seem

at once like something in the far, far past, and as if it had been but the other day,—for so many things have happened since, and yet it all comes back so vividly. The most striking result, my darling, of being here again, is to make me realize more strongly than ever that I am happier,—yes *infinitely* happier than I was or ever dreamed of being in those days, or in all the days of my life before! I wish, dearest, that I could *show* you the difference, could in some way bid you "look on this picture and on that" for then you would be so glad for my sake that you would never again waste a moment's regret on the little incidental troubles and sufferings that are the small price I pay for it. Then I often thought I was happy and so I was for I had an elastic disposition and the world was very beautiful; but below it all was an infinite sadness. But now "an infinite content keeps house with happy thought." Ah my husband you have been everything to me,—you *are* everything. If I could but tell you how devotedly, absorbedly, passionately I love you in return for all this happiness! I am like the lark, happiest of living creatures, who "sings and he sings & forever sings he, I love my love and my love loves me."

Your own wife   Ellie.

ALS (WC, NjP).
  [1] Bonaventure and Thunderbolt are identified in ELA to WW, Feb. 11, 1884, ns. 4 and 5, Vol. 3, p. 17.
  [2] Apparently Dripps's son.

Two Letters to Ellen Axson Wilson

My own precious darling,   Princeton, Sunday, 13 March, '92

A Sunday without you and spent in an hotel is as dreary an affair as I can imagine. Sunday is the only day in the week that I can devote entirely to my heart, to loving and letting love grow; but what can I do with my heart when you are away? Shall I sit and think how sweet it *would* be if I had you in my arms to kiss and overwhelm with caresses; shall I dream of what your eyes are like and of the ecstatic things they suggest when they melt and glow and fill up with laughing flames under my gaze? Shall I think of sitting close by you and holding your hand while we chat and chat in that perfect intimacy and harmony which so lightens and strengthens our hearts? Shall I keep intimate company with thoughts of your tenderness, your quick sympathy of intelligence and sudden delights of suggestive comment, your beauty, your caressing ways, your sweet voice, your whole wifely charm? Shall I *wish* for you all the time and yearn all day for what I cannot have? I dare not do that. It seems to burn my heart up to dwell thus long and intimately upon the qualities I so love in my darling. My desire for her presence grows so passionate that it frightens me and makes me tremble. What can compare with the pleasure that a man may get from married intimacy with the woman he loves as I love you, my wife, my darling; and how shall he dare think about those pleasures when it is impossible, and must long be so, for him to see her! His heart would surely break with sheer longing! It delights me to dwell upon thoughts of you, but it often fills me with terrible fears, too: when I realize how my life has been surrendered, *given*, wholly to you. What would become of me if—But dear, dear, this will never do! This is morbid. I'll rack myself to pieces sure enough, if I am not careful. Why not love my darling as equably as strongly, with as much courage as devotion, with such sunniness and gladness as her own sweet nature is full of! Sometimes I think—I fear—Eileen, my queen, that I have in part spoiled your sweet, serene, nature by bringing it into contact with my sombre, morbid nature—that I have frightened you with anxieties and perplexed you with fears that you never would have known had I not brought you into my troubled life! Certain it is that your sweet courage and hopefulness, your calm-eyed love of beauty and of duty, have done me unspeakable service. You have taught me—I never knew before you came to me—what happiness is—and, oh, how can I ever love you enough for it, my sweetheart! But it gives me keen pain to remember how often I have troubled your spirits and brought settled looks of care into your face, which was surely meant to reflect nothing but sunlight and speak nothing but *brave* love and purpose; how often I have injected a dash of my own morose moods into your naturally happy ones. Ah, darling, love and forgive me! Remember how much easier you have made it for me to feel cheer by the way: what a sweet guide to happiness and provoker to courage you have been—and perhaps this will compensate you for whatever you may have sacrificed to

> Your own Woodrow

Love and kisses as ever. Ah, my precious little girls!

My precious darling,   Princeton, 14 March, 1892

I took tea with the Fines last evening (Sunday) and enjoyed myself very much. I was a trifle tired of Mrs. Fine (as I am prone to be, you know), for she went to New York on Friday on the same train that carried me and I had to talk to her pretty steadily for a tediously long time; but last night the conversation was general (Billy Magie was there, too) and that fact made it very easy and amusing. That is the only 'event' that I have to record. The news may be almost as briefly told. Miss Wikoff is still confined to her room, though slowly recovering, and Dr. Wikoff,[1] though going his rounds, is suffering torture from a felon on his wrist. That's one item. The other is of a very different sort. Somebody (whose name I heard but can't recall, for I never heard it before) has given the College $100,000 for a new recitation building and our classes may now be comfortable.[2]

That's all the news, I believe.

I hope that you have not seen Mrs. Green[3] yet, on her way back home, for I have been forgetting to tell you all this time that when I called on her to bid her good-bye she gave me two little silver forks for Margaret and Jessie and a silver spoon for Nellie. They are perfect little beauties, of course, with the childrens' (first) names engraved upon them in full. The dear little folks will have good reason to treasure them, on all accounts. (I had a call, by the way, from Mr. Richard Fisher, Mrs. Green's brother, just after you left—while I was in the midst of shaving, in preparation for the calls I was about to set out to make,—the first of the nineteen!).

That *is* a *delightfully* sweet letter from Florence Hoyt and I shall hereafter love her for writing it. It is so evidently and so sweetly genuine. In such effusions it is quite impossible to mistake a false note for a genuine one. Art cannot do *that*: the heart must do it.

And so there *are* no pretty girls in Savannah? That is indeed hard luck! I suppose I must content myself with (a task of rather doubtful expediency, if you were not so delightfully and perfectly free from jealous suspicion) describing the pretty girls *I* see—for the sake of seeing them over again in words,—if for nothing else, why then for the satisfaction of saying at the close of every description—what I can always say with hearty enthusiasm—that you are more beautiful than any of them. Nobody else—whatever perfection of form or colour or texture individual beauties may have—*nobody* can compare with you in your wonderful *variety* of beauty—as if all the virtues and all delights of mind or sense took turns in looking out through your changing expressions—your eyes, your play of colour, your subtly mobile mouth! Oh, my darling, how can I ever get time to look at you *enough* when you come back—how can I solve that old problem: how can I both devour you with my eyes and strain you close to my heart: how can I both see you and kiss you. To look at you provokes me to kiss you—to kiss you provokes me to look at you:—I don't know *which* way I most ardently wish to possess you—and make sure

that you are mine and that you accept and welcome me to your
arms as   Your own Woodrow

ALS (WC, NjP).
¹ Anna Wikoff and her father, James Holmes Wikoff, M.D., who lived at 22
Nassau Street.
² The bequest of Daniel Burton Fayerweather, a wealthy but little-known
leather merchant of New York, who died on November 15, 1890. In his will,
Fayerweather made specific bequests totaling $2,100,000 to twenty institutions
of higher learning (Princeton was not among them). After provision for his
wife, relatives, and employees, the balance of his estate was to be distributed
by his executors as they saw fit, evidently—with the understanding, however,
that it would be divided among educational and charitable institutions.
Fayerweather's widow contested the will in court, but a compromise was arranged by which the executors provided more generously for Mrs. Fayerweather
than had the will itself.
The newspapers announced on March 29, 1892, that a total of $4,335,000
(the specific bequests of $2,100,000 plus the bulk of the residue of the estate)
had been granted to thirty-six educational institutions and ten hospitals and
charitable organizations. In addition to its $100,000, Princeton was to receive
one tenth of whatever additional residue might remain from the final disposition
of the properties of the estate.
Wilson presumably heard about the bequest at a faculty meeting or elsewhere
on the campus some two weeks before the public announcement of the alloca-
tions. However, he was mistaken as to how the $100,000 was to be spent, as
no new classroom building was constructed on the Princeton campus during
this period.
³ Aminta Green, widow of Charles Green, of Baltimore and Savannah and
an old friend of the Axsons.

From Ellen Axson Wilson

Savannah, Monday
My own darling,   [Tuesday, March 15, 1892]¹
I was so rushed all through yesterday that I failed entirely
in my efforts to get a letter written. I am writing now before
breakfast so that this may leave on the same mail as usual.

I had a nice little budget of letters yesterday. Two from you,
Miss Hubbell's,² one from Rose³ besides Stock's photo. Rose writes
begging me to visit her on my way home. Speaking of photographs, it is singular that those of mine have never turned up.

I am *so* glad, dearest, to hear about the New York lecture! I
know it was simply a *grand* success when you are willing to
admit as much as the mild statements in your letter. Ah but
it's me thats proud of my darling! Your successes make me so
happy, dear; and I think it is delightful for you to have an opportunity to score some in New York.

You know people down here are asking me too if you are
going to Baltimore! It seems to be all over the country.⁴ Have
they been attacking you about it in Princeton? Have you seen
Dr. Patton?—how is he? Have you made the strike for the other
five hundred⁵ as you said you were going to at this juncture? It
is certainly a good time to do it, and I hope your courage won't

fail you, for you know, dear, if we have another baby how many heavy expenses it will involve. Suppose you tell them to try to "fix" you by building a house to suit you and giving it you rent free instead of that four or five hundred! Did Mr. McCormack write a satisfactory letter?[6] I have been curious to know what he *would* answer.

Please give my love and sympathy to the Murrays. Has Mrs. Armstrong[7] been there. That was certainly a distressing "experience" of yours in connection with it, poor dear! I am glad you had such a pleasant evening at the Arnolds. I hope people will invite you out a good deal while I am gone. Am much obliged to the Arnolds for *jumping* to such pleasant conclusions about me without troubling themselves to wait for such a trifling matter as evidence! But everyone is not as logical as Bagehot who insisted on a persons making a joke before he would believe him witty! The children send scores of kisses. All are quite well. With a whole heart full of love for you & pride in you and devotion *to* you I am as ever

Your little wife   Eileen

ALS (WC, NjP).

¹ Ellen was confused. She was actually writing on Tuesday, as the contents of her letter and WW's reply of March 17, 1892, indicate.

² Mary C. Hubbell to EAW, March 8, 1892, ALS (WP, DLC). Miss Hubbell was a friend in Middletown.

³ Rosalie Dubose's letter is missing.

⁴ The *New York Times*, February 21, 1892, had reported that Dr. Richard T. Ely had submitted his resignation as Associate Professor of Political Economy at the Johns Hopkins to accept a professorship at the University of Wisconsin. "Two prominent graduates of the historical department," this account went on, "Prof. Woodrow Wilson of Princeton and Prof. Henry C. Adams of the University of Michigan, are among those mentioned as Dr. Ely's successor." Other newspapers, including those in Savannah, undoubtedly carried the same story.

⁵ During the negotiations in late 1889 and early 1890 over Wilson's appointment at Princeton, the most difficult issue had been the one of salary. Patton had offered $3,000, explaining that the highest professorial salary of $3,400 went only to the older professors, and that $400 of this sum was regarded as a housing allowance. WW to R. Bridges, Feb. 18, 1890, Vol. 6. Another issue in the negotiations was Wilson's lecturing at the Johns Hopkins, which of course required him to be absent from Princeton for six weeks during the academic year. Patton and the trustees finally agreed that Wilson should be permitted to continue his lectures at the Hopkins. However, Patton said that the time might come when the trustees would want Wilson to end his Baltimore affiliation. F. L. Patton to WW, March 5, 1890, *ibid.* Wilson may have interpreted the reassuring if ambiguous closing sentences in Patton's letter to mean that Princeton would compensate Wilson for his loss of income if it insisted that he give up his Hopkins appointment.

⁶ McCormick's letter is printed at Jan. 28, 1892; for Wilson's comment on it, see WW to EAW, March 17, 1892.

⁷ Mrs. Andrew Campbell Armstrong, Jr., sister of Julia Murray.

To Ellen Axson Wilson

My own sweet darling,   Princeton, 15 March, 1892

This is the day, apparently, when *I* have to do without a letter from my sweet one. Of course it's unreasonable for me to fret about that—because there are two days, Sunday and Tuesday, in each week on which I get no letter, when every other day brings me one and two days bring me two. And yet, so lonely and so love-sick am I,—so keenly do I pine for my sweet little wife, that constantly repeated messages of love from her seem nothing less than indispensable to me. That day seems blank and wasted, without life, which does not bring a letter from her. I must think about other things. And assuredly there are enough things to think about, and to spare! I am in the midst of written recitations and examination of delinquent students, who failed at the regular examinations, or were absent. A most cheerful and distracting occupation, scarcely compatible with writing lectures. But you must not be too anxious about me, my precious little lover. I am so selfish that I hate to say this—so dearly do I value *every* indication of your devoted love. But there is no cause for anxiety. I am quite well, and, although rushed beyond measure, not overwhelmed or at all in danger of breaking down. Only my social standing is likely to suffer—for I simply *cannot* call on the people (like Dr. Shields,[1] for instance) whose invitations to dinner I have to decline. At least I cannot for the present—and I am afraid that they do not understand. I *am* taking care of myself to the best of my ability. *I* am just as anxious as you can be to preserve my health and vigor. I love you and our precious children too much to want to leave you or to burden you with an invalid. I *do* seek amusement and I do loaf as much as I possibly can in such odd moments as offer. Perhaps I will stay over night once and again in New York; but I don't know. Sometimes I am afraid of myself, my little wife. I can tell you so because you have *so much sense* and know that what I say and fear argues not one whit of real infidelity to you—is anatomical and not of the heart. Sometimes these imperious passions of mine make me tremble at thought of what I *might* do were temptation to come in my way. Perhaps, I say to myself, it is just as well to spend my nights here when I *must* keep out of mischief. Forgive me for writing all this to you, my darling, if it pains you. When I write to you, as when I talk to you, I must out with anything that is in my thoughts. It does me good to make you a confidante in absolutely everything. Ah, me, if you were not so wholly, so charmingly sane, so without morbidness or affectation in your mental make-up, such a genius for *seeing* things, I might have been the closest, unhappiest fellow in the world. Your sweet candid nature has acted upon my nature like sunshine, both purifying and expanding it. Oh, my darling, how I love, how I *love* you! What would I be were I not

                              Your own Woodrow

Love and kisses to all. To-morrow I shall write from New York

ALS (WC, NjP).
[1] Charles Woodruff Shields, Professor of the Harmony of Science and Revealed Religion, one of Wilson's professors when he was an undergraduate.

From Ellen Axson Wilson

My own darling   Sav Mar. 15/92

I have heard from Aunt Lou again today.[1] She has gotten a cook and wants me to come. I wrote before begging her to let Maggie[2] meet me in Atlanta & go to Rome with me,—(that seemed almost the only chance to see enough of her to get acquainted, and I know Aunt Florence [Hoyt] would be glad to have her.) Aunt Lou says she would be glad to let Maggie go but she has no nice clothes; she wants me to come first to Gainesville, and when Maggie is ready take her on to Rome. That would be a delightful plan for it would enable me to see so much of Maggie,—but!—as things stand of course it is impossible for it would probably end in my not going to Rome at all, for I would probably be sick before the Gainesville visit was over and would have to rush home. And I *must* go to Rome; my *first* object in coming south was of course to see to that neglected grave;[3] I doubt if I ever have another opportunity; and besides it has already been unmarked so long that I feel it a keen distress, and even disgrace to all of us. So you see what a dilemma I am in; it is very embarrassing, for I don't know what in the world to say to Aunt Lou. However I have decided to do as I first intended and leave here for Rome early Friday morning reaching [t]here late that afternoon. When I thought I could not go to Aunt Lou's I had almost decided to stay here longer, but now of course I must hurry on as I have only two weeks more,—only one before the courses are due. Do you remember the exact date by-the-way? I mean what day of the week and month they started last. I am afraid, dear, I shant be able to send anything much in the way of a letter after this from Sav., for I have still thirteen visits to make; and prayer meeting will take up one afternoon & a drive with Mrs. Neufville[4] one morning, then there is packing and several other little matters; so you see I will be rushed.

I have been interrupted three times in writing this—now it is quite late at night, so darling I must add only a hurried good night. I *love love love* you my own Woodrow with all my heart.

                              Your own   Eileen.

I asked Uncle R. to give me a suggestion as to the inscription & he made out the enclosed which I think will perhaps do quite well.[5] Won't you *please* make any change which you think would improve it and arrange the *lines* properly for engraving. I know you have skill at that, as shown in those dedications. And then will you send it on to Stock for his approval and tell him to send it back to me at Rome *as soon as possible*?

ALS (WP, DLC).
    [1] This letter is missing.
    [2] Her sister, Margaret Axson.
    [3] Of her father, the Rev. Samuel Edward Axson.
    [4] Harriet Fenwick Tattnall Neufville, widow of Edward H. Neufville.
    [5] This enclosure is missing, but see WW to EAW, March 19, 1892, with Enclosure.

From Joseph Ruggles Wilson

My precious son   Clarksville, March 16/92

    I am sorry to learn, through your last letter to Josie—received to-day—that you are enduring the pangs of solitude—a state of life in which I am enabled, by long experience, to sympathize. I had not known that Ellie & the children were away from you, in the South; but seeing that this is best for *them* you will be all the more easily reconciled to the separation; and then it will be not long before you shall all be reunited.

    As you may have guessed, from what you have heard of my continued illness, (since January 14), that the winter has been dreary enough to me. I am still confined pretty much to the house and the bedroom. I go to my college duties every day,— going and returning in a close carriage—but during the afternoon and nights my situation is—well, not delectable. I don't continuously *suffer*, but my main complaint remains having yielded only partially to remedies. Of course it will be absolutely necessary for me to resign my position here at the end of the present college year. I *ought* indeed, in justice to myself, to do so at once, but this would inevitably occasion the break up of my department; and I have not the courage to do what must disband the most hopeful, as well as largest, class I have ever had—and so I hang on at considerable sacrifice and personal risk—hoping simply that God will favor me with strength enough to get through until June, which now seems to be likely. What principally troubles me is an answer to the puzzling question, what am I to do with myself afterwards for the little time that may remain before I join your sainted mother.

    Thus do I write selfishly about my old self; a poor subject at best; a poorer one at worst. But then I am sure you will take an interest in it, and not allow yourself to be troubled—for indeed I am not unhappy, although much broken.

I had hoped to hear from my beloved son directly and often during my critical days—but you had other calls upon your valuable time. I have not written just because I could'nt; or because I didn't wish to occupy your mind with my griefs.

Your affectionate & devoted   Father.

ALS (WP, DLC).

To Ellen Axson Wilson

My own darling,   New York, Wednesday, 16 March, '92

Again I am writing from New York, before the delivery of my lecture, this time from the office of the Law School in the Equitable Building—last time from the Astor House. Just before leaving Princeton—I can't say 'home'—I received your Sunday letter, written after your tea at the parsonage, and closing with that sweet, *sweet* passage about the increased happiness of your life since we left that parlour married. Oh, my darling, for once at any rate, I will put away that skeptical feeling that always haunts me about the possibility of *my* giving one any happiness, and abandon myself to the delight—the keenest I ever enjoyed or can enjoy—of *believing* that I have made you happy! How much better I shall lecture for the presence of that comfort in my heart. I think I shall get this passage in your letter by heart, in order that I may carry it about with me these lonely days as a sort of glorious intoxicant. Oh, my love, if you can say all this—if you can call what you have suffered a *small* price to pay for what you have enjoyed, how exalted should my heart be all the time— and how purged of all morbidness! The only trouble is that your *presence* has become so indispensable to me that *happiness* without it seems a sort of counterfeit,—a sort of unreal *play*—a sort of imitation of life amidst a condition of suspended animation. And yet *thoughts* of you go a long way towards making me actually light-hearted and happy. How literally true is it, my darling, that you *constitute* my life!

But I can't write a thoughtful letter amidst these surroundings. I can only send you a passionate love letter and once more tell you how entirely I am   Your own Woodrow

Love and kisses to all

ALS (WC, NjP).

From Ellen Axson Wilson

My own darling,   Sav. Mar. 16/92.

Just a hasty line before I start out to the *dentist's*—alas! *That tooth* has been giving me a good deal of trouble the last few days and I must see what the matter is before I travel again. I am just a little blue about the Rome trip, it turns out to be so long and troublesome. I shall either have to leave here at 7.10 in the morning, spend the night in Atlanta & then on to Rome; or leave here at 8.30 at night reaching Atlanta at 7.45 & Rome at 11. A.M. after making two changes. I suppose I shall do the latter, though I did hope to avoid the trouble and expense of night travel.

I have been visiting all the morning,—could not take the drive because the weather was threatening. I did not tell you by the way what a charming one I had with Janie Garmany, George's sister.[1] We left the shell road and followed the most *exquisite* little forest road you ever saw; it was a perfect mass of yellow jasmine on both sides; we came home with the cart laden. Our scenery is certainly the most picturesque in the world; and everything is in such perfect harmony; there are no "Queen Anne villas" among the oaks and grey moss to set your teeth on edge with the incongruity; but only little mossy grey cabins almost hidden among magnolias &, at this season, surrounded with a rosy cloud of peach blossoms.

Was interrupted! Now it is night & you will be glad to hear the result of my visit to the dentist. The trouble was with the back tooth,—the one whose nerve he killed last. It threatens an abcess but he says it is in the first stage and he thinks he can check it. I asked him too about that swelling you saw in Balt. and he says it is "only a fistula—a safty valve"; the tooth is safe as long as it is there, he wishes one would come over the other. But we are to have visitors to tea & I have yet to get the children to bed & dress so must close in great haste. Believe me darling though I don't have time to talk about it that I love you with all my heart & strength and am altogether   Your own   Eileen.

ALS (WC, NjP).
    [1] Jane and George Larcombe Garmany (College of New Jersey, '93) were children of George Washington and Jane Champion Garmany of Savannah. Three other sons of this family had been graduated from Princeton: Francis Champion, '79, Jasper Jewett, '79, and Howard Hunt, '83.

To Ellen Axson Wilson

My own darling,   Princeton, 17 March, 1892

This letter that came from you this morning contains a budget of questions which I must try to answer. I will follow your own order: The first lecture in New York was *not* a "grand success" at all, but only a success; the second one, of yesterday, was, I think, rather more of such a success as is legitimate before a law class: it was much more concrete, specific, detailed, *legal* than the first, and made, I judge, a more definite impression. The audience fell off a little. (By the way, I did *not* stay in New York over night, but came back to Princeton, *like a good* boy)

Yes, they have asked me here about the Baltimore business; but I have quite disposed of that and am asked no more questions now,[1] except once and again by students.

I have not seen Dr. Patton. No one but the Dean sees him, except on imperative business; for he is still very weak and very easily upset by any sort of exertion. It disturbs his stomach *to talk.* Consequently I of course have not made the *strike.* But Dr. Murray told me the other day that he had spoken to Dr. Patton about it (his text was the fact that the house Senator Stockton occupies is to be assigned to one of the newly elected Seminary professors, our stable, therefore, vacated, and our rent probably increased),[2] saying that he thought it high time I should receive the $400 allowance for rent. Dr. P., he said, agreed instantly, and he got the impression that the matter would be attended to (indeed Dr. P. said he would attend to it) so soon as possible (the next meeting of the Board?)—*if Dr. P. did not forget it*! I shall try to find means of keeping him in mind of it!

McCormick answered, before you left Baltimore, that he would reply to my letter fully after he had had time to consider its contents as their importance demanded; but his detailed answer has not come yet.

I believe that Mrs. A[r]mstrong was present at her sister's funeral, but I am not sure. I take it for granted that she was. 'Andy'[3] was here, I know.

'People' *are* inviting me out as much as you could wish (West invited me to come and live with him!) but I am too busy to accept more than half the invitations I get. 'It's hard grinding, gentlemen, it's hard grinding," but I can stand it as long as necessary.

Is it only my imagination, darling, that this letter, written before breakfast, was written by a little woman suffering a trifle from low spirits? I devoutly hope so! Or is there really something on her heart that she is holding back, upon a false principle of love? Oh, my darling, *don't* do anything like that!

I have a suggestion to make, sweetheart; if, by next Wednesday evening, the 23rd., the 'courses' have shown themselves, please ma'am (or as much sooner as may be) send me a night telegram as follows (this will be our *cipher*) "Will consider Rose's invitation to go to Asheville[.] All well." I do not feel any confidence, of course, but I cant repress a hope, and I want to know as soon as possible. I will understand what *no* telegram means! Oh, my sweet darling! God bless and protect you in all things. Your husband yearns over you, would cherish you, adores and longs for you almost to the breaking of his heart.

Your own Woodrow

Long, loving kisses for the children—love to all.

ALS (WC, NjP).

[1] There is no evidence that Wilson was ever offered the professorship at the Hopkins, and it is a safe assumption that he would not have accepted this position in economics had it been proffered. This is probably what Wilson had said to persons in Princeton.

[2] John Potter Stockton, United States Senator, 1865-66 and 1869-75, and Attorney General of New Jersey, 1877-97, had lived in the house at 73 Stockton Street, adjoining the Wilsons' house on Steadman Street. Stockton had rented the stable of the Wilson house from the Wilsons' landlord, Dr. John Dale McGill. The new Seminary professor who moved into 73 Stockton was the Rev. Dr. George T. Purves, Professor of New Testament Literature and Exegesis.

[3] Andrew C. Armstrong, Jr.

From Ellen Axson Wilson

My own darling,   Sav. Mar. 17/92

I have been rushing around so all day that I am "all tired out" & so sleepy too that I fear I must content myself with the briefest line.

I heard from Stock today,[1] he says he is getting so *fat* that he can't wear any of his clothes; weighs 167! No other news from him.

My tooth is all right today;—he looked at it again this morning & put iodyne on again; he is also making me take *quinine* for it,— says it was the result of cold. Says to put on more iodyne if it inflames again & I need have nothing more done to it until I get home. It was funny,—I told Leila I would not go to Dr. Hopps,[2] I wanted a cheaper one, and I certainly found him for he charged nothing!

I leave tomorrow night at 8.30, and I don't believe I will have much trouble after all, for the agent says the trains draw up in Atlanta side by side & I have only to step from one to another, and of course the change at quiet Kingston will be easy enough. I am to have two opposite lower berths and the upper ones are not to be lowered unless necessary—which isn't likely. They are those nice Central R.R. sleepers and not horrid Pullmans.

I am *delighted* to hear of the $100,000—though I do wish

everything did not have to go in buildings. Goodnight darling, I *wish* I could write a love letter tonight for my heart is *so* full of love for my own Woodrow; but I am *so* tired that I have no vocabulary, no ideas, no *nothing!*—except mere *love*—in the abstract! But darling I am in every fibre of my being,

Your own,   Eileen.

ALS (WC, NjP).
¹ His letter is missing.
² Dr. Daniel Hopps, dentist, whose office was at 51 Bull Street.

To Ellen Axson Wilson

My own darling,   New York, 18 March, 1892
   This time I am writing *after* the lecture (the third) at the ferry-station waiting-room. The lecture 'took' rather better, I judged, than either of the others.
   Your letter announcing your intention to go to Rome to-morrow morning reached me just as I was going to the train this morning. Several of my letters will have to follow you: I wish I had known sooner.
   The courses are due, Tuesday, the 22nd, I feel quite sure. In a recent letter I made a request which I shall repeat here. If the courses have *come* by Wednesday night send me a night telegram as follows (this will be our *cipher*) Will consider Rose's invitation to Asheville. All well. (The last words will mean all *normal*).
   I should think that you could make a perfectly *frank* explanation to Aunt Lou. If not, allege your promise to Florence to go at once to Rome. If the courses come, you can *return* to Rome with Maggie. Ah, if the courses come! God be merciful to my darling! How my heart *burns* with solicitude and how it aches with pain when I think what I may have brought upon you! God keep and bless you, my darling, my treasure!

Your own   Woodrow

ALS (WP, DLC).

From Ellen Axson Wilson

My own darling,   Savannah, Mar 19/92
   Won't you be surprised to get another letter from Sav. after all! I went to bed Thursday night fully intending to start the next night; but there had been a cold, damp change in the weather and Nellie and Margaret had both taken what seemed slight colds. But most of Thursday night Nellie was really quite sick, vomiting, running off at the bowels, & coughing a great

deal. So ot course I had to decide to wait over until Monday night. Nellie seemed very much better yesterday and last night she had a splendid night;—did not cough at all,—and seems quite well to-day except that her bowels are still a little loose. I sent for the Dr. yesterday and he said there was "nothing much the matter" and would not even give them any medicine. Margaret seems quite well too today[.] I am *very* glad that I was detained for yes-terday and today have been excessively cold even here—"the coldest days of the year" the paper says, and I should have been sorry to have chosen them for travelling—*northward* too—with the children. The prediction is for warmer weather tomorrow

Nellie was such a little tyrant yesterday that I really *could* not write,—thought I would write a long letter at night, but having been up with her all of the night before, I found myself very headachy and exhausted, so I went to bed instead,—very selfishly I fear. This is only a hasty note written early so as to catch my usual mail. I shall try and write a real letter tomorrow. So with much love from all your little girls and a whole heart full from your little wife, I am dearest   Your own Eileen.

ALS (WP, DLC).

To Ellen Axson Wilson, with Enclosure

My precious darling,   Princeton, 19 March, 1892

I cannot tell you in what a state of mind I have been all yes-terday and to-day about that journey of yours from Savannah to Rome, particularly to-day since I learned what the journey was to be like, running through the night and including two changes! Oh, my darling! My anxiety has increased so during the day that I just now went out and telegraphed to uncle Will.[1] to ask whether you have arrived safely. I suppose you travelled without a nurse, too! Oh, dear me! I wonder how long it will be before I get an answer to that telegram! By the way, did you lose your nurse *before* leaving? (You spoke of having to put the children to bed). Is Maggie [Hulsey] to come to you in Rome? You must not take another journey without anyone to help you. By the way, sweet-heart, what money do you need? Your purse must be pretty low by this time. I got $82 from the text-book the other day, and, unless I hear from you that you need more, I will send you $50. next week.

Just as I sat down to write this, after coming in from the telegraph office, I remembered of what a colossal piece of stu-pidity I was guilty yesterday! Before starting for New York I put an envelope in my pocket addressed to you in *Savannah*. I got your letter, saying that you would leave on Friday, on my way down to the train, and then, when I had scribbled my note in the ferry station, I put it *in that envelope* and mailed it on my way out, *without changing the address!* Oh, I am *so* sorry, my sweetheart. Just when you may need letters most! And that reminds me to repeat the answer to your question as well as a suggestion of my own which I have already put, now, into *two* belated *Savannah* letters. Your courses, I feel quite sure, will be due on Tuesday, the 22nd. My suggestion is this, if they come by Wednesday evening—or at all, for that matter—send me the following (cipher) telegram: "Will consider Rose's invitation to Asheville. All well." The last words will mean, all *normal.* Make it a night message, if necessary to avoid explanations why such a message should be sent with haste—otherwise make it a day despatch. Ah, *if they come!* I do not *dare* to *expect* that they will; I only venture a desperate *hope!*

I have read the epitaph which uncle Randolph prepared several times without seeing how it could well be bettered. The only suggestion I have to make is, that the quoted words put into the mouth of the Master ("It is enough," "Come up higher") be omitted and the lines divided as shown in the copy which I enclose. In that form it seems to me that it would be in all respects satisfactory. I will send uncle R's copy to Stock (with my own) and ask him to write to you at once.

No: I have changed my mind: I would end it much more simply (I enclose two forms, marked 1, 2).[2]

My sweet love, I am afraid I cannot stand your stay in Rome as well as I stood your stay in Savannah. I shall not feel that *you* are so comfortable or so happy. But cannot you take some of the rides or walks *we* took? This is almost the season in which I first met you—and fell so deep, so delightfully in love—to my own infinite happiness and good, beginning to live by becoming altogether   Your own Woodrow.

Warmest love to all—devouring kisses for the babies.

ALS (WC, NjP).
    [1] Dr. William Dearing Hoyt.
    [2] Wilson's copy for the first version of the epitaph (an edited version of Randolph Axson's text) is still enclosed with Wilson's letter and is printed as an Enclosure. This version was not used. Wilson's copy of the second version is missing. Slightly edited by Ellen Axson Wilson (as subsequent letters will reveal), it was used as the epitaph and is printed in EAW to WW, April 5, 1892, n. 1.

(I)
In memory of
Rev. S. E. Axson,
who departed this life
May 28th., 1884
Aged 47 years 5 months.
A faithful servant of Jesus Christ
For eighteen years paster of the
Rome Presbyterian Church.
While yet in life's meridian
The Master called him
to exchange
"The Conflict"
for
"The Crown"
And he entered into
Rest.

WWT MS. (WC, NjP).

From Ellen Axson Wilson

My own darling,   Sav. March 20/92.

We have a beautiful bright day again,—much milder too, and the children seem really quite well, so all looks favourable for our getting off tomorrow night. I am very glad they are enjoying two or three days more of this sunshine. They still look well; have not been pulled down by these little attacks. One lady says Nellie is the most perfectly beautiful human being she ever saw. She is charmingly sweet and affectionate to the whole family;—is especially devoted to Aunt Ella. We were talking about you the other day in bed, and I said "Mama wants to see Papa *so* much, poor Mamma!" and you should have heard the caressing *reassuring* tone in which she said "Papa will come to see 'ou, Mamma;—he'll come!" Bless her little heart!

Thanks, dear, for telling me so much about the New York lecture. I hope you will never let your modesty stand in the way of giving me full satisfaction on all these points,—of telling me what everybody said and appeared to feel about you and your speeches &c. That is very satisfactory as regards the "raise," as far as it goes. Let us hope that Dr. Patton may be prevented from "forgetting." And what about the professor of economics? Surely something is to be done about that![1] Can't Dr. Patton be persuaded under the circumstances to leave the matter in the hands of you and Mr. Sloane?

I have no recollection, dear, of being "depressed" on the morning in question or any morning indeed; I assure you darling that my spirits are all that could be desired.

You may count on me to send you the telegram if circumstances permit!

I am very sorry you did *not* stay in New York. I am *perfectly sure*, dear, that nothing dreadful would have happened. I *know* that even if you wanted to you would never really arrive at the point through all the hateful preliminary stages; and apart from that I believe, darling, that I know you better in this respect than you know yourself and I would have the most *absolute confidence* in you under *any* circumstances.

I had a singular example the other day of the *cruelty* of gossip and the impossibility of the public being able to judge of the private affairs of others. Janie Garmany's engagement seems to be a standing joke in the place, even such good people as Aunt Ella laughing about the number of times the day has been appointed, making cruel remarks about his wanting to be rid of her, &c. The other day in the course of a long drive the poor girl was moved to be confidential and then I found what a pitiful tragedy the wise public had converted into a roaring farce. It is too long a tale for the present, but they have been engaged eight years,—since she was a child indeed,—three years ago she became *stone blind* on the day on which she was to have been married, and remained so for a year. This was caused by ill health and many sleepless nights spent nursing a dying father. And just to think that the people in my circle here who presume to judge of her most private affairs are really so ignorant of her that they did not even know she had been blind! Then the day was appointed again and he became desperately ill, and the marriage was "indefinitely postponed[.]" Says the wise public "why *"indefinitely,"*— "singular that they were not married as soon as he recovered, he evidently wants to be out of it;—and 'they say' the engagement *is* finally broken." Whereas the sad and simple fact is that he never *has* recovered but is dying of consumption. They are both anxious to be married anyhow,—she wants to take him to the South of France, but her family oppose the "sacrifice." Evidently Mamma's way of absolutely refusing ever to "sit in judgment on her neighbour" is not only Christianity but common sense, for how is it possible for us to see into his *heart*; and "out of *it* are the issues of life"

Will you please do me a favour, viz write to Mr. Kennard and ask him to send to Mrs. Julia McLeod, 167 Barnard St Savannah all the facts that he conveniently can about the workings of his "New South B. & L. Ass."[2] You know about the Woman's Exchange here? The church ladies have themselves undertaken the enormous task of making the money to rebuild the burnt "S. S. & Lecture-room[,]" the general resources of the church having been entirely exhausted in restoring the main building. They are doing splendidly—making many weeks $100.00, & averaging very high. But all this money lies idle in bank, & Mrs. McLeod is much excited over my report of this Association. Of course though they must be *very* conservative in their investments. Will you ask Mr. Kennard if he honestly thinks his institution *safe* enough to receive trust moneys of this kind? Ask him if he has any idea of being here soon; they would like extremely to meet him. I would write to him for them but I havn't his address. And will you please write at once,—if you have not done so,—to Balt. about those photographs? There is still no sign of them and I fear it is a total loss. It is *so* provoking. I have not that address either.

But it is almost dinner-time, I have been interrupted by two visitors—though it *is* Sunday, and so I must bring this long chat to a close. How I wish, love, that it was a chat! Wouldn't you like a long talk and a long walk with me in this sweet sunshine? Oh how I wish you could have been here too! I want so much for people here to know you. How I should have liked to take you to church this morning and let everyone see you, though I fear my feelings during the services would not have been as devout as they might be; *pride* would have been the prodominant feeling. In fact I am crazy to "show you off," as I am doing the children, to all my friends! Of course I tell everybody about you & show them your picture; but seeing is believing you know; as it is I suppose they consider me partial. They all admire your picture though as much as my heart could wish. (By the way, it is *very* inconvenient to have it only in a book,—have you ordered those others?) If you could hear what they say you would never think again that you are not handsome; you dear noble-looking, splendid, brilliant *magnificent* man! There isn't any word or combination of words in the language which would do you justice or tell you more than the smallest fraction of what your little wife thinks and feels about you. With all my heart & thought & life,

Your own   Eileen.

ALS (WP, DLC) with WWhw notations on env.: "6 Wh.   2 & 7 Pet.   3 Dal."
    1 She refers to Dr. Patton's promise, made during the negotiations over Wilson's appointment, that Princeton would soon appoint a man in political economy, thus relieving Wilson of the necessity of giving courses in that subject.
    2 That is, Kennard's New South Building and Loan Association of New Orleans.

To Ellen Axson Wilson

My precious darling,   Princeton, 20 March, 1892

So you did not go to Rome on Friday, after all! My telegram must have surprised and amused uncle Will. not a little. I said 'Did Ellie and the children arrive safely?' He replied 'Letter received to-day will come Tuesday'—and so I spent my dollar and my trouble for very little[.] Still I should have been in wretched ignorance and suspence (not knowing your change of plan since you wrote me that you would start on Friday) if I had *not* telegraphed. It made me much "easier in my mind." Ah, but this is a strenuous, trying business, this of having your whole life and thought bound up in the life of another person who is hundreds of miles away from you, and whose messages are always three days old when they reach you! What a painful range those three days afford a lonely fellow for speculation and anxiety! It's lucky for him when he has no leisure at all, but *must* be working always, and so driving his thought, whether it will or no, away from dangerous places. It's well this New York job is to last as long as it does. What a hold it has given you, my little pet, upon me to have been my wife these seven blessed years! How inextricably thoughts and plans and hopes are connected with you! How central your sweet face is in every picture, whether of the past or of the future, that either my memory or my imagination forms! It sometimes seems almost one and the same thing to live and to think of you. How quickly my heart would die, were there no hope of seeing you familiarly and constantly again!—of perceiving and *knowing* your presence in my life! My sweet guardian, guide, inspirer, how lovely you are in the influence you have exercised over my life; how much you have purified and sweetened and quickened and broadened it, spite of these terrible, imperative passions, dark temptations, horrid moods that remain! Your love has ennobled me; your mind has educated and liberalized me, besides delight-ing me always; your sweet sunny disposition and your charming knack for hoping have lightened my heart of its worst burdens; your enthusiasm has been like wine to my mind! When I get you again in my arms, I shall get, with you, all my courage, insight, strength, gladness, motive back again—and I shall not easily let you go! Oh, for a few tones of my sweet one's voice this Sunday afternoon, surely meant for such music—what would I not give for a kiss, a caress, a direct love message from your eyes! What a difference it makes in everything when you are away—how the old *difficulties* crowd back into everything one tries to do! How the *work* side of everything becomes prominent!

But how much sweeter it will all make your home-coming—like a burst of Spring after a close Winter! There's more *joy* than anything else in loving you, even when you are away from me and I feel the separation most desperately—you are so *provocative* of love: it is so sweet to think of you and to think of you as loving *me*; it is such a delight to think of all the secure past and all the inspiring future, to think that all your charms are for me and my life—and that I am *acknowledged* as

Your own Woodrow.

Love to all, and kisses without number to our blessed little pets.

ALS (WC, NjP).

From Ellen Axson Wilson

My own darling   Savannah Mar. 21/92

The day is perfect,—bright and mild, the children all seem *quite* well & had a splendid night so all seems favourable for the journey tonight.

I have a pretty story on "Marga-Dessie." Yesterday they went to Sunday-school and coming home they were separated, Jessie being with Ellen & M. with Leila. Margaret was very uneasy about Jessie but Leila consoled her by telling her that she would probably find Jessie here. "Where's Jessie" were her first words when Aunt Ella opened the door; and when told that she was not here her face fell sadly. She sat very quiet & wretched-looking for a few minutes and then suddenly jumping up she threw her arms about Leila & said, half-crying, "Cousin Leila, I *can't* stay here without Jessie!" So Leila had to take her out to look for Jessie. In the meantime Ellen says Jessie was worrying in the same way about Margaret. They stopped at a cousin's and when they left Jessie literally *ran* all the way home "to see where Margaret was." But alas for sentiment!—Jessie explains that she was afraid Margaret would eat up all the supper! But it is breakfast time & I must stop. I will telegraph you of our safe arrival in Rome.

I love you, dear, "with all the smiles, tears, *breath* of all my life" and am in every thought,   Your own   Eileen.

All send love & the children kisses

ALS (WC, NjP).

Two Letters to Ellen Axson Wilson

My own darling,   Princeton, 21 March 1892

I took dinner yesterday after chapel with Prof. Packard (and the Fines), and as I was coming away he sent his regards to you in a most earnest and cordial manner. Mr. Arnold has done the same several times—and Mrs. McCosh—and the Fines—and the Greens[1]—and Miss Ricketts[2]—in short, everybody who has had a chance. You are very much beloved, my sweet darling (You should have heard Mrs. Bird[3] of Baltimore sounding your praises when I went to tell her good-bye!) Perhaps its fortunate for me that nobody but myself has the chance to know *how* lovable and charming you are: there might be some combination formed to take you away from me! Do you think that you would be as charming then as you are now? Does your devotion to me make you *more* charming, I wonder, by bringing out the sweet *woman* traits that you possesses in such delightful perfection.

Ah, my love, how I dote on this diminishing calendar from which I tear a leaf for each day that is gone! If only it did not bring threats, fears, of sickness for you! How I love to see the time passing which separates you from me! How my hope dwells upon the moment when I shall see you and the precious baby girls once more! But, I find I must not dwell on that—for all it is couched in *words* of joy. I must change the subject.

Maggie Foley's[4] father lingered until Sunday, the 13th, when he died—the *disease* cured, they said, but too late for his strength. He was buried on Wednesday. Already they have made arrangements to continue to work the farm with the assistance (and, I suppose, under the direction) of a man who agrees to do it for his board—devoting, I presume, only a part of his time to it. Mrs. Harris[5] told me all this. I have not seen Maggie or any of her sisters. I will try to see her this week if possible—though my two days in New York make it difficult. I hope that after this week I shall have to go only once a week. I have seen very few people indeed since I got back, I have been obliged to keep so constantly and so closely to the task of preparing lectures. One afternoon I made some calls, but that's all. I called on Mrs. Brown,[6] who seems about as usual, on Mr. and Mrs. Green, and on Prof. Shields, who had invited me to dine with him the very evening I dined with the Arnolds and Miss Clarke. That evening, by the way, was my only "evening off" so far.

You will be glad to know that I consulted Dr. Wikoff about that pain I used to imagine to be in the region of the vermiform appendage, and that he concludes that it is only a partial obstruction of the *bile duct* (it is nowhere near the said appendage)—the duct which conveys the bile from the liver to the bowels. I am now, therefore, duly taking medicine before every meal.

If I could venture on a love letter to-day, I could tell you of some sentiments which ought to make you very happy if you like to be loved passionately,—even tragically; but I believe that I had better wait until another time. Kiss the children for me as often as you think of me and give all a great deal of love, keeping for yourself all you can possibly want from

Your own Woodrow

1 Undoubtedly the Rev. Dr. and Mrs. William Henry Green of 38 Stockton Street.
2 Henrietta Ricketts, 80 Stockton Street.
3 Mrs. William Edgeworth Bird.
4 A servant who had earlier worked for the Wilsons.
5 Probably the widow of William Wirt Harris, late Treasurer of the college, of 342 Nassau Street.
6 Susan D. Brown, a widow who lived at 65 Stockton Street.

My own darling,   Princeton, 22 March, 1892

I went to call on the Ricketts[1] yesterday afternoon, carrying the children's photographs with me. I wish you could have seen her delight (I mean Miss Ricketts', of course) with the pictures! It would have done your heart good: it was delightful—as spontaneous and complete as a mother's. She did not look as *you* did when you first saw the proofs—nobody can look as you do because nobody is so beautiful or can summon their whole soul into their eyes as you can, looking more like a glad angel than anything else—but she was as much excited in look and manner and exclamation as nature (a very generous nature in respect of enthusiasm) would permit, and I was immensely gratified. She made a very interesting remark about Jessie, by the way. She said that when she first saw that little mixture of boyishness and maidenly sensibility she had the most vivid and "singular" impression that here was a child "who had a *career* ahead of her." Had she ever told you that?

I saw Maggie Foley on the street yesterday. She is looking *better* than I ever saw her look—says she received your letter (what was it about?), that she will come back to us when you return, and the family is getting on very nicely. Mrs. Harris told me a rather touching thing. Mary [Foley] told her that before her father died he charged them to be good to their mother, "because, you know, Mrs. Harris," she added, "he knew that we loved him better than we ever loved her."

I met Mrs. St. John[2] at the Ricketts. She seems a good deal more quiet, and somewhat older, than she did before her recent critical illness, but her health, apparently, is quite restored. She walks, she says, two or three miles at a time. She repeated, by the way, a compliment which had been paid you by "a very talented, interesting man." Someone asked where you were and he replied "She's down among the roses, where she belongs." Wasn't that as pretty (I am sure it was as appropriate) a compliment as you ever received, my little treasure?

This is a three lecture day, as yesterday was—I am writing between lectures 5 and 6, in a somewhat fatigued condition, as you may imagine—but I am not half so tired speaking as I am waiting for the telegram which ought some hours since to have announced your arrival in Rome. Is it possible that you can have forgotten me temporarily—and how anxious I would be to learn how that journey ended that has kept me upon such tenterhooks ever since I learned of what sort—with how many changes—it would be? I shall wait a little while and then telegraph to ask.

The medicine Dr. Wikoff gave me is evidently doing me good. I am still *indigestive*, so to speak, but I am not so much so as I was.

To-morrow I shall be in New York and shall have to send you one of those scribbled notes which I so hate to send, and which, I am afraid, you hardly care to receive, so little of myself or of anything else can I put into them. Would you rather I should not write at all on those days?

Oh, how passionately, yearningly, desperately I love you, my sweet, sweet Eileen, my little wife!   Your own Woodrow

ALS (WC, NjP).
    [1] Henrietta and her mother, Eliza Ricketts, widow of Palmer Chamberlaine Ricketts.
    [2] Julia Stockton (Mrs. Richard C.) St. John, 73 Stockton Street.

From Stockton Axson

Middletown Conn
My dear Brother Woodrow: March 23 1892
    I forwarded to Sister at Rome yesterday (Tuesday) the ideas for Father's epitaph together with such suggestions as I had to offer.[1] I agree entirely with you that the inscription should be brief.

I daresay you find it desolate enough living a bachelor's life now, and, though sorry to hear that you are suffering with your stomach, am scarcely surprised when I remember how sensitive you are in that quarter, especially when living on hotel diet. I suppose however it will not have to last much longer, will it?

I fear that you are working too hard. How do you prosper

with your New York lectures? By the way, if you stay over in New York at night at all, you had better take an evening off and go to see Daly's company in Tennyson's new play,[2] which according to the papers seems to really be making a sensation. Perhaps you have already seen it.

Professor West promised to send me some sort of circular,[3] stating the requirements for the degree but he has not yet done so. If it is no trouble to you will you see that something of the kind is sent me.

I dont want to add an iota to the burden of your present duties, but if at faculty meeting or elsewhere you happen to see Professor West I should be glad if you will find out something for me on the following points.

1. How large a proportion of philology will be required of me in working up my major. And what do they mean by *philology*. I have come to find that of all terms this is one of the most indefinite. If they mean a mastering of some of the larger principles of philological science such as I can get from Müller, Whitney &c, this will be a great relief.

2. For a minor what sort of work will they require in History; my idea of the sort of history which I will need as a student of literature is I suppose somewhat popular. It seems to me that what I most want is a clear understanding of the most salient features of modern European history, together with a comprehension of the varying (or growing) temper of the general public as it is manifested in succeeding periods.

3. What is meant by the History of Philosophy? Anything more than the grinding up of some good text-book (Schwegler, for instance)?

Lastly, and altogether most important, what sort of thesis will be required? If they require a philological thesis I fear that that will settle matters finally with me. Or will they allow me to write a purely literary thesis?

In thinking over the matter recently I have thought that something might be done with a subject something like this: The History of English Literary Criticism. This would probably begin with Sidney and come down through Matthew Arnold, a subject broad enough in all conscience, perhaps too broad.

The object would be to point out the various methods of criticism (including of course varying literary ideals) which have prevailed among English writers. For example, to take three very distinct periods, in the time of Dryden, Temple, Swift and Pope there was a continual squabble about the relative merits of the "Ancients" and the "Moderns"; the ideal being Classicism, naturally literary criticism was based for a large part on Aristotle and the classic writers.

Later on we have the narrowly subjective and arbitrary rules laid down by such men as Kames and Blair.

And lastly, I suppose that the prevailing type of broader and loftier modern criticism may be said to be inductive and inter-pretive. The idea is very loose in my head yet and it may not do at all (I havent had an opportunity of speaking with Professor Winchester about it), but I mention it merely to ask if *any* such broad, general "merely literary" topic would be accepted at Prince-ton as subject for a thesis. I know that the Hopkins authorities would turn pale at the thought of allowing a candidate for a degree to waste his time in such trifling.

I hope that you will manage to at least *exist* until the return of Sister and the children.

With warmest love I am

Very affectionately yours   Stockton Axson

ALS (WP, DLC) with WWhw notation on env.: "*Ans.*"; also WWhw and WWsh notes for a reply on letter and env.

¹ Stockton's letter to Ellen is missing, but his suggested copy for the epitaph, written on a loose page, is still in WP, DLC.

² Lord Tennyson's comedy, *The Foresters*, based on the legend of Robin Hood and with music by Sir Arthur Sullivan, had opened at Daly's Theatre on March 17, 1892, and had been warmly praised by the critics.

³ Stockton had obviously talked to Professor Andrew F. West about the possi-bility of coming to Princeton for graduate study and about the requirements for the Ph.D.

To Ellen Axson Wilson

My own darling,   New York, 23 March, 1892

This time I am writing, before the lecture, (my topic is 'Sover-eignty' and I am going to read that *paper* on Sovereignty which I prepared for the Philosophical Club of the Faculty—a great serv-ing of *comfort*) from a most delightful place. I am sitting at a table which stands in the gallery of the Law Library of the Equitable Building—where the rooms of the Law School are—by a window, practically in the sixth storey, which looks *down* upon Trinity churchyard and *out* upon the bay. On a clear day the view is glorious. To-day is not clear, but wet and foggy and wretched in all respects.

I shall try to make this the last *Wednesday* (till the latter part of April) on which I shall lecture—coming *once* a week, on Fri-days only.

I came up here to study law. I have six volumes of law reports before me—and I have studied *some*—but thoughts of you fill both my head and my heart so full that I can think of and do nothing else. I must go down and get my lunch, for wh. there's just about time enough before the lecture. But here's the fullest love message you ever had, darling! And how much that is to say, it would be impossible for me to express. My love for you, and yours for me, are indeed the breath of my life. With a full heart,

Your own Woodrow

Love to all. Your telegram about your safe arrival was a *great* comfort.[1] Oh, for another! My heart feels as if it were about to *break*.

ALS (WC, NjP).
  [1] This telegram is missing.

From Ellen Axson Wilson

My own darling,   Rome [Ga.] Mar 23/92
    You have of course received my telegram and know we are safe. Indeed I think I crowded a good many facts into those ten words. The journey was *much* pleasanter than the one South because we had those delightful sleepers with no upper berths and with *large* comfortable dressing rooms. There was but one other passenger, (excuse pencil—the pen was intolerable) an old gentleman from Boston who was going to Marietta. He devoted himself to the children. I had paid the porter beforehand to help "change" at Atlanta. The conductor & this old gentleman also assisted so I had help enough and to spare. We had to sit for an hour in the waiting room & really you yourself could not have been more thoughtful & attentive than this old man. He is a great friend of King Cooper, who married Josie Sibley; was his confidant in all his love troubles. When he left us at Marietta I told him to tell Mr. Buttolph & Mrs. Sibley that he had seen us, & just a minute after in rushed Mr. Buttolph & King Cooper to see me,—our old friend having found them at the station. And do you know that Josie has left her husband,—temporarily of course—& gone to New York to study art again! Isn't it a shame? It seems she married him only under agreement that she should never have any cares of housekeeping &c, & should be perfectly independent to come & go as she pleased.
    Nobody met me here because it seems Uncle R. had telegraphed only when I would leave *Sav.* not when I would reach here, & the station-master here told them I could not get here until three. But of course I had no trouble, just took a carriage & came up. My trunks though have not come yet, but I hope for them on this morning's train.

All are well & look natural except of course Margie[1] who is immensely grown & improved. She is quite handsome. You need not be worried about my visit, dear, for you know our old Martha is cook now & that insures good and clean food, & I am so perfectly at home with them that I don't hesitate to ask for anything I want. I keep a fire in my room all the time for instance. The spring seems to be quite as far advanced as in Sav.—gardens full of flowers, trees in blossom &c, so you need not be anxious about the climate. The weather was ideal yesterday, but it is raining today.

Miss Ida called yesterday & drove me all about the town & East Rome; there has been a great deal of *building* but no special improvement. The Tedcastles[2] have a great *mansion* on the highest point of the Brower[3] property overlooking the river. It has fine *grounds*, a splendid drive leading up to it and, they say, all the latest "Yankee improvements" inside. They touch a button, for instance, lying in bed & light the gas anywhere in the house. Agnes has called to see me twice,—before I came & yesterday, when I missed her as I was driving.

I saw Aunt Annie & two of her boys,[4] honest looking ugly little chaps. Birdie[5] is with her Uncle in S. C.

A nice nurse was awaiting me here when I came, Rosa, Martha's niece. She is a school-teacher & a very pleasant looking girl. You asked about the Sav. nurse: oh yes, she staid with me until I left, and she was good-natured & the children liked her, but so green & stupid that I did not trust her to put them to bed or do anything for them alone except watch them at play. I expect to get Maggie [Hulsey] when I go to Gainesville.

When I waked this morning I found that the courses had begun! I decided to wait a few hours though before sending the telegram so as to be perfectly sure they were normal. I *am* sure now—at eleven or twelve,—and will send the telegram as soon as possible. I won't say how glad I am, darling, for your sake more than my own. Now I shall write to Sister Annie.[6]

Can you send me Nellie's old* cloak? I need it *dreadfully*. I think it is hanging up in your room behind the curtain but if not it is in one of those two wooden boxes in the trunk room & *near the top*. And you could put my photo. colours inside the bundle. But I am worn out trying to write with this stub. There are apparently no pen no knife no paper & no stamps in the house. I must wait to write more till my trunk comes. Your letter so fortunately *mis*directed reached me in Sav. just before I left. I have had two here, *such* sweet ones, but I can't answer them today. But I love you Woodrow, darling, devotedly passionately entirely I am forever   Your little wife,   Ellie

*The brownish one with faded velvet collar & cuffs.

ALS (WP, DLC).
   [1] Margaret Bliss Hoyt, daughter of Dr. William D. Hoyt. Margaret was seventeen.
   [2] Agnes and Arthur Tedcastle.
   [3] That is, the property formerly owned by Abraham T. H. Brower, husband of Wilson's first cousin, Jessie Bones Brower. The Browers had moved to Chicago.
   [4] Anna Cothran Hoyt, widow of Robert Taylor Hoyt. She had three sons, Nathaniel, Robert Motes, and Wade Cothran.
   [5] One of the two living daughters of Anna Cothran Hoyt, Elizabeth Cothran or Mary Mitchell Hoyt.
   [6] About the possibility of their visiting the Howes in Columbia.

From Ellen Axson Wilson

Rome Ga. 3/23 1892

Will consider Roses invitation to go to Asheville. All well
                                        E A Wilson

Hw tel. (WP, DLC).

To Ellen Axson Wilson

Princeton, 24 March, 1892

Oh, my precious, precious darling, how shall I express the profound joy, the infinite, unspeakable relief I experienced upon receiving that cipher telegram! I found it waiting for me when I got back from New York yesterday afternoon: and how much sunnier the world has seemed ever since—how much easier my work, how much surer all plans and hopes! I did not realize the dreadful weight of the anxiety that had been making all my days and all their work a wearing struggle. Now I can work with a light heart, an unhesitating courage—with certainty, ease, speed—everything that will keep me in health and hope! Oh, how fervently do I thank God for his mercy in delivering my darling from that long toiling illness! *That* is what was slowly breaking my heart. *I* did not deserve anything—this is a mercy to *you*, and I am grateful to the bottom of my heart.

Now, darling, all your plans may be reconstructed. You shall go to Gainesville and take Maggie [Axson] somewhere with you afterwards, if Aunt Lou will permit,—after staying in G. as long as Aunt Lou's plans permit. You shall go to Columbia (write to sister *at once*, please, dearest, to ascertain her plans) and then— (or before, if it would suit sister's plans better, and our own,) to Asheville—for you *must* make good the statement of that telegram, you know! Oh, how happy I am! How glad I can be *always* now, thinking of my precious little wife and incomparable sweetheart and of my delightful little girls among those who love them and whom they love. Be sure, darling, to enjoy everything and every moment, so that when I see you again (ah, me!) I shall find you looking as I wish, your eyes fuller than ever of joy and sweetness, veritable windows of delight, your cheeks full of the richest colour, your whole system quickened, to meet me with higher pulse and keener, more open joy than ever. Make it your chief business to gain in spirits and in flesh—worry about nothing, knowing that you are thereby storing up delight for your husband's eyes and heart when he shall see you again. Oh, love, I feel like a boy to-day! I could not, if I tried, find terms extravagant enough in which to express my spirits—my joy, my ecstatic love for you and delight on your account. I mean to keep that telegram among my treasures. It has given me a new lease of life. Ah, if I could only cover you with kisses—smother you with caresses, overwhelm you with both together! I should ask nothing more. I hate (pardon me for saying it, my love!)—I hate the thought of the thing that put you in jeopardy—I mean I hate the thought of being so selfish as ever to indulge myself again at your expense by never so remote a possibility. I have suffered nothing short of torments of desire lately—am suffering them daily now (what I am made of or what is to become of me, I can't imagine)—but I know that I love you with absolute purity and devotion—I know that I am happy in nothing so much as your safety and happiness—that except as it might affect you, I don't care what I suffer—that I am just now the happiest man in the world, glorified by your love, my own love for you, your happiness, my own identification with you! My matchless wife and queen! God bless you!   Your own Woodrow

ALS (WP, DLC).

Notes for a Letter to Stockton Axson

[c. March 24, 1892]

Mem. for Stock[1]
English Lit.

Thesis approved—special examination + general on Eng. lit.
Philology

   Anglo-Saxon (Sweet's grammar & reader) general gram. knowledge, and ability to read ord. prose and poetry.
   Mid. Eng.—special knowledge of 14th cent'y Eng. with ref to Chaucer—rest of M. E. more general.

"Elizabethan Eng.["]—general knowledge.
Philosophy
　　Prelim. Logic (Jevons) Psy. (Sully). Hist'y of Phil. Schweg-
　　　　ler + Locke, Berkeley and Hume (Ency Brit)
　　If minor, These authors (Eng. empirical movement) with thor-
　　　　oughness, reading their works and being able to give his-
　　　　torical connexions, expound, criticise,—*or* some other equal
　　　　period.

WWhw MS. (WP, DLC).
　1 Wilson had just talked with West and was preparing to answer the questions raised in Stockton's letter of March 23, 1892.

From Ellen Axson Wilson

My own darling,　　　　　　　　　　　Rome [Ga.], Mar. 24/92
　I received *two* sweet letters from you yesterday, & that was
indeed a red letter day; though I fear I shall have to pay for it
by having none today. I am in despair now because one of those
is *lost*; I laid it on a table for a moment and it vanished into thin
air!—and I had only read it hastily *once*! But the disorder and
confusion of this house are so stupendous that I suppose I should
be glad if I don't lose the children—if they escape being buried
under some pile of rubbish. But between my lost letter & my lost
trunks I am like a wandering spirit today seeking rest and finding none. I have been out myself this morning to try and trace
those trunks, & they declare that they have now heard from them
in Atlanta & that they will be here tonight. I went to both stations
to look for them. Then I had to go and buy paper, pen, stamps &
a flannel shirt for Nellie. The poor child has been wearing *mine*
this morning[,] she having come to grief with her own. Don't
be alarmed,—I have on one of Aunt F's![1] I had one of Will's[2] for
her but being a dirty looking *red* she screamed violently when I
tried to put it on her!
　I had a very pleasant visit yesterday from Anna Harris & we
are to spend the day there[3] Sat. Another old class-mate also called
with a very pretty little girl; she has five—has had *seven*.
　It seems that Aunt Annie is at odds with Uncle Will, *most* unreasonably. It is of course too long a story to burden a letter
with. But it is going to make things rather unpleasant for me.
Aunt Annie does not visit here & she wants me to go up there &
stay with her.
　I had a letter this morning from Cousin Emma Sibley, Josie's
mother, begging me to make her a visit in Marietta, but of course
I don't want to and shall make some excuse.
　I went this morning to see about the stone. It will cost about

$40.00 I believe, so that if *you are sure* you can spare it now you had better send me a little more than $50.00. Stock will pay half but I don't know how soon I will get it from him. Uncle R. cannot give me any from the children's estate for such a purpose without an order from the court. He spoke of getting one but as the sum is not very large anyhow, I don't like to seem to him to grudge it, and will say nothing more to him about it. The stone mason thinks he can have it finished and put up next week in order that I may see it. I hope Stock will write promptly about the inscription for the man must have it by Tuesday. I like No. 2 *much* better, it is very good. Don't you think it would sound better though to leave out the words "he was." If you do, will you re-arrange the lines properly & return? Perhaps it would be more *consecutive*—so to speak—to have it something like this,—"For eighteen years pastor of the Rome Presbyterian Church. A faithful servant of Jesus Christ who while yet in life's meridian was called by the Master to his exceeding great reward." This is merely a suggestion for you to work out if you think best. I wish I could write you a *nice* letter, dear; my heart so overflows with love that I should like to try and put some of it into words, but I really can't in this confusion. But my *heart* is speaking to you at all times, darling, and trying to tell you how I love *love love* you.   Your little wife   Ellie

Will that little silver watch of yours run? If so will you send it to me in the bundle with the cloak? It is in the basket of silver at Mrs. Ricketts. I find it extremely annoying to travel without a timepiece.

The marble man has just sent me word that the headstone is $45.00.

ALS (WC, NjP).
    [1] Aunt Florence Hoyt.
    [2] William Dana Hoyt, age twelve at this time.
    [3] That is, at Anna Harris's home in Rome. She lived with her father, Judge R. R. Harris.

Report of a Lecture at the New York Law School[1]

[March 25, 1892]
[V. *Sovereignty and the Nature of Government,*
according to the Decisions of the
Supreme Court of the United States][2]
Almost all the cases which concern this topic are the early

    [1] For the provenance of this document, see the Editorial Note, "Wilson's Lectures at the New York Law School."
    [2] The title comes from Wilson's notes for this lecture.

cases decided by the Supreme Court of the United States and in them the judges had the habit of giving their opinions seriatim, and we have the awkward condition of individual opinion containing authentic law so that in head notes of the cases you will find a specific root [rule?] held out, each one of which is an authorized root. Each set of premises is part of the law of the case, consequently you find idiosyncrasies creeping in.

In the first place, something of the French philosophy has crept into that court. The early cases speak of government as if it were resting upon an actual agreement of the persons forming it. In Calder vs. Bull, 3 Dallas 388, Justice Chase gave the opinion of the court: "An act of the legislature contrary to the great first principles of the social compact cannot be considered a rightful exercise of legislative authority: the genius and the spirit of our state government amount to a prohibition of such legislation. Our constitutions are formed according to choice and not according to an abstract philosophy of politics." He says a law which would punish a citizen of Connecticut would be inconsistent with the original compact and out of keeping with our constitutional law. An act of the legislature making a man judge in his own case would also be unconstitutional, and so Mr. Justice Chase weaves out of his imagination other legislations seeming to him contrary to justice. This was an *obiter dictum* and we are not bound to it because it had nothing to do with the case in hand, in which the legislature of Connecticut had undertaken to intervene in the probation of a will. The legislature passed a special act re-opening the question, and allowing a period of six months after the new decision for an appeal, and the question was whether this was a constitutional act. It was decided by the court that it was a legitimate proceeding, and Mr. Chase proceeded to reflect on the original compact and said: "If the legislature had done something inconsistent with the original compact, it would have been unconstitutional." In the same case, p. 395, the customs of the community not only might, but did form part of the constitution of Connecticut. It ran back to deliberate choice. An integral part of it was made out of the habits of the community. The 109 U.S. 513 decides that the right of eminent domain belongs to every independent government, is an incident to sovereignty, and requires no constitutional provision. This statement infers that our courts hold that the government, as well as the people, is a sovereign body and maintains that the right of eminent domain attaches to every independent government because, incident to sovereignty, the courts hold with regard to the original nature of government that in the construction of the Constitution we must look to the history of the times and examine the things which then existed to ascertain the old law, the mischief, and the remedy. We must regard them as a product of past circumstances; as James McIntosh said: "A government grows and is not made." The history of the times is not the constitutional act, the assembling of a constitutional convention which forms instruments to be adopted by the vote of the people. But in order to find out what the people wanted we must look to the history of the times, and the generating principle is experience. In 3 Dallas, it said usage is part of the Constitution.

Look to the Supreme Court's definition of a state. Justice Paterson said (in 3 Dallas 93): A distinction was taken at the bar between a state and its people. I cannot comprehend such a distinction. By a state forming a republic I had not meant the legislature of a state but all the citizens who are integral parts of it. All taken together form the body politic. In a great republic the sovereignty resides in the great body of the people, not as so many individuals but only in their political capacity. If the commonwealth of Pennsylvania consisted of, say, for example, 100,000 persons, 99,999 of them would not constitute a state because one was missing. You would not then have present the state, because the whole citizenship constitutes the state. Because of considerations of convenience, though waiving considerations of principle, it has been arranged that the majority should rule and that it should not be necessary to have the assent of all, only of such part of them that could agree in greater numbers than the other side. In Texas against White, 7 Wallace 700, Justice Chase says: "A state is a people or community. The people in whatever territory dwelling, either temporarily or permanently, and whether existing under regular government or looser ties constitute the state (a sort of movable changing state, like the waves of the sea). This is undoubtedly the fundamental idea upon which our constitutions are established." In another case where the decision was rendered by the Chief Justice, 7 Wallace 39, Luther vs. Borden, the court decided that a change of constitution was a question to be decided by the political and not by the judicial authority. It was a Rhode Island case. Rhode Island had retained her colonial charter as her state constitution without going through any change,—the old charter was the new constitution. By the year 1842, so many changes had taken place that the people were discontented. The charter formed something like a monopoly in which it was possible for a minority of the voters to control the government. The government being a monopoly had no idea of consenting to any change; but the body of the people were so discontented that about 1842, by an outside movement independent of the existing government, they elected representatives who formed a new constitution for the state, setting aside the old charter government. The old government interfered with force and continued the charter, but subsequently they themselves called a convention and modified the old constitution. The question was brought about by that general situation. Fundamental to the case the Supreme Court had to decide which was the legal government of Rhode Island. The court said it cannot be decided. Such a question is a political question, not a judicial one. It must be determined by the predominance of the best party in Rhode Island; the party that can whip the other by peaceful means will decide the question. It had been decided the people were sovereign. The people of Rhode Island wanted the change but were prevented from realizing it by the intervention of a minority. The court said, we cannot give to the majority their sovereignty because the minority are in a better strategic position, which means that the court is driven to the principle that constitutions are not created by popular choice but by situation, by contest, and by compromise of forces, are brought into existence by political powers which may or may not derive their support and sanction from the majority of the people. The case was settled by the government which proved to be sovereign notwithstanding it was not backed by the mass of the people in Rhode Island. Theory here went to pieces. 17 Howard 393. The court decided with reference to the government of South Carolina that certain prerogatives of the English sovereign remained with the government of the state, and the powers are *parens patriae*. The King is the father of his country, the guardian and elder of the people. His decisions were a decisive determination of what was justice among his subjects. It was a question of the administration of justice, and the court decided that the old prerogatives of the crown had remained with the people. This implies that the government had a history aside from the framing of the constitution. The other theory was that nothing which the people had not put into the constitution remained there, but here the courts said that this was the projective part of the government of England, and in so far as the people had not modified the government it retains the prerogatives of the English crown.

The court proceeds a step farther and asserts the absolute despotism of the body politic. The power existing in every body politic is an absolute despotism. In constituting the government, it distributes that power as it pleases and imposes what checks it pleases. Livingston vs. Moore, 7 Peters 546. This opinion affected the divisions of powers, especially the exercise of certain judicial powers by the legislature of Pennsylvania under its constitution. The people can mix the judicial with the legislative or the executive as it pleases, may do just as it chooses.

According to Marshall, the government of the Union is a government of the people, in form and in substance. It emanates from them and is to be exercised directly on them and for their benefit. (My will being supreme creates an agent which is to boss me. This seems to be inconsistent.) This government, though limited in its powers, is yet supreme in its sphere of action. This would seem to result from its nature. It represents all and acts for all. This language is found in 4 Wheaton 405.

This sovereignty residing in the people is nevertheless subject to division. In this declaration we here say according to the Austinian theory: We have whole sovereignty, also divided sovereignty. The powers of the general government and of the states, said the Supreme Court, are separate and distinct sovereignties acting separately and independently of each other within their respective spheres (which are marked in the air). They are exercised as separate powers in the same territory (they have ideal differences only). Abelman vs. Booth 62 U.S. 506. A man was arrested by a marshal of the United States, committed by a commissioner of the United States to prison, released by a state judge, was tried in a district court of the United States, convicted by the court, was imprisoned and again released on *habeas corpus* by a state court, and the case was appealed to the Supreme Court of the United States. Wisconsin and the United States act in the same territory and independently of each other. It is intolerable that the United States' sovereignty should be interfered with by the sovereignty of Wisconsin in respect to a person, acting under the authority of the United States marshal. This says that the United States forms a single nation and the federal government can legitimately control all individuals or governments. 6 Wheaton 413-14. For all governmental purposes, the states and the citizens thereof are under the same sovereign authority and are governed by the same law. In all other respects the states are necessarily foreign and independent. They are under common subjection, under common laws subject to common authority, but yet necessarily foreign and independent to each other. The opinion is rather incidental. 2 Peters 509. See also 18 Howard 350, where the same opinion may be found.

The people are checked in the exercise of their sovereignty. This is very singular. The Constitution of the United States says the Supreme Court is supreme over the people of the United States aggregately and in their separate sovereignties because they have excluded themselves from the immediate agency in changing the law, and have directed that amendments be made by representation for them. The Constitution is supreme, binding the people as it binds all the governments over the people. Dodge vs. Woolsey 18 Howard 347. This was a question of jurisdiction— whether a stock-holder could sue in the United States courts an Ohio corporation of which he was a member.

Certain of our prohibition friends tried to do certain things. The State of Illinois tried to pass a prohibitory amendment to its constitution which required that the legislature should pass an amendment, submit it to the people, and then repass it by another legislature subsequently to the ratification by the people. In the course of passage through the legislature the bill was wrongly engrossed, fraudulently or negligently, and those who opposed it came to the supreme court and said it was unconstitutional, and the supreme court of Illinois upheld them. The prohibitionists claimed that it was a lot of red tape and asked what is the government of Illinois, and what is it for? Is it not the sentiment of the people that the amendment should pass, and is it not absurd to say the bill should go by the board merely because of a clerical mistake? But the supreme court said the people have tied their own hands. Here the sovereign has created a regency and abdicated. Is the regent sovereign or the man who has abdicated? We are face to face with the picture of a divided and limited sovereign, divided and limited by itself, which resigns its presidency over affairs and takes position in the background.

We have a people limited by their own contract. The states, though making contracts and the law of contracts, are nevertheless themselves bound by contract. The court said: "The state constitution has been changed since the passage of the act chartering the bank." It was a question of the Bank of Ohio. The state chartered the bank and agreed that if the bank paid over a certain part of its receipts it should be released from the payment of taxes. The arrangement was not satisfactory, and the state proceeded to tax the bank notwithstanding the agreement. It was shown that the state constitution had been changed and contained a clause which made it impossible for the legislature to enter into any such an agreement, but the Supreme Court said the state was bound by the old contract. The union of the states was made by each of them conceding a portion of their sovereignty for the benefit of all. The same principles of justice which bind individuals must bind the state. They bind all, through the mutual acquiescence of all in the Constitution. This is not, says the court, because their sovereignty is impaired, but because the exercise is diminished in quantity (when the exercise of my will is diminished I am put into a lunatic asylum) because they have put restraint upon its exercise, in virtue of a voluntary engagement. Dodge vs. Woolsey, *idem.*

In one case the Supreme Court of the United States had to face this question. In a maritime prize case, one of the points brought up was whether the Congress of the confederation before the Articles of Confederation had been made could erect a court of admiralty of any sort, original or appellate jurisdiction; because if it could not erect such a court, certain important rights would have been abrogated. The Continental Congress before and after the Articles of Confederation had authority to constitute a court of appeals with jurisdiction to hear and determine all appeals from courts of admiralty in the several states. The powers of the Continental Congress were revolutionary in their nature, arising out of events, adequate to every emergency and coextensive with the objects to be attained. The Continental Congress was the supreme council of the Union, a body having no constitution—simply a committee of representatives from various states meeting under incongruous instructions. Nevertheless by its own exercise of power, it became the sovereign council of the Union, to exercise any power it could get hold of, and because it got hold of the war powers, it could erect courts of appeal and put into operation all the judicial machinery connected with the administration of prize cases. Government comes into existence by reason of historical circumstances and not by reason of any constitution whatever. Constitutions are the formulations of experience; not originative but formulative in their character. We must find the origin of sovereignty in government actually erected. The Supreme Court when it comes to a case where it would have broken down our system of order must fall back upon the colonial historical idea of government, which forms as crystals form because of the operations of the laws of nature. Its institutions are regulated by this principle, 3 Dallas 55. A self-sovereign power could arise of itself without legal commission or constitutional act.

Chief Justice Marshall says: America has chosen to be a nation, and for many purposes her government is complete, for all objects. It is adequate to the objects to be attained, but the circumstances called for and the nature of the government demand that it is (and in order to find out what the Continental Congress was in respect to power we must inquire what it did).

The people have declared by assent, that in the exercise of all powers given to these objects, it is supreme. It can legitimately control all governments within American territory. The states are members of one empire, for some purposes sovereign and for other purposes not sovereign. 6 Wheaton 414.

To Ellen Axson Wilson

Law Library, P. O. Building,[1] N. Y.,

My own darling,   25 March, 1892

I have just come from the Law School—it is now a quarter to four o'clock—and my last two-law-lecture week, for the present, is over. I can write only the merest note, of a line or two, because of a raging headache—for which West is responsible. He made me drink some California claret last night, which made me wake up with one of my old fashioned headaches—the sort I used to have when city tired. I shall sleep it off to-night—but it made the lecture go hard, I can tell you! But it was a good—an effective —lecture, nevertheless, I believe.

I've had no letter to-day yet (one may be waiting for me in Princeton) and I had none yesterday—but that telegram keeps me in spirits.

Ah, my darling, how I love you, and how sweet it is to live knowing that I am some day to be with you again.

Your own Woodrow

ALS (WC, NjP).
[1] The library of the New York Law Institute, in the United States Post Office Building at Broadway and Park Row, not to be confused with the Law Library of the Equitable Life Assurance Society in the Equitable Building, where the New York Law School had its rooms, and mentioned by Wilson earlier and later in this series of letters.

Two Letters from Ellen Axson Wilson

My own darling,   [Rome, Ga., March 25, 1892]

I write in *desperate* haste for I was prevented by visitors from writing this morning & now I have run from the dinner table to scribble a line before the mail leaves at 3 P.M. My trunks actually came last night after we had spent the whole of three days "stirring" up the officials. I never saw such creatures! The argument of the "unjust judge" proved the only one strong enough to move them. The trunks were in Atlanta all the time, & the officials there not only kept them three days without cause but made me pay 50¢ storage! Was not that adding insult to injury?

We are all very well though we are having "Rome weather."

It has rained most of the time since the day we came, but it is warm and there are also fires all over the house.

I enclose Stock's note so.[1] Wish he had sent them to you. I shall wait for your answer to this before giving the mason the inscription. Please give me your unbiassed judgment, which I shall abide by. His letter has but *this moment* come, and I have not had time to consider his suggestions myself.

I love you, dear, "with the passion put to use in my old griefs; & with my childhood's faith"; and am altogether

Your own   Eileen

My pictures have just come. The little ones are good but the large one poor, *I think*[.] Will send some on to you.

ALS (WC, NjP).
  [1] This enclosure is missing.

My own darling   [Rome, Ga.] Saturday [March 26, 1892]
    Alas, another hasty note today, for I am to spend the day—literally!—with Anna Harris; she is to send for us at *ten o'clock*! It is already half past nine & I am not dressed, having been very busy getting "the wash" together &c. &c.

It is very warm and pleasant this morning, not clear but *promising* to be so before twelve. I am *so* anxious to have a little bright weather so that I may get out to the cemetary, &c.

I received your dear little note from New York yesterday; today I must wait I suppose until I come back from Anna's to hear. You will be glad by the way to know that I found my lost treasure —that letter. The little people all send you scores of kisses, they are as usual winning golden opinions from all sorts of people. I am very glad to come to the old place "and bring my babe and make my boast"(!) but oh! I will be so glad when it is over! It seems to me sometimes that I simply *cannot bear* the separation another week,—that it is just *killing* me. "Oh that I had wings like a dove for then would I fly away and be at rest." Never, *never, never* will I of my own will leave my love again. With all my soul,—with every heart-throb,

Your own wife,   Eileen

ALS (WP, DLC).

To Ellen Axson Wilson

My own precious darling   Princeton, 26 March, 1892
    I want you to sit down before the mirror, if you can find time and place in that disordered house, and describe your appearance

for me. Are your cheeks rosy? Are there lines of fatigue about your
eyes, or do they shine clear and fresh? Do you look plump or is
much travelling and much nursing and much managing making
you look thin,—pulled down? Are the lines of your cheeks rounded
or straight, dragging a little? Please ma'am tell me just how you
feel. Do you feel tired much of the time; or do you feel fresh
and elastic? I am anxious to have *all* of these questions answered,
—and just as much more added of self-description as I can induce you to write,—as you know I should like to have you write.
(I wish you would have a tin-type taken every week and send
them all to me!)

I have tried to get a photograph of myself for you, but Pach
wont turn up. If he does not come the first of the week, I will
order from New York.

I enclose a draft on New York for $75. A week from now the
first of the Quarter will have come and I will send you some
more. I wish, sweetheart, you would let me know how much you
want. I'll send it in big sums occasionally or in small sums regularly, just as you prefer.

I did not understand from uncle Randolph when he wrote
about the division of the money that there was something that
could come out of the portions of the other children to pay for the
stone on papa's grave, but that he held back a certain sum, about
$100, as I recall his letter, *undivided*, to see what the Rome
people might propose doing. I am afraid, therefore, that it will be
necessary to tell him, sooner or later, what the stone cost, in order
that he may complete his division of the money and straighten
out his accounts as executor. I should much rather tell him than
Stock. Stock can't spare any money at all just now, I imagine—
and, if uncle R. hasn't an *undivided* hundred which would cover
Stock's portion of the cost as well as Ed's and Maggie's, you
had better pay the whole sum yourself and say nothing about it
to anybody. But I am afraid uncle R. will have to know,—for,
as a man of business, he will be worried about that undistributed
balance. I think that what he has to get an order of court for is
to sell a security for the purpose—of the sum required. For I think
he said that he held back some one stock with a view to applying
it in that way. However, I am perfectly willing that you should
act upon your own discretion in the whole matter.

My headache is entirely gone, to-day. I slept it off, as I expected, and am feeling all right again.

I got baby's old cloak from the house and sent it off by express
this afternoon with the colours inside—the only ones I could find—
orange and crimson,—except a dark brown. I saw no yellow at all.

I am puzzled over the quiet way in which you speak of, what made me so wild with delight, the coming of the courses. Did you want a baby, so that you might have the last trial over and done with? Are you dreading my threat of another trial—for a boy? If you are, I withdraw it. You shall have no dread that I can remove. I will forego any hope—any instinct—even the greatest, to make you happy. For I love you—oh, I *love* you with all my heart and am altogether   Your own Woodrow

Much love to all—passionate kisses for the sweet little ones.

ALS (WC, NjP).

From Ellen Axson Wilson

My own darling,   Rome [Ga.], March 27 '92

That *delightful* letter written after the receipt of the telegram I found awaiting me on my return from Anna's yesterday. You may be sure I enjoyed it. I fairly laughed aloud with pleasure as I read; your happiness in the fortunate issue out of our scrape was so contagious and I was so happy for your sake and so charmed with your high spirits. Perhaps I should again assure you, by the way, that it has all been perfectly normal.

I went to church this morning and took the children and held quite a reception afterwards. The children were immensely admired and my "youthful" appearance excited as usual general astonishment. It is really absurd by this time for I have not met a single person either here or in Sav. who has not begun the conversation with exclamations over my youth & unchanged appearance. The Warren's in Sav. declared that they "had not thought there was much room for improvement (!) but that I really was prettier than ever." Mr. Baker[1] too expresses the same opinion. But pah! I thought I would try to gratify you by reporting "compliments,"—as you requested, but it's no go—it makes me feel too sick. I will strain a point though and tell you Anna's comment "Well, I should think Mr. Wilson would be proud!" and Martha's,—repeated every time she sees me "La, Miss El-Lou how you does *favour yourself!*" It is funny and pleasant to see Martha's adoration of me and her faithful attachment to all our family. They say that ever since she has been here she has had the habit of frequently looking up my picture in the album and *talking* affectionately to it.

A great many people here and some in Sav. think Jessie looks like Mama. Today for the first time someone said she was like "the Bones girls";[2] they all think your picture is like Mrs. Bones.

By the way did you know that Jessie[3] was South? in Aug. I
suppose. She has been in Atlanta. How I wish I could see her!
If I knew her address I would write her and try to arrange a
meeting.

Minnie Hoyt is coming home soon! The poor child has had an
attack of scarlet fever. You remember she went to Atlantic City
while we were in Balt. for a few days rest? While there she
co[n]tracted this fever; it has been a long though not very severe
case. She has lost so much time that she has apparently given up
the struggle for this year,—poor child! But as she can't write herself yet they know nothing about her plans except that she will
come home soon.

I go to Aunt Annie's on Wed. for three days probably. The
family here are "fighting mad" about it. It is pleasant but at the
same time embarrassing to be so struggled over. I shall leave
here a week from Tuesday I think,—if we get that matter of the
inscription settled in time. I have been so rushed that I have not
written to Sister Annie yet but will certainly do so tomorrow.

Uncle Will is reading "The Little Minister"[4] aloud and we
find it delightful. I was so busy in Sav. that I had time to read
only the first chapters.

It seems to me that I have "supped on horrors" ever since I
came to Rome but the saddest of all the tragedies I have heard
today. You know beautiful Mary Parks who married "Hice"
Howell? They are of course unhappy; it was a case of Beauty &
the Beast,—one of those ["]utterly inexplicable matches." He is a
coarse, brutal, selfish creature & has treated her badly;—that was
to be expected,—but the terrible part is to follow,—it has driven
her to *drink*! Did you ever hear of such a thing? She was actually
on one occasion brought home intoxicated from somewhere on
the street. But Mr. Geochious[5] (!) says she is now fully conscious
of her danger and is making a determined effort to escape. She
has *five* little children.

But it grows late and I must bid my darling 'good-night[.]' Ah
love, what would I not give for a goodnight kiss! The longing to
see you, these latter days especially has been so intense that it
almost seems as though my soul would escape from the more
sluggish body to go and seek you. I find myself unconsciously
reaching out my arms to you and finding alas, only space. Ah
me! I was reading just now in "Ruth" & when I came upon
those wonderful love words of hers you may imagine the echo
they found in my heart. "Entreat me not to leave thee or to return
from following after thee; for whither thou goest I will go and
where thou lodgest I will lodge; thy people shall be my people &

thy God my God. Where thou diest I will die and there will I be buried; the Lord do so unto me and more also if aught but death part thee and me." When she once more finds herself in your arms such will indeed be the heart cry of

Your little wife.

ALS (WP, DLC) with WWhw notation on env.: "College Bill—I. Benet."
  ¹ An old suitor of Ellen's.
  ² The daughters of James W. and Marion Woodrow Bones.
  ³ Jessie Bones Brower.
  ⁴ James Matthew Barrie, *The Little Minister* (London and New York, 1891).
  ⁵ The Rev. George Thomas Goetchius, pastor of the Rome Presbyterian Church, 1885-1900.

To Ellen Axson Wilson

My own darling,   Princeton, Sunday 27 March, 1892

I wish I could believe that you are moderately comfortable where you are. I don't like to think of you as having to worry and manage, even when you are with those whom you love and who love you. I like to think of you as a guest around whom all the establishment turns, for whose pleasure all the household is organized. When you are at home, the work that you do dignifies you—though you do too much of it—and it does not often worry you, for you are mistress, and take such a sweet, beautiful pleasure in making those who depend upon your care comfortable and happy. Oh, what a *sweet*, what an ideal little housewife you are! But when you are away from home I want you to have a veritable vacation and rest. It's hard work taking care of a sensitive fellow like me: and I want you just now to be petted and amused and 'played to' all the time. I shall feel much happier when you are in Columbia and Asheville,—and Gainesville, if things there are following an ordered course. I can't tell you, my darling, how my heart yearns *to have you have a good time*,—a holiday pleasure outing, away from all worry,—even the worry of my too solicitous love! I really believe that I love you well enough to deny myself wholly for your sake.

But I do *not* believe that, if I were King Cooper I could love my wife—a woman who had married me on the condition that I should have no real claim to her—on condition that she should live with me only when she had nothing more attractive to do,— that she should assume no responsibilities that would create a home, and take none but the inevitable risks of personal inconvenience which are inseparable from living with a man at all! That is not love in which there is no capacity or instinct of self-sacrifice[.] I should not want a woman I loved to *make* sacrifices for me; but I should not love, but despise her if she were not *willing* to make them if love should prove to involve them. Mrs. Cooper is stricken from my list.

How different my sweet love is from all these creatures! How complete and womanly, how surpassingly sweet is her love—how full of sacrifices that do not seem such to her, and which, consequently glorify her, and make me feel that there is nothing I would not undergo or suffer to save her from pain. Oh, how it did torture me to think that I had spoiled this trip of yours, this opportunity for rest and recreation, by my selfish self-indulgence! How supreme is the relief and the thankfulness that now fill my heart to overflowing with gladness! Ah, my darling, my whole heart is yours, my whole life—and nothing that I can give is half enough to offer in exchange for your sweet love and wifely devotion—by which I am so wonderfully exalted and strengthened and bettered every way! My conduct ought to be a thousand times more yours than it is. I ought to do *much* more (I *could*, were I not so selfish in my enjoyment of you, do *much* more) for your happiness than I do. And I mean to when you come back— after this terrible proof of how indispensable you are to me—this awful time of waiting and thinking. With all my heart

Your own Woodrow.

Much love for all. Hundreds of kisses for the sweet, *precious* girlies.

ALS (WC, NjP).

From Ellen Axson Wilson

My own darling,   Rome [Ga.] March 28/92

How very, very sorry I am about that dreadful headache! It makes my *heart* ache to think of my poor dear lecturing in the midst of such suffering. It must have been an awful effort! Ah, if I had only been there to try and do something for you afterwards! And to think of your making a really good lecture under such circumstances! What splendid self command! You dear brave fellow, you don't know how proud I am of you!

We have at last a really glorious day. The morning—it is just twelve now,—has passed writing to Sister Annie and Mrs. Sibley[,] making candy—chocolate creams and peppermints—for Mrs. Stevens, and receiving a long call from an old friend Mrs. Whittemore. This afternoon at three I am going driving with Agnes,— and will I suppose miss half a dozen or so calls in the meantime. My friends and I seem to be playing a game of hide and seek. I missed among others, Mr. & Mrs. Goetchious when they called, but they saw the children and she was *raving* then and yesterday over Nellie's head, "It is the head of a genius"; she has seen but one to equal it—a marvellous child of Prof. Joe LeConte's.[1]

But as usual I have been interrupted and must close in haste. I love you darling, I love you with every heart-beat I literally think of you *every* moment, my soul side is always turned toward whatever distractions surround me.

As ever   Your own Eileen

All quite well.

ALS (WC, NjP).
[1] Joseph LeConte, the distinguished geologist, who had formerly taught at the University of Georgia and was at this time a professor at the University of California.

To Ellen Axson Wilson

Princeton, Monday 28 March, 1892

Oh, my sweet, *beautiful* darling! The photographs came this morning and I have been 'taking on' over them, every spare moment, in a way that it would, I suspect, both touch and delight you to see. Oh, they are so pretty, so wonderfully sweet and delightful. Perhaps the smaller one *is* the better—the most wholly unobjectionable—but there is *very* little difference between them in point of excellence, and the bigger one brings out these glorious eyes of yours to much better advantage. The *expression* is what gives the smaller one a slight advantage,—so ineffably pure and sweet and natural and attractive. If I did not have her already, I would barter anything to marry a girl with such a face as that—so *perfectly* pure and so completely bewitching at one and the same time—such a lovely and wholly lovable type of beauty. You are certainly the prettiest girl in the world! The smaller photograph has *another* advantage, and that a very great one[:] *I can carry it in my pocket*—and there it shall always be till I get another which is better, if a better be possible. It has been in my pocket all morning—and I have *felt* it there all over. I am sorry you don't like the larger one. I am altogether satisfied with both.

Ah, sweetheart, what an absorbing passion is this of mine for my peerless darling! How I pity all other men! How I wonder at my own good fortunate [fortune], and feel inspired to live better on account of the sweet trust imposed in me.

Ah, my little lady, how wise is your love—your method of loving. If I did not know by sweet experience how devoid, how totally devoid, of artifice your whole feeling for me is, I should suspect you of shrewd policy in one thing. When you say, in one of your letters, that you trust me *absolutely* and have not the slightest fear of my being betrayed by the terrible temptation to which I am most exposed by nature and temperament, you say the wisest as well as the sweetest thing that a little wife could say. Knowing, as I do *know*, that I might yield to that temptation without any real infidelity to you, and feeling that temptation, as I have recently, more terribly, more overpoweringly than ever before in my life, I wrote the simple truth when I said that I did not *dare* to stay in New York over night. But after you have said that you *do* absolutely trust me to *refrain*—that you would not be afraid to see me go anywhere—what could I do that would not be a betrayal of your love! You tie me hand and foot. I believe I should have resolution enough to *burn up, body and soul*, rather than betray your love! That is my crown—that sweet love of yours—I should forfeit *every*thing, were I to forfeit one iota—one throb of that. I should have nothing more to live for—I should be *ashamed* to live any longer. Your trust seems to me like nothing less than an *awful* responsibility!

"It seems to me sometimes that I simply *cannot bear* the separation another week—that it is just *killing* me." *Ought* I to be sorry that you feel that way? I can't for the life of me help feeling glad! Oh, how shall we *not* enjoy each other when this terrible season of separation is over!   Your own Woodrow

ALS (WC, NjP).

From Ellen Axson Wilson

My own darling,   Rome [Ga.] March 29/92
    We are to have people to "spend the day," so of course I must write a hasty note at break-neck speed;—having had to write two other necessary letters already this morning! I *am so* rushed and hurried here, I fear I shall have to give up trying to write real letters until I reach the quiet of Gainesville.
    I had a charming drive yesterday. It was the one bright day since the day we came. (It is cloudy again today.) Mrs. Stites the mother of Will McKee, who was engaged to Marion Bones, is visiting Agnes and was with us. We found by comparing notes that we were on *the same train* coming south, and both got off at Savannah. And we were both in church together the following Sunday. Will met her there and another singular thing happened then; on the Monday after I met Mrs. Hopkins and she told me she had heard I was in Sav. from "Will McKee"! I asked in surprise "who he was," and was told that he was the stepson of Mr. Stites[,] president of the Poet Society and a prominent northan minister;—Will had recognized me in church.

I heard a great deal about Jessie from Agnes;—her wonderful "smartness" as a housekeeper, and semp[s]tress and amateur photographer &c. She does all the sewing for Helen[1] and the rest and "the girls look as though they had come from the hands of the best professional." She also makes quantities of the most beautiful photographs going through all the processes of development herself, and much of the time she does her house-work because she can't keep servants in the suburb where she lives. She is said to be well but "quite thin from hard work." An interruption—must close abruptly. I love you Woodrow darling deeply, tenderly, passionately, devotedly. I am forever   Your own   Eileen

ALS (WC, NjP).
    [1] Jessie's little sister, Helen Woodrow Bones.

To Ellen Axson Wilson

My own sweet darling,   Princeton, Wednesday 30 March, 1892

Forgive me for not sending you a letter yesterday. It was three-lecture day, and crowded with other engagements besides. Had I *foreseen* all the engagements, I could probably have economised my time better and found an opportunity to write; but, as it was, I was euchered out of my letter altogether. Neither did I receive a letter from you, it being Tuesday,—so that it was a desolate day, with no sort of communion with my darling. I shall take care that it does not happen so again. It makes me feel so dreary—seeming somehow to *add* to our separation.

One of the things that occupied me yesterday was a call upon Dr. Patton, the first I have made. I met George Patton[1] on the street, and he told me that his father was feeling a good deal better and that he was sure he would be glad to see me, if I would call. I went, of course, just as soon as possible. Mrs. Patton received me, most cordially, saying that the Dr. saw almost no one, but was now glad to receive "congenial spirits." She took me upstairs, where I found him sitting in his bed-room, *not* looking very badly, but changed enormously in appearance by the full beard which has grown during his illness. I stayed only about six or eight minutes, because Dr. [William Henry] Green had just seen him, and I was fearful of fatiguing him. He talked principally about my affairs, saying he was anxious to assure me that he knew that I was not as comfortable as I ought to be (he had had a talk, he said, with Cyrus McCormick about me in February) and that he meant to see what could be done so soon as he could attend to anything; that he *hoped* they were not going to lose me to any other institution, and meant to do everything to keep me. I got the impression that he had wanted to see me in order to say these things. Apparently he is at least sure to recover completely; the length of the process is alone doubtful. *He* hopes to preside at Commencement.

Our Committee is just now in the midst of some distressing matters of discipline. There are a couple of loose women (strangers) in town, and some of the boys have been discovered entertaining them in one of the college rooms. As usual, the men we have caught are not the most guilty, but they are guilty enough to deserve severe discipline, and we are not without hopes of catching the rest of at least one of the 'crowds' concerned. It's an ugly business altogether.[2]

I spent a very pleasant evening calling on the Arnolds recently. Mr. Arnold was not at home, but I saw Miss Susie and Mrs. Arnold. The latter was down stairs, her arm out of its sling, going about, apparently, without any pain. She was in excellent spirits and very agreeable indeed. I took your photographs over and Miss Susie spent the whole time I was there looking at them. Mrs. A. did not like them—'they were not as pretty as you were, and the smaller one made you look too old'; but I think this last judgment was due to the fact that she did not have her glasses. Miss Susie agreed with me that the little one was a trifle the better of the two, and was as sweet as possible, though she, too, thought that neither of them did you justice. Oh, how I do love to talk to other people about you, when they know you and how pretty and delightful you are! And, by the way, darling, I shall be seriously vexed if you do *not* repeat *all* the compliments paid you that you remember: you are doing it for my sake, at my entreaty, because it contributes to my happiness. Isn't that enough? I repeat the few that are paid me, not without a grimace, of course, but because I know you want to hear them. *Dont* go back on me, love.

We had a play last night, in the gymnasium, from the Dramatic Association, and it was exceedingly enjoyable—really excellently done,—a hundred *per cent.* better than the 'Pokahontas' of last year. The play was "Katharine," a travesty, by John Kendrick Bangs,—a sort of parody on the *Taming of the Shrew*.[3] In so far as it was a 'take-off' on Shakspere, I did not like it: instead of being delicate, it was done with a broadax. But as a pleasant, bright, entertaining piece of acting it was good. Both the make-up and the acting of the boys was really wonderfully good.[4] The only thing that marred my pleasure was your absence. Every minute that threatened to give me the blues. Nearly every laugh was extinguished with a sigh, that you should miss so much fun— that I was obliged to enjoy myself *alone*!

I am so much obliged to you, my pet, for all these details about what you are doing and the persons you are seeing—about taking the children to church—about the reception afterwards—even about the sad family histories such as that of Mrs. Howell's. All such details give me a realization of your visit that nothing else could. And then, when the passionate love passage comes how the life leaps in my veins! Every word of love you write, my darling, is a word of gold for me. If you should some day find a quiet space of time and leisure of spirit in which to write me a *whole* love letter, nothing *but* love, love, love, from beginning to end, I believe I should sing, and laugh, and walk on air for a week on that single intoxicating draft! I sat at table this morning and read that exquisite quotation which you took from Ruth—and I dared not look at any one for a time after that, for I knew that my eyes were full to overflowing with the sweet tears of unspeakable happiness. Oh, how deep those words did go into my heart—what a sweet song they have been there all day! Bless you, my precious darling, for this incomparable love, this ravishing sweetness of wifely devotion. Sometimes your passionate sentences of tenderness make me almost mad with joy. It seems to me, as I read, that, so long as you love me that way, no sorrow or trial or struggle can ever daunt my heart for a moment. So calm and silent and commanding a peace comes into my life! I love all men more, I am juster, more urbane, and tolerant, and hopeful, and trustful, because my little wife loves me with her pure and perfect heart, watches me with affectionate approval and admiration out of her deep clear eyes—because my spirit has won your spirit to its close companionship—because I am loved by the little woman whose nature most delights me, whose mind most excites my admiration and confidence[,] whom my love and my taste pick out as the most perfect of her sweet kind. Oh, darling, I *love* you,   Your own Woodrow.

Warm regards to Martha—kisses for the children—love for all.

ALS (WC, NjP).

[1] George Stevenson Patton. Born Nyack, N. Y., March 13, 1869. A.B., College of New Jersey, 1891. Studied at Princeton Theological Seminary, 1892-95. Assistant Professor of Biblical Instruction, Princeton University, 1895-1900; Assistant Professor of Moral Philosophy, 1900-1902; Secretary to the President of Princeton University, 1895-1902; Professor of Moral Philosophy, 1902-14. Director of Education, Crown Colony of Bermuda, 1914-24; member, Colonial Parliament of Bermuda, 1916-37. Died March 25, 1937.

[2] For the reports of the Discipline Committee and the action of the faculty on these cases, see the Princeton Faculty Minutes, printed at March 30 and April 6 and 13, 1892.

[3] Reviewed in *The Princetonian*, xvi (March 30, 1892), [1].

[4] According to *The Princetonian*, the success of the play was largely due to the acting of Booth Tarkington, '93.

From the Minutes of the Princeton Faculty

[March 30, 1892]

... The Committee on Discipline reported that Messrs. —— &
——, (Sc. Sci.) for gross misconduct in the College Dormitories,
had been directed to return home pending further investigation
of their conduct and to await the action of the Faculty. . . .[1]

1 Hearings on these cases, dated March 26 and 28, 1892, are recorded in the
body of WWsh notes described in Princeton Faculty Minutes, Sept. 23, 1891,
n. 1.

From Joseph Ruggles Wilson

My precious son—   Clarksville, March 31/92
    Accept my commiseration in the matter of your loneliness. I
think that solitude is all the harder to bear when it is voluntary
(as in your case) and not compulsory (as in mine). For in the
one case it has a term which may be anticipated, and yet, however near, seems hopelessly far off—whilst in the other the inevitable is present to summon up all of one's grit to bear it. An
imprisonment which shall end in a month or two makes each
day interminable: but if it is never to end, then resignation
does not count the days.
    Do you spend all your time (when not officially or socially
employed) at that wretched caravansery? I should suppose that
your "study" on Steadman St. would find you some relief.
    Is there a probability that you will be called to the vacant
chair (Ely's) at Johns Hop.? One of the daily papers so stated
some weeks ago. Or would you accept of an "assistant" professorship, which I think that is?
    Have you yet finished your lectures at the law school in N. York
which I saw by "The Times" you were to deliver sometime in
March? And pardon if I ask the further question, what is the condition of your new book (on American History)? Everything that
concerns you equally concerns me.
    I have reason to hope that my health is improving—slowly but
surely. It is still necessary to use a close carriage in my going
to and returning from College. But in a week or two I shall try
to dispense with this means of locomotion. I must endeavor to
get strong enough to go to Hot Springs (Ark) by the middle of
May, when our General Assly meets there[.][1] I am desirous of
trying the effects of the baths in that place which *may* do me
good, and can do me no harm.
    Josie is well although he has been threatened with an attack

of fever. His chief business is that of courting at which he seems to be a model expert. He sends much love to you.

I must now close—and have written these rambling lines more for the pleasure of a short chat with my darling son than in the hope of giving to him any special pleasure. Love to Ellie when you write next.   Your loving   Father

ALS (WP, DLC) with WWhw notation on env.: "Ans. 10 April/92."
  [1] It met in the First Presbyterian Church in that city, May 19-28, 1892.

To Ellen Axson Wilson

My own darling,   Princeton, 31 March, 1892
    When you go to church (the to-morrow after you get this let-ter) can't you sit near where you sat that first time I saw you—it was about where uncle James Bones's pew used to be—and (will it be wrong in church?) think of me, of all the sweet things that that first glimpse of you made possible for both of us, of all the sweet love time that has come after. Forget all the suffering and hard work and anxiety, and think only of that wh. has illumi-nated and beautified everything, our perfect love for each other. Have you gone any of the ways we went walking, or any of the ways we went driving, together—and have they recalled anything? If you please, ma'am, you may now recollect (by association of ideas) all the details of your falling in love with me which you so cruelly forgot when I (more than once) cross-questioned you, with such yearning curiosity, about your feelings towards me at the several stages of my wooing, in those never-to-be-forgotten times and places. Ah, how I should delight to take those walks with you *now*, darling—now that I love you so much more—now that you are so much *more* beautiful, and interesting, and charm-ing than you were then.[1] For the Warrens and Mr. Baker and the rest are right: little room as there then seemed to be for im-provement in you in any respect, you are prettier and sweeter now than ever. By the way, I've been reading Herrick, and here's a little poem, entitled "Of Love. A Sonnet," which comes so near my present mood and meaning in one or two particulars that I must quote it:

> "How love came in I do not know,
> Whether by the eye or ear, or no;
> Or whether with the soul it came
> (At first) infused with the same;
> Whether in part 'tis here or there,
> Or, like the soul, whole everywhere,

> This troubles me: but I as well
> As any other this can tell:
> That when from hence she does depart
> The outlet then is from the heart."

Though, if I were *looking* for a poem to express both what I felt when I first saw you and what all our subsequent life has shown me of yourself and of the sweet things of love, I should adopt Wordsworth's "She was a phantom of delight," line for line, word for word, dropping not a syllable, except to fit the colour of your hair! That poem almost perfectly expresses both my mind's and my heart's judgments of you, my Eileen.

Do you stop with wishing at night for *one* good-night kiss—and would you stay out of my arms to receive that one, if that were all. Ah, my little queen, how like our love and our impulses grow! Do *you*, too, catch yourself stretching out your arms to embrace *me*? Why that's what I do almost every time I let my thoughts dwell upon you when I am alone. I believe that if I could hold you in my arms for just five minutes every day, look into the depths of those sweet eyes—cover their lids, your sweet, sweet lips, your cheeks, your chin, your neck, your brow with kisses, and make just one attempt to put my love in words—I could endure the rest of the twenty-four hours, as I cannot now! Oh, darling, *when you come*! Your own Woodrow.

Love and kisses to whom they belong.

ALS (WC, NjP).
¹ See the Editorial Notes, "Wilson's Introduction to Ellen Axson" and "Wilson's Early Courtship of Ellen Axson," both in Vol. 2.

From Ellen Axson Wilson

My own darling, Rome [Ga.] March 31/92

I failed altogether to write yesterday and I am *so* sorry, but it was unavoidable. I had to come here to Aunt Annie's—early in the morning before Uncle Will left with the buggy. I hoped to write after I reached here but Aunt Annie's sister and her daughter were already here to spend the day with me. Cothran, her son also came in to dinner, and immediately after dinner the whole Cothran & Smith clan began to come to see me; there were eight or ten ladies calling at once, and I hadn't a free moment until night, when it was too late for any train that day.

I received two sweet letters from you yesterday, having failed to get one the day before. Am so *charmed* that the pictures have given you so much pleasure. You dearest and most delightful of lovers! How *can* you like me so much? Such praise from you is a sort of sweet intoxication to me,—but an innocent one, for no one was ever spoiled but only humbled, yet strengthened to greater effort by *such* praise—praise born of a great love.

I have been much interested in Annie Laurie's[1] work on "art!," to which she had been for sometime devoting herself. She really showed extraordinary talent. She seems to have been a remarkably lovely girl too and a most devoted Christian,—she wanted to be a missionary. Everyone whom I meet is earnest in praise of her exquisite character. It was almost the hardest blow that could have fallen on Aunt Annie. Yet she bears it nobly.

Minnie Hoyt has been heard from at last; she will be back in two or three weeks, is going back to Hull next summer but says nothing about her plans regarding the degree,—was not able to write much. Poor girl, I am so sorry for her—and for Florence too, whose whole girlhood, from eighteen to twenty-three, has already been given up to the task of sending Minnie to college. She is the most self-denying—the most perfectly unselfish young person I ever saw. So lovely in character in *every* way! She says she can't & won't go to college, even if Minnie were well enough to send her, before Margie is through school because she can't be spared from home;—her mother would be too lonely. And as Margie has two more years at school poor Florence will be rather old when she begins.[2] But there is so much confusion that I must give up trying to write more today. I love you Woodrow dearest I love you until it *hurts!* I am in all things

Your own Eileen.

ALS (WC, NjP).
[1] Annie Laurie Hoyt, Aunt Annie's daughter, who had died in 1891.
[2] She was born in 1864.

A Review

[April 1892]

DROIT ET LIBERTÉS AUX ÉTATS-UNIS: LEURS ORIGINES ET LEURS PROGRÈS. By ADOLPHE DE CHAMBRUN. Paris: Ernest Thorin, 1891. Pp. ii, 542.

The last few years have been rich in foreign commentaries on our institutions. Everybody knows of Mr. Bryce's *American Commonwealth*, with its extraordinary masses of detail about every portion of our life and organization as a nation and its great abundance of intelligent comment. Hard on the heels of Mr. Bryce's three volumes come Mr. Carlier's four, *La République Américaine: États-Unis*,[1] more exhaustive even than the English work, and, in the fullness and significance of the historical matter which it contains, much more satisfactory. The Duc de Noailles has given us his *Cent Ans de République aux États-Unis*;[2] and Prof. Boutmy devoted a large part of his stimulating little volume of *Études de Droit Constitutionnel*[3] to a consideration of the significant peculiarities of our system of public law. M. de Chambrun had already published *Le Pouvoir Exécutif aux États-Unis: Étude de Droit Constitutionnel*[4]: the volume before us is another contribution to the same department of study. These two volumes must surely make every student of institutions deplore the recent death of their distinguished author. His long residence in this country, as *conseil avocat* of the French Legation, had enabled him to acquaint himself, with a lawyer's thoroughness, with our legal institutions. He had become enough of an American to catch the points of view of English-American law, and had had the industry and intelligence to acquaint himself with the more significant portions of the history and literature of our law; but in becoming an American lawyer he had not ceased to be a French lawyer, and he had a very keen appreciation of all the points wherein our law differed in thought and method, either wholly or in part, from the law of the Continent.

In some respects M. Boutmy's *Études* and this latest work of M. de Chambrun's are most significant and more helpful to the student than any of the others that I have mentioned. They not only show a notable advance in the methods of French writers in the study and estimation of legal and political institutions; they also enrich the literature of their subjects as it could not have been enriched by writers of any other race. Frenchmen have hitherto been compelled by their language to be logical and by their lack of political experience to be doctrinaire. It must always be a slow process by which men of such wit and such coherency of mind as theirs are made to understand that the institutions that make for liberty are neither logical nor subject to doctrine: that a good system of politics need not be systematic. Frenchmen like these of whom we speak have found this out, and have set to expounding the facts which seem to them equally strange and important in that striking language of theirs, for which point is as inevitable, it would seem, as grammatical construction. It is thus that the matter gets enriched: nothing could be more suggestive or more stimulating, more emphatic of old points or more disclosive of new than the way in which they apply their wit and their style of setting forth the things in English and American political thought and practice which strike them by reason of their contrast with what has been thought and done in France.

There is rather less vivacity and felicity in M. de Chambrun's manner of treatment than in M. Boutmy's, but his matter is, in its way, hardly less satisfactory. His object in the volume before us has been to give the natural history of certain things which a Frenchman of the last generation would have deemed to have no natural history at all, but to be axiomatic—namely, the ideas of political equality and popular sovereignty. He shows very clearly that our institutions rest in the main on English custom and statute, that is, English experiment; that where they differ in form or conception from English practice, practical conditions, rather than theoretical notions, have effected the modification; that many of the tenets of our abstract political doctrine are a foreign gloss upon our institutions rather than legitimate inferences from them; our sovereign people, for example, meekly submitting to history in respect of its division into State groups, oddly determining what it should *not* do by tying its powers up in written constitutions, agreeing, though itself a δῆμος that it had better put checks upon democracy—in a word, developing and adapting English institutions, not Rousseauite doctrine. The result, a government, practical, unique, admirable! Then he turns to the consideration of those portions of our law which offer the most instructive contrasts to French legal practice; discusses at some length our criminal procedure, our jury system, our laws of property, our provisions for religious freedom, liberty of speech, of the press, and of petition; and, with the question, "What government affords a like body politic?" he closes a book which deserves translation and a large body of English readers.

  Princeton.   WOODROW WILSON.

Printed in the Philadelphia *Presbyterian and Reformed Review*, III (April 1892), 396-98.

 [1] Auguste Carlier, *La république américaine États-Unis* (4 vols., Paris, 1890). [All notes Eds.']

 [2] Jules Charles Victurnien, Duc de Noailles, *Cent ans de république aux États-Unis* (2 vols., Paris, 1886-89).

 [3] Émile Gaston Boutmy, *Études de droit constitutionnel; France, Angleterre, États-Unis* (Paris, 1885 and 1888). Wilson's review of the English translation of the second edition of this work is printed at August 22, 1891.

 [4] Charles Adolphe de Pineton, Marquis de Chambrun, *Le Pouvoir exécutif aux États-Unis* (Paris, 1876).

To Ellen Axson Wilson

                  New York,
         Gallery of Law Library, Equitable Building—
My own darling,   Window overlooking harbour, 1 April, '92
  Don't be alarmed at my extravagance in buying you a new watch. Though real silver and fully guaranteed, it cost only $6,

and that was only a little more than it would have cost to put the old one in working order. Of course you ought to have a time piece when travelling, and this is the most convenient form. One word of explanation. It winds by the stem, like any other watch— may need a little shake to start it—and is set by turning the stem *firmly pressed in*, or down. I hope it will prove to be what is promised of it.

The lecture has not come off yet—I wish it had, so that I could go out in this glorious sunshine. There's still a good deal of winter in the air, but there's some Spring too—enough to make a most delicious and invigorating mixture, delightful to take into the lungs.

I did not get a letter as I usually do before leaving home, and so my heart is not quite as light as it would be if it had a new message from its little mistress, but love is a wonderful blessing, when one is permitted to love a precious little woman like you— "a Spirit, yet a Woman too"—it keeps the heart singing always, alike young and strong and full of hope

Your own Woodrow.

ALS (WC, NjP).

From Ellen Axson Wilson

My own darling   Rome [Ga.] April 1 1892

Just one hasty line to tell you that we are well and happy today. I am just leaving Aunt Annie's & of course it would not "do" to spend the last moments writing to you. But as I go from here to spend the day with Agnes,—returning at night to Uncle Wills,—I will have no opportunity later in the day to write. The weather is glorious—has been now for three days.

With a heart full to overflowing with passionate love I am as ever   Your little wife.

ALS (WC, NjP).

To Ellen Axson Wilson

My own darling,   Princeton, 2 April, 1892

No letter either yesterday or to-day—what *can* have happened! I shall not know until Monday, for this is Saturday. I shall do my best to stand it, my best *not to think*,—for that is my only salvation. Has going to Aunt Annie's put you 'beyond the pale'; have those "ugly but manly boys" pocketed or lost your letters; have you lost your nurse, or has something happened to the children;

worst of all—has anything been the matter with *you*, my precious one? But I said I would not think—and I must keep to my resolution. I will suppose it all due to some hindrance not in the least tragical: shall rely on that last assurance, of "splendid health, plump and rosy," and wait until Monday as best I may.

That lecture yesterday did not 'go off' quite so well as some of the others, I am afraid,—but it was the sixth and only four more remain to be given. That's a comfort.

It now seems pretty evident that it is not to be within my *choice* to stay over night in New York, whether I feel that I can trust myself or not. My duties here are too pressing to allow of any longer absence from Princeton than may be absolutely necessary. Possibly after my lecturing at the Law School is over I may run over once or twice for a frolic; but, so long as I have two lectures for the classes here and one for the men there to prepare every week, frolics will be out of the question. I should only drain my energies further by attempting to make room and occasion for them. And I have no idea of doing that: I am nursing myself assiduously.

I have not told you how kind my friends here have been to me in my loneliness. Magie and Dulles[1] have fairly compelled me to take meals with them again and again; I have a standing invitation, already twice enforced, to take tea with the Fines on Sunday evenings; Dr. Shields has invited me several times and Sloane twice, though I have been obliged to decline both; I have dined with Dr. Packard, as I told you—altogether, I have been most generously treated (the Richardson's,[2] among the rest, having pursued me with invitations). If I were not so busy, I could have a very jolly, sociable time. As it is, I by no means feel isolated or neglected.

I love you, darling, so passionately, so tragically,—I think my heart would break were I to try to tell you how much.

Your own Woodrow

ALS (WC, NjP).
   [1] The Rev. Joseph Heatly Dulles, Librarian of Princeton Theological Seminary, 1886-1931, a bachelor who lived at 27 University Place.
   [2] Mr. and Mrs. Ernest Cushing Richardson of 69 Prospect Avenue. Richardson was Librarian of the College of New Jersey.

From Ellen Axson Wilson

My own darling   Rome [Ga.], April, 2/92

As usual someone—Mrs. Bowie,—is coming to spend the day and I am writing in desperate haste to get through before they come. I have just been writing to Minnie Brown[1]—in Atlanta,—

replying to an invitation to visit her. I shall go over Thursday morning and stay with her until late the next afternoon,—then on to Gainesville. That will give me the wished for glimpse of my other Atlanta friends,—Mrs. Duncan,[2] Miss Carrie & the Bowies. I find it impossible to leave here before Thursday, there are so many visits,—and besides I must get my washing done. I had a delightful day with Agnes yesterday. They have a lovely home and the most *perfectly* beautiful situation I ever saw *anywhere*. It is not a 'view' but a whole panorama of them—a different one from every window and all equally lovely. Yesterday was a charming day—a day of hurrying clouds and a sweet rain-washed atmosphere, of violet shadows on the hills and a soft radiance over all,—and it would be impossible to give you any idea of the beauty of those views! The *lines* of the hills are peculiarly lovely about Rome. The *composition* of each picture is perfect. I would *almost* be willing to live in Rome—or at any rate just *out* of it,—for the sake of such a feast as Agnes has always spread before her.

Nellie is sitting beside me and she has just remarked "I am writing to Papa, you know?" Margaret is also writing on a slate, & Nellie says she wants me to get her "a *wall* like Margarets"! She was chattering in bed yesterday morning and observed "Jessie sinks me is a little gurl." "And aren't you[?]" "No, me is a *miss*." "Is Jessie a little girl?" "No Jessie is Mamma & Marga is Papa." "And what is Rosa[?]" "I isnt sinking about Roses." "And what is Mamma[?]" "I isn't sinking about you too!" She always calls the nurse "Roses," saying it in the most beautiful way.

I was almost on the point of telegraphing you last night. I was so 'scared' having gotten no letter for two days. When I came from Agnes last evening and found that none had come by the last delivery I was so miserable that Florence slipped away down town, made them let her look for herself at the office, and came back triumphant. And it was such a delightful letter too—so sweet and so long! Your interview with the Dr. was all that could be desired. It means the $400.00 at once and certainly, and perhaps if we make known our desires it may mean the *house* built for us. If it only *would* result that way how happy I should be! I am indeed delighted that things are so satisfactory.

Have been interrupted by a long call & must now close abruptly. All well,—the weather lovly. The children send love & kisses—so does your little wife—an ocean of *it* & a *shower* of them! Now and ever   Your own Eileen

ALS (WC, NjP).
 [1] Her first cousin, Minnie Brown Henderson, the recently married daughter of Ellen's Aunt Louisa.
 [2] Martha Deloney Berrien Duncan, formerly of Savannah.

To Ellen Axson Wilson

My own darling,   Princeton, 3 April, 1892

It is one month to-day since I saw you off in Baltimore—*one* month! Why it seems six months at least! How much a fellow can suffer in one month! There's a great deal of philosophy in what dear father said in a letter I received from him yesterday: loneliness like mine is really harder to bear than loneliness like his: "an imprisonment which shall end in a month or two makes each day interminable: but if it is never to end, then resignation does not count the days." My days do fairly seem interminable, short as they are for the work which must be crowded into them. Work is the only blessing under such circumstances. Ah, my lovely darling, how can we ever part again? It now seems to me quite impossible that I should leave home—i.e. *you—at all* this summer. It will take at least a year spent close by your side to get this soreness out of my heart. I am afraid that when once I do get you back again, I shall *bore* you with my kisses and caresses,—so long will it take me to work off this present feeling of starvation— of *impotent* love, that can make no adequate demonstration of itself, that is nine parts unsatisfied yearning. I have always made love to you as diligently as was at all compatible with your doing any house-keeping or any work of any kind; but I rather think that when you come back you will have to give up all work and simply devote your time to receiving my attentions, to being kissed and made love to as long as you are awake.

Of course I am not without comfort even now, or without some keen delights which proceed from you. It is such a *satisfaction* to love you! Everything about you is so delightful to dwell upon, your sweet tenderness, your exquisite capacity for understanding and sympathizing with things both expressed and unexpressed, whether of the mind or the heart, your sure insight, your unerring instinct for what is true and lovable, that unique combination in you of deep poetry and strong sense at which I have so often wondered and rejoiced; and then your beauty, so suitable to it all, so sweet an advertisement of what your mind and nature contain,—oh, when I think of you, of what I conceived you to be from the first and have now proved that you are by nine years of happy intercourse with you, my heart swells with a joy and exaltation which are altogether inexpressible and perfect. And so I am *not unhappy*—how could I be?—even now, but only suffering exile a while from the joys of that companionship that makes up my life. I should be a churl and should not deserve your love, should I really fret and repine because of your absence; could

I not be glad and content to think of you and the precious babies where you *must* be both giving and getting so much pleasure, and where you will all get rosy health for the time of the happy, happy home-coming—where it does you good to be—where you *ought* to be, and to stay till all the plan is carried out. I *am* glad, darling; I cannot be otherwise than glad when I think of you where you will have some of the satisfactions you deserve. Oh, I love you, devotedly, passionately, to distraction!

Your own Woodrow.

Kisses as many as they will take, for the children—love to all.

ALS (WC, NjP).

From Ellen Axson Wilson

My own darling,   Rome [Ga.] April 3rd 1882 [1892]
    I *have looked* with longing eyes at that part of the church where we used to sit, both last Sunday and this, but I did not succeed in sitting there. What would seem to be the corresponding pew was filled with a large family of strangers and I did not know how to manage it. But the interior of the church is so changed,—four aisles instead of two, new pews of a different shape and style &c. &c.—that it would have been little satisfaction had I accomplished it.
    I have taken the drive by the "river-road" and around; and of course I have been over the East Rome paths. And how vividly those dear old days came back to me as I did it. The strangeness, the wonder, the doubtfull delights of that time seemed suddenly made real again and brought into sharp, sweet contrast with the familiar happy present,—with its perfect love and confidence, its full knowledge of you and pride in you, it *ineffable* joy. Ah dearest love, what a difference between the old and the new,—how sweet was that—how infinitely sweeter this! The former had the charm of *mystery* hanging about it. I cannot satisfy you fully about those days because they are still enveloped in something of that mystery to me. All the thoughts and feelings, even the events, of that time seem to lie in the "doubtful light" that comes between the darkness and the dawn. But it is such a lovely light,—that rose of dawn,—so fresh and fair and filled with such sweet promise for the coming day that I cannot find it in my heart to wish the mist dispelled. I have not taken the river path to the great stone yet, but I *must* do it. I think these days of sunshine have perhaps made it dry enough now and I mean to slip away and attempt it, malgré my thirty-six calls and other engagements.
    How sweet your lines from Herrick are!—and by the way I

might adopt them as another answer to your request for all the "details" of my falling in love with you! No, dearest, I won't grieve because I had not my wits about me enough to describe the details of the plunge, but I *would* like to find the "great heart-word" which would reveal to you how *deeply in* I fell,—which would tell with what a *passion* of love and joy and pride in you my heart is swelling. Dearest it is my deliberate conviction,—nay I do not *believe* it, I *know*—that the combination of qualities found in you is the rarest, finest, noblest, *grandest* of which human nature is capable. It is a combination which if put in a book in all its naked truth would be censured by every critic as impossible, —an unwarrented idealism. What!—such strength and nobility of character combined with such ineffable tenderness, such un-selfishness and thoughtfulness in things great and small, & a nature so exquisitely gifted in power of sympathy,—of under-standing others:—social gifts such as you describe, and the ora-tor's gift,—the "personal magnetism" and *all* those gifts which go to make a born leader of men, combined with powers of thought of such a kind that he must undoubtedly rank as a *genius*, no less than Burke himself; and added to all this a strength of pur-pose and of will and powers of application which result in achievments so great that while yet in his earliest manhood his rank is now among the foremost thinkers of his age!—well! no wonder the critics scoff and disbelieve! It would be incredible if it were not *true*; for truth is indeed stranger than fiction. You may smile if you will and call me 'partial' but you cannot deny, sir, that a wife has excellent opportunities for becoming acquainted with her husband; and the mere *impulse* to make the best of him which we call 'partiality'—"a poor thing sir but 'tis mine own!"— won't carry one through unlimited trials of patience. A wife always finds her husband out sooner or later! On the other hand no one ever knows *how* good a good man is except his wife. It is false that we turn our best side to the world; we keep it only for our nearest and dearest. The "critics" will never know of what beautiful things our human nature is capable. But *I* know my darling, for I know *you*, heart and soul and all, and *love* you with a perfect love. And I saw it all "as in a glass darkly" when first I met you and chose as best describing you those lines; do you remember? "A mouth for mastery & manful work, a certain brooding sweetness in the eyes, a brow the harbour of fair thought."[1] Ah if I could *tonight* kiss again & again & yet again those eyes, that mouth and brow, I would indeed be as perfectly happy as I am perfectly blest in being

Your little wife.

ALS (WC, NjP).

1 Ellen first called Wilson's attention to the aptness of this quotation from Jean Ingelow's "Laurance" during their courtship days. See EAW to WW, March 10, 1884, Vol. 3, pp. 75-77. It recurs in EAW to WW, June 20, 1892.

Two Letters to Ellen Axson Wilson

My precious love,   Princeton, 4 April, 1892

I am sorry to say that I must send you only a line or two. I could not study on Saturday, because of indigestion: to-day, therefore, I must rush—for it is three lecture day.

I received a letter and a note from you to-day, and you can imagine how relieved I was, after these days with no letter at all, to hear that you are all well and happy. Your words are sweeter than the jasmine leaves in the note! Ah, my sweet one, you carry my life about with you. My love follows and dwells with you all day, and in my dreams at night. Always and in every (worthy) thought, I am   Your own Woodrow.

Indigestion *much* relieved yesterday and to-day.

My own sweet darling,   Princeton, 5 April, 1892

I am belated, alas! to-day again. Indeed the time I am taking for this note *ought* to be devoted to the completion of that third lecture of the day, which must be delivered only two hours hence, and which is not yet ready! But I'd rather cut the lecture hour short than not write to my darling. Love has claims which are paramount to those of International Law, and I mean to write *some* words of love to my pet, though the lecture should go by the board in consequence. I could not get along did I not allow some vent for the love that is surging in my heart all the while. Thoughts of you fill my mind and heart all the time: I am all the while taking your sweet picture from my pocket and kissing it—making love to it: I am all the while beguiling my loneliness with thoughts of you, with silent love-making, with eager efforts to *imagine you* where you are and live close to you even in your absence. And I *must* have out with these longings and ecstacies of affection. Oh, my love, my ideal little wife, my sweet heart's mistress, my lovely companion and mate, in what way do I *not* love you—in what way shall I not make love to you when I have you again by my side! It's the present passion of my life to see and kiss you.

Kisses those blessed babies for me and imagine yourself strained to the heart of   Your own Woodrow

Much love to all.

ALS (WC, NjP).

From Ellen Axson Wilson

My own darling,   Rome [Ga.] Tuesday [April 5, 1892]

I am so *very* sorry that you failed to get a letter Saturday! Don't know what could have happened to my Thursday one; it was written and mailed *quite* early in the morning,—earlier than usual. Too *bad* that it should have been that one of all others that failed when there was none to reach you the day before and none *could* reach you the day after! It was odd though that we should have had the same experience, on exactly the same two days, only thanks to Florence's enterprise *I* did not have to wait over Sunday. I did not *write* a letter yesterday either, though I mailed my Sunday one. I was paying calls all day, from half past ten to six,—paid eighteen! And immediately after breakfast I had to go downtown to see the stone mason;[1] so I thought I would write at night when I had more time. But alas by night I was so worn out that I went to sleep immediately after supper sitting bolt upright in my chair, and had to retreat ignominiously to bed. I write now before breakfast, and of course in haste, for immediately after breakfast I must meet the stone mason at the cemetary, and then I have to make calls again. This stage of my visit is almost too busy to be pleasant; I am glad I have no "friends" in Gainesville.

I *have* really enjoyed my visit here extremely though; everyone has been so nice to me, and the family are simply devoted to me. They show—*all* of them—such unfeigned *delight* in having me here, and such constant desire to do *everything* possible to please me—that I would be hard to please indeed if I were not happy with them in spite of their little peculiarities of domestic arrangement. If you want me to be an honoured guest—"the person around whom everything else revolves" (!) you would certainly be satisfied with their attitude towards me. Did I tell you that I had heard from Sister Annie and she insists upon my coming there. The girls[2] are still with her though and I fear that I will crowd her dreadfully.

Many, many thanks darling for the little watch! It has not come yet;—I can write more when it does. All well. I love you darling with *all* my heart and am in all things and altogether,

                              Your own Eileen

I leave here at 8.50 Thursday morning, reaching Atlanta at 11.03.

ALS (WC, NjP).

[1] By this time Ellen had received the final draft of the epitaph from Wilson, which he had either sent in a separate envelope or enclosed in one of his letters in late March or early April. The text, copied from the gravestone, follows:

In Memory of Rev. S. E. Axson
who departed this life May 28, 1884
aged 47 years 5 months,
For seventeen years pastor of the Rome Presbyterian Church.
While yet in the noonday of life
In the heat of a well-fought fight
The Master called him to his exceeding great reward.

2 Mrs. Howe's nieces, Jessie Kennedy and Marion Green, and perhaps a sister of Marion Green. Annie W. Howe to WW, May 20, 1893, Vol. 8, says that Dr. Green had come to take the "girls" home.

From the Minutes of the Princeton Faculty

[April 6, 1892]

. . . The Committee on Discipline reported that they had directed Messrs. —— and —— who had been guilty of gross misconduct in the College Dormitory to return home as soon as possible. The cases of these students and the others guilty of the same offence are to be reported to the Faculty for action at the next meeting. . . .[1]

1 Hearings on these cases, dated March 31 and April 2 and 5, 1892, are recorded in the body of WWsh notes described in Princeton Faculty Minutes, Sept. 23, 1891, n. 1. The two students just sent home were not the same as those whose cases had been reported to the faculty on March 30, 1892.

To Ellen Axson Wilson

Princeton, 6 April, 1892

Oh, my precious, precious darling, what a letter this is that I have just received,—that love letter you wrote last Sunday! What would I not give if I could write such a love letter to you—a letter that would give you such an exquisite passion of delight as this of yours has given me! What a *wonderful* letter—a *perfect* expression of its sweet, its supremely sweet thoughts! Darling, I verily believe that the moments spent reading that letter were among the most perfectly happy I ever spent. For this is the first time you have ever fully told me your love *in words*. I have known it, felt it, read it in your eyes and in your whole life as a perfect wife, been transported by it in your tender kisses and passionate embraces: but I never before *heard* it. What I have been waiting and praying for has happened: the *vocabulary* and imagery of love that I knew were pent up in that sweet heart and wonderful little brain of yours, the homes of all sweet and beautiful things, have at last broken over all restraints of timidity or reserve, and here is a veritable prose poem of love, full of the most exquisite expression of the most subtle sides of the boundless affection of a little woman of the profoundest gift for loving! I can't describe to you the effect it has had upon me. It *is*, my darling, take it as a whole, that "great heart-word" for which you long. If it would not wear it out, I should carry it with me for the rest of my life. I verily believe that it is the most perfect love letter ever written. It's forms of expression ravish me quite as if the meaning had no special application to myself. And it comes to me as a proof of my own knowledge of you, and so is all the sweeter to me. I knew that, along with such rare gift of expressions you have always exhibited upon other subjects, there *must* go an unequalled gift for putting *love* into words:—and here's the triumphant proof. Oh, darling, will you *talk* to me with a perfect freedom and sweet poetic license of phrase like this when you are in my arms once more? It is because I knew the treasure of love-words that was in you that I have so often plead with you to make love to me as freely in words as you did in kisses and caresses, that I begged for a "*whole* love letter, every word love," —that I *plagued* you to *talk* to me of your love for me. Now that I have what I wanted, and even more than I dreamed was possible, I am simply *transported*. Now that her reserve of demonstrative speech is broken, her interjections and exclamations expanded into sentences, perhaps my darling will again and again thrill me through and through with this surpassing delight of being made love to with the sweetest words in the language, as well as with the sweetest looks and the sweetest caresses that ever wife bestowed on husband. Ah, Ellie, my delightful little wife, my ravishing little sweetheart, my little genius of a wife and companion and lover, how hallowed for me are those spots, those walks, those scenes where first my bliss began, where first I found out the treasures of mind and heart and life that you had in store *for me* (as a generous God willed it)! If only I can live up to the pride and strength and great courage that your love and companionship have put into me, it will be the *achievement of my life* that I am   Your own Woodrow.

Sincerest, deepest love to dear little Maggie, to Aunt Lou, and our inimitable babies, the pledges of our love.

ALS (WC, NjP).

Two Letters from Ellen Axson Wilson

My own darling,   Rome [Ga.], April 6/92

What sort of weather are you having this morning I wonder! I see in the paper that the thermometer at the north has dropped 40° in three hours! It is still warm here,—but *such* a rainstorm!

People are already getting anxious about the rising rivers. And *my* plans are all broken up for the stone mason was to get the stone in place this morning and I was to see it this afternoon; and now of course he can't work in this weather, so I won't see the work finished after all. I saw the stone though and it looks very well indeed. I have had a tiny little wind-fall which will pay for my half of the expense. Old Aunt Francis in Springfield[1] died recently, you remember. She left to Uncle Henry, her name-sake, $200.00 and to each of Grandmother's other children or their heirs $100.00, which of course gives each of us $25.00.

But I have *so* much to do today that I must cut this very short. I am bored about the rest of my calls with which the weather is interfering. The worst of it is that having taken them in districts, I have been to see a number of comparative strangers and left some of my best friends—the Bowies, Agnes, &c. I went to see dear old Mrs. Gardner the other day and she brought in Mr. Wright. The last time I saw him was in a very peculiar interview in which I told him I was *engaged*, and he behaved rather badly![2] He was awfully embarrassed the other day, I am sure I don't know why. *I* felt perfectly at ease.

Mrs. Gardner told me I was as "bonny as ever." And now 'good-bye,' darling until tomorrow in Atlanta. We go as we came on the Rome road & not on the E. T. & V.[3] so you need not fear accidents. All well and send love. Remember that I love you more than tongue can tell,—almost more than heart can hold, and am forever   Your own   Eileen

    A
kiss from
Jessie.

1 She is unknown to the Editors.
2 James Wright, another former suitor. For an account of the "very peculiar interview," see ELA to WW, May 12, 1884, Vol. 3, p. 175.
3 The East Tennessee, Virginia and Georgia Railroad.

My own darling,   Atlanta   April 7/92
    Before this reaches you will have gotten my telegram and will know that we are safely out of Rome.[1] I hope you won't have seen before that anything about the terrible rains there. They are the worst they have had for forty years, and they say the water will go into the second story windows soon. I never heard of anything like the rapidity of the rise. After the one night's rain the trains were cut off on the Rome road. Florence came from school about 12 o'clock yesterday and reported the town in the wildest excitement—the school broken up, people

moving out of their houses &c. &c. We ran to the telephone and enquired if the Rome road would run trains the next morning; were told that they were already stopped. Then we telephoned to the other station,—the E. T. & V. & asked if their trains were still running: "Yes." "Would the 4 P.M. train go through to Atlanta?" "Yes." "Was it *perfectly* safe?" "They would not try it if it were not." So I immediately decided to take it, for I knew it would be my last chance to escape for nobody knew how long. It was doubtless rather reckless to attempt it, but they were,—or seemed— sure it was safe and I felt that it was only justice to Aunt Lou to avoid if possible any postponement of the visit. If she had not been about to move I should have remained in Rome. Well, I drove downtown in the pouring rain and saw the headstone, finished; the man had written up to ask me to see it *there*, since it was impossible for him to put it in place in such weather. It is a beautiful piece of work,—perfectly satisfactory in every respect. Then I went to East Rome & told Agnes and the Bowies 'goodbye,' then I went back and we sent the man to Forestville, with the buggy for my 'wash,'—which he brought rough-dry and damp! Then, after dinner I hastily finished my packing and we went in a close carriage to the station, and were really off a[t] 4 o'clock,—were due in Atlanta at 6.40 P.M. But,—about half an hour after we started we came to a very long halt beside a broad and furious yellow stream, known as "Dry Creek"! Great excitement seemed to prevail in the car especially as we finally crept across the bridge. As we passed a certain point I heard some one exclaim "*Thats* the place!" I ventured to enquire what was the matter and was told that one of the bridge piers was about to wash away; it was very dangerous but they had decided to risk it "this once"! But we got safely over & went on for another half hour; then came another halt for perhaps ¾ of an hour. "What was the matter?" "The road-bed had washed and the tracks were out of line; they were repairing them." After that we *crept* along for a time and then, at about the time we were due in Atlanta we stopped again; and now we were told that there was a bad washout above & that we would have to stay there until nine, perhaps until twelve, possibly until morning! I hoped they *would* stay 'till morning for I did not like the idea of going in the dark over a road in such condition. But we did get off at nine and reached here safely at ten. Mr. Henderson[2] was still awaiting us, and we reached the house perfectly dry and well. The children were *lovely*; they did not *whimper once* the whole time—went to bed in the best of spirits and slept until ten this morning. They had a good supper on the car, bread & butter & milk, I must tell you about that tomorrow;—it is dinner-time now & I *must* close at once. Everyone was *so* good to us on the car! Though you would not suppose it, the journey is, on that account, really a pleasant memory,—now that it *is* over: I am glad now that I came, though I would never do such a thing again—with children. They did not catch cold & there are no bad results of any kind. We go on to G. tomorrow *if it clears*. It is still pouring rain. We had a *hard* storm here this morning. There is *no* trouble about the road to G.

I love you, my precious one more than life itself, I am always & altogether,   Your own   Eileen

ALS (WC, NjP).
  [1] This telegram is missing.
  [2] Minnie Brown Henderson's husband. His full name is unknown to the Editors.

To Ellen Axson Wilson

My own lovely darling,   Astor House, N. Y., 8 April, 1892
I follow your plan of writing for an earlier mail than usual, because I could not write yesterday. You could hardly guess how I spent yesterday. There was a meeting of ladies (wives of nabobs) here in N. Y. yesterday morning at Mrs. Cuyler's house,[1] to consult about means—financial and other—for aiding Evelyn College,[2] and the McIlvaine ladies[3] induced me to come over and address it, as an expert upon the subject of women's education![4] I came, however, with an unfinished lecture in my bag, (for the Law School to-day) which could be finished only where law-books were accessible wh. I could not get in Princeton. After the meeting, and my lunch, therefore, I spent the rest of the day in the law-library in the P. O. building writing my lecture. In the evening I went to the theatre. And now here I am just through with my breakfast (*I can't* write *before* breakfast!), thinking of you and writing to you with a heart swelling with ineffable love. You are in Atlanta and I am with you there, if ever a man's heart and thoughts were away from his body. My sweet love! I've just read your love letter of last Sunday over again, for the nth time; and I would not change places with anybody in the world, who could not be your husband.

At 12 o'clock to-day I am to go down to the Café Savarin in the Equitable Building, where the Law School has its quarters, and lunch with the Princeton men in the School—with how many of them I don't know. The invitation was informal and gave one no hint of how much of a "spread" to expect. I'll tell you about it afterwards—for I shall try to write again this afternoon.

For the present I can only think of how happy I am in your

love. You have not sat before the mirror and described your appearance for me, sweetheart. If you are looking well, and blooming with the fullness of that loveliness that I never saw in any other face but yours, please ma'am don't hesitate to say so: you wont *dare* say *how* pretty you are, and the description will only delight me beyond measure. I do long to *see* how much colour there is in your cheeks, how much light and clear spirits in your eyes. The happiness of being your husband, dearest, is sometimes so great as almost to overcome me. That I should *possess* so much loveliness—that I should be *married* to a woman so perfectly fitted to my ideals of what a woman should be, seems almost too good to be true. But it *is* true and I am the happiest, most deeply blessed man in the world in being

Your own Woodrow.

Is not the enclosed the most extraordinary thing you ever read?[5]

ALS (WC, NjP).

[1] Mrs. Theodore Cuyler, at 214 Madison Avenue.

[2] Evelyn College, housed in a large frame structure that stands off Nassau Street, at what is now Evelyn Place, in Princeton, was opened in 1887 under the leadership of the Rev. Joshua Hall McIlvaine (College of New Jersey, 1837), Professor of Belles Lettres at Princeton from 1860 to 1870. The institution was incorporated in 1889 with McIlvaine as president and a Board of Trustees that included Francis L. Patton, James O. Murray, William Henry Green, and other professors and trustees of the College of New Jersey and Princeton Theological Seminary. The liberal arts faculty was composed largely of faculty members from the college. There was also a preparatory school, a "School of Music," and a "School of Design."

The founders of Evelyn College hoped that it would be an independent but co-ordinate institution affiliated with the College of New Jersey, and Mrs. Cuyler and her friends were at this time trying to raise money for endowment as well as an emergency fund of $5,000 to keep the institution alive. As a pamphlet issued probably in the autumn of 1891 explained: "To accomplish this result, an association, which has for its name the Evelyn Association, has been organized among the women of New Jersey, aided by women from other states who are interested in this young college. Its plan of work is simple and practical. A president and a large board of vice-presidents chosen from the various townships, are seeking each in her own locality, to enroll members for the association who shall pay a yearly fee of one dollar each, and who shall form themselves into a branch association or club, to use their influence, as they have time and opportunity for the interests of the New Jersey College for Women. An executive committee of fifteen ladies, meets every month in New York City, at the New York Ladies' Club, 28 East 22nd St., to receive reports from the vice-presidents, and to direct and control the whole work. Branch associations have been already organized in Jersey City, Newark, Orange and Morristown. Before the end of the coming winter, it is hoped that no town or township in the State will be without its Evelyn Association and that no woman who has at heart the education of her own sex, and a true pride in her own State, will fail to become a member of it." *Higher Education of Women in New Jersey* (n.p., n.d.), p. 8.

Evelyn College managed to survive with the support of the Evelyn Association during the lean years following the Panic of 1893. However, the college closed its doors after the death of President McIlvaine in 1897. See Evelyn College for Young Women, annual catalogues, 1887-97.

[3] Elizabeth D. and Alice M. McIlvaine, daughters of Dr. McIlvaine, "Principals" of Evelyn College.

[4] The single extant account of this meeting, in *Evelyn College, 1891-92, Annual Report* (n.p., n.d.), says only that the meeting at Mrs. Cuyler's house "was

From Ellen Axson Wilson

My own darling,   Atlanta April 8/92
I am in a great rush this morning as you may imagine for we leave at four o'clock for Gainesville, & I have several calls to make this morning besides packing, &c. &c.—so I must put you off with a line; will try to make up for it in the quiet of Gainesville. The weather has cleared off *gloriously*. All well and having a *very* pleasant time. With a heart full of love I am, dearest,
                    Your devoted little wife   Eileen

ALS (WC, NjP).

To Ellen Axson Wilson

My own darling,   Princeton, 8 April, 1892
Here I am back in Princeton again (I never can say 'back home'!). I could find neither time nor place to write this afternoon before leaving New York.

The lunch went off most pleasantly. Eight or nine Princeton men connected with the Law School sat down with me, including the two Princeton men who are professors.¹ Everything was most informal—stories of our college days went round in a jolly way—and I enjoyed myself very much indeed. The only drawback was that it was just before my lecture hour, and the meal was rather too substantial to lecture on!

Of course I'm tired out. I always come back from New York in excellent humour to go to bed; but bed's always a perfect cure.

Having been absent two days, your telegram from Atlanta waited twenty-four hours for me. At first its contents startled me—"to escape a freshet"! but, upon second thought, the freshet *was* escaped, and I was reassured. And you increased the length of your stay in Atlanta by so much? I shall anxiously expect your Gainesville telegram.

Oh, my lovely pet, how my heart travels with you! I shall be *so* glad to have you *resting* in Gainesville, with less of that fatiguing calling to do. *There's* your chance to *get fat*! Be sure to use it for that purpose!

I love you, darling, oh, I love you! How selfishly I do wish for you when I am worn out. Your sweet presence always soothes and rests and cheers me so! I must try to get to dreaming of you as quickly as possible!   Your own Woodrow.

Warmest love to all.

ALS (WC, NjP).
  [1] Robert Davison Petty, '83, and Alfred Gandy Reeves, '84.

From Ellen Axson Wilson

My own darling,   Gainesville [Ga.] April 9/92.

We came over, as we expected, yesterday afternoon,—had a pleasant and uneventful little journey of two hours and found Minor Brown, one of those dreadful stepsons,[1] waiting for us. And we are now very comfortably settled at Aunt Lou's. She seems well and looks perfectly natural, and Maggie is *lovely*. She *looks* the picture of health and *is* very well and much stronger. Her beauty seems to me of a very fine type—so much character as well as sweetness. There is nothing *conventional* about it,—though her colouring, complexion, &c are exquisite too. She has very sweet manners but is rather quiet so of course I will be able to write more fully about her a little later when we become more acquainted. Uncle Warren is of course in Athens, and, —I have had one great shock—Fannie[2] is here! will be here for three weeks. Isn't that hard luck?

I didn't have time while in Atlanta to tell you how much I was pleased with Mr. Henderson. He is *very* nice looking, rather handsome, has excellent features,—a fine nose &c. His face is smooth shaven and has a good deal of character about it. He is a perfect gentleman in manner. They have a sweet pretty little home— quite new; they have been in it only two or three months. They are only partly furnished as yet but what they have is really handsome & in excellent taste. Minnie is a nice housekeeper, and it was certainly a comfort to be in a place again where cleanliness and system prevailed.

I was quite successful in carrying out my plan. I saw Miss Carrie, Miss Rosa, Mrs. Duncan, Mrs. Bowie and Mrs. Bones,— also Miss Sophie Bowie who is visiting Rosa. I took a cab, & all the children, & spent most of the morning at it. It was a *perfectly* lovely day. They all "took on" excessively over the children—and *me* too! Miss Carrie lives just around the corner from Minnie and has a beautiful, large new house into which they have just moved. Her husband bought a large tract of land there for $1800.00 & afterwards refused $20,000.00 for it; and it is now worth so much that Mr. Henderson says he would be a well-to-do man with it alone. The other Mr. Kingsbury,—Miss Rosa's husband—is worth at least a quarter of a million. She was looking splendidly & has several handsome children. Miss Carrie too looks *so* well & happy, it was an *especial* pleasure to me to see her again, but *so* tantalizing! She is the *sweetest* thing! Mrs. Duncan is just as lovely and beautiful as ever; I wouldn't have missed seeing her for *anything*. She sent all sorts of affectionate messages to you;—told the children that you were her sweet-heart!

Do you know that Jessie Bones [Brower] has been in Atlanta, and left Thursday morning at eight o'clock! I arriving, you know, the night before at ten! Isn't that too bad? I was excessively disappointed. Mr. [James W.] Bones was at the station to see me off, but I scarcely had a glimpse of him owing to a rather ill-timed streak of economy. Acting on Mr. Henderson's advice we went down on the street-car instead of in a hack, just missed a car, had to wait fifteen minutes for another and barely reached our train in time.

I found that *sweet* letter in which you are "taking on" so over mine awaiting me here; but I won't try to answer *it* today, darling, because I am writing in the bosom of the family & of course amid much confusion and noise. It has turned suddenly cold this morning so that I am afraid to sit in the other rooms; and Nellie insists upon leaning against my right arm most of the time!

The little watch, I am sorry to say did not arrive before I left Rome and will have to be forwarded. I was afraid to pay the stone mason before I made this journey but I shall send him the $45.00 now and then I shall have just one dollar left! All the rest has gone in the necessary expenses of travel, servant, washing, &c. I have not had time yet to write to Stock for his share. All send love. All well. I love you darling, *passionately*,—I am in every thought   Your own Eileen.

ALS (WC, NjP).
    [1] A son of Warren A. Brown by an earlier marriage.
    [2] Ellen's first cousin, Frances Hoyt, daughter of the Rev. Henry Francis Hoyt.

To Ellen Axson Wilson

My own sweet darling,   Princeton, 9 April, 1892
    Even though it assured me of your safety and was written after all danger was passed, your account of that journey from Rome to Atlanta filled me with the greatest consternation. My darling in such danger, in peril of her life—all that is dearest, most indispensable to me on earth exposed to risk of absolute destruction! Oh, I dare not realize in my *heart* what might have happened—it might break my heart to think of it! I have chosen the

other part of it all to dwell upon, my darling's calmness and quiet bravery throughout all the trying experience. For *I* see, between the lines of your letter, just how you acted and bore yourself. Ah, how I do admire—*adore* you, my incomparable little wife. How admirable—how adorable you are in every situation! And those sweet, splendid little *ladies* who were with you—what charming pieces of *you* they are—how it delights me to think that perhaps there's much more of *you* in them—much more of what is purely sweet and serenely strong in them—than of me. If, by having children we can multiply *your* traits, it is our duty to the world to have as many as possible! How I love the little darlings— how I should like to kiss them to my heart's content. By being sweet with you they can have anything they want from me!

I have not yet received any telegram from Gainesville: I wonder if storms delayed you again?

Nellie, sweetheart, I wish I could give you some idea of how much you are in my thoughts,—and in what way! "She is a winsome wee thing, This sweet wee wife o' mine."

> "I never saw a fairer
> I never loe'd a dearer
> And neist my heart I'll wear her
> For fear my jewel tine."

> "The world's wrack, we share o't,
> The warstle and the care o't;
> Wi' her I'll blithely bear it,
> And think my lot divine."[1]

◊

> "There wild woods grow, and rivers row,
> And many a hill between;
> But day and night my fancy's flight
> Is ever wi' my Queen."

> "I see her in the dewy flowers,
> I see her sweet and fair;
> I hear her in the tunefu' birds,
> I hear her charm the air:

> "There's not a bonie flower that springs
> By fountain, shaw, or green,
> There's not a bonie bird that sings,
> But minds me o' my Queen."[2]

Why is it, love, that I feel the need, the appetite for poetry so much more when you are away, and appreciate the uses of it so much more keenly, than when I have you constantly with me? I think I know the reason. It is surely because your love and presence supplies a profoundly poetical element to my life. You *are* my poetry. You appeal when you are by my side to just those elements of my mind and nature that poetry appeals to. Your love, our sweet confidences, your caresses, all the penetrating *romance* of our attachment for each other ravish me just as poetry does—take my breath, elevate my heart to a delicious exaltation of feeling, fill my eyes with tears and my mind with pure purposes. I *live* my poetry when you are by! You have brought into my life all the keen elements of *living* and experiencing that the best literature imparts. That's a secret I had not fathomed before; but now I see it. Ah, love, if I could only give in return something like the same pleasure to you, if I could only be sure of putting the same ecstasy into *your* life by the simple force of my personality and of being with all the ardour of my personality

Your own Woodrow!

Love to all—extravagant love to the babies—and kisses, including dear Maggie.

ALS (WP, DLC) with EAWhw list of names on env.
  1 Robert Burns, "My Wife's a Winsome Wee Thing."
  2 Adapted from Burns's "Of A' the Airts."

To Albert Bushnell Hart

My dear Professor Hart,   Princeton, New Jersey, 9 April, 1892
    The letter enclosed, from the Longmans, in your note of the 5th.,[1] has made a painful impression upon me. Doubtless it may have been meant to be courteous in expression, but in *undertone*, at any rate, it is very far from being so. . . .
    Should nothing prevent the carrying out of my present plans, it ought to be easy for the publishers to get my volume ready for sale by the middle of the Winter. In that way it would be ready for those who wanted to use it in course with yours as soon as they could be ready to use it.
    With much regard,

Sincerely Yours,   Woodrow Wilson

TCL (R.S. Baker Coll., DLC, from a torn TLS).
  1 Both Hart's letter and its enclosure are missing.

To Ellen Axson Wilson

My own darling,   Princeton, Sunday 10 April, 1892

I am *so* glad that you are at last in Gainesville, which will, I hope, be a sort of haven of rest for you, and where you will, I know, derive so much happiness from being with dear Maggie. I like to think of you there. It is such a sweet thought to me that now you have *a sister* in a sense in which you never have had one before,—a companion and intimate of that sweet and closest sort,—giving you a joy such as you have never had since Mama died, and such as *my* love (with its too selfish aspects) can never supply. Ah, how devoutly do I hope that that dear sister's health will permit her to be with you constantly some day! It makes me so happy, dear, to think of new forms and prospects of pleasure and happiness for you! I love to look forward to a companionship for you which will bring new light into your eyes and add still more elasticity to your spirits,—and I've pleased myself constantly ever since receiving your telegram from Gainesville[1] with thoughts of your being a sister now at last! Somehow this does not make me in the least jealous—though I have once and again been almost jealous of Nennie and Marga-Jessie; it only humbles me, to think that there is some happiness that even love such as mine cannot give you—that there is a side of your nature that I cannot satisfy—and fills me with a joy (which, thank God, I know to be unselfish, so much does it seem to enlarge and better my heart!) beyond expression that you *can be satisfied*. I love Maggie anyway, for her own sake: how devotedly will I love her, if she prove the sister you want! Nellie, if you could see my heart as I write these things, you would know how I love you!

I wonder *which* letters of mine you found awaiting you in Gainesville—was that one among them in which I poured out my heart about that exquisite love letter you wrote last Sunday? I've forgotten whether that was addressed to Rome or to Gainesville. I specially wanted that letter to reach you because I would not for the world have *that* letter of yours go without its special answer! I wonder whether you are writing me another Sunday letter to-day, saturated, as that one was, with the very essences of your wonderful little lover's-heart? I think that another letter like that one would permanently turn my head, intoxicate my heart for the rest of my life! Ah, what a rare little genius you are, my Eileen, mavourneen!

I am about to go out to dinner with Magie and Dulles—who have been as good to me, as thoughtful and attentive, as *you* could wish them—as true friends could be—dragging me off to meals at all stages of the week, and keeping me both in good cheer and in good food! I believe I have not taken either dinner or supper at the hotel any Sunday, except the first, since I got back. Last Sunday I dined with the Cornwalls (the first time I was ever *inside* the house[2]) and had a pleasant (tho.' very mild and quiet) time, besides a good dinner. In the evening I took tea with Sloane, and found fewer causes of irritation in his presence than ever before. *This* evening I go to the Murrays'—Mrs. [Mr.] and Mrs. Armstrong being here on the Spring vacation of two weeks which they are fortunate enough to have—ours is to be less than a week! Kuhns and Miss Conn[3] were married last Wednesday, the 6th. They are to live for the present with the Conns.[4] I believe that that is the only Middletown news of any consequence that I have heard. Both the Armstrongs look unusually well, it seems to me, and 'Campbell' does declare himself in uncommonly good health. I wish I found him a little less trying; but I have little doubt about having a good time to-night when the whole family circle is together.

Nothing satisfies me away from you, though, nor can till you come back.

> "When I think on the happy days
> I spent wi' you, my dearie;
> And now that lands between us lie,
> How can I but be eerie!
>
> "How slow ye move, ye heavy hours,
> As ye were wae and weary!
> It was na sae ye glinten by
> When I was wi' my dearie.["][5]

Somehow, my darling, I cannot find a love poem anywhere which does not, if only it ring true, speak some part of my feeling towards you. I seem to have run the whole gamut of love in loving you. I am afraid you would not *like all* the poems that seem to me to speak for me—I am *so* bad in some things, so incurably passionate and out of tune with your sweet, pure nature! But you wont mind their speaking for me, will you?, if only I don't let them speak to you. I realize, my darling, when I am away from you (and realize it with pangs of remorse that are beyond all mercy keen and destructive of my peace!) how deeply I must often bore, if I do not pain, you when you are with me. I realize it by the struggles which I have to keep certain things out of my letters which I should not hesitate to say were you present. If I know anything I know that my love for you is pure and exalted and that, for me, with my intensely passionate nature, these things are no contradiction of that, but only an expression of a love both exalted and profound. But my letters go to you cold— simply on their own merits. I am filled, when I write them, with a keen, absorbing desire to make them speak only what will make you happy; and I instinctively shun a certain part of my thoughts for fear that part might in the cold letter offend my sweetheart's taste. Ah, were I always to write in the mood of the day, what passionate letters I should sometimes write you: and to write in that way would be more candid, more truthful once and again, perhaps. How I do *hate* myself often because it costs me an effort to write what you will like to read! What a keen and torturing pain it is, that there is something in me that I instinctively know, when I am thus cool and away from you, must be hateful to my love! How I wince under her praises, and feel obliged to remind her of those things which she cannot love, but only endures, in me! Darling, it is nothing less than terrible to have to remind you thus; but I dare not do otherwise. I know that you forgive me: oh, how many and how unspeakably sweet are the proofs that you love me *perfectly* all the same! And what a comfort it is *to know how I love you,*—with what ardours of everything that is best in my nature. I am not ashamed *of the way in which I love you,* but only of the way in which, in my rude demonstrations of my man-like love, I must often pain you! I know, too, what an elevating pleasure it is to try to write such a letter as will convey some portion of my absorbing love to you in such shape as will delight my pet. *Does* it not sometimes delight you, darling? I do try so hard to speak my real heart's meaning to you. I do so hard try to write myself down in some adequate phrase as what I am,   Your own Woodrow.

ALS (WP, DLC).
    [1] It is missing.
    [2] At 51 Nassau Street.
    [3] Oscar Kuhns, Associate Professor of Romance Languages at Wesleyan in 1892, and Lillie Belle Conn.
    [4] Professor and Mrs. Herbert William Conn of Middletown.
    [5] "When I Think on the Happy Days," a song formerly attributed to Robert Burns and found in early editions of his works.

From Ellen Axson Wilson

My own darling   Gainesville April 11/92

    I did not get my letter written last night as I expected & am doing it now in great haste as the man is about to go to the office. I have no nurse yet and the children keep me so busy and *distracted* all day that I thought I would wait until evening so as to write a *real* letter instead of one of these horrid scrawls. But I had caught a little cold, thanks to the wretched weather, and so when I got the children to bed I was so tired and so hopelessly *sleepy* that I scarcely had sense enough to go to bed. So my plan about writing you a nice long letter I was *forced* to give up. I feel *quite* well again this morning except for a stiff neck. The children are still quite well except that Jessie coughs a little at night. She seems perfectly well during the day; I rub her chest thoroughly and give her cough medecine, and don't think she will be sick.

Loula and her three children[1] came over Sat., the children are not pretty but 'cute.' Hoyt is a nice, manly, sensible boy. They were very much excited over some new kittens, & Hoyt amused us by telling us with great pride that he "found them before the old cat did." The cat was temporarily absent at the time and he hunted her up and presented them to her.

Loula is looking wretchedly and they are anxious about her. She has hemmorrages from the bowels and is very weak,—has been in this condition for a year.

Oh, I forgot to tell you why I haven't a nurse. Maggie's sister "miscalculated" & her baby is only a few days old now, but I think she will come to me in a few days more. I have had no letter from you since Friday,—will doubtless get one or two this morning.

I love you my dear husband, my own Woodrow, more than life itself & I am oh *so hungry* for a sight of your dear face!

Your own Eileen

ALS (WC, NjP).
 [1] They are identified in Louisa C. H. Brown to EAW, March 5, 1892, n. 7, printed as an Enclosure in EAW to WW, March 7, 1892.

To Ellen Axson Wilson

My own darling,   Princeton, 11th April, 1892

Only a line to-day, alas, because I am overrun with engagements. I enclose a draft on New York for $50. Don't run so low again, sweetheart, but let me know *before* you are 'strapped.' I will send the money at any time you say—I can only *guess* at the state of your purse.

What hard luck to find *Fanny*, of all people in the world, at Gainesville! Oh, it is *too* bad—I am so distressed.

Did you find Maggie, the nurse, waiting for you? I am so glad to think of your being able to settle down now to a *permanent* nurse arrangement. I *love* you darling, "more than tongue can tell, almost more than heart can hold"—to use your own sweet words—and am wholly   Your own Woodrow.

ALS (WC, NjP).

From Ellen Axson Wilson

My own darling,   Gainesville   April 12/92

Just think I had *four* letters from you at once yesterday! Was not that a treat? though to be sure I should have preferred to get them each on its appointed day. My mails have been very irregular ever since I came to the up-country. One of these was forwarded from Rome as also one from Florence; which shows that communication is again established with that unfortunate place.

By the way that reminds me that I have never had time to finish telling you my adventures on that train. I wanted especially to tell you about how I got our supper because oddly enough a Princeton boy is,—remotedly—concerned in it; and I would be *much* obliged if you would look up said boy, John Bowman,[1] by name and be 'nice' to him. When we came upon the wash-out some of the gentlemen went to reconnoiter for supper. They found a little farm-house close by the track & getting the promise of supper there came back to tell the rest. Half a dozen of them came to me to ask if they could help me. I asked them to bring me some cold bread and milk for the children. Back they came in a few moments to announce that there was *neither* to be had— nothing but corn-bread & bacon. Then, without my knowing it, one of these men went out to find some milk, took a long walk through the storm to a distant farm-house and came back triumphant with a large pitcher full, which he insisted upon giving the children free, gratis, for nothing. There proved to be a Pullman sleeper along and some of the people were in the meantime trying to get supper there. They were refused however for it was their rule that only their passengers could use their "buffet." Someone tried to get milk for the children there but they had none; then I suppose they put in a plea for the little children for the next thing I knew they sent me word that I could bring them all in and get supper there. (I had sent to beg them to let me have some bread for them.) The sleeper was different from any I have seen before; it was *all* divided into little compartments, private rooms as it were; I was put into one that was empty but bore marks of occupation and there we had to wait about an hour for our supper, so many 'orders' were there ahead of us. In the meantime one of the occupants returned, a large, fine-looking young man of the Henry Grady type. His manners were not bad except that he was a little *too self-posessed*, so to speak. He began immediately to talk to the children and then to me. I was of course disturbed in mind at being an intruder upon him and so though I did not quite like him I concluded that good taste required that

I should not be ungracious. In answer to one of his questions I told him I was from Princeton. A few moments after his travelling companion appeared, an older and very pleasant looking man with "*Scotchman*" writ large all over him. No. 1 immediately informed him that I was from Princeton whereupon he became much excited, said he had a son there, produced his picture and bragged about him at great length. He is the only child and is evidently adored. He is a freshman, took first group in everything,—is very big and strong, is in the "scrub," &c. &c. He is of course the afore-mentioned John Bowman. They live in Plainfield, N. J. and know Dr. Murray there. He and John Wanamaker (!) married sisters the *same night*;—it was a double wedding. Well, Mr. Bowman immediately took charge of us & was kindness itself. I had intended to take a berth if we were detained all night, but while I was waiting to find out positively about that we actually started off. Then my dilemma was what to do when I reached Atlanta, for we were six hours late and I did not suppose Mr. Henderson would be awaiting me, besides I had never seen him. Worse still none of us in Rome had known his *home* address,—only the *business* address, which of course would do us no good at that time of night. So I decided to go to the Kimball House until morning & Mr. Bowman was going to take me over and manage things for me. But fortunately that was not necessary for I had scarcely gotten out of the car when a gentleman, who turned out to be Mr. Henderson asked if I was Mrs. Wilson. He had been waiting for us all the evening, and had been about to make "a night of it" himself. But I have made a longer tale of this than I intended and now the man is about starting for town & I must close in haste. We have at last beautiful weather again. I am almost entirely rid of my cold & the children seem quite well. I have a nurse today, a *very* nice one I think named Georgia. Maggie's sister is not doing well & she cannot leave her until we leave here.

Oh, I have been so dreadfully home-sick for you darling the last few days;—it seemed as though I could not *bear* it! But I am behaving better today. I had a *good* time dreaming about you all night. I really spent it with you sweet-heart. If I only could dream so *every* night! I love you, Woodrow, my husband, devotedly passionately and am forever   Your own Eileen.

ALS (WC, NjP).
¹ Of the class of 1895.

To Ellen Axson Wilson

My own darling,   Princeton, Tuesday 12 April, 1892

It seems to me extremely hard luck that no-letter day and three-lecture day should be one and the same, as they are on Tuesday! Still, I know that nothing is the *matter*, and the lack of a letter does not seriously affect my spirits: it only increases my loneliness.

I was very much amused and delighted, darling, to notice how perfectly your preliminary report about Maggie (in the only letter I have yet received from Gainesville) would suit her dear sister. I should say of *you*, were I set to describe you briefly. She "is *lovely*. Her beauty seems to me of a very fine type—so much character as well as sweetness. There is nothing *conventional* about it,—though her colouring, complexion, &c. are exquisite too." I should heighten the touches a little, but all the essential points suit you. I have no doubt that it is because Maggie is very much like you and of just the same type exactly.

You will please ma'am sit down upon the receipt of this and tell me exactly and in full what those Atlanta friends said about you, unless you want to wait and have it begged and worried out of you by a series of letters. I shan't let you off a single compliment. I liked so much what Mr. Wright's dear old Scotch mother said, 'You are as bonny as ever.' Bonny seems to me to be an adjective that particularly suits you, you sweet, *bright* beauty, you!

> "When I thy parts run o'er, I can't espy
> In any one the least deficiency;
> But every line and limb diffused thence
> A fair and unfamiliar excellence:
> So that the more I look the more I prove
> There's still more cause why I the more should love."

Ah, my darling, I have to use poetry when you are away, but it does not satisfy me—as you do. I do so love you! I love to let my thoughts dwell close about you in all your lovely person,—as close as a caress. I have kissed you oftener in imagination, I believe, since we parted, than I kiss you when you are with me. I wonder that your lips and cheeks and eyelids do not *burn* sometimes from the sheer intensity of my love-thoughts about them!

I don't know whether or not I have answered your question about going to Columbia. I should say, go by all means. The visit to sister Annie was, in *my* mind, one of the chief objects of your going South, and I should be bitterly disappointed, should you not go. Sister can make room for you in that big house: and if she said 'Come' she certainly meant it. Even if you should find after getting there that it resulted in uncomfortable crowding you could make your stay brief—but at least get a glimpse of sister and the rest of the dear ones there.

How about the visit to Asheville? What did you reply to Mrs. Dubose?

I must go out and vote (in the borough election) before going to my four o'clock class, so good-bye, my precious love. I go to New York this week on Thursday, instead of (Good) Friday. Next week I go Wednesday and Friday and finish the job! How glad I shall be, to be through with it! I have not enjoyed the course: it has been an effort to me all through.

I love you, I adore you, I am altogether and in all things
Your own Woodrow

A *great deal* of love to dear little Maggie (with kisses) and to all; and for the babies what you would give them from yourself.

ALS (WC, NjP).

From Ellen Axson Wilson

My own darling,   Gainesville April 11 [13]/92

Pray excuse the pencil this morning; there is but one bottle of ink in the house and Fannie has it. This suggests to me my many tribulations in regard to letter-writing. It is a continual trouble to me, darling, that I do not—*can* not send you the sort of letters that I know you wish and expect. I feel really miserable every day when I send off these wretched scrawls, and yesterday when I read your *delightful* Sunday letter in which you were hoping that I too was writing you a "love-letter," I felt sick at heart to think of the excuse for a letter that went to you instead of what you longed for. But I never have a *moment* to myself here, and it is no exaggeration to say that I could not to *save my life* write a love-letter in a noisy crowd. I must sit and brood & dream about you, dearest, before the right words come. It is still so *very* cool here and the house is so very "airy" that I cannot sit in my room at all. There is in it a little wood stove which makes a blaze for half an hour while I dress the children and then it grows as cold as ever. There is but one warm room in the house and there we all stay together. I tried last night with great exertion to keep up my fire, bringing arms full of wood upstairs myself &c. in order that I might write to you when I came up to bed. Then when I came there was not a spot in the room except the floor where the light would not shine in the children's eyes. I tried finally to shade them with my body while I wrote,—and I had just written the second line when the baby began to cry. And she was so very indignant—so *outraged* by my conduct that she cried and fought and thrashed the bed for an hour and a half by the clock—that is 'till half past eleven. I began to think she must be sick, but she is so perfectly well this morning apparently that I have been forced to abandon that theory. But the attempt to write a "love-letter" was certainly an ignominious failure. I grow utterly hopeless of sending you anything worth while. I am not my own mistress at all, especially since I am really "roughing it" among these good southern relatives of mine. The letter you liked so much, you dear partial thing, I managed to write only by beginning it when I should by all means have been in bed (that is when everyone else had gone to bed & left me the family sitting room) and finishing it somewhere in the neighborhood of *one* o'clock.

That was such a sweet letter that came yesterday, my love: Ah love you don't know how I *delight* in these precious letters of yours; what priceless treasures they are to me. Yet, darling, I fear that you are expending too much life-energy and time over them, busy as you are with your work. I feel it must be so from my own experience. If I am right I beg you will write me a love-letter only on Sunday & for the rest send me a hasty line just [?] to say how you are and what you do. I will be content merely to know that my darling is "well and doing well." I love you, dear,

> "I love you to the depth and breadth and height
> My soul can reach in feeling out of sight,
> For the end of being and ideal grace.
> I love you to the level of every day's
> most quiet need by sun & candle light"[1]

I am always & *altogether*   Your own Nellie.

ALS (WC, NjP). Postmarked April 13, 1892, 10 p.m.
  [1] From Elizabeth Barrett Browning's "How do I love thee?"

To Ellen Axson Wilson

My own darling,   Princeton, 13 April, 1892
    There certainly must be something the matter with the handling of the mails between Princeton and Gainesville, if you received no letter between Friday and Monday. It *ought* to take only twenty-four hours for a letter to pass between us: Your Mon-

day letter left Gainesville at three o'clock and was delivered here at the same hour on Tuesday—just after I wrote my letter to you. To-day no letter has come (and it's already after four o'clock). I hope nothing has come of my darling's cold and dear little Jessie's cough! Do you have to sleep in a room without fire these chill nights?

The weather here is beginning to moderate. For about a week it has been quite like November weather. Last Monday we had a base-ball game here played amidst constant flows of snow. To-day is more like "base ball weather," though it is still quite cool.

I think that as soon as settled warm weather comes I will open the house every day, or at any rate as often as possible, and maybe use my study. It is such a constant inconvenience to be away from the various working conveniences which I can have there but cannot transfer to this little box of a room here in the hotel.

Westcott, by the way, is going abroad again this summer and I am to have the use of his room[1] for my writing, as I did last summer. Probably it will be an all-summer job again. Indeed I think it pretty certain that it will be, now that I come to look more closely at what remains to be done to complete the 'Epoch.'

There is to be a veritable exodus of our men to Europe this summer—indeed it is beginning already. Westcott and Thompson[2] sail to-morrow morning (on the same ship with Frank[3] and George Patton); in May Harper and Frothingham[4] go; and later Sloane, Cameron,[5] Marquand, perhaps West (and his wife). I am sure my list is quite incomplete—I have heard of some eight or ten, it seems to me—but my head is thick to-day and I cannot think of any more now. Dr. Patton will go, if he is strong enough by that time to stand so much travelling.

I am afraid, darling, that with Fanny in the house, and a boor or two like Minor Brown,—and with no nurse!—Gainesville will be anything but the haven of rest for you that I had hoped and prayed it should be. The absence of a nurse is a really serious matter and makes me quite anxious about you. You will get anything but health and improvement out of your trip at this rate, my poor little pet. If you were of my worrying disposition, instead of your own sunny and sanguine temperament, you would come home thin and worn out! Perhaps you will, anyhow—who knows! Oh, I pray that it may not be so. It's useless for me to beg you to take care of yourself—you never will if there is any work to be done for anyone else.

But I must be off to Faculty meeting—with a heart-breaking wish for a glimpse of your lovely face[,] a touch of your sweet lips.

Ah, darling, if I had always to be away from you, I should die of love,—and should be glad to die.

Your own Woodrow.

ALS (WC, NjP).
¹ 12 West Witherspoon Hall.
² Henry Dallas Thompson, Assistant Professor of Mathematics.
³ Francis Landey Patton, Jr., '93.
⁴ George McLean Harper, Assistant Professor of French, and Arthur Lincoln Frothingham, Professor of Archaeology and the History of Art.
⁵ Henry Clay Cameron, Professor of Greek Language, Clerk of the Faculty, and one of Wilson's teachers when he was an undergraduate.

From the Minutes of the Princeton Faculty

[April 13, 1892]

. . . In the cases of Messrs. ——, ——, —— and ——, found guilty of disorderly conduct by introducing women of bad character into a College room, after a statement of the facts, upon recommendation of the Committee of Discipline it was "Resolved, That the parents of ——, ——, and —— (Members of the Soph. Class in Sc. Sci.), be required to remove their sons from College; with the understanding that they will, at the beginning of the next College year, be granted, upon application, such letters as will enable them to enter another Institution."

"Resolved, That —— (Soph. Cl. Sc. Sci.) be suspended for the rest of the present College year, with permission to return during the period of the final Examinations at the end of the term"

From Ellen Axson Wilson

My own darling,   Gainesville April 14 [1892].

Many thanks for the check which came safely yesterday. I did not send off the $45.00 last week after all because I was afraid that the mails were not getting safely into Rome. So I collected the check and sent off the money-order yesterday. I am having some of the children's sewing done here because this travelling around is robbing me, of course, of all my usual time for spring sewing and the children bid fair to be in rags in a week or two;— am also very busy sewing myself. Have had to get new shoes and spring hats too; so I am glad to get the money.

I wish you could see Nellie now, she looks *splendidly*; her cheeks are like roses. I tried to find a hat for her to play in, could find nothing I liked and finally took a little boy's straw cap with straw visor; you don't know how cunning she looks with it over her curls. The children are all looking especially well since we came here. Nellie *seemed* quite well in Rome but yet her bowels were loose all the time, I suppose owing to the lime-water. Here is her latest speech; as Aunt Lou went out of the room she said "peoples call that yady Mamma; *isn't* peoples funny?"—laughing heartily. I suppose she thinks I have an exclusive right to the name "Mamma."

I have been very busy this morning washing the hair of the crowd,—had to do it just after breakfast while the room was warm; the consequence is I am writing this so fast to get it off in time that my words are almost tumbling over each other. Dear little Maggie sends love to you, so do the babies, and everybody; and so does your little wife, just as much of it as you can possibly want or as your heart can possibly hold.

Your own Eileen.

How do the New York lectures 'go' these days? You have said nothing about them of late.

ALS (WC, NjP).

To Ellen Axson Wilson

New York, Equitable Law Library

My sweet darling,　　　　　　　　Thursday, 14 April, 1892

My eighth lecture is over—next week two more, and then I shall be free of the job. The lecture to-day went rather more easily than usual. I enjoyed speaking a little, and I judged that the audience enjoyed themselves also more than formerly. Doubtless this was one of my best lectures.

But I have been able to think of little else since yesterday but that you *dreamed of me all Monday night*—oh that you had told me *what* you dreamed! Probably that was one reason why I spoke more effectively to-day: it so fills my spirits with all elevating influences to know that my darling loves me in so absorbing and vivid a wise! Bless you dearest, for your love: it *constitutes my life*: it is my motive force—more than ambition or all other motives put together. And I *return* your love with a passion of affection which I am wholly unable to express—even in kisses, caresses, thoughts, ways of service. I am wholly, eagerly, joyously, passionately,　　　　　Your own Woodrow

ALS (WC, NjP).

From Ellen Axson Wilson

My own darling　　　　　　　　Gainesville, April 15 [1892]

There seems a fatality about it!—something happens *every*

morning to make it necessary for me to write you in a "tearing hurry." This morning we are to go to Loula's to spend the day—starting at the usual unearthly hour. And before I go I must write two other letters beside this. One to Atlanta for Aunt Lou giving directions about Maggie's new dress, and one to Sister Annie to see if she can throw any light on the question how to get to Columbia. We interviewed the ticket-agent yesterday and he says we must go to *Seneca City*, leaving here at eleven A.M. & reaching there at 1.45; then we must stay there until 8 o'clock the next morning! there being but one train a day. Isn't that appalling? Or if we prefer we could leave here at ten P.M. getting off at Seneca City at *one*. Fanny declares that there is a better way by some *new* road which her father, who is one of the directors of the Seminary[1] takes. But she can throw no further light on it. So I will see what Sister A. knows about it.

I am trying to persuade Aunt Lou to let Maggie spend the summer with me. I caught her well the other day; she was speaking of how delicate Mamma had been as a child; they hardly thought she would live: "but she spent the summer at the north when she was twelve years old and came back a new creature—perfectly well and strong." I asked her if she did not think it would have the same effect on Maggie and told her how much Aunt Ella said little Ellen's short visit had done for her. She hadn't a word to say. Dr. Baily[2] was here the next day and I asked him if he thought it would do her good. He answered "Yes *ma'm*, I *do*" most emphatically. So you see I have a strong case, but Aunt Lou looks so broken-hearted whenever I speak of it that I have scarcely the heart to press it. She says she can't live without her; and I think from what she says is afraid Maggie would get weaned away from her, or as she says "not want to come back." She says she can go when she is twelve. Though Stockton apparently did not notice it Maggie has all the dreadful Gainesville peculiarities of speech. She says "You was" & "I come" instead of "came"; she has no final "g's" &c. &c. I am almost afraid to speak to so sensitive a child about it & besides what good would it do when I am to be with her but a few days. What would you do? Do you think there would be more chance of correcting it if I had her for the summer now than if I waited until she is twelve? She may improve in Athens, but I doubt it, for the worst of it is that Aunt Lou herself has dropped into the same careless ways & speaks as badly as her neighbours. I don't think I ever knew before of a case where one who inherited the speech of a gentlewoman afterwards degenerated into a distinctly illiterate style.

What would you do about the visit? Would you press the point? Of course there is the difficulty of getting her there. If I were going straight from here she could go with me but as it is she would have to meet me at Asheville—if I go there.

I told Rose and Beth[3] both that I would try to spend a few days with them if nothing in the meantime happened to prevent.

And now a hasty good bye darling. I love you more almost than heart can hold, and oh how I *long* to see you!

Your little wife   Eileen

ALS (WP, DLC) with WWhw names on env.
 1 The Columbia Theological Seminary.
 2 J. W. Bailey, M.D., an obstetrician of Gainesville, who had cared for Ellen during the birth of her first two children.
 3 Elizabeth Adams Erwin of Morganton, N. C.

To Ellen Axson Wilson

My own sweet Nellie,   Princeton, Friday 15 April, 1892
    I have just received that plaintive pencilled letter of Wednesday in which you explain why you cannot write *leisurely* letters, like my own. You must not think, my lovely sweetheart, that I am *a whit* dissatisfied with the hasty notes you sometimes send me. I *know* how hard it must be for you to write at all—though I admit I did not realize quite the extent to which you are "roughing it." The detailed revelations of your letter have filled me, indeed, with a new anxiety about your health in that chill house. Please, darling, tell me just how bad your cold is. I shall be very unhappy till I hear. As for your letters, my darling, let them be never so brief or hasty—let them consist of but a line, like a telegram, assuring me of your health and welfare,—and I shall be *perfectly satisfied*. This is said in all soberness and earnestness, pet,—and not under a mere generous impulse. You *must* not *worry* about not being able to write the sort of letters you would like to write—to do that would prove that you did not know how to make me happy; and *you must never sit up after bed-time to write to me*—if I never get another letter as long as I live. I feel like apologizing for asking you to write another love letter like that precious one, which ought to satisfy a fellow for the rest of his life, like an exquisite poem. *I don't want another.* Just so you can once and again tell me the leading details of what is happening to you and the girlies, I shall be delighted. You are to take all this literally, my Eileen—for I mean every word of it, with an intense earnestness which you *dare* not neglect, if you love me. I *know* how you love me: I don't need to be told elaborately—just one sentence is enough—you are a matchless little

lover, and I *live* on your love every moment of my life. Save all your eloquence on the subject till you are safe in my arms again and can pour it all into my ear and fairly make me beside myself with delight! Then you can have the pleasure of seeing how elaborated love-making *tells* upon me—makes an extravagant boy of me, turns and *keeps* me young and in high spirits. Love *talk* and caresses are a sure prescription against all my maladies of spirit. Your business *now* is to worry about nothing—least of all about me—to be light hearted and plump for your home-coming! See to it that you do your duty!

As for me, I am in the best of spirits, and don't need you at all—not a bit!—for the present! What I need is that you should be happy, should enjoy yourself and all that you do and see among your loved ones—and I am wretched only when that need is not filled—Remember that, miss!

As for writing love-letters, that does not hurt me! *I* do not write in a family sitting-room (if I did, I should go crazy!) with the children romping about and pulling at me; I do not have the constant care, and the dressing and undressing, of three boisterous young misses. *I* can 'brood' (that's a happy word!) over the words I need to tell you my love *all the time*—and I do. The hours when I am not writing to you are a continuous preparation for the hour when I am. My letters but pour out the words of love that have been accumulating in my heart during the silence of twenty-four hours spent for the most part alone and in the constant consciousness that I am   Your own Woodrow.

Love to all—kisses to Maggie and the babies. Does your nurse prove a good one?

ALS (WC, NjP).

From Ellen Axson Wilson

My own darling,   Gainesville April 16/92
This is little Margaret's birthday! it seems very suitable that it should be spent *here*.[1] How glad I am that it is not literally her *birth*-day, but that *it* is six years past! The little people are all very happy over *three* tiny little red trunks with keys to them and three mites of—ten cent—dolls;—bought in order that there might be some clothes small enough to go in the trunks!

I had a pleasant day with Loula yesterday. She is certainly a fine girl,—and the most *cheerful* sufferer I ever saw. We feel very anxious lest she may have some fatal disease, and what makes it worse is that the doctor does not seem quite to understand the case. She has suffered terribly for a year, at intervals; yet she is the one who keeps up the spirits of all the rest.

She says she is *sure* it would do Maggie good to go home with me and it seems a splendid opportunity too; besides Maggie is wild to go. She thinks it would be "the making of her." Yet she thinks we will have to give it up for the present because she believes it would almost kill Aunt Lou. Just now it would be harder than at any other time because she is leaving her old home and parting from Loula & her children; and that itself is almost more than she can bear. I had almost come to this conclusion myself so I suppose I must yield gracefully and say no more about it. I am shocked to find how expensive the trip to Columbia will be. If I take the nurse it will be $25.00 at least. I have already spent seven of my fifty on shoes &c. for them, and when I pay my nurse, my washerwoman, & my semptress there will be *very* little margin left, scarcely enough I fear for the hotel-bill for twenty-four hours for the crowd which this trip involves. Don't you think perhaps I had better give it up? And yet I suppose I have gone too far now, in writing to Sister Annie, &c. to retreat gracefully.

Do you remember the little beauty Martine Saunders, whom we used to admire so much? She is a young lady now and called on me a day or two ago. She is still a beauty, though I think not quite so lovely as when she was a child. Her father is old Col. Saunders, Uncle Warren's crony;—you remember how they entertain each other night after night by going to sleep together in their respective easy chairs? He says, by the way that your humble servant is the most beautiful woman he ever saw! He is president and proprietor of the bank, and when I went in to draw the check the other day I noticed that he seemed on very cordial terms with Maggie, but I noticed nothing else. It seems however that the younger men in the bank have a great joke on him about it; for they declare that he made desperate efforts to keep up a steady conversation with Maggie in order that he might thereby gain more time to look at *me*, forsooth! and they say that so distraite was he, so little did he have his mind on what he was *saying*,—that finally it became nothing but "oh, Maggie, Maggie, Maggie, Maggie!" an indefinite number of times! I hope you won't be jealous of my venerable conquest!

How is it that those men can leave Princeton so early as this? It is very odd but I am glad of it for then you can do it yourself next year! *I* think you had better move directly to Mr. Westcott's room instead of to the study. Why not? Oh darling if I were only there with you! Nellie was so sorry for me this morning because

I wanted to see you so much that she volunteered to "go today & bring you" to me. Dear little soul! We all love you darling, oh so dearly and I am in every thought,   Your own Eileen

ALS (WC, NjP).
¹ In her birthplace.

To Ellen Axson Wilson

My precious little Nellie,   Princeton, Saturday 16 April, 1892
    What a relief it is to turn away from the Supreme Court Reports, over which I have been toiling all morning, to you, my charming little sweetheart, every thought of whom is so sweet and restful! Sometimes it is hard for me to decide whether pain or pleasure predominates in my thoughts,—the pain,—the *intolerable* pain,—of separation,—the pleasure, the *unspeakable* pleasure of loving you and thinking of you *as mine* and as someday to be back in my arms, nestling close, with quickened breath because of your love for me! I've found some lines of a song in Shakspere that almost exactly fit this double mood:

> "Nor shines the silver moon one half so bright
> Through the transparent bosom of the deep,
> As doth thy face through tears of mine give light:
> Thou shinest in every tear that I do weep;
> No drop but as a coach doth carry thee."¹

Again and again do tears fill my eyes when I think of your [you]—sweet tears of love, hot tears of longing—and, oh, how beautiful you look through those tears!

    It's still cool here—*quite* cool—but there are some thrills of spring in the air, and as they come I think, with such ecstasy, of the sweet summer we shall spend together,—of reading to you as you sketch, of sitting with you on the piazza in the twilight, of being close by your side all evening, your presence dominating everything, both within me and about me! Ah, how happy I shall be—if you are—and what a training I am going through now for that time! What am I *not* learning of the charm and delight of your presence!

    But there are two matters of business which I must speak of, and I shan't find time or place for them unless I break off, and bring them in despite my thoughts of you. First, as to money. What I sent you can't last you long, and wont you, sweetheart, let me know *in plenty of time* when you need the next remittance? Let me know, particularly, as far ahead as possible, the date at which you expect to leave Gainesville. (Where are you going next, by the way, to Columbia or to Asheville?)

Next, as to the watch. It was sent, by express, to Rome, on March 31, and should have reached there four or five days before you left. I have gotten the agent here to write on about it, and I hope it will be forwarded soon. Did you not receive Nellie's cloak either, with the colours inside? You have not spoken of their arrival. I trust they did not miscarry too.

Thank you, pet, for repeating Nellie's speeches to me: they are so sweet, and so characteristic. Are you penetrating dear little Maggie's reserve and learning to know her familiarly, so that you can give me some further report of her character—or does being cooped up by the cool weather in the same room with Fannie and the rest prevent the progress of any real acquaintance or intimacy?

You don't know, darling, how much it sharpens the edge of my loneliness to go into our house here,—and yet whenever I enter it I want to *stay*, so strongly, so sweetly does every foot of it suggest *you*. If I dared sit down in one of the rooms, I could sit there, I am sure, absorbed by the hour in the sweetest and yet saddest dreams conceivable—of you and the children and all our delightful life together—penetrated through and through with the consciousness of being,   Your own Woodrow.

ALS (WC, NjP).
    1 *Love's Labour's Lost*, Act IV, Scene 3, lines 30-34.

From Ellen Axson Wilson

My own darling,   Gainesville April 17 [1892]
    This is of course the nurse's "afternoon out," & I have the children, but as they are busily playing just now I will try to scribble a little note because I believe if I do and can manage to get it mailed it will leave tonight. I had the unexpected treat of a letter from you today, for Uncle Warren is here and went to the office after church. He ran over from Athens last night to spend Sunday and see me; he is the same dear kindly old soul he always was. His devotion to Maggie—his positive infatuation about her is really touching. He loves all children though, and is paying devoted attention to mine; and they have taken a desperate fancy to him. He gave me a shock just now at dinner by declaring *to their faces* that he did not know which was the prettier, Nellie or Jessie. I did not know whether to be most concerned for Jessie or *Margaret*. I protested vigourously; whereupon Aunt Lou gave me another shock by quoting Mrs. *Bones* as saying "Mrs. Axson

you ought to *praise* Ellen more, it would do the child good to have some *little* idea how perfectly beautiful she is!" Did you ever hear of anything funnier than that? Aunt Lou must have gotten "awfully mixed" in some way. It is odd, by the way, how many people about here say that Ed's wife[1] and I are alike. Did I tell you that she was "expecting" any day now. It seems she did not want any children, kept it off from the first, but finally decided to have *one* because Ed was so crazy for them. Now however Loula says her "receipt," whatever it is, seems to have failed. Though I do her the credit of supposing that regard for Ed, or perhaps for the sad condition of an only child has again triumphed. I am afraid she is rather too much of a society woman. They say she never occupies herself with domestic affairs or sewing, in fact that she doesn't do any sort of work. Yet after all I suppose there is no *virtue* in the mere *doing* of such work when it isn't necessary. She must have the most extraordinary social gifts. For instance they went one summer on a round of visits among Ed's half-brothers & country cousins. They all dreaded her coming but declare now that they will never mind it again,—she was so pleasant and adapted herself so easily to everything. Aunt Lou says she finds something to please and interest her in every situation. I am excessively sorry that I can see nothing of her on this trip, for I have a great curiosity about her. I have seen two pictures of her here and confess that I was a good deal disappointed; the features and expression are not especially good; I suppose it is the wonderful colouring that gives the impression of such dazzling beauty. But the children are "carrying on" so now that I really don't know what I am writing so I think I had better stop and read them some Bible stories. At present they are all three singing "Jesus loves me" in chorus. It is an open air concert for we have at last a lovely warm, bright day & I am writing on the front piazza and watching them at their play in the garden. They are *all* looking splendidly & the older ones *are* perfectly well. Nellie has quite a little cold just now, but does not seem at all sick with it. My cold is only a slight one in the head & throat,—nothing of the least consequence. I will be better now that the weather is good. I assure you that apart from that I am as well as can be—plump and rosy and not in the *least* tired. I am sure I have abundant evidence to all this for I think at least five hundred people have told me since I came south that I was "looking splendidly," "like a fresh young girl," "better than ever!" &c! &c! &c!! And *you* have now golden opinions from them all for taking such good care of me. And now good-bye my own darling. Ah me, I love to be with these little people, but I *would* like to put them to sleep for a bit for I *feel* like making love to my darling this afternoon. Remember dear how *constantly* I am doing so down in my heart of hearts.   Your own   Eileen

ALS (WC, NjP).
[1] Mary Celestine Mitchell Brown, wife of Edward T. Brown.

To Ellen Axson Wilson

My own precious darling,   Princeton, Sunday 17 April, 1892
    I feel sure that when this separation is over it will always seem to me the longest season of my life,—longer even than those twenty-six years that I waited to find you. Now that I have known you and possessed you these seven blessed years, my life penetrated through and through with your sweetness and your love, I can do nothing without you. I wait for my life to begin again. My work goes dully without inspiration—might be *any*body's work, so much does my individuality seem to be merged in you. How ridiculous it was for me to think of going to Europe alone—and doing effective work there![1] I cannot even enjoy myself normally —I cannot enjoy my*self* at all! Last Thursday I stayed in New York all afternoon (taking the last train back) in order to visit the Metropolitan museum; but I did not half enjoy it. Every beautiful thing I saw but made me think the more longingly of you. I wondered whether it was one of the things *you* had seen there, and what you thought of it. For *that's* the rub: my *mind's* loneliness. All my best and most intimate thoughts I must keep to myself: my mind is a hermit, imprisoned in a dreary silence. Accustomed to expand in the sunshine that goes with you, it now feels benumbed, withered, incapable of the healthier sort of growth

> "A solitary fagot will not burn:
> Bring two, and cheerily the flame ascends."[2]

That gallery seemed empty without you. If I had just *come* from you—that morning, say—it would have been different. But the solitariness has taken hold upon me, and the solitary fagot will not burn. The best pictures and figures for me are in my head.

> "If men but knew the mazes of the brain
> And all its crowded pictures, they would need
> No Louvre or Vatican: behind our brows
> Intricate galleries are built, whose walls
> Are rich with all the splendors of a life."[3]

And no painter ever painted love or womanhood in half so sweet a wise as they are displayed in the gallery behind my brows. If my thoughts did not have that retreat there would be no happiness for me at all; but as it is I can sit and brood among those pictures till my heart burns and my eyes glisten with the deepest pleasure, surely, that it is given a man to know. Wordsworth has come as near as possible to describing one of the faces in that sweet retreat—or rather one phase of the beautiful face that dominates it everywhere, being present in *all* pictures there that are most dear and most delightful:

> "And she hath smiles to earth unknown;
> Smiles, that with motion of their own
> Do spread, and sink, and rise;
> That come and go with endless play,
> And ever, as they pass away,
> Are hidden in her eyes."[4]

Was there ever so *perfect* a description of those smiles, so subtle, so deep, so constant, so changeful, and yet always so charming, that "come and go with endless play" upon that face I love so, and which even when they pass away lie "hidden in her eyes"? When I came upon those lines this morning they fairly snatched my breath away. I don't believe that Wordsworth ever saw a face that deserved or matched those lines quite as perfectly as yours. Oh, if I could only write poetry such as that, or paint like one of the old masters, to immortalize that face—a face *meant* for poetical treatment: for poetry or painting—not for sculpture—meant to be described in whatever depicts sweet spiritual elements. Ah, darling, when you brought poetry into my life, why did you not make a poet of me? 'Twas almost cruel to fill a fellow's heart so full of poetical emotion and then leave it to ache for very fullness, without any vent but poor quotation for all its eager impulses. Perhaps it was selfish calculation on your part. You knew that, if I could not relieve myself of the sweet ecstacies of loving by writing verse or painting pictures, I should spend my fervor and delight in kisses and caresses, and all extravagancies of love-making—that I should pour out upon *you* all the ardour of my nature! Ah well! I know that that is the *sweetest* way of all; but just now, when it is forbidden me, and I have nothing to give even you but these very words which I cannot mould to my purpose, what am I to do, what is to become of me! At any rate, it is some relief to write the simple words, '*I love you*,' and to 'take on' about you in the most adequate words I can find. "Shame," says Mr. Sill,

> Shame! that a man with hand and brain
> Should, like a love-lorn girl, complain,
> Rhyming his dainty woes anew,
> When there is honest work to do!"[5]

But it's in the same poem that he says "a solitary fagot will not burn"—and the same poem ends by his being rescued from his hermitage by his lady-love. So there's no shame about it, but an honest, blessed fact,—of the strength, that best strength, that comes from heart-companionship. 'Tis this "treading among flowers of joy" that

> "Shalt show us how divine a thing
> A Woman may be made."[6]

This stubborn dullness of spirit and mind that I experience while you are away from my side—while all the sweet strength of communion is taken away—is not proof of weakness, but of strength and blessedness, inasmuch as I am to have you, and live at my full, again! I can't tell you how proud and happy it makes me to realize my dependence upon you, because you are so worthy of being depended upon by the strongest of men: "A spirit yet a woman too,"—a spirit to purify, strengthen, exalt a man,—a woman to delight him! Ah, darling, how shall I ever tell you what is in my heart about you! It is a delightful pleasure to *try* to tell you; but it always ends in comparative failure. I can only give you some faint conception of what I mean when I say '*I love you!*' I never knew how much could go into a few simple words— how much of life and soul and all there is in a man—until you loved me and I could say them *to you*! It is my sole title to you that I can love you as much as you deserve to be loved. Whatever other limitations I have, there are none at all on that side. I have an infinite capacity for loving; and the whole of that capacity is exerted upon you—my peerless little wife. It is beyond measure delightful to give you all of *something* that you deserve. My *life* is not what it should be for your sake, but *my love is*. In heart, if not in character, I am wholly and without limitation

Your own Woodrow.

Give what messages and kisses you will to our precious babies and our sweet little sister, Maggie. Please, ma'am, give aunt Lou my love too—and give Fannie some message, if you can think of any that would be at once suitable and truthful!

Your W.

ALS (WC, NjP).

[1] The subject of many letters in 1886-87, printed in Vol. 5.

2 From Edward Rowland Sill's "The Hermitage."
3 *Ibid.*
4 From "Louisa."
5 From "The Hermitage."
6 From Wordsworth's "To a Young Lady."

From Ellen Axson Wilson

My own darling,   Gainesville April 18/92

The little watch has come at last this morning,—forwarded from Rome. It is a little beauty, so very chaste! I am *so* much obliged to you, dear! You were of course a naughty boy to get it when the old one *could* have been fixed, at least to serve my temporary purpose, but I *love* you for doing it all the same. It will be my birthday present. The baby's cloak came promptly & has been most useful. I have never had time to use the paints. That reminds me of "Sims Autobiography"!—Dr. Marion Sims![1] Did you ever read it? It is *fascinating.* Uncle Will lent it to me in Rome but I hadn't time to read a word of it there. I left it on the table of my room there and told Uncle Will where he would find it. A week after it *followed* me *here*, Florence having supposed that it was a book of my own that I had forgotten. So *now* I am reading it with great interest.

We seem to have nothing but extremes in the way of weather, it has been uniformly cold since I came here, and now all at once we are suffocating with heat. I hope the change will enable Nellie to throw off her cold; mine is already getting better.

I am *especially* busy today preparing some work for the semptress, and *must* cut this short, dear.

I have had another *good* night, darling, through the whole of which I dreamed of you! I could not tell you *what* I dreamed, it was all inarticulate love-making;—but I was in your arms and it was oh, so sweet! and I could see your dear face so plainly. Yet after all scarcely more plainly than in my *day*-dreams, for even *then*—that is *now*—I can see those beautiful eyes shining on me so clearly that it seems scarcely possible they are so many miles away. Ah if she could only *kiss* them again and yet again what a happy little wife would be   Your own Eileen

ALS (WP, DLC) with WWhw notation on env.: "Jenkins v. Culpepper Co., 1 Hugh., U. S. Circ. 568."
1 James Marion Sims, *The Story of My Life* (New York, 1884).

To Ellen Axson Wilson

My own darling,   Princeton, Monday 18 April, 1892

Here's a passage from a letter which will interest you (I've gotten singularly few letters recently). It is from Dr. Albion W.

Small,[1] now President of Colby University, Waterville, Maine, but Professor-elect of Sociology at Chicago, where he is to go in the Fall. I met him in Baltimore, where he took his degree, and where he attended a portion of one of my courses on Administration. I wrote him about another matter, of course (a place for a boy[2] who wants to teach), but added to the business the 'pleasure' of congratulating him, with some cordial words of appreciation, on his appointment to Chicago. This will explain his language. "My dear Friend, Reversing the order of your note, I will make pleasure precede business. Your hearty words of congratulation were most acceptable, but it would be still more agreeable to me if I could in return congratulate the University and myself with you on your acceptance of the Chair of Political Science at Chicago. I have kept hoping that this arrangement would be made and do not yet give it up. For months I have been telling President Harper that no appointment could, in my judgment, be more satisfactory than yours to that position. Whether you would accept or not, of course I do not know. But I have just returned from looking over the ground and it seems to me that no such field can be opened in this country during our life for work that will count the most in raising the political intelligence of the people."[3] President Harper, for some reason, does not seem to take kindly to suggestions concerning me! Perhaps it's just as well for me not to be tempted away from a place so ideally fitted as Princeton for the quiet, contemplative study and slow-paced thought that must go into my *magnum opus.*[4]

Of course I knew that you must have a good deal more money to go to Columbia, my pet. Don't worry about that—only tell me *when* you will need it and give me a rough (but ample) estimate of the amount.

And so you *are* going to Asheville, *and* to Morganton! Dear me! Of course I *wanted* you to do this: I don't mean to complain a bit; but it makes my heart sink to think how long it is to be before you start for home! I'm getting a bit desperate. But all right—I can stand it,—after what I *have* stood. I may get a little hardened to the slow torture of it! Of course you must go. There's no telling when you will make another chance, and it would not be kind to leave *such* friends out of your itinerary.

It almost makes me ready to counsel you to press your wish to bring Maggie north with you, what you tell me about the opinion of the doctor, and of every one else whose opinion is valuable, with regard to the effect it would probably have upon her health. The case of mama is indeed in point—and is most impressive—perhaps as a *warning*. But possibly it *would* be inhuman to urge it just now upon Aunt Lou. Perhaps you must let it drop (unless the doctor should actually think the change *necessary* for the child). It goes hard with me to say so, though— so many imperative arguments (in addition to our pleasure) are there for bringing her.

I love you darling, with a full—an aching, heart and am in every thought,   Your own Woodrow

Much love to all

ALS (WC, NjP).
    ¹ Albion Woodbury Small, born Buckfield, Maine, May 11, 1854. A.B., Colby University, 1876; student, Newton Theological Institution, 1876-79; studied at the Universities of Berlin and of Leipzig; Ph.D., the Johns Hopkins, 1889. President, Colby, 1889-92. Served the remainder of his academic career at the University of Chicago from 1892 to 1924 as head of the Department of Sociology, Dean of the College of Liberal Arts, and Dean of the Graduate School. Prolific author, founder of the *American Journal of Sociology*, and president of the American Sociological Society, 1912-14. Died March 24, 1926.
    ² Winthrop More Daniels. See WW to W. M. Daniels, May 1, 1892.
    ³ This letter is missing.
    ⁴ A reference to his projected "Philosophy of Politics." See the Editorial Note, "Wilson's First Treatise on Democratic Government," Vol. 5.

From Ellen Axson Wilson

My own darling,   Gainesville, April 19/92
    I write this morning before breakfast, for having been waked early by the children I thought I would gain a little time and quiet in that way. It is deliciously cool and fresh now; the garden which I look out upon is full of old-fashioned, sweet scented flowers,—lilacs & pinks &c. Some exquisite doves are there too, distracting my attention badly with their pretty play. So that the prospect is altogether fair, and I feel very peaceful and serene. And that reminds me dear, to say that you must not suppose I am at all uncomfortable here. In the first place Fannie has improved I think, certainly there has been no back-biting in my presence, and very little of the old-time "palaver";—and none of the "boors" live in the house as you supposed. Minor is the only one in town and I have seen him but once since the night I came. As for the fare I wish you could share with me the nice chickens and Aunt Lou's *delicious* butter, fresh every day, as yellow as gold and sweet as a nut. I never saw anything so nice. I can scarcely resist eating it all up "plain so."
    You ask more about Maggie and indeed I have been intending to write but have always been so hurried. I am quite sure that I have never seen a more interesting girl or one of more unusual mental promise. She is so companionable, talks so well, in spite of her slips in grammer,—and her little mind is so thoroughly

alive and wide awake that it is a constant pleasure to be with her and to study her. She is, I am glad to add, a simple child at the same time,—devoted to dolls &c.,—will play for an hour with her rubber ball. She is very sweet and affectionate, and at the same time very *spirited*. I think she has unusual force and decision of character. There is not one trace of *pertness* about her which I think is rather remarkable considering how bright she is and how much noticed. Indeed she is remarkably little spoiled *considering*; for she is the centre around which everything revolves here, Aunt Lou saying, for instance, about certain dishes, "Maggie doesn't like them *and so we* never have them"! I think she is really quite a good child in spite of it all, though there is nothing *angelic* about her. She doesn't impress you with any special *lovliness* of character as Ellen[1] used to at her age. But she is, on the other hand, better than Ellen is now for most of her "heavenly-mindedness" was "the early dew of morning." In short Maggie is a little sister to be delighted with in every respect. At the same time Stockton's rather extravagant praise had the usual, *inevitable* result. My expectations were *unreasonably* raised and I was of course a little disappointed. There is nothing *brilliant* about either her beauty or her mind. She is *very* pretty but not by any means "the most beautiful child I ever saw";—perhaps she *is* the prettiest of her age though. Jessie and Nellie are both much prettier now, but there is no telling what they will be at the ungainly age of ten.

I did not save as much time as I hoped by coming down early for before I had finished my second page the family came in, & I am finishing as usual after breakfast, and I must close in haste for Loula is coming to spend the day & I have several things to attend to before her arrival. Nellie's cold seems better. I love you darling more than life & I long to see you with a longing unutterable. I am counting the days now 'till it will be possible for this parting to end. With my whole heart

Your own Eileen

ALS (WP, DLC) with WWhw on env.
[1] Ellen Axson, daughter of Randolph Axson.

To Ellen Axson Wilson

My own darling,   Princeton, Tuesday 19 April, 1892
The college sprang into life again at ten o'clock this morning, after the Easter recess, which began last Thursday at noon. It relieved me of four of my six lectures for this week: so that I had *no* lectures for this week: so that I had *no* lecture yesterday,

and this is a *two*-lecture, instead of *three*-lecture, day. It happened so very opportunely; for I lecture twice this week in New York (Wednesday and Friday), to finish up the job there, and I needed an extra free day for the extra preparation needed. This week ends the *stress* of work under which I have been laboring since I left Baltimore—and I shall be very thankful to strike into a more leisurely pace. Most of the examination papers of last term still remain to be read; but, after the pull I have had during the last three months, I look forward to the job of reading them almost as if to a respite! It will be a *bore*, but there will be so much less *out-put* called for: it will be an endurance, not an exertion.

That was indeed a delightful story you told about Col. Saunders and your experience in the bank! It ought to go into a plot: the "Maggie, Maggie, Maggie" is an exquisite touch! No, indeed, I am not jealous of the old gentleman: I admire his taste: he is assuredly right about your looks—*they* are simply a fact, and a man would be blind who did not see (what I have seen ever since the very first time I saw you) that you are the most beautiful woman in the world!

What you say about Maggie's illiterate ways of speaking is indeed alarming, especially in view of the fact that that has become aunt Lou's method of talking too, so that the child hears nothing else. The only possible way of curing a child of such a habit is, not precept (at any rate, not precept alone), but association, constant and unbroken, with those who habitually speak correctly. It's heart-breaking to think that she has no present prospect of that; for the habit grows harder and harder to break, of course, as she grows older. We *must* get her away *soon*, and *keep* her just as long as possible when we get her. 'She can come when she is twelve'? How old is she now? Does she read much—and does she show no consciousness of her habit? But of course she does not! I would not speak to her *now* about it, not only because of her sensitiveness, but also because it could do no good unless you could stay with her and gently train her in the matter.

But I must stop: I have two lectures to finish—one for this afternoon, the other for New York to-morrow. I have written this letter just as fast as I could scratch and must now precipitate the close (so to speak!).

I love you, darling, oh, I love you—how I wish I had time to dwell on my phrases and tell you just how passionately and consciously I love you all the time!   Your own Woodrow.

Scores of kisses to the precious babies and to Maggie. Love to all the rest.   W.

ALS (WC, NjP).

From Ellen Axson Wilson

My own darling,   Gainesville April 20 [1892]

I have heard from Bro. George with regard to schedules to Columbia. He says the best way is to go to Augusta and sends me the schedule. By it I can reach Columbia the same day that I leave here; but it makes a terrible day's journey for babies! We would leave here at 6.28 A.M., would have to rise at 4.00—& reach Columbia at 10.40 that night! However I shall try it if I can get through tickets & checks here. But if I must find my trunks & recheck them & buy tickets, as well as change cars with my little crowd in Atlanta, the route will be impossible, for the connection is close there,—only ten minutes delay. Uncle Henry says it is best to go the *Greenville* way and that is the one I shall take if I don't go to Augusta. I leave here at 11.03 A.M. & reach Columbia at 3.50 P.M. the *next* day, (exactly as I would if I went to Seneca,) remaining in Greenville from 3.00 P.M. one day to 9.00 A.M. the next. But there is no change except at Greenville & it is better than Seneca because Cousin Jimmie Hoyt[1] and his family live there, and Aunt Lou is going to write to him to meet me & see me to a hotel &c. They are very nice people;—you remember Stockton visited them last summer. They were the girls that he turned the hose on in Rome! I am going down as soon as I can today, to find out about through routes and then I shall write at once to Bro. George and settle this puzzling business. I have postponed going from Thursday to Friday in order to make more sure of some more money coming from Princeton in answer to my statement on that subject. Even if I take the two-day route that will still enable me to get there Sat. afternoon.

Nellie was stung by a wasp a little while ago but seems perfectly easy again now. But it has reminded me of those wasp nests at home,—the huge one in the honey-suckle and the small ones in various windows about the house. You know we were going to be so sure to get rid of them while the weather was cold and they were dormant; and we never did! Perhaps if you send a man around *very promptly* it is not yet too late. Won't you please see to it? We can't get at those in the vines after the leaves have gotten thick. And please make him devise some way to kill those bees in the bank; perhaps a burning fagot stuck in would do it. Finally and *especially* please *don't* do any of it *yourself*! When are the Stockton's going to give up the house and stable? How I hope that stable will be vacated before the fly season begins. Everyone says our troubles with them are due to that stable. Now that they have begun to tease here I am continually racking my brain to think of some way to keep them out at home. I think another all summer struggle with them would be the death of me!

Dear me this *is* a dull letter indeed—worse than all its predecessors! I would like to make up for it a little on this last page but there is a Bedlam broke loose in the room, and I feel perfectly dazed & incapable of thought. Nellie's cough is still better I think, though since the storm last night the weather is again very damp & cold & I am a little anxious about them. Am so glad I am going to leave here soon! No letter from you yesterday of course,—but there will I expect be two today. Oh darling I am just heart-sick for a sight of your dear face! I feel as though I *could* not bear it longer. Much as I want to see Sister Annie I have to fairly *make* myself go there. But it will not be much longer now. I will stay a week in Columbia, three days in Morganton & three in Asheville, then start from Asheville for home the ninth of May. I love you darling *passionately* and I am with every heart-throb,

Your own Eileen

ALS (WC, NjP).
  [1] Son of Henry Francis Hoyt.

To Ellen Axson Wilson

My own darling,   Equitable Law Library, N. Y., 20 April '92
    My ninth lecture just over. One more, on Friday, and then *some* relief. I wish I had the strength to write you a love letter—but I have not. I feel as if I *could* write such a letter as would make your eyes shine, your pulses race, your heart rejoice: for the love *thoughts* people my mind just now like the liveliest company imaginable. I do love you *so* ardently! But somehow lecturing here tires me specially—and you know how fatigue robs me of *words* first of all.

    But I am *quite* well—*very* well,—by no means too tired to be good for me. And I do love, love, love my precious, my matchless little wife.   Your own Woodrow

ALS (WC, NjP).

From Ellen Axson Wilson

My own darling,   Gainesville, April 21/92
    Just a hasty line today for of course I have my packing to do and am busy, and besides must give as much time as possible to the family.

    I go by way of Greenville, for it is as I expected,—I could get tickets and checks no farther than to Atlanta on the Aug. route.

I don't dread this journey at all: Cousin Jimmie was written to yesterday—has probably gotten the letter by this time. And if some of them meet me it will simplify things a great deal. I see from your letter received yesterday that you did not realize how soon we were to leave here,—but you need not worry about my not getting the money. I shall borrow ten dollars from Loula and then I will have more than twenty to start with and will be quite comfortable. It does not make a *particle* of difference.

What a sweet *precious* letter was that other that came yesterday, darling! It almost made me cry, it was *so* sweet,—and you are so lovely and so splendid,—and it is so delicious to be loved thus. Oh it is impossible to describe the exquisite pleasure and pain with which I read such letters,—the joy in our love and the longing for my lover's dear presence. Oh dearest how I do love *love, love* you!

Well, this parting will soon be over & as I live it is the *last* time that I will ever leave *you*. With all my heart,

Your own Eileen.

All well.

ALS (WC, NjP).

To Ellen Axson Wilson

My own darling,   Princeton, Thursday 21 April, 1892

I wonder if you wrote me a letter last Sunday which I did not get? A letter written on Monday and one written on Tuesday have reached me, but I have heard nothing of Sunday—not even that you did not write. I ask because I don't want to lose a line of your dear writing. I have an affection for every line of your writing—I have hesitated sometimes to tear up an old memorandum of yours—dearly as I love to tear up memoranda!

I enclose a draft on New York, my darling, for $100. There has not been time for you to answer my request for an estimate of how much you would want; but I send this in order that you may be in no uncertainty about money in case you are fixing upon a day for leaving Gainesville. Don't fail, however, to *keep* me informed of the state of your purse, so that I can remit promptly the sums you may need.

I have just come from a meeting of the Special Committee[1] at West's house, where the committee first lunched and then worked; and the committee business—and talk, coming in the middle of a depressing day of east wind and misting rain, and after a morning of 'grinding' among the Supreme Court reports in the library, has left me feeling rather tired and dull,—more like dozing than like writing letters, and I am afraid I must send you a very lifeless epistle. Some of the phrases in your letter—about dreaming all night of being in my arms, have so charmed me, though, that my heart is by no means heavy like my mind, but supplies me with light and cheer enough even for this dull day. Oh, you sweet, precious little wife! You are a continual delight and inspiration to me. It just *carries me away* to have you think, and dream, such things about me. Your love for me is *so* wonderful and delightful!

What you tell me about Maggie is extremely interesting—makes a charmingly attractive picture of our little sister. It all seems to me to be just what *I* would have expected from Stock's description: perhaps my imagination was not so much excited as yours was. And it all makes me *very* glad; it shows what an interesting, what a delightful companion you will have when Maggie comes to stay with us. I will try not to be jealous of your not wanting me as much as you do now when you have such a satisfying little companion at hand as you will have then! Give the dear little woman a great deal of love and a great many kisses from me, and try to think of something to tell her about me that will make her like me a good deal.

There's one rather startling piece of news, which, I judge, has hardly reached Gainesville: the "Woodhull House" (Mr. Patterson's) at Lawrenceville was entirely destroyed by fire on Sunday morning last![2] The boys, with one or two exceptions, were out, it being vacation, so that no lives were endangered; but I suppose most of the contents of the house was consumed. I don't know what they are to do with the boys.

I love the girlies, my pet, oh *so* dearly—and I love *you* with a longing, a devotion, and a passion that I can give you no adequate *hint* of until you are in the arms of   Your own Woodrow.

ALS (WC, NjP).

¹ Wilson was probably referring to the Committee on Special and Delinquent Students, of which West was chairman.

² Woodhull House at the Lawrenceville School was built in 1885 and named for Henry Woodhull Green, brother of the school's founder, John Cleve Green. It burned down during Easter vacation in 1892 and was immediately rebuilt. James Lawson Patterson, Sc.D., taught mathematics at Lawrenceville from 1883 to 1894. Roland J. Mulford, in *History of the Lawrenceville School, 1810-1935* (Princeton, 1935), p. 95, n. 1, called him "perhaps the greatest teacher the School has had."

From Ellen Axson Wilson

My dear W.   Gainesville April 22 [1892].

We leave this morning at eleven. All are well and in good form for the journey. The weather is warmer and promises to clear off beautifully. We are all ready to start, & I anticipate a very easy, pleasant journey. With best love from all and as much as you can dispose of from myself. As ever

Yours, E. A. W.

Have just heard from Cousin Jimmie Hoyt. He will be glad to take charge of us at Greenville.

API (WP, DLC) with WWhw notation on card: "Solutio Quaestiones legati delinquentis judice competente."

Three Letters to Ellen Axson Wilson

Equitable Law Library,
My own darling,   New York, 22 April, 1892
   I cannot express my chagrin at finding that my delay in sending you money has interfered with the carrying out of your plans! I might just as well have sent it earlier—the only reason I did not was that this has been a week of positively *feverish* work with me—the culmination of the preparation for my lectures here —and almost all matters of business have been neglected in consequence. You did not give me the least *hint*, you know, of the time at which you expected to leave Gainesville, until the letter, written on Wednesday, which I received *this morning*, and read on my way over here on the train; and I had no idea you expected to leave this week. I thought that you intended to stay longer in Gainesville than in Savannah or Rome, and I looked forward to your going, probably, about the middle of next week. Oh, I am *so* sorry, so *mortified* that I should have caused you all this trouble. I will send you fifty dollars more to Columbia.
   Darling, don't grieve sister Annie by *too* brief a stay. It breaks my heart very nearly to give the advice: but stay *two* weeks to make sure of being generous to her. I love her so much that you must act as I would in the case—except, of course, in the improbable event of your stay positively inconveniencing the household. But don't *imagine* that!
   Of course Maggie, the nurse, is to go with you? You can't manage that journey without her, or the visits to Asheville and Morganton. I could not think of consenting to your trying all that alone.
   Will $50 more be *enough* to send to Columbia? If not, I can easily send you more than that.
   Your Sunday letter reached me this morning! It left Gainesville the same time your Wednesday letter did.
   I am writing *before* my (last) lecture. I hope I wont think of that money delay while I am lecturing! I have already worried

myself nearly sick about it! To *think* of my doing anything to worry *you*, or to delay your home-coming! But I must try to put it out of my head.

It provokes me to have you compared with Ed's wife—you are so incomparably her superior in every respect—*particularly* in *beauty*. I am tempted to say in this connexion, though it is particularly in everything!—that I have nothing but impatience for these absurd comparisons! You are perfectly beautiful and perfectly lovely—she is imperfectly good looking and most imperfectly lovely. You are incomparable, my own, precious little treasure of a wife—and, in spite of my stupid, unpardonable derelictions, I am with growing gratitude, delight, devotion, passion,

Your own Woodrow

A great deal of love to all.

My own darling,   [Princeton, N. J.] Saturday [April 23, 1892]

The lectures in New York are finished! I did *not* think of the money during the lecture yesterday, and it went off, probably, better than any of its predecessors. So far as I can judge from the expressions of opinion I was permitted to hear, I believe the course must be put on record as, on the whole, a satisfactory success. They want me to become (to all intents and purposes) a regular instructor next year and conduct an extended *recitation* course in constitutional law, with a text-book, but of course I probably could not manage so big a job at such long range. The question as to my acceding to the proposal is nominally "left open," but the way in which it must be decided is pretty clear. It would probably be an intolerable burden.[1]

I am still dreadfully chagrined about my failure to understand your plans and send you that money—though it was hardly lack of intelligence that I should not understand: for not only did I not "realize at what time you were to leave Gainesville," as you mildly put it, but no direct *intimation* of the date was I given until the letter received yesterday informed me that you had "put off" starting from Thursday till Friday! Ah, you monkey! Remember that a person of my degree of intelligence can't divine dates at this distance. It was like you, you brave, executive little woman to go *anyhow*,—but I don't like to think of the narrow margin of means on wh. you are travelling *to-day*. Ah, how I pray for your safety, my precious treasures!

How will this do for a schedule, darling? Leave Columbia May 6th for Asheville (that is your *direct* way—by the new railway that runs through Arden Park); remain in Asheville till Monday or Tuesday, the 9th or 10th; leave Morganton on the 13th—and get here in time for your birth-day: I can't spare you then! I will have the house aired and cleaned, and sufficiently in order to suffice till Monday. In the meantime tell me where the bed-clothes are, please ma'am—*and my summer garments*. I will have the wasps attended to at once. Not many of the leaves are out here yet—none at all upon most of the trees. I should not be surprised if you would see most of the Spring here yet. Nothing but the grass has shown green so far.

I can't move into Westcott's room now, by the way, because Crosby[2] is to have it till the end of the year, his family having already gone away.

I suppose that the Stockton's have gone, for I have received the P.P.C.[3] cards of the whole 'crowd' some days ago. I shall go around to the house to-day some time and see whether the horses are out of the stable. If they are, there is much hope on the fly question, for I doubt whether more than a few scouts of the race have put in their appearance yet—even at a stable.

Oh, how sweet it is to have a *definite* idea of how long I shall have to wait for my darling's home-coming—to be able to say "three weeks" and to begin to plan the necessary preparations! It makes me inexpressibly happy! What a sweet summer we shall have, my lovely one! Do you think you will be able to stand all the kisses, all the involved and various love-making that I shall insist upon. To judge by these precious phrases in your letters you *probably can*. Ah, how delightful it is to be in such real earnest, with such precious proofs of your sweet love,

Your own Woodrow.

A heartful of love to the dear ones in Columbia. I love them from the bottom of my heart. Please tell me if the money is forwarded to you. Did you leave your address with Aunt Lou?

[1] About Wilson's lectures at the New York Law School in 1893, see WW to H. E. Scudder, March 27, 1893, Vol. 8.

[2] Nicholas Evertson Crosby, Instructor in Greek and Latin.

[3] *Pour prendre congé* cards, left during this period at neighbors' homes when one permanently changed his address.

My own darling,   Princeton, Sunday 24 April, 1892

I had a very narrow escape from spending a wretched day to-day; for your telegram from Columbia[1] did not reach me until ten minutes of eleven last night, being brought to my door just as I was in the act of getting into bed. If the telegraph office had not been kept open much beyond its usual time by an unusual rush of business, I should not have received it at all, I suppose, till to-morrow, Monday! All of which illustrates the tragedy of the sort of loneliness in which I am living. There is nothing to mitigate anxiety or to divert worry: all my happiness is involved in the fortunes of a sweet little woman and her sweet little company of babies who are hundred of miles away and about whom I can find out absolutely nothing *of my own motion*. There could be no more painful situation in a moment of anxiety for a man disposed, as I am, to brood and brood till my heart is fairly ready to break.

But of course all that was averted this time. I know that my treasures are safe—and that they are safe in a home which I dearly love. It gives me specially keen delight to think of you *with my people*, not only because I love them, but also because your being with them, as my sister's sister, gives me additional evidence of your being mine. Anything that identifies you as a Wilson is particularly delightful to me—just because your identification with me is the sweetest fact in all the world. Stay the two weeks, if you can, my darling, just because I wish it.

It seems to have cost you an effort to go to Columbia; but I am sure that you must *feel* your welcome now that you are there, and that it will not be hard for you to stay: you will not need to fall back upon my wish as your motive. *I* know how much and how genuinely sister Annie loves you—and how much her love means.

Give them *all* as many love messages as you can frame, and kiss sister Annie for me again and again. Try your best to get her to promise to come to see us this Summer, or, at any rate, next Fall. Don't *let* her say 'No'—and don't let brother George refuse to come for her, and pay us at least a little visit himself.

Only two more Sundays to spend without you! What a blessed thought that is. I seem to have grown so much older waiting for you to come home! But one hour spent with you will rejuvenate me. It will be so easy and so delightful to be light-hearted and to laugh when you are in my arms again, to answer all my kisses, return all my caresses in that exquisitely sweet way of yours, to share my laughter and provoke me to light-heartedness with those sweet eyes of yours. With your breath on my cheek as we exchange confidences, in that sweet intimacy of love which is the best spiritual tonic that ever man was blessed with, all my gayety and strength will come back to me with a rush, and I shall be young and happy again! Ah, my love it's thus that I look upon you! I never *enjoyed* my faculties till you quicked all my life with your sweet loving presence, your perfect companionship—of sympathy, of understanding, of spiritual and mental stimulation; and now your love and presence are indispensable to me. I don't believe I have lectured once at my best—with dash and confidence —since you left me. My mind and heart alike pine for you, my sweet genius, my wife! When you come you will bring every-thing to   Your own Woodrow

ALS (WC, NjP).
1 It is missing.

From Ellen Axson Wilson

My own darling,   Columbia, April 25/92
    Here we are, you see, safely in Columbia and having a de-lightful time. Everybody is so charming and everything is so nice that we could not be otherwise than happy. They are all looking well, though Sister Annie isn't feeling very strong,—has head-aches a good deal. She is just as pretty as ever, and doesn't look a day older. The baby [Annie] is *lovely*, the cutest, brightest, merriest little thing,—very much the sort of baby that Jessie was at her age. You know she is just one year old now. Bro. George hasn't changed a particle, and is as nice as ever;—"little" George is the only one who *has* changed. He is much thinner & more quiet;—*very* handsome and one of the nicest boys I ever saw any-where. I have quite fallen in love with him.
    I really think Columbia at this season is the lovliest town in the world,—*must* be! The streets and the gardens are both *so* beautiful. I was surprised to see how much more advanced the season was than in Gainesville. The foliage is full grown and of the richest green, and it is the height of the rose season. I don't know when I have seen so many before or such lovely ones. This house and garden are both *full* of them; you ought to see the vine on the end of the piazza, or the great "rose-tree" that my eye rests on as I sit at the table! They are "a perfect dream," espe-cially when the afternoon sun is on them. I don't think I ever saw anything so sweet and *restful* as the whole effect from the front piazza, of the garden & street. Oh, if you were only here! I want you more than ever *here*, darling. It seems so unnatural to be among *your* people without you. I did not suppose I *could* think of you more constantly than I have been doing heretofore, but it seems that it was possible after all. For existence here is *one unbroken longing* for you. For one thing I know of course that you would enjoy it here so much more than at the other places, and that makes me wish for you with a more perfect longing. I feel as though I must,—I *must* have you *now*,—that it

is really impossible to do without you. I positively pant and tingle all over with the desire to see you, my own, *my own* love! It seems as though the feeling is so intense that it must draw you here like some strange irresistible magnet, conquering time and space and every other obstacle. Oh I want you, I *want you*.

I have been interrupted, & now must close for the carriage is at the door to take us driving, & everyone is waiting! Sister A. sends love & *begs* you to see if you can't come down for me here. It seems she had taken it into her head that that was your plan & *counted* on seeing you, so is greatly disappointed. I shall leave here for Asheville on Sat.–if you don't come(!). With dearest love

Your own   Eileen.

I have no nurse, and will bring none north. Will tell you about it tomorrow. Had a *very* pleasant journey here.

ALS (WC, NjP).

To Ellen Axson Wilson

My own darling,   Princeton, Monday 25 April, 1892
I am grieved to say that I shall be obliged to put you off with just a line or two to-day, not so much because of the three lectures–I could have managed a letter in spite of them–as because of the numerous interruptions of which I have been the victim, and the engagements of other sorts which have run me into a corner. I must study now because to-night is to be stolen away from me. Richard Malcolm Johnston is to lecture[1] *and I am to introduce him*–isn't that a grind? I am perfectly well, and your lover to the very bottom of my heart.

Your own Woodrow

ALS (WC, NjP).
[1] A popular lyceum lecturer and writer of fiction full of southern local color. Actually, as WW to EAW, April 27, 1892, reveals, Johnston gave a reading rather than a lecture.

From Ellen Axson Wilson

My own darling,   Columbia April 26/92
I am sorry to be obliged to report trouble in our little camp this morning. Don't be startled though,–it is not so *very* bad! Poor little Jessie has broken her collar-bone! But now that Bro. George has bandaged it she is not suffering at all, and is sitting up in bed this morning, playing, and as bright as possible–altogether herself. It was Jessie Kennedy's fault. She had been told expressly

by both Sister Annie & myself *not* to lift any of the children; never-the-less, when they happened to be out of our sight for a few minutes she took Jessie on her back and then fell down with her—with this result. That was yesterday soon after dinner. Bro. George was in the house at the time and she was attended to at once. Of course she suffered terribly at first and during the examination, but, though of course she cried terribly for a while, was very brave & showed splendid self-control while he was bandaging it &c. Bro. George said he had thought he might have to give he[r] cloroform, he often has to give it to children in such cases. It isn't a bad fracture, indeed the bones staid in place so perfectly that he had great difficulty in finding the break. He says it will be nicely healed in two weeks. In the mean time she will have to be kept *very* quiet; which of course gives me my hands full. I am afraid my letters are going to be rather more unsatisfactory than ever,—I feel that I really ought to be with her now!

By the way, I have a nurse now who promises well, and I am so glad because now the other children will not have to be confined too. Maggie, in Gainesville behaved very strangely indeed: she came to see me soon after I reached there and I told her I would leave in two weeks & wished to take her with me. She seemed *very* anxious to go with me,—and then I *never saw her again*! At last I sent to tell her to come to see me & she said she would, but did not. I heard *of* her saying that if I could wait another week she could go, but her sister was not doing well and she could not leave her then. But she did not come to tell *me* that or anything! As Aunt Lou says "it was a real nigger trick"— ["]the way they *always* do in Gainesville,"—but she had thought Maggie was different. It is all for the best, a fortunate escape for me. I have felt dubious all along about taking her north. Where the negros are so inconceivably worthless as they are in G. it really seemed impossible that any *one* of them could wholly escape the taint. I could have brought my other nurse with me to Columbia but I expected Maggie up to the day before I left; then it was too late to get the other one;—she wanted to go but had no clean clothes! But it was just as well; I did not need her at all on the trip, and it would just have been a waste of money.

The letters, with the check enclosed, came from G. this morning. Many thanks, dear. I did not need Loula's ten dollars after all, but reached here with twenty odd. Fifty dollars more will be the greatest abundance to get home on I should say. I doubt if I go to Asheville & Morganton now. If I do it will only be to spend one night in each place. Perhaps I had better do *that* though, for

I feel now more than ever that I will *never* leave home again & must see my friends now or never!

Sister Annie says I must tell you that *she* thinks this accident ought to be excuse enough to bring you here!—to take the invalid home, you know! But don't come *just* for that, for pity sake, for she is going to be *quite* well before I leave & I don't mind the trip *at all,*—thats *honest*! But if you could come for the two weeks, or ten days, that would be worthwhile. I should think you could come south as well as the others could go to Europe! Besides *I* need you to massage me for I hurt *that* hip & side carrying Jessie up those winding stairs yesterday! I am quite lame today;—but of course, dear, *that* will wear off soon. But I *must* go to my little pet! I do hate to send off a letter that will worry you as I know this will my darling. Try to be philosophical, dear, it is really *not* serious. Oh I love you, dear, devotedly, & I am altogether

Your own   Eileen

ALS (WC, NjP).

To Ellen Axson Wilson

Princeton, Tuesday 26 April, 1892

Alas, my precious little sweetheart, I must again confine myself to the merest note—this time for a very interesting reason: because my morning hours, during which my afternoon lecture should have been prepared, were stolen from me by a committee[1] of the Board of Trustees of the University of Illinois whom came to look me over for the presidency of that institution! I'll tell you about it—and about Col. Johnston's lecture—to-morrow.

I have not had any letter from Columbia yet; but I hardly expected one.

I am quite well and in good spirits; but oh, my sweet, my *precious* little wife, how I do long for a dream about your home-coming—how passionately do I *love you*!

Your own Woodrow.

A heart-full of love to all.

ALS (WC, NjP).
[1] Francis M. McKay and Nelson W. Graham.

Reading Recommended for Undergraduates

[April 27, 1892]

COLLATERAL READING.

A list of books for parallel reading in some of the junior and senior electives, which are more especially adapted to the purpose, has been obtained from the different professors.

Prof. Woodrow Wilson recommends the following:

In Administration: "The Central Government," by N. D. Traill; "Local Government," by M. D. Chalmers; "The State in Its Relation to Trade," by T. H. Farrer. All three of these books belong to the English Citizen Series, published by Macmillan.

In International Law: Selected chapters (particularly the introductory chapters) in Lorimer's "Institutes of the Law of Nations"; Books I and II of W. O. Manning's "Commentaries on the Law of Nations"; and Sir Henry Maine's "International Law."

In Political Economy: Bagehot's "Economic Studies"; Toynbee's "Industrial Revolution"; and Walker's "Money, Trade and Industry." . . .

Printed in the *Daily Princetonian*, April 27, 1892. (The *Princetonian* began to appear daily on April 11, 1892; henceforth, it will be cited as a newspaper rather than a periodical.)

From Ellen Axson Wilson

My own darling,   Columbia, April 26 [27]/92

Our little invalid is up today and seems to feel quite bright—suffers very little. Indeed she has complained of it only twice since it was first hurt. Bro. George says she is doing very nicely indeed. This is the Sunday-school picnic day, and the lady across the way had a house picnic for her little girls & some others so as to beguile them into staying at home. I took Jessie to it & was very glad of such an opportunity to divert her mind. She is the sweetest, most patient little thing you ever saw, is very quiet, which of course with Jessie is so unnatural as to be pitiful, but yet seems cheerful and happy. She is now busy over some toys I got for her this morning. They were promised her during the ordeal of examining the arm night before last but I could not get them yesterday because I was teased with constant visitors,—Mrs. James Woodrow, Mrs. McKay,[1] Mrs. Wright, Uncle James [Woodrow] & the minister Dr. Smith.[2] And,—I forgot,—Allie Cozby. She by the way is a pretty, attractive, girl, very popular with the school-girls & others. Jennie Woodrow[3] came to see me the day before. She is very nice;—has a sweet manner and is really pretty. Her children are healthy and rather good-looking. She looks delicate herself. I hope you will see her while she is in this country.[4] I wonder if you have heard from father and know that he has been here and at the north very recently. He went there to bury that old blind friend,[5]—the name has escaped me at this moment. They took the body to Wilmington. And then father had to hasten back to Clarksville. He has fully determined now to leave Clarksville at the end of this year. Indeed is already "breaking up,"—has sent a few things here & a few to *New York!* Sister Annie was rather concerned at that last, but says that he does not seem to expect to live there because he asked them if he could not build a little house in the *yard* here, and they all discussed adding a wing to the house and almost decided to do it. He seems to have given up his idea of living with us,—or perhaps his restlessness demands several homes. They feel like yourself very anxious about his loss of occupation but say that his illness this winter has so enfeebled him that perhaps it is as well.

What *is* the name of the president at Lawrenceville?[6] It has escaped me entirely. Won't you drop him a postal & ask him to send a catalogue here as soon as possible? I would write if I could think of his name. George is *wild* to go there, but they say they can't afford it. Still they want to look at the catalogue. Their idea is for George to enter freshman here[7] next year & at its end enter the Princeton freshman class. But George says he couldn't get into Princeton then, that he would still not be prepared in Latin & Greek, that the year here would do him very little good. Sister Annie says his one ambition is to get to Princeton but he thinks as matters stand that he will never succeed. He wants to be a professor of the classics and it seems to me on that account an especial pity that he can't go to Lawrenceville next year because he has had to study in a rather make-shift way and the thorough drill there in the classics would be invaluable to him.[8] They are all longing to "talk it over with you." One thing they wish to know is whether he could arrange to take some preliminary examinations *here* either in June or next fall?

The lameness which was troubling me so yesterday is *very much* relieved today. I have taken a severe cold and have now a tremendous *quinine* head-ache. But Bro. George is attending to all that and I am sure I shall be nearly well tomorrow.

I wish I could tell you, dearest, how constantly you are talked about and wished for—how much you are loved, by everyone in this house. As for me I love you so, my darling, that I can scarcely *bear* it. It is a sweet torture. I feel as though I should literally *die* if I had to look forward to—say—another *month* of separation. I cannot cannot *live* without you my Woodrow my husband. You are all in all to   Your little wife   Eileen

ALS (WC, NjP).
    [1] Probably Elizabeth C. (Mrs. Robert B.) McKay, mother of Wilson's old Columbia friend, Douglas McKay.
    [2] The Rev. Dr. Samuel Macon Smith, pastor of the First Presbyterian Church of Columbia.
    [3] Janie Wilson Woodrow, Dr. Woodrow's daughter, who had married the Rev.

Samuel Isett Woodbridge in 1884. For a fuller identification of Woodbridge, see JRW to WW, May 25, 1892, n. 1.
   4 The Woodbridges, Presbyterian missionaries in Chinkiang, China, were home on furlough.
   5 Dr. Moran, who had died on April 4, 1892.
   6 He was James Cameron Mackenzie.
   7 South Carolina College, now the University of South Carolina.
   8 George Howe III did enter the Lawrenceville School in September 1892. See WW to J. C. Mackenzie, Sept. 9, 1892, n. 5, Vol. 8.

To Ellen Axson Wilson

Princeton,
My precious little darling,   Wednesday 27 April, 1892
   Your first letter from Columbia reached me yesterday afternoon, and it would be hard to tell which feeling predominated in my mind after reading it,—pleasure because of the delightful time you are having, or consternation because of your being without a nurse. My darling, how *can* you go to Asheville and Morganton without a nurse? I shall be miserable to think of it—for I simply *cannot* get away from my engagements here to come for you,—unless, of course, there is an absolute necessity—as there will not be if you can get a through sleeper back. I am thrown into a veritable 'frame of mind' by the anxiety caused by the situation. If you actually need my assistance, why of course you must telegraph for me in time for me to come and make the journey with you. Oh, this is hard—almost too hard to bear—that I cannot come in answer to the call contained in your letter here—it is so ardent as almost to frighten me!
   But it is a comfort to think that you are having so delightful a time in Columbia. You could hardly have any other sort with those sweet people. How I do love and *want* them! Remind sister Annie that, though I cannot come now, it is my plan to meet Mr. and Mrs. 'Dode'[1] there when they visit her in June—and June is *almost next month*. Please make love to them *all* for me in the mean time.
   I send the $50 I promised to send; but I want you to stay another week all the same, my precious one. *Oh, how I love you!*
   Col. Johnston's reading (the love story of Mr. Absalom Billingsly and 'The Early Majority of Mr. Thomas Watts') was a complete success; everybody was delighted. He really read *perfectly* in that delicious *patois*. My introduction, too, is said to have been everything that it should have been.[2] I had a long talk with the Col. afterwards, and found him charming. He knew all about us, of course; and said he had been specially anxious to meet you. Grandfather Hoyt had been "a great friend of his," and he knew that you were the daughter of "Miss Jeanie" ("a *lovely*

creature") and was very sure you must be worth knowing and *seeing*. I wish you *could* have met him: you would have enjoyed him as a perfect type of the old Southern gentleman.

The Illinois University matter, about which I promised to tell you, is quite amusing. The two Trustees waylaid me at my classroom door, told me immediately that they had come to look me over for their vacant presidency, and—proceeded to do so! I was not embarrassed simply because I did not *care* what impression I made. They were in the East, it turned out, to look at *several* men to whom their attention had been directed! They did not make me any proposition; but, since they can offer as much as $6,000, I consented to wait to hear from them, and to 'consider' the matter! They were very intelligent men indeed, and made a most favorable impression upon me. Isn't the situation amusing? Would you like to move to Urbana, Ill.?

Oh, I love you, darling, and the sun is so much brighter now that I *know* when you are coming to

Your own Woodrow.

ALS (WC, NjP).
  [1] He is referring to the coming marriage of Joseph R. Wilson, Jr., and Kate Wilson.
  [2] The *Daily Princetonian*, April 26, 1892, reporting on Johnston's performance (held, incidentally, in the Second Presbyterian Church), said: "The speaker was gracefully introduced by Prof. Woodrow Wilson."

Wilson Announces His Courses for 1892-93

[April 28, 1892]

NEW ELECTIVE COURSES.

. . . In Jurisprudence, Prof. Woodrow Wilson will give a course during the second term on Comparative Constitutional Law. This course follows that in General Public Law, and is intended to serve as a continuation of that course in the special field of constitutional law.

Prof. Wilson offers another new course in the History of Law. In this course an attempt will be made to give a general sketch of the history of law, by means of such a comparative study of the origins of law among the Aryan races and of the best known national systems of law as may serve to bring out features common to legal development. The general purpose of this course will be to indicate the essential character and natural sources of law: its place and function in the history of political society.[1]

Still another new course will be given by Prof. Wilson on the History of Legal Philosophy.[2] This course will consist of a critical exposition of the opinions of representative writers upon Jurisprudence, as to the nature, function and sanctions of law. The object of the lectures will be critical rather than constructive; but an attempt will be made throughout to indicate those portions of theory which may be regarded as permanently established because of their correspondence with the facts of political experience. . . .

Printed in the *Daily Princetonian*, April 28, 1892.
    1 For additional comment, see the Editorial Note, "Wilson's Teaching at Princeton, 1892-93," Vol. 8.
    2 Wilson did not give this course, perhaps because Professor Sloane, who offered a course on the history of political theory, objected.

From Ellen Axson Wilson

My own darling,   Columbia April 28/92
    Your little family is doing *very well indeed*. If you are still feeling any anxiety about us I hope you will allow it to be entirely and at once dispelled. Jessie seems perfectly comfortable and happy and has adjusted herself to the situation with remarkable facility. The weather is delicious and she is out of doors or on the piazza constantly & so is not going to suffer at all in general health. The others are perfectly well. There is scarcely a trace left of that little lameness of mine. I still have a severe cold in the head & throat, but that is an old story and of no consequence. Doubtless it adds to Sister Annie's cares, already too heavy, to have us here, but we are so evidently welcome that I won't mind it especially as it was your wish to have us stay longer. And we are not crowding them, for they still had a guest room. You know there are five rooms upstairs, Jessie & George each have theirs & the large new billiard room up stairs had been given up to the girls at the first of the season. The house has been *very* much enlarged and improved since we—or at least *I*—were here. I would hardly know it. It is a *lovely* home. I would rather live here than anywhere in the south. And yet they were rather in earnest when they asked us,—in a letter you remember?—if there was an opening for a physician in Princeton. It is on account of Sister A's health; it is not strong & they think she needs a more bracing climate. Still there is nothing seriously wrong with her and they are by no means prepared to run serious risks. And of course it would be a serious risk to go to Princeton or anywhere else without some definite arrangement like partnership with, or succession to a leading physician. How are Dr. Wykoff & his daughter now, by the way? Do you hear anything new about the situation as regards physicians? And what is the population of Princeton? Bro. George asked me and I hadn't an idea. Would

it not be ideal to have them there,—yet of course we could not dare to try and tempt them to the step.

That is *very* interesting about the Ill. Presidency! The more good offers you have the better so that our Princeton friends may be frightened into raising your salary in spite of "precedents"— or at least building *that house* and giving it you rent free! How I hope the Chicago University people will ask you so that you may have the pleasure of refusing,—in revenge for their dilly-dallying! I have been *so* pleased with your success in New York, dear. Just think, it was *days* ago you were writing of that & I have been so busy & "upset" that I havn't had a word to say about it. Now I must say a hurried good-bye for I have been interrupted & it is dinner time. I love you darling with all my heart & life & am forever   Your own Eileen.

ALS (WC, NjP).

To Ellen Axson Wilson

My own sweet darling,   Princeton, 28 April, '92
The news of our sweet little Jessie's accident reached me this morning: the effect it has had upon me you can imagine—particularly since there is added to it your distressing strain—which is really more serious than Jessie's hurt. Can you not get massage in Columbia? If you can (and can get it *intelligently* done) *you must* do so at once. I hope that you will consult brother George about it constantly and let me know immediately exactly how serious it is, and how much my assistance is needed. Oh, my poor, poor little girls! It nearly breaks my heart! My present *thought* is to go to Columbia on Wednesday or Thursday of next week and bring you back the week following when Jessie can travel—though I *must*, if possible, avoid taking the time and the money, if it breaks my heart! You can telegraph me at any time if you feel that you need me sooner. If I come, we can hardly go to Asheville and Morganton. I don't see how you *can* go by yourself.

Meantime I need your advice desperately, and may have to come to you for that: it is about that Illinois offer. It is now practically an offer: to preside over the development of the State Univ. into something like the efficiency of Wisconsin and Michigan: salary $6,000, *plus* the assistance of a general business manager, a short-hand secretary, etc.—no teaching, and ultimately a good deal of time for literary work. It seems a really great opportunity of its kind. I don't want a presidency, as you know, but I *must* increase my resources, to provide for you and the children—

and I am going to New York this afternoon, to consult Bridges and several members of the Finance Committee of the Board of Trustees. Then I shall have a definite basis for seeking the advice which will conclude the whole matter,—your own!

And so I must break off my letter, leaving it to sound like a mere business letter simply because I *dare* not give leave to the love and deep concern which the news of the morning has filled my heart with! I love you—admire you—adore you—yearn for you—with the ardour, the *agony* of a heart which is absolutely yours. I have not lost a whit of self-possession (I am not even unhappy) but I am *possessed* with such feelings as *must*, under the circumstances, fill the heart of   Your own Woodrow.

ALS (WC, NjP).

From Ellen Axson Wilson

My own darling,   Columbia April 29/92

Sister Annie wishes me to go driving with her in a few moments and I *must* answer a letter from Rose [Dubose][1] before I start, so I am afraid I must put you off today with a line.

Jessie is still doing nicely, Bro. George says the bone is already beginning to knit. I have an excellent nurse—the best of the *four* I have had since I left you. She is so very careful and watchful of Jessie.

And by the way you will have to ask our friends there to look out for a nurse for me. Perhaps you had better drop Maggie Foley a line. I think I would. Tell her the coloured girl's sister was sick & she could not come, and ask her to try and find someone. It is a bad season of the year to get any one in Princeton. If we *must* try the city let it be Phila. rather than N.Y. I had a sweet little letter from Mrs. Hazen yesterday.

Have you heard anything from Stock lately? Do you know if he ever applied for his degree at Princeton?

All send their dearest love. With a heart *full*—full to overflowing with love for my darling, I am as ever

                          Your own Eileen.

ALS (WC, NjP).
    [1] It is missing.

From Francis M. McKay

Dear Sir: Fifth Avenue Hotel, New York.   Apr. 30—1892

Mr. Graham and I have decided to recommend calling you to the Regency of the University of Illinois at a salary of $6000.

provided that you indicate at the earliest practicable moment your readiness to accept such a call. We believe there is a great oportunity there for the right man. In a few years, with proper management, it can be made one of the first state universities in the land.

I am sure that you would also find time and oportunity to carry on any special lines of work that you may desire outside of your duties as Regent.

Hoping for an early and favorable reply I am,

Truly yours.   F. M. McKay
134 Warren Ave.
Chicago Ill.

ALS (WP, DLC) with WWhw notation on env.: "Ans. 12 May, 1892."

To Ellen Axson Wilson

My own darling,   Princeton, Saturday 30th April, 1892

I don't know that I accomplished very much in New York yesterday: I saw Mr. Jno. A. Stewart[1]—one of the most conservative of the Trustees, as well as one of the most influential—who said that the Trustees would very cheerfully give me $3,500 (to cover my present house rent), and that a somewhat general rise in salaries would come as soon possible. The Trustees would not, he thought, be willing to give one man more than any of the others, but he felt that I "could afford to wait" for what Princeton would do, for me and some others. I saw Mr. James W. Alexander,[2] who was very much stirred up; said he would himself do a great deal to keep me from leaving Princeton and asked me to "give him two or three days" to look the situation over and see how some other men felt. I have stirred the best men up very pleasantly; but don't know what will come of it. If nothing more than the $3,500, *that* will be *one* hundred more than any one else.

I saw Shaw and Finley (who is from Ill.) and Bridges and canvassed the question of my accepting the invitation very thoroughly. There is certainly a very eminent career opened there: but would it end or permanently embarrass my literary work? That's the real question.

I saw Stock. in New York, too. He had come down to see the President of the University of Kansas,[3] who practically offered him a place: but it was to teach nothing *but* composition and Stock. evidently don't want it. The poor boy, by the way, has suddenly been brought to the necessity of looking for something to do, because the (temporary) collapse of the Central R. R. leaves him with only $250![4] I wonder how this will affect Ed's[5] schooling, by the way. Did uncle Randolph say anything about the matter to you while you were in Savannah? Stock says he got a *very* blue letter from him not long ago.

Your letters, my darling, about dear little Jessie's condition since the accident and the rapid decrease of your lameness have lifted from my heart a great part of the load of anxiety that rested upon it, and my spirits have come up famously. But I am still puzzled what to do about coming for you. Not my college work only, but the preparation of the house, and the further conduct of negotiations in the matter of Illinois v. Princeton, make it seem a sheer impossibility to leave at present: and yet my heart commands me to go in a way that I see no way to resist. *I will make no plans about it for a few days*, but wait and see what the nature of the news from you is—especially about your own lameness and cold. Both my conscience and my judgment tell me that, if you can, *without risk or anxiety*, get along without me, you must do so: but if the news sets a certain way I shall throw both judgment and conscience overboard! For I simply could not endure the thought of your actually needing me. I love you with a consuming, masterful love which commands my whole nature. If I had known what this separation would cost me I don't know that I should have had the courage and the unselfishness to consent to it at all. Oh my little wife, my precious, matchless, altogether lovely darling, my heart is fairly breaking under its load of love for you!

Your own Woodrow.

Unbounded love to all the dear household! How I do love and *thank* them all!

ALS (WC, NjP).
¹ John Aikman Stewart, a New York banker and member of the Princeton Board of Trustees since 1868. Stewart, born in 1822, served as a trustee until his death at the age of 104.
² James Waddel Alexander, another trustee, identified earlier in this series.
³ Francis Huntington Snow, Chancellor of the University of Kansas.
⁴ The Central Railroad of Georgia went into receivership in April 1892 as the result of a suit filed the preceding month. The case remained in litigation for several years, and the railroad was not reorganized until 1895. A large part of the Estate of Samuel Edward Axson was invested in Georgia Central bonds.
⁵ Her brother, Edward Axson, then completing his last year at the Bingham School in North Carolina.

From Ellen Axson Wilson

My own darling, Columbia, April 30/92

Your letter written after hearing of Jessie's accident came to hand this morning. Ere this however you have received later letters from me and are doubtless reassured as to all of us. I am entirely over that strain, and Jessie is doing nicely; so there is no necessity whatever for you to come on. I will not leave until she is *quite* well, so that it will be as easy to travel alone as it was before. And I assure [you] I have not minded the other trips a *particle*.

Ah how I wish I *were* with you to talk over this new situation! There are a thousand questions I want to ask. Of course I can *say* nothing about it now because I know absolutely nothing about it, except the salary. And I don't quite know that either! I mean is it *just* $6000 or $6000 & the the [*sic*] usual president's perquisites, so to speak; a nice house and grounds; the grounds kept up by the college; & his travelling expenses when on college business? How large is the faculty & how many are the students? What sort of an endowment have they? Do you think enough to compete with the Chicago University. What is & has been the spirit of the legislature towards it? In fact tell me all you know about it & have time to write. Have they nice buildings? What sort of a place is Urbana?—how large &c. &c. You will be obliged to go out there, won't you?—before you decide. They can't expect you to decide a matter like this without *plenty* of time to consider. We will want to look over the ground *very* carefully in order to determine which position would give you most time for original work. It seems to me that that is *the* most important question. All others are dwarfed to insignificence beside it. Is the "business manager" something *more* than Mr. Osborne is at Princeton; a more important official—one who would relieve you of more care & work. It seems to me that with such an official & with affairs properly systematized a president *might* have more time to write than a professor. Yet I feel perfectly in the dark on the subject. I have always thought that there must be something very *distracting* about the duties of a college president; yet with the committee meetings, faculty meetings, &c. &c. &c. the professor seems to be about as much in "the thick of it." But I won't keep on writing of what I know nothing about.

All send their dearest love. As for myself I really don't know what to do with mine, there is too much of it to send,—the mails would not hold it; yet my heart is so full that I cannot keep it. What would you do about it? With perfect love & devotion,

Your own Eileen

ALS (WP, DLC) with WWsh on env.: "Something really worthwhile could be made out of it." (Wilson used this phrase in his letter to Ellen of May 2, 1892.)

To Ellen Axson Wilson

My own sweet darling,   Princeton, Sunday evening 1 May, 1892

I have been so much occupied for a week with important, as well as distressing, matters which needed both to be thought about and written about—and *seen* about—that it now seems to me an age since I had the leisure of spirit to write you a real love letter. And yet I have so longed to do so. Nothing so contents my heart and head as to make love to you—and *this week*, when there were matters of the first importance to be decided, I have somehow *realized* my love for you more than ever. I have *needed* you so much—for counsel and sympathy and sustaining love—and have been made so *vividly* conscious of the intimate part you play in my life! I am so hopelessly incomplete without you: nothing vital, nothing but routine, is possible for me in your absence. Ah, my darling, I just constantly repeat to you, just because their truth is so constantly new, and so continually renewed in experience, the sweet facts of my debt of love to you. My whole nature does homage to you—and I love to run over the details of my admiration and devotion. I am passionately fond of beauty, and you have beauty of a type which seems to me the *sweetest*, and the most provocative of love that it is possible to imagine. I am extravagantly devoted to intellectual pleasure such as is afforded by the companionship of a mind endowed with great store of broad, sane sense, with quick powers of sympathetic perception, and with a pervasive quality of imaginative thought and ardent love of beauty—and yours is such a mind: that extraordinary, that almost incredible combination which it exhibits, of practical wifely sense and helpfulness with the atmosphere of perfect literary perception and an incomparable womanly charm and loveliness, fills me sometimes with an overwhelming sense of delight and obligation which it would be impossible for me to put into words at all! And you promise to *stay young* so delightfully! You make daily progress in the art and in the thoughtless delights of love-making! You manage your children like a matron and your husband like a lover. There is all the charm of a romantic courtship thrown about my life by the way you look at me, and seek me out in the house, and smile into my eyes, and caress and cling to me; and there is all the dignity of matronly success in the way you manage our little household. You make me feel at one and the same time like a settled married man, possessing a home grown old in comfort and happiness, and a young lover, every day finding new charms and some new form of beauty in his mistress, living in perpetual romance! And on still another side, the intimacy of intellectual companionship, you fill my life with equal success and equal sense of pleasure and power! Do you wonder that, in such three-fold perfection, you seem to me the loveliest, sweetest, most wonderful, and most satisfying little woman that the heart of man ever desired? I am yours, my darling, to the full extent of both my mind and my heart—when I get you again I shall be the happiest man in the world—until I get you again it is one and the same thing to be miserable and

Your own Woodrow.

The usual messages to all.

ALS (WC, NjP).

To Winthrop More Daniels

My dear Mr. Daniels,   Princeton, New Jersey, 1 May, 1892.

I have been prevented by innumerable things from writing to inform you of the answer which President Small of Colby made to the inquiries I promised you I would make with regard to the future provisions there for the work in Economics. I wrote to him almost immediately after I saw you. In his answer he says: "I presume that the work will be expected of my successor in the presidency. I see no probability that another position, including the work in Sociology, can be made at once, although it must come eventually. I should like to know more about the young man: I should like to keep him in mind in reference to possible vacancy in Chicago." I will, of course, write him soon something more about the "young man." In the meantime, as I sent you word the other day about the matter by Axson, please do not conclude any arrangement with Wesleyan for next year before communicating with me again.[1]

In haste,
Yours with much regard,   Woodrow Wilson

WWTLS (W. M. Daniels Coll., CtY).
    [1] Wilson had Daniels in mind for the appointment in political economy at Princeton.

From Ellen Axson Wilson

My own darling,   Columbia, May 1/92

It is after ten o'clock and I havn't time to write much but I must scribble a few lines before I go to bed. I have of course had the care of the children today & so could find no good opportunity to write. This evening Uncle James and his wife spent

with us. We had a very pleasant evening,—except that Uncle
James again overwhelmed me with confusion by calling the attention of the company to my "remarkable resemblance to the
'Sistine Madonna' "! How *can such* a man say such a thing! He
is the last person in the world I would expect to say anything
extravagant;—and said in that quiet, even, matter-of-fact tone of
his it is all the more *dreadful!*

By the way, speaking of that family I did not tell you what
a *lovely* baby Jennie has. It is perfectly wonderful for a three
months old child,—the sweetest, brightest, prettiest thing I almost
ever saw. And to crown its attractions it is named *Woodrow!* I
really want to run away with it. I asked her if she would not
give him to me, and she said she would!

I asked Uncle James if he thought a college president would
have much time for writing and he said he thought he would,—
instanced the number of presidents who had done important
literary work. He said he would certainly go out there and find
out all about *everything*—especially everything about the *trustees,*
before accepting. He says he has understood that those Ill. towns
outside of Chicago were very wretched, semi-barbarous places!

He suggested that if you had any fancy for going to the
"J. H. U." this might precipitate matters in that direction. You
know I had thought of that. I would certainly let it be known
at once both in Baltimore & *New York* as generally as possible
that you had had this call and were considering it seriously.

I think, apart from this view of it, that Dr. Gilman would be a
good person to consult, I mean as to the opportunities for literary
work that you are likely to have in such a position as well as
regards the position and prospects of this college. Tell him how
you have conceived and planned literary work of a large and
serious kind & that whatever position you attained or however
much you accomplished as an "educator" you would feel that
life had been something of a failure unless you found time and
opportunity for that particular thing.

You know it strikes me that this is a most serious crisis, not
only for us but for the college. They have practically to decide
now whether they will continue to be "the College of New Jersey"
or become the great "University" they are always talking about.
They cannot rise to the first rank unless they can contend with
others of first rank for the best men, in open market on equal
terms; that is unless they can break through this absurd precedent of putting an equal value upon what is *worse* than worthless—what no one of course wants,—and what is most valuable
and most in demand. If they continue that they will very rarely

get the best men and when they do they *must always* allow them quickly to slip through their fingers, just as poor Wesleyan must from sheer weakness. If I were you I would push this issue unhesitatingly to the end *for the good of the College* no less than for my own, for I firmly believe that the whole future of the college is at stake. But I *must* stop. With a heart full almost to breaking with love & longing for a sight of your dear face I am always & altogether,   Your own Eileen

ALS (WC, NjP).

To Ellen Axson Wilson

My own sweet darling,   Princeton, 2 May, 1892
    I am in the usual Monday rush—writing a lecture between hours—but perhaps I can find time to answer your questions about the Illinois offer. I don't wonder you ask them, you sweet thing—*you* must wonder that I made it necessary for you to ask them. I would have given you all the particulars last week, if I had not had a sort of expectation of seeing you this week.
    The $6,000 would *not* include a house: there *is* no president's house. But cost of living is about one third less than it is here (the best meats, for example, being 10¢ *per* pound). All traveling expenses on college business would be paid. The business manager would be much more than Mr. Osborn—would relieve me of *all* the care of material superintendence. My letters would be dictated, not written, for I would be given a short-hand secretary. The faculty now numbers about twenty-two; the students over five hundred—male *and female*. Several of the faculty are women, too. The endowment is small, derived from the sale of government lands granted the college; but the legislature has always granted the institution what it has asked; the feeling of the state and the organization of the schools are back of it; and they seem confident of generous support in the realization of the wish to equal the Universities of Michigan and Wisconsin. They expect to supplement rather than rival Chicago, which will be *graduate* predominantly, whereas the work proposed for the State institution would be for the most part undergraduate. Urbana is quite a small place; but it is, it seems, a twin town with Champaign, from which it is separated by less than a mile, with which it is connected by means of an electric railway, and which has a population of about 12,000. It is on two railways—3 hours distant from Chicago. There are about 5 good (though, I judge, *plain*) buildings—and 3 more are now being planned. This is exclusive of dormitories, of which they have none, the students boarding in

the two towns. The work done, so far, has been principally technical and agricultural; but their wish is to develop the literary side upon a generous scale under the guidance of some man of Eastern training and traditions. This is really almost all I know of the place—except that I got the impression from Shaw and the Illinois men I saw in New York that something worth while could be made out of this opportunity. It would, however, involve an *immense* amount of executive work (to the exclusion of everything else at first—for a couple of years at least)—and *that*, as you say, is *the* question. I may go out there in a day or two, but I have formed no plans at all about it. I am waiting to hear from Mr. Alexander.

Although it is in violation of almost every wish and instinct I have, my sweetheart, not to come for you, my *judgment* tells me that I can be of a *great deal* more service to you by staying here and making ready for your home-coming. There is *so* much to do that simply could not be done without my superintendence.

Oh, I love *all* in that dear home yonder with all my heart—and you with a tenderness and passion beyond all reckoning.

Your own Woodrow.

ALS (WC, NjP).

From Ellen Axson Wilson

My own darling,   Columbia, May 3/92

Your letter of yesterday—of course I had none this morning—was certainly very interesting. Oh how how I wish I could see you and hear in detail what all these men said,—what Finley said about Ill. for instance! You know you have given me *no* facts as yet about the university? Your interview with Mr. Alexander was quite satisfactory I should say. I do not see why even if the *College* raised your salary any of those other men would have the *remotest* cause to resent it until *they* too had $6000 offers and the college refused, in spite of it, to raise *theirs*! But of course they *could* not resent *friends* of the college making that sort of outside effort to keep you, for they would have *nothing whatever to do with it*. How would it do to suggest, at this juncture, the building of that ideal house? Of course to be given rent free to you as long as you stay in Princeton!—of course too in *addition* to the $3500! They might buy your lot to build on it(!).

I am concerned about Stock. I wish he *would* write to me—haven't heard from him in an age. I don't understand at all about his money. Do you mean the money that he had *first*, from Papa, was invested in C. R. R. stocks? That from Grandfather is safe;

part of it is of course in "debentures" but they are of the nature of bonds and are not expected to be affected by all this confusion. I heard nothing but "Central R. R." talked while I was in Sav. Uncle R. spoke quite freely of his own possible losses but said not a word of the children's money being involved. Don't you suppose that Stock, who is extravagant you know, has simply *spent* all of the capital from Papa except the $250.00? Or perhaps Uncle R. as we always supposed, has been paying the children interest on their money himself, and owing to his own heavy losses can't return any more of the capital just now. I asked him expressly about Ed's schooling;—if these troubles would interfere with it. As usual he did not answer directly but I got the impression that it was all right as regards that.

I should not think that under the circumstances Stock could afford to reject *any* position that would serve to give him his first foot-hold in the academic world. I fear he is too fastidious a youth! How are his health and spirits by the way? And by the way I heard a singular piece of gossip about him in Rome, viz. that that beautiful Miss Hardeman who died last year was deeply in love with him! You remember they were great friends and he has her picture. But this is the merest gossip and almost certainly false, I suppose. All over Georgia I had to contradict reports of his engagement to Miss Howell.[1] That is a sad piece of business, I fear.

Though I *mailed* a letter to you yesterday I did not write one, dear. Everything conspired to prevent—among other things I had a little surgical operation. Bro. George found last week that I had a big "polypus"—some sort of mucus growth—up my nose; he removed it Sat. and completed the operation yesterday. It was not very painful because he used coccaine. It must have been growing there for years & its removal will increase my breathing capacity & decrease my tendency to take cold. All send love, darling. Remember that I love you more than words can tell. I am almost afraid now-a-days to think *how* much, or to let my mind dwell on my almost unendurable longing for you. With all my heart,   Your own   Eileen

I forgot to say that I am feeling no inconvenience today from that little operation, and that my cold too is almost gone.

ALS (WC, NjP).
   [1] Emily Howell, identified in S. Axson to WW, June 10, 1889, n. 2, Vol. 6. Her romance with Stockton had obviously come to an end.

To Ellen Axson Wilson

Princeton,

My own sweet darling,   Tuesday afternoon 3 May, 1892

Just a little love note to-day: there is no news, and I should hardly have time to tell it if there were any. But I love you, ah how I love you—and just now I feel a sort of triumphant satisfaction in having proved (to myself, at any rate) that I love *you* better than I love myself. If I had loved myself more than I loved you, I should have started for Columbia to-morrow; but the house is to be made ready, and the way to love you is to help you.

Let me know the *dates* of your plans, darling, as soon as you can: so that my plans may make connexion.

Are you getting *well*, and are you preparing to be suffocated with kisses by   Your own Woodrow.

ALS (WC, NjP).

Francis Landey Patton to Cornelius Cuyler Cuyler

My dear Mr. Cuyler,   [Princeton, N. J.]   4th May, 1892.

I am anxious that some provision should be made as soon as possible for an increase of Professor Wilson's salary. It is very important, on account of his position in the College, that he should be made comfortable. I could not ask the Board of Trustees to increase his salary at this time without seeming to make invidious distinctions, and we are not ready for a general increase in salary.

I hope in the near future that we shall be able to raise Professor Wilson's salary out of the funds of the College, but if there is any way,—either through some appropriation which could be made from the Alumni Fund or from private funds, whereby an amount equal to $400. or $500. per year could be placed in the hands of the Treasurer for the purpose of supplementing Professor Wilson's salary, I should feel that it was of great advantage to the College, and it would be a great relief to me.

I write this to you confidentially, and shall be glad to receive any suggestions from you about it. If you feel that it is not wise to make any appropriation from the Alumni Fund for this purpose, or that it is not practicable to secure the amount necessary from private contribution, do not hesitate to say so to me. It is only my deep anxiety for the permanent connection of Professor Wilson with the College, and to promote his comfort that leads me to write in this frank manner about it.

As I expect to be out of the Country during the Summer, I

would be very glad if any provision looking toward the supply of this necessity could be made so that I should be able to set Professor Wilson's mind at rest upon the subject before Commencement.

This suggestion, I ought to say, is made to you without any knowledge on the part of Professor Wilson. I have simply told him that I was interested in securing an increase of salary for him.

I am,   Very faithfully yours,   Francis L Patton

ALS (Patton Letterpress Books, University Archives, NjP).

From Joseph R. Wilson, Jr.

My dearest brother: Clarksville, Tenn.   May 4 1892
I have time for only a few lines. I want to tell you of my plans. Unless something happens to prevent, we will marry on the 14th or 15th of June at noon and at home. At 3.35 P. M. the same day, we will leave for Columbia, reaching there the next night about ten oclock. We will stay there a week or ten days and then return home. We postpone for a week because sister Annie has young ladies with her who will not leave until June 15th, and Kate and I feel that it will be more pleasant to visit her new relatives without having strangers about. Now, my precious brother, I *must* have you with me when I marry if possible. If the dates I name dont suit you and you could come to C'ville. any later, let me know at once, for I *must* have my only and my dear, true & noble brother. He is too dear to me for me to do without him if he can possibly come. If you do not come here, you can go to Columbia, cant you? Let me know as soon as possible, please. I think I will have a photo. of Kate's to send you before long. She is in Springborough, Ohio, now visiting relatives. Will probably not be home much before June 1st.

Father is pretty well but not strong, by any means. I am O. K. Love unbounded to your dear self, sister Ellie & the children.
                    Your devoted bro   Joseph.

ALS (WP, DLC).

From Cyrus Hall McCormick

Prof. Woodrow Wilson,   [Chicago] May 4, 1892
Letter received. After careful consideration advise against new plan.   Cyrus H. McCormick.

T tel. (C. H. McCormick Letterpress Books, WHi).

From Cyrus Hall McCormick

My Dear Wilson: 329 Wabash Ave. [Chicago] May 4, 1892

I have read your letter[1] carefully and have digested the subject, which is not at all surprising to me, and I can well imagine many an Institution that would be proud to secure your leadership. In what I have to say, I shall have no reference whatever to Princeton, or to my connection with it as a Trustee or otherwise, nor with your present position, but simply that of my friend who is offered the position at Champaign.

In the first place, the University of Illinois has very little standing in this Community: It is regarded as only a high school, and a very ordinary one at that. I do not believe the authorities of the State contemplate any large endowments or forward movements, which will be sufficient to warrant a man of your prospects in giving up his specific work for the sake of the interests of the University of Illinois. Personally, I do not believe that the Institution at Champaign will even supplement what will be done here in Chicago, and this will be so far the center of everything that very little public attention can be attracted to any other Institution here except Lake Forest, which already has a permanent hold upon the Community. I believe that should you undertake the Presidency, it would mean the abandoning of your specific work which you have so ably planned for yourself, and the undertaking of a certain amount of business developement and push which would be necessary to coordinate the elements at Champaign and add to them sufficiently to make an important Institution. For that work, it does not seem to me that you are nearly so well suited as for the special branch in which you are now engaged, and it would seem to me like surrendering the brilliant plans which you have in mind,[2] and which I am satisfied in time will be realized. There are many Institutions that I could name which would offer you far greater facilities than the one you have under consideration, and the very fact that they offer you so large a salary is an indication to me that they would expect to place upon you the burden of establishing the whole Institution, and thus the Trustees and others will be relieved of work which they would probably have to do under other and less enthusiastic leadership.

On the question of salary, I can say but little. That, of course, is very tempting to you, but I do not believe that even by securing that you would be able to do the work you contemplate, for with it would be coupled the necessity of doing so much other work that little time would be left for your own developement and study.

Turning now to the Princeton side of the case for a moment, were I in your place, I think I should not consider a change unless it was a matter of absolute and imperative necessity, for I cannot conceive of a place in this Country where you would be more harmoniously placed* for the developement of that specific and important work which you have in mind, and which must, if successful, bring you great satisfaction and reputation.

In order to give you promptly the result of my thought, I have telegraphed you thinking that a day or two might make some difference, and after all, what I have said is simply my personal judgment.   Very sincerely yours,   Cyrus H. McCormick

P.S.

By a curious coincidence, since writing the foregoing I have had an opportunity of consulting Tom Hall '79[3] and T. D. Jones,[4] of '76, today at lunch time, and without going into any questions which would be improper for them to know, I discussed the situation at Champaign with them, and they fully and heartily concurred in the views which I had already formed, and which are mainly outlined above. You may depend upon it that they will not repeat any questions which I have asked them, and you therefore have the benefit of their judgment as well as my own.

* this, of course, with the hope that financially matters will improve for you at Princeton

TLS (C. H. McCormick Letterpress Books, WHi).
    [1] Wilson's letter is missing.
    [2] Undoubtedly a reference to Wilson's plans for a law school at Princeton and for his future scholarly writing.
    [3] The Rev. Thomas Cuming Hall, at this time pastor of the Forty-first Street Presbyterian Church in Chicago; afterward a distinguished theologian and professor at the Union Theological Seminary and the University of Göttingen.
    [4] Thomas Davies Jones, born Mifflin, Wis., Aug. 13, 1851. A.B., College of New Jersey, 1876; A.M., 1879. Admitted to the Illinois bar in 1879, he practiced law in Chicago until 1900. President of the Mineral Point, Wis., Zinc Company, and director of several firms, including the International Harvester Company and the New Jersey Zinc Company. Trustee of Princeton University, 1906-12. President Wilson named him to the Federal Reserve Board in 1914, but the Senate refused to confirm the nomination. Member of the War Trade Board, 1917. Died Sept. 27, 1930.

From Ellen Axson Wilson

My own darling,   Columbia May 4/92

It is just two months today since I left you!—the very longest two months I ever spent. Oh how glad I am though that they are over & the end of this separation draws near! The days now seem as long as weeks did at first;—I don't know how I am to bear the one week remaining. It is I hope just one week and a day now before I see my love. Though if in the meantime you find you must go to Ill. to look about, and had best go at once, I suppose I had better wait here until your return. I think Jessie will be well enough to travel by the middle of next week, and if so I expect to reach Princeton on Thursday at 2.06 P.M. Bro. George has found out the schedule for me. I leave Columbia at 4.10 P.M., arrive in Salisbury at 9.45 P.M. and there change to the fast vestibule train, which reaches Washington at 8.38 A.M., leaves at 9.00 A.M. arrives in Phila. at 12.30 & leaves at 12.44 P.M. It makes good connections you see all through. Of course I must change at Washington & Phila. I have given up going to Asheville and Morganton.

I have a little plan to propose. When Bro. George said Jessie's arm would be *knit* in two weeks I, in my ignorance supposed, that he meant it would be *quite well* in two weeks. But it seems it will not be really strong for five or six weeks; and it must be bandaged for about a month; and she has to be watched *constantly* to keep her from running around and risking fresh injury. She *feels* so well & lively that it takes the whole time of one person to keep her sufficiently quiet. Now I don't mind the journey north *at all*. I can accomplish it without any risk or trouble (and I do *not* need you!) but I do dread excessively the first week in Princeton when we will be "getting settled" and there will be no nurse to watch Jessie while I am attending to all my other necessary duties. I want to spend that week at the *hotel* & let Maggie [Foley] devote herself to the children while I work at the house. That would solve the problem entirely & take an enormous weight of care and anxiety off my mind. Then we would get really comfortably settled for the summer so much sooner & with so much less annoyance. The carpets *must* be taken up, you know, for it was not done last spring,—they having been put down so late the fall before. All the spring cleaning could be easily & thoroughly done that week (without driving you out of your study.) All I would want you to do before I come is to engage the workers, one man—who knows how!—to beat carpets & wash windows; I would probably need him two days,—& two women. Let one of them be *Catherine*. It is hard to get anyone the first part of the week on account of the laundry work, so be sure to engage them for the Friday & Sat. after my arrival. I *especially want Catherine for those days*. The white woman who does our sweeping would do for the other one. Let Mr. Titus[1] go in *beforehand*, whenever he had time & loosen all the carpets including the hall & staircase;—or perhaps you could get a cheaper man who could do it without tearing them.

The postman!—*must* mail this! With *dearest love*
Your own   Ellie

I shall reach home with nearly $100.00.

ALS (WC, NjP).
¹ Nelson W. Titus, carpet layer.

To Ellen Axson Wilson

My own darling,   Princeton, Wednesday 4 May, 1892
How sweet and sensible and practical you are in what you say about the Illinois matter—and how I admire you in it all! Unquestionably it is true, as uncle James says, that college presidents have been among our chief writers—but not presidents of western agricultural colleges, asking to be developed. The more I think about the question, the more pronounced does my instinctive dread of the work I should have to do out there—and of the atmosphere it [in] which it would have to be done—become. It would be an entirely different thing from taking charge of an institution already literary and scholarly in its traditions: and, without the proper atmosphere, my literary plans would, I am sure, prove impossible of execution. Besides, I am not at all in sympathy with co-education. And, above all, there is this question of conscience: Ought any man who is not willing to devote the best years of his life to the task to accept a call to the function of developing the State University of a great State like Illinois? It cannot be done without an expenditure of the very best thought and energy, and it cannot be done within less than ten or fifteen years—a break of administration in the midst of the process would delay, if it did not endanger the defeat of, its successful completion. Now I am quite sure that I do *not* wish to devote the best of my life and energy to a task of just that sort. To do so because the pay is liberal (*if I can get enough here*) would be to sacrifice my highest aims to material comfort. Does not that settle the question, and make it a duty of *conscience* to decline (since I could not give them my *heart* for the work) and take, for the present, whatever they will give me here?
I have written to McCormick, a very frank letter, asking what he thinks I ought to do, and what he knows about the status and prospects of the State University; and I might run down to Baltimore and consult Gilman in person; but you know how I am constituted. The question I ask myself is, If I do not mean to accept the Illinois call in any event, ought I to '*work*' it in this

way? Having done as much as I have already done to stir things up, would you think me foolish, darling, if I did nothing more in that direction? I want to satisfy *you* in the matter—to be guided by your judgment, and by all your wishes in the matter.

It seems to me, my dear little queen, that I ought to consider myself under great obligations to uncle James for making full and public statement of your "remarkable resemblance to the Sistine Madonna" (and I conclude, from your saying that he 'again' called attention to the fact, that he had said the same thing at least once before!). Just because it is the deliberate judgment of so cool-headed a man, familiar with the original picture, and delivered, not emotionally, but in a "quiet, even, matter-of-fact tone," it furnishes me with the backing you have always demanded for *my* opinion of your incomparable face—the judgment of a very careful and perfectly competent witness who is *not* in love with you—hopelessly, passionately, life-deep in love with you, as is   Your own Woodrow

Unbounded love to all

ALS (WC, NjP).

From Ellen Axson Wilson

My own darling,   Columbia, May 5/92

I wonder if you are as *hot* as we are today; think of the thermometer at 90° already! I begin to *feel* in still another sense that it is time to go home. I wish I could take Sister Annie with me; she is very much 'run down' with the care of the baby and her large family,—has headache most of the time. The baby too is troubled with her teeth & they have very broken nights. But Sister says she must stay at home this summer unless she is forced to take the baby off because she can't afford to leave; they have had such an expensive winter. These girls and Jessie have been a great care to her, she says she feels twenty-five years older than before they all came. Jessie is a very bad child; you can't believe a word she says; and strangest of all when she is found out in her stories she doesn't show the least sense of shame! She is very disobedient and passionate too. Sister Annie seems to be in dispair about her.

Bro. George is having a good deal of practice in our family! I asked him to examine Margaret's ears, and he found yesterday that she was decidedly deaf in one. It is a case that is easily cured though by dilating the drum. It is the result of cold. He is going to blow up the nostril every day, & we must get the little instrument and continue it afterwards. She could only hear the watch at four inches when he examined & a moment after,—when he had "blown her up"—she could heard [hear] at eighteen. He says he can help mine, to some extent at least, by taking out a great lump of wax. He will probably do it today. Jessie has had a little sick turn this morning but seems to feel well again now. I have not had a chance to write before and now I am making extreme haste so as to give this to the postman when he comes at twelve.

Your letter yesterday about Ill. was quite satisfactory,—that sweet, *charming* love-letter still more so, of course. I can never get over the wonder of it, darling, that you can think and feel so about me. It makes me *so* happy and yet it humbles me so deeply too; for how can I *help* knowing and feeling how far short I fall of that description. It is the love-light in your eyes that blinds you, dear! But oh how I long to *be* all that you think me,—all that my darlings wife should be! May God help me to grow more into that likeness!   Your own Eileen.

ALS (WC, NjP).

To Ellen Axson Wilson

My own darling,   Princeton, Thursday 5 May, 1892

I received a rather amusing telegram from Chicago yesterday. It ran as follows: "Letter received. After careful consideration advise against new plans. Cyrus H. McCormick." I suppose a letter will follow. I am inclined, however, to take the telegram seriously. In the first place, the telegraph seems to be Cyrus's favorite means of correspondence; and, in the second place, after a talk I had with Bridges the other day in New York about McCormick, I am sure that his advice in such a matter is both sober and disinterested. Bridges is an admirable judge of character; he is intimate with McCormick; and he advised me to write to him, on the ground that he is perfectly familiar with the condition of educational affairs in Illinois, more clear-headed in advice upon practical matters than any other man of his (Bridges) acquaintance, and sure, because of the quality of his heart, to advise as a friend and class-mate, and not as a Princeton trustee.

The last time I saw Dr. Patton he told me that when Cyrus was here in February they had had a long talk together about me: which doubtless meant, about the subject of that letter I wrote Cyrus from Baltimore, concerning the Law School, etc.[1] Dr. Patton probably *suggested* as much to McCormick as he dared; for he has several times intimated to me that my class-mates ought to endow my chair. Possibly the "careful considera-tion" of McCormick's telegram refers to a consideration of my prospects of advantage here as well as of the situation in Illinois. But I am quite in the dark, and can only guess what may be in the wind.

No word from Mr. Alexander yet; but he may be doing some-thing.

I know that it must have seemed extraordinary to you, darling, that I told you nothing of what I knew of the University of Illi-nois; but I expected to *see* you before this: I should of course never decide such a matter without detailed conference with you. I expect, maybe, to telegraph you in a day or two *for permission to decline the call*. I've found it impossible to get my *heart* in-terested in the Illinois projects for a moment.

I am doing all that you have suggested by way of preparation for your coming—but, alas, I've heard of no one for nurse yet. There is no one you could bring from Columbia, is there?

If you need more money, darling, (by the way did you receive that $50 remittance?) please telegraph me, if there is not time to write, how much I should send. Are you going to Asheville and Morganton?

My darling!—and you, too, have undergone a surgical opera-tion! Oh, how glad I am that brother Geo. discovered the trouble and removed it! I should rather trust him than any one else I know of—and yet how it makes my heart ache to think of my darling having to suffer so! It makes me unspeakably wretched to think of it even now, when I know that it's over! That poor little nose! I hope it will now be able to get along with less assist-ance from the mouth. How opportune it is by the way: for when once my lips come into contact with that sweet mouth I don't see how I can withdraw them again even to let you breathe. My sweet love!   Your own Woodrow.

Besides unbounded love to all in that dear household, please give a great deal for me to uncle James and the rest of that family.

                                        W.

ALS (WC, NjP).
  ¹ See C. H. McCormick to WW, Jan. 28, 1892, n. 1.

From Ellen Axson Wilson

My own darling,   Columbia, May 6/92
    We were out until one last night at a party,—had a very pleasant time, and saw some pretty girls and very pretty costumes. "Cousin

Jimmie"[1] was my escort, his baby[2] being too sick for his wife[3] to go. Of course after such dissipation I don't feel very wide awake at this rather early hour, but I suppose I will be even more stupid in the heat of the day, so I will get my letter written while I am still equal to it.

Uncle James has been 'looking up' the University of Ill. & has given me a lot of statistics about it;—which of course contribute very little to ones real knowledge on the subject. I agree with Uncle James that it will be absolutely necessary for you to go out there before you can form any judgment in the matter or decide the question intelligently in *either* way. In thinking of the matter I am trying hard to drop my prejudices—very strong ones I must admit—against the West. My *reason* tells me that a great deal of it is doubtless due to pure ignorance, for do I not see every day exactly similar prejudices in southern people against the north & vice-versa, and perceive at once their absurdity because I know both sections. After all those Ill. people are doubtless the same as ourselves, most of them of eastern origin, and at worst the *professors* will be gathered from everywhere, and will furnish cultural society.

But to return to the point, don't you think you had better go out there now before I come home? I have been in many moods about this call of course, and the only thing I continue sure about is that we ought by all means to find out all about it before we decide. It would be so much *easier* just to decide against it,—"and be done with it!" That I think that is our chief temptation. But if it *should* be, peradventure, a great opportunity we don't want to lose it for want of courage to grasp it. It *might* give you a great deal *better* opportunity for literary work than you can ever have as a professor, more independence of position, more power to mould times and events to suit yourself;—and then the freedom from class-work—what a *great* thing that would be. *All* your *intellectual life* would flow in the one great channel, without impediment, whereas now it is divided into numerous small streams, —half a dozen courses on half a dozen subjects,—lectures in Balt, lectures in New York &c. &c. And not one of all the "courses" on the exact subject on which you wish to write! That is the worst of the present situation; your intellectual energies are exhausted before you come to the "main point.["] But the work of a president is so different that it might well take *half* your time, or more, yet leave your mind fresh for thinking & writing during the other half. You know that so far all your serious original work has been to do in vacation; there has been *no* time for it during the college year;—and I sometimes fear there never will be. For you havn't your lectures written out, & if you *had* you could never simply "turn the barrel over." You would have to get in touch again with every topic, expend so much thought upon it and so much nervous energy in its delivery,—that there would be none left *that day* for "the great work." And even "free days" are of small service when they alternate with *full* ones. The current of thought cannot flow steadily enough. Too many "mental somersaults," as you describe them, are demanded. But you have discovered of course that I am echoing *you*, especially as you expressed yourself when we were in Balt. last & you had "the blues" about your future in Princeton, & your chances for original work there. I remember how dissatisfied you were because Mr. Sloane had the department you wanted,[4] & you could *never* teach and write on the same subjects. But the postman will be here in a minute. I love you dear *devotedly, intensely.*

Your own Eileen.

I would consult about this matter with *everyone* of judgment, especially & at once with Mr. Gilman.

Will you please find this number of Babyhood[5] for Bro. George? They are in the medicine closet.

ALS (WC, NjP).
[1] James Hamilton Woodrow, Dr. Woodrow's son.
[2] Fitz William McMaster Woodrow, born May 2, 1891.
[3] Katharine McGregor McMaster Woodrow.
[4] Sloane and Wilson were the two professors in what was now called the History and Political Philosophy Section of the Department of Philosophy. Ellen meant that Sloane was giving some courses—specifically, English constitutional history since 1688, comparative politics, and the history of political theory—that Wilson wanted to offer.
[5] *Babyhood, the Mother's Nursery Guide* was published monthly in New York from 1884 to 1909.

To Ellen Axson Wilson

My own darling,   Princeton, Friday 6 May, 1892

A letter from McCormick came this morning, which I enclose.[1] It constitutes the only 'news' touching the Illinois matter. By the "specific and important work" I have "in hand" I understand him to mean the Law School—as also where he expresses the conviction that it will "in time be realized." I am more and more inclined to think that our decision must be as he suggests.

Princeton is filling up with guests very rapidly this afternoon—and oh, how I wish my darling might have been here for all the fun that is attracting them! To-night we are to have a concert from the Yale Glee and Banjo Clubs, and, after that the "Senior Assembly"[2]—to say nothing of the two receptions this afternoon—

one at the Ivy Club, the other at the new Athletic Club House, to mark its formal opening.[3] And then to-morrow we are to have, in the morning the annual "handicap games,"[4] and in the afternoon our first match game of base-ball (for some seasons) with Harvard![5] Isn't that a cluster of attractions?

I wish I enjoyed it all more; but, it has come to this, that, without you, I can enjoy nothing—nothing seems either natural or worth while.

Now even letter writing comes hard—it seems so poor a method of communication—so pitiable a substitute for genuine love-making now that your home-coming is so near at hand, and I shall have you in my arms *next week*—only six days from this very moment! Ah, me! how cruelly slowly time moves at such a crisis of love as this!

Surely, darling, you must be mistaken in saying that, after catching the through vestibule train at Salisbury you will have to change *twice*, both at Washington and Philadelphia. Telegraph for places on some through car—pay *any*thing that is necessary to avoid the change at Washington—even if you have to engage a section from New Orleans to New York. You *must* do this, darling, or I shall be wretched beyond measure!

I have engaged rooms here, as you wished; have seen Maggie; and have almost completed the other preliminary arrangements you suggested in the letter that came yesterday: so you may rest easy about the carrying out of that plan. I can't help dreading the work you will insist upon doing: I fear that it, on top of dear little Jessie's accident will undo whatever good effects your journey may have had upon you! For I know by sad experience that I cannot control you in respect of the amount of work you undertake at all. I shall feel almost ready to run away to avoid the distress of it.

But I can't scold you (by anticipation) with my heart bursting full of love as it is. Sometimes my love for you, my Eileen, seems to me fairly entitled to be called tragical—so intense is it—so masterful of all my moods—so powerful in all its effects. If your ineffable *sweetness* did not act as a delicious *comfort* to my highwrought feelings, I think they would break my heart with their sheer intensity. My love, my love! I am waiting for you with a heart too full for anything but an infinitude of kisses!

Your own Woodrow.

Unbounded love to all!

ALS (WC, NjP).

[1] The enclosure is missing, but see the letterpress copy printed at May 4, 1892.
[2] The senior class dance held in the gymnasium on the evening of May 6, fol-

lowing a concert given ("for the first time in intercollegiate history") by the Yale Glee and Banjo Clubs in the lecture room of the Second Presbyterian Church. *Daily Princetonian*, May 6 and 9, 1892.

3 Henry Fairfield Osborn, College of New Jersey, '77, and Professor of Comparative Anatomy at Princeton since 1883, resigned in May 1891 to become head of the Biology Department at Columbia College. As a parting gift to his Alma Mater, Osborn presented a clubhouse to the newly formed Princeton University Athletic Association, for the use of the various teams during training. The clubhouse was constructed in the autumn and winter of 1891-92, and all members of the college were invited to attend the formal opening on May 6.

4 The third annual handicap games were a variety of track events held by the Princeton University Track Athletic Association at University Field in Princeton on May 7. Students from Princeton, Yale, Williams, the University of Pennsylvania, and elsewhere participated. According to the *Daily Princetonian* of May 9, 1892, "The events were closely contested by Princeton. Yale also made a very good showing, but no records were broken."

5 See WW to EAW, May 8, 1892, n. 1.

From Ellen Axson Wilson

My own darling,   Columbia, May 6/92

I expect to be so busy tomorrow that I am taking time by the fore-lock & am writing tomorrow's letter tonight, though memories of the party last night urge me to make it a hurried one and get to bed!

I began to tell you a piece of news the other day when I was interrupted by the postman, & since then it has been constantly crowded out. I did not know before I came that Dr. Dubose,[1] Mac's only brother, had moved to Columbia. They live very near, on this street. His wife is an old Sewanee friend of mine as well as Rose's & of course came to see me as soon as I arrived. And now Rose is there! Rose and Mac and all three of the children! They came today & will stay until Tuesday. Rose's children are *lovely*, little Julia is especially pretty. The baby too is a beauty and very bright for four months. Rose is just as sweet as ever,— though not so pretty. While her figure is much stouter, her face has lost its roundness and colour,—but it is as sweet as ever. The oddest change is in her *hair*; you know it was a lovely rich bronze, —now it is jet black! I suppose she must have lost it in some illness & that it came back a different colour. Well, I should like to write pages about a subject of so much interest to me as Rose & her children, but I must deny myself.

The letter that I sent you today was almost an answer to the one that I received containing as it did my misgivings about your future chances for independent work while in a professor's chair, —misgivings derived both from observation and experience and also *directly* from yourself. I am *very* far from wishing to take a brief for Ill.—but I *would* like to hear your answer to those misgivings before the question is settled! The subject of that letter and of that conversation in Balt. has been constantly in my mind for the last day or two. I think the questions it raises are certainly of sufficient importance to make it wise for you to continue for a time to *weigh* and *canvass* the subject, to collect evidence and opinions on it; especially to consult Dr. Gilman & any other college presidents you may know. There are Dr. White of Cornell and Dr. Andrews,[2] both writers. I wish you would write to them, & ask them how the two positions of professor & president compare in opportunities for work.

I would not let the question of salary weigh with me *at all*,—except indeed as a larger income would contribute to your success as a writer. Of course with an income of $6000, and equivalent to $8000, you could get a fine library & go to Europe every summer. And with the presidential power in your hands you could doubtless make the vacation one of four months. But though this may sound like it I repeat that I *am not really* pleading the cause of Ill. This pen is driving me *wild* & it is late besides—so I will close abruptly.

With the passionate love and devotion of all my life I am

Your little wife,   Eileen.

ALS (WC, NjP).
  [1] Theodore M. Dubose, M.D., who lived on Blanding Street.
  [2] Andrew Dickson White, former President of Cornell University, and Elisha Benjamin Andrews, then President of Brown University.

To Ellen Axson Wilson

My own darling,   Princeton, Sunday. 8 May, 1892

I hope you did not laugh *too* much over that postal card I sent you yesterday: to lose such a game, and so overwhelmingly, is, as you know, a tragical matter for me.[1] I think that last night I was—I *must* have been—the most profoundly 'blue' man on the continent. I was worn out with fatigue and emotion—and, besides that, your letter—that *very* strong and wise letter you wrote Friday—on the Illinois question had quite unsettled the convictions that were coming to a head in my own mind, and I was hopelessly upset on that score. To-day I am calmer and my convictions again begin to assert themselves—even as against my darling's excellent reasoning in favour of a further and very careful consideration of the advisability of accepting the call. If the University of Illinois had an *assured income* sufficient to secure any considerable part of the new developments to which its trustees are looking forward, I should be very strongly inclined to accept their proposals. But it *has not.* Its income from permanent sources does not cover its *present* expenses. It depends, and must depend, upon legislative grants—and no legislative grant can, under the Constitution of Ill., be made to run longer than two years. Every two years the arrangements for legislative backing would have to be renewed—and one of the trustees who visited me here *said* that they *needed* a man of popular powers, who could manage the Legislature. The only assurance they can give of legislative support they give on the strength of what they believe to be the public opinion of the State—and upon the willingness of the Legislature in the past to give them what they asked—and they had asked, they said, very little. You see, therefore, that my task *would never be done*: and I do not wish *such* a political function. I would give an ounce of my blood if I could put off the preliminary decision of this matter until Thursday; but some indication of what I mean to do must be sent off by Wednesday: and, if I do not mean to play with them, I had better say no at first. (By the way, the trustees of the University are elected *by popular vote*, on party tickets!)

But I *will* not take up *all* of my Sunday letter with business! I've just heard some compliments paid you which delighted me. Mrs. Owen[2] reports that her brother, Ed. Sheldon, whom you liked so much, and found it so easy to become acquainted with, reported, after meeting you, that he had found you *perfectly charming*. She told me, too, that you were a great favorite with the students who knew you (as well as with the young ladies of the town) and that Phinizy[3] said he would rather talk to Mrs. Wilson than to any young girl he knew! *There's* a compliment for you from a young sport! There's proof, too, of my thesis of last Sunday, the unspeakable charm of *sympathy* there is about your mind. That, combined with charm of manner such as yours, with broad and sunny intelligence such as I never found in any one else, and with beauty of the exquisite Southern type of yours, constitutes all that either the heart or the mind of a man could desire. Kisses to all—with love unbounded—and for yourself, the whole thought and life of   Your own Woodrow.

ALS (WC, NjP).

[1] Wilson's postal is missing. Harvard defeated Princeton 11 to 5 in the game played on May 7.

[2] Elizabeth Sheldon (Mrs. Henry James) Owen, a widow who had just moved to 10 Mercer Street with her two daughters, Alice Proctor and Isabel Sheldon Owen.

[3] Bowdre Phinizy, '92, from Augusta, Ga.

From Ellen Axson Wilson

My own darling,   Columbia May 8/92

Your letter with Mr. McCormack's enclosed came today. That is strong testimony against Ill. I *think* it will probably be best for you to decline—yet *not in too great a hurry*. I would still collect other evidence and consult other authorities, especially Mr. Gilman. I was talking to Cousin Jimmie just now;—he thinks you would have a *great deal* more time and more *mind* at your disposal for original work as president than as professor. I simply give that opinion for what it is worth,—I don't quote him as authority. Yet it would be the very irony of fate for *you* to be breaking your heart because a *western co-educational* college did not prosper! Certainly we are prepared by birth and training, by education and association, to be supremely indifferent to the fate of all such. Yet of course in such a position your happiness would depend to a great extent on the success of the institution which you represented. I think it won't do.

I think it is very "mean" in Mr. McCormack to say nothing,— or the same as nothing, about increase of salary at Princeton! It is a *shame* that he don't do something definite about it at once. If he expects you to devote your life to Princeton's interests, at enormous pecuniary sacrifice, he ought to show some practical devotion to it himself, especially when he can do it *without* sacrifice. He could without feeling it a particle endow your chair so liberally that you would never be *tempted* to leave as long as you live. I think it is his plain *duty* to Princeton to do it. Now if ever is *the* time when he should give the college something besides *advice*!

This is commencement Sunday for the Seminary,[1]—we have just come from church where we heard Dr. Jerry Witherspoon[2] preach a rather poor sermon. He had a good idea but it was not well worked out. The gay flower-garden effect presented by the congregation was very striking after the severe taylor-made styles of the north.

Have you heard from Stock?—whether he is going to Kansas. *What* a pity it is for him thus to postpone indefinitely getting his degree. Don't you suppose that if he came to Princeton, and had neither board nor tuition to pay he could get through on his $250.00 and what he could make by working for the "Review of Reviews"? What do you think of writing to him to that effect? Of course with the proviso that we remain in Princeton. If it does strike you favourably, darling, I would be grateful to you for writing to him about it before he makes his plans. But this may be such a good opening in Kansas that he ought to accept it. Do you know what he is going to do this summer?

But it is now after dinner; I have the care of the children & they require such constant watching that I must close. All send love; & remember that I love you, my own Woodrow, just as much as you would want me to,—more than even you know, now and always   Your own Eileen

ALS (WC, NjP).
  [1] That is, the Columbia Theological Seminary.
  [2] The Rev. Dr. Jere Witherspoon, pastor of the First Presbyterian Church of Nashville.

To Frank Irving Herriott[1]

My dear Mr. Herriott,   Princeton, New Jersey, 9 May, 1892.
    I wish very much indeed that I could go to the meeting of the Academy to which you refer, and stand by you, if you should come under fire.[2] But my little family, which has been in the South since the first of March, is coming home, and there is so much to do by way of preparation that I cannot possibly get away.
    I don't think that you need fear savage criticism from the Philadelphia men. Stand by your guns and I feel sure that you will come out all right. You have your subject well in hand; and when that is the case a man can stand fire without fear.
                        Very sincerely Yours,   Woodrow Wilson

WWTLS (Ia-HA).
  [1] At this time a graduate student at The Johns Hopkins University, where he took his Ph.D. in 1893.
  [2] Herriott's paper, "Sir William Temple on the Origin and Nature of Government," read before the American Academy of Political and Social Science in Philadelphia on May 13, 1892, was printed in the *Annals*, III (Sept. 1892), 150-79.

To Ellen Axson Wilson

My own darling,   Princeton, Monday 9 May, 1892
    Unless I hear that you have changed your plans about starting on Wednesday, I shall write you no more letters after this one. Remember, darling, that you are to *telegraph* me any change of schedule you may decide upon: otherwise I could not meet you at the Junction or make any of my arrangements properly.
    One word in answer to the letter I received this morning: I don't think that the evidence of such men as President White and Mr. Gilman would be at all conclusive as to my opportunities for original work in Illinois, because Cornell and the Johns Hopkins have both had assured (or at any rate *calculable*) incomes. The same is true of Brown, where Andrews is. I *have* heard President Angell, of Michigan, speak very fully of the life of a President who has to extract grants from a Legislature and manage a political board of Trustees; and Stock. told me the other day in

New York that [James Hulme] Canfield (formerly a writer and professor in my own lines in the University of Kansas with three times the number of hours of class work that I have here), now president of the University of Nebraska (which is much further advanced in development than the Illinois institution, though originally of much the same sort) had said to him that he had once had great plans for original and literary work; but that since he had taken charge of the Nebraska University as president he had given up all idea of ever returning to books again. In short, I am convinced that what we are considering is, not the general question of *a* college presidency, but the special question of *this* college presidency. That the University of Illinois has (potentially) a great future before it I am quite ready to believe. I even think that I could secure that future for it, by devoting all my energies (including those of the latent politician within me) to the task, in many ways a very inviting one. But to do this would be to forego during the best years of my life my literary plans, with the likelihood of losing during those years—by reason of the new mental habits created by such a life of executive initiative—the literary faculty—at any rate in its fineness,—if not the literary impulse itself. I am—after abundant reflection, as you may suppose,—deeply convinced upon these points. And I know that you will regard these considerations as conclusive.

And now, my darling, good-bye till I have you once more in my arms—and all my life comes back to me *with you*! Oh, how sweet it will be to exchange *this* intercourse for *that*—for *you*! How my heart leaps and throbs to think of the unspeakable delight of having you once more close by my side and renewing all the sweet happiness of our perfect companionship! My precious darling! my ideal little wife! my matchless little lover!: the delay in seeing you becomes intolerable as the necessity for endurance grows less. Impatience and happiness together are making me fairly quiver with suppressed emotion! Give the dear one's in Columbia a loving farewell *for me*—with unbounded tenderness and love. *Cant* sister spend part of her summer here? Oh, my darling—my darling—come quickly to

Your own Woodrow.

ALS (WC, NjP).

From Ellen Axson Wilson

My own darling,   Columbia   Monday, May 9 [1892]
    Rose is coming over with the children this morning early so I have only time for a hasty line before she arrives.

I am going to leave here *tomorrow* afternoon,—I shall see you on *Wed.*! Bro. George says it is *quite* safe. Isn't that *glorious*?

I have decided not to take the vestibule. The gain in time would not pay for the great trouble involved in changing at Salisbury at ten o'clock at night. The man told Bro. George expressly that I should have to change at Washington on any and all trains; but he is going to see about it again, today,—see if telegraphing back will secure such a sleeper (he will telegraph for me *anyhow*). But that is the only change before I get to Phila. Will you meet me there or not? Do as you think best and find convenient, dear. I will be detained there two hours. This is the schedule.

No. 12—Leaves Columbia 4.10 P. M.
Arrive Washington 10.25 A. M.
Leave   "   11.00 A. M.
Arrive Philadelphia 2.20 P. M.
Leave   "   4.00 " "
Arrive Princeton   5.36 " "

Oh darling, I am so happy and so excited that I can scarcely keep still enough to write;—for you know all this has *just* been decided. To think that I will see my darling the day after tomorrow! Then this death in life—this dreadful separation is almost over! It seems almost too good to be true! Oh my love, my love, my Woodrow, I am *so* happy & will be so much happier *soon*! Only two nights more,—"and nights are short this time of year!"

But the bell rings[.] I think it is Rose. I must say "good-bye"— a short "good-bye." I love you, *love* you, dear, and am now and forever,   Your own Eileen

Later

Sister Annie has just told me something of importance. Bro. George has a patient that he sent to New York possibly for a serious operation. If the operation is to be done she is to telegraph for him & he is going on. He expects to hear today; and he thinks that if he goes I had better wait a day or two & go with him. I suppose that on Jessie's account I had better do so. But it almost breaks my heart to think of waiting. What do you think? If you would prefer that I should come anyhow tomorrow telegraph me; but if you think I had better wait I will understand silence to signify that.   Your little wife   Eileen

What a *goose* I am,—*of course* you won't get this in time to telegraph! But I will telegraph you *tonight* if I decide to *wait*.

ALS (WC, NjP).

Francis Landey Patton to James Waddel Alexander

My dear Mr. Alexander,   [Princeton, N. J.] 10th May, 1892.

I received your kind letter in regard to Professor Wilson, and write now to say that before I heard of the proposal that had been made to him, I had written to Mr. Cuyler in reference to an increase of Prof. Wilson's salary, by the appropriation of some of the Alumni Fund or by private subscription and have received from Mr. Cuyler a very favorable reply. If the money, say $500. per annum, can be raised through friends of Prof. Wilson or from the Alumni Fund, it would be a great deal better than for the increase to be made by a vote of the Trustees out of the current funds of the College, because it will save us from the appearance of making invidious distinctions, but in any event, I consider it essential to the Institution's wellfare that Prof. Wilson be made comfortable, and I should be in favor of adding $400. or $500. per annum from the funds of the College if it cannot be obtained in any other way,[1] and I have said so to Prof. Wilson in an interview I have just had with him. I think there is no doubt that he will stay with us.

In regard to Mr. Daniels, I am heartily in favor of inviting him to become Assistant Professor in Political Economy in the College at a salary of $1,500. per year. I think it safer to take a young man with his reputation to make than to take a man who has already made his reputation either as a doctrinaire protectionist or a doctrinaire free trader. Mr. Daniels is the choice of Professors Sloane and Wilson—the Professors immediately interested in the Department, and in our interview with Mr. Charles Green[2] a few days ago, he expressed himself as being in favor of our appointing Mr. Daniels. Professor Wilson will consult with Mr. Daniels, and try and keep him from committing himself prematurely to Wesleyan University. . . .

Very sincerely yours,   Francis L Patton

ALS (Patton Letterpress Books, University Archives, NjP).
    [1] One can only conclude from E. R. Craven to WW, June 30, 1892, Vol. 8, that Patton did not succeed in raising the supplement to Wilson's salary from outside sources.
    [2] Charles Ewing Green, '60, a Trenton lawyer, trustee of the Estate of John Cleve Green (his uncle), and chairman of the Finance Committee of the Board of Trustees.

To Daniel Coit Gilman

My dear Mr. Gilman,   Princeton, New Jersey, 12 May, 1892.

I take the liberty of writing to you upon a matter of great importance to myself, because I know of no one from whom I could more wisely seek the advice of which I stand in need.

I have been offered the presidency of the University of Illinois upon conditions which make the offer very attractive indeed. The salary would be $6,ooo; but in addition to that I should have the assistance of a business-manager who would relieve me of the superintendence of the material detail of administration, and of a short-hand secretary who would relieve me of the drudgery of correspondence. I should, moreover, have no teaching to do.

The University is at present quite undeveloped, except upon the technical side of the agricultural and mechanic arts, having originated, like so many other institutions in the West, in the federal land grants made in aid of the establishment of agricultural colleges. Now, however, the educational leaders of the State feel that they are ready to make their University what the universities of Michigan and Wisconsin have already become. They feel, moreover, and the facts seem to me to warrant their confidence, that the legislature and people of the State will support them in their effort.

Their intention is not at all to enter into rivalry with the institution about to be established at Chicago, but rather to supplement such institutions by the most ample provision possible for the best undergraduate instruction in all branches of a liberal education,—a wise and moderate programme.

Now, devoted as I have already become to Princeton, I should like to superintend such a task of development, for I have some ideas about the way in which it ought to be done; but there is one important proviso: *provided* it did not involve the surrender for an indefinite period of my ambitions as a writer. I have some literary tasks at heart which I could not afford entirely, or even for a very long time, to forego; and you would confer a very great favour upon me if you would express your frank opinion upon the probable effect of such a presidency upon a literary career.

Which, in your opinion, is the more likely to have sufficient freedom of time and mind for effective literary work, a professor or a college president? The tasks which I have laid out for myself are large, and will require protracted, sustained, and systematic effort: are the duties of a college president who has no teaching to do so essentially distracting, do you think, (when compared with those of a teacher) as to be fatal to the successful prosecution of such undertakings?

Mrs. Wilson joins me in cordial regards both to yourself and to Mrs. Gilman and your daughters.

Very sincerely Yours,   Woodrow Wilson[1]

WWTLS (D. C. Gilman Papers, MdBJ).

¹ In light of the letter that follows, written on the same date, one can only speculate as to whether Wilson wrote this letter to President Gilman in order to please Ellen, who had of course been urging him to write thusly, or in order to make sure that Gilman knew about the Illinois offer. It is also possible that Wilson thought that he would receive other invitations to be a university president and was seeking Gilman's advice for general consideration of the relative merits of a professorship and a presidency.

To Francis M. McKay

My dear Sir: Princeton, New Jersey, 12 May, 1892.

I of course received your letter of April 30th., written from New York. I need not apologize for having taken two weeks to answer it: were there not special re[a]sons for my coming to an early conclusion, on your own account, I might, rather, apologize for coming to a conclusion upon so important a matter in so short a time.

I have given the matter of the regency of the University of Illinois very serious consideration indeed during the two weeks which have been at my disposal; and the advice which my friends, —but more particularly my own reflections,—have given me is, I now feel confident, the wisest and best. My first impulse not only, but my first reflections as well, strongly inclined me to accept the nomination which you and Mr. Graham so flatteringly offered me. Almost everything that you had told me, or that I learned from other quarters, of the University of Illinois made me feel that I could find a career in its regency that would call forth my best powers and reward me in every way. Even the fact that the University was obliged to depend so largely upon the Legislature for its means of support and growth constituted, in its way, an attractive element in the situation, for it aroused the latent politician within me.

But one imperative consideration has turned the scale of my judgment decisively in the other direction. I do not believe that anyone ought, in the exercise of a good conscience, to accept the position of regent of the University of Illinois who would not be willing from the outset to devote his life to the tasks of development which it involves,—and I have not been able to form such a resolution. It is a function to which a comparatively young man ought to devote his life-time,—all his best and most active years, all his best constructive faculties; and I,—to be perfectly frank,—have become conscious, as the question has more and more definitely shaped itself in my mind, that, were I to accept the position, I could not accept it with my mind made up that it was my final and only field of work. It is quite evident to me that my literary plans would, in such a post, have always to be subordinated to executive duties: and I know that I would always find them asserting themselves in my preference as my principal interest; and the resulting warfare of duty and preference would make me either an indifferent regent or an indifferent writer.

I can say these things without even a suggestion that I do not think the offer you have made me worthy of the acceptance of the best man in the country. I regard your preference of me as much the greatest compliment that has been paid me. I decline only upon the ground that I do not feel that I could make such an office my exclusive life function, and I think that you ought to have a man who could and would make it the single duty and distinction of his life. I regard this decision,—though it is now so clear and unalterable in my mind,—with some satisfaction just because it has been arrived at by overcoming a strong temptation. In declining your kind overtures I have overcome selfishness.

It is a sincere pleasure to me to have gained the acquaintance, and I hope the esteem, of two such men as yourself and Mr. Graham, and I trust that there may some time occur an opportunity of making that acquaintance closer and more intimate. Please accept my warmest expressions of regard and gratitude. I give up with sincere pain the opportunity of associating myself with you in the work of your State University.

Most sincerely Yours,   Woodrow Wilson[1]

WWTLS (WC, NjP).
[1] A shorthand draft of this letter is in WP, DLC.

An Examination

14 May, 1892.

Special in Jurisprudence.

1. What is meant by the term 'Positive' Law? What is Professor Clark's generic definition of Law?

2. What is the derivation of the terms for Right and Wrong, and what is the double significance of the terms meaning Right in German, French, and Italian? Explain that double use.

3. Give the classification of Law according to the nature of the subject-matter.

4. Give Merkel's definition of Right; give also Holland's definition. How is legal right to be distinguished from moral right?

5. In what way, and for what reason do actual relationships give rise to legal relationships; and in what sort of cases only can actual relationships give rise to jural relationships?

6. What is involved (i.e., what processes of fitting the law to the facts) in the action of the courts in the adjudication of cases?

7. Under the subject of Personal Relationships not of Contract, what are the four kinds of constructive obligation? Give illustrative examples.

8. What does Puchta say, by way of introduction, of nature, spirit, reason, and freedom; and why does he call freedom "the foundation of Right["]?

9. What, according to Puchta, is the two-fold conception and meaning of the term Right?

10. What does Puchta say of Right as a principle of equality?

WWT examination (WP, DLC).

To Winthrop More Daniels

My dear Mr. Daniels,   Princeton, New Jersey, 16 May, 1892.

I would have answered your letter before, had it been possible to do so in the midst of house-cleaning. My little family have just returned, and we got into our house again only this afternoon.

I have something to say that is very satisfactory to myself: I hope that it will be as satisfactory to you. Both from Dr. Patton and from one of the Trustees I have information which warrants me in saying that there is every probability that you will be offered an appointment here next year as Assistant Professor of Political Economy at a salary of $1500.[1] I sincerely wish that the salary were to to be more, to start with; but it is as much as others of the same rank are receiving, and there is this difference about their position and the one that will be offered you, that the Assistant Professorship of Political Economy will certainly be made, within a reasonably short period, a full chair.

Now of course this is only a violent probability; I write it as a "pointer," for the purpose of ascertaining whether you would be likely to accept such an offer. If you would not decline a Wesleyan proposal for less than an *official* assurance that you will be elected here, Dr. Patton will, I feel sure, get the proper committee of the Trustees together and assure you of their recommendation to the Board, which would be to all intents and purposes an election.

Please write to me as soon as you can about this matter. I am sincerely anxious to see you here. You would be sure of a cordial welcome on all hands; and I think, from my own experience, of a most pleasant and profitable life besides. I sincerely trust that you will feel disposed to come. But you will, I am sure, be perfectly frank about all aspects of the matter.

Excuse haste, under the circumstances, and believe me

Most cordially Yours,   Woodrow Wilson

WWTLS (W. M. Daniels Coll., CtY).

[1] Documentary evidence on the point is missing, but it seems very likely that Wilson was able to use the Illinois offer to persuade Patton to consent to the immediate appointment of a man in political economy, as well as a modest salary increase for himself.

An Examination

May 19th, 1892.

College of New Jersey.

Examination in International Law.

1. What is the relation of a new state to the contract rights, and to the property, of the parent state; and what are the effects of cession upon the contracts, rights, and obligations, and upon the property, of the state ceding, and the state acquiring?

2. What are the general conditions of the legality of intervention; and what are the grounds which are alleged to be sufficient for intervention?

3. What are the various sorts of agents of a state; and what are the rules as to the reception of diplomatic agents, the commencement of their mission, their rights, and the termination of their mission?

4. What are the limits to the rights of violence against the persons of enemies; the rules as to non combatants, and as to combatants?

5. What are the rules as to private property not within the jurisdiction of any state?

6. In what does Postliminium consist and what are the limits to its operation?

7. What has been the practice in the nineteenth century concerning contraband, and what does contraband include, according to that practice?

8. Why was it possible for one man to do as much as Grotius did towards the creation of International Law? What two systematic writers preceded Grotius? What were the plan and scope of his work? What conceptions constituted the philosophical basis of it?

9. Contrast Vattel with Grotius in the plan of his work, its fundamental philosophical conceptions, and its significance and use for the student of International Law.

10. Which are the Five Great Powers of Europe since the Peace of Paris of 1763? What were the principal international arrangements effected by the Congress of Vienna? Give the date of that Congress and the occasion of its assembling.

Printed examination (WP, DLC).

To Winthrop More Daniels

My dear Mr. Daniels,   Princeton, New Jersey, 24 May, 1892.

I think that everything will turn out here to your mind.[1] I saw the President yesterday, and he is to present your name to the Curriculum Committee to-morrow for formal recommendation to the Board. They will certainly accept your nomination without objection. That much is practically assured.

As for the length of time you will have to wait for your promotion to full rank as Professor, the President, with his usual caution, would not commit himself to a formal promise on that head; but I received from him the same sort of assurance that he gave me with reference to my being relieved of the work in Political Economy at the end of two years. He 'confidently expects that your promotion will come without difficulty at the end of three years, both sides being satisfied in the mean time,' and I think that that is as much of a promise as we shall get or need desire. It practically assures you the most considerate and liberal treatment: gives you a definite basis of calculation.

I, it seems, am to remain 'Professor of Jurisprudence and Political Economy' and so be head of the Department[2] of which you will be the other member: in short, I am to be, for the trial heat, your 'chief.' I am sure that I need not assure you that this arrangement will not involve any real curtailment of your liberty in your work. It will be pleasant to be thus consulting colleagues.

This, I trust, simplifies the whole matter for you, and insures your acceptance. Unless I write you to the contrary within a couple of days (by Thursday night) that the Curriculum Committee did something unprecedented, you may take our part of the programme as complete, minus only the action of the Board itself,—which would follow the recommendation of the Committee as of course.   Faithfully Yours,   Woodrow Wilson

WWTLS (W. M. Daniels Coll., CtY).
    [1] Daniels' letter is missing.
    [2] The History and Political Philosophy Section of the Department of Philosophy was divided in 1892 into the History and Political Science Section under Sloane and the Jurisprudence and Political Economy Section under Wilson.

From Joseph Ruggles Wilson

My precious son—   Hot Springs, Ark.   May 25, 1892

Your charming letter was duly received, and has cheered me as I needed to be amid the fearful monotonies of Gen. Ass. commonplace. Besides this place of meeting is a mere hole for invalids and for gamblers, so that at every turn the eye is offended and the moral sense pained. The hotel pictured above [the Arlington Hotel] is a big wooden structure that looks well only in lying picture. Nevertheless my health continues pretty fair, so that I can reasonably hope to take rail road accommodation for my return, about Monday next, the 31st. It is simply a question of endurance. Meanwhile I love you and Ellie to the utmost of my tolerably large capacity for entertaining in the "living room" of my heart these objects of my affection. And I do feel grateful, with a warmth of gratitude I am unable to express, for the affection felt for me at the Princeton home, as likewise at the Columbia corner.

You certainly acted wisely in declining the Illinois venture— i.e. so far as I can see the case in your brief notice of it. To dance attendance upon a legislature, to entreat for money to carry on one of its own institutions, would be intolerable to the fine nerve of my noble boy. Besides, you would be diverted from the specialty which you are so desirous to lift into conspicuity.

You need not have troubled yourself to write that $100 check, for which I was not looking—but I can make it up to you.

I find here, Rev. S. I. Woodbridge[1] who you know married Jeanie Woodrow. He seems a nice little fellow whom one cannot help liking even though there is not much about to call forth swift admiration.

I need not *send* my love to you all—for my love is always with you. I hope to meet you at Columbia.

In haste and deep affection   Your devoted   Father

ALS (WP, DLC).
[1] The Rev. Dr. Samuel Isett Woodbridge. Born Henderson, Ky., Oct. 16, 1856. A.B., Rutgers College, 1876; studied at Columbia Theological Seminary, 1879-80, and at Princeton Theological Seminary, 1880-82. Ordained on Oct. 7, 1882, by Charleston Presbytery, he served as a missionary in China for the rest of his life, first in Chinkiang, 1882-1902, and then in Shanghai, 1902-26. Founder and editor, 1902-26, of the Shanghai *Christian Intelligencer*. He wrote several books about his experiences in China and translated a number of Chinese works into English. Died in Shanghai, July 23, 1926.

To Winthrop More Daniels

My dear Mr. Daniels,   Princeton, New Jersey, 30 May, 1892.

Your letter of Saturday has just reached me,[1] and I hasten to reply, in order that you may not be kept in any doubt about the situation here.

You need not wonder at your having received no official notification of the resolution taken by the Curriculum Committee for I find that things are done here most informally. Of course, too, the action of the Committee is hardly formal until presented to the Board. I think that the President has relied on me to conduct the whole correspondence in the matter. The nomination was adopted without the least objection by the Committee, and I am informed that Dr. Patton said to the Committee very explicitly that this nomination looked toward the establishment of a full chair of Economics and a promotion.

When Dr. Patton said to me that he "confidently expected that your promotion will come without difficulty at the end of three years, both sides being satisfied in the meantime," he said it not only for my information but to be repeated to you. It therefore constitutes as much of an assurance as I think we can get, from this particular President. I say this out of my own experience. When I was approached by Dr. Patton with reference to my election here, he expressed the same sort of 'hope' with regard to my being relieved of the work in Economics at the end of a couple of years; and that was the most that he said. And yet I find that he has regarded that as substantially a promise. I think his fear is, that he may give a promise which may bind him officially to some course which might prove impossible. All that he means to say is, that he has every reason to believe that a promotion will take place at the end of three years, and will feel himself bound to propose it unless some imperative reason why it should not, or rather could not, be done should disclose itself. This, it seems to me, practically assures you the promotion.

You can certainly count, too, on me to remind the President, should it become necessary, of this assurance.

I think that their inclination here is to be liberal with the corps of instructors; and, it seems to me, that in your case, the general prospects for a career would be better here than at Wesleyan, and the pecuniary and hierarchical prospects not inferior, even if a shade less definite.

Most sincerely Yours,   Woodrow Wilson

WWTLS (W. M. Daniels Coll., CtY).
¹ Daniels' letter is missing.

An Examination

2 June, 1892.

Princeton College.
Examination in Elements of Political Economy.

1. What is Production, and who are producers? Prove, as well as State, the latter.

2. What is Exchange? Why does the discussion of value fall

under Exchange? What are the various kinds of value? What are the individual, what the social, aspects of value? What relation has money to value?

3. What are the four shares in distribution, and by what general laws is each share determined?

4. What effect has rent upon the price of commodities? What effect has rent upon wages?

5. What was the industrial revolution? What is the Labour Question; and how far was the labour question created by the industrial revolution? Under what general division does the discussion of the labour question fall?

6. Discuss the question: what can be done to help the labouring classes?

7. What is the entrepreneur, and what are his functions? For what does he receive profits?

8. What is an industrial crisis, and how is it occasioned?

9. Give the marks by which you would distinguish essentially socialistic legislation from mere state interference.

10. What conditions give rise to modern socialism; what features of the present industrial system does it chiefly attack; and what modern conditions created opportunities for its propaganda?

11. State and criticise the theoretical basis of socialism.

Printed examination (WP, DLC).

From Stockton Axson

[Middletown, Conn.,

My dear Brother Woodrow: c. June 7, 1892]

I am just in receipt of your letter which is very welcome to me. I should be delighted to see you all in Princeton during commencement, but to do this will be impossible because of my work here. We dont get through until the 29th and the amount of work which I shall have to do between now and that date terrifies me.

Daniels told me that you have definitely decided not to go to Illinois. I am sure that time will witness the wisdom of this decision. It is leaking out that he is to go to Princeton next year, and the knowledge is causing wide spread and loud lamentation. You are fortunate in getting him. He is a magnificent man.

I suppose that you are rejoicing over the situation in the Republican camp.[1] If splits must come I am glad that we had ours some months ago so that time has been in a measure to heal the breach. Surely our prospect of success is better now than it has been in months.

Please thank Sister for a photograph of herself which I received some time ago. I did not acknowledge the receipt of it at the time because I didnt know how long she was going to remain in Columbia or where she was going from there. I am very glad to have the picture which to me seems first rate. I am very glad that little Jessie's collar-bone has healed so nicely.

I have had nothing from Ed[2] for a long time but suppose that he will be starting home soon.

And now let me thank you again for the invitation which I should much like to accept. I write in great haste

Affectionately yours   Stockton Axson

ALS (WP, DLC).
  [1] Stockton was referring to the confusion and division in the Republican party caused by Secretary of State James G. Blaine's peremptory resignation from the Cabinet of President Benjamin Harrison on June 4, only three days before the Republican national convention was to open. This, Blaine's last effort to win the Republican presidential nomination, failed ignominously, and Harrison was nominated on the first ballot.
  [2] Edward Axson, who was still at the Bingham School.

From the Minutes of the Princeton Faculty

5 5′ P.M, Wednesday, June 8, 1892.
. . . The Report[1] on the Monitorial System was then taken up, considered, amended and adopted and is as follows, viz: *Resolved* that

1.   *A Monitorial System*
be introduced for the benefit of those Professors who wish to avail themselves of it, and that the system apply to Classes or Divisions of Seventy (70) members and upward.

2. That monitors be secured from those students having room-rent or tuition free.

3. That the Regulations for Monitors be in substance as follows, viz:

Rules for Monitors.

A person accepting a monitorship is understood to engage to observe faithfully the following rules:—

1. He shall always (unless detained unavoidably) be present in season when he is to officiate as monitor.

2. He shall in no case appoint a substitute to act in his stead, nor permit any other person to make a mark upon his rolls. When he foresees the necessity of absence he shall inform his Class officer (or in his absence some other officer who shall approve of an offered substitute for the time[)].

3. He shall mark those who are punctually present, those who are tardy, and those who leave before the close of the exercise.

4. He shall write on each roll its date, giving both the day of the week and the day of the month.

5. He shall *himself* render the roll to the Class officer or to the College Registrar.

ALS (WC, NjP).

1 For the appointment and first report of this committee, on which Wilson served, see the Princeton Faculty Minutes, Nov. 20, 1891, and Jan. 8, 1892.

ADDENDA

Two Letters to Azel Washburn Hazen

[Middletown, Conn.]
Monday evening, Nov. 25[26]/88

My dear Mr. Hazen,

With very deep misgivings, I accept the part you proposed I should take in the exercises of the Bible Society next Sunday evening. If I were to decline it would be merely through diffidence—I am not at all sure that I can make an address that will be satisfactory even to my friends; and I am by no means certain that one has a right to decline a part in such exercises merely through diffidence. Beyond a doubt I can say *something* about the Bible—who cannot among those who have come into vital contact with it?—and perhaps my something ought not to be withheld when it is asked for.[1] I shall sympathize very keenly, however, with those who were responsible for asking me.

Very sincerely Yours,   Woodrow Wilson

[1] A brief account of the meeting of the Middletown Bible Society on December 2, 1888, in the Middletown, Conn., *Penny Press*, Dec. 4, 1888, says about Wilson only that he spoke.

My dear Friend,   Princeton, New Jersey, 22 September, 1891

We were beyond measure distressed to learn of Mrs. Hazen's illness.[1] I sincerely trust that the attack continues to be of the less aggravated type, and that you may *very* soon write us that she is convalescent. We shall be heavy hearted till you do; for the illness of so dear a friend weighs on our spirits very grievously. Give her warmest messages of love from us both.

My father spoke in warmest terms of his meeting with you in Saratoga. He spoke of getting from you a sense of worth and of high spiritual and intellectual gifts such as very few other men had so soon made him feel. "The man makes me *love* him," he said, in his impulsive fashion. You see, therefore, that you have equal attractions for both father and son.

I am delighted to think that my last letter gave you so much gratification: it is a satisfaction to pay one's just debts—and I owe you all the gratification I can possibly give.

We have spent the entire summer at home,—never going further away than an afternoon's drive would take us. For I had a job to do which could not be any longer postponed: that 'Epoch of American History' of which you may have heard me speak. I got about two-thirds of it into shape to be revised—and hope that the remaining third and the revision may be accomplished this Winter,—even though there be new courses of lectures still to be prepared. Our college year begins tomorrow.

Please remember us to all our valued friends in Middletown that you may see. Accept once more our assurances of deep sympathy and affection.

Yours most Sincerely,   Woodrow Wilson

ALS (in possession of Frances Hazen Bulkeley).

1 Wilson is replying to A. W. Hazen to WW, Sept. 17, 1891, printed in this volume at that date.

NOTE ON THE INDEX

THE alphabetically arranged analytical table of contents at the front of the volume eliminates duplication, in both contents and index, of references to certain documents, such as letters. Letters are listed in the contents alphabetically by name, and chronologically within each name by page. The subject matter of all letters is, of course, indexed. The Editorial Notes and Wilson's writings are listed in the contents chronologically by page. In addition, the subject matter of both categories is indexed. The index covers all references to books and articles mentioned in text or notes. Footnotes are indexed. Page references to footnotes which place a comma between the page number and "n" cite both text and footnote, thus: "624,n3." On the other hand, absence of the comma indicates reference to the footnote only, thus: "55n2"—the page number denoting where the footnote appears. The letter "n" without a following digit signifies an unnumbered descriptive-location note.

An asterisk before an index reference designates identification or other particular information. Re-identification and repetitive annotation have been minimized to encourage use of these starred references. Where the identification appears in an earlier volume, it is indicated thus: "*1:212,n3." Therefore a page reference standing without a preceding volume number is invariably a reference to the present volume. The index supplies the fullest known forms of names, and, for the Wilson and Axson families, relationships as far down as cousins. Persons referred to in the text by nicknames or shortened forms of names can be identified by reference to entries for these forms of the names.

A sampling of the opinions and comments of Wilson and Ellen Axson Wilson covers their more personal views, while broad, general headings in the main body of the index cover impersonal subjects. Occasionally opinions expressed by a correspondent are indexed where these appear to supplement or to reflect views expressed by Wilson or by Ellen Axson Wilson in documents which are missing.

INDEX

Abelman *v.* Booth, 516
Adams, Charles Kendall, *3:501,n1; *4:331n3; 71, 72, 76, 92, 159, 160
Adams, Henry Carter, *2:391,n1; 73, 486n4
Adams, Herbert Baxter, *1:15,n20; *2:391,n1; 93, 101-2, 104, 113, 159, 168, 226n2, 230, 271,n8, 320, 379n1
Adams, Louis Bartholomew, 193
administration, WW lectures on, 381-436
Administration de la France. Histoire et mécanisme des grands pouvoirs de l'état, fonctions publiques, conditions d'admission et d'avancement dans toutes les carrières, privilèges, et immunités (Haas), 119
Aiken, Charles Augustus, *1:191n,1; *74,n1
Alden, Edmond K., 271,n2
Alexander, James Waddel, 176, 178n2, 192-93, 374n1, 602,n2, 609, 619, 630
Alexander Hamilton (Lodge), 284
Alfred, King of the West Saxons, 31n10
Allendale, S.C., 54n2
Allgemeines Staatsrecht (von Gareis), 429, 431
Allgemeines Verwaltungsrecht (von Sarwey), 116, 119, 167
American Academy of Political and Social Science, 96-97, 106-7
"American Ballot Reform" (Shaw), 230n4
American Commonwealth (Bryce), 167, 283, 284, 291, 343-44, 370, 371, 376, 379, 534
American Commonwealth Series, 194, 211, 234, 236, 245
American Economic Association, 234
American History Series, 274,n1, 277, 291
American Institute of Christian Philosophy, 97
American Political Ideas (Fiske), 282, 283, 284
American Review of Reviews, see Review of Reviews (New York)
American Society for the Extension of University Teaching, *209,n1,2; WW memorandum, 223; 316
Ames, Knowlton Lyman, 172,n2
Ancient City (Fustel de Coulanges), 283, 284
Ancient Law: Its Connection with the Early History of Society and Its Relations to Modern Ideas (Maine), 14n, 139, 283, 284
Ancient Régime (Taine), 284
Ancient Régime and the Revolution (Tocqueville), 284
Andrews, Elisha Benjamin, 239,n2, 624,n2, 627
Angell, James Burrill, 627

Annals of the American Academy of Political and Social Science, 97,n1, 106-7, 186, 339,n9, 386n4, 627n2
Anne, Queen, 43
Areopagitica (Milton), 358,n10
Aristotle, 132, 193, 210n2, 223, 280, 283, 284, 350
Arkansas College, Batesville, 11n5
Arlington Hotel, Hot Springs, Ark., 637
Armstrong, Andrew Campbell, Jr., 191,n3, 492,n3, 557; Mrs. (Mabel Chester Murray), 191,n3, 486,n7, 492, 557
Arndt, Ernst Moritz, 326
Arnold, Carrington Gindrat, 468n1
Arnold, Louise, 372,n5, 469
Arnold, Matthew, 505
Arnold, Richard J., 467,n1, 480, 486, 502, 529; Mrs. (Minnie S. Clarke), 372,n5, 467,n1, 480, 486, 502, 529
Arnold, Susie, 480, 529
Ashby *v.* White, 151
Ashton, Mary Jane, *2:66on1; *4:196,-n4; *5:264n1; 45,n2, 103, 189
Astor House, New York City, 470, 490, 549
Athletic Organizations of Princeton University: Their Histories, Records and Constitutions, June 1891, 243,-n1
Atlantic Monthly, 164, 165, 176, 203, 211n2, 288, 289, 290, 315, 370
Aucoc, Léon, 119, 385, 386, 387, 388n7, 392, 403, 405
Augusta (Ga.) Presbytery, 53,n2
Austin, John, 292, 318, 326,n3, 327, 328, 329, 334, 336, 455, 516
Avon-by-the-Sea, N.J., 97
Axson, Carrie Belle, first cousin of EAW, *2:557n2; 449, 450n2
Axson, Edward William, brother of EAW, *2:372,n2; 181,n3, 452,n8, 521, 602,n5, 610, 640,n2
Axson, Ellen, first cousin of EAW, *2:557n2; 278,n1, 285, 288, 449, 450n2, 568, 574, 581,n1
Axson, Isaac Stockton Keith, paternal grandfather of EAW, *2:334n2, *2:547,n3, *2:557n2; 461, 609; Mrs. (Rebekah Randolph), *2:334n3, *2:547n3; 461
Axson, Leila, first cousin of EAW, *2:557n2; 448,n2, 501
Axson, Margaret Randolph ("Maggie"), sister of EAW, *2:417n1, *3:118n1; 450,n1, 451, 452,n3, 466-67, 488,n2, 509, 521, 546, 555, 556, 562, 563, 567, 568, 570, 571, 573, 577, 579, 580-81, 582, 586
Axson, Randolph, Sr., paternal uncle of EAW, *2:557n2; 278,n1, 284, 285, 288, 445,n1, 446, 452, 481, 489, 496, 507, 512, 521, 581n1, 603, 610;

Mrs. (Ella Law), *2:557n2; 448,n1, 449, 497, 498, 501, 568
Axson, Samuel Edward, father of EAW, *2:334,n3; estate of, 603n4; grave, 488,n3; gravestone and inscription, 489,n5, 496,n2, 497, 504, 511-12, 520, 521, 523, 544,n1, 547, 548, 553, 566; 609-10; Mrs. (Margaret Jane Hoyt), *334n2,3; 556, 568, 573, 579, 597
Axson, Stockton (full name: Isaac Stockton Keith Axson, II), brother of EAW, *2:386n1; 4,n3, 45-46, 50, 56, 178, 181,n3, 182, 183, 183-84, 187, 248, 278, 285, 316, 344, 369, 450,n2, 461, 485, 489, 493, 496, 504-6, 510-11, 512, 520, 521, 553, 568, 581, 583, 586, 601, 602, 603, 606, 609, 610, 626, 627, 639-40

Babyhood, the Mother's Nursery Guide, 621,n5
Bagehot, Walter, 88, 168, 173, 210n2, 223, 281, 282, 283, 284, 315, 354, 486, 595
Bailey, J. W., M.D., 568,n2
Baker, 522,n1, 532
Baker, Ray Stannard, 341n11
Baltimore: Lyceum Theatre, 443; Princeton alumni, 443
Baltimore Sun, 443n
Bangs, John Kendrick, 529
Bardwell, Joseph, 323n2
Baring-Gould, Sabine, 284
Barrie, Sir James Matthew, 523,n4
Batbie, Anselme Polycarpe, 119
Bayless, George A., 207n2; Mrs. (Sarah W.), 207n2
Bazard, Saint-Armand, 83
Beach, Charles Fisk, Jr., 173
Bede, 18
Beecher, Henry Ward, 376n1
Behördenorganisation des Verwaltung des Innern (Meyer), 167
Bellamy, Edward, 86
Bellevue Hotel, Philadelphia, 164
Benham, George M., 296,n5
Bennett, Charles Edwin, 218,n4
Bentham, Jeremy, 280, 326, 327
Berkeley, George, 511
Besant, Annie (Wood), 225,n3
Berg, Guenther Heinrich von, 118
Bibliographia Hopkinsiensis, 320n1
Biddle, John Craig, 164,n2, 445
Biggs, John, 445
Bill, Alfred Hoyt, 96n2
Bird, William Edgeworth, Mrs. (Sarah Baxter), *3:605,n3; 502,n3
Birrell, Augustine, 326,n2, 353,n6, 362,n15
Blackstone, Sir William, 133, 151
Blaine, James Gillespie, *3:391n1; 640n1
Blair, Hugh, 506
Blanc, Jean Joseph Charles Louis, 83, 194, 439

Blavatsky, Helena Petrovna, 230,n3
Bloch, Maurice, 120
Bloomfield, Maurice, 214,n2, 218
Bluntschli, Johann Kaspar, *2:391,n2; 153, 432, 454
Blydenburgh, Benjamin Brewster, 289,-n1
"Bob," "Bobby," see Bridges, Robert
Bodin, Jean, 132, 334, 436
Bonaventure (cemetery), *3:16,n4; 481,n1
Bones, James W., uncle-in-law of WW, *1:39n4; 524n2, 532, 553; Mrs. (Marion Woodrow), *1:39,n10; 522,-n2
Bones, Maria, *2:392; 552, 573
Bones, Marion McGraw, first cousin of WW, *1:487n2; 527
Book News (Philadelphia), 246, 284
Bornhak, Conrad, 119, 416n19, 427
Boughton, Willis, 316
Bourinot, John George, 284
Boutmy, Émile Gaston, 275-76, 283, 284, 535,n3, 536
Bowie, Mr. (Rome, Ga.), 547, 548; Mrs., 538, 547, 548
Bowie, Mrs. (Atlanta), 539, 552
Bowie, Sophie, 552
Bowman, James, 561
Bowman, John Hall, 560,n1, 561
Bracton, Henry de, 29,n9
Bradlaugh, Charles, 225,n3, 229
Bragdon, Henry Wilkinson, 242n
Brashear v. Mason, 152
Brennan, John Menifee, 342,n5
Bridges (cousin of Robert), 82
Bridges, Eleanor, 290, 309
Bridges, John Miller, *61,n2, 69, 92, 95-96, 102, 179, 290, 309-10
Bridges, Mary (Mrs. John), 61
Bridges, Robert ("Bob," "Bobby"), *1:284,n1; 61, 69, 78, 82, 92, 95-96, 102-3, 105-6, 179, 193, 194, 242, 289-91, 308-9, 309-10, 315, 376n2, 380, 601, 602, 618
Bridgman, Howard Allen, 240
Brie, Siegfried, 59-61, 76,n4
Bright, James Wilson, 50,n1, 204,n2
Brodnax, James Maclin, 343,n5
Brooklyn Institute of Arts and Sciences, 369
Brower, Abraham Thew H., first cousin-in-law of WW, *2:17,n3; 508,n3; Mrs. (Jessie Bones), *1:39,-n4; *2:17n3; 508,n3, 523,n3, 528, 553
Brown, David, Mrs. (Susan Dod), 502,-n6
Brown, Edward Thomas, cousin of EAW, *2:519,n1; 452,n6; Mrs. (Mary Celestine Mitchell), *5:528,-n2; 574,n1, 588
Brown, Minnie, see Henderson, Minnie Brown
Brown, Minor, 552,n1, 565, 580
Brown, Warren A., uncle-in-law of

EAW, *2:401,n2; 452,n5, 552, 553n1, 571, 573; Mrs. (Louisa Cunningham Hoyt; "Aunt Lou"), maternal aunt of EAW, *2:402n2; 450, 451-52, 466, 467, 469, 488,n1, 494, 509, 539n1, 546, 547, 552, 567, 568, 571, 573, 574, 577, 580, 581, 582, 583, 589, 593
Brown University: coeducation proposed, 442, 443, 444; Diman Memorial Fund, 239,n1; Historical and Economic Association, 372,n4
Browne, Francis Fisher, *5:468,n1; 310, 318, 440
Browne, William Hand, 204,n1
Brownell, William Crary, *61,n3
Browning, Elizabeth Barrett, 564
Browning, Robert, 326, 358,n9
Brunswick Hotel, New York City, 176
Brusa, Emilio, 113n3
Bryce, James, Viscount Bryce, *2:547,-n2; 89, 167, 283, 284, 291, 343-44, 370-71, 376, 379, 534
Bryn Mawr College, 7
Buckley, James Monroe, 79,n3
Buena Vista, N. C., WW purchases lot in, 248,n1
Bulkeley, Frances Hazen, 228n
Bulmerincq, August von, 454,n1
Burgess, John William, 164, 274,n1, 474; WW marginal notes on his Political Science and Comparative Constitutional Law, 169-71; WW review of, 164, 165, 166; text, 195-203
Burke, Edmund, 122, 151, 210n2, 223, 245, 280, 283, 284, 305n1, 334,n8, 352,n5, 365,n19, 542
Burlingame, Edward Livermore, 242,-n2, 289, 290
Burns, Robert, 554,n1,2, 557,n5
Buttolph, Mr., 507
Bynkershoek, Cornelis van, 453

Caesar, Julius, 18
Café Savarin, New York City, 549
Calder v. Bull, 513
Calhoun, Samuel, 301,n10
Cambridge University: Lecture Syndicate, 209n1
Cameron, Henry Clay, *1:191,n1; *565,n5
Campbell, Robert, 326n3
Canfield, James Hulme, 628
Cannon, John Franklin, 270,n2
Carey, Henry Charles, 439
Carey, Martha Ward (Mrs. James Carey), 45,n3, 50, 227, 271, 274
Carlier, Auguste, 534,n1
Carlyle, Thomas, 362,n14
Carr, Dr., 290, 309
Carrie, Miss (Atlanta, Ga.), 539, 552, 553
Catherine (servant), 615
Cecil, Sir Robert, 400
Cent ans de république aux États-Unis (Noailles), 535,n2

Central Government (Traill), 105, 167, 283, 284, 400, 595
Central Railroad of Georgia, 602,n4, 609, 610
Central University, Richmond, Ky., 323n2
Century Dictionary, 293
Century Magazine, 232,n5, 245
Chalmers, Sir Mackenzie Dalzell, 283, 284, 595
Chamberlin, Thomas Chrowder, 218, 222, 224, 247
Chambrun, Charles Adolphe de Pineton, Marquis de, 534-36
Chapin, Aaron Lucius, 237
"Character of Sir Robert Peel" (Bagehot), 354,n7
Charlemagne, 18n
Charles I, 26, 43
Charles II, 401
Charles VII, 404
Charles IX, 335
"Charles Bradlaugh" (Besant), 225,n3
Charleston (S. C.) News and Courier, 54n2
Charleston (S. C.) Presbytery, 53,n2
Chase, George, 372n3
Chase, Salmon Portland, 250
Chase, Samuel, 513, 514
Chaucer, Geoffrey, 510
Chautauquan, 40n, 44, 461,n2
Chéruel, Pierre Adolphe, 119, 395n13
Chesnut, William Calvin, 241
Chicago: Princeton alumni dinner, 159n1
Chicago, University of, 188, 189, 190, 191-92, 271,n8; EAW hopes for offer of chair to WW, 600; 604, 606, 608, 613, 631
Church Union (New York), 270n3
Cicero, Marcus Tullius, 404, 455
Civil Government in the United States (Fiske), 282, 283, 284
Civil War and the Constitution, 1859-1865 (Burgess), 275n1
Clarence, Duke of (afterward William IV), 399
Clark, Edwin Charles, 292, 293, 455
Clark, John Bates, *5:564,n1; 49, 51, 68, 75, 80
Clarke, Susan C., 467,n1, 480, 502
Clarksville, Tenn., 55; JRW Jr. on, 77, 78; Arlington Hotel, 3
Clarksville (Tenn.) Democrat, 97-98
Clarksville (Tenn.) Progress, 3, 77, 78, 97, 98, 324
Clarksville (Tenn.) Progress-Democrat, 98, 220n2
Clay, Henry, 272
Clemens, Samuel Langhorne, 376n1
Cleveland, Grover, *3:247,n2; 148n9
Cobden, Richard, 214
Cocceji, Samuel von, Baron, 418
coeducation, 442-43, 444
Coffin, Seward Vincent, 171-72, 243; Mrs. (Della Maria Brown), 243

Coke, Sir Edward, 151, 305

Colbert, Jean Baptiste, 395, 405

Cole, Hugh Laing, 177

College of New Jersey, see Princeton University

Colonies, 1492-1750 (Thwaites), 175,-n1, 176, 206, 272

Columbia College, 192,n1, 372n3; Law School, 372,n3

Columbia (S. C.) State, 249

Columbia (S. C.) Theological Seminary, 54n2, 568,n1, 626,n1

Commentaries (Caesar), 18

Commentaries on the Law of Nations (Manning), 595

Commons, John Rogers, 68,n2, 181,n2, 317,n2

Comparative Administrative Law (Goodnow), 120

Comparative View of the Executive and Legislative Departments of the Governments of the United States, France, England, and Germany (Wenzel), 175,n2

Coney, John Haughton, 440,n1

Conferences sur l'administration et le droit administratif faites à l'école des ponts et chausées (Aucoc), 119, 385, 386, 387, 388n7, 392, 403, 405

Congregationalist, 240

Congress Hotel, Saratoga, 238,n3

Congressional Government (Wilson), 283, 284. See also Wilson, Woodrow: Writings

Conn, Herbert William, 557,n4; Mrs. (Julia M. Joel), 557,n4

Connecticut Valley Economic Association, 49n2, 51, 69n, 75, 80

Constitutional History of the United States as seen in the Development of American Law, 149

Constitutional Law of England, see Introduction to the Study of the Law of the Constitution (Dicey), 473

Constitutional Legislation in the United States (Ordronaux), 153,n12

Contemporary Review (London), 71

Cook, A. D., 294,n1, 295

Cook, Joseph, 316,n1

Cooley, Thomas McIntyre, *4:357,n2; 105, 212, 291

Cooper, King, 507, 524; Mrs. (Josie Sibley), 507, 511, 524, 525

Cornell University: A. Shaw elected to chair, 62, 71; turns down offer, 160; C. K. Adams suggests WW, 160

Cornwall, Henry Bedinger, *1:605,n2; 179,n1, 192, 294, 557; Mrs. (Mary Hall Porter), 557

Cours de droit administratif (Ducrocq), 119

Cours de droit public et administratif (Laferrière), 119

Cowie, James A., 70n

Cox, Henry Bartholomew, 212n, 309n

Cozby, Allie, 595

Craig, John Newton, *2:548,n1; *47,n1, 51, 52, 71

Craven, Elijah Richardson, *6:526,n1; 48,n1, 57, 58-59, 445

Creasy, Sir Edward Shepherd, 283, 284

Critical Period of American History (Fiske), 187

Cromwell, Oliver, 401

Crosby, Nicholas Evertson, *589,n2

Cursus der Institutionen (Puchta), 293

Cuyler, Cornelius Cuyler, *1:440,n1; 180n1, 219-20, 611, 630

Cuyler, Theodore, Mrs. (Mary DeWitt), 549,n1

Cyclopedia of Political Science, Political Economy, and of the Political History of the United States (ed. Lalor), 49

Dabney, Richard Heath, *1:685,n1; 67, 85, 233-34

Daily Princetonian, see Princetonian

Daniels, Winthrop More, *205,n3, 317, 579,n2, 606, 630, 634, 636, 637-38, 639

Davis, Jefferson, 185

Davis, John Davis, *1:138,n5; 46,n3

Dean, the, see Murray, James Ormsbee

Decatur v. Paulding, 152

"Decay of Local Government in America" (Patten), 386,n4

Deems, Charles Force, 97

Delaware & Raritan Canal, 373

democracy, WW lecture on, 344-69

Democracy in America (de Tocqueville), 284

Demosthenes, 347

Denison, George A., 68,n1, 75, 82n1

Dennis, Alfred Pearce, 83,n1, 439n1, 440

Deutsche Litteraturzeitung (Berlin), 61, 76

Development of Constitutional Liberty in the English Colonies of America (Scott), 283, 284

Dewey, Davis Rich, *3:36,n5; 239

Dial (Chicago), 310, 320, 440

Dicey, Albert Venn, 187, 275, 283, 284, 473; Mrs. (Elinor Mary Bonham-Carter), 275

Dickinson College, 179,n2

Dictionary of Greek and Roman Antiquities (Smith), 141

Dictionnaire de l'administration française (Bloch), 120

Dictionnaire historique des institutions, moeurs et coutumes de la France (Chéruel), 119, 395n13

Dilke, Sir Charles Wentworth, 284

Diman, Jeremiah Lewis, 239,n1

"Dode," see Wilson, Joseph R., Jr.

Dodge v. Woolsey, 517, 518

Dohm, Mr., 300

Dohm, M. E., Mrs., 297,n7, 298

Donnan, Elizabeth, 239n1

Donovan, Caroline, 184n1
Dougan, Peter, Mrs. (Elizabeth Mills), 449,n7
Doyle, Sir Arthur Conan, 376n1
Dripps, Joseph Frederic, 468,n2, 481; Mrs. (Emily Dunning), 468,n2, 481
Dripps, Robert D., 481,n2
Droit et libertés aux États-Unis: Leurs origines et leurs progrès (Chambrun), 534-36
Dryden, John, 505
Dubose, Julia, 623
Dubose, McNeely, *3:12,n1; 623; Mrs. (Rosalie Anderson), 459,n2, 466, 485,n3, 563, 569, 601, 623, 628, 629
Dubose, Theodore M., M.D., 623,n1
Ducrocq, Théophile, 119, 403
Duffield, John Thomas, *1:133,n3; *92,n2, 96, 112, 294, 342
Dufour, Gabriel, 119
Dulles, Joseph Heatly, *538,n1, 556
Duncan, Martha Deloney Berrien Nesbit (Mrs. William), *3:15,n1; 539,n2, 552, 553
Dunlop, George Thomas, Jr., 342,n5
Dupriez, Léon, 426n21
Durham, N. C., WW gives lecture on "Democracy" at, 368
Dwight, Theodore William, 372n3; Dwight Alumni Association, 373n3

East Tennessee, Virginia and Georgia Railroad, 547,n3, 548
Easton, John William, 207-8
Eaton, Clement, 54
Economic Studies (Bagehot), 595
Educational Review, 276n
Edward I, 27
Edward the Confessor, 42
"Elemente der allgemeinen Rechtslehre" (Merkel), 249-69, 292, 293
Elements of Jurisprudence (Holland), 291, 293
Elements of Law Considered with Reference to Principles of General Jurisprudence (Markby), 293
Elements of Politics (Sidgwick), 310, 318-20, 332,n7
Elizabeth I, 30
Ella (nurse), 469
Elmira College, 345n2, 368
Ely, Richard Theodore, *2:448,n1; 102, 320, 379n1, 486n4
Emerson, Alfred, *3:125,n7; 247
Encyclopædia Britannica, 416n19, 511
Encyklopädie der Rechtswissenschaft in systematischer und alphabetischer Bearbeitung (ed. von Holtzendorff), 119, 249n1
Englische Verfassungsgeschichte (von Gneist), 119
Englische Verwaltungsrecht der Gegenwart in Vergleichung mit dem deutschen Verwaltungswesen (von Gneist), 119

English, Virginia Shaw, 63n, 76n, 95n, 184n, 226, 245
English constitution, WW on, 12-44
English Constitution (Bagehot), 282, 283, 284
English Constitution (Boutmy), 283, 284
English Constitutional History from the Teutonic Conquest to the Present Time (Taswell-Langmead), 88
Epoch of Reform (McCarthy), 284
Epochs of American History, 165, 175-76, 210, 213, 221, 227, 233, 242, 272-73, 274, 277, 285-86, 290, 378, 565
Epochs of Modern History, 286
Equitable Building, New York City, 373n3, 490, 519n1, 536, 549; Equitable Life Assurance Society Law Library, 506, 519n1, 536, 567, 584, 587
Erwin, Elizabeth Adams, *2:399,n1; 569,n3
Eshbaugh, D. O., 160
Essay on the Principles of Population (Malthus), 439
Études de droit constitutionnel; France, Angleterre, États-Unis (Boutmy), 535,n3
Evans, Hoyt Brown, 452,n7, 559
Evans, James Philip, Mrs. (Loula Brown), first cousin of EAW, *3:306; *5:158,n1; 452,n4,7, 559,n1, 568, 570-71, 581, 585, 593
Evans, Jeannette, 452,n7, 559
Evans, Kathleen, 452,n7, 559
Evelyn College, Princeton, N.J., 549,n2; Evelyn Association, 550n2
Ewing, Esmond, 277-78
Ewing, Robert, 77,n1, 248, 277-78; Mrs. (Harriet Hoyt), first cousin of EAW, *3:267,n4; 278,n3

Falkner, Roland Post, 222,n1, 224
"Fanny," see Hoyt, Frances
Farrand, Max, *172,n3, 222, 243
Farrer, Thomas Henry Farrer, 1st Baron, 595
Fay, Edwin Whitfield, 214
Fayerweather, Daniel Burton, *484,n2
Federal and State Constitutions, Colonial Charters, and Other Organic Laws of the United States (Poore), 129n6
Federal Government in Canada (Bourinot), 284
Federal Government of Switzerland (Moses), 284
Federalist Papers, 90, 129,n6, 367, 479
Fentress, David, 343,n5
Fentress, James, Jr., 343,n5
Ferron, Henri de, 120
Field, Stephen Johnson, 148n9; Field-Terry Case, 148,n9

Fifty Years of the Class of 'Seventy-Nine Princeton, 380n1
Filmer, Sir Robert, 132
Fine, Henry Burchard, *223,n3, 322, 483, 502, 538; Mrs. (Philena Fobes), 222-23, 483, 502, 538
Fine, John, 223,n4
Finley, John Huston, *271, 602, 609
Finley, Robert Johnston, 184,n2, 187, 271
"First Century of the Constitution" (Johnston), 187
First Lessons in Political Economy (Walker), 105, 291, 379
First Principles of Political Economy (Chapin), 237
Fisher, John Crocker, M.D., 73-74, 93
Fisher, Richard, 484
Fiske, John, 187, 282, 283, 284
Flemming, James Ralston, 287,n1
Flemming, Woodville, Maj., 287; Mrs. (Ella Ralston), 287
Flinn, John William, 54n2
Flood, Theodore L., 12n
Foley, Maggie, 103n, 502,n4, 503, 601, 615, 622
Foley, Mary, 503
Folwell, William Watts, 73
"Food-aided Education," 230,n4
Foresters (Tennyson), 505,n2
Formation of the Union, 1750-1829 (Hart), 175,n2
Forum magazine, 230
France as It Is (Lebon and Pelet), 283, 284
Francis, Aunt, 547
François I, 335
"Freedom" (Tennyson), 362,n13
Freeman, Edward Augustus, *3:124,-n3; 86, 89, 90, 91, 284
Freeman, Mary, *5:277,n1; 240
French Revolution (Gardiner), 284
Friedrich II ("the Great"), 419
Friedrich Wilhelm I, 418, 426
Friedrich Wilhelm ("The Great Elector"), 418
Frothingham, Arthur Lincoln, 565,n4
Fustel de Coulanges, Numa Denis, 283, 284

Gaines, L. W., 77, 98
Gardiner, Bertha Meriton (Cordery), 284
Gardiner, Samuel Rawson, 284
Gardner, Henry Brayton, 271,n4, 372,n6; Mrs. (Mabel Richmond), 271, 372,n6
Gardner, Mrs. (Rome, Ga.), 547
Gareis, Karl von, 429, 431
Garmany, Francis Champion, 491n1
Garmany, George Larcombe, 491,n1
Garmany, George Washington, 491n1; Mrs. (Jane Champion), 491n1, 498
Garmany, Howard Hunt, 491n1
Garmany, Jasper Jewett, M.D., 491n1

Garrett Biblical Institute, 237
Gates, Mr., 187
Gautier, Théophile, 462n1
General Principles of Constitutional Law in the United States of America (Cooley), 105, 291
Genesis of a New England State: Connecticut (Johnston), 187
George, Henry, 86
George I, 43
George II, 43
George III, 43, 367
George IV, 43
Georgia (nurse), 561
Georgia, University of, 4
Germany, Present and Past (Baring-Gould), 284
Gesetz und Verordnung (Jellinek), 119, 132
Gibbs, Frederick S., 69,n2
Gibby, William Dwight, 205,n4
Gide, Charles, 303,n1
Gilbert, Charles M., 449,n5; Mrs., 449
Gildersleeve, Basil Lanneau, *2:335,-n1; 189, 218
Gilman, Daniel Coit, *1:593,n1; 3-4, 168, 182-83, 184, 189, 191-92, 203-4, 320, 379n1, 607, 616, 624, 626, 627, 630-31; Mrs. (Elizabeth Dwight Woolsey), 631
Girardeau, John Lafayette, *2:131,n2; 52n1; Mrs., 52,n1
Gneist, Rudolf von, 89, 93, 118-19, 393,n10
Gods and Little Fishes (Dennis), 83n1
Godwin, Harold, *1:249,n3; 242
Goebel, Julius, Jr., 373n3
Goetchius, George Thomas, 523,n5, 525; Mrs. (Antoinette Wingfield), 525
Goldie, Matthew, 294, 295, 296, 297, 300
Goldsmith, Oliver, 356,n8
Gonzales, William Elliott, 249n1
Goodnow, Frank Johnson, 120
Gorham Company, 380n1
Grady, Henry Woodfin, *2:125n; 560
Graham, Nelson W., 594,n1, 598, 601, 632, 633
Grannis, Elizabeth Bartlett, *6:358,n1; 270n3
Grant, Hugh John, 69n1
Grant, Mr., 78
Grant, Ulysses Simpson, 149
Gray, Emma Larimore, first cousin of WW, 287
Green, Charles, Mrs. (Aminta Fisher), *2:582; 484,n3
Green, Charles Ewing, 630,n2
Green, Eddie, 79
Green, Edward Melvin, 71,n1,79, 545n2; Mrs. (Sarah Emily Howe), 71, 79
Green, George, 79
Green, Henry Woodhull, 586n2
Green, John Cleve, 586n2, 630n2

Green, John Richard, 88; Mrs. (Alice Sophia Amelia Stopford), 284, 398-n16
Green, Marion, 79, 544,n2
Green, William Henry, *6:527,n1; 502,n1, 528, 550n2; Mrs. (Elizabeth Hayes), 501,n1
Greene, William Brenton, 57
Greene, William Brenton, Jr., 481n1; Mrs. (Katharine Porter), 480,n1
Grinnell College, 229,n1
Grotius, Hugo, 453, 635
Growth of the English Constitution from the Earliest Times (Freeman), 284
Grundsätze der Polizeiwissenschaft (von Justi), 118
Grundsätze der Polizey, Handlung und Finanz (Sonnenfels), 118
Guild, William Alexander, 342-43,n5
Guizot, François Pierre Guillaume, 284

Haas, Claude Pierre Marie, 119
Hageman, John Frelinghuysen, Jr., 441,n1
Hall, Thomas Cuming, *614,n3
Hall, William Edward, 291, 292, 379, 454,n2, 456
Hallam, Henry, 355
Hamilton, Alexander, 90, 201, 479
Handbuch der politische Oekonomie (von Schönberg), 119
Handbuch der Verwaltungslehre und des Verwaltungsrechts (von Stein), 118
Handbuch der Verwaltungslehre, mit Vergleichung der Literatur und Gesetzgebung von Frankreich, England, Deutschland und Oesterreich (von Stein), 118
Handbuch des Oeffentlichen Rechts der Gegenwart, in Monographien (ed. Marquardsen), 119, 120, 167, 345n1
Handbuch der teutschen Policeyrechts (Berg), 118
Hanna, John Hunter, 342,n5
Hardeman, Miss (Rome, Ga.), 610
Hardenberg, Friedrich Leopold, *Freiherr* von, 50,n2
Hardenberg, Karl August, Prince von, 420
Harno, Albert J., 65n7
Harper, George McLean, *3:571,n1; 565,n4
Harper, William Rainey, 190,n1, 579
Harris, Anna, *2:505,n1; 511,n3, 520, 522
Harris, R. R., 511,n3
Harris, William [Wirt], Mrs. (Christina Van Alen Butler), 502,n5, 503
Harrison, Benjamin, 239n1, 640n1
Harrison, Thomas Perrin, 50,n3
Hart, Albert Bushnell, *5:472,n1; 164,n2, 165, 175-76, 210-11, 213, 221, 272-73, 274-75, 276-77, 285-86,

370, 375-76, 377-78, 438, 550,n5, 555
Hart, Thomas Riego, 472
Hartford Theological Seminary, 369
Harvard University, 4, 444; baseball game at Princeton, 622, 624,n1; Law School, 65
Haskins, Charles Homer, *6:118,n1; 218,n5
Hastie, W., 293, 313
Hazen, Azel Washburn, *6:15,n2; 181, 228-29, 269-70, 289, 317; Mrs. (Mary Butler Thompson), 181, 229, 289, 317, 601
Heath, Daniel Collamore, and D. C. Heath & Co., 70, 76-77, 172-73, 175, 239, 302-3
Heffter, August Wilhelm, 326
Henderson, Mr., 548,n2, 552, 553, 561; Mrs. (Minnie Brown), first cousin of EAW, *3:306; 538,n1, 548n2, 552
Henderson, George, 209,n3
Hendrickson, George Lincoln, 222
Hengist, 21
Hening, William Waller, 312
Henry, (James) Bayard, 378,n1, 443n, 445
Henry, Patrick, 367
Henry I, 42
Henry II, 23, 30
Henry II (Green), 284, 398n16
Henry III, 27, 31n
Henry VI, 26, 31
Henry VIII, 30
Henry Clay (Schurz), 284
Herbert B. Adams: Tributes of Friends, with a Bibliography of the Department of History, Politics, and Economics of the Johns Hopkins University, 1876-1901, 320n1
"Hermitage" (Sill), 575,n2, 577,n5
Herrick, Robert, 532, 541
Herriott, Frank Irving, 627,n1
Hibben, John Grier, Mrs. (Jenny Davidson), 207n2
Higginson, Thomas Wentworth, 288
Higher Education of Women in New Jersey, 550n2
Hildebrand, Bruno, 439
Hills, Mrs. (Baltimore), 103
Histoire politique interne de la Belgique (Poullet), 181
Historian's World (ed. Donnan and Stock), 239n1
History and Origin of Representative Government in Europe (Guizot), 284
History of American Politics (Johnston), 284
History of Historical Writing in America (Jameson), 271,n6
History of Methodism in Utah (Merkel), 180n1
History of Political Economy (Ingram), 291
History of the Eighteenth Century and of the Nineteenth till the Overthrow

of the French Empire (Schlosser), 57,n2

History of the English Constitution (von Gneist), 93n

History of the Law of Nations in Europe and America, from the Earliest Times to the Treaty of Washington, 1842 (Wheaton), 455, 456

History of the Lawrenceville School, 1810-1935 (Mulford), 586n2

History of the Louisville Presbyterian Theological Seminary, 1853-1953 (Sanders), 323n2

History of the School of Law, Columbia University (Goebel), 373n3

Hobbes, Thomas, 326

Holland, Sir Thomas Erskine, 291, 293, 633

Holst, Hermann Eduard von, *2:472,-n3; 91

Holtzendorff, Franz von, 126, 249n1, 292

Home, Henry, Lord Kames, 506

Homer, 280

Hooker, Richard, 352

Hopkins, Mrs. (Rome, Ga.), 527

Hopps, Daniel, 493,n2

Horsa, 21

Hosmer, James Kendall, 283, 284

Hot Springs, Ark., JRW on, 636-37

Houghton, Mifflin & Co., 194

House Called Morven (Bill), 96n2

"How do I love thee?" (E. B. Browning), 564

Howard, George Elliott, 271,n9

Howe, Annie, niece of WW, 591, 617

Howe, Annie Wilson (Mrs. George Howe, Jr.), sister of WW, *1:3,n6; 10,n2, 47, 51-52, 70, 71, 79, 80, 82-83, 248, 249, 442, 508,n6, 523, 525, 544, 562-63, 568, 571, 584, 587, 590, 591, 592, 593, 594, 596, 597, 599, 601, 612, 617, 628, 629

Howe, George, Jr., M.D., brother-in-law of WW, *1:39,n8; 47,n2, 52, 70-71, 79, 80, 83, 195, 238, 248, 249n1, 583, 590, 591, 592, 593, 595, 596, 599, 600, 601, 610, 615, 617, 619, 621, 629

Howe, George, III, nephew of WW, *1:220n1; 47,n3, 52, 83, 591, 596,-n7,8, 599

Howe, James Wilson, nephew of WW, *1:128,n3; 82,n1

Howell, Emily, 610,n1

Howell, "Hice," 523; Mrs. (Mary Parks), 523, 530

Hoyt, Annie Laurie, first cousin of EAW, 534,n1

Hoyt, "Birdie," first cousin of EAW, 508,n5

Hoyt, Elizabeth Cothran, first cousin of EAW, 508,n5

Hoyt, Florence Stevens, first cousin of EAW, 468-70, 484, 534, 539, 544, 547, 560, 578

Hoyt, Frances ("Fanny"), first cousin of EAW, *3:315n1; 552,n2; 559, 563, 565, 568, 573, 580

Hoyt, Henry Francis, maternal uncle of EAW, *3:307,n2; 547, 553n2, 568, 583, 584n1

Hoyt, James ("Jimmie"), first cousin of EAW, 583,n1, 585, 587

Hoyt, Margaret Bliss ("Margie"), first cousin of EAW, 508,n1, 534

Hoyt, Mary Eloise ("Minnie"), first cousin of EAW, *2:495,n3; *3:576-n3; 448,n2, 523, 534

Hoyt, Mary Mitchell, first cousin of EAW, 508,n5

Hoyt, Nathan, grandfather of EAW, 597

Hoyt, Nathaniel, first cousin of EAW, 508,n4

Hoyt, Robert Motes, first cousin of EAW, 508,n4

Hoyt, Robert Taylor, Mrs. (Anna Cothran; "Aunt Annie"), aunt-in-law of EAW, 508,n4, 511, 523, 533, 534, 537

Hoyt, Sadie (Saidie) Cooper, "Aunt Saidie" (Mrs. Thomas Alexander Hoyt), aunt-in-law of EAW, *3:484,-n1; 57, 61,n1

Hoyt, Thomas Alexander, maternal uncle of EAW, *3:268n4; 57, 61,n1, 277,n2, 451,n3

Hoyt, Wade Cothran, first cousin of EAW, 508,n4, 533

Hoyt, William Dana, first cousin of EAW, *3:220,n1; 511,n2

Hoyt, William Dearing, M.D., maternal uncle of EAW, *2:476,n1; 495,n1, 500, 509n1, 511, 523, 533, 537, 578; Mrs. (Florence Stevens), *3:226n1; 469,n1, 484, 488, 511,n1

Hubbell, Mary C., 485,n2

Hug, Lina, 284

Hulsey, Maggie, *5:526,n1; 451,n4,1, 452, 453, 495, 508

Hume, David, 511

Hunt, Theodore Whitefield, *1:76,n1; *6:528,n1; 54, 57, 342

Hunter, Ida M., 240

Hurt, Miss, 445

Huston, Joseph Miller, 342,n3, 445

Hutton, Maggie, 103n

Hyde, William DeWitt, 218,n3

Ida, Miss (Rome, Ga.), 508

Illinois, University of: C. H. McCormick on, 613; presidency offered to WW, 594, 598, 600-1, 601-2, 603, 604, 608-9, 612-13, 615, 616-17, 618, 619, 620, 621, 623, 624-25, 627, 628, 630, 631; declines offer, 632-33; 635n1, 637, 639

Imbrie, Andrew Clerk, 292, 293, 304n1

Indian affairs, 84n2

Industrial Revolution (Toynbee), 595
Ingelow, Jean, 543n1
Ingram, John Kells, 291
Institutes of Common and Statute Law (Minor), 293
Institutes of Roman Law (Sohm), 293
Institutes of the Law of Nations (Lorimer), 595
Institutions municipales et provinciales comparées (Ferron), 120
International Law (Hall), 379
International Law (Maine), 595
Iowa College, *see* Grinnell College
Irvine, William Mann, 205,n5
Isham, William Burhans, Jr., 78, 380n1
"Isham Dinners" (Kerr), *5:200,n1; 78,n1, 380n1

Jacobsen, Edward Percy, 303n1
James, Edmund Janes, 73, 96-97, 106-7, 203, 209n1, 246n1; Mrs. (Anna Margarethe Lange), 203
James, George Francis, 246,n1
James II, 29, 43
Jameson, John Alexander, 329,n5, 330, 331, 336, 341,n10, 351,n3
Jameson, John Franklin, *2:448,n2; 226-28, 238-39, 270-71, 273-74, 371-72, 442-43, 444, 470
Jellinek, Georg, *6:170,n2; 90, 119, 132, 133, 435
Jenkins *v.* Culpeper Co., 578n
Jephson, Henry, 440n1
Jessup, Henry Winans, 67n13, 14
Jevons, William Stanley, 511
John (King of England, 1199-1216), 27, 42
Johns Hopkins University, 4, 5, 6; English seminary and journal meetings, 56,n1; WW plan for school of public affairs, 64; Donovan professorship, 184, 191-92, 204, 372; 192, 219n1,2, 227,n1; House of Commons, 241; 271n8; Bibliography, 320,n1; Seminary of Historical and Political Science, 325n1, 369; 372, 607. *See also* Wilson, Woodrow: The Johns Hopkins University
Johns Hopkins University Studies in Historical and Political Science, 284
Johnson, Percy Lincoln, 79,n1
Johnston, Alexander, *2:558,n1; *4:-324,n1; 46, 49, 187, 284
Johnston, Richard Malcolm, *592,n1, 594, 597,n2
Joline, Adrian Hoffman, *6:683,n1; 48, 54-55, 57, 58-59, 166
Jolly, Ludwig, 119
Jones, Richard, 194, 439
Jones, Thomas Davies, *614,n4
"Josie," *see* Wilson, Joseph R., Jr.
Journal of Southern History, 54n2
Joy, James Richard, 26n, 40n
Judson, Harry Pratt, 73
Juilliard *v.* Greenman, 148
Juridical Review, 66

jurisprudence, WW notes on, from Merkel, 249-69
Juristische Encyclopädie (Merkel), 292
Justi, Johann Heinrich Gottlob von, 117, 118

Kames, Henry Home, Lord, 506
Katharine (Bangs), 529
Kennard, F. C., 224n, 235, 247
Kennard, John Hanson, Jr., *3:62,n1; 223-24, 235-36, 247, 498-99; Mrs., 224, 235, 247
Kennedy, Anderson Ross, brother-in-law of WW, *1:66n1; 11n1,3,5
Kennedy, D. N., 323,n1,2
Kennedy, Jessie, niece of WW, *5:315,-n1; 10,n1, 47,n2, 52, 70, 79, 544,n2, 592, 595, 617
Kennedy, John W., 10,n3; Mrs., 79,n1
Kennedy, Joseph Leland, nephew of WW, *5:315,n1; 10,n1,4, 51
Kennedy, Marion Wilson (Mrs. Anderson Ross Kennedy), sister of WW, *1:3,n5; 10,n1, 79,n2
Kennedy, William Blake, nephew of WW, 10,n1
Kennedy, Wilson Woodrow, nephew of WW, *5:315,n1; 10,n1
Kent, Charles Artemas, 149
Kerp, Robert P., 316
Kerr, Alexander James, *1:141,n2, 380n1
Kimball House, Atlanta, Ga., 561
King, Clarence, Mrs. (Daisy Anderson), *3:31,n3, *3:195n1; 459,n1, 466
Kingsbury, Mr., 552; Mrs. (Rosa), 552
Kuhns, Oscar, 557,n3; Mrs. (Lillie Belle Conn), 557n3

Laband, Paul, 90, 130, 138, 139, 435
Lafayette College, 441; *The Lafayette*, 441n3
Laferrière, Firmin Julien, 119
Lake Forest College, 247, 613
Lalor, John Joseph, 49,n1
Langdell, Christopher Columbus, 65
Lassalle, Ferdinand, 83, 439
"Laurance" (Ingelow), 543n1
Lavake, Thomas William, 297,n6; Mrs. (Juliet Stratton), 297,n9, 298, 300
Lawrenceville School, 297, 298, 596,-n6; Woodhull House, 586,n2
Lawton, Alexander Robert, 449,n6; Mrs., 449,n6
Learned, Marion Dexter, 50,n1
Lebon, André, 120, 283, 284, 403, 404, 406
LeConte, Joseph, *526,n1
Lectures Introductory to the Study of the Law of the Constitution (Dicey), 187, 283, 284, 473
Lectures on Jurisprudence, or the Philosophy of Positive Law (Austin), 326,n3

Ledlie, James C., 293
Lee, Fitzhugh, 247
Lee, Francis Bazley, 181,n1
Legal Education in the United States (Harno), 65n7
Leggett, William, 295,n3, 301, 302
Lehrbuch des deutschen Verwaltungs-rechts (Loening), 119
Lehrbuch des deutschen Verwaltungs-rechtes (Meyer), 119
Lehrbuch des deutschen Verwaltungs-rechts (Rösler), 119
Leibnitz, Gottfried Wilhelm, Baron von, 453
Leslie, J. D., 323n2
"Letter to a Member of the National Assembly" (Burke), 352,n5
Libbey, William, *176,n1
Liberty, Equality, Fraternity (Stephen), 283, 284, 361,n12
Lieber, Francis, 329, 351,n2
Life and Times of Stein (Seeley), 284
Life of Cicero (Trollope), 284
lightning-rods, 216
Lincoln, Abraham, 153
Lioy, Diodato, 293, 313
List, Friedrich, 108
Little Minister (Barrie), 523,n4
Livingston v. Moore, 516
Local Government (Chalmers), 283, 284, 595
Locke, John, 130, 132, 133, 136, 223, 283, 284, 350, 352, 511
Lodge, Henry Cabot, *1:476,n1; *2:-48n1; 284
Loening, Edgar, 119
London Society for the Extension of University Teaching, 209n1
Long, Isaac Jasper, 10,n5; Mrs. (Callie Kennedy), 10,n5
Longmans, Green & Co., 285, 550,n5, 555
Lorimer, James, 66, 595
Louis XI, 335
Louis XII, 404
Louis XIV, 405, 406
"Louisa" (Wordsworth), 576,n4
Louisville Presbyterian Theological Seminary, 323n2, 324
Low, Seth, 192,n1, 372n3
Luria: A Tragedy (Browning), 358,n9
Lumholtz expedition in Central America, 176
Luther v. Borden, 514

MacAlister, James, 164,n3
McCarthy, Justin, 284
McCay, LeRoy Wiley, 192,n2
McCormick, Cyrus Hall, Jr., *5:767,-n3; 112n1, 158-59, 379, 486,n6, 492, 528, 612-14, 616, 618, 619, 621, 625, 626; Mrs. (Harriet Bradley Hammond), 159
McCosh, James, *1:133,n4; 325n1, 341,n11; Mrs. (Isabella Guthrie), 502
McCulloch v. Maryland, 152

McFee, Charles Wolf, 104
McGill, John Dale, M.D., 188, 215-16
Machiavelli, Niccolò, 210n2, 223
McIlvaine, Alice M., 549,n3
McIlvaine, Elizabeth D., 549,n3
McIlvaine, Joshua Hall, *550n2
McIntosh, James, 514
McKay, Douglas, *1:22,n1; 595n1
McKay, Francis Marion, 594,n1, 598, 601-2, 632-33
McKay, Robert B., Mrs. (Elizabeth C.), 595,n1
McKee, Will, 527
Mackeldey, Ferdinand, 326
Mackenzie, James Cameron, 596,n6
Mackintosh, Sir James, 353
McLaughlin, Andrew Cunningham, 176,n4
McLean, Alexander, 238,n1; Mrs., 238
McLeod, Julia, Mrs., 499
Macloskie, George, *1:76,n2; 192,n1, 294
McMichael, Charles Barnsley, 444
McMillan, Charles, 192,n1
MacNair, Theodore Munro, *46,n1,2
McNair, Thomas Ferguson, 180n2
McRae, Alexander, 459,n3, 466
McRae, Carol, 459,n3, 466
McRae, Jack, *3:194,n1; 459; Mrs. (Julie Anderson), 459,n3, 466, 470
"Madame Blavatsky" (Stead and Sinnett), 230,n3
Mademoiselle de Maupin (Gautier), 462-66
Madison, James, 129, 201
"Maggie," *see* Axson, Margaret Randolph
Maggie (nurse), 467, 494, 559, 561, 587, 593
Maggie (servant), 445,n2
Magie, William Francis, *1:360,n6, 46,n3, 179, 483, 538, 556
Maine, Sir Henry James Sumner, 14, 89, 139, 283, 284, 328, 352, 454, 455, 456, 457, 595
Mallard, Robert Quarterman, 274,n1
Malthus, Thomas Robert, 439
Manning, William Oke, 595
Marbury v. Madison, 152
Marion, 287
Markby, William, 293
Marquand, Allan, *1:134n4; *51,n2, 551n4, 565
Marquardsen, Heinrich, 113n3, 116, 119, 120, 167, 345n1, 403, 416n19, 429, 454n1
Marshall, John, 152,n11, 477, 516, 518
Martha (servant), 469, 508, 522
Marx, Karl, 83, 108, 439
Mason, Edward Campbell, 149n10, 185-86
Mead, William Edward, 190,n2
Meier, Ernst von, 119, 126, 388
Memphis, Tenn., Second Presbyterian Church, 323n2
Memphis *Appeal-Avalanche*, 277
Merkel, Adolf, 340, 633; WW trans-

lation and digest from his "Elemente der allgemeinen Rechtslehre," 249-69, 292, 293; *Juristische Encyclopädie,* 292
Merkel, Henry M., 180n1
Merrill, Charles Edmund, 49
Metropolitan Museum of Art, 575
Meyer, Georg, 119, 167
Meyers, James Cowden, 195n1
Middle Period, 1817-1858 (Burgess), 275n1
Middletown, Conn.: Conversational Club, 10n; Eclectic Club-house, 375; Methodist Church, 10n; North, or First, Congregational Church, 229; Russell Library Hall, 344, 374; WW lecture on "Democracy" at Opera House, 368
Mifflin, George Harrison, 271,n7
Miles, Frederick B., 209n1
Mill, John Stuart, 283, 284, 361,n11
Miller, Marion Mills, 84,n1, 195
Miller, Philippus William, *104,n1, 377, 381
Milton, John, 280, 357, 358n10, 367
Ministres dans les principaux pays d'Europe et d'Amérique (Dupriez), 426n21
"Minnesota" (proposed volume for American Commonwealth series), 194, 211, 234, 236, 245
Minnesota, University of, 72-73, 74
"Minnie," see Hoyt, Mary Eloise
Minor, John Barbee, *1:581,n3; 293
Mohl, Robert von, 118, 124
Money in Its Relation to Trade and Industry (Walker), 595
Montesquieu, Charles de Secondat, Baron de la Brède et de, 129,n6, 133, 134, 210n2, 223, 283, 284, 367
Montfort, Simon of, Earl of Leicester, 27
Moran, Robert Sanford, 285, 595,n5
Morgan, Forrest, 354n7
Morley, John, Viscount Morley of Blackburn, 284
Morrel, T., 445
Morse, Anson Daniel, *75,n1
Morse, John Torrey, Jr., *2:48n1; 284
"Morven," Princeton, N.J., 96n2
Moses, Bernard, 284
Mount Holyoke College, 369
Mulford, Roland Jessup, 586n2
Müller, Wilhelm, 181, 284
Munro (of Norwood Park), 238
Munro, Wilfred Harold, 271,n3
Murray, Hamilton, 61n1
Murray, James Ormsbee ("the Dean"), *1:205,n3; *96,n1, 191n3, 192, 294, 295, 296, 297, 299, 300, 446,n3, 458, 486, 492, 550n2, 557; Mrs. (Julia Richards Haughton), 446, 458, 486, 557
Murray, Julia, 446,n3, 458, 486n7
Murray, Nicholas, 204,n3
Murray, William Haughton, M.D., 561

Mustard, Wilfred Pirt, *217,n1-218, 222, 224, 247
"My Wife's a Winsome Wee Thing" (Burns), 554,n1
Myself (Commons), 317n2

Napoléon I, 353, 386
Nashville, Tenn., WW gives lecture on "Democracy" at, 369
Nashville *American,* 277
Nassau Hotel, Princeton, 294, 295, 296, 460, 531
Nation (New York), 70,n1, 76
"National Sovereignty" (Jameson), 325,n5, 351n3
Nebraska, University of, 628
Neufville, Edward H., Mrs. (Harriet Fenwick Tattnall), 488,n4
New Princeton Review, 187
New South Building and Loan Association, New Orleans, 499,n2
New York City: Daly's Theatre, 505,-n2; People's Municipal League, 69n1; Tammany Hall, 69,n1,2; Trinity Churchyard, 506
New York Ladies' Club, 550n2
New York Law Institute Library, 519,-n1, 549
New York Law School, 372,n2, 460n4, 519n1. *See also* Wilson, Woodrow: New York Law School
New York Times, 69n2, 177n, 531
Newton, Charles Bertram, 342,n1
Nicoll, DeLancey, 478
Niebuhr, Barthold Georg, 326
Nithard, 18,n6
Noailles, Jules Charles Victurnien, Duc de, 535,n2
North, Alfred, 207-8
North, Eric McCoy, 8,n2
North, Frank Mason, 8,n1, 10; Mrs. (Louise Josephine McCoy), 10
North, Roy Lorton, 208
North American Review, 370,n1
Northrop, Cyrus, 74
Norwood Park, Long Branch, L. I., 237
Novalis, 50,n2

Oberlin, Ohio, WW gives lecture on "Democracy" at, 369
Obiter Dicta (Birrell), 326,n2, 353,n6, 362,n15
"Ode on the Death of the Duke of Wellington" (Tennyson), 368,n21
"O'er the wide earth . . ." (Wordsworth), 362,n17
"Of A' the Airts" (Burns), 554,n2
"Of Love. A Sonnet" (Herrick), 532-33
Öffentliche Recht und die Verwaltungsrechtspflege (von Sarwey), 119
Old Sarum, Wilts, 31,n10
Olden, Mary C., 207n2
On Civil Liberty and Self-Government (Lieber), 329, 351,n2
On Liberty (Mill), 283, 284, 361,n11
"On the Alleged Obscurity of Mr. Browning's Poetry" (Birrell), 326n2

"On the Conception of Sovereignty" (Ritchie), 339,n9
Ordronaux, John, 153,n12
Orelli, Alois von, 345n1
Origin and Growth of the English Constitution (Taylor), 284
Ormond, Alexander Thomas, *6:528,-n2; 96,n3
Orris, Samuel Stanhope, *1:330,n2; 458,n1
Osborn, Edwin Curtis, 48n1, 59, 207-8, 604, 608
Osborn, Henry Fairfield, *1:330,n3; *623n3
Otis, James, 367
Outline History of England (Joy), 26n, 40n
Owen, Alice Proctor, 625n2
Owen, Henry James, Mrs. (Elizabeth Sheldon), 625,n2
Owen, Isabel Sheldon, 625n2
Oxford University: University Extension Delegacy, 209n1

Pach Brothers (photographers), 461n1, 521
Packard, William Alfred, *1:193,n1; 96,n2, 112, 294, 502, 538
Page, Thomas Nelson, 441,n2
Pall Mall Gazette (London), 71
Palmer, Benjamin Morgan, *3:13,n1; *4:552,n1; 323,n3
"Paris, the Typical Modern City" (Shaw), 232,n5, 245
Parker, J. P., 232n
Partch, Arthur W., 237, 241-42
Patrick Henry (Tyler), 284
Patten, Simon Nelson, 386,n4, 387
Patterson, James Lawson, 586,n2
Patton, Francis Landey ("the President"), *3:114,n3; 48n1, 54, 57, 62, 63; on establishment of law school, 64; 65, 67, 73, 74; favors call to A. Shaw, 75, 94; 76, 106, 164; on WW and salary, 192-93, 486n5, 497, 539, 611-12, 630; 225, 226, 244,n1; illness, 440,n1, 443n, 444, 485, 492, 528, 565; 497n1, 550n2, 618, 634, 636, 638; Mrs. (Rosa Antoinette Stevenson), 528
Patton, Francis Landey, Jr., 565,n3
Patton, George Stevenson, *528,n1
Paxton, William Miller, 445
Peel, Sir Robert, 354
Pelet, Paul, 283
Pepper, William, 209n1
Petty, Robert Davison, 372n3, 551,n1
Phelps, Edward John, 79,n2
Phi Kappa Psi fraternity, 218,n6
Philadelphia: Bellevue Hotel, 444; WW lecture on "Democracy" at, 369
Philip Augustus, 404
Philosophy of Right (Lioy), 293, 313
Phinizy, Bowdre, 342,n2, 625,n3
Physics and Politics (Bagehot), 281-82, 283, 284

Pittsburgh, WW gives lecture on "Democracy" at, 369
Plantation Life Before Emancipation (Mallard), 274,n1
Platform: Its Rise and Progress (Jephson), 440,n1
Poe, Edgar Allan (Princeton '91), 172,-n2, 374n1
Po-ka-hon-tas, produced by Princeton Dramatic Association, 194, 529
Political History of Recent Times, 1816-1875, with Special Reference to Germany (Müller), 181, 284
Political Science and Comparative Constitutional Law (Burgess), WW marginal notes, on, 169-71; WW review of, 195-203
Political Science Quarterly, 178, 179, 330n5, 343, 351,n3, 371
Politics (Aristotle), 283, 284
Polizeiwissenschaft nach den Grundsätzen des Rechtsstaats (von Mohl), 118
Pond, James Burton, 376,n1,2
Poole's Index, 181
Poore, Benjamin Perley, 129n6
Pope, Alexander, 505
"The Pope's Encyclical on the Labor Question," 230,n4
Poullet, Edmond Ives Joseph Marie, 181
Pouvoir exécutif aux États-Unis (Chambrun), 535,n4
Practical Jurisprudence, A Comment on Austin (Clark), 292, 455,n4
Pradier-Fodéré, Paul Louis Ernest, 120, 167
Précis du Cours de droit public et administratif professé à la Faculté de droit de Paris (Batbie), 119
Précis de droit administratif (Pradier-Fodéré), 120
Presbyterian and Reformed Review (New York), 87, 91, 233, 536
Presbyterian Church in the United States [southern], General Assembly, 195,n1, 204, 531,n1, 636; Synod of Alabama, 54n1; Synod of Arkansas, 54n1, 323; Synod of Kentucky, 53n1, 322,n2, 324; Synod of Memphis, 54n1, 323n2; Synod of Mississippi, 54n1, 323; Synod of Missouri, 323n2; Synod of Nashville, 54n1, 322; Synod of South Carolina, 54n2; Synod of Texas, 54n1
Presbyterian College of South Carolina, 11n3
President, the, see Patton, Francis Landey
Preussisches Staatsrecht (Bornhak), 119
Princeton, N. J.: Ladies' Club, 369; Second Presbyterian Church, 178n2, 598n2, 623n2
Princeton Alumni Association for the Northwest (Chicago), 106,n1, 159n1

Princeton Alumni Association of Philadelphia: WW address to, Jan. 1891, 67, 104, 106, 168, text, 161-63, newspaper report, 164; WW address to, Feb. 1892, 377, 378, 381, 440n1, 443, newspaper report, 444-45
Princeton Alumni of Maryland, 443
Princeton Club of New York, see Princeton University: New York Alumni
Princeton Club of Philadelphia, 104n1
Princeton Inn, 220,n1,2
Princeton Press, 58n3, 61n, 164, 310
Princeton Theological Seminary, 74
Princeton University: WW sees at threshold of her university career, 62; EAW on continuance as college or development into university, 607-8; loose women entertained in college room, 529, 531; faculty offended by American Review of Reviews, 225-26, 229, 231-32, 243-44

Albert B. Dod Hall, 112, 207-8; Alumni Fund, 611, 630, proposed, 177; Athletic Club House, see Osborn Field House; Athletic Organizations, 243,n1; baseball: Princeton vs. Harvard (1892), 622, 624,n1; boating, 373-74; Bonner-Marquand Gymnasium, 529; Boudinot Fellowship in History, 48; Caledonian Games, *1:145n1, 219; Cap and Gown Club: WW made honorary member, 342; Carnegie Lake, 374n1; Catch-as-Catch-Can Club, 92n1; Chancellor Green Library, 426n1; Chapel Stage Speaking, *1:220,n1, 51n3; Class of 1876 Memorial Prize Debate, 84,n2; Class of 1883 Library of Political Science and Jurisprudence, 67; College Offices (now Stanhope Hall), 300, 301-2; Committee on the Allotment and Rental of Rooms and the Disposal of Furniture in the Rooms by the Students: appointment, 96, report, 108-12, 159,n2, 162,n2, 207; Committee on Discipline: established, 294, WW minutes, 294-302, 529, 531, 545, 566; Committee on Special and Delinquent Students, 585,n1; Committee on the Curriculum, 636, 637, 638; Committee on the Difference in the "Passing Mark," 192,n2; Department of History and Political Science, 636; Department of Jurisprudence and Political Economy, 636; Department of Philosophy, 325n1; Dickinson Hall, 69n1; Dramatic Association, 194, 529; East College, 302; Edwards Hall, 302; electric lights, 301-2; Faculty Minutes quoted, 11, 51, 84, 96, 108-12, 192, 195, 294, 322, 342, 373, 531, 545, 566, 640-41; Faculty Philosophical Club, 325n1, 471, 506; Fayerweather Bequest, 67, 484,n2, 485n2, 493-94; finances, 94; football, 46,n2; Football Association, and captaincy of 1889, 172,n2; "handicap games," 622,n4; Ivy Club, 622; Joline Prize in American Political History, 48, 54-55, 57, 58-59, 166; Law School, 1847f, 64; Liberal Debating Club, 84,n2; Library Committee, 106; library in summer chaos, 245; Lyman H. Atwater Prize in Political Science, 204,n1; Lynde Debate, *1:145,n1, 195; Marquand Chapel, 51,n3, 187-88; monitorial system, 342, 373, 640-41; Murray Hall, *61n1; Osborn Field House, 622,n3; Philadelphian Society, *61, 58; political economy professor, 497n1; requirements for Ph.D. in English (1892), 505, 510-11; Reunion Hall, 302; School of Jurisprudence proposed by WW (1902), 68; School of Political Science proposed (1890), 64; Senior Assembly (1892), 621n2; Southern Club, 342,-n1; Theodore Cuyler Prize in Economics, 180,n1, 215; Track Athletic Association, 623n4; University Athletic Association, 623, WW elected to graduate advisory committee, 303,n2; University Hall, 300; West College, 301-2; Whig Hall, 301; White Elephant Club, 297, 298, 299; Witherspoon Hall, 565,n1

Albert Shaw and proposed chair of economics: 62, 72, 73, 74, 75-76, 92-95, 225-26, 229, 231-32, 243-45

Baltimore alumni, 443

Chicago alumni, 106, 159n1

Class of 1879: Decennial Record, 214; gives punch bowl to W. B. Isham, 380n1

New York alumni, 193; WW address to, March 1891, 176-77, 178; dinner of March 1886 referred to, 161,n1

Philadelphia alumni: WW address to, Jan. 1891, 67, 104, 106, 161-64, 168; WW address to, Feb. 1892, 377, 378, 381, 440n1, 443, 444-45

Proposed School of Law: WW plans, 7, 63, and editorial note, 63-68; WW suggests Morven site, 96; urges school before Philadelphia alumni, 163, before New York alumni, 177, 178; WW's dearest scheme, 234; 379n1; predicts law school to Baltimore alumni, 443; C. H. McCormick and WW plans, 613,n2, 618, 621

See also Wilson, Woodrow: Princeton University

Princetonian (after April 11, 1892, Daily Princetonian), 51,n3, 58n3, 69n, 83, 84, 105, 166,n2, 172n2, 178, 179, 180, 187, 189, 195, 219, 303n3,

325n1, 373-74, 379, 445, 530, 595n, 598n2, 599n, 623,n2,4
Principles of Political Economy (Gide), 303,n1
Principles of Sociology (Spencer), 330,-n6, 352,n4
Problems of Greater Britain (Dilke), 284
"Progress of the World," 230,n4
Puchta, Georg Friedrich, 293, 308n3, 437, 634
Pufendorf, Samuel, Baron von, 453
Puritan Revolution (Gardiner), 284
Purves, George Tybout, 493n2
Pyne, Moses Taylor, *5:132,n2; 67n15

Queen, John Wahl, 205,n2

Ramsay, David, 362
Rayburn, Calvin, 445
Raymond, Bradford Paul, 68, 191; Mrs. (Lulu A. Rich), 68
Reay, Sir Donald Mackay, 1st Baron, 362
Rechtsstaat (von Gneist), 118, 393,n10
Reconstruction and the Constitution (Burgess), 275n1
Reed, Thomas Brackett, 370
Reeves, Alfred Gandy, 372n3, 551,n1
Reiley, Mr., 375, 377-78
Reiley, DeWitt Ten Broeck, 375,n2
Republican party: confusion and division in, 639,n1
République américaine États-Unis (Carlier), 534,n1
Review of Reviews (London), 71, 230, 232n3
Review of Reviews (New York), 71-72, 76, 92, 93, 160, 183, 187, 225-26, 229-32, 236, 243-44, 626
Ricardo, David, 108, 194
Richardson, Ernest Cushing, *538,n2; Mrs. (Grace Duncan Ely), 538,n2
Richardson, Hugh, 343,n5
Ricketts, Henrietta, 502,n2, 503
Ricketts, Palmer Chamberlaine, Mrs. (Eliza Getty), 503,n1, 512
Rise and Progress of the English Constitution (Creasy), 283, 284
Ritchie, David George, 339,n9
Riverside Press, Cambridge, 271
Roberts, William Charles, *4:370,n1; 247
Rodbertus, Johann Karl, 83, 108
Rockwood, Charles Greene, Jr., 179,n1
Rome, Ga., Presbyterian Church, 512, 541, 544,n1
Rommel, William Cooper, 445
Roosevelt, Theodore, 79
Rosa (nurse), 469, 508
Röscher, Wilhelm Georg Friedrich, 108
Rosemont, Penn., postmaster, 240
Rösler, Hermann, 119
Rousseau, Jean Jacques, 86, 133, 536
Rümelin, Gustav von, Sr., 119
Ruskin, John, 157,n13, 364,n18

Russell, Frances Ann, 270,n1
Russell, Samuel, 270n1
Rutgers College, 375

Sagaponack, Long Island, 10n2
St. John, Richard C., Mrs. (Julia Stockton), 503,n2
"St. John of England. On the Centenary, of the Death of John Wesley" (Stead), 225,n3
Saint-Simon, Claude Henri de Rouvroy, Comte de, 83, 439
Salmon, Lucy Maynard, *4:336,n1; 176,n4
Sampson, Mr. and Mrs. (Charlottesville), 82
Sanders, Robert Stuart, 323n2
Saratoga Springs (N. Y.) *Saratogian*, 270n2
Sartor Resartus (Carlyle), 362,n14
Sarwey, Otto von, 116, 119, 122, 124, 131, 143, 153, 155, 167, 383, 390, 416
Saunders, Colonel, 571, 582
Saunders, Martine, 571
Savannah, Ga.: Independent Presbyterian Church, 449,n4, Women's Exchange, 499; Laurel Grove Cemetery, 460
Savigny, Friedrich Karl von, 327
Scharf, John Thomas, 227,n1
Schlegel, August Wilhelm von, 326
Schlosser, Friedrich Christoph, 57,n2
Schönberg, Gustav Friedrich von, 119, 167
Schulze, Hermann Johann Friedrich, 416n19
Schurz, Carl, *2:74n1; 284
Schwegler, Albert, 505, 511
Science of International Law (Walker), 454n3
Scott, Austin, *2:447n3; 376
Scott, Eben Greenough, 283, 284
Scott, Francis Markoe, 69,n1
Scott, Winfield, 286
Scovel, Sylvester Fithian, 218
Scribner's Magazine, 242n2, 289
Scribner's Sons, Charles, 274,n1, 277, 291, 376
Scudder, Horace Elisha, *3:149n1; 164, 165, 211, 234-35, 236-37, 240, 245, 290, 308-9
Seeley, John Robert, 284
Selden, John, 453
Selfgovernment, Communalverfassung, und Verwaltungsgerichte in England (von Gneist), 118
Semple, Samuel, 84n2, 195n1
Seven Lamps of Architecture (Ruskin), 157,n13, 364,n18
Seward, William Henry, 250
Shafer, Willis Drake, 472
Shakespeare, William, 281, 529, 572,n1
Sharon, William, 148n9
Shaw, Albert, *3:214,n1; elected to Cornell chair, 62, 71, declines, 92-93, 159-60; possible call to Prince-

ton chair of economics, 62-63, 64, 72-74, 75-76, 92-95, 184, 225-26, 229, 243-45; made editor of American *Review of Reviews*, 92, 160, Princeton shocked by first issue, 225-26, 229-32, 243-45; on American clergymen, 230; on W. T. Stead, 230; mentioned, 187, 194, 236, 240, 271, 278, 602, 609

Shaw, William B., 232n4

Sheldon, Edward Wright, *1:240,n7; 310, 625

Shields, Charles Woodruff, *1:211,n1; *487,n1; 96n2, 538

Short History of Anglo-Saxon Freedom (Hosmer), 283, 284

Short History of the English People (Green), 88

Sibley, Emma, 511, 525

Sibyl (Elmira College), 345n2

Sidgwick, Henry, 310, 318-20, 332,n7

Sidney, Algernon, 132, 350, 352 [*erroneously called Sir Philip*]

Sidney, Sir Philip, 505

Sill, Edward Rowland, 349, 575,n2,3

Simon de Montfort, 27

Sims, James Marion, 578,n1

Sinnett, A. P., 232n3

"Sir William Temple on the Origin and Nature of Government" (Herriott), 627n2

Sketch of the Germanic Constitution from Early Times to the Dissolution of the Empire (Turner), 284

Sloane, William Milligan, *2:91,n2; *5:418,n1; 62, 76, 84, 94, 166, 193, 195, 204-5, 225, 226, 291, 322, 378, 440, 443, 444, 445, 498, 538, 557, 565, 599n2, 621, 630

Small, Albion Woodbury, *6:135,n1; *578,n1, 579, 606

Small, Samuel White, 180

Smith, Adam, 108, 194, 439

Smith, Charles Sidney, 481,n2

Smith, Edwin Oscar, 314n1, 322, 342, 344

Smith, Samuel Macon, 595,n2

Smith, Sir William, 141

Snow, Francis Huntington, 602,n3

Sohm, Rudolf, 293

Sonnenfels, Josef von, 118

South Carolina College, 596,n7

South Dakota, University of, 167n1

Southern Iron Company, 277,n1

Southern Presbyterian (Columbia, S. C.), 54n2

Southwestern Presbyterian (New Orleans), 274,n1, 323n2

Southwestern Presbyterian University, Clarksville, Tenn., 10-11, 322-23, 323n2, 324; Theological School, 54n1

"Southwestern Presbyterian University and 'The Proposed Theological Seminary for the Southwest'" (Bardwell), 323n2

Southworth, James H., 70n

sovereignty, 325-41

"Speaker as Premier" (Hart), 164, 165, 210,n2, 213, 221, 370

Speirs, Frederic William, 166-67

Spencer, Herbert, 330,n6, 331, 336, 352,n4

Spirit of Laws (Montesquieu), 283, 284

Sprague, Henry L., 69,n2

Springfield, Mass., WW address in, 80-82

Springfield Republican, 82, 188

Staatsrecht der französischen Republik (Lebon), 120

Staatsrecht der schweizerischen Eidgenossenschaft (von Orelli), 345n1

Staatsrecht des deutschen Reiches (Laband), 130

Staatsrecht des Königreichs Italien (Brusa), 113n3

Staël, Anne Louise Germaine (Necker), Baronne de Staël-Holstein, 353

Stamford, Conn., WW gives lecture on "Democracy" at, 369

Stanley, Henry Morton, 75,n1, 376n1

State, The (Wilson), 283, 284. See also Wilson, Woodrow: Writings

State and Federal Government in Switzerland (Vincent), 283, 284

State and Its Relation to Trade (Farrer), 595

Statutes at Large; Being a Collection of All the Laws of Virginia (Hening), 312

Stead, Richard, 284

Stead, William Thomas, 71, 72, 74, 76, 93, 225,n3, 226, 230,n3, 231, 243, 245

Stein, Heinrich Friedrich Karl, Baron von, 420

Stein, Lorenz Jacob von, 115, 118, 124, 167

Stengel, Karl Michael Joseph Leopold, *Freiherr* von, 119

Stephen, Sir James Fitzjames, 283, 284, 361,n12

Stephenson, Andrew, 68,n2, 181,n2, 205-6, 317

Stevens, Mrs. (Rome, Ga.), 525

Stewart, John Aikman, *602,n1

Stewart, William Adams Walker, 310; Mrs. (Frances Gray), 310,n1

Stewart College, Clarksville, Tenn., 54n1

Stickney, Albert, 396,n15

Stites, Mrs., 527

Stock, Leo F., 239n1

Stockdale *v.* Hansard, 151

Stockton, John Potter, 492,n2, 583

Stockton, Samuel Witham, 96n2

Stockton estate ("Morven"), Princeton, 96

Story of My Life (Sims), 578,n1

Strong, Mr., 289,n1

Stubbs, William, 89, 398

Studies, National and International (Lorimer), 66

Studies in Constitutional Law: France-England-United States (Boutmy), 275-76, 283

Sullivan, Sir Arthur, 506n2

Sully, James, 511

Sunderland, Robert Spencer, 2d Earl of, 30

Sweet, Henry, 510

Swift, Jonathan, 505

Switzerland (Hug and Stead), 284

Sydney, *see* Sidney

"Synod of Memphis" (Leslie), 323n3

System der Präventiv-Justiz (von Mohl), 118

Tacitus, Cornelius, 18, 346

Taine, Hippolyte Adolphe, 284

Taming of the Shrew (Shakespeare), 529

Tarkington, Booth, 530n4

Taswell-Langmead, Thomas Pitt, 88

Taussig, Frank William, 73

Taylor, Charles H., 178,n1

Taylor, Hannis, 88, 89, 91, 284

Taylor, James Monroe, 321

Taylor, Zachary, 286

Tedcastle, Arthur W., *2:461n1; 508,-n2; Mrs. (Agnes Vaughn), *2:334; 508,n2, 525, 527, 528, 537, 539, 547, 548

Temple, Sir William, 505

Tennyson, Alfred, 1st Baron Tennyson, 362,n13, 368, 505,n2

Terry, David Smith, 148n9; Mrs. (Sarah Althea Hill), 148n9

Texas *v.* White, 514

Thibaut, Anton Friedrich Justus, 327

Thomas, H. T., 376,n2

Thomas Jefferson (Morse), 284

Thompson, Henry Burling, 374n1, 445

Thompson, Henry Dallas, *565,n2

"Thoughts on the Cause of the Present Discontents" (Burke), 365,n19

Thunderbolt plantation, nr. Savannah, *3:16,n4; 481,n1

Thwaites, Reuben Gold, 176n1, 206, 377, 378

Titus, Nelson W., 615,n1

"To a Young Lady" (Wordsworth), 577,n6

Tocqueville, Alexis de, 127, 210n2, 284

Todd, Henry Alfred, 271,n10

Tolman, Albert Harris, 188,n1

Tolman, Herbert Cushing, 222

Toynbee, Arnold (1852-1883), 595

Tracey, Capt. (of Clarksville, Tenn.), 248

Traill, Henry Duff, 105, 167, 209, 283, 284, 400, 401, 402, 595

Traité de la jurisdiction administrative et de recours contentieux (Laferrière), 119

Traité général de droit administratif appliqué ou exposé de la doctrine et de la jurisprudence concernant l'exercise de l'autorité du roi, des

ministres, des préfets, etc. (Dufour), 119

"Traveller" (Goldsmith), 356,n8

Treatise on International Law (Hall), 291, 454,n2, 456

Trinity College, Durham, N. C., 368

Trollope, Anthony, 284

Trotter, Edward Hough, *1:412n1; 104

True Republic (Stickney), 396,n15

Turner, Frederick Jackson, *6:58n1; 176,n4

Turner, Samuel Epes, 284

Tuttle, Herbert, 160,n1

Twain, Mark, 376n1

Two Treatises on Government (Locke), 283, 284

"Two Views of Madame Blavatsky" (Stead and Sinnett), 230,n3

Tyler, Moses Coit, 176,n4, 284

typhoid fever, 8

University Club, New York, 69, 468,n1

University Extension, 316

" 'University Extension' and Its Leaders" (Adams), 225,n2, 230

Utah University of the Methodist Episcopal Church, 180,n1

Vanderbilt University, 369

Vandiner, Lucy, 452

Van Dyke, Henry Nevius, *1:157,n1; 92, 106, 193, 440

Vanuxem, Louis Clark, *1:204,n1; 104

Van Vleck, Clara, 191,n1

Van Vleck, John Monroe, *5:734,n1; 191n1

Vassar College, 368; invitation to WW to lecture, 321

Vattel, Emmerich von, 453, 635

"Verwaltungslehre" (Rümelin, *et al.*), 119

Verwaltungslehre (von Stein), 118

"Verwaltungsrecht" (von Meier), 119

Veto Power: Its Origin, Development and Function in the Government of the United States 1789-1889 (Mason), 185-86

Victoria, Queen, 43

Vincent, John Martin, *5:466n3; *6:-59-60n1; 283, 284

Völkerrecht oder Internationales Recht (von Bulmerincq), 454,n1

Walker, Francis Amasa, 105, 217, 291, 379, 595

Walker, Thomas Alfred, 454n3

Walker, Williston, 80

Wallace, George Riddle, 195

Walpole (Morley), 284

Walpole, Sir Robert, 26

Waltham, Gussie, 47

Wanamaker, John, 561

Wanamaker, Rodman, 445

Wanamaker, Thomas Brown, 445

Warfield, Benjamin Breckinridge, 91n3

Warfield, Ethelbert Dudley, 441
Warren, Frederick Morris, 45,n1
Warren, J. L., and daughter, 448,n3, 522, 532
Warren, John, 296,n4
Warren, Minton, 218,n2
Warren & Axson, 450n3
Waterville, N. H., 317
Wayland, Francis (1826-1904), 80
Wealth of Nations (Smith), 439
Webb, Robert Alexander, 54n2
Welldon, James Edward Cowell, 283
Welcker, Friedrich Gottlieb, 326
Wellington, Arthur Wellesley, 1st Duke of, 368
Wells College, 321
Wenzel, John, 175
Wesley, John, 225,n3, 229
Wesleyan University, 4, 7, 68; athletics, 171-72; Foot-Ball Association, 172n1; 190, 191, 192, 205-6; Russell House, 270; 278n2; Y.M.C.A., 314; Olla Podrida, 314, 374; 317; WW lecture on "Democracy" at, 374-75; Wesleyan Argus, 375; coeducation at, 442, 444; 608, 630, 634, 638
West, Andrew Fleming, *6:528,n3; 310, 437, 438, 492, 505,n3, 511n1, 519, 565, 585,n1; Mrs. (Lucy Marshall FitzRandolph), 207n2, 310n3, 565
West, Randolph, 310,n3
Westcott, John Howell, 207n2, 234n1, *437-38,n1, 441, 565, 571, 589
Wheaton, Henry, 455, 456
"When I Think on the Happy Days" (Burns), 557,n5
White, Andrew Dickson, 624,n2, 627
Whittemore, Mrs. (Rome, Ga.), 525
Wikoff, Anna, 484,n1, 599
Wikoff, James Holmes, M.D., 484,n1, 502, 504, 599
Wilder, William Royal, *1:253,n2; 214, 269, 270, 380
William III, 30
William IV, 43
William the Conqueror, 23, 24, 30, 398
Williams, Jesse Lynch, 303,n1
Williams College: Mark Hopkins Memorial Hall, 237n1, 240
Willson, Robert Newton, 444
Wilson (father of Kate), 55
Wilson, Eleanor Randolph, daughter of WW and EAW, 446, 448, 449, 460, 461, 468, 484, 494, 495, 497, 501, 508, 511, 526, 539, 553, 556, 566, 571, 573, 574, 581, 583, 584
Wilson, Ellen Axson, 3, 8, 10, 47, 50, 56, 57, 61, 68, 70, 71, 76, 78, 79, 80, 82, 83, 85, 95, 103, 105, 168, 172, 174, 178, 179, 181, 184, 187, 191, 204, 207, 214, 220, 223, 224, 226, 227, 228, 229, 232, 236, 238, 239, 242, 243, 245, 248, 249, 270, 271; sketching, 273; 277, 278, 285, 288, 289, 290, 291, 292, 312, 317, 321, 323, 344, 369, 379n1, 380, 441, 442, 443, 444, 445-46; journey to Savannah with children, 446; 447-48, 448-50, 450-51, 457-58, 459-62, 466-70, 480-89, 490-504, 506-10, 511-12, 519-30; photographs of, 526, 530; 532-34, 536-55; escapes flood in Rome, Ga., 547-48; 556-94, 595-98, 599-601, 602-6, 606-11; EAW resemblance to Sistine Madonna, 607, 617; 612, 614-29; return journey to Princeton, 629; 631, 637, 640

AND WOODROW WILSON

love for WW, 447, 449, 460, 461; always happy in his love, 466; 469; WW has been everything to her, 482; love for WW, 488, 491, 494, 509; heart overflowing with love, 512; intense longing to see WW, 523; loves WW with every heartbeat, 526; love for WW, 528; WW's personal magnetism and gifts which go to make a born leader of men, 542; love for WW, 544, 549; loves WW passionately, 553, 584; dreamt of WW all night, 561, 567, 578, 586; loves WW so that she can scarcely bear it, 596

HEALTH

grippe, 179, 443; possible fourth conception, 448, 492, 493, 494, 496, 498, 508-10, 522; trip to dentist's, 491, 493; lameness, 594, 596, 599, 603; colds, 559, 565, 574, 599, 603, 610; polypus in nose, 610, 619

READING

Sir James Matthew Barrie, The Little Minister, 523,n4
Book of Ruth, 523, 530
Elizabeth Barrett Browning, 564
James Marion Sims, The Story of My Life, 578,n1

Wilson, George Grafton, 271,n5; Mrs. (Lily Rose), 271
Wilson, Janet Woodrow, mother of WW, *1:3,n1; 219n1
Wilson, Jessie Woodrow, daughter of WW and EAW, 446, 448, 449, 459, 484, 501, 503, 522, 539, 556, 559, 565, 573, 578, 581, 591; breaks collar bone, 592; 593, 595, 599, 600, 601, 603, 604, 615, 618, 622, 629, 640
Wilson, Joseph Ruggles, father of WW, *1:3,n1; 3, 10-11, 52-54, 55, 56, 82, 85, 98; lends WW $200, 105; 159n1, 168, 174, 195; and purchase of Washington Street property, 204, 206; 219, 220, 237-38, 248, 269-70, 271, 273-74, 278, 284-85, 287-88, 289, 311-12; church affairs, 322-23, 323n2; 324; prostate trouble, 380;

441-42, 489-90, 531-32, 540, 595-96, 612, 636-37

Wilson, Joseph R., Jr. ("Dode," "Josie"), brother of WW, *1:3,n8; 3, 11,n6, 53; engagement to Kate Wilson, 55-56; 77-78, 84-85; purchases *Clarksville Democrat*, 97-98, 206, venture fails, 220; mentioned, 168, 204, 248, 277, 288, 312, 323, 324, 380, 441-42, 489, 531-32, 597,n1, 612

Wilson, Kate, fiancée of JRW, Jr., 3, 53, 55, 77, 78, 85, 98, 220, 248, 324, 442, 598n1, 612

Wilson, Margaret, daughter of WW and EAW; 446, 451,n2, 459, 468, 484, 494, 495, 501, 539, 556, 570, 573, 617. *See also* 6:13, 15, 24, 95, 113, 121, 122, 125, 127, 134, 140, 142, 144, 146, 150, 155, 160-61, 388, 391, 539

WOODROW WILSON

AND ELLEN AXSON WILSON

returns from Baltimore without family: terrible loneliness, 445; heart aches to breaking with love and longing, 445; unspeakable sadness at separation, 447; heart chilled by visit to empty Steadman Street house, 448; EAW love an inexhaustible well of pure happiness, 450; heart-hungry almost to desperation, 461; yearning for EAW, 462; not alive without EAW, 470; complete surrender to EAW fills him with fears, 483; EAW love of beauty and of duty have done him unspeakable service, 483; EAW more beautiful than any pretty girls he sees, 484; lonely and love-sick, 487; longs for EAW almost to the breaking of his heart, 493; influence exercised by EAW over his life recounted, 500; passionate yearning, desperate love for EAW, 504; desire for son mentioned, 522; absorbing passion for his peerless darling, 526; life leaps in his veins at love-passage in EAW letter, 530; courtship remembered, 532,n1; love has claims which are paramount to those of international law, 543; happy in her love, 549-50; EAW adorable in every situation, 554; EAW's love supplies poetical element to his life, 555; WW has run the whole gamut of love in loving EAW, 557; love-making makes an extravagant boy of him, 570; intolerable pain of separation, 572; WW passionately fond of beauty and EAW's beauty the type most provocative of love, 605; heart bursting full of love, 622

Woodrow Wilson, cont.

APPEARANCE

Pach Brothers photograph (1889), 461,n1; photographs of, admired in Savannah, 499; "handsome . . . dear noble-looking, splendid, brilliant *magnificent* man!" (EAW), 499

FAMILY LIFE AND DOMESTIC AFFAIRS

WW and family move into rented house at 48 Steadman Street (now 72 Library Place), Princeton, about Sept. 1, 1890, 4n-5n; family goes to Baltimore for period of WW lectures at the Johns Hopkins, 102, 103, 105; repairs to bath-tub, safe in dining room, paraphernalia of fireplaces at Steadman Street, 188; WW purchases large lot on Washington Street (now Washington Road) in Princeton, 204, 206,n2, 441; J. H. Westcott offers to purchase portion, 437-38; family all sick with *grippe*, 210; repairs to Steadman Street house and lightning rods, 215-16; WW purchases lot in Buena Vista, N. C., 248,n1; WW takes room at Nassau Hotel on return from Baltimore, 445; new silver watch, 512, 536-37, 544, 553, 573, 578; EAW on opening Steadman Street house, 615-16, 622

HEALTH

la grippe or influenza, 83,n3, 84, 96, 372; nervous illness, 274; obstruction of bile duct, 502-3; indigestion, 504, 543; drinks A. F. West's California claret: headache next day, 519, 521, 525

THE JOHNS HOPKINS UNIVERSITY

WW lectures on administration, 1891-1893, editorial notes, 112-14, 381; notes for lectures, first year course, 114-58, second year course, 381-436; mentioned, 6, 93, 101-2, 104, 158, 165, 193, 213, 221, 471, 486n5; required reading for minor in administration, 1891, 167

possible invitation to chair, 379n1; mentioned for chair, 485,n4; WW not offered professorship, 492,n1; JRW inquires about call to chair, 531

Seminary of Historical and Political Science: *2:447n3; WW reads "The Literary Politician," 168; "The Development of Law," read March 1889, mentioned, 325n1

NEW YORK LAW SCHOOL

WW lectures, editorial note, 470-72; report of a lecture, 472-79; lecture on sovereignty and nature of gov-

Woodrow Wilson, cont.
ernment, March 1892, text, 512-19; lectures mentioned, 467, 468, 470, 480, 485, 490, 492, 494, 497, 500, 502, 505, 506, 519, 531, 537, 538, 549, 551, 563, 567, 582, 584, 587, 588

OPINIONS AND COMMENTS

book reviewing, thoughts on, 165
John William Burgess, 165, 195-203
coeducation, 442, 444
college curriculum: new methods of education putting in new topics of practical moment, 163
faculty committee work: torture, prolonged and horrid, 162; a tiring imposition, 164
Mrs. H. B. Fine, tiresomeness of, 483
in-breeding in American colleges, 244-45
New England: self-regarding narrowness of, 62
F. L. Patton: an extraordinary man intellectually, 62
pretty girls, 458, 469, 484, 619
science: excessive attention paid to in colleges, 236,n2
southern college towns: dangers of for young ladies, 467
no state can safely develop by revolution, 18
William Thomas Stead, 245
Sundays dreary in a hotel, 482
Caleb Thomas Winchester, 182-83

PRINCETON UNIVERSITY

WW on faculty committees, 51, 84, 96, 108-12, 192, 195, 294, 322, 342, 640-41; talk before Philadelphian Society, 58, 61; plans for School of Law, 63, and editorial note, 63-68; prospects of development in WW lines of work most encouraging, 165; notes for Chapel talk, April 1891, 187-88; on committee for Lynde Debate, 195; examination for Theodore Cuyler Prize, 1891, 215; referee for Caledonian Games, 1891, 219; summer study in Witherspoon Hall, 1891, 233,n1, 236, 242; elected to graduate advisory committee of University Athletic Association, 303,-n2; on committee to arrange for restoration of billiard tables, 322; made honorary member of Cap and Gown Club, 342; on committee for monitors for the large classes, 342; salary, 379n1, 485,n5, 602, 611-12, 626, 630
teaching: WW's teaching at Princeton, 1890-91, editorial note, 5-7; description of course in jurisprudence and political economy, 1890-91, 5; course in public law, 1890-92, 6-8, 9; en-

Woodrow Wilson, cont.
rollment in WW class in public law, 58n3; condition examinations in political economy and constitutional law announced, 69; notes for advanced course in political economy, 83; readings for Princeton classes during absence at Johns Hopkins, 105; examination in political economy, Jan. 1891, 107-8; examination in public law, Jan. 1891, 161; WW resumes classes, March 1891, 173; notes for a course in American constitutional law, 174-75; notes for elementary course in political economy, 177; announcement of lectures on administration, March 1891, 178, 179; announcement of junior and senior electives in constitutional law, April 1891, 187, 189; special examination in history of political economy, 193-94; examination in administration, May 1891, 208-9; examination in constitutional law, May 1891, 212-13; examination in political economy, June 1891, 216-17; notes on jurisprudence from Merkel, 249-69; WW's teaching at Princeton, 1891-92, editorial note, 291; course on jurisprudence, 1891-94, editorial note, 292-93; notes for a course in jurisprudence, 303-4; notes for a classroom lecture: outlines of jurisprudence, I, 304-8, II, 312-14; 180 students in elective jurisprudence class, 1891, 310; classes for second term, 1891-92, 379; examination in the outlines of jurisprudence, Feb. 1892, 436-37; examination in the history of political economy, Feb. 1892, 439; announcements of examinations, 445; resumption of classes, March 1892, 445; notes for a course in international law, 453; notes for a classroom lecture on international law, 453-57; collateral reading in administration, international law, political economy, 594-95; announcement of new elective courses for 1892-93, 598-99; examination in jurisprudence, May 1892, 633; examination in international law, May 1892, 635; examination in elements of political economy, June 1892, 638-39
Syllabi compiled and published by students: Syllabus on International Law Taken from the Lectures of Prof. Woodrow Wilson 1892 [n.p., n.d.], 292,n4; *Syllabus on Jurisprudence. Taken from Lectures of Prof. Woodrow Wilson* [n.p., n.d.], 293,n11; *Syllabus on Public Law, 1891* [n.p., n.d.], 6
See also main entry Princeton University

Woodrow Wilson, cont.

PROFESSIONAL ACTIVITIES AND
CAREER

mentioned by president of Cornell for
vacant chair, 159-60
remarks on his choice of a profession,
162
considered for professorship at Columbia, 192
urged by A. W. Small for chair at
University of Chicago, 579; EAW
hopes for offer, 600
offer of presidency of University of
Illinois, 594, 598, 600-1, 601-2, 603,
604, 608-9, 612-13, 615, 616-17, 618,
619, 620, 621, 623, 624-25, 627,
628, 630, 631; declines offer, 632-
33; 635n1, 637, 639
See also Wilson, Woodrow: The Johns
Hopkins University, New York Law
School, Princeton University, Public
Addresses and Lectures, Writings

PUBLIC ADDRESSES AND LECTURES

Worcester Polytechnic Institute Commencement Address, 1890, mentioned, 167; *see report,* 6:675-78
"How to Prevent Legislative Corruption," *see the next title*
"The Evils of Democracy," delivered
before the Connecticut Valley Economic Association, Nov. 24, 1890,
69n, 75; newspaper report, 80-82
"College Work and the Legal Profession," address to Princeton Alumni
Association of Philadelphia, Jan. 30,
1891, text, 161-63
Address to New York Alumni of Princeton, March 12, 1891; newspaper report, 176-77
"Leaders of Men," delivered before the
Kent Club of Yale Law School in
Osborn Hall, March 18, 1891, 80n4,
181,n1; *see text,* 6:646-71
"Political Sovereignty," read before
the Faculty Philosophical Club,
Princeton, Nov. 1891, text, 325-41;
read to class at New York Law
School, March 23, 1892, 506
"Democracy," a lecture, 321,n2, 322;
editorial note, 344-45; text, 345-68;
delivery record, 368-69; S. Axson on
lecture as delivered at Wesleyan,
369; newspaper report, 374-75
Response to toast at dinner of Balti-
more alumni of Princeton, Feb. 18,
1892, 443
"The Future of Princeton," address to
Princeton alumni of Philadelphia,
Feb. 19, 1892, notice of, 444-45
Letter of J. B. Pond on public lectures,
376

READING

*authors and works read, cited, alluded
to, etc.*

Woodrow Wilson, cont.

Aristotle, 132, 280; *Politics,* 283, 284;
350
Ernst Moritz Arndt, 326
Léon Aucoc, *Conferences sur l'administration et le droit administratif
faites à l'école des ponts et chausées,*
119, 385, 386, 387, 388n7, 392, 403,
405
John Austin, 327, 328, 329, 455
Walter Bagehot, 88; "The Character
of Sir Robert Peel," 354,n7; *Economic Studies,* 595; *The English
Constitution,* 282, 283, 284; *Physics
and Politics,* 281-82, 283, 284
Sabine Baring-Gould, *Germany, Pres-
ent and Past,* 284
Anselme Polycarpe Batbie, *Cours de
droit administratif,* 119
Bede, 18
Jeremy Bentham, 280, 327
Guenther Heinrich von Berg, *Hand-
buch der teutschen Policeyrechts,*
118
Augustine Birrell, 326,n2; *Obiter Dicta,*
353,n6, 362,n15
Sir William Blackstone, 133, 151
Jean Joseph Charles Louis Blanc, 439
Maurice Bloch, *Dictionnaire de l'ad-
ministration française,* 120
Johann Kaspar Bluntschli, *Allgemeine
Statslehre,* 432; 454
Jean Bodin, 132
Conrad Bornhak, 416, 427; *Preuss-
isches Staatsrecht,* 119, 427
John George Bourinot, *Federal Gov-
ernment in Canada,* 284
Émile Boutmy, *The English Constitu-
tion,* 283; *Studies in Constitutional
Law: France—England—United
States,* 275-76, 283, 284, 535,n3, 536
Henry de Bracton, *De legibus et con-
suetudinibus Angliæ,* 29,n9
Robert Browning, 326; *Luria: A
Tragedy,* 358,n9
James Bryce, Viscount Bryce, 89; *The
American Commonwealth,* 167, 283,
284, 291, 343-44, 370, 371, 376, 379,
534; "A Word as to the Speakership,"
370,n11
August von Bulmerincq, 454
John William Burgess, *Political Sci-
ence and Comparative Constitutional
Law,* 164, 165, 169-71, 195-203; 474
Edmund Burke, 122, 151, 280; *The
Clarendon Press Selections from
Burke's Works,* 283, 284; "Letter to
a Member of the National Assem-
bly," 352,n5; "Thoughts on the
Cause of the Present Discontents,"
365,n19
Robert Burns, 554,n1,2, 557,n5
Julius Caesar, *Commentaries,* 18
Henry Charles Carey, 439
Auguste Carlier, *La république améri-
caine États-Unis,* 534,n1

Woodrow Wilson, cont.
Thomas Carlyle, *Sartor Resartus*, 362,-
n14
Sir Mackenzie Dalzell Chalmers, *Local Government*, 283, 284, 595
Charles Adolphe de Pineton, Marquis de Chambrun, *Droit et libertés aux États-Unis: leurs origines et leurs progrès*, 534-536; *Le Pouvoir exécutif aux États-Unis*, 535,n4
Aaron Lucius Chapin, *First Principles of Political Economy*, 237
Pierre Adolphe Chéruel, *Dictionnaire historique des institutions, moeurs, et coutumes de la France*, 119, 395n13
Marcus Tullius Cicero, 455
Edwin Charles Clark, *Practical Jurisprudence, A Comment on Austin*, 292, 455,n4
Sir Edward Coke, 151
Thomas McIntyre Cooley, *General Principles of Constitutional Law*, 105, 291
Sir Edward Shepherd Creasy, *The Rise and Progress of the English Constitution*, 283, 284
Albert Venn Dicey, 275; *Lectures Introductory to the Study of the Law of the Constitution*, 187, 283, 284, 473
Sir Charles Wentworth Dilke, *Problems of Greater Britain*, 284
Théophile Ducrocq, 403; *Cours de droit administratif*, 119
Gabriel Dufour, *Traité général de droit administratif appliqué*, 119
Encyclopædia Britannica, 416n19, 511
Thomas Henry Farrer, 1st Baron Farrer, *The State and Its Relation to Trade*, 595
Federalist Papers, 90, 129,n6, 367, 479
Henri de Ferron, *Institutions municipales et provinciales comparées*, 120
Sir Robert Filmer, 132
John Fiske, *American Political Ideas*, 282, 283, 284; *Civil Government in the United States*, 282, 283, 284
Edward Augustus Freeman, 80, 90, 91; *The Growth of the English Constitution from the Earliest Times*, 284
Numa Denis Fustel de Coulanges, *The Ancient City*, 283, 284
Bertha Meriton Cordery Gardiner, *The French Revolution*, 284
Samuel Rawson Gardiner, *The Puritan Revolution*, 284
Karl von Gareis, *Allgemeines Staatsrecht*, 429, 431
Théophile Gautier, *Mademoiselle de Maupin*, 462-66
Charles Gide, *Principles of Political Economy*, 303,n1
Rudolf von Gneist, 89, 93; *Englische Verfassungsgeschichte*, 119; *Das*

Woodrow Wilson, cont.
englische Verwaltungsrecht der Gegenwart in vergleichung mit dem deutschen Verwaltungswesen, 119; *History of the English Constitution*, 93; *Der Rechtsstaat*, 118, 393,n10; *Selfgovernment, Kommunalverfassung, und Verwaltungsgerichte in England*, 118
Oliver Goldsmith, "The Traveller," 356,n8
Frank Johnson Goodnow, *Comparative Administrative Law*, 120
John Richard Green, *A Short History of the English People*, 88
Mrs. John Richard Green, *Henry II*, 284, 398n16
François Pierre Guillaume Guizot, *The History and Origin of Representative Government in Europe*, 284
Claude Pierre Marie Haas, *Administration de la France*, 119
William Edward Hall, *A Treatise on International Law*, 291, 292, 379, 454,n2, 456
Alexander Hamilton, 90, 201, 479
William Waller Hening, *The Statutes at Large: Being a Collection of All the Laws of Virginia*, 312
Patrick Henry, 367
Robert Herrick, "Of Love, A Sonnet," 532-33
Sir Thomas Erskine Holland, *Elements of Jurisprudence*, 291, 293, 633
Hermann Eduard von Holst, 91
Franz von Holtzendorff, 126, 249n1, 292
Homer, 280
Richard Hooker, 352
James Kendall Hosmer, *A Short History of Anglo-Saxon Freedom*, 283, 284
Lina Hug and Richard Stead, *Switzerland*, 284
John Kells Ingram, *A History of Political Economy*, 291
John Alexander Jameson, "National Sovereignty," 351,n3
Georg Jellinek, 90, 133, 435; *Gesetz und Verordnung*, 119, 132
Johns Hopkins Studies in Historical and Political Science, 284
Alexander Johnston, *The Genesis of a New England State: Connecticut*, 187; *History of American Politics*, 284
Ludwig Jolly, 119
Richard Jones, 439
James Richard Joy, *Outline History of England*, 26n, 40n
Johann Heinrich Gottlob von Justi, 117; *Grundsätze der Polizeiwissenschaft*, 118
Charles Artemas Kent, "The Supreme Court since 1864," 149
Paul Laband, 90, 138, 139, 435; *Das*

Woodrow Wilson, cont.
Staatsrecht des deutschen Reiches, 130
Firmin Julien Laferrière, *Cours de droit public et administratif*, 119; *Traité de juridiction administratif et de recours contentieux*, 119
Ferdinand Lassalle, 83, 439
André Lebon, 403, 404, 406; *France as It Is* (with Paul Pelet), 283, 284; *Das Staatsrecht der französischen Republik*, 120
Francis Lieber, 329; *On Civil Liberty and Self-Government*, 351,n2
Diodato Lioy, *The Philosophy of Right*, 293, 313
Friedrich List, 108
John Locke, 130, 132, 133, 136, 350, 352; *Two Treatises on Government*, 283, 284
Henry Cabot Lodge, *Alexander Hamilton*, 284
Edgar Loening, *Lehrbuch des deutschen Verwaltungsrecht*, 119
James Lorimer, *Institutes of the Law of Nations*, 66, 595
Justin McCarthy, *The Epoch of Reform*, 284
James Madison, 129
Sir Henry James Sumner Maine, 89, 328, 352, 454, 455, 456, 457; *Ancient Law*, 14n, 139, 283, 284; *International Law*, 595; *Lectures on the Early History of Institutions*, 14n; *Roman Law and Legal Education*, 14n
Thomas Robert Malthus, *An Essay on the Principles of Population*, 439
William Oke Manning, *Commentaries on the Law of Nations*, 595
William Markby, *Elements of Law Considered with Reference to Principles of General Jurisprudence*, 293
Heinrich Marquardsen, 113n3, 116, 167
John Marshall, 477
Karl Marx, 83, 108, 439
Edward Campbell Mason, *The Veto Power: Its Origin, Development and Function in the Government of the United States*, 149n10, 185-86
Ernst von Meier, 126, 388; *Das Verwaltungsrecht*, 119
Adolf Merkel, 340, 633; "Elemente der allgemeinen Rechtslehre," 249-69, 292, 293; *Juristische Encyclopädie*, 292
Georg Meyer, *Die Behördenorganisation der Verwaltung des Innern*, 167; *Lehrbuch des deutschen Verwaltungsrecht*, 119; "Verwaltungslehre," 119
John Stuart Mill, *On Liberty*, 283, 284, 361,n11
John Milton, 280, 357, 367; *Areopagitica*, 358,n10

Woodrow Wilson, cont.
John Barbee Minor, *Institutes of Common and Statute Law*, 293
Robert von Mohl, 124; *Die Polizeiwissenschaft nach der Grundsätzen der Rechtsstaats*, 118; *System der Präventiv-Justiz*, 118
Charles de Secondat, Baron de la Brède et de Montesquieu, 129,n6, 133, 134, 367; *The Spirit of Laws*, 283, 284
John Morley, Viscount Morley of Blackburn, *Walpole*, 284
John Torrey Morse, Jr., *Thomas Jefferson*, 284
Bernard Moses, *The Federal Government of Switzerland*, 284
Wilhelm Müller, *Political History of Recent Times*, 284
Barthold Georg Niebuhr, 326
Nithard, 18n6
Jules Charles Victurnien, Duc de Noailles, *Cent ans de république aux États-Unis*, 535,n1
John Ordronaux, *Constitutional Legislation in the United States*, 153
James Otis, 367
Simon Nelson Patten, "Decay of Local Government in America," 386,n4, 387
Benjamin Perley Poore, *The Federal and State Constitutions, Colonial Charters, and Other Organic Laws of the United States*, 129n6
Edmond Ives Joseph Marie Poullet, *Histoire politique interne de la Belgique*, 181
Paul Louis Ernest Pradier-Fodéré, *Précis de droit administratif*, 120, 167
Georg Friedrich Puchta, 437; *Cursus der Institutionen*, 293
David Ricardo, 108, 194
Johann Karl Rodbertus, 83, 108
Wilhelm Georg Friedrich Röscher, 108
Hermann Rösler, *Lehrbuch der Verwaltungsrechts*, 119
Jean Jacques Rousseau, 86, 133, 536
Claude Henri de Rouvroy, Comte de Saint-Simon, 439
Gustav von Rumelin, Sr., "Verwaltungslehre," 119
John Ruskin, *Seven Lamps of Architecture*, 157,n13, 364,n18
Otto von Sarwey, 122, 124, 131, 143, 153, 155, 383, 390, 416; *Allgemeines Verwaltungsrecht*, 116, 119, 167; *Das oeffentliche Recht und die Verwaltungsrechtspflege*, 119
Friedrich Karl von Savigny, 327
August Wilhelm von Schlegel, 326
Gustav Friedrich von Schönberg, ed., *Handbuch der politischen Oekonomie*, 119, 167
Hermann Johann Friedrich Schulze, 416n19
Carl Schurz, *Henry Clay*, 284
Eben Greenough Scott, *The Develop-*

Woodrow Wilson, cont.
  ment of Constitutional Liberty in
  the English Colonies of America,
  283, 284
John Robert Seeley, *The Life and Times
  of Stein*, 284
William Shakespeare, 281, 572,n1
Henry Sidgwick, *The Elements of Politics*, 310, 318-20, 332,n7
Algernon Sidney, 132
Edward Rowland Sill, 349, 575,n2,3
Adam Smith, 108; *The Wealth of Nations*, 439
Sir William Smith, *Dictionary of Greek
  and Roman Antiquities*, 141
Rudolf Sohm, *Institutes of Roman
  Law*, 293
Josef von Sonnenfels, *Grundsätze der
  Polizey, Handlung und Finanzwissenschaft*, 118
Lorenz Jacob von Stein, 124; *Verwaltungslehre*, 118, 167
Karl Michael Joseph Leopold, *Freiherr
  von Stengel, Wörterbuch des deutschen Verwaltungsrecht*, 119
Sir James Fitzjames Stephen, *Liberty,
  Equality, Fraternity*, 283, 284, 361,-
  n12
Albert Stickney, *A True Republic*, 396,-
  n15
William Stubbs, 89, 398
Cornelius Tacitus, 18
Hippolyte Adolphe Taine, *The Ancient
  Régime*, 284
Thomas Pitt Taswell-Langmead, *English Constitutional History from the
  Teutonic Conquest to the Present
  Time*, 88
Hannis Taylor, *The Origin and Growth
  of the English Constitution*, 87-91,
  284
Alfred Tennyson, 1st Baron Tennyson,
  The Foresters, 505,n2; "Freedom,"
  362,n13; "Ode on the Death of the
  Duke of Wellington," 368,n21
Anton Friedrich Justus Thibaut, 327
Alexis de Tocqueville, 127; *The Ancient
  Régime and the Revolution*, 284;
  Democracy in America, 284
Arnold Toynbee, *Industrial Revolution*,
  595
Henry Duff Traill, 400, 401, 402; *The
  Central Government*, 167, 283, 595
Anthony Trollope, *The Life of Cicero*,
  284
Samuel Epes Turner, *A Sketch of the
  Germanic Constitution from Early
  Times to the Dissolution of the Empire*, 284
Moses Coit Tyler, *Patrick Henry*, 284
John Martin Vincent, *State and Federal Government in Switzerland*, 283,
  284
Francis Amasa Walker, *First Lessons
  in Political Economy*, 291; *Money
  in Its Relation to Trade and Industry*, 595

Woodrow Wilson, cont.
Friedrich Gottlieb Welcker, 326
Henry Wheaton, *History of the Law
  of Nations in Europe and America,
  from the Earliest Times to the
  Treaty of Washington*, 1842, 455,
  456
William Wordsworth, 576,n4, 577,n6;
  "O'er the wide earth . . . ," 362,n17

RELIGIOUS LIFE

talk before Philadelphian Society, Oct.
  30, 1890, 61, notes, 58; Sunday
  afternoon talk in Marquand Chapel,
  April 5, 1891, notes, 187-88

SELF-ANALYSIS

lonely at Princeton: has not yet found
  the companion he wants, 228;
  sombre, morbid nature, 483; imperious passions make him tremble at
  what he *might* do if temptation came
  his way, 487; terrible temptation to
  which he is exposed by nature and
  temperament, 527; intensely passionate nature, 558; the latent politician within him, 628

TYPEWRITERS AND OFFICE
EQUIPMENT

Caligraph: example of WW typing, 9,
  in use by WW since 1883, 221; A. B.
  Hart asks for recommendation, 213;
  WW suggests a Hammond, 221;
  apology for writing letter on typewriter, 233, 236

WRITINGS

"The Author Himself" (1891), 211,n1,
  234,n1; T. W. Higginson on, 288,n1;
  R. Bridges on, 289; 290; C. T. Winchester on, 315
"Character of Democracy in the United
  States" (1889), mentioned, 344
Congressional Government (1885),
  *4:6-179; 85, 176, 189, 206, 282,
  283, 284; J. Bryce on, 343; 370
Division and Reunion, 1829-1889 (in
  progress; published 1893), 165,n1,
  176,n3, 206,n3, 210, 213, 227, 233,
  242, 273, 274-75, 277, 286, 288, 290,
  375, 377, 378, 531, 555, 565
"The English Constitution" (1890-91),
  text, 12-44; 91n3
"A Literary Politician (Walter Bagehot)" (1889), read to J. H. U. Seminary, 168; reported unpublished, 173
"The Modern Democratic State"
  (1885), *5:54-92; mentioned, 99,-
  n1, 344
*An Old Master and Other Political
  Essays* (1893), 325n1, 435n25
"The Philosophy of Politics" (projected), 7; outline, 98-101; 579,n4, 621.
  See also Index to Vol. 5
"Political Sovereignty" (1891), text,
  325-41; 344, 435n25, 471, 472. *See*

Woodrow Wilson, cont.
also the entry under Wilson, Woodrow: Public Addresses and Lectures
Review of Charles Adolphe de Pineton, Marquis de Chambrun, *Droit et libertés aux États-Unis:leurs origines et leurs progrès*, 534-36
Review of Edward Campbell Mason, *The Veto Power*, 185-86
Review of Émile Boutmy, *Studies in Constitutional Law: France–England–United States*, 275-76
Review of Hannis Taylor, *The Origin and Growth of the English Constitution*, 87-91
Review of John William Burgess, *Political Science and Comparative Constitutional Law*, 195-203
The State (1889), 137, 138, 139, 142, 167, 205,n1, 233, 239n1, 283, 284, 325n1. *See also the indexes to Vols. 5 and 6*; advertising circular for, 70,n1, 76; review by Richard Heath Dabney, 85-87, 233; review by Siegfried Brie, 59-61, 76; royalty statements, 172n1, 302-3; study-guide by John Wenzel, 175
The State and Federal Governments of the United States. A Brief Manual for Schools and Colleges, royalty statement, 173n1
"The Study of Administration" (1887), 178, 179
"The Study of Politics" (1891), 246n2; text, 278-284
Translation from Théophile Gautier, *Mademoiselle de Maupin*, 462-66
"The True American Spirit," proposed article, 240,n1

Winans, Samuel Ross, 294
Winchester, Caleb Thomas, *5:753,-n1; 4, 181; WW on, 182-83; 184, 188, 189-91, 191-92, 203, 278, 314-17, 321, 372, 506; Mrs. (Alice Goodwin Smith), 191, 317, 321
Wisconsin, University of, 218, 379n1
Withers, William Alphonso, 246
Witherspoon, Jere, 626,n2
Witherspoon, Mrs., sister of R. Bridges, 69
women, education of, 442-43, 444, 549
Woodbridge, Samuel Isett, 595,n3, 637,-

n1; Mrs. (Janie [Jeanie, Jennie] Wilson Woodrow), first cousin of WW, *1:487n2; 595,n3, 637
Woodbridge, Woodrow, 607
Woodrow, Fitz William McMaster, 620,n2
Woodrow, James, maternal uncle of WW, *1:41,n1; 47, 52,n2, 53, 54n2, 214, 286-87, 595, 606, 607, 616, 617, 619, 620; Mrs. (Melie or Felie S. Baker), *1:42n1; 595, 606
Woodrow, James Hamilton, first cousin of WW, *1:576,n2; 619-20,n1, 626; Mrs. (Katharine McGregor McMaster), 620
Woodrow, Marion, first cousin of WW, *1:649,n4; 52
Woodrow, Mary Charlotte, first cousin of WW, *1:593n1; 287,n2
Woodrow Wilson: Life and Letters (Baker), 341n11
Woods, Frank Churchill, 214,n3
Woods, Hiram, Jr., *1:133,n3; 214; Mrs. (Laura Hall), 214
Woods, Lawrence Crane, 6
Wooster, University of, 218
"Word as to the Speakership" (Bryce), 370,n1
Wordsworth, William, 362,n17, 533, 576,n4, 577,n6
Works (Bagehot), 354,n7
Works (Burke), 334,n8, 352,n5
World's Columbian Exposition, Chicago, 1893, 380n1
Wörterbuch des deutschen Verwaltungsrechts (von Stengel), 119
Wright, George, 248
Wright, Jacob Ridgeway, *1:412n1; 104
Wright, James, *2:651; *3:83,n1; 547, 562
Wright, Mrs., 595
Wyman, Isaac Chauncey, 67n17

Yale University, 444; Glee and Banjo Clubs, 621,n2; Kent Club of Yale Law School, 79, 181; Law School, 79; Osborn Hall, 80n
Yorkville, S. C., 54n2
Young, Charles Augustus, 51,n1, 294

Zouche, Richard, 453